What Kind of Death

Many books have been published about physician-assisted death. This book not only offers a comprehensive and in-depth examination of that subject, but it also extends the discussion to a broader range of end-of-life decisions, including suicide, palliative care and sedation until death.

In every jurisdiction that has laws permitting some kind of physician-assisted death, a central point of controversy is whether such assistance should only be available to dying patients, or to everyone who wants to end his life. The right to determine the manner and time of one's own death, however, does not necessarily mean that physicians should be permitted to cooperate in ensuring a quick and peaceful death. In this book, Govert den Hartogh considers the fundamental and practical matters – including concrete issues of legal regulation – related to end-of life decision-making. He proposes a two-tiered system. Everyone should have access to humane means of ending his life, if his decision to end it is voluntary, well considered and durable. But doctors should only participate in a joint action of ending the patient's life on his request if they also are convinced of acting in the patient's best interests, in particular by ending intolerable and unrelievable suffering. And perhaps there is a reason to restrict that second service to dying patients. The whole argument, however, depends on the extent to which, in both tiers of the system, we can design legal safeguards that will enable us to trust judgements about the requesting person's request and about his suffering. The book considers much new evidence in regard to this issue.

What Kind of Death will appeal to researchers and advanced students working in bioethics, applied ethics, philosophy of law and health law.

Govert den Hartogh is Emeritus Professor of Moral Philosophy at the University of Amsterdam, the Netherlands.

Routledge Research in Applied Ethics

Corporate Responsibility and Political Philosophy
Exploring the Social Liberal Corporation
Kristian Høyer Toft

Sexual Ethics in a Secular Age
Is There Still a Virtue of Chastity?
Edited by Eric J. Silverman

The Ethics of Virtual and Augmented Reality
Building Worlds
Erick Jose Ramirez

The Ethics of War and the Force of Law
A Modern Just War Theory
Uwe Steinhoff

The Philosophy of Online Manipulation
Edited by Fleur Jongepier & Michael Klenk

The Ethics of Political Dissent
Tony Milligan

Why Conscience Matters
A Defence of Conscientious Objection in Healthcare
Xavier Symons

The Ethics of Agribusiness
Justice and Global Food in Focus
Shane Epting

For more information about this series, please visit: https://www.routledge.com/Routledge-Research-in-Applied-Ethics/book-series/RRAES

What Kind of Death

The Ethics of Determining One's Own Death

Govert den Hartogh

Routledge
Taylor & Francis Group
NEW YORK AND LONDON

First published 2023
by Routledge
605 Third Avenue, New York, NY 10158

and by Routledge
4 Park Square, Milton Park, Abingdon, Oxon, OX14 4RN

Routledge is an imprint of the Taylor & Francis Group, an informa business

ISBN: 978-1-032-24796-0 (hbk)
ISBN: 978-1-032-24995-7 (pbk)
ISBN: 978-1-003-28111-5 (ebk)

DOI: 10.4324/9781003281115

Typeset in Sabon
by KnowledgeWorks Global Ltd.

For Lya,

sine qua non

Contents

Acknowledgements

My interest in the subject of decisions at and about the end of life started in 1991 when I had to teach it to medical students. Most of them thought that their views could simply be justified by an appeal to the right of self-determination but responded to actual cases in a way that betrayed other concerns. I have always been interested in the tension between the principles of respect for autonomy and beneficence, and this is a subject that is shaped by that tension. This book is the latest of a series of attempts to articulate it.

I have tried to address the issues that the wish to determine the manner and time of one's own death globally raise. This is a difficult task because the discussion about these issues is everywhere highly dependent on details of a specific cultural and institutional environment. Inevitably my own perspective is determined by my own environment. But I have had the good fortune of living in a country that has both a long experience with legalized euthanasia and a long tradition of research on its practice. That my focus is admittedly 'Benelux-centred', as an anonymous reviewer for Routledge commented, may therefore not be a mere disadvantage. (The reviewer didn't think so.)

The time (1998–2010) that I functioned as a member of the Regional Review Committee for Euthanasia South Holland-Zealand was a formative period for the development of my understanding of the Dutch euthanasia practice, both from the point of view of patients and of medical practitioners. Membership involved intensive discussions about hundreds of cases, in particular with Jan Suyver, Maria Wildenburg and Gerrit Kimsma, who were my colleagues during the whole period. I have also learned a lot from my interactions, often in a counselling role, with the protagonists of the Dutch research tradition, Gerrit van der Wal, Agnes van der Heide, Bregje Onwuteaka-Philipsen and their colleagues, as well as with the legal scholars who collaborated with them, Sjef Gevers and Johan Legemaate.

Throughout the years I have discussed the issues with many other friends and colleagues, including Maurice Adams, Eva Asscher, the late Ron Berghmans, Henk Blanken, Ineke Bolt, Miriam de Bontridder,

Theo Boer, Hilde Buiting, Martin Buijsen, Gijs van Donselaar, Gert van Dijk, Jurriaan de Haan, the late Helen Keasberry, Bert Keizer, James Kennedy, the late Henk Leenen, Anne Ruth Mackor, Theo Matthijssen, Paul Mevis, Esther Pans, Pieter Pekelharing, Judith Rietjens, Klaas Rozemond, Mette Rurup, Peter Rijpkema, Maartje Schermer, Eugène Sutorius, Willie Swildens, Ghislaine van Thiel, Donald van Tol, Margo Trappenburg, Suzanne van de Vathorst, Ton Vink, Tim Vis, Laura de Vito, Koo van der Wal, Heleen Weyers, Eric van Wijlick and Els van Wijngaarden. Inez de Beaufort gave me in addition invaluable moral and practical support during the final stage of writing and preparing for publication. These are all Dutch persons, and Peggy Battin who can't be missed on this list should count as an honorary Dutch person. But I also had illuminating discussions with Sarah and Bill Ruddick during my term as a visiting scholar at New York University (2004). The reviewer whom I already mentioned made some very perspicacious terminological and methodological comments on the manuscript.

Four men deserve a place in a personal gallery of honour because they have had the strongest influence on my own way of thinking. The late Andries van Dantzig, one of the pioneers of the Dutch euthanasia movement, used to be sceptical about the whole idea of self-determination. As a psychiatrist he was much more interested in the complex motives for death wishes. What is it about death that for a particular person makes it seem preferable to life? The late John Griffiths taught me that it is basically not the lawgiver and the courts but society that determines to what extent legal rules will affect actual practice. But the law can have some influence on the further development of that practice if its rules are, to begin with, in line with the way in which people already think and act. Over the years Boudewijn Chabot has made me realize that it is an open question to what extent, in determining the manner and time of your own death, you need to rely on doctors. Suicide is therefore the basic issue, not physician-assisted death. Finally, Henri Wijsbek showed me how, in thinking about a person's interests, we can take her own perspective seriously without attributing final authority to her judgement. He also read most of the chapters of this book, offering sentence-by-sentence comments on language and argumentation.

The cumulative impact of these influences has been a threefold ambition: to introduce a new argumentative complexity, take, as much as possible, the whole gamut of available empirical data into account, and propose a modestly de-medicalized perspective.

Haarlem, March 2022

1 Introduction

1.1 What kind of death?

We die in different ways. Sometimes suddenly, as a result of an accident or crime, a stroke or a heart attack. More often at the end of a period of illness that may be more or less prolonged and involve more or less misery. Sudden, non-violent death has its attractions, if it is not felt to come much too early. It may, however, be traumatic for one's relatives and friends. Knowing that death is inevitable we prefer it to arrive at the end of a long, happy and fulfilling life. If we have a lethal illness, we hope that it will not cause us much suffering. Some of us prefer to die in a state of full awareness, surrounded by close relatives and friends. Others prefer gently to slide away into eternal sleep. By now much is known about the preferences people have regarding the manner and time of their own death. I will summarize that knowledge in Chapter 2.

What can we do to make our death approximate the kind of death we prefer? The question applies both to the manner and the time of our death, but these issues are related to each other. Sometimes we have to choose between an earlier but better and a later but worse death.

Human beings have always had some means to alleviate their suffering, including opium since the time of the Sumerians (but in Europe only available since the sixteenth century). They have always had the option of ending their own life or having it ended by another, although in earlier times it was almost impossible to die peacefully at your own or another person's hand. Most poisons that were known to be effective in procuring death did so in a painful manner. Old and ill people have also always had the option of stopping eating and drinking, although they didn't have the present opportunities to ensure the humane character of this kind of death. Presumably, however, they knew how important it is to keep the mouth moist.

In recent times the options have increased. Palliative care has become a medical specialism of its own, employing a rich array of interventions. One possible intervention is so-called palliative sedation, lowering the patient's consciousness more or less deeply, temporarily or permanently. One variety of palliative sedation is deep sedation that is meant to go on for the remainder

DOI: 10.4324/9781003281115-1

of a patient's life. If this option is chosen, an additional choice must be made to provide or not to provide artificial hydration. By now we also know a substantial number of drugs that can be used to end your own or another person's life in a quick, safe and painless way. If a person decides to stop eating and drinking, the process can be monitored and complications (a delirium, for example) can be prevented or stopped by medical intervention.

Because the power of medicine to prolong life has grown enormously, the option to stop life-saving treatment or abstain from starting it has become much more prominent. This option raises a number of important questions of its own. It is generally accepted that the decision can be made on the patient's request, or because the burdens of treatment can be disproportionately large. But is it also possible for a life-prolonging treatment to be 'futile'? There is growing consensus that overdiagnosis and overtreatment are common phenomena, but in order to identify particular cases of overdiagnosis and overtreatment, we would need to agree on the proper aims of diagnosis and treatment and perhaps on the meaning of 'health'. Unfortunately, we don't. These are important questions indeed but discussing them would require another book.

Decisions about the manner and in particular the time of a person's death are everywhere heavily regulated by the law, and, if doctors and nurses are involved, by their professional morality. Suicide is, by now, outside the Islamic world, forbidden in only 15 countries (Section 2.5), but even elsewhere, it is often considered an unqualified duty of everyone to try to prevent it. Access to drugs that would enable a person to end her own life in a safe and humane way is normally blocked, although well-informed people know the ways to sidestep such blockades, for example by ordering the drugs on the internet. If you ask your relatives or friends to help you to end your life, such assistance will also be forbidden in most places. There are by now seven countries and five Australian states in which doctors are permitted to end a patient's life on his request when a number of conditions have been satisfied.[1] In some other jurisdictions doctors are permitted, under similar

1 The Netherlands (2001), Belgium (2002), Luxembourg (2009), Colombia, Canada (2016), New Zealand (2021), Spain (2021), and the Australian states of Victoria (2017), Western Australia (2019), Tasmania (2021), South Australia (2021) and Queensland (2021). The Colombian Constitutional Court decriminalized 'mercy homicide' already in 1997, but it hardly occurred in practice before a further judgement from the Court (T-970) in 2014 and more specific regulation in Resolution 1216 from the Ministry of Health in 2015, Benavides 2018. Victoria's *Voluntary Assisted Dying Bill* (2017) permits the administration of a lethal drug by a doctor only when the patient is unable to self-administer or digest the drug. The other Australian states that I mentioned permit administration by a physician in all cases. On 29 January 2021 the Assembly of the Portuguese Republic approved a law permitting euthanasia and physician-assisted suicide, but the country's Constitutional Court declared the bill unconstitutional. An amended bill was vetoed by the Portuguese president on 30 November 2021. In 2021 a Peruvian court allowed euthanasia in the individual case of Ana Estrada.

conditions, to provide access to lethal drugs, normally only to patients suffering from a fatal illness (Chapter 5, footnote 28). Many drugs that are used in palliative care, including opioids and the benzodiazepines that are needed for palliative sedation, are usually also only accessible to doctors. Palliative sedation, including deep sedation until the end of life, is also regulated in most places, sometimes by law, more often by professional guidelines.

In considering such regulations we always have to be aware of the extent to which they are upheld in practice. For example, in most countries your friends and relatives are forbidden to help you to end your life, but it is quite rare that such actions lead the authorities to initiate investigation or legal action (Section 5.1). When you order a barbiturate from abroad, in most countries, the risk of getting in legal trouble is also quite remote. It is important to be aware of such facts, because so many participants in the debate about legal regulations argue as if a legal prohibition is sufficient to avoid the dangers supposed to be implied in the prohibited practice. It is equally important to realize that, although almost everyone is in favour of providing high-level palliative care to all dying patients, the actual level provided even in countries in which palliative care as a medical specialism is most highly developed is often insufficient. Often even an adequate dosage of morphine is withheld from dying patients, because it is supposed to have either an addictive or a life-shortening effect.

Nevertheless, individuals have, increasingly, some choice as regards the kind of death that they prefer. Legal authorities and professional organizations of doctors have choices as regards the kind of death they want to permit. In this book I discuss the choices of individuals from the point of view of their personal interest and private morality. What would really be a good death? What can we do to bring it about? I also discuss the choices of legal authorities and organizations from the point of view of public, including professional morality. I start with suicide, because it invites us to focus on the basic question whether it is ever, and if so when, prudentially wise and morally permissible to prefer death to life. It is, moreover, the one option in the spectrum of options to be discussed that doesn't necessarily involve a second person. We need to be clear about the issues involved in morally assessing suicide and its legal regulation before we complicate things by adding considerations about the proper role of others, including relatives, doctors and nurses. The choice of this starting point will turn out to have important consequences for my discussion of other kinds of death. We should not assume without argument that the involvement of physicians is essential for the safe and effective implementation of any decision to end one's life.

The subject of this book is determining the manner and time of one's own death. I will therefore not consider the even more difficult and controversial issue of mercy-killing in the case of severely suffering but categorically incompetent patients: newborns, very young children, the severely mentally handicapped and people in an advanced state of dementia who have not recorded a request for euthanasia in an advance directive.[2] Perhaps I should have discussed whether and in what way minors should be allowed to participate in decision-making about the manner and time of their death, but in the present state of the debate I have not much to add to it. And this book is long enough as it is.

The proper use of concepts in this area is essential for a clear, unbiased discussion. I will consider conceptual issues in the appropriate theoretical context: issues concerning 'suicide' in Sections 3.6 and 4.1, concerning 'euthanasia' in Section 5.6. It may help to clarify at the outset that I will define 'euthanasia' as ending someone's life on her request, not: in her (presumed) interest. According to this definition the intentional terminating of the life of a newborn is not to be called euthanasia. From Chapter 5 onward I will avoid the term 'physician-assisted suicide', but not for the presently fashionable reason that in cases referred to by that name people are not actually committing suicide (Section 3.6). Rather, as I will explain in Section 5.4, in those cases the doctors involved are either doing less or more than providing assistance. I will try to avoid euphemisms as much as possible, with the exception of the term 'euthanasia' itself, for which no short equivalent exists. I consider it euphemistic because it is always an open question whether ending a person's life on her request actually results in a good death. 'Medical Aid (or Assistance) in Dying' (MAID) is equally euphemistic but also imprecise, because, fortunately, care-providers can often somewhat ease the hard work of dying for a person without hastening her death. That the term is euphemistic and imprecise may no longer be a real problem, however, because by now it has a clear special meaning in common use in North America. But 'MAID' has additional problems, as I already indicated: it suggests that killing oneself isn't suicide as soon as a doctor is participating in the action (Section 3.6). And it refers to a class of medical actions that should not all be considered forms of aid or assistance (Section 5.6).

'Euthanasia', on the other hand, has its own problems. As I defined it, it is only in common use in some European countries (the Netherlands, Belgium, Spain, Portugal, Italy). Readers from other countries have to consider my definition – ending someone's life on her request – as a mere stipulation. Moreover, I called it a euphemism, but in many places, including Germany and North America, it rather has strong negative connotations. But in discussing ways of ending one's life that require the involvement of a doctor, we simply don't have a universally satisfactory terminology. Any author writing in this area for an audience that isn't restricted to his own country will therefore have to make some difficult terminological decisions. (See in particular Sections 5.6; 7.1; 9.1.)

2 Cf. den Hartogh 2014b on severely handicapped newborns.

1.2 The basic structure of the argument

The ordering of the material that I described may seem to be a natural one for any book on moral and legal aspects of end-of-life decisions. But as a matter of fact, it has a more specific rationale. In this section I will not offer an outline of the argument of the book as a whole, but I will describe a skeleton of that argument that is meant to explain its structure.

I will start by arguing that people have a right to decide about the manner and time of their own death, because such decisions belong to the core of self-regarding choices that each person has the authority to make for himself (Chapter 2). Such decisions can only be considered ways of exercising that particular right if they are made without undue pressure and after due reflection, preferably in open dialogue with intimates. Chapters 3–5 in Part I consider what this right implies. If people want to expedite the *time* of their death, most of them have the option of stopping eating and drinking (Chapter 4). But people also have the right to determine the *manner* of their death, and most people who consider ending their own lives will prefer to die in other ways, in particular by the use of drugs that secure a quick and peaceful death. These drugs aren't publicly available because of the obvious risks involved in public availability, in particular the risk that they will be used by people who are coerced or manipulated to use them, or who use them in a moment of deep despair. But if people have a right to end their own lives, the state is obligated to provide access to these drugs to them, if they have made their decisions in the proper way. That is not really a way of 'assisting' or even of 'facilitating' suicide; it is standing out of the way of legitimate use (Chapter 5).

If, however, we consider the way in which suicide is 'assisted' by doctors in the Netherlands and Belgium, this turns out to be a very different kind of action. These doctors do not merely lift a barrier, rather they take on the responsibility to ensure that death comes quickly and painlessly. In these cases, it is also mistaken to speak about mere 'assistance', but for the very different reason that these are cases in which the doctor and the patient cooperate in bringing about the death that the patient desires. Morally it doesn't matter at all who of them performs the final action in the series of required actions. Legally, it shouldn't matter either (Chapter 5).

Can the physician's participation be justified by appealing to the right of the patient to decide about the manner and time of his own death? That is the most common way in which authors try to justify the legalization of either physician-assisted suicide or euthanasia or both. It presupposes that a person can *waive* her right to life, thereby authorizing another person to take it. But if we consider legal systems all around the world, we discover that, by now with the possible exception of Germany and Austria,[3] the right to life cannot be waived in any of these systems, any more than the right to personal freedom. Such legal systems are often accused of being paternalistic in this respect, but I will argue that the paternalism involved is of a special kind, indirect paternalism, that isn't vulnerable to the usual objections to paternalism (Chapter 9). I conclude that the right to life doesn't only protect our authority to make decisions in regard to our life but also our basic interest in survival. That means that the right can only be set aside if two conditions have been satisfied: the person freely decides to end her life, and it is in her basic interest to end it. That is why it is proper for the law to make requirements, not only on the patient's request but also on his condition, for example unbearable and unremittable suffering.

In most permissive jurisdictions doctors are only allowed to help patients in ending their lives in any way, if these patients suffer from a fatal illness that is expected to kill them within a limited time frame, mostly put at six months. This requirement excludes certain categories of patients who, in its absence, would be eligible for some kind of assistance and would regularly request it, in particular psychiatric patients, very old people and patients suffering from dementia. (A fourth category consists of patients in an advanced stage of a degenerative disease, who still have a life expectancy of more than six months.) In all permissive jurisdictions, whether or not they have posited a time limit, these three categories are at the core of the ongoing moral and legal debate about 'physician-assisted death' or 'medical aid in dying'.

Can we justify a physician's participation in the joint act of ending a person's life in those cases? Even if we can be sure enough that the patient's request for such participation has been voluntary and well-considered, we might still not be sure enough that acting on his request is in his basic interest. It may, for example, be doubtful whether or not there still is any way of making his life liveable for him (Chapters 14 and 15). The solution to the problem of the extension of permissible 'assistance' to the problematic cases could therefore be a two-tiered system in which different requirements are made for different categories of peoples. In such a system it may be justifiable to introduce a time limit for a doctor cooperating in ending a patient's life, as long as people beyond that limit still have access to lethal drugs (Chapter 16).

This is the basic plot of the book. But it also has a subplot. By now the main argument against the legalization of either physician-assisted suicide or euthanasia consists of two parts. First it is suggested that legalization is not necessary if sophisticated forms of palliative care, including deep sedation that is meant to continue until the end of life, are available to all dying patients. In Part II (Chapters 6–8) I will therefore

3 See Section 16.1. But in Germany and Austria it is still forbidden to end a person's life on her request.

discuss the aims and limits of palliative care and sedation until death. Second it is held that legalization is undesirable because of the risks it will create, in particular for specific categories of people, to be 'assisted' in ending their lives, even though they have not voluntarily and competently decided to end it, and their suffering cannot be considered intolerable and unrelievable. Part III (Chapters 10–12) will investigate whether these risks can be managed by a system of legal safeguards.

1.3 Some matters of method

Advocates of legalizing either physician-assisted suicide or euthanasia almost invariably argue in favour of their position by appealing to the need for some fairly radical revision of commonsense morality. Opponents likewise tend to believe that in addition to pointing out slippery-slope concerns, their only task consists in defending the same tenets of commonsense morality that the other party wants to reject or revise.

By 'commonsense morality' I do not refer to the moral views of the majority. In many countries, in particular in Western Europe and North America, the majority of the population is now in favour of the legalization of either physician-assisted suicide or euthanasia or both, and most of these people will defend their view by appealing to people's right to self-determination. But these people will commonly understand their own belief to be a departure from a traditional view that they also know to have been legally enshrined everywhere a mere generation ago.

The most prominent of those revisions are the following. Most advocates of physician-assisted suicide and euthanasia argue that the prohibition of these actions conflicts with people's right to self-determination.[4] That right is supposed not only to allow a person to end her own life but also others to do this on her request. Others have attempted to show that there is no morally relevant distinction between killing and letting die, or, more precisely, between killing someone and allowing him to die from an independently originating threat. Therefore, anyone who allows doctors to abstain from life-saving treatment on the request of the patient should accept the legitimacy of euthanasia under the same conditions.[5] Similarly, advocates have argued that there is no morally relevant distinction

4 Margaret Battin gives the following list of the "first philosophical voices in the new debate about euthanasia and physician-assisted suicide", beginning around 1980: Beauchamp, Frey, Brock, Mayo, myself (Battin), Harris, Glover, Prado, Kuhse and Singer, and says that these authors "largely supported an autonomy-based view", Battin 2005, 19–20. She could have added Feinberg, as well as other pioneering European authors in addition to Glover and Harris, including Hoerster and van der Wal.

5 Appealing to a "preponderance of the evidence from ethicists", the Canadian Supreme Court stated in *Carter v Canada* [2015 SCC 5 at para 335] "that there is no ethical distinction between physician-assisted death and other end-of-life practices whose outcome is highly likely to be death".

between ending a person's life in order to prevent further suffering and using some medically indicated way of alleviating that suffering that is known to have the shortening of the patient's life as a probable side effect. Because opponents almost always permit actions of the second kind, it is, advocates suggest, inconsistent for them to oppose euthanasia. The most comprehensive expositions of the liberal view combine these three lines of argument, from Jonathan Glover, *Causing Death and Saving Lives* (1977), to Wayne Sumner, *Assisted Death* (2011).

In this book I will take a different line. Although I will argue that the right to self-determination implies, indeed, a right to end one's own life (Section 2.5), I will also contend, as I already indicated in the last section, that an appeal to the right to self-determination is insufficient to justify ending the life of another person on her request. It would only be sufficient if we accepted the principle *Volenti non fit iniuria* – you cannot wrong a person by an action to which she has consented – without any restriction. As a matter of fact, however, no legal system accepts consent as a justification for killing, and I will argue that at least part of the explanation is that no legal system recognizes the *Volenti* principle to apply to acts of killing, not even any of the systems that presently permit euthanasia under certain circumstances. And I will show that the moral objections to this limitation of the applicability of the *Volenti* maxim – all variants of the accusation of paternalism – are mistaken (Section 9.5).

Although, as I said, most recent arguments in favour of the legalization of euthanasia appeal exclusively to the right to self-determination, there always have been authors (including Battin and Sumner) arguing that this appeal can be or has to be supplemented by an appeal to a principle of mercy or benevolence.[6] But it has rarely been discussed why exactly we need these two principles, and what exactly are their complementary roles.

It could also be shown that the distinction between killing someone and allowing him to die is legally relevant in all legal systems. Even in legal systems that recognize a duty to rescue, the penalties for failing to rescue are much lower than those for homicide. The same point can be made about the distinction between ending a life in order to prevent further suffering and acting on a medical indication in a way that predictably has a life-shortening effect. Even in permissive jurisdictions actions of the first kind are much more heavily regulated than actions of the second kind. In the case of these two distinctions, however, I will not discuss whether or not any moral rationale for making them can be found. I can afford to remain agnostic about the issue, because I don't need to take a position on it for my own arguments to succeed. In this sense my arguments are *minimally revisionist* ones: they do not appeal

6 E.g. Young 2007; Sumner 2011; Jackson 2012; Miller, Truog 2012; Smith 2012; Battin 2016; Birnbacher 2017, ch. 4. Miller, Truog, as well as Birnbacher, point out that purely autonomy-driven views are incompatible with the role morality of doctors.

to any of the three revisions of commonsense morality that people who defend the justifiability of 'physician-assisted suicide' and 'euthanasia' usually appeal to. By choosing that starting point I aim to find as much common ground between opponents and defendants of a permissive legal regime as possible. Of course, my argument will at various points result in a specification of that common ground that is more controversial.[7]

In explicating the idea of minimal revisionism I have also demonstrated another distinctive aspect of my argumentative strategy. On the whole my method is the usual one in bioethical discussions. It starts from convictions that I suppose to be shared by almost everyone and argue for principles that are best suited to accommodate those shared convictions, without privileging my own personal ones. Occasionally I offer some considerations that support those convictions or show the weakness of alternative views. The distinctive element that I want to point out is that to this *corpus* of the "considered judgements of competent moral judges",[8] I add a number of views that are structural elements of all legal systems, the fact, for instance, that consent is not accepted as a defence in cases of homicide, or battery, or incarceration (Sections 9.1; 9.5). However, in such cases in particular, as I indicated already, I will not be content with pointing to the universal acceptance of such structural elements by legal systems, I will also consider whether they have some plausible moral rationale or at least can withstand seemingly relevant moral objections.

Authors who try to identify justifiable legal arrangements by moral argument normally recognize, at best, the limits of the implementation of morality by legal means, created by the nature of the law as an instrument of maintaining social order. In my approach not only does ethics instruct law, law also informs ethics.

Taking the law into consideration in this way has some consequences regarding the third of the views that I ascribed to traditional common sense: the distinction between terminating someone's life and administering palliative medication that may also have the effect of hastening his death. It is often supposed that one can only make this distinction if one subscribes to the *Doctrine of Double Effect*, the view that there is an important moral distinction to be made between intending something to happen, either as one's final aim or as part of the means one chooses to achieve that aim, and allowing it to happen as a mere side effect. However, although all legal systems accept the distinction, many of them have a conception of the guilty mind that is incompatible with Double Effect. They make the distinction, not in terms of the intention of the agent but of the availability of proper indications justifying his actions. Or they should make the distinction in that way in order to avoid

7 See for example Sections 4.3; 7.3, on the distinction between killing and letting die.

8 Rawls 1951.

inconsistency and confusion[9] (Section 10.5). I will therefore not commit myself to the Doctrine of Double Effect.

I will not presuppose any particular ethical theory, either some form of direct or indirect consequentialism, contractualism, act or rule deontology or whatever. If my conclusions fit with any particular theory, that may well strengthen the theory rather than my conclusions. My ambition is rather to get fairly strong normative conclusions from fairly modest and relatively uncontroversial normative assumptions, by appealing to conceptual arguments and empirical data. As we will often have occasion to observe, however, the debate about end-of-life decisions is hampered by a lack of empirical data about the way people actually die. Only from the Netherlands and Belgium, in particular Flanders (the Dutch-speaking part of Belgium), we seem to have an abundance of empirical data, but a permanent problem with the appeal to these data is that they depend on a classification of medical end-of-life decisions (in terms of the intentions of the doctor) that is ethically controversial and legally irrelevant, at least in the Netherlands, Belgium and many other countries. When this is taken into account, the available data tell us a different story than both advocates and opponents of the legalization of euthanasia have assumed. This applies in particular to the hypothesis, already suggested by Yale Kamisar in 1958, that a legal regime that permits the ending of lives on request will necessarily cause the spreading of a practice of ending lives without request (Chapter 10).

9 I have defended this interpretation of the law in den Hartogh 2019a.

Part I

Suicide

2 Determining the manner and time of your own death

2.1 Preferences about death

What kind of death do we actually prefer? There is by now a rich literature answering that question.[1] Its topic is usually said to be 'the good death', but we might wonder whether that is an appropriate concept. Isn't death always a bad thing for you to happen, even when all other accessible alternatives are even worse?[2] Let's therefore take 'a good death' to mean: a comparatively good death, a way of dying that is better for you, or at least not worse, than all other ways.

The scholars who have studied people's views, good sociologists as they are, standardly accentuate the individual and cultural variability of those views. Actually, however, a remarkable finding of their research is that about many components of the good death, and particularly about most components considered highly important, there is a widespread consensus among individuals and among members of different cultures. The consensus includes Europe, Australasia, Eastern Asia, North and probably Latin America. Nor do we find large differences between the perspectives of patients at the end stage of a lethal illness, people who have recently lost a close relative and the general population. On the importance of some components doctors and nurses have somewhat deviating views. What we also find, of course, is individual and cultural variation in the ranking, even of the elements that are on everyone's list.

1 For the following summary I mainly rely on surveys by Steinhauser et al. 2000 (USA); Rietjens et al. 2006 (the Netherlands); Miyashita et al. 2007 (Japan); Haishan et al. 2015 (China); Yun et al. 2018 (South Korea); and meta-reviews of the existing literature by Kehl 2006; Meier et al. 2016; Krikorian, Maldonado, Pastrana 2020. Tayeb et al. 2010 (Saudi-Arabia) show that ideals of the good death in (some parts of) the Muslim world are markedly different in many respects.

2 'A good death is an oxymoron', Scarre 2012. According to many authors finitude is a necessary structuring element of a good life. If true that would mean that in order to live well we have to die once, but not that there has to be any particular moment at which death is good.

DOI: 10.4324/9781003281115-3

As one would expect everyone finds it important to be free from pain, shortness of breath, anxiety, gloom and other forms of physical and emotional distress, but it is only in the USA that this is the most important element, at least in the view of the general population. Chinese physicians and nurses mistakenly think it is people's highest priority. A related, but actually often competing, concern is to die in a calm and quiet environment, not being connected to tubes and ventilators, not being subjected to aggressive and invasive treatment, receiving warm and affectionate care. Most people like to be hugged. They also like not to have multiple and changing care-providers, but a professional nurse and a physician who knows them and their family well, who is open to discussions about treatment and care, but also prepared to attend to other concerns, including existential ones.

Relations with one's family are high on almost everyone's list. People want to spend time with their relatives, to be able to express their feelings, to give and receive support. They want to die in the presence of their intimates. This is an essential element in Europe and North America, but it is the top priority in Asian countries. One aspect of it is not being a burden on one's family, but this is much more important in Japan and South Korea than it is in China, where people expect to be cared for by their relatives. And whatever philosophers think of the possibility of posthumous benefits, most people want to be assured that their family members will do well after their death.

There is a salient cluster of preferences surrounding the value of being in control. First, there is general agreement about the importance of the ability to stay in one's favourite place. For most people this is home, although the (large) majority will actually die in a hospital or a place of residential care.[3] The preference for home is less prominent in urban areas in the USA. People also agree about the importance of independence from others, the ability to move around and take care of oneself unsupported. This is more highly valued by older than by younger people. The ability to participate in making decisions about one's treatment and care is one of the top priorities in North America and Europe, but it is only valued by a (substantial) minority in Asia. Related to this is the wish of many (even in Japan 57% of the population), but by no means all, to be able to control the time of one's death, if necessary by suicide or euthanasia.

There is another cluster of preferences surrounding the value of a sense of closure. People generally want to be able to say goodbye to a selected group of others. Completing unfinished business, on the other hand, is much more important to some people than to others, and it is on the average more important in Western than in Asian countries. People want to get their financial affairs in order and make arrangements about their funeral and their estate. In the USA this is much more important

3 In Australia only 14% of deaths occur at home, Swerissen, Duckett 2014.

than medical personnel think it is. For many people it is also critical to have no regrets. Remarkably it is only occasionally mentioned that completing one's life can also mean to seek reconciliation and forgiveness.[4]

As a group, physicians also tend to underestimate the extent to which people value being respected as a person, not being treated as an object or a child. In Western countries this respect includes having one's individual values acknowledged, whether or not these correspond to majority values. It ranks among the highest priorities of almost everyone to maintain one's dignity and a sense of self-worth. In addition, many people value to be in a physical condition in which they are not the object of pity and don't feel ashamed of their looks. In particular in Asia people don't want to appear physically or mentally weak to their families.

An element that is highly valued by some but hardly by others is a sense of achievement. Looking back on their life as a whole some people want to feel that it was meaningful, and hence worth living, that they have contributed something to the well-being of others or society. Some people even care about leaving a legacy to posterity. In South Korea medical professionals overrate the importance of life's achievements to the general population, but in the USA they underrate it.

Religious factors are, of course, also highly variable, both on the individual and the cultural levels. 'Peace with God' is very important in the USA and South Korea, but much less so in the Netherlands, Japan and China.

Most people, particularly in Europe and North America, prefer to be fully aware of their situation until the end. That these people are not prepared 'to sacrifice lucidity for analgesia'[5] is not always sufficiently appreciated by doctors. A substantial minority, however, prefers to slide away into eternal sleep. This group is much larger in Asian countries. Even some people who prefer full awareness consider it an element of a good death not to think about their imminent death during their last days. Many of them don't even want to know that they are going to die shortly; they expect their doctors, nurses and family members not to inform them, and to make the necessary decisions about treatment and care without consulting them. This was, of course, the general practice in Western countries until the 1960s as well.[6] This is another element on which the perspectives of doctors and the general population may diverge: in China more people prefer not to be lied to than doctors think, but in Japan the reverse seems to be true.

Basically the same death-denying attitude is shown by the ideal of many people – the large majority in Japan – of 'fighting against disease' until

4 Patrick, Engelberg, Curtis 2001.

5 Steinhauser et al. 2000.

6 A landmark in this process of changing attitude is Glaser, Strauss 1965. Both modern bioethics and the hospice movement started at about the same time.

the very end.[7] They believe that 'as long as there is life there is hope', are fond of stories of miracle cures, and consider it a part of the professional morality of doctors and nurses never to dash their hope and try out every available treatment. For them there is no such thing as a transition from a curative to a palliative phase. For other people, however, it is essential to prepare for death, to know their actual situation, trying to respond to it in appropriate ways, and finally to die accepting death, or at least being resigned to it. This is an ideal with a long history, both in Hellenistic and in Christian thinking. Roberto Bellarmino claimed prisoners facing execution to be fortunate: knowing that they will die shortly, they can confess their sins and pray with an alert mind, unclouded by illness.[8]

In the Introduction I have already described some of the actions which people can take in order to come closer to their individual ideal of a (relatively) good death. Some of these actions result from a trade-off between a preference for a better and a preference for a later death. In this chapter, from Section 2.3 on, and in the next three chapters, I will focus on the clearest and simplest case of this kind: suicide.

2.2 Motives for wanting one's life to end

A number of jurisdictions permit a doctor to assist a patient who wants to end his life when some conditions have been satisfied. Even in jurisdictions in which any kind of assistance is forbidden such requests are sometimes made, and occasionally granted. Is there any correspondence between the reasons why people make such requests and the components of the 'good death' listed in the first section?[9] Many people have some wish to die, but the wish that is expressed in requests for assistance tends to be less ambivalent and more persistent than other wishes. In these respects such requests resemble the decision to end one's own life without any medical aid, but for reasons that I will discuss in the next chapter we know very little about the motivations for 'rational' suicide. That is why in this section I focus on the reasons for seeking medical aid in ending one's life.

It is often assumed that pain that cannot be controlled adequately is the major reason. But pain is actually only one in a large range of physical symptoms, lack of breath, nausea, physical exhaustion and many others that may motivate a request for physician assistance, including symptoms

7 See also Miyashita et al. 2015.

8 *The Art of Dying Well*, 1619.

9 For the following summary I mainly rely on Lavery et al. 2001; Kelly et al. 2002; Mak, Elwyn 2005; Pearlman et al. 2005; Wilson et al. 2007; Georges et al. 2007; Ganzini, Goy, Dobscha 2008a; Ganzini et al. 2009; Nissim, Gagliese, Rodin 2009; Dees 2011; Nuhn et al. 2018; Gaignard, Hurst 2019; cf. Dees 2010 for a list of relevant studies; Monforte-Royo et al. 2012; Hendry 2013 and Rodriguez-Pratt et al. 2017 for meta-reviews. Ebenau, Hasselaar, van Gurp 2017 list ideals of the good death of cancer patients.

that are side effects of medical treatment or care.[10] Normally a patient will have several of those physical symptoms, and suffering from them may be aggravated by a perceived lack of understanding by others. Nevertheless, such symptoms are rarely the only reason, and, on most reports,[11] are the most prominent concern in a minority of cases only.

Loss of autonomy or control is a more prominent motive, perhaps the most prominent one of all. Actually, the concept covers two different, although related motives: loss of elementary bodily functions (speaking, swallowing, walking, eating, getting up, going to the toilet), and as a result being dependent on the care of others, and loss of the ability to mentally cope with one's circumstances (Section 6.7). This is of course characteristic of cases of cognitive decline, but the erosion of a sense of self is also common in patients who are dying from a lethal illness.

In the last section we have seen that the wish to be able to look back on a meaningful life is an important element of a good death for a minority of people only. But the irreversible loss of meaning and purpose is a second highly prominent reason to request assistance in procuring death. It encompasses the loss of social roles, including roles within the family. It is difficult to retain your personal relations when you can hardly speak. Activities that give meaning to life are also essential for maintaining a sense of one's identity. Therefore loss of meaning tends to imply a loss of that sense as well. A third prominent reason is loss of dignity. This also covers two rather different motives: lack of social recognition and a low self-esteem but also feeling ashamed of one's appearance and condition, because of incontinence, fecal vomiting or stinking wounds. 'I don't recognize myself' is the common element. This reason is strongly connected to being dependent on the care of others.

As regards all these elements it is not only the person's present condition that counts but also, sometimes primarily, her fear for the future: more extreme suffering, increased loss of function, of independence, of social roles or of mental capacity. These expectations are strongly determined by people's personal experiences, in particular of the dying process of close relatives.[12] Things can only get worse, no hope of improvement is left, and even people who wanted to fight disease to the end may actually throw in the towel at this stage. As regards physical symptoms, the

10 See Ruijs 2012 for the full range.

11 Exceptions include Meier et al. 1998; Wilson et al. 2007; Fischer et al. 2009; Deliëns et al. 2011, 181–182. The importance of physical symptoms probably has decreased since 1998 due to improved palliative care. The importance of physical symptoms found by Fischer et al. may be due to the eligibility requirements of Swiss organizations for assisting suicide, as the authors suggest. Deliëns' report is based on physicians' reports to the Belgian Federal Commission for Euthanasia Control and Evaluation. It is well-known that doctors tend to stress physical symptoms in these reports (Section 12.3).

12 Norwood 2009, 34–38.

fear that they may become uncontrollable may even be more prominent than the experience that they are. If fear of this kind motivates an actual death wish, this may show a lack of trust.

Feeling oneself a burden on others, in particular on one's family, is also an important motive, albeit more important in American than in European reports.[13] This may reflect differences in welfare state arrangements, but another, somewhat related explanation might be that a Dutch or Belgian doctor is not likely to grant a request that is primarily motivated by this concern. If informal caregivers are overburdened, in their view, that is not a problem that should be addressed by euthanasia.[14] Nevertheless, even in Europe, death is often not only seen as a way of escaping from one's own suffering, but also of reducing the suffering of one's family. Excepting this, concerns about family relations are strangely lacking in the available reports.[15] As a quick scan of reports to the Dutch Regional Euthanasia Review Committees tells us, however, the loss of a partner, of a child, or, more generally, loneliness and social isolation are not at all uncommon motives for a euthanasia request, albeit rarely the only motive. Loneliness is also one of the most common elements in the motivation of wishes to die of people who are suffering from an accumulation of old-age ailments (Section 14.2). Moreover, most people who consider hastening their death don't want to make any decision that is not acceptable to their closest relatives and only want a euthanasia to take place if they agree to be present.[16]

Loss of meaning, independence, social recognition and a sense of self are largely consequences of the loss of functional abilities, including communication abilities. But the causal relation may sometimes be indirect, because the loss of abilities makes it more difficult or impossible to compensate for losses in social contact (Section 14.2). People often accommodate to ability impairment over time, until the accumulation of impairments reaches a threshold where they feel that they can no longer cope with it.

One element of the ideal of a good death that really hasn't any counterpart in reported motives for requesting physician-assisted death – excepting peace with God – is a sense of closure. This seems to belong to the more lofty part of the ideal that people can most easily do without. On the whole, however, we find a clear correspondence between the elements of the ideal and the reasons why people take active steps for ending

13 For a survey of available data see McPherson et al. 2007, 121–123.

14 The motive is rarely mentioned in reports of euthanasia to the Dutch review committees, Buiting et al. 2009.

15 Exceptions include Lavery et al. 2001, about patients with HIV or aids; Wilson et al. 2007. The review of available Dutch data by Roest, Trappenburg, Leget 2019 confirms the importance of family relations.

16 Norwood 2009; Roest, Trappenburg, Leget 2019; Boer, Groenewoud, de Jonge 2021 (case descriptions by relatives).

their lives with the assistance of physicians. The idea that such people have quite distinct views of the good death is mistaken.

So what differentiates people who actively pursue death from others? One might expect that they are in a worse state, suffering more severely, in particular in the final stage of a fatal illness. A Dutch study suggests that this is not the case either: both the nature and the severity of the suffering of people with and people without persistent and active death wishes may be the same.[17] If this is true, the difference is probably more a matter of a general style of coping with adverse circumstances. People who decide to end their own life may be more in the habit of taking things into their own hands in all cases.[18] They also seem to have been more actively involved than others in decision-making about their own treatment and care during their illness.[19] These may be the people who most value to be able to determine the manner and time of their own death.[20]

Against this factual background – the most common ideals of a good death, the most common motivations for actively pursuing death – I will discuss some normative questions and questions about values in the remainder of this chapter. Can it ever be prudentially wise, all things considered, to decide to shorten one's life, with or without the assistance of others? Even if it can be, and even if there is this large correspondence between ideals of the good death and the reasons for a persistent and active death wish, that doesn't mean that all such death wishes are really prudentially wise. Should we then still respect them, at least if they are voluntary and well-considered? Do people have a *right* to end their own life, even if it is unwise or immoral to do so?

2.3 Can death ever be preferable to survival?

In 1557, when, in the town of Delft, he climbed the stake on which he was about to be burned alive by the Holy Inquisition, the Zwinglian priest Angelus Merula was struck by a heart attack, from which he died instantly.[21] It seems hard to deny that this was a blessing for him.

17 Ruijs et al. 2014; cf. Kjölseth, Ekeberg, Steihaug 2010. This conclusion is more convincing as regards the nature than as regards the severity of the suffering. People may give their own suffering the highest possible score because they still haven't experienced a degree of suffering that would make them prefer death.

18 This hypothesis is confirmed by the detailed case descriptions given by the three ethnographic studies of euthanasia that have been performed in the Netherlands: Pool 1996; The 1997; Norwood 2009.

19 Ganzini et al. 2009.

20 Another differentiating factor will be whether or not physician-assisted suicide or euthanasia is accepted and a fairly common way of dying in one's social environment (Section 16.6).

21 He left a legacy to build an orphanage in his hometown of Brielle, which can still be seen there today.

Perhaps it could be objected that this is not really a case of preferring death to survival, but rather, of preferring one kind of death to another when death is imminent anyway. But if someone enters into a phase of such extreme suffering that will go on for the remainder of his life, a preference for ending that phase as quickly as possible will be only the more understandable, the more that phase will otherwise be extended over time.

Some people believe that existence itself is a benefit that has to be taken into account. Even if you have irreversibly lost all higher brain functions, including the capacity for consciousness, it will, in this view, still be good for you that your brainstem functions are still intact, supporting the ongoing capacity for spontaneous respiration and circulation. Or even, still more controversially, that respiration and circulation are artificially maintained, allowing a substantial number of other biological functions to go on.[22] The contrary and in my eyes more plausible view is that mere biological life has no intrinsic personal value at all, but only the value of a vehicle of all things that are intrinsically good for you, possibly only excepting some posthumous benefits.[23] But even if existence, whether conscious or not, is itself an element of human flourishing, that doesn't mean that Merula's death wasn't a blessing for him. That conclusion would require the stronger assumption that existence is a benefit that cannot be trumped by any amount of harm. Some philosophers accept that view, arguing that death can never be preferable on balance because life itself is a basic and therefore incommensurable good.[24] Considering the case of Merula, this is an intuitively implausible view.

Moreover, these authors subscribe to the *Doctrine of Double Effect* (Section 1.3). They hold that it is always wrong to violate, by action or omission, a basic human good *directly*, either as your final end or as a means to that end. But according to them it can be all right to act in a way that you know to cause harm to a basic good as a side effect. Hence it is always wrong to intend to end a person's life, but it can be all right to offer a patient pain-killing medicine, knowing that this will

22 As in particular Alan Shewmon has shown to be possible, Shewmon 2001, cf. den Hartogh 2019b with further references.

23 Aristotle, *Eudemian Ethics* 1214b, referred to by Echénique 2016; Glover 1977: 45–46; Raz 2001, ch. 3, Section 3; Kagan 2012, 258–262, 325–328. This view allows for the possibility, to be discussed in Chapter 9.2, that mere biological life has an intrinsic impersonal value. Gorsuch 2006, ch. 9, and many others fail to make this distinction.

24 Grisez 1970, ch. 6; Ramsey 1978; Grisez 1978; Finnis 1980, ch. 4–5; Finnis, Boyle, Grisez 1987, ch. 10–11; and many other works by these authors. In their view 'human life' refers to a bundle of valuable elements, including freedom from pain and psychological health. But each of these aspects is equally worth preserving, including the life of a patient in an irreversible comatose state (Terry Schiavo). This view has been adopted by Pope John Paul II in the encyclical *Veritatis Splendor* (1993) and can therefore be considered part of the doctrine of the Catholic church.

shorten her life. That permission, however, is subject to a proportionality requirement. And this can only mean that it has to be shown that the person's death is the 'lesser evil' in comparison with a continuation of her suffering. Ascribing an incommensurable value to anything seems to be inconsistent with a proportionality requirement.[25]

It is a more plausible view that biographical life, characterized by both consciousness and self-consciousness, has a value of its own to you, irrespective of what you are conscious of[26] (see also Section 8.5). Again, if that is true, it doesn't mean that the goodness of being (self-) conscious cannot be outweighed by the badness of the contents of your consciousness. It can be objected to the view itself that a consciousness that is absorbed by the awareness of continuous suffering that is not redeemed by any meaning that you can ascribe to your life has no personal value for you at all to begin with, not even a value that is outweighed by disvalues.[27] But this objection doesn't show that living consciously and self-consciously never has any value of its own for you, only that this value cannot properly be taken into account by mere addition. Perhaps the value of your consciousness and the value of the contents of your consciousness are to be seen as the factors x and y in the product xy. (If either of the factors is zero, the product is zero.) Suffering and meaninglessness could then bereave your biographical life of all personal value up to a threshold, but in the area beyond that threshold living a life could still have some value of its own. If you succeed to some extent, however modest, in making something of your life, coming up to its challenges, that formal achievement may add something to the value of your life, in addition to what it is that you have made of your life. An intrinsic value need not be an unconditional value.[28]

If death is sometimes preferable to survival, how do we decide whether this is the case or not? Philosophers and psychologists often talk about a 'life worth living'.[29] That phrase suggests that we consider what the

25 McCormick 1977, 110–111; den Hartogh 2019a. Grisez 1978, 56; Finnis, Boyle, Grisez 1987, 263–267, reply to this objection that determining the moral acceptability of bad side effects doesn't require the weighing of the non-moral value of goods. But the principle of fairness and similar principles they appeal to instead (that, by the way, seem to me all to require such weighing) all apply to cases in which the good and the bad effects concern different people. It is hard to see how a weighing of values can be avoided when a proportionality assessment has to be made in a single-person case. That may be the reason why the *Doctrine of Double Effect* is rarely applied to other single-person cases (Section 8.5).

26 Nagel 1970; 1986, 224–225; Frankfurt 2004, 47; Kaufmann 2016; Scheffler 2013, 198–201.

27 Raz 2001, 101, Section 5 (a consciousness that wholly consists of the permanent experience of pain); Tugendhat 2006, 28–36 (being conscious of having a completely empty life).

28 Fumagalli 2018.

29 For a systematic criticism of this concept see Fumagalli 2018.

future has in store for us, score the positive net value of the good things and the negative net value of the bad things, and calculate which of the two total scores is the highest. We get a somewhat similar picture when we consider the famous Epicurean argument against the possibility of death having any value whatsoever for us, positive, negative or even zero value. According to Epicurus death – meaning the state of being dead, not the process of dying – can have no value for us, because if you are dead you do not exist, it is not a state that can be ascribed *to you*. 'If you are, death is not, and if death is, you are not'. There is something approaching consensus in contemporary philosophy that it is true that death cannot have any intrinsic value for you. However, it is claimed, it can have a comparative value. Epicureans object that the comparison to be made is a comparison between a state of existence and a state of non-existence, but the second state is not a possible state of *you*. The standard answer is that what we are actually comparing is a longer and a shorter life, and these are both possible lives that you can live. Both scenarios will, it is suggested, have the same value during the period that is common to both. From the moment of your death in calculating the total value of the shorter scenario, no positive or negative value will be there to be taken into account. Hence everything depends on the total net value to be expected from that moment on in the longer scenario. (More on this reply to Epicurus' argument in Section 15.3.)

One problem with this account is that it presupposes at least a rough comparability of the value of the good and bad aspects of a life.[30] I already rejected the suggestion that these aspects are absolutely incomparable, but it doesn't follow that they are comparable to the extent required by the idea of a 'life worth living', or by contemporary attempts to measure that worth, for example in terms of QALY's. Goods such as autonomy and freedom from suffering may be incommensurable to a large extent. Or consider happiness and meaning as dimensions of human flourishing. The proper analysis of both concepts is controversial in itself, and it may be the case that both the questions whether a life is overall a happy one and whether it is overall a meaningful one have to be answered by taking very disparate data into account and hence themselves have no determinate answers in a large number of cases. It seems even more plausible that it is hard to measure on a single scale the contribution that happiness and meaning in a person's life make to her well-being. When Ivan Ilyich on his deathbed got into a state of despair realizing how empty his life had been, should we have tried to comfort him by pointing out that he had always been quite content with that life? Would that make him better off than a person who has made such important

30 The incommensurability of dimensions of the good life is a constant theme in the work of Joseph Raz, cf. Raz 2013 on its relevance for the morality of suicide and euthanasia.

contributions to art and science as Tchaikovsky or Wittgenstein, but has been unhappy for most of his life, or even depressed to an extent bordering on suicidality?

This problem is aggravated if it is true that living a biographical life has some value of its own, because it will again be difficult to measure that value on the same scale that is also used for measuring the value of the contents of consciousness. And even if it is true that non-existence has no positive, negative or zero value for us, it is hard for many people to fully face up to the prospect of death. We saw already that many people consider it a part of a good death never to think of their imminent death, even during their last days. The loss of one's life is, indeed, different from all other possible losses. Losses of control, coping ability, hope, meaning and dignity, as we have considered them in the last section, are all losses that are suffered by me. But how do I respond to the prospect of the loss of me? As Samuel Scheffler says:

> My only resources ... seem to involve turning back on myself a set of attitudes—such as sadness, grief, rage, anxiety—that are tailored to circumstances in which the self endures and undergoes a loss. But those attitudes become unmoored when directed toward their very subject. And this induces, or can induce, panic.[31]

There may be remnants of infantile solipsism involved in this attitude, but it is very real nonetheless, not something that people can be cured of by any dosage of Epicurean medicine. 'Nothing to be afraid of'.[32] If the prospect of non-existence has this kind of negative value for someone, how do we factor it in assessing whether survival still has a net value for him?

For these reasons it is plausible that there is often a large zone in which it is indeterminate whether someone's life is or isn't worth living, or even worth not living. In addition it can be very uncertain what the future has in store for us. Therefore there is not only a metaphysical but also a large epistemic grey zone. People often don't know for sure whether their suffering is beyond relief, but the decision to end one's life is irreversible. Hence there is often only one safe side to err on. The extent to which it may be indeterminate whether death or life is to be preferred may also help to explain the finding I reported at the end of the last section that of people in the same irreversibly bad condition, some decide to go on with their lives and other to end it. None of them need to be irrational. These considerations also help to explain why most people who after careful deliberation decide to end their lives do so with a residual ambivalence.

31 Scheffler 2013, 86; cf. Nagel 1986, 212; de Beauvoir 1972, 44; Kamm 1993, 59–60, 64–65.

32 Title of Barnes 2008.

All this, however, doesn't exclude that there are clear cases on either side of the grey zone, including cases in which death is strongly to be preferred. The death of Angelus Merula is an example. Suppose it is true that of two people in a comparable state of extreme suffering, one may decide to end her life and the other to continue living, without either of them being irrational, the choice being determined by the kind of person they are. It may then still be valuable to both of them to be able to die as they have lived,[33] or even, at this final stage, to become the kind of person they always have wanted to be. Looking back, we could then possibly say of both of them that their choice made their life as a whole more worth living (Section 16.6).

In this section, I have argued that some possible reasons for preferring death to survival are really good reasons, or at least no less valid than reasons for continuing life. But in Section 2.2, I listed the reasons why people actually prefer death, and it is still an open question whether any of these reasons are good ones. This will be the subject of the next section.

2.4 The art of dying

In Section 2.1 I have identified some points of divergence between medical professionals and the general population as regards their view about a (comparatively) good death. Elements that people valued more than doctors and nurses included maintaining mental awareness, making funeral arrangements (USA), a sense of achievement, not being a burden to one's family (USA, South Korea), freedom from pain (China) and dignity. Such discrepancies cause concern whether end-of-life care is sufficiently in line with the actual priorities of people. It should, however, be stressed that the area of convergence between professional and popular views is much larger than the area of divergence. It has been claimed that, due to the hospice movement, medical professionals have adopted an ideal of 'dying with dignity, peacefulness, preparedness, awareness, adjustment and acceptance', which is now used to discipline individual people and constrain their choices.[34] It is much easier for care-providers to deal with patients who die in the 'right way'.[35] This criticism fails to acknowledge that this ideal actually is widely shared by people, even on a global scale, and requires physicians to overcome to some extent their traditional biomedical short-sightedness.

However, the criticism is not totally unfounded either: there has been a tendency within the palliative care movement to prescribe to patients 'correct' preferences about death and dying. One element of the movement's conception of the good death that is sometimes imposed

33 Raz 2013.
34 Hart, Sainsbury, Short 1998.
35 Cottrell, Duggleby 2016 with further references.

on people is the idea that suffering is something to be avoided at all costs. The pursuit of that aim may easily become counterproductive, for example because patients may blame themselves for not being a good patient if the pursuit fails, or because the permanent assessment of their condition that the pursuit requires may be experienced by them as burdensome and intrusive.[36] Some patients may be tired of dying rather than tired of living. More fundamentally, people may have good reasons for preferring to retain full consciousness in spite of its painfulness (Section 8.3).

The conception of the good death that in many countries is still dominant in palliative care may also become oppressive by denouncing all death wishes as signs of mental illness, or at least as resting on a lack of appreciation of the proper value of life[37] (Section 6.8). In the last section I argued that this view is mistaken. Nevertheless, it is not always an easy question whether the aim of professional medical activity should be fixed by individual choice, rather than by individual benefit. Isn't there sometimes something to be said for good old medical paternalism? To be sure, many of the priorities that I have listed in Section 2.1 will meet universal recognition and sympathy. Who will dispute that people should, if possible, be left to die at home, in the company of their family and friends, that they should be treated with concern and respect, and that it is to be welcomed if they are able to complete unfinished business? Other preferences, however, are more controversial. Even these preferences cannot simply be brushed aside, of course, but it is not self-evidently true either that doctors should always respect them. A clear example is provided by a dying person's supposed wish to die in ignorance. How do we verify the assumption to begin with, if we didn't have the opportunity to do so at an early stage of his illness? Another clear example is the wish to try out every available treatment option, whatever the balance of possible benefits and burdens. Arguably doctors should adhere to the maxim 'first, do no harm' in these cases (Section 9.5).

Other elements of people's conception of a good death may be quite understandable in themselves, but questionable when they lead to death wishes. As we have seen, a major motive of people requesting medical assistance in ending their lives is the loss of the ability to take care of oneself, even as regards the most basic elements of self-care. You may be bedridden and incontinent, you may not be able on your own to take food or drink, or even to remove a fly that tickles your nose. When this happens, professional

36 Streeck 2019, with further references.

37 That many people don't let themselves be 'disciplined' by this element of the ideal of the good death of end-of-life care-providers is observed by Cottrell, Duggleby 2016, but then criticized by them as a product of neo-liberal ideology that has no space for a 'natural' dying process. This two-pronged criticism seems to leave dying patients in a Catch 22-predicament.

or informal caregivers have to step in. As a result they will largely determine what happens within the most intimate sphere of your life. But if that is a reason for you to say 'I'd rather be dead', we might want to argue with you. Look, we might want to say, you seem to have lived your whole life in an illusion of self-sufficiency. But human beings are always vulnerable, every moment they may be the victim of an accident that makes them dependent on the compassion and care of others, good Samaritans or professionals. As the Stoics could tell you, it is precisely this illusion of self-sufficiency that makes you a slave of Fortune. Rather you show true independence if you are able to cope with your condition, and with the cutbacks on your privacy it implies, even to the point of being able to be thankful to your nurse, or to correct her if she is unduly paternalistic.[38]

A related aspect of suffering, both of the very old and of the dying, is being ashamed of one's physical appearance because of incontinence or disfigurement. Such problems are aggravated if you need others to handle them.[39] But again a Stoic would observe that it isn't your fault that you have got into that condition, you cannot be blamed for it and therefore it cannot be a proper object of feelings of guilt or shame. You don't lose your dignity at all; you may rather uphold it by the composed way in which you respond to the situation. It is a mistake to think that 'dignity resides in the bladder and the rectum'.[40]

And if you are no longer able to do what you always did, the activities that gave meaning to your life and opportunities for enjoyment: climbing mountains, writing books, directing the canteen of your soccer club? That can also happen at every moment of your life, and it is part of the task of living to cope with such losses. Even if you irreversibly lose every possibility of being of use to others? Perhaps you never completely lose that possibility. It may be of value to others to see you retain some kind of inner peace and harmony even in very difficult conditions. But even if you have to withdraw from the stage of your life into the wings altogether, one way of going on is to stay there and observe with interest how the world is going on without you.[41]

Such considerations could be generalized. At the end of your life it is to be expected that illness will cause a continuous series of deprivations: of social relations, of autonomy, even of the ability to provide elementary

38 Boer 2012. "Loss of control is part of life", according to a Dutch physician who refused a patient's request for euthanasia for that reason, ten Cate et al. 2017; cf. van Tol et al. 2011, 132.

39 Cf. case 2016–74 on the website of the Dutch Regional Euthanasia Review Committees: facial disfigurement experienced by a patient who highly valued her looks.

40 Ackerman 1998, 151. She refers to human dignity, but the point rather applies to one's dignity as an individual person, not as a human being. Human dignity cannot be lost.

41 Cf. Tugendhat 2006, 51.

self-care and of feeling well in your own body instead of burdened and 'filthy'. And every time again you have to go through a mourning process in order to cope with the loss. But perhaps you could cut short that whole process by realizing and accepting that this is what happens in the final stage of human life and that it makes no sense to resent the unavoidable. The only proper response is *amor fati*. With the exception of pain and other physical symptoms all these conditions concern the absence of a good, not the presence of an evil. What is positively bad is only your emotional response to them.

You could describe a basically similar attitude in terms derived from the Christian rather than the Stoic tradition. The *Ars Moriendi* (ca. 1415) describes the typical 'sins' of old age: lack of faith ('my suffering is senseless'), despair (instead of acceptance), greed ('I have to hand in everything I had'), lack of patience, and pride (resenting being dependent on the care of others, resenting your bodily decay).[42]

If someone succeeds in accepting the unavoidable, or at least to resign to it without bitterness and anger, that is admirable. But that attitude is not only compatible with a stance of perseverance but also with a well-considered choice for death.[43] For the *Ars Moriendi* that is of course the summum of impatience, 'ending your life as the pagans do'. But for Lucretius it is rather a kind of greed or gluttony always to want more of life.[44] 'I had a good life, life has nothing more to offer me than serious suffering, I have to die soon anyway, so why not now?' That your life is completed is, as I will argue (Section 14.3), an odd reason for preferring death to life, but it may well describe a possible response to the existence of better reasons. A decision to end one's life is not necessarily a weak protest against Fate of people who are unable to take their losses. Whether you decide to soldier on or not, both decisions can be either a successful exercise of the art of dying or a failure in that respect, and this in basically similar ways. To accept the unavoidable requires a high level of self-reflection and inner freedom, both if it leads you to quietly wait for death, or if it leads you to greet death as an old friend and go gently into that good night.[45] What old age requires is graceful disengagement, and a choice for death can be the ultimate form of letting go.[46]

One possible reason for you to prefer that option is that it can be a realistic prognosis that you will lose your coping ability: because of pain, breathlessness or other physical symptoms that cannot adequately be

42 *Tractatus artis bene moriendi*, Chapter 2.

43 Kjölseth, Ekeberg, Steinhaug 2010.

44 Lucretius, *De rerum natura*, 3, 935–936.

45 As Vink 2016a observed, all 26 people interviewed by Van Wijngaarden 2016 (see Chapter 14, footnote 37) had a disaffected and fearful attitude to their life. Vink comments that this isn't necessarily the case with all people who 'consider their life to be completed'.

46 Nissim, Gagliese, Rodin 2009.

relieved, permanent physical and mental fatigue, loss of cognitive abilities and even emotional changes, sometimes as a result of medication. Such circumstances also underline that it may be possible to describe an ideal way of dealing with the conditions of a fatal illness or old age, but that it would be unreasonable to derive any practical conclusions for the individual case from that ideal. It is probably superhuman not to feel any shame if your facial expression has been changed by paralysis, even if there is nothing that you can be blamed for. And if you have lived in an illusion of self-sufficiency for your whole life, at an age of 90 you can hardly be expected to acquire a Stoic conception of autonomy. The very fact that loss of meaning, of control and of personal dignity are such common motives for people to long for death should be a reason for others, including doctors and nurses, not to be moralistic about the values underlying that desire. We should recognize that there is a plurality of basic goods that cannot all be realized within one life, and that can make mutually exclusive options equally eligible for choice.[47]

This does not mean that we should abstain from judging people's priorities altogether. For example, old people should not go into the wings too quickly, but a certain amount of disengagement is appropriate in the 'fourth phase' of life.[48] Whether a person's suffering is 'unbearable' is to a certain extent a normative question: it is unbearable if we cannot reasonably expect her to bear it.[49] And we may indeed expect old people to give up on some of the goods of life without immediately wanting to be dead. On the other hand, the psychological resources people need for timely and appropriate disengagement are unevenly distributed.[50] Inner freedom is largely a gift. The choice for death is not beyond critical assessment, but in making such assessments, we have to take into account both the plurality of values and the point of view of the particular person making that choice, as it is determined by his personality and biography (see also Sections 8.5, 12.7).

2.5 Is there a right to suicide?

Values are important, but so are rights. Your choice for death may be open to criticism, but what follows from that? In particular, in pursuing a good death, do you have, or should you have, the right to decide to end your life and act on your decision? This question is largely independent of the prudential and even the moral evaluation of your decision: if you

47 Raz 1997.

48 Callahan 1990 rightly recommends detachment, but perhaps at a too early stage.

49 Wijsbek 2012b.

50 You would need a thorough knowledge of a person's personality and life history in order to determine his place in this distribution, often a more thorough knowledge than you can possibly acquire in a way that is compatible with respect for his privacy. But in this section I have abstracted from such epistemic limitations.

have the right to end your own life, you are free to do so, whatever others, wrongly or even rightly, think of it. You need no right to make a proper decision. Nevertheless, whether you have such a right is also partly a moral question: are there, all things considered, decisive reasons for recognizing such a right? If there are such reasons, but the right is nevertheless not recognized by the law, you have only a moral claim, not a full-blooded right. Rights are political creatures. If, on the other hand, the law assigns you a right, but without sufficient moral justification, you have an inverted commas' 'right' only. A right, properly so-called, requires both moral legitimacy and social recognition.[51]

By now many states recognize a competent patient's right to refuse life-prolonging treatment. It may seem that most jurisdictions also acknowledge a right to suicide, although suicide is still illegal in most, probably all predominantly Islamic countries, and in some other ones, including the Bahamas, Cyprus, Georgia, Ghana, Guyana, Malawi, Myanmar, North Korea, Papua New Guinea, St Lucia, Singapore, South Sudan, Tanzania, Tonga and Uganda.[52] However, that an action is not punishable doesn't mean that you have a right to act in that way. The lawgiver may believe that suicide is always something to be deplored and, if possible, prevented, but at the same time consider that penalizing it is not an effective way of reducing its incidence, perhaps because it is in many cases, if not all, to be considered an expression of mental illness. If a right to suicide exists, there must be at least some suicides that the state has no moral opinion about. If you plan to end your own life, you could claim others not to interfere in the implementation of your plan, at least when there is no doubt that your decision has been freely made after due reflection. Whether recognition of the right should have other normative consequences, I will consider in Chapters 4 and 5.

Do we have such a right, or at least the corresponding moral claim? If we have, the right is most plausibly considered an element of the right to self-determination.[53] That right should be understood as a bundle of normative assets that together delineate a private domain within which it is up to you to decide what you do. You are not only free to make these decisions, you also have the authority to make them. That means, in the first place, that other people have corresponding duties, at least the duty not to interfere in the execution of your plan. In the second place it means that the reasons why they shouldn't interfere are *content-independent* ones. They do not depend on the prudential or moral quality of your decisions.[54]

51 Feinberg 1973, 63–64; O'Neill 1996, 131–135; Beitz 2009, 194–195.

52 Mishara, Weinstub 2016. In some of these countries (Guyana, Lebanon) the law is rarely if ever enforced.

53 It could also be seen as an element of the right to life, if that right is understood, perhaps on a choice-theory of rights, as being exercisable, or at least waivable (Section 9.5).

54 Hart 1958, 102; 1982, 18, 254; Raz 1972, 95; den Hartogh 2002, 114.

Why are these reasons content-independent? The primary explanation is that your right is meant to protect an area of private sovereignty, and private sovereignty is highly valuable, both in itself and because of the social status it implies, of being an equal among equals. It is in itself an essential element of a good life. A secondary explanation might be that we wouldn't trust others, in particular the state, to make correct judgements.[55] Even if we know by now that in identifying their own good and the best ways to realize it people are very prone to make mistakes,[56] they may still do better than others. In this case, allowing people to act on their own ideal of the good death may increase their opportunities to come closer to it.

It is important to observe that the authority, assigned by a right, need not be unlimited. As a matter of fact it never is.[57] For example, property-rights are always an important element of your right to self-determination, but your authority to decide what to do with your possessions is limited in all kinds of ways. If you are the owner of a registered monument, you are not permitted to tear it down. Even your right to bodily integrity is limited: the police may require you to undergo a blood-test in order to check whether you have drunk too much before starting to drive. The state may introduce mandatory vaccination against a very dangerous virus like Ebola. All such limitations, however, have to be explicitly stipulated by the law. You are allowed to do everything you want to do with your monumental mansion that is not prohibited. It is within that area that your decision has a content-independent authority.

Such limitations do not only have to be explicitly stated, they must also be justified. The default is always that you are free to do what you want, and there have to be good reasons for restricting that freedom. And it is much easier to justify restrictions on property-rights than on the right to bodily integrity. The moral force of the default is much stronger in the second case than in the first. In order to forbid you to tear down your house, it is enough that the house contributes to the aesthetic value and historical identity of a townscape, but in order to coerce you to undergo a blood-test, it has to be shown that drunken driving endangers other people's lives. So there is a hierarchical order of layers within your private domain: your body is more stringently protected than your goods. It is more essentially yours. But within that order your existence is the apex. If it is asked what is most essentially yours, the answer is: your life.

Consider the following analogy. Of any possible system of rights the right to personal freedom is an essential element. If you are a chattel slave, you have no rights at all, even if your master permits you to make all those decisions that bearers of the right to personal freedom are

55 See Griffin 2008, 79–80, on the reasons why rights resist trade-offs.
56 Tiemeyer, Thomas, Prast 2009.
57 Den Hartogh 2002, Chapters 6 and 7.

permitted to make. For you are only conditionally permitted to make those same decisions, the permission can be withdrawn at any moment. In a somewhat similar way it might be claimed that your right to end your own life is an essential element of any possible bundle of rights that can constitute a right to self-determination. The analogy is not perfect, because if you don't possess this particular right, that doesn't mean that you have no other rights, because the option to exercise any of them would be merely conditional. But if you don't have the option to end your life, that implies a restriction on all other options you have. For every decision you make it makes a difference whether it is of your own free will or not that you are there to make that decision. You may be free to stay in your own house or move to a hospice, but perhaps what you really want is not having to make that decision at all, but to be left to die. You are then not really the owner of your own life, but at best only a trustee. If people have no moral claim to kill themselves, they may still be permitted to make all kinds of important self-regarding decisions, but not the one important decision that is logically prior to all those other decisions.[58] "These people are trapped".[59]

If the right to end one's own life is part of the right to self-determination, it is only available on the same conditions as other parts: you can only exercise it by a decision that is voluntary and competently made. It is also possible for your right to conflict with the rights of others, or with other basic moral considerations, for example about human dignity, that cannot be cashed out in terms of individual rights. These issues remain to be discussed at a later stage (Section 5.2; Section 9.3).

It is a stock-in-trade criticism of this conception of personal sovereignty that it reflects an individualistic illusion of autonomy that has nothing to do with the actual realities of living, or dying.[60] That criticism, however, fails to distinguish between the ideal of an autonomous life and the right to self-determination.[61] Being autonomous requires a modicum of independence from the views and wishes of others, for otherwise your decisions wouldn't display any consistency, but the degree of independence required is only a moderate one.[62] Moreover, it is undeniable that in order to be autonomous you actually, and even necessarily, have to live in interaction with others, to communicate with them, sometimes to

58 I don't claim that the decision to continue or discontinue living is necessarily the most important decision for you to make. Whether to die now or in three days or three weeks, time doesn't really determine the overall shape of your life like the decision to have children or the decision to have your uterus removed. It is therefore also false that euthanasia is the most momentous decision a doctor can ever have to make, van Dantzig 1999.

59 Benatar 2013, 241.

60 E,g. Cottrell, Duggleby 2016.

61 Feinberg 1986, ch. 18.

62 Feinberg, *ibid.*

compete with them and often to be supported by them. Almost all decisions that you autonomously make are largely a function of the influence of others, accumulated throughout your life. Hence the truly autonomous person conceives of himself in decision-making as a social being, not only because he owes duties to others, but primarily because relations with others are constitutive of his personal identity.[63] These relational aspects of autonomy will turn out to be essential to a proper understanding of what is involved in the right to suicide (Section 5.1). It is also a characteristic of a well-considered decision to end your life that it is made in dialogue with others, attributing a lot of weight to their views (Section 3.5). Nevertheless it should be up to you to determine that weight. A relational conception of autonomy doesn't imply that you don't have an exclusive authority to make your own self-regarding decisions. On the contrary, the essential social relations between autonomous persons will be symmetrical ones, relations between equals, and this requires each of them to have this authority. Some people have a stake in you, but they don't own you. It is the free interaction between adult people that best promotes their autonomy, as well as, at least in some cases, their other interests, including their interest in dying well. That requires the mutual recognition of individual rights to self-determination. Hence the supposed antithesis between recognition of a right to suicide and of the relational character of autonomy is spurious.

Does the law anywhere recognize a right to suicide? Jurisdictions that criminalize suicide clearly don't, and we have already seen that jurisdictions that don't criminalize it do not necessarily recognize it either. In its landmark decision *Vacco v Quill* (1997) the US Supreme Court explicitly denied that such a right was protected by the US Constitution, and in particular by the 14th Amendment.[64] It was therefore a bold step when the European Court of Human Rights in *Haas v Switzerland* (2011) admitted that the right to respect for a private and family life (Art. 8 of the *European Convention of Human Rights*) implies 'the right to determine the manner and time of one's own death'. The Court added that this right, like any other right, is 'concrete and effective', not merely 'theoretical and illusory'.[65]

63 Mackenzie, Stoljar 2000; Rössler 2017, ch. 8.

64 *Vacco v Quill*, 512, U.S. 793 (1997). In *Obergefell v Hodges*, 135 S. Crt 2584 (2015) on same-sex marriage the Court subscribed to a more expansive understanding of protected liberty interests, but it is improbable that the Court in its present composition would overrule *Vacco*.

65 In *Pretty v UK* (April 29 (2002), nr. 2346/02) the ECHR already agreed that mrs. Pretty "is prevented by law from exercising her choice to avoid what she considers will be an undignified and distressing end to her life", adding that "the court is not prepared to exclude that this is an interference with her right to respect for private life." But 'is not prepared to exclude' doesn't seem to be interchangeable with 'acknowledges'.

Unfortunately, until now the right *is*, on the whole, merely theoretical and illusory, at least in the case law of the Court. Art. 8 also stipulates that interference by a public authority with the exercise of the right is allowed if it is in accordance with the law and necessary in a democratic society for a limited number of policy aims, including 'the protection of the rights and freedoms of others'. And the Court, perhaps inevitably, recognizes that states have a 'wide margin of appreciation' in determining which limitations of the right to suicide are 'necessary' for this reason. The Court, therefore, has rejected the claims of the appellants in all the cases in which an appeal to this right has been made, starting with Mr. Haas' claim to get access to lethal drugs with no other condition than cooperating in a test of his mental capacity (Section 5.6). Even the claim of Mr. Nicklinson to get such access was rejected, although it was considered legally valid by the English Supreme Court, which only decided not to enforce the claim in deference to the authority of Parliament to reconsider the prohibition of physician-assisted suicide itself.[66] We may hope that the Court would accept the claim of a citizen of Cyprus that the prohibition of suicide in that country violates Art. 8. But a claim for compensation for interference in an attempted suicide would almost certainly be rejected, as would any claim for access to lethal drugs, or for allowing close relatives and friends to play an active role in the implementation of a suicide plan. Hence even in Europe the right to suicide is still hardly anything more than a moral claim. Canada's *MAID* law (2016), on the other hand, arose out of the finding of its Supreme Court in *Carter v Canada* declaring the blanket prohibition of Medical Assistance in Dying to contravene Section 7 of the *Canadian Charter of Rights and Freedoms*. Echoing the language of *Haas*, the Court considered that people should not be deprived of 'the ability to bring a peaceful end to their lives at a time and in the manner of their own choosing'.[67]

In this chapter I have first shown that there is a clear correspondence between common ideals of a (comparatively) good death and the most common motives of pursuing death. That is a reason to believe that these motives are often at least intelligible. It doesn't by itself show that they are also rational. I considered and rejected one argument purporting to show that they are never rational. Of some of these motives, however, for example the wish not to be dependent on the care of others or the dislike of physical disfigurement, one might wonder whether they would be recognized in the best defensible account of the art of dying. But even such motives can often be traced to constitutive aspects of a person's

66 *Nicklinson & Lamb v UK* (July 16 (2015) nrs. 2478/15, 1787/15). See also *Pretty* (footnote 65), *Gross v Switzerland* (May 14 (2013), nr. 67810/10), *Koch v Germany* (July 19 (2012), nr. 497/09).

67 2015 SCC 5, at para. 14. For Germany see Section 16.1, for Austria *ibid.*, footnote 6.

identity as it has been determined by her personality and biography. We should also take into account that there is a plurality of basic goods that cannot all be realized within one life, and that can make mutually exclusive options equally eligible for choice. Some reasons for preferring death to survival, e.g. the wish not to lose one's coping resilience, may be elements of such packages.

But appealing to a structural account of the idea of a personal domain, I have also argued that people have a right, or should have a right, to end their own lives as an integral part of their right to self-determination. Hence, even if your choice for death is rationally criticizable in terms of your own basic values, that choice, as long as it is voluntary and made with sufficient decisional capacity, is protected by that right. In Chapters 4 and 5, I will discuss what it should mean to recognize your right to determine the manner and time of your own death. At that stage I will also start to consider whether this right also implies the power to give other people, either friends or other intimates, or care-providers, in particular physicians, permission to assist you in ending your life. That discussion will only be completed in Chapter 9.

3 The invisibility of rational suicide[1]

3.1 The problem

Read any number of texts on suicidology.[2] The picture you will get of suicide is the following. A 'suicidal ideation' normally is the result of a psychiatric illness, rarely a psychosis, sometimes borderline or an anti-social personality disorder and most often a form of treatment-resistant depression or bipolar disorder. In the majority of cases people who seem to attempt to kill themselves do not unambiguously want to be dead. The action should rather be understood as a 'cry for help', or as a gamble: it is okay if they die, but also okay, perhaps better, if the people around them understand that they really are in a miserable condition requiring help, or at least recognition. Even if they really intend to kill themselves, they don't act on a settled plan, but most of the time impulsively, having made the final decision less than an hour before the actual action.[3] Of course, they have considered it many, many times before, they have longed for death, but until now shied away from bringing it about. Or they have only made unsuccessful attempts. Because of this lack of planning, they tend to use means of killing themselves that happen to be at hand, and these are almost always violent means, means that cause considerable damage to their bodies or some severe suffering before they actually die. Drowning, shooting, hanging themselves, throwing themselves from a high building or a bridge or before the train. They almost never discuss their plans with friends or family. Whether a 'rational suicide' ever occurs is controversial, but if it does, at most in 5–10% of the cases. "Suicide

1 An earlier version of this chapter has been published before (den Hartogh 2016d). It is a pleasure to thank an anonymous referee of *Bioethics* for his or her exceptionally thorough and helpful comments.

2 For example, such classical works as Shneidman 1996; Jamison 1999; Joiner 2005.

3 Joiner 2011, 73–74; Simon et al. 2001. The literature about suicide and impulsivity is somewhat confusing because the concept of impulsivity is neither clearly defined nor consistently operationalized, Gvion, Apter 2011.

DOI: 10.4324/9781003281115-4

is a complication of psychiatric disorders".[4] In the tradition of Western thought about suicide since Augustine, this is the end point of a development, beginning with the Puritans – for example Richard Burton, *The Anatomy of Melancholy*, 1621 – in which suicidality was no longer primarily understood as a sin but rather as an illness.[5]

Read any number of files from the Dutch review committees for euthanasia,[6] and you get a totally different picture. In all cases in which a request for euthanasia has been granted, both the doctor and at least one independent colleague who has been consulted have judged the request to be well-considered.[7] Most of these cases concern patients suffering from a lethal illness, the large majority being in the terminal stage of that illness, the minority already suffering from severe physical symptoms. Most members of the remaining group are very old people, handicapped by an accumulation of the typical ailments of old age, in particular restricted sight, hearing and mobility (Section 14.2). All these people have considered their condition and possible options for the future explicitly, realistically and repeatedly, and have arrived at the stable conclusion that there is no other way out of their suffering but death. They may have some residual ambivalence about this decision, but that is only an indication of the fact that the decision really is the outcome of a process of weighing pros and cons. During that process they have talked a lot with their family and friends, and usually also with their doctor. They have not even considered killing themselves by violent means. Family members remember these days as strongly reinforcing their mutual connectedness, often as a kind of celebration of family bonds.[8] Normally there is no history of mental illness, but if there is, both the doctor who has to decide about the request and the independent colleague who has to be consulted by legal requirement have established that at present they are sufficiently competent to make the decision. Often that judgement has also been confirmed by at least one psychiatrist.

The combination of these two findings is puzzling. Suicide and euthanasia (in the Netherlands supplemented by a small number of cases of physician-assisted suicide) are both ways of implementing a decision to end one's life; the only difference between them being that in the case of euthanasia carrying out that decision is delegated to a physician.

4 Mann 2002, 308. In a meta-review of 154 psychological autopsy studies, Lonnqvist 2009 found a median proportion of 91% of suicides identified as being committed by people diagnosed with mental disorder.

5 Ferngren 1989; Minois 1999; Baumann 2001; Watt 2004.

6 The files are available in Dutch on http://www.toetsingscommissieseuthanasie.nl; for English summaries of the most interesting cases see the link *Annual reports*.

7 Whether a decision or request is rational or well-considered is a matter of the role of the agent's beliefs and values in his decision-making, not necessarily in his conscious deliberation, Brandt 1975; Wittwer 2013; cf. Section 11.6.

8 Norwood 2009.

How is it possible that suicides are seldom rational and requests for euthanasia that have been granted almost without exception are? In 2020 the number of registered suicides in the Netherlands amounted to 1825, the number of reported cases of physician-assisted death to 6938, on a total number of 169,000 deaths.[9]

In most countries in the world physicians are legally prohibited to help a patient to end his life. That doesn't mean, of course, that they never do it, but the available data, limited though they are, suggest that such assistance is far more often given in the Netherlands and Flanders than it is elsewhere.[10] But if doctors don't help, we would expect a substantial number of the patients who get no such help, or don't ask for it because they already anticipate a refusal, to help themselves. In that case, how is it possible that in these countries 'almost everyone who has a physical illness and subsequently commits suicide also has a psychiatric illness'[11] and therefore should be presumed to have made up his mind in an irrational way? Suppose that in the Netherlands physician-assisted death would be forbidden in all forms and that only 25% of the patients who now receive assistance would then decide to end their own lives. That would already almost amount to the number of suicides registered at present. Presumably their decision would then be as rational as it is now.

Why am I interested in this problem? We have seen in the last chapter that a shorter life is sometimes to be preferred, at least not dispreferred, to any longer life that is still accessible to the agent. We have also seen that everyone has, or should have, the right to make that kind of judgement and act on it by ending his own life, on his own free will and after due reflection. These conclusions would, however, be of limited interest if in actual practice rational suicides hardly if ever occurred. But that is still the dominant view in suicidology, and in many countries, also in both medicine and law, as well as probably in the general population. By discussing the problem that I have outlined I hope to be able to test that view.

3.2 The rationality of requests for euthanasia

Is it true that requests for euthanasia that are granted by Dutch doctors are mostly well-considered? The question is almost never considered by suicidologists. This is also true as regards requests that are granted by doctors in any other jurisdiction that permits euthanasia or physician-assisted suicide

9 RTE Annual Report 2020.

10 van der Heide et al. 2003; Emanuel et al. 2016.

11 Jamison 1999, 102–103, with references. Jamison adds that some medical conditions, in particular temporal lobe epilepsy, Huntington's disease, multiple sclerosis, spinal cord injury, brain cancer, HIV/AIDS and other STD's significantly increase the risk of suicide. On his view that is to be explained by the fact that these conditions assault the brain. He doesn't consider the possibility that the very *prospect* of that assault may provide an intelligible reason to kill oneself.

under some conditions. One interesting exception is a passage in Thomas Joiner's important book *Myths about suicide*.[12] According to Joiner it is a robust finding of suicidology that no more than 10% of suicides can be considered rational ones. His own belief is that this figure is too high: there are no rational suicides at all. The only fact that tempts him to back off from this position is that under the Oregon *Death with Dignity Act* a number of patients – 49 in 2007, 245 in 2020[13] – have been given drugs to end their lives by physicians who have screened these patients on mental disorders. But at the end of the day Joiner remains sceptical about the rationality of these requests. He points out that patients who do not fully satisfy the criteria for a psychiatric diagnosis, in particular the diagnosis 'depressive disorder', may satisfy some of these criteria and therefore can be said to have a partial syndrome, even if not a full-blown disorder. The Oregon patients may for example satisfy the following criteria: suicidal ideation (by definition), sadness and sleep disturbance, even if they don't exhibit anhedonia, appetite disturbance, concentration problems, guilt feelings, psychomotor retardation or agitation. But even if only this partial syndrome can be ascribed to them, we have reason, Joiner thinks, to doubt the rationality of their decision.

Now it seems that if your terminal illness[14] causes you to suffer to such an extent that you decide that death is to be preferred to survival, you can hardly be expected to be merry and cheerful. In that case sleeping problems will also be normal, if they are not already to be explained as symptoms of your physical illness.[15] Hence Joiner's quasi-diagnosis appears almost fully to rest on the mere fact of 'suicidal ideation'. This means that his ascription of a subthreshold depressive syndrome to the Oregon patients is a tautology.[16]

Joiner believes that his analysis is confirmed by the fact that many cancer patients in the same stage of their illness as the people who make requests for lethal drugs do not make such requests. The major motives of the people who do are loss of autonomy, decreased ability to participate in activities that make life enjoyable and loss of dignity. Most people, he concedes, readily understand these motivations, but the fact remains that they are not endorsed by those other patients who are equally ill and in pain.[17] This difference, however, only shows that it is not illness and its symptoms as such that determine a person's suffering, but the meaning these symptoms have for her, and that this meaning depends on her values, biography and

12 Joiner 2011, 186–193.
13 Out of an annual number of deaths of 40,200, Oregon Health Authority 2020.
14 In Oregon prescriptions for lethal drugs can only be obtained by patients with a life expectancy of max. six months.
15 Block 2000.
16 As Joiner more or less concedes, without drawing any consequences.
17 Cf. Jamison 1999, 86ff, for a similar argument.

personality (and the quality of the care she receives), including, as Joiner recognizes, her mental strength and resilience. It doesn't show that the people who make the requests are mentally disturbed after all. Why is it pathological for a person to consider it unbearable suffering to have a face disfigured by stinking wounds, if she has been a model all her life and has always very much valued her appearance (Chapter 2, footnote 39)? The larger part of our thoughts and actions are to be explained by personal factors. That doesn't make these thoughts and actions pathological.

Some relevant personality traits could be described as personality disorders. A person may for example be more prone to being and feeling lonely than people with normal social capacities. But when these traits are virtually unchangeable and co-define that person's identity, this diagnosis by itself doesn't make a choice for death irrational.[18]

Suicidal ideation and behaviour do indeed belong to the most prominent criteria for a diagnosis of depressive disorders, but in the *DSM-V* (2013), it is also seen as a cross-cutting issue of a range of mental disorders, including anorexia nervosa, schizophrenia and posttraumatic stress disorder. For that reason the *DSM-V* introduced a separate 'suicidal behaviour disorder', mainly identified by a suicide attempt within the last two years, as a subject for further study.[19] One of the reasons is that about 10% of the people who commit suicide have not been diagnosed as having any other mental disorder. Obviously, this proposal presupposes that suicidality as such is pathological. Hence in the future we may expect it to be a 'robust finding' of suicidology that rational suicides do not exist.

On Joiner's view all suicides are motivated by a combination of two facts: that one doesn't truly 'belong', that is to say: has no significant social relations, and that one is a burden to others. He immediately stresses that these are only 'facts' in the agent's own perception; actually, these perceptions are always mistaken.[20] Are they? Did Captain Oates make a mistake when he thought he endangered Scott's expedition? In the town of Rotterdam recently the body of a woman was found who had been dead for ten years and had not been missed by anybody. Would she have been mistaken if she had considered herself socially isolated on the day of her death? These are extreme cases. The sober fact is that many people, in particular many sick and elderly people, are extremely lonely, and fully dependent on the care of others that they will never be able to reciprocate, often seven days, 24 hours a day. Similar observations can be made about other perceptions that motivate death wishes, as we have seen: loss of meaning, loss of autonomy, loss of dignity. These perceptions are not always veridical, but, unfortunately, they often are. If they weren't, not only the choice for euthanasia but also the choice for refusal of treatment or for deep sedation

18 Wijsbek 2012a.
19 *DSM-V*, 801.
20 Joiner 2005, 99, cf. van Orden et al. 2010.

until death (which implies a biographical death) would much more often be irrational than is commonly supposed.[21]

The same unexamined assumption can be found in the work of the eminent suicidologist Edwin Shneidman. Interestingly in his book *The Suicidal Mind* he never mentions mental illness.[22] Rather he considers suicide to be an understandable response to a condition of frustrated psychological needs (for affiliation, recognition or autonomy), leading to immense psychological pain. Nevertheless, he agrees with Joiner that this response always involves a defect in deliberation that he identifies as constricted, black-white thinking, disabling the person to consider possible alternatives to death as a way out from her dire condition. But how does he know that there always are such alternatives to be considered and preferred?

In his *Psychological Pain Survey* Shneidman takes a certain episode from a Nazi camp, now generally known as Sophie's Choice, as his reference point, the highest point on a scale of 1–9, on which subjects with suicidal thoughts are asked to score themselves, reporting thereby, as he says, their 'pain of excessively felt shame, guilt, fear, anxiety, loneliness, angst of growing old or of dying badly'.[23] But the choice of this reference point itself reflects an acknowledgement that the highest possible level of psychological pain is an appropriate response to that particular vignette case. So how can he be sure in advance, without considering the condition to which any particular score is a response, that the negative emotions it reports are 'excessive'? The answer must be that it is the very fact that the person has suicidal thoughts that tells him this. 'Never kill yourself while you are suicidal'.[24] That is a nice summary of the tautology involved in this way of thinking.

As I reported in Section 2.2, it is only in a minority of the cases that pain, lack of breath, fatigue and other physical symptoms are at the core of a person's motivation to request euthanasia or a physician's assistance in ending her life. It has occasionally been argued that this very fact 'proves' that most of these requests are caused by mental illness after all.[25] That argument relies on the same presupposition: you must be mentally ill either to think that meaning, autonomy, dignity and hope have gone forever from your life or to conclude from that thought that it would be better for you to die. "Much of the decision to die is in the constructing of events, and most minds, when healthy, do not construe any event as devastating enough to warrant suicide".[26]

21 Mayo 1986, 150.
22 In Shneidman 1981 he called the supposedly strong correlation between suicide and mental illness, one of the 'fables around suicide'.
23 Shneidman 1996, 13.
24 Shneidman 1996, 166.
25 E.g., Emanuel 1997.
26 Jamison 1999, 91.

The view that in all, or even most of the 6900 Dutch cases, the patient's decision-making authority has been compromised by mental illness, at least of the partial syndrome variety, is implausible, because it depends on taking the very request of the patient as an indication of pathology. This conclusion is compatible with the view that in some cases Dutch GPs miss out on signals of depressive disorders that really should throw doubt on the patient's authority, or that they too quickly agree with the patient that his suffering can only be ended by death.[27] That view may be true in some cases, but it is unlikely to be true in most.

3.3 A presumption of irrationality

Perhaps it is not the Dutch doctors who are mistaken, but rather the suicidologists. Perhaps it is a mere prejudice to believe that states of mental illness, in particular major depressive disorders, tend to compromise the patient's decision-making capacity and authority.

Is it really? A core characteristic of such disorders is a mood disturbance: the patient is extremely unhappy, and his negative emotions cannot be understood as an appropriate response to his actual condition or events that have happened in his life. He is "fearful without danger, sad without loss, suspicious without persecution".[28] It is fully understandable that the person's primary concern is to escape from this condition of unhappiness, but the condition itself is an expression of his mood disturbance, and therefore his death wish is as well. That is one reason to doubt whether the patient's decision can be considered sufficiently competent to require to be respected.

Generally speaking, it is true that depressed persons haven't lost their cognitive abilities. Although their judgements about the future are, given the same evidence, more negative than other people's judgements, it is even controversial whether they are more often inaccurate.[29] But if they aren't, this is only true as regards the whole population of depressed patients. People with the highest scores on depressive symptoms really are unduly pessimistic and have difficulty discriminating between more and less likely events.[30] Even if a death wish as such doesn't prove distorted thinking, Shneidman's description of the constricted, dichotomous way of thinking he ascribes to the 'suicidal mind' as such appears

27 Van der Lee et al. 2005; Breitbart et al. 2000; Kim, Lemmens 2016 (Section 13.5). For a similar suggestion about Oregon see Ganzini, Goy, Dobscha 2008b. According to Passik et al. 1998 GPs in general often miss out on such signals. Such claims are hard to evaluate because of the unclarities surrounding the diagnosis of a depressive disorder, as discussed in Section 11.6.

28 Koerselman 1998.

29 Schuklenk, van de Vathorst 2015. In this section I use some formulations from my comment on this article, den Hartogh 2015a.

30 Strunk, Lopez, DeRubeis 2006; Hindmarch, Hotopf, Owen 2013.

indeed to be characteristic of severe depressive disorders.[31] Such patients underrate their successes and overrate their failures and are unable to appreciate or even recognize alternatives to the decisions they are prone to make. But even if their characteristically negative judgements could still be seen as sufficiently sensitive to evidence, if they still have the highest possible score on the MacCAT instrument for measuring competence, that would not be enough to attribute decision-making authority to them, because decisions do not only depend on judgements but also on affective states, and in their case, these are distorted by mood disturbances. Even if they are able to recognize the possibility of a better future, they may be indifferent about the prospect.

It cannot be denied that mental illness often has an undue influence on a person's decision-making capacity and authority. However, the mere fact of a *history* of mental illness does not imply that the person's decision-making authority as regards life or death should be doubted forever. Even most patients who at present still suffer from depression go through intermediate periods in between episodes of deep depression and during these periods may be capable of a sober assessment of their condition and prognosis.[32] They may then conclude that a future life consisting of episodes of deep depression and waiting for them is a prospect so bleak that it is reasonable to want to avoid it, by death if there is no other way. Of course, we have to make sure that this decision is the outcome of an adequate weighing process and is stably enduring through time. It may be difficult to make sure, or sure enough (Section 13.5). But it is not always impossible.

It is not, by itself, the presence of mental illness that signals irrationality. But reconsider the way in which the decision to end one's own life is often made and carried out, as described in the opening paragraph of Section 3.1. The agent thinks about suicide long and often, indeed obsessionally. But she has not only a wish to die, but also to live, and the relative strength of these wishes varies from day to day. "Ambivalence saturates the suicidal act".[33] On a day on which she is strongly drawn to action, she may decide upon a particular way of acting and even start making preparations. From that moment on the chosen plan is mentally available to her, resting on the shelf until the time that she takes it from there and acts on it. At that

31 According to Baumeister 1990 it is characteristic for the suicidal mind to escape from painful self-awareness by a state of 'cognitive deconstruction', focussing on the here and now. That would explain the remarkably mundane character of most suicide notes, as well as the lack of attention the suicidal person often has for the consequences of his act for others.

32 Nederlandse Vereniging voor Psychiatrie 2009; Spittler 2017.

33 Jamison 1999, 39. This is also a central theme in Shneidman 1996. The ambivalence is also shown by the remarkable fact that many people who kill themselves until the last moment have other plans. And by the equally remarkable fact that if their attempt is stopped, for example because a barrier has been put on the bridge or alongside the railway, they normally go home without making another attempt elsewhere, Seidel 1978.

moment the actual decision is in the majority of cases made and acted upon within an hour. We could call such actions *quasi-impulsive*. The means that are then chosen are almost always violent ones. These are often the only means that have been contemplated.

It is not always clear whether suicidal people fully appreciate what it means to be dead. Even if they don't believe in an afterlife, they may concentrate on the negative aspects of their life that death will free them from, without fully realizing that it will free them from everything else as well. That is why death may be inordinately seductive to them.

It is not only the ongoing battle between the wish to live and the wish to die that explains why the final decision tends to be postponed again and again. In addition, the agent often has to overcome strong inhibitions to really use the violent means she contemplates. Why do some people succeed in overcoming their inhibitions and other people do not? Thomas Joiner has made a substantial contribution to the literature by suggesting that people have to work up themselves to being able to act, and actually acquire this ability as a result of a habituating process of self-injury. For example, many people with suicidal thoughts relieve their tension (and release euphoria-producing endorphins) by cutting their arms and legs with knives. Such non-lethal forms of self-injury do not themselves lead to suicidal thoughts or plans, but they help a person who has such plans to execute them.[34]

If this is really the normal way for people with suicidal thoughts to proceed, it raises doubts concerning their decision-making capacity at several points. The first point is the ambivalence of their attitude, finally only resolved by the quasi-impulsive decision to act. In the second place, some form of planning is almost always involved, but the planning tends to be elementary and defective because done in a state of emotional turmoil that interferes with its quality. As a result, only plans that can be quickly taken from the shelf are executed, and these usually involve the use of violent means, in the sense of 'violent' that I have stipulated: disfiguring and painful.[35]

Joiner's account of the necessary habituating history gives us an additional reason for doubting the rationality of the paradigmatic kind of suicide that I described in Section 3.1. However, his account is ambiguous on a central point: the nature of the inhibitions to be overcome. In many places Joiner suggests that the inhibitions are given with our natural drive to survive, but in other places, the inhibitions seem to concern the violent nature of the means chosen.[36] It may be that we have to

34 Joiner 2005, 2011.

35 Joiner 2011, 39, 70ff.

36 For example, when he says that if you only needed to turn a little switch in your arm, it would not be a problem to kill yourself, Joiner 2005, 50. Or when he calls it a relevant effect of habituation to self-harm that one's pain-tolerance is increased, *ibid.*, 76–78.

overcome both obstacles before we can act on a decision to end our lives (cf. Section 16.2). But the euthanasia cases clearly show that, in order to overcome our fear of death, we need not accustom ourselves to acts of self-injury. That is also shown by the much larger number of decisions to stop treatment. The evidence Joiner provides may only confirm the hypothesis that such a history facilitates a person to overcome his inhibitions against the application of violence to his own body.[37] If that is true, the obviously pathological nature of going through this preparatory course adds to our suspicions of the act it prepares for.

A final characteristic of such suicides that is inimical to the well-considered character of the decision is the common lack of communication with friends and family, let alone with doctors or other professional consultants.[38] Consulting others is always the best way to test the rationality of your beliefs and intentions, in particular when so much is at stake as the end of your life. But people will fear, and most of the time fear with reason, that any information they provide about their plans to others will only lead to interventions thwarting those plans. (At the same time they normally betray their ambivalence by giving hidden clues of their plans. Unfortunately, these are mostly only afterwards recognized for what they are.) In the descriptions of Joiner and other suicidologists this lack of communication, like the use of violent means, is so self-evidently involved in suicidal action that they do not even explicitly discuss it.

When a psychiatric patient, in particular a patient with a major depressive disorder, is on a suicidal course that exhibits these characteristics – the suicide, when finally decided upon, will be quasi-impulsive, violent and lonely – we have every reason to presume that the decision will not be a well-considered one. Suicides exhibiting these characteristics are very frequent. Therefore we cannot solve our problem by insisting that, contrary to the common belief in suicidology, most suicides, even those committed by psychiatric patients, are to be considered rational after all.

The reason we cannot, however, is that these suicides exhibit the characteristics I mentioned, not the mere fact that they involve psychiatric patients.[39] Suicide, whether assisted by or delegated to physicians or not, *can* be well-considered, a fully intelligible response to the dramatic circumstances some people find themselves in, as a result of physical illness, traumatizing events in their life, but also of mental illness (or a combination of these factors).

37 Confirmed by Anestis, Khazam, Law 2015. According to them people acquire the capability to die by suicide by a history of non-suicidal self-injury because thereby their fear of bodily harm is decreased.

38 On A.T. Beck's *Suicide Intent Scale* (Beck, Kovacs, Weissman 1979) the degree of isolation (no notification, locked doors) is even a criterion for serious intent.

39 Wyatt et al. 2016 found poor Iowa Gambling Task performance by older suicide attempters who used violent means, not by elderly people with suicidal behaviour in general.

3.4 Explaining the mystery

If suicidologists are right, no more than 10% of all suicides, at best, can be considered rational ones. If Dutch doctors and consultants are right, almost all granted requests for euthanasia are rational. At first sight these supposed 'facts' seem to be incompatible. I considered and rejected two proposals to explain the mystery. So, what *is* the explanation? I have four suggestions to offer.

1 The first explanation follows from my argument in Section 3.2: people may be classified as mentally ill for the very reason that they have 'suicidal ideation'. If we resist such tautological classifications, we do not only have a reason for accepting that in most cases in which requests for euthanasia have been granted, the request has been well-considered, as I concluded in that section. We also have a reason for distrusting the 'robust finding' of suicidology that no more than 5–10% of suicides can be classified as rational ones.

2 The second explanation is closely related to the first one. If you have a stable death wish, however well-founded in the circumstances in which you find yourself, in a climate in which the wish itself is already considered a clear sign of mental illness, in which you cannot communicate about it with others without endangering the very possibility of acting on it, and in which it seems to be generally acknowledged that you can only do so by using violent means, it is only to be expected that you develop mood disturbances and other symptoms of mental illness, perhaps including a tendency to acts of self-injury. The pathologization of suicide as such, which finds its pinnacle in the recent proposals of the *DSM-V*, may to some extent have a self-fulfilling character, as (surely to a fuller extent) the pathologization of homosexuality and BDSM had since Krafft-Ebing and Havelock Ellis.[40] It may even partly explain why people prefer to die with the assistance of a doctor: if a doctor gives his blessing to your death wish, it can't be a sign of madness.

3 A relatively minor point: the fact that a person had a history of mental illness may have led the coroner to classify her case as a suicide. After all, it was precisely in order to enable coroners to make such decisions in equivocal cases that psychological autopsies were originally undertaken.[41]

40 This is the element of truth in the full-scale attack of Szasz 1971 on the medicalization of suicide.

41 This also relativizes to some extent the finding from psychological autopsy studies that in 90–95% of suicide cases there is a history of mental illness, Robins 1981; Cavanagh et al. 2003. Taylor 1982 called this a secondary suicide clue. On the other hand, if the person's death wish existed for a longer time before his suicide, the very fact may have contributed to the diagnosis of a depressive disorder.

4 My final and most important explanation also concerns the registration of suicides. It is well known that not all cases of suicide are actually registered as such.[42] In particular drownings, fallings from high places, collisions and medication poisonings are notoriously difficult to classify as either accidents or suicides (or, occasionally, murders).[43]

Long ago the English sociologist Maxwell Atkinson did some fieldwork on the classificatory decisions made by coroners.[44] He discovered that in equivocal cases they attributed the death to accident rather than suicide. And they often did not classify deaths as suicides, even if they suspected them to be suicides, if there was no obvious evidence making this classification inescapable, as, for example, the presence of a suicide note or of the very means used for the killing, a gun, a rope or arsenic. As we have already seen, they tend to make the same decision if there is no history of mental illness, for if there is no pathology, suicide is *ipso facto* doubtful.[45] They gave a verdict of 'heart failure' or 'old-age frailty' or 'unknown illness', allowing the death to be registered as a natural one. Or they gave an open verdict, a class almost as large as suicide verdicts in the UK.[46]

Why do they proceed in this way? The main reason seems to be that coroners understand their principal task to consist in identifying felonies, not in producing correct statistics of causes of death.[47] It would require much time, money and expertise to identify, for example, every case in which death has been caused by an overdose of drugs, and even then the drugs can have been taken by accident. If there is no suspicion of crime, coroners (and physicians in countries in which certificates of natural death need not to be given by legal officials) do not consider the

42 Sainsbury, Barraclough 1968 discovered that the suicide rate of immigrants in the UK was similar to the rate in their countries of origin. Barraclough, Holding, Fayers 1976 could not find any significant variation in the number of suicide verdicts between coroner's offices and pathologists. Such findings have been used to conclude that the estimations of suicide rates must be largely correct, de Leo et al. 2006. But they do not exclude the possibility that some subcategories, e.g. 'rational' suicides, are systematically underrepresented in all suicide statistics. In any case, the evidence about the unreliability of such statistics has recently grown, Tait et al. 2015.

43 Battin (1980) 1994, ch. 14, footnote 27, already suspected that what she called 'surcease suicides' tend not to get reported and registered as suicides.

44 Atkinson 1978.

45 Tait et al. 2015.

46 In many epidemiological studies this class is included in the category of suicides, as it is in the English national targets for suicide reduction, de Leo et al. 2006. This leads to overestimation. But English coroners have to make sure that it is 'beyond reasonable doubt' that a death was caused by suicide, Australian ones only that this is probable on balance, Tait et al. 2015.

47 Confirmed by Das 2004 for the Netherlands.

effort worthwhile. Most of them probably believe that suicide requires an intention to kill and do not know that the law doesn't make that requirement in many countries, and not consistently in others (Section 4.1). But in many cases the deceased did not unequivocally aim to die, and in those cases, it will not only be hard to establish his intention, but even the antecedent probability of death.[48]

In addition, these officials usually want to save the family from the nasty consequences of an identification of a suicide: police investigations, news reports, stigmatization, community blame, refusal of life insurance or of a burial with full religious ceremony.[49] After all, family members are usually the only living persons the officials meet in their work, and these family members have just been hit by a catastrophic event. It is normal to have a concern for their feelings, if there is no reason to suspect a crime. Finally, coroners tend to share the general public's inclination not to classify suicides as such if they do not fundamentally disapprove of them, in particular when the horror of the use of violent means is lacking.

Further exploration by Boudewijn Chabot has shown that in particular two non-violent ways in which people carry out a decision to end their own lives tend not to be registered as suicides.[50] The first kind, stopping eating and drinking, is almost never registered as such.[51] (In Section 4.3, I will discuss whether this really *is* a kind of suicide.) To my knowledge it nowhere gets an entry of its own in the suicide statistics, alongside drowning, shooting, poisoning etc. It is almost never even mentioned by suicidologists. Typical is a remark made in passing by Joiner, "that there are documented instances in which people ... have retreated to isolated areas like remote woods, denied themselves water, and thereby died by suicide".[52] Obviously he is unaware of the fact that many people in suburbia die that way.

The second kind of suicide that tends not to be registered as such[53] occasionally gets into the statistics under the heading of 'poisoning', together with the use of cyanide, arsenic and carbon monoxide. It consists of the use of drugs that kill painlessly, for example chloroquine, amitriptyline or pentobarbital. By now there are plenty of books giving information about drugs that can be used to end your life in a safe

48 Cf. Andriessen 2006.

49 Goldney 2009. Catholic medical examiners in Canada report lower number of suicides than others, Jarvis, Noldt, Butt 1991.

50 Chabot 2007, ch. 8; Chabot, Goedhart 2009.

51 In Chabot's research only in 4 of 97 cases, Chabot 2007, 227.

52 Joiner 2011, 198.

53 A third method is asphyxiation by the inhalation of helium, nitrogen or another inert gas, Varlet et al. 2019; Chabot 2019, ch. 9. If the equipment that has been used has been removed after the agent's death, the cause of his death will not always be properly identified.

and humane way (Section 5.3). Even in France and Australia where the publication and dispersion of such books is legally forbidden, the information is of course available on the internet for anyone who makes a serious effort of finding it. The drugs can sometimes be acquired by having them prescribed by one's physician and not using them for the aim for which they were prescribed, whether or not the physician has any suspicion of these proceedings or can even be considered a secret accomplice to it.[54] In addition the drugs can now be ordered from elsewhere, for example from China or Mexico. Addresses can be found on the internet, their reliability in some countries checked with volunteers from right-to-die societies.

Chabot was also the first who, in collaboration with the statistician Arnoud Goedhart, tried to find out how often these methods had been employed, in his case in the Netherlands during 1997–2003 (when the average number of reported euthanasia cases was only ca. 1800). They found an unexpectedly high number of 2100 cases a year of voluntarily stopping eating and drinking (on about 140,000 deaths).[55] The number of cases of suicide by the non-violent use of drugs that they found was 1600. Chabot and Goedhart used information from witnesses identified in a random selection from the general public. Later two national surveys of end-of-life decisions (2010, 2015) arrived at estimations of resp. 600 and 730 cases of stopping eating and drinking (0.4–0.5% of deaths), and of resp. 300 and 280 suicides by the use of painless medication.[56] The difference between these estimations is hard to explain, but one relevant fact is that people often take care of not informing their physician about their plans, partly because they fear that he will interfere, but perhaps also because they want to avoid the death to be identified as a suicide, with the attendant negative consequences of this identification for their family. Both reasons apply in particular to the use of drugs.[57]

54 Quill, Lo, Brock 1997; Meier et al. 1998.

55 Corrected from the original calculation of 2800 in order to take account of the possibility that some of these cases concerned dying patients who had lost their appetite as a result of the spontaneous disruption of metabolism in the dying process, cf. KNMG/V&VN 2014, 27; Elzenga 2016. Perhaps the correction has been too conservative.

56 Van der Heide et al. 2012, 111–118; Onwuteaka-Philipsen et al. 2017, 130–131; cf. Hagens et al. 2021 for a more extended account of the same research and a comparison with the incidence of suicide by violent means (0.7%). According to Chambaere et al. 2015, in 0.5% of deaths in Flandres 2013, people died by stopping eating and drinking. This percentage is also based on reports from doctors. Stängle, Schnepp, Büche 2020 found that 1.1% of all deaths occurring in Swiss nursing homes and private homes resulted from stopping eating and drinking. In addition, we know that 34% of a sample of Oregon nurses, and 62% of a sample of German doctors, had come across at least one case of stopping eating and drinking in the past four to five years, Ganzini et al. 2003, see also Chapter 16, footnote 34; Hoekstra, Strack, Simon 2015.

57 For another possible explanation of the difference see footnote 55.

3.5 Two kinds of suicide

So how is it possible for suicides to be mostly irrational, while the similarly motivated requests for euthanasia are mostly well-considered? The solution to the problem I proposed in the last section consists of several elements, but the main point is the following. We should not say that most suicides are irrational, but only that most *registered* suicides are. But why should we think that most suicides that aren't registered are well-considered?

Suicides tend to cluster into two groups with common characteristics, only one of which is visible to the authorities and the public. The first group consists of the suicides that satisfy the standard picture of suicide in suicidology, as I have described it in Section 3.1 and elaborated it in Section 3.4: quasi-impulsive, executed by violent means and without any communication with family or friends. The other group consists of suicides by non-violent means which are carefully planned and carried out, in consultation with friends and relatives, and often with their assistance.[58] In these cases it may be the presence of others that makes death less daunting, rather than a history of self-injury. These very characteristics explain why suicides in this cluster tend not to be registered as such. Because non-violent means have been used, it is hard to distinguish the body of the suicidee afterwards from the bodies of people who have died from natural causes. Careful planning and the involvement of family and friends make it possible to suppress other signs. In addition, the coroner or the physician who has to make up the death certificate does not feel the need to investigate the matter in these cases, even if he suspects suicide. Stopping eating and drinking he will not even classify as suicide.

Some suicides from the first cluster will not be registered as such because the people who have found the body, friends or relatives, succeed in concealing the cause of death, in particular when this falls under the heading of 'poisoning'. On the other hand some cases from the second cluster, mainly involving the use of drugs, will be registered as suicides, for example because the decedent and his family have decided that they have nothing to hide and want to take full responsibility for their actions. But, pending further research, the conclusion seems warranted that the correlation between the clustering and the probability of registration is pretty robust.

So is the clustering itself, although it is not perfect.[59] It is for example possible for a person with suicidal thoughts to order drugs from abroad,

58 Suicides from the second group answer to the description given by Michel de Montaigne of a 'Coustume de l'Isle de Céa', *les Essais, Livre II*, 3.

59 Spittler 2017 found a strong correlation between loneliness and a short period of decision-making.

without having decided to use them and then use them in a quasi-impulsive way and without prior communication with others. On the other hand it is not impossible for a person to prefer to use a gun, for example because he considers the use of drugs to be unmanly,[60] and to execute his decision after careful planning and communication with friends. Clearly these matters depend to some extent on cultural variables.

I have argued that, as suicidologists suggest, there is an important class of suicides that we should presume to be irrational, but that these are to be identified by their characteristics, not by a history of mental illness. I have also argued that there is a second, significant class of suicides which are to be presumed rational, well-considered ones, a class that has escaped being noticed by suicidology, *precisely because* they lack the characteristics of the first class. These are evaluative claims, because 'rational' and 'irrational' are evaluative concepts. But the evaluations involved are not moral ones. Nevertheless, they have important moral consequences.

In discussions of suicide it is often suggested that it is hardly a subject for ethical evaluation, because the suicidal mind is almost always in the grip of mental illness and therefore insensitive to any moral considerations.[61] This is simply false as regards suicides from the second cluster. The idea may also be too simplistic in regard to suicides from the first one. If a person is subject to distorted thinking, she may be unable to give some considerations their proper weight, but that doesn't mean that she is unable to give them any weight at all. Whatever one's state of mind it is blameable to kill oneself knowingly by flying an airplane with 150 passengers against a mountain.

If a rebuttable presumption of irrationality is justifiable in the case of suicides from the first cluster, in the absence of special countervailing evidence, we are justified to intervene in order to prevent a suicide attempt to succeed. We are justified not only for paternalistic reasons, but also because such suicides normally have harmful, often devastating consequences for others. Even when friends and relatives are aware of suicidal ideas, which is by no means always the case, they will usually not expect the action at the moment it is done, and it is of course horrifying to find your loved one hanging from the ceiling or shot. The violent character of the action is also shocking for third parties, for example the driver of the train that destroys a body before his eyes. Nor is it an implausible thought that the offense against human dignity that such violent acts involve give us an independent additional reason to try to block them (Section 9.4).

60 For a similar attitude see *Judges 9:53* (about Abimelech). Lester 2006 calls the suicide by a firearm of Ernest Hemingway at least consistent with his lifestyle.

61 See, e.g. Cholbi 2011, Epilogue. It is probably the major reason why suicide has been taken out of the criminal law in most jurisdictions.

But if the presumption that suicides from the second cluster are well-considered ones is also warranted, that has moral consequences as well. A decision to stop eating and drinking can be taken impulsively, for example when a request for physician assistance has been refused. But it cannot be executed impulsively. Collecting lethal drugs requires planning, in order to acquire information about efficient and safe means and ways to get and use them, and the execution of the plan requires some skill and some patience. It is true that the decision to use the drugs can eventually still be quasi-impulsive, but this probability is low when the decision has been discussed with intimates or friends. If it is very probable that the decision has been made in a rational way, that probability gives us at least one highly relevant reason not to intervene in its execution. Only for intimates it may not necessarily be a decisive reason.

This is as true in regard to psychiatric patients as to others. In Section 3.2 I argued that suicidal thoughts do not as such indicate mental illness. I now add that suicidal thoughts in people suffering from mental illness do not as such show that these thoughts are irrational ones. More important than a history of mental illness is what kind of suicide is being considered: a quasi-impulsive, violent and lonely act, or the execution of a plan that is carefully made, in dialogue with others and involving the use of non-violent means. This distinction is not only relevant for the decision to prevent the successful execution of the plan or abstain from interventions, but also for the decision to provide or not provide any requested aid.

If the argument of this chapter is accepted, one important conclusion follows for the aims of healthcare systems. At present all societies, including societies that permit euthanasia or suicide assistance under some conditions, consider it one of those aims to prevent as many suicides as possible. But if in a substantial number of cases, a person who kills herself has the basic right to do so, it cannot be an unqualified duty of the healthcare system to prevent her from doing so. In many individual cases, prominently including cases of mental illness, it will be difficult to determine whether the person who wants to end her life has sufficient decisional capacity to appeal to this right (Section 13.5). But the aim of the general policy should be revised.[62]

This chapter had to be written because of a lingering doubt. In the last chapter I argued that the right to self-determination includes a right to suicide. That would, however, be a conclusion without any practical consequences, if it would be true that any person who commits suicide by the very fact shows that, being in the grip of mental illness, she isn't competent to exercise that right. I have argued that suicidologists tend

62 Kious, Battin 2019. But I fail to understand why this revision would require us to agree on an objective measure of suffering, den Hartogh 2019d.

not to recognize the existence of rational suicides, because they don't meet them. Actually, the evidence for their existence is strong enough. Hence we can continue our argument by asking: if there is a right to suicide, what exactly does it imply?

3.6 Postscript: comments on a proposal

In 2017 the American Association of Suicidology (AAS) published a position statement on the meaning of 'suicide'.[63] In this document the organization argues, as I have done, that there are two kinds of suicide, but also that these are so different from each other that it is misleading to speak of 'suicide' in both cases. The very word has strongly negative overtones, calling to mind the paradigmatic cases that I described at the beginning of the chapter and characterized in the last section as quasi-impulsive, lonely and violent. The AAS statement offers a more comprehensive résumé of the 'typical' characteristics of 'suicide in the conventional sense'. But these characteristics are normally absent in cases in which a person has been assisted by a doctor to end her life. Hence, we should stop calling such actions 'physician-assisted suicides' and speak of 'physician aid in dying' instead. This statement is the most extensively argued explanation of a position that is by now widespread, in particular in North America. American right-to-die societies don't refer to 'assisted suicide' anymore. The Oregon *Death with Dignity Act* (1998) already explicitly stipulated that no action taken in accordance with it counted as suicide. But at the time this probably was a mere legal fiction, introduced to avoid undesirable legal consequences, in particular in regard to life insurance. The argument of the AAS presents itself as a conceptual one.

In this concluding section I will offer some criticism of this argument. At the end of this chapter my first criticism will be fairly obvious. If we accept the argument, it implies an easy solution to the problem that I described in Section 3.1: unassisted suicides are 'typically' irrational, but if a doctor assists a person in ending her life, that very assistance guarantees the rationality of the action. But medical assistance cannot define the difference between the 'two kinds' of action. Suppose two persons decide to end their lives, who are in exactly the same physical, psychological and social condition and also share the same relevant values. One of them lives in California and is able to secure a prescription for a barbiturate from his doctor. The other lives in Arizona and has to travel over the border to acquire the same barbiturate in Mexico. Clearly it would be mistaken to speak of suicide in the second case but not in the

63 American Association of Suicidology 2017. For the same view see already American Public Health Association 2008.

first. And the implication that the first person is rational, but the second irrational is also clearly wrong.

As a matter of fact, the AAS acknowledges that there is some 'overlap' between suicide in the conventional sense and physician aid in dying. But 'overlap' doesn't seem the proper term for actions that don't satisfy the criteria of either 'suicide' or 'physician aid in dying'. Moreover, suicides that have a great deal in common with 'physician aid in dying' are clearly considered a marginal phenomenon. However, even setting aside for the moment the controversial case of stopping eating and drinking that I will discuss in Section 4.3, I have presented evidence in this chapter confirming that it is a mistake to suppose suicides without physician assistance that are not quasi-impulsive, lonely or violent to be exceptional and rare. Even if they were, they would, however, still block a conceptual argument to the conclusion that physician involvement is itself a defining characteristic of actions that we shouldn't count as suicides. If a doctor in Oregon writes a prescription for lethal drugs, that doesn't at all exclude the possibility that the patient swallows the drugs a year later impulsively and without consulting others. This may only rarely occur, but it is a realistic possibility, not a conceptual impossibility. For a proper conceptual argument we should even take into account possibilities that may not have been realized but conceivably could be. If someone hangs himself, it will clearly be suicide, even when a doctor has provided him with the rope.

The involvement of a doctor is neither a necessary nor a sufficient reason to exclude an action from the class of suicides. If there is any kind of actions to be singled out from that category, it should be identified by the relevant characteristics directly, not by a characteristic like physician involvement that is only correlated with them, and as a matter of fact only correlated imperfectly.

An additional problem is that the term 'assisted suicide' rightly refers to two agents involved in a joint action, the suicidee and his assistant. But the term 'physician aid in dying', besides being euphemistic and imprecise (Section 1.1), only focuses on one agent, as if he is the only one whose rights and responsibilities we have to consider. Because of this the AAS proposal reinforces the medicalization of the debate about the right to choose the manner and time of one's own death: the only options to be considered involve a doctor in a performing or contributing role.

Should we then decide to require suicides, properly so-called, to be committed quasi-impulsively, lonely and violently, and exclude actions that do not satisfy these conditions? Perhaps it is possible to coin a new term like 'auto-thanasia' for the excluded actions,[64] that is not so obviously euphemistic and imprecise as 'physician aid in dying' and does

64 Van Hooff 1990. Or consider the German 'Freitod'.

not focus on the doctor. I don't deny the advantages of this proposal: it would be nice to have a term that is not burdened by negative associations. One obvious problem with the proposal is that, as I observed in Section 3.5, the clustering between these three characteristics – quasi-impulsive, lonely and violent – is not perfect. Hence we have still to decide how to classify actions that satisfy one or two of these conditions only, but not all three. Perhaps the most basic problem with the proposal is the following. If a person ends her life by taking a barbiturate after due reflection and intensive consultation with relatives and, perhaps, her doctor, our reason for not calling this a suicide is that we don't want this action to be tainted by the usual associations this term evokes. But these associations themselves rest on a mistake, as I argued in this chapter: the mistake of disregarding the invisibility of rational suicide. We should rather concentrate our efforts on dispelling the illusion that suicides are commonly, if not invariably, quasi-impulsive, lonely and violent acts. That is a necessary step before we can even hope the introduction of new terms to be widely accepted.

It is interesting to remind oneself of the history of the very concept of 'suicide'. It is not a word known to antiquity but a neologism, coined in the seventeenth century,[65] as an alternative to the term 'self-murder', equivalents of which are still in common use in the other Germanic languages.[66] In these languages the use of the almost technical term 'suicide' to some extent neutralizes the extremely negative associations attached to 'self-murder'. Responsible media should ban that word, because these associations are almost always inappropriate.[67] For one thing, 'murder' as it is used in common parlance and in many legal systems is incompatible with consent. But one could speculate that, precisely because of the disappearance of that word in English, 'suicide' to a larger extent has inherited the associations of a sin, in addition to the connotations of a pitiful illness.

65 "In Cicero's ears *suicidium* would have sounded as 'swine-slaying'", Van Hooff 1990. According to Daube 1972 the neologism has been introduced by Walter Charleton in *The Ephesian Matron*, 1651 or 1652. Charleton followed John Donne who in *Biothanatos* (published ca. 1645, but probably written in 1607) had introduced the term 'self-homicide' for the same reason: to accentuate that self-killing is not necessarily a sin. Griffin 1986 found the term 'suicide' already in Thomas Browne, *Religio Medici*, 1643. However, van Hooff 1990 refers to the use of *suicida* (self-killer) in a work by Gauthier de Saint-Victor from 1177 or 1178.

66 'Selbstmord', 'zelfmoord', 'selfmoord', 'selvmord', 'självmord', 'sjálfsvíg', resp. in German, Dutch, African, Danish and Norse, Swedish, Icelandic.

67 In 2019 the Dutch quality newspaper *NRC* rejected an opinion piece proposing such a ban because the proposal would "lack practical urgency".

4 Which actions should we count as suicides?

4.1 The definition of suicide

If we have a right to suicide (Section 2.5), what exactly is it that we have a right to? A clear discussion of the right is hampered by the fact that the definition of 'suicide' has been a controversial subject for a long time.[1] Many kinds of death have been classified as suicides by one author but excluded from this class by others. The main reason for this dispute, as has become increasingly clear, is that questions of definition and of evaluation have been mixed up.[2] The term 'suicide' may have been invented in the 17th century in order to get rid of the negative connotations of 'self-murder', the idea of suicide is still coloured by pity and horror, and, inevitably, as a result the originally neutral term has acquired negative connotations of its own. One result of this is a tendency in the literature to deny that any act one approves of really is a suicide. The death of Captain Oates who walked out from his tent into the Antarctic blizzard in order to enable his comrades to stop caring for him and to focus on their own survival is a typical example. A related tendency is to prefer euphemisms – self-chosen death, self-deliverance, death with dignity, auto-euthanasia, *Freitod* – in order to avoid the burden of the negative connotations of 'suicide'. I prefer to question the general appropriateness of these connotations (Section 3.6).

Because of this accretion of negative connotations to the concept, we cannot expect to find a definition simply by requiring it to satisfy all the intuitive classifications we share. Our intuitions may be biased. To some extent we will therefore have to regiment them by keeping in mind the aim of the enterprise: to delineate a class of actions that share a number of important characteristics and thereby invite us to consider them for evaluative and regulative aims, and for empirical study, as a class.

Why is it so important to discuss matters of classification? They may be relevant for life insurance companies that have an exclusion clause

1 An excellent discussion of this issue is Cholbi 2011, ch. 1. For surveys of the debate in suicidology see de Leo et al. 2006; Goodfellow, Solves, de Leo 2018.

2 Beauchamp 1978; Cholbi 2011, 18–19.

DOI: 10.4324/9781003281115-5

for suicides, but even these companies could be allowed to decide these issues by whatever stipulations they like to make, or by leaving it to the law to make them. When an Oregon resident uses the pills that he has acquired on a receipt from his doctor according to the provisions of the Oregon *Death with Dignity Act*, he is clearly committing suicide, but the law itself, as we saw, in order to avoid unwanted legal consequences, states that he doesn't (Section 3.6). Why bother? The moral evaluation of an action that results in someone's death, one could suggest, depends on its specific characteristics, for example its effects on the interests of the agent and others, not on its classification as either a suicide or a non-suicide. But the indirect effects of such actions, for example, for the way people draw lessons from their experience, really *do* depend on the way they classify the actions. And in a legal context or the quasi-legal context of professional morality, issues of classification are undeniably relevant for the determination of appropriate responses, and not always so easily solved by stipulation. For example, in countries in which no right to suicide is recognized, the very fact that a person plans an act classified as a suicide may be a reason to consider him to be 'a threat to himself' or 'a vulnerable person in need of help', and therefore to hospitalize him, or to make it obligatory for everyone to interfere, if possible, in the execution of his plan. If only acts one doesn't consider 'rational' are classified as suicides, it seems easy to draw conclusions about the justifiability of preventive measures and interventions. Of course, consensus about the definition of suicide would be very helpful for medical and legal scholars. It is by now commonly recognized that suicidological research is hampered by the fact that the results of studies cannot be compared, because they rely on different definitions of suicide.

We can find satisfactory solutions to most of the definitional questions if we follow two guidelines. The first is that we should avoid shortcutting questions of evaluation by definitions.[3] 'That is (not) suicide' should not be acceptable as an argument why an action that results in the death of the agent is either right or wrong.[4] Our second guideline follows from the recognition that suicide is a species of killing, its specific difference being that it is a killing of the self. We are therefore well-advised to take over the core of common elements in the legal definitions of homicide, accepting deviations from it only for very good reasons.

3 This guideline doesn't presuppose or imply that conceptual issues in this area should always be kept distinct from evaluative or normative ones. In Section 4.3 we will meet a counterexample to that view: the distinction between killing and letting die.

4 Beauchamp 1980; Tolhurst 1998 (1983), 111; de Leo et al. 2006, 8; Cholbi 2011, 18–19. Kupfer 1998 (1990), 80, doesn't classify an action as a suicide if death is imminent anyway, for example within two weeks, but in an honest footnote concedes that he may be reluctant to call such acts suicides because they seem morally permissible to him.

Killing may be done for all kinds of reasons, prudential, malevolent, even altruistic ones. These reasons are relevant for evaluation, not for classification. If it is possible to kill another person for altruistic reasons, it is equally possible to kill oneself for such reasons. Yes, we admire Captain Oates, as well as Friar Maximilian Kolbe, who, during the second world war, volunteered to die in the place of a fellow prisoner, a Jewish father of a family.[5] But that is no reason to deny that their actions were suicides.

Similarly, if it is possible to be coerced to kill another person, it is equally possible to be coerced to kill oneself. That coercion was involved is also only relevant for evaluation, not for classification. Surely the deaths of Socrates and Seneca were suicides.[6] It is true that the coercer is morally responsible for the death in such cases; hence we can understand Plato when he says that it was the Athenian court that killed Socrates. But if you are coerced to hand over your money, you hand over your money, it is not the robber who hands it over, though he is responsible for making you do so. A coerced suicide is not an oxymoron any more than a suicide for altruistic reasons is.

Almost all proposed definitions of suicide require the agent to *intend* to end his life, and it cannot be denied that this view has some intuitive support.[7] But we have already seen (Section 1.3) that, generally speaking, the law considers an act an act of killing if death is its foreseen effect; it need not be intended. The volitional element in the definition is only that the foreseen effect is no reason for the agent to abstain from the action; in that sense he endorses the effect. It is being caused knowingly and willingly (cf. Section 10.5).

It can be argued that the law has good reasons not to rely on the agent's intentions. One such reason is the indeterminacy of intentions.[8] In the case of Captain Oates, for example, it has been argued that he did not intend his own death, but only to save his comrades by removing himself from the place where they felt duty bound to take care of him.[9]

5 See O'Keeffe 1998 (1981), 141, who argues that Fr. Kolbe did not kill himself because he had not the intention to die. The case resembles the famous fictional case of Sidney Carton from *A Tale of Two Cities*, referred to by Kupfer 1998 (1990), 167.

6 Frey 1978, discussed by Beauchamp 1980, 72; Smith 1980; Tolhurst 1998 (1983), 109–110; McMahan 2002, 456. In the case of Socrates one could even argue that he was not coerced to kill himself, but only to kill himself or to go into exile.

7 An early exception is Durkheim 1897. His argument was that intentions are hard to verify, in particular the intentions of a person who is no longer there to inform us about them. Egel 1999 omits intention from his definition for the same reason. Cholbi 2011, ch. 1, defines suicide as intentional self-killing, but classifies as 'intentional' all self-killings in which the result was foreseen and endorsed. Some definitions do not clearly distinguish between 'intentional' in this sense and 'intended', see e.g. de Leo et al. 2006. I discuss a similar mistake about euthanasia in Section 10.5.

8 Den Hartogh 2019a, Section 5, with further references. The problem was for the first time described in general terms by Foot 1979 (1968).

9 Cf. Tolhurst 1998 (1983), 108.

If Amundsen had accidentally come along with his sledge dogs and saved him, he would have been all too happy.[10] Similarly, Fr. Kolbe would not consider himself to have failed if he had not been executed. And the soldier who saves the lives of his fellow soldiers by throwing himself on a grenade, did he not merely intend to use his body as a shield? But if such moves are accepted, there are many paradigmatic cases of suicide in which we could also redescribe the object of the agent's intention in such a way as to make death a mere side effect. Augustine thought that some Christians, who solicited too openly for martyrdom, were really committing suicide, but presumably they all knew that if they survived their execution in some miraculous way, they would have an even better chance of being canonized. Or think of the spy who swallows a cyanide pill in order to make sure that he will not betray his comrades under torture.[11] Couldn't one argue that he doesn't intend to die, but only to temporarily incapacitate himself to speak up? Similarly, consider the person who arranges his suicide to look like an accident in order to enable his family to collect life insurance money and start a new life elsewhere. Couldn't he be said to intend only to *look* dead until the moment at which the insurance company cannot recover the money any longer?[12] Perhaps we could even say that the large majority of people who kill themselves do not really intend to be dead but only to put an end to their sufferings. A depressed person who in despair takes an overdose of pills would not be disappointed if he woke up with a peaceful mind.

And as Shelly Kagan says, if that particular soldier would not have thrown *himself* on the grenade but another soldier, we would not hesitate to call it an act of killing.[13] Following my second guideline that is a decisive argument to call his present action a suicide.

An act is only a homicide or a suicide if death actually occurs; if it doesn't occur, the action can only be an *attempted* homicide or suicide.[14] If nobody dies, there hasn't been a killing. Long ago Erwin Stengel famously argued that in most cases in which the agent seemed to attempt to end his life he did not really endeavour to do so, because he did not intend that outcome, nor, we could add, even foresaw it. In such cases

10 Here and in the following examples I use the so-called Failure Test (Jansen 2010) for identifying the 'real' intention. On limitations of this test see Chapter 10, at footnote 53.

11 Kupfer 1998 (1990), 165.

12 Cf. Bennett 1995, 210.

13 Kagan 1989, 242–246; cf. McMahan 2002, 456; Cholbi 2011, 30–31.

14 Cholbi 2011, ch. 1, classifies unsuccessful attempts as suicides. But he is not fully consistent in this, in particular he misclassifies his own example on p. 22: a man swallows a drug that actually would not kill him, but for the fact that he has also just drunk a bottle of vodka, without knowing the lethal effect of the combination of the drug and the vodka. On my view this is an attempted suicide and an accident, but not a suicide, but Cholbi could not agree to this classification.

the 'attempt' should be understood as a dramatic way to focus the attention of the people around him on his plight which he thinks they neglect at present.[15] It is now commonly believed by suicidologists that cases in which the attempt merely is a 'cry for help' and cases in which the agent without any ambivalence tries to end his life as surely and effectively as he can are only the ends of a continuum. Very often the agent is aware of the fact that his action can have two possible outcomes: death or being saved in time. If the last outcome occurs, he expects, usually not without reason, that his bargaining position will be improved.[16] The agent may rank these outcomes equally or differentially, but he considers both to be better than the status quo. Whether we should classify such cases as attempted self-killings only depends on the probability the agent attributes to the outcome of death.

The same is true about attempts that succeed. It is possible that in a case at Stengel's end of the continuum, in which the agent neither really intends to end his life nor even foresees that he has a significant probability of doing so, he nevertheless more or less accidentally causes his own death. It is true that even in such a case death is more than a mere accident, for even if the real aim is to demonstrate to others that the agent is in such a dire state that he needs help, this is done by showing, or at least pretending to show, that a choice for death is a real option for him. But if the antecedent probability of death is not greater than in the case of dangerous sports like bungee jumping or mountaineering, the case should not be classified as a suicide. We are only in the neighbourhood of suicide.

So how probable should the outcome be, in the agent's perception, for his action to be classified as a suicide? No definition of suicide could possibly answer that question in a non-arbitrary way. Michael Cholbi makes a perspicacious comment on the issue when he observes that it is a virtue, not a defect of a definition that it explains why seemingly hard cases really are hard cases.[17] However problematic this may be for the work of the coroner, we can only accept that there is a grey zone between real suicides and risky actions. (In reality, as we have seen in Section 3.4, he may welcome the indeterminateness as giving him room for manoeuvre.)

Does suicide always require an action? Consider the case of an otherwise healthy patient who refuses a life-saving treatment, e.g., of his appendicitis, even though that treatment itself would not cause him any disproportionate additional burdens of its own. It cannot be denied that this agent has a suicidal mind. But the case differs in two possibly relevant

15 Stengel 1964. Daube 1972 shows that this fact was already known to the ancients.

16 In some, perhaps many cases the person's motivation may be less instrumental than that; she rather wishes to make a statement, cf. Wood 1980 on expressive suicides.

17 Cholbi 2011, 35.

respects from a paradigmatic case of suicide. The first difference is that this agent will die as a result of a life-threatening process, his appendicitis, that he has only allowed to proceed but not initiated himself.[18] The second difference is that this independent process can only be stopped by someone else, a physician. Allowing the process to proceed in this case doesn't mean abstaining from action oneself but refusing someone else to act who needs one's consent for acting. That these two differences are relevant, in particular in combination with each other, has some intuitive support, though I would not claim that support to be decisive.

Rather this is one question that we cannot hope to decide merely by appealing to our linguistic intuitions. But if we classify such cases as suicides because of the intention of the agent, it will be hard to identify any clear borderline distinguishing them from other cases of refusal of treatment. As a result, in countries where a right to refuse life-saving treatment is recognized, but a doctor is professionally obligated to prevent a suicide if he can, the law would be indeterminate. If, on the other hand, we make it obligatory for a doctor to decouple life-saving equipment in all cases in which the patient refuses further treatment, we are not thereby committed to make it obligatory for him to assist that patient to kill himself when he requests such help. It seems therefore advisable to distinguish between refusals of treatment and suicides. As we have seen, the distinction is not without intuitive support. Grey zones may be unavoidable, but if we *can* avoid a particular grey zone, that is to be preferred, certainly from the point of view of the law or professional morality. The important thing again is to realize that if we decide not to classify these refusals of treatment as suicides, in spite of significant similarities as regards the mental state of the agent, that need not prevent us from taking these mental states into account in evaluating the refusals, morally if not legally.

It seems, therefore, defensible to take the question whether death has been caused by a life-threatening process that has not been initiated by the agent and that can only be stopped with the aid of another agent as decisive for our classification. As we will see below in discussing death by self-imposed dehydration (Section 4.3), however, accepting these criteria need not imply that only actions can be classified as suicides.

Perhaps the most difficult definitional question is whether or not getting oneself to be killed by another person is to be considered suicide. Think of 'suicide by cop', of a soldier who stands up from a trench that hides him from a nearby enemy,[19] or of an aged cowboy who arranges a duel with

18 Beauchamp 1980, 74; O'Keeffe 1998 (1981). Tolhurst 1998 (1983), 107, rejects the criterion. Gert, Culver, Clouser 1998 rightly point out that we call it suicide if a person dies from a process that he did not initiate himself but could easily have blocked. More on this in Section 4 at footnote 39.

19 Baechler 1981, 19f.

a vastly superior gunman.[20] One could argue that the agents in these cases do not strictly initiate the series of events that will kill them, because one of those events consists of the killing action that the other person 'freely' but predictably decides upon, in response to their 'invitation'. But if this is not suicide, it is clearly very close to it, at least as close as the refusal of treatment of an appendicitis is. It is engineering one's own death. And shouldn't we recognize at least some cases of martyrdom as suicides?

In such cases it is clear that a homicide takes place, hence, if you believe that a death cannot be the outcome of a homicide and a suicide at the same time, you cannot classify the cases as involving suicides, but only as victim-precipitated homicides. But why should you believe that? Intuitively, it has to be conceded, both intention and probability seem to be relevant for deciding on the proper classification. If the cowboy goes to the fight with unloaded guns or shoots into the ground when the duel begins, it seems more plausible to say that it is a case of suicide than when he starts fighting to the best of his capacity, albeit with no expectation of winning. It could be suggested that if the agent intends to get killed, it is always a suicide if he succeeds, but if he merely foresees that he will be killed, it is only suicide if he foresees this outcome with virtual certainty.[21] This ruling would allow us to deny that Fr. Kolbe committed suicide, or that a soldier does who dies on a very dangerous mission that he has taken on as a volunteer. But the ruling would also draw us into the intractable problems of the proper individuation of intentions. I am therefore inclined to reach the same results by classifying none of these actions of causing oneself to be killed by another's hand as suicides. That would also mean that we do not consider it a suicide when a spy refuses to divulge any information under torture, although she knows that she will die as a result. That result also conforms to our intuitions,[22] but I do not deny that there is an element of stipulation involved, in particular in cases in which we believe death to be the intended outcome and not a mere side effect.

As I already warned the reader at the beginning of this discussion, in the case of such highly contested concepts it is unavoidable that in the end we have to cut the Gordian knot. If the truth about them cannot be established by inspecting a Platonic heaven of concepts, no definition is likely to be able to accommodate all our intuitive classifications smoothly.

Catching our results in a single formulation is not easy. The following formulation comes close: suicide is acting in such a way that one causes

20 Frey 1998 (1981), 131–132; cf. Clint Eastwood's *Gran Torino* (2008). Or consider the fictional case of the death of Ronald Opus, *Wikipedia*. In my view this isn't a case of suicide: Opus arranged for someone to be shot, but he didn't foresee that this someone would be he.

21 In English law an action is a killing if death is the intended result; if the result is merely foreseen it is only a killing if it is foreseen with virtual certainty, Kennedy, Grubb 2000, 2002.

22 Graber 1998 (1981), 152.

one's own death, knowing that this is the probable outcome of one's action, and without anticipating that another person will knowingly be the proximate cause of that effect. But the concept of 'acting' used here is imprecise. We will have to consider it more closely in order to decide whether ending one's life by stopping eating and drinking is or isn't suicide (Section 4.3).

4.2 Stopping eating and drinking[23]

One way in which a person who has decided to end her life can carry out that decision is by stopping eating and drinking. Though the contrary has been known to be true since antiquity, most people believe that self-starvation always leads to an inhumane, even gruesome death. Actually, feelings of hunger and thirst are limited and controllable.[24] The body starts producing ketone bodies which reduce the feeling of hunger, and after a few days endorphins which even tend to cause a mildly euphoric state.[25] At that time hunger is no longer felt at all. The feeling of thirst is largely caused by dehydration of the oral mucosa that can be effectively counteracted by keeping the mouth moist. Further factors determining feelings of thirst are at present only the object of unconfirmed hypotheses, but it is clear that these factors vary with age and state of health and play hardly any role in the case of the very old and sick. The progressive disturbance of renal functions leads to a kind of dumb condition that is not unpleasant.[26] If sleeping and pain medication are available and you are helped to change your position in bed in order to prevent decubitus, the most important complication that should be taken into account is the occurrence of delirium or agitation in the end stage of the process, when you are getting into a state of diminished or variable consciousness. In that case continuous or intermittent sedation will be necessary. Of course,

23 In this section and the following ones I use some formulations from den Hartogh 2020c.

24 Cf. Ahronheim, Gasner 1990. According to Ganzini et al. 2003 the medium score for the quality of this kind of death, given by hospice nurses in Oregon was 8 on a scale from 0–9. See Bolt et al. 2015 for a similar outcome, based on reports from Dutch physicians. These results correspond to the experience of physicians, nurses and counsellors from right-to-die societies, as appears from many anecdotal reports, cf. Vink 2013, 87; 2018, 117–130. Overall 74% of the witnesses interviewed by Chabot 2007, 165–169, reported to have experienced the process as leading to a humane death. According to Chabot planning and care may have been defective in the other cases.

25 This paragraph mainly relies on Sullivan 1993; KNMG/V&VN 2014.

26 Pathophysiological research about the effects of stopping the intake of fluids has been limited (Phillips 1984; Burge 1993; McCann 1994; Terman 2006) and is in need of confirmation, Suchner 2018.

if you suffer from any physical symptoms of an illness, standard palliative care has to be provided.

The process takes time, 7–15 days, and longer if the intake of fluids is not fully stopped from the beginning. If death occurs before 4–7 days, depending on age and medical condition, it is probably caused by illness rather than by dehydration (Section 7.2). In the beginning the process requires resolve and discipline. It also requires careful planning and the well-informed support and care of others, either relatives and friends or nurses. These facts go a long way to guarantee that a decision to die in this way will be both voluntary and well-considered.[27] You can decide to start the process impulsively, but you cannot implement your decision impulsively. And in most circumstances it is hardly conceivable that your decision will be implemented with the perseverance needed if you do not fully endorse it. In a few cases the attitude of others may tip the balance when you are tempted to give up, and in such cases the process can be expected to be a tough one. If you have a strong desire to remain in control, you may not like being dependent on the care of others to the extent that is needed, and the fact that the process ends with a period of diminished consciousness and coma may also be a problem for you. But the necessary support and care of intimates often strengthens mutual bonds. That is one reason why these intimates often look back on it as a period that has enriched their lives. During the first days you also have the time to reflect on your life, say goodbye and make some final arrangements.[28]

People can use this method of ending their lives without requesting a prescription from a physician and without transgressing any law that requires such a prescription for the acquisition and possession of lethal drugs. The option is available to some persons, for example patients with a spinal cord injury, who don't have other options of ending their own lives. It is less suitable for the young and healthy.[29] And it requires a determination that we cannot expect very fragile elderly people to have at their command (Section 14.6).

27 Bernat, Gert, Mogielnicki 1993; Quill, Lo, Brock 1997; Miller, Meier 1998; Gert, Culver, Clouser 1998; Ivanovic, Büche, Fringer 2014; Quill et al. 2018; Jansen, Wall, Miller 2019.

28 Eddy 1994, 272: 179–181; Chabot 2007, 173–176; Vink 2013, 85; Bolt et al. 2015b; Birnbacher 2015; Quill et al. 2018. For some information about the incidence of the decision to stop the intake of fluids, see Chapter 3 at footnote 55–56.

29 Overall 81.6% of people using this method of ending their life were 80+, Hagens et al. 2021. According to Bolt et al. 2015b their median age was 83 years. 76% depended on others for everyday care, 74% had a life expectancy of less than one year. As reported by Hagens et al. 2021 44.7% had requested euthanasia; cf. Chabot 2007, 127 (47%); Bolt et al. (19%).

4.3 Is it suicide?

People who decide to take this route to a self-chosen death usually are indignant when it is labelled suicide. ('Mother would never commit suicide, she considered it a sin'.)[30] Are they right?[31] The question is legally relevant in some jurisdictions, because they recognize a legal obligation for everyone to prevent any suicide, if possible. It is more commonly relevant because you need others to avoid unnecessary risks and burdens, and these others might be accused of assisting with suicide, if it is suicide.

If it is not, what is it? The usual suggestion is that it should be classified with refusals of life-sustaining treatments.[32] The first step in this direction is made by the redescription, common in the literature, of stopping eating and drinking as 'refusal of food and fluids'. But stopping eating and drinking does not necessarily involve *refusing* anything that is offered by others. You may, unwisely, act on your own, or the people supporting you may not offer you anything unless you ask for it. Moreover, handfeeding by a relative, or even by a nurse, is not a kind of medical treatment, and therefore even refusing an offer of food and drink is normally not refusing treatment.

A major argument for classifying stopping eating and drinking as a kind of treatment refusal rather than suicide is the following. If someone has started to stop the intake of fluids and cannot be convinced or seduced to give up his plan, the only way to prevent his death is by forced hydration. But that would not only violate his right to self-determination but also his right to bodily integrity. That is the very same reason why we should respect a refusal of treatment.[33]

However, if a person uses any kind of poison to kill herself, it is equally true that her life can only be saved by a bodily intrusion, emptying her stomach. That is no reason to deny self-poisoning to be suicide. And that we have the same reasons for respecting certain decisions that hasten

30 Cf. Chabot 2007, 228.

31 This is denied by O'Keeffe 1998 (1981); Hallenbeck 2000; Walther 2010; Ach 2011; Birnbacher 2015; Jox et al. 2017; Menzel 2017; Keown 2018, 253ff; Moskop 2021; de Leo 2022; and with some qualifications by Jansen, Sulmasy 2002b and Jansen 2004 (but cf. Jansen, Wall, Miller 2019). Cantor 2006 is also inclined to deny it.

32 Bernat, Gert, Mogielnicki 1993; Miller, Meier 1998; Gert, Culver, Clouser 1998; Quill, Lee, Nunn 2000; Pope, Anderson 2011, 420; Neitzke et al. 2013; Ivanovic, Büche, Fringer 2014; Schwartz 2014; KNMG/V&VN 2014; Quill 2015 (but cf. Quill et al. 2018); Feichter, Weixler, Birklbauer 2018. According to Bickhardt, Hanke 2014 it should be considered a class of actions on its own. Sumner 2021 doesn't call it suicide but agrees that it 'hastens death, rather than merely allowing it to happen'. Of Swiss health-care professionals 63.5% considers it a natural form of dying, 5.4% suicide, Stängle et al. 2021.

33 Gert, Culver, Clouser 1998, 187; Pope, Anderson 2011, 421; Feichter, Weixler, Birklbauer 2018; McGee, Miller 2017; Birnbacher 2017, 323. McGee, Miller and Birnbacher don't conclude that cessation of taking fluids isn't suicide.

death doesn't show that these decisions all belong to the same category, either of suicides or of refusals of treatment. That a way of acting is protected by a right doesn't entail that it cannot be suicide. Otherwise, we couldn't recognize a right to suicide without implying that it is not really suicide that we recognize a right to. This is a clear example of evaluative considerations intruding upon the discussion of a classificatory issue.

In Section 4.1 of this chapter I indicated two significant differences between refusals of treatment and suicides. If you die because you refuse to use antibiotics, your death will be the primary effect of a life-threatening process that you haven't initiated, pneumonia. You have 'only' allowed that process to follow its course without blocking it. But by abstaining from drinking you initiate the process that will kill you, dehydration.[34] A second relevant difference is that medical treatment requires a doctor who takes co-responsibility for the course of events. But for the maintenance of your bodily functions by the provision of food and drink you are responsible yourself, in free interaction with your intimates and market parties. Continuing normal self-care is different from consenting to the intervention of a doctor in a case of illness.

The relevance of these differences comes into sight when we look at the most fundamental objection to the classification of stopping eating and drinking as suicide, an objection already presupposed in the idea that it rather resembles refusal of treatment. Suicide is an action, but when you stop eating and drinking you only omit doing something. You do not kill anybody, only allow yourself to die. The distinction between killing and letting die is, however, not simply a subdivision of the distinction between actions and omissions. On the one hand it is an action to decouple life-saving equipment, but if it is done because the patient refuses further treatment or because continuing it is no longer considered to be in his interest, it is a case of allowing him to die. His treatment is invested in a technical device, hence in order to discontinue the treatment you have to switch off the device. That is why there is no morally or legally relevant difference between withholding and withdrawing treatment. On the other hand when a doctor fails to administer antibiotics to a pneumonia patient who requests treatment and is otherwise completely healthy, that doctor kills her patient, just like a mother kills her new-born baby when she doesn't give it food and drink. These examples show that we classify a policy, whether it consists of actions or of omissions, as killing or letting die, by comparing that policy to some baseline of 'normal' action. In the examples that baseline is determined by duties of care. As long as you have such a duty, an omission to act that results

34 This is agreed to by Gert, Culver, Clouser 1998, 193 ("an electrolytic imbalance caused by a lack of fluids"); and Cantor 2006; but denied by Pope and Anderson 2011, 420: "The patient's natural state is to dehydrate unless fluids are affirmatively introduced."

in death will be a killing, but as soon as the duty ends, the action that is needed to stop caring will have to be classified as letting die.[35]

If we consider actions and omissions with deadly consequences for the agent, the baseline is determined by all those elementary forms of spontaneous self-care that you need to maintain your life from moment to moment and from day to day. If by an immense effort you would succeed to hold your breath forever, we would not say that you didn't kill yourself because you merely 'omitted breathing'.[36] When you remain sitting on the former tidemark when the tide comes in, you are as much drowning yourself as when you walk into standing water.[37] That is why consciously stopping to provide yourself with food and drink is suicide.

By the way, the reason why ceasing to breathe as well as ceasing to eat and drink are killings is not that effort is involved. It can require much effort to abstain from aggression against someone who has deeply insulted you. But that doesn't make abstaining from aggression an action.[38]

I have pointed to two elements that differentiate refusing treatment from stopping eating and drinking: the presence of a life-threatening process that the subject has not initiated, and the fact that only another person could stop that process. It now turns out that both are necessary. The incoming tide is a process that no-one has initiated. So is an avalanche, but if you consciously wait until it has reached you without making the few steps aside that would save you, that is suicide.[39] Somewhat more realistically, if you accidentally ingest a deadly poison, but knowingly fail to do what is necessary to empty your stomach, that is also suicide. As it is suicide if in spite of freezing cold you don't put clothes on when your central heating system falls out, with hypothermia as a foreseen result.

Stopping the intake of fluids has a number of characteristics that differentiate it from paradigmatic cases of suicide. These characteristics have also been advanced as reasons for denying it to be a form of suicide. To mention but one example: the decision is reversible during the first days, and death doesn't occur abruptly.[40] But if you lock someone up in a shed in your garden and allow him to die there from lack of food and water, you certainly kill him (Section 7.3). Similarly, if you kill yourself

35 According to the Supreme Court of South Australia self-starvation is not suicide because there is no duty to feed oneself, *H Ltd v J* 2010, SASC 176.

36 "The cessation of the physiological influx of nutrients and water ... parallels the cessation of the physiological influx of oxygen in hanging or drowning.". Jox et al. 2017. Would Pope and Anderson (cf. footnote 34) consider deoxygenation to be our 'natural state'?

37 Justice Scalia of the US Supreme Court, *Cruzan v. Director, Missouri Department of Health* 497 US 261 (1990) at 296, quoted by Keown 2018, 255.

38 Birnbacher 1995, ch. 6.1.

39 *Pace* Tolhurst 1998 (1983), 109. See Section 4.1 at footnote 18.

40 Neitzke et al. 2013; Feichter, Weixler, Birklbauer 2018.

by means of a slowly working poison that you could but don't neutralize by a counterpoison even after several days, that is still suicide.

If most suicides are different from voluntary dehydration in some respect, for example by being done in a quasi-impulsive and violent way by absolutely lonely people,[41] that doesn't mean that they are different by definition. It means that they are not, as long as some suicides are not different in those very respects[42] (Section 3.6). I have, moreover, argued in Section 3.4 that non-violent suicides that are the outcome of a process of reflection and dialogue only *seem* to be rare because they tend not to be registered as suicides.

A final set of arguments that purport to show that abstaining from the intake of fluids is not suicide are explicitly normative: if it would be suicide, we should morally condemn and perhaps legally prosecute doctors, nurses and relatives who help people to go through the process. But most people rightly prefer to leave those doctors, nurses and relatives in peace.[43] Arguments of this kind show what is wrong with short-cutting evaluative questions by definitions. If we cannot identify any relevant differences between stopping eating and drinking and at least some suicides, we should rather conclude that we have to accept that suicide assistance is not necessarily impermissible in all cases.

4.4 Legal consequences

Many doctors and nurses believe, for reasons that I have discussed in the last section, that stopping eating and drinking is not a kind of suicide.[44] Recently some professional medical organizations have also taken that position.[45] These organizations thereby avoid having to address some difficult moral and legal issues. They conclude that on the request of a person who has decided to stop the intake of fluids a doctor is at least permitted, perhaps even professionally required to provide care to that person. That duty includes providing her with relevant information about the process

41 KNMG/V&VN 2014. As Jox et al. 2017 point out, the dying phase resembles that of a natural dying process which also involves some degree of dehydration. They suggest that this may partly explain the widespread acceptance of the practice.

42 Jox et al. 2017 ('a discrete form of suicide'); Keown 2018, 253.

43 E.g., Alt-Epping 2018.

44 In 93 of 97 cases the doctors who established the death of the person registered it as a 'natural death', Chabot 2007, 227.

45 Quill, Byock 2000 (for the American College of Physicians-American Society of Internal Medicine, End of Care Consensus Panel); Hospice and Palliative Nurses Association 2011; KNMG/V&VN 2014; American Nurses Association 2017 (reporting a growing consensus); Feichter, Weixler, Birklbauer 2018 (for the *Österreichische Pallativgesellschaft*). Nauck, Ostgathe, Radbruch 2014 (*Deutsche Gesellschaft für Palliativmedizin*); and Radbruch, de Lima 2017 (International Association for Hospice and Palliative Care) implicitly take this position.

and about the further care she will need, in particular mouth care, to be given by the person herself and by others. It also includes monitoring that care and supplementing it when necessary, by providing sleeping pills and pain medication and by sedating her when delirium occurs.

If, however, as I concluded, stopping eating and drinking is a kind of suicide, it seems that doctors who act in such ways are guilty of assisting with suicide, which is still a crime in most countries and states.[46] Some authors have argued that, even if stopping eating and drinking is a form of suicide, the prohibition of providing assistance doesn't apply to these doctors. Even in countries that have introduced an exception to this prohibition for doctors who satisfy certain requirements, they do not need to appeal to that exception. For it is, these authors argue, fully up to the person to decide whether or not to end her own life in that way, she doesn't need the doctor either to authorize or to implement that decision. The only thing that the doctor supplies is information and comfort.[47]

It is true that in providing care to a person who has discontinued the intake of fluids, or information about the process to someone who seriously considers the option, the doctor in no way authorizes her decision. He can be neutral about it, or even disagree with it.[48] However, it cannot be denied that a doctor by monitoring the process and intervening when necessary, at least makes it easier for that person to kill herself in this way. He lowers a threshold for carrying out and therefore for making that plan. It may even be the case that a person only decides to go down this road because her physician assures her to make her comfortable on the way. That is the clearest case of causal co-responsibility, but it is not the only one.[49] In jurisdictions in which assisting with suicide is legally forbidden, all or most actions that merely facilitate the suicide without being necessary for performing it, are covered by the prohibition. If it is only difficult but not impossible for you to stir the natrium-pentobarbital through the custard, in taking over that task your son or daughter is surely assisting you, both in the colloquial and in the legal sense.

That a doctor in providing care to a person who has decided to end her life by stopping eating and drinking similarly facilitates her suicide,

46 In some countries no such legal prohibition exists, e.g., in Germany. In the past it was, however, considered punishable to leave a person in a state of life-endangering risk without interfering. But court decisions (e.g. OLG München NJW 1987, 2940: *Hacketal*) have made it clear that this doesn't apply when a person has voluntarily waived his claim to such 'aid', as he does by voluntarily stopping eating and drinking, Birnbacher 2015.

47 McGee, Miller 2017; Feichter, Weixler, Birklbauer 2018.

48 Cf. Jansen 2004 on cases in which she considers stopping eating and drinking to be a suicide and hence impermissible. On her view it is always a professional duty of doctors to provide palliative care to the people involved, but if it is a case of suicide, the doctor cooperates in that person's wrongdoing if she provides information, either about the option itself or about the care she will be given. Cf. Section 5.3.

49 As Jox et al. 2017 suggest.

and therefore should be considered to assist her, doesn't necessarily mean, however, that his action is actionable. That is fairly obvious if the person has a legally acknowledged right to end her own life, or to end it in this particular way.[50] It is true that even in that case it may still be open to the law to restrict forms of assistance in order to protect the rights and freedoms of others. But we have already seen that this justification of restrictions on the execution of the right does not apply to this particular case. It is almost unthinkable that someone will end his own life in this way, who has decided to do so either involuntarily or incompetently. Hence, if a doctor is allowed to give the necessary care during the process, there will be no reason for anyone to be afraid of being 'helped' against his own will and judgment.

Consider the analogous case of a patient who refuses a life-saving treatment in order to end his life. If the physician thinks his decision to be mistaken, she can, in a respectful way, argue with him, but she cannot force him to undergo treatment. Moreover, whatever her personal views, during the dying stage that starts now, she still will be responsible for providing care, including the palliative care needed to avoid suffering. She has a professional duty, often explicitly recognized by the law, not to leave her patient in a helpless state.[51] To some extent she will thereby facilitate the implementation of the patient's decision, but that is irrelevant, for the patient is within his rights in making that decision. Palliative care is medically indicated because of the condition of the patient and, given that justification, the fact that it may facilitate the implementation of the patient's plan is a mere side effect. That the doctor fulfils his professional duty of relieving his patient's distress doesn't make him an accessory.

But even in a jurisdiction in which no right to suicide is recognized, the kind of palliative care that we are presently discussing need not be punishable. It is permissible for a doctor to offer a painkilling drug to a patient that he knows will probably shorten her life in addition to ending her suffering, even though his action will in many jurisdictions satisfy all conditions for classifying that action as some kind of homicide. As long as he acts on a proper medical indication and satisfies a proportionality requirement, what he does will be morally and legally all right. His action will be considered a justifiable homicide, or not

50 Cantor 2006, 111, refers to two unpublished New York cases in which the courts refused nursing homes the authorization they requested to intervene in the process of stopping eating and drinking of two chronically ill elderly women in their mid-eighties. Quill et al. 2018, footnotes 24–26, mention three other judicial precedents (1984, 1992, 2010). Cf. footnote 35.

51 According to the French *Claeys-Leonetti law* of 2016 the patient will even have a legal right to receive continuous deep sedation until death when he has a serious and incurable condition, his decision is life-threatening in the short term and is likely to cause unbearable suffering.

a homicide at all. (As we have seen already in Section 4.1, this need not depend on the doctor's intention.) In this case the doctor may properly judge alleviation of the patient's suffering to be more important than the foreseeable shortening of her life. The same reasoning applies when someone decides to end his life by abstaining from taking fluids. If a doctor provides the necessary care in such a case, the law and professional morality could and should recognize a similar exception to the prohibition of assistance and consider the doctor's action either a justifiable assistance or no assistance at all.[52]

Some final comments. First: it has been argued that food and drink are not only to be considered life-saving nutrients. They are also focus points of social interaction. Sharing food and drink is an essential element of our being connected to each other. Therefore, merely to consent to your loved one's decision to stop eating and drinking would already mean to sever your connection to him, leaving him to his social death.[53] This conclusion is in clear contradiction with the actual experience of people who make this decision and carry it out in close cooperation with their relatives. It rests on a reification of symbols: you can't have the thing without the symbol. But surely people can abstain from some symbolic means of expressing their connectedness for good reasons without sacrificing their connectedness. When people can no longer greet each other in the customary way because of the infection risks in a pandemia, that doesn't mean that they are all socially dead.

A second comment: some important questions about this particular way of ending one's life have to be left open until further stages of my argument. A first question is the following: it would be much easier for you to carry out a decision to stop eating and drinking if your doctor consented to start continuous deep sedation, either from the start or when you have shown your resolve by pressing on for the first few days.[54] That it is easier is not an indication for sedation that is recognized by the existing guidelines for palliative sedation,[55] but it is questionable whether these guidelines aren't too restrictive in regard to the indications they authorize. This is an issue that I will discuss in Section 8.3. It could, second, be argued that sedating a person who has a life expectancy of more than a few days and failing to give her food and fluids from that same time on is equivalent to killing her at her request. If a doctor thinks

52 Jansen 2004 (see footnote 48); Jox et al. 2017. Keown 2018, 257–258, accepts this argument, but only when the doctor doesn't act with intent to facilitate suicide.

53 McInerny 1992; Loewy 2001; Jansen, Sulmasy 2002b.

54 Unless doubts about the efficacy of deep sedation in eradicating awareness are warranted (Section 8.2).

55 Feichter, Weixler, Birklbauer 2018. They also argue that this means disabling the person to exercise her right to self-determination. But the person's request implies waiving that right.

that euthanasia is always wrong, but that this is an acceptable alternative, he may be merely deceiving himself.[56] Whether this is true I will consider in Section 7.3. Conclusions as regards the proper use of deep sedation in the care for a person who has started a process of voluntary dehydration will be drawn in Section 8.7.

A second question will also have to wait. It sometimes happens that at a later stage in the process the person, perhaps in a delirious state, loses her decision-making capacity and repeatedly requests a glass of water. Let's assume that before she started the process the person has explicitly declared that her present wish should be disregarded. Should it be?[57] Should her prior decision, competently made, overrule her later decision, incompetently made? I will address that question in Section 15.4 on the authority of advance directives.

In Section 2.5, I argued that people have, or should have, a right to determine the manner and time of their own death. Voluntarily stopping eating and drinking is clearly a way of exercising that right, whether we consider it a kind of suicide or not. In this chapter I have appealed to a proper understanding of the concept of suicide to argue that stopping eating and drinking really *is* a form of suicide, and the medical surveillance that is required to avoid severe suffering during the process, a form of assisting suicide. But assistance of that kind is nevertheless justified by the professional morality of doctors and nurses, even in jurisdictions in which assisting with suicide is a crime.

What about the care provided by relatives and other informal caregivers? I will discuss this question in the next chapter (Section 5.1).

56 Magnusson 2009; Rady, Verheijde 2010.

57 KNMG/V&VN 2014. Quill, Byock 2000 believe that water should be given in this case; Quill et al 2018 see it as a dilemma, with arguments for and against giving water.

5 What is implied by the right to suicide?

5.1 Assistance by loved ones

Mrs. Heringa was 99 years old. She suffered from heart failure, back and renal problems, was almost blind and permanently tired, had impaired hearing and mobility and as a result of all these problems thought that she could no longer spend her days in a meaningful way. Her second great-grandson was expected but she didn't want to wait for him. She decided to end her life and when her GP refused to help her, she made her own plans. Her son Albert discovered that she did no longer use any of the many medicaments she received for her ailments but saved them all in order to kill herself with them. On reflection he could sympathize with her plan, but he realized that the means she intended to use for carrying it out were ineffective and dangerous. By coincidence he happened to have a surplus of the anti-malaria-drugs that he used to take on his many travels through tropical countries. He had acquired those drugs on prescription; to possess them is not illegal anyway. By consulting the literature and his apothecary he found out that the drugs were sufficient to allow his mother to end her life in a safe, efficient and painless way. He also helped her to make further preparations, but she took the pills without help. That the initiative was hers and that she was in full control of the procedure could be verified by looking at the video her son made of her last hours.[1]

In Germany and Sweden help of this kind is not forbidden by law, though we seem to have almost no information about the extent to which it is actually provided. In the Netherlands, as in most other countries, the penal code contains an explicit provision prohibiting suicide assistance. The Dutch code adds an exception to that prohibition, but the exception only applies to physicians who meet a number of requirements of due care. But, as long as the assistance is provided by friends or family, this crime is rarely prosecuted. Even when, in some of the six cases in which a counsellor of a right-to-die society has been brought to court for assisting suicide, it turned out that some family members had given similar assistance, they

1 Cf. the case of Mr. Kalisvaart, described in Section 14.1.

DOI: 10.4324/9781003281115-6

were not prosecuted. When the counsellor's lawyer protested about unequal treatment in one of these cases, the court replied 'that it was understandable that the prosecution had taken the emotional involvement of the children with the death wish and death of their mother into account'.[2]

Nevertheless, when Heringa's video was shown on television two years after his mother's death, the Public Prosecutor decided to act, although only after three more years of hesitation. The District Court duly convicted him but didn't impose any penalty. The Court of Appeal in Arnhem dismissed the criminal charge, but the Supreme Court nullified that decision and referred the case to the Court of Appeal in den Bosch. That court convicted him again and gave him a suspended sentence of six months with a two years' probation. Finally, six years after Heringa's first trial, that decision was upheld by the Supreme Court.[3]

Much of the argument in these procedures is of local interest only, because it appeals to specific elements of the Dutch legal tradition. But one particular defence that counsel increasingly relied on is of broader interest. As we have seen (Section 2.5), the European Court of Human Rights has accepted that people have the right to determine the manner and time of their own death. Interestingly the Court derives that right from the right to respect for one's private and *family life,* recognized in Art. 8 of the *European Convention of Human Rights.* Arguably, therefore, what the right protects is not only the interest of a person to make decisions about her own life, but also the interest she has in making these decisions and carrying them out in the intimate sphere of her own close relations.[4]

It is by now generally accepted in philosophical thinking about autonomy that an autonomous being is not an isolated mushroom. Although

2 Rb Almelo 29 mei 2009, ECLI:NL:RBALM:2009:BIS891, confirmed on appeal.

3 Rb Zutphen, 22/10/2013, ECLI:NL:RBGEL:2013:3976; GRH Arnhem-Leeuwarden, 13/5/2015, ECLI:NL:GHARL:2015:3444; Hof den Bosch ECLI:NL:GHSHE: 2018:345; Hoge Raad 16/4/2019, ECLI:NL:HR:2019:598. For a similar case see Rb Limburg, 26/2/2019, ECLI:NL:RBLIM:2019:1740. The court convicted a son who had helped his father to end his life with the use of helium and imposed a suspended sentence of three months.

4 ECRM, *Koch v. Germany* 19/07/2012, nr. 497/09, confirms the special standing family members may claim on account of their personal connectedness to the person who ends her life, thereby revising its earlier judgment that the right to a private and family life is untransferable, *Sanles Sanles v Spain*, 26/10/2000, nr. 48335/99. Mrs. and Mr. Koch claimed the right of access to lethal drugs. When their claim had been rejected, Mrs. Koch ended her life with the help of *Dignitas* in Switzerland. After her death the German courts rejected Mr. Koch's appeal to the original decision, because he couldn't appeal to the rights of his dead wife under Art. 8 anymore. But the European Court decided that he *could* appeal to his own right because of his "exceptionally close relationship" to his wife "and his immediate involvement in the realization of her wish to end her life." His appeal was nevertheless rejected because on account of the wide margin of appreciation it was up to the German legal authorities to decide on it. In 2017, however, the *Bundesverwaltungsgericht* accepted the appeal, see footnote 47.

social influences can have both positive and negative effects on the quality of our decision-making, that quality can normally be improved by a dialogue with the right people. Such a dialogue provides us both with a reality check of our own ideas and with the awareness of a wider horizon of alternative options. You may therefore hope that when you inform your loved ones that you plan to take your own life they will not automatically resign themselves to your intention 'because it is your decision to make', but consider whether this really is the best choice left to you, and remonstrate with you if they are not convinced. Even if you decide to go against the common views of your social environment, the confrontation may have crystallized your decision. If your decision lacks all social support, it will be hard for you to maintain the self-confidence that is necessary for truly identifying with that decision.[5] Loneliness tends to pathologize: that is the basic reason for promoting rather than disturbing the social embedding of suicide.

This doesn't mean that either the state or the medical profession could require your decision to be supported by your intimates. Your social relations are only autonomy-supporting if they are symmetrical, and this means that at the end of the dialogue you should be left to make up your own mind (Section 2.5). If this is denied, your self-respect is endangered in yet another way.[6] And more may be at stake than your self-respect. At a certain moment your partner could come to the insight that you are absolutely determined to end your life, even though he is still not fully convinced that there are no alternatives. He might then conclude that further resistance would be of no avail and might threaten to undermine your relationship at the very end of its history. That could be a defensible reason for him, though not necessarily a decisive one, to show his unbroken solidarity by some form of assistance.

It is up to the people involved to weigh such considerations; the law should respect their weighing. If a person's right to a private and family life implies a right to make decisions about her own death, and the right extends its umbrella of protection to her family and close friends, the forms of assistance it permits therefore cannot be restricted to cases in which it is beyond reasonable doubt that death is in that person's best interests, for example because it ends intolerable suffering that cannot be relieved.

5.2 The rights and freedoms of others

Assistance is of course rightly forbidden as long as it is not beyond reasonable doubt that it doesn't compromise the voluntary and well-considered character of the person's decision. Your family can be your worst enemy, more than any third person. Think of a person who hasn't really consented

5 Anderson, Honneth 2005; Mackenzie 2008.
6 Nys 2016.

to ordering Pentobarbital from Mexico, but doesn't dare to deny it. But it is also in the interest of society at large to provide people with guarantees that they will not be manipulated in more or less subtle ways to make a choice for death. Both general safety and the general sense of safety belong to the important external effects of safeguards against abuse.

These social interests may co-determine the framing of the safeguards. Even if it follows from Art. 8 *ECHR* that your right to determine the manner and time of your own death implies a right to involve your family in making these decisions and acting on them, neither of these rights is an absolute one. For Art. 8 goes on to stipulate that these rights can be interfered with in accordance with the law, if that interference is necessary in a democratic state for one or more of the reasons mentioned on a limitative list. The relevant reason in a case like this is: to protect the rights and freedoms of others.

Can we ever be sure that no impermissible pressure has been exercised and shouldn't that be a reason to forbid assistance in all cases? The remarkable thing about the *Heringa* case is that nobody, not even the Public Prosecution or any of the courts that convicted him, had the slightest suspicion that Mrs. Heringa's decision to end her life wasn't fully her own. And if her rights under Art. 8 *ECHR* include her right to be assisted by her son, this right cannot simply be taken away by a blanket prohibition that is motivated by reasons that by general acknowledgement do not apply to her case. A legal instrument of that kind is too blunt.

In all recent cases in which an argument of this kind has been presented to the European Court, it has replied that national legal authorities are in the best position to decide what is 'necessary in a democratic state in order to protect the rights and freedoms of others', and that they therefore have a 'wide margin of appreciation' in this area.[7] Because most European states at the moment impose a blanket ban on suicide assistance, we cannot realistically expect the court to take any other position, even though it means that the right to determine the manner and time of one's own death in many places is merely 'theoretical and illusory', not 'concrete and effective' (Section 2.5). But it doesn't follow that a blanket ban is justifiable anywhere.

In the *Heringa* case, the Court of Appeal den Bosch replied as follows to the appeal of the defence to Art. 8 *ECHR*. It is true that a right to suicide is implied by the right to a private and family life, and it may be

7 *ECHR*, *Haas v Switzerland* 20/1/2011, no. 31322/07 (Section 2.5), *Gross v Zwitserland*, 14/5/2013, no. 67810/10, *Koch v Germany* (footnote 4), *Nicklinson and Lamb v the UK*, 23/6/2015, no. 2078/15. In *Pretty v the UK* (29/4/2002, nr. 2346/02) the court itself argued that the general prohibition on assistance could be considered as 'necessary' to protect weak and vulnerable people, and that the prohibition applied to Mrs. Pretty, even though she could not be considered either weak or vulnerable. Since *Haas* the Court hasn't repeated that it is unavoidable to draw the boundaries of the prohibition so broadly, cf. Black 2012.

true that this right implies a right of family members to provide assistance. We need not decide whether this actually is true, because, even if it is, it is open to the lawgiver to limit the right in order to protect the rights and freedoms of others. The Dutch lawgiver has done this by a blanket prohibition. The European case law makes it clear that the European Court considers this to be within the wide margin of appreciation it accords to national states. The appeal therefore fails. We may expect the present appeal of Albert Heringa to the European Court to be equally unsuccessful.

This turns out to be the usual way in which Dutch courts decide when the European Court grants a margin of appreciation to national states.[8] The courts translate the margin into an area of discretion for the legislative and the executive. In a number of cases applicants have, for example, argued that provisions of fiscal law violate the principle of equal treatment because of the arbitrary way in which they distribute fiscal burdens and privileges. In one of those cases the Dutch Court of Appeal conceded to the applicant that a rule of fiscal law was substantially unjust for this reason, but, because the European Court recognizes an 'exceptionally wide margin of appreciation' in fiscal matters, left it to the lawgiver to redress the injustice.[9]

This attitude of the Dutch courts may be understandable at a time when the judiciary is habitually accused of usurping democratic powers. But the result is that the courts largely abdicate their task to protect the basic rights of individual citizens, in particular against the institution that has the greatest power to infringe upon those rights.[10] In states that are parties to the European Convention, the courts should always decide a claim that a legal provision violates one of the rights recognized in that convention on its merits, not by merely anticipating the outcome of an appeal to the European Court. If that is done, a blanket ban on assisting suicide is clearly indefensible. How such a ban should be narrowed down will of course depend on details of the relevant legal system and other contextual matters. In the Dutch case the Supreme Court could simply have decided that the prohibition doesn't apply when it is beyond reasonable doubt that the person's decision to end her life is voluntary

8 Happé 2014 (on fiscal law); Barkhuysen 2013.

9 ECLI/NL/GHDHA/2017/3602. In *Dudgeon v UK*, 22/10/1981, no. 7525/76, on the other hand, the Court decided that the scope of the margin will be restricted in cases concerning "a most intimate aspect of private life", see also *Dickson v UK*, 4/12/2007, no. 44362/04, Vis, Zuurveld 2021, no. 151–152.

10 Dutch courts are not permitted to assess whether Dutch laws are in accordance with the Dutch Constitution. This is often defended by pointing out that the courts are permitted to assess whether a law is in accordance with a treaty, in particular with the European Convention, because the Convention and the Constitution contain similar lists of human rights. But this defence doesn't take the actual practice of assessment into account.

and well-considered.[11] In addition the Court could have designed some procedural rules for deciding whether or not this is beyond reasonable doubt. Or it could have left this task to the legislature.

Pioneering work along these lines has been done in the UK. In *Purdy v DPP* (2009) the House of Lords required the Director of Public Prosecutions to produce guidance for people who contemplate ending their lives with assistance from others, by specifying which factors would determine a decision to prosecute or not.[12] The Lords gave some hints about such factors: the choice for death should be a genuine exercise of autonomy, the presence of pressure or coercion should count in favour of prosecution, as should an improper, for example financial motive. In response the Director issued a policy for prosecutors.[13] The leading idea of the policy is that prosecution should be in the public interest, and this means that its aim should be the prevention of abuse and harm. The policy applies to all kinds of assistance, but a professional is more likely to be prosecuted than a relative, in particular when he has a professional duty of care as regards the requester. Of course, a permissive regime created by a prosecution policy offers less legal certainty and protection than a regulatory system introduced by the legislation or the courts.[14] But it is clear that Albert Heringa would not have been prosecuted in the UK.

Anyway, if the courts fail to protect the right to a private and family life sufficiently, it is the task of the lawgiver to change the law, recognizing that this right implies some right to assistance by loved ones, however specified and limited.

In Section 4.3 I argued that stopping eating and drinking should be recognized for what it is: suicide. It follows that, even though in such cases the provision of palliative care by physicians could be justified by the medical indications for such care, any assistance by friends and relatives,

11 Cf. the "modest proposal" put forward by Rachels 1980 to permit mercy killing with the only condition that the mercy killer proves that the person killed had made a voluntary and well-considered request. If the proposal is restricted to family members in a home setting, the objections made by Feinberg 1986, 347–351, don't apply.

12 UKHL 45. Debbie Purdy, a patient with multiple sclerosis, planned to travel to Switzerland in order to end her life with the assistance of *Dignitas* and wanted to be sure that her husband would not be prosecuted for helping her to make the journey. Without that assurance she intended to travel when she could still do so unaided. She died in 2014, having intermittently refused food during the year before.

13 Director of Public Prosecutions, *Policy for Prosecutors in Respect of Cases of Encouraging or Assisting Suicide*, Feb. 2010, updated 2014. An application for judicial review by disability campaigners was rejected by the Court of Appeal in 2017. Up to January 2019 144 cases of assisted suicide had been referred to the Crown Prosecution Service. Three cases of encouraging or assisting suicide had been successfully prosecuted, one case had been charged and acquitted, seven cases referred onwards for prosecution for homicide (Data from cps.gov.uk).

14 Lewis 2011.

for example by moistening the person's mouth, would actually be covered by a blanket prohibition on assistance, although in many jurisdictions prosecution is extremely unlikely. But such actions seem to belong *par excellence* to the sphere of family life protected by Art. 8 *ECHR*. They should be explicitly decriminalized. That would also encourage professional associations of doctors to recognize the provision of palliative care in such cases as a professional task and to offer guidance for the proper fulfilment of that task.

5.3 A right to information?

Some other exceptions to the general prohibition of assistance are more or less generally recognized.[15] In the first place it is plausible that the mere presence of relatives and friends providing moral support makes it easier for people to overcome their fear of death, and in that sense facilitates suicide. But even if you reject the existence of a right to suicide, you should agree that it is inhumane to condemn people to die lonely.[16] In most countries, secondly, providing general information about non-violent ways to kill oneself will be considered to be covered by the right to freedom of expression.[17] If it belongs to the core of people's rights to make that decision in a well-considered way, it is obvious that the provision of relevant information cannot be forbidden.

In 1991 Derek Humphry published his famous *Final Exit*, in which he gave general information, in particular as regards the use of a plastic bag for realizing painless asphyxiation. In the following year the use of that method increased by 31% in the USA. That fact led some authors to accuse Humphry of irresponsible behaviour.[18] But even when the use of this method increased as a result of the publication, the total number of suicides did not. We should welcome every case in

15 As they have been in Dutch case law in a series of six cases between 1995 and 2008 in which volunteers from right-to-die societies have been charged with providing unlawful assistance, cf. Griffiths, Weyers, Adams 2008, 46–47. Two of these cases ended with an acquittal, two others with a partly unconditional prison sentence.

16 Since 2004 volunteers of the Final Exit Network are willing, after checks, to sit with persons suffering from chronically painful illness as they choose to end their lives. After unsuccessful efforts by the states of Arizona and Georgia to prosecute some of those volunteers, the state of Minnesota obtained a felony conviction from a grand jury on 14 May 2015. The Supreme Court of Georgia found the Georgia statute against assisting suicide in violation of the First Amendment protection of free speech, and struck down the statute in its entirety, 6/2/2012. But physically helping a person to commit suicide or physically providing the means is still a felony in Georgia.

17 *Final Exit* is banned in France; attempts to ban it in Australia and New Zealand failed.

18 Marzuk 1993.

which non-violent means have been used instead of violent ones, and effective means instead of unsafe ones, that will only cause irreparable damage to the brain. (Incidentally, we know by now that the plastic bag method actually *is* unsafe.[19]) We have no reason either to assume that the provision of the information invites more impulsive suicides, because the methods described require planning. It is even possible that the fact that a person has this information will give her the knowledge that she can act effectively at a later time, and thereby the confidence that she needs to go on with her life. The main point, however, is that so much misinformation is provided, by oral communication, the social media and many books and articles, even with a scientific pretention. It is then always helpful to publish what is reliably known. Even if the law doesn't recognize a right to suicide but doesn't forbid it, it is always to be preferred that people who make that choice do so as carefully as possible.

5.4 Two kinds of assisted suicide[20]

In the literature about physician-assisted death the distinction between assisted suicide and euthanasia – helping someone to kill himself or killing him on his request – is generally considered to be of fundamental moral importance. In many of the jurisdictions that legally permit some kind of physician-assisted death, only assisting suicide is allowed; in jurisdictions that forbid both, the maximum penalty for assistance is usually much lower; and in most jurisdictions in which some form of legalization has been proposed and debated, it is only assistance that has been under consideration.[21] Until now only seven countries also allow euthanasia.[22] In the Benelux-countries physicians generally prefer euthanasia to assisting suicide.[23] This preference is something of a mystery. In the past doctors may have been right in expecting more complications when they chose assisted suicide, but by now this is probably only a consequence of lack of experience and hence a self-fulfilling

19 Chabot 2014, 88–90.

20 Sections 5.4–5.6 are an updated version of den Hartogh 2017a.

21 For example Nevada, North Carolina, New York and other American states, listed in http://www.deathwithdignity.org/advocates/national.

22 Chapter 1, footnote 1. In Belgium the law of 2002 formally only permits euthanasia, but the Federal Control and Evaluation Commission on Euthanasia (FCECE) stated in its first biennial report (2004) that it considered assisting suicide to fall within the definition of euthanasia. But see footnote 40.

23 In 2020 the Dutch review committees received 6938 reports of euthanasia, 216 reports of assisted suicide, and 17 reports of a combination of both actions, RTE Annual Report 2020. In 2013 in 98.7% of reported Flemish cases barbiturates had been administered intravenously, with or without neuromuscular relaxants, Dierickx et al. 2016. Self-administration of medication is forbidden in Quebec; across Canada it occurred less than seven times in 2020, Health Canada 2020.

prophecy.[24] Anyway it is clear that these doctors don't recognize the distinction to have the fundamental importance attributed to it elsewhere.

This is understandable. In both cases the doctor acts on the initiative of the patient. That is confirmed by the fact that before administering the lethal drugs or giving the lethal injection, she will always ask the patient whether he still wants to go on with the procedure. In both cases the willing cooperation of the patient is needed throughout the whole process. And in both cases the proceedings are under the final control of the doctor, because she has the responsibility to ensure that death occurs, safely, relatively quickly and painlessly. She acts and tells the patient how to act effectively. Even if the plan is that the patient drinks something, she will use an alternative way of ensuring his death if he cannot hold the drink. In such a close cooperative scheme, why should it matter who is performing the last action of the whole series?[25] In penal law the answer to that question is normally irrelevant for deciding whether an act should be classified as co-participation or as mere complicity. In this case the contribution that the doctor makes is so essential that we should consider his action a kind of co-participation, whether he performs the last action or not. If she intends to perform a euthanasia she will use an infusion needle in order to induce a coma, and sometimes she will ask the patient to open it. Occasionally the patient then turns out to have died already before the doctor can administer muscle relaxants, thereby turning a planned euthanasia into a suicide. The most one could say is that if the last action is the patient's, that underlines that it is his autonomous choice that is implemented, but that is only a matter of symbolic meanings.[26] In either case, if death follows, doctor and patient will be jointly responsible for that outcome. The doctor does not merely assist, but rather participates in a joint action of ending the patient's life.[27]

24 Kouwenhoven et al. 2014. The reasons mentioned by doctors in research are only practical ones. For example, the intake of barbiturates is often considered less safe because they can be disgorged. According to Groenewoud et al. 2000 in 18% of the cases in which a doctor had decided to assist a patient's suicide, she ended up in giving a lethal injection, cf. Magnusson 2002. Dutch doctors who administer barbiturates still always insert an IV, enabling them to administer euthanatics if necessary. But the present guideline for the oral method enables doctors (and not only doctors) to prevent almost all the complications that occurred in the past, Stallen, Marlet 2018. Only the use of opioids may be a contraindication for administering barbiturates. Another reason for preferring euthanasia may be that in that case death follows the administration of drugs more quickly.

25 McMahan 2002, 460; Dworkin 2012.

26 As such understood by most Dutch doctors, Kouwenhoven et al. 2014. Paradoxically, as the authors say, the choice for assisted suicide is predominantly made by the physician. Most patients prefer to be killed by doctors to killing themselves (Section 16.2).

27 "Suppose a physician supplied a lethal dose to a patient with the knowledge and intent that the patient will wrongfully administer it to another. We would have no difficulty in morality or the law recognizing this as a case of joint action to kill for which both are responsible" (Brock 1992).

In Oregon, as in the other American states that permit assisted suicide,[28] on the other hand, all the doctor does, after having ascertained that the patient has voluntarily expressed his wish to die, is capable of making and expressing health-care decisions and cannot reasonably be expected to live longer than six months, is to give the patient a prescription for a lethal drug. When the patient has acquired the medication, it is his own responsibility to procure his own death in a safe and effective way. The prescribing physician can be present if she wishes but is so only in 12% of the cases.[29] The patient can decide not to use the drugs, and in about one third of the cases actually decides not to.[30] More often a volunteer from a right-to-die society, in Oregon named *Compassion and Choices*, will be present. In the Netherlands and Belgium the doctor is not even allowed to leave the patient alone with the drugs. He may go to the next room but must be continuously available to intervene if the drugs are not sufficiently effective.[31]

So, even when a case in Oregon and a Dutch case are both classified as 'physician-assisted suicide', the cases are fundamentally different.[32] Pentobarbital and similar lethal pharmaca are not freely available on the market. There are obvious reasons for limiting the access to such drugs: they can be used impulsively, to commit suicides that cannot be regarded to be well-considered, or fully voluntary. In addition, they can be used for killing others. When a patient approaches a doctor in Oregon, the doctor ascertains whether these risks are absent, or minimal, and, if they

28 Oregon (*Death with Dignity Act* 1994), Washington (*Death with Dignity Act* 2008), Vermont (*Patient Choice and Control of End of Life Act* 2013), California (*End of Life Option Act* 2015), Colorado (2016), District of Columbia (2017), Hawaii (2018), New Jersey (2019), Maine (2019), New Mexico (2021). In *Baxter v. Montana* (Dec. 6, 2009) a trial court allowed a defence of consent for a doctor charged with assisting a suicide. To my knowledge all presently proposed bills also conform to the Oregon model. Outside the USA assisted suicide, but not euthanasia, is at present not punishable under certain conditions in Switzerland, Uruguay, Austria (2022) and the isle of Jersey (2021). In its ruling no. 242/2019 the Italian Constitutional Court found that assisted suicide was permissible when a competent patient was in a state of overwhelming pain. In November 2021 a quadriplegic patient succeeded in getting his assisted suicide approved by a regional health authority. On Germany see Section 16.1.

29 Oregon Health Authority 2020.

30 Lewy 2011, 134.

31 Griffiths, Weyers, Adams 2008, 100–101. In 1994 the disciplinary measure of a warning was imposed on a doctor who had left a lethal drug in the possession of a patient, whose depressive husband then used it for committing suicide, *Tijdschrift voor Gezondheidsrecht* 1994, 433–435; Weyers 2004, 301–302.

32 One reason for preferring 'physician-assisted suicide' to euthanasia that has often been adduced is that in the case of assistance it is easier for the patient ultimately to change his mind, Glover 1977, 184; Brody 1993; Lewis, Black 2012. But whether this is a real difference depends on the doctor's role: merely to write a prescription or to direct and supervise the joint action that both agents have agreed to participate in, as Watts, Howell 1992 already observed.

are, makes the drugs accessible to the patient. That is not really a form of assistance, it is lifting a blockade when the acknowledged rationale for the blockade doesn't apply. In a 'state of nature' people would have unlimited access. Then the state comes along, limiting access, for whatever reason. If the state then makes an exception for people who have chosen death without undue pressure and after ample consideration, it only stops interfering with their freedom. It stands out of the way.[33]

In a similar way there are excellent reasons why civilized countries restrict private people's access to guns. But if the state allows access in some cases, for example for shooting sports or hunting, it does not facilitate these activities, it only abstains from hindering or thwarting them. The default is unlimited access; access is only limited for some acknowledged reasons, to the extent that these reasons require. If they don't apply, access is free again.

5.5 The relevance of the distinction

Suppose that the right to self-determination is recognized by the law to extend to decisions regarding the manner and time of one's own death. If a person exercises this right, the only basic requirements she has to satisfy for her decision to stand will concern her freedom from coercion and manipulation and her decision-making capacities, including her state of information. It is a proper concern of the law to make sure that these requirements have been satisfied and it could delegate this task to doctors. If it has been established that the requirements have been satisfied, the doctor could 'lift the barrier' to the acquisition of a lethal drug by writing a prescription. A regulatory system of that kind would be exclusively justified in terms of the right to self-determination. That is, indeed, the common way in which the inhabitants of Oregon, Washington, Vermont and California understand these laws, both opponents and supporters of the 'death with dignity' acts of these states.

It is true that most Dutchmen and Belgians understand their own laws to be an expression of respect for self-determination as well, no less than the citizens of those American states.[34] But in order to actually justify those laws in that way, we would not only need to recognize the right to self-determination to include the authority to end one's own life, but we also would need to appeal to the *Volenti* principle: *Volenti non fit iniuria*, no injury is done to a consenting person (Section 1.3).

33 As Gijs van Donselaar suggested to me long ago.

34 Van Holsteyn, Trappenburg 1995, summarized in Griffiths, Weyers, Adams 2008, 26; van Delden et al. 2011, ch. 2–4, in particular pp. 31, 54. At the time of those studies most people nevertheless were in global agreement with the legal requirements of due care (to the extent they knew them).

For it is not contradictory to permit you to cause harm to yourself by doing something, but not to permit anyone else to cause similar harm to you on your request. The *Volenti* principle is best known as a principle governing some particular legal domains, in particular tort law. The question is whether it should also be seen as a general moral principle that covers all actions, including the exercise of those basic rights that are traditionally considered to be 'inalienable': the right to life, to bodily integrity and to personal freedom. In Section 9.5 I will argue that these rights are indeed unwaivable.

If, on the contrary, they could be waived, the distinction I have made between two kinds of doctor's involvement in procuring death would lose some of its interest. But although both kinds of involvement could then be justified by appeal to the same principle of respect for autonomy, they would still be justified in a different way. Access to humane means of suicide would be something any agent could demand,[35] but full cooperation of a physician in executing a decision to end one's life would still only be something that, applying *Volenti*, the law permits but doesn't require.

The law could go further, giving people a right, both to access to lethal drugs and to the participation of a physician in the joint act of ending the patient's life (Section 16.5). But even in that case a difference might remain. Access to humane means would basically be a negative right, a right to non-interference. By appealing to it you demand to be restored to your default-freedom to use those means, because the reasons for limiting that freedom do not apply to you.[36] Full cooperation of a doctor in executing your plan to end your life would, however, be a positive right, a right to the provision of some good or service. Positive rights are often considered, not only by libertarians, to be less urgent than negative ones. Even if one thinks that at least sometimes it can be equally urgent to secure a positive as a negative right,[37] one will need different types of argument to establish either of these rights. The conclusion of these arguments may be that everyone has the negative,

35 It could be disputed whether this is recognized by the law in Oregon *etc*. It is clear that no individual doctor has a duty to provide access to lethal drugs, but it may be enough that you can always easily find a doctor prepared to give you a prescription when you satisfy the legal requirements. This, however, doesn't seem to be the case either (Section 16.1).

36 X has a negative right to p, if X is permitted to do p and to abstain from doing p (a Hohfeldian liberty), and others, including the state, have a duty not to prevent X from doing p, as well as a duty not to force X to do p. The notions of 'preventing' and 'forcing' are in need of specification: if I set out to buy some delicacy and someone else buys the last item in stock, he prevents me to buy it but does not violate my negative right. But these complications do not threaten the point of this section.

37 It is for example arguable that professional positive duties of care are on a par with negative ones in terms of urgency (Section 4.3, at footnote 35).

but only some people the positive right. Or that the negative right corresponds to duties of all persons, but the positive right only to duties of some, for example doctors. (Even if either right also corresponds to duties of the state to enforce it.)

Hence the difference between the two kinds of 'assistance' has normative consequences in a wide range of cases. But the relevance of the difference is most prominent if the right to suicide follows from the right to self-determination, as I have defended (Section 2.5), but the *Volenti* principle doesn't apply to the right to life, as I will contend in Section 9.5. In that case the permissibility of an active, even directive role of the doctor cannot be argued for in terms of the principle of respect for autonomy alone.

In Section 5.4 I have argued that 'physician-assisted suicide' has a different meaning in regulatory systems of the Oregon- and of the Benelux-type. In the first case it means that the doctor gives someone access to humane means to end his own life, in the second case she takes co-responsibility for the safe and effective implementation of that plan. In this section I indicated that these two kinds of 'assistance' may be in need of different justifications, and in Chapter 9 I will argue that, indeed, they are. I do not claim, however, that laws of the Oregon- and of the Benelux-type actually appeal to different justifications. At first sight that may seem true, because in Oregon the doctor has only to make sure that the patient is well-informed, is competent, and acting voluntarily, in the Benelux also that he is in a state of intolerable and intractable suffering. But that neat picture is actually blurred in many ways.[38] At most it seems defensible to claim that the right to self-determination has a more prominent role in the justification of the American laws,[39] the professional duty of beneficence of doctors a more prominent one in the Benelux laws. Correspondingly the American laws only permit the doctor to 'lift the barrier', the Benelux laws only to offer full participation in the joint act of ending the patient's life.[40] But this correspondence between the

38 As analysed more extensively in den Hartogh 2017a.

39 Most of these laws do not explain their moral basis. But New Jersey's *Death with Dignity Act* (2019) starts by declaring the right to obtain lethal medication as an extension of the patient's right to decide about whether to have life-prolonging medical procedures provided, adding only to the list of aims 'to assist capable, terminally ill patients who request compassionate aid in dying'.

40 On 26 April 2019 an Antwerp court (*Raadkamer*) decided that doctor Marc van Hoey, president of the Flemish right-to-die society, could not be prosecuted for violating any requirement of due care stipulated by the Belgian Euthanasia law because his patient had drunk herself the cup of poison he had given her. Hence he had not poisoned her. This verdict seems to annul the decision by the Federal Control and Evaluation Commission on Euthanasia (2003, see footnote 22) to extend the legal regulation of euthanasia to physician-assisted suicide. But in its ninth biannual report (2020, p. 30–31), the FCECE reiterated its position. The legal status of physician-assisted suicide in Belgium is therefore at present in need of clarification.

moral basis of the law and the task they entrust the doctor with is patchy at best.[41] The claims I made in this section are therefore normative ones; I don't pretend that they correspond to the actual legal facts.

5.6 Deblocking access

In Switzerland the role of the doctor is like his role in Oregon: to lift the barrier to the non-violent means a person needs in order to implement his decision to kill himself.[42] The usual procedure for such a person is to approach an assisted suicide service like *EXIT Deutsche Schweiz* or *Dignitas*. If the organization decides to provide assistance, it will ask a physician to assess the person's competence and to write a prescription for pentobarbital or a similar drug. The right to self-determination is supposed to provide the moral justification for this act, which by itself is not considered a medical task.[43]

The Swiss Criminal Code (Art. 114) prohibits causing the death of a person for commendable motives, and in particular out of compassion, at the victim's own genuine and insistent request, attaching a maximum penalty of three years to it. Any person who for selfish motives incites or assists another to commit or attempt to commit suicide is liable to a custodial sentence of maximally five years (Art. 115). No further requirements are specified for lawful assistance. In writing prescriptions, however, doctors also have to take professional guidelines into account. And the relevant guidelines not only stipulate that the patient should be competent and his decision voluntary, persistent and well-thought out, but also that his symptoms and functional constraints cause unbearable suffering and that medical and non-medical alternatives have been tried out or rejected by the patient.[44] Structurally this is an amalgam of the Dutch and the

41 The *Voluntary Assisted Dying Act* of Victoria (2017) doesn't fit the pattern at all.

42 On the Swiss regulatory system, see Bosshard in Griffiths, Weyers, Adams 2008, ch 4; Lewy 2011, ch 4; Bartsch et al. 2019.

43 Schweizerische Akademie der Medizinischen Wissenschaften 2018. According to a position statement of the *Foederatio Medicorum Helveticorum* (FMH) from 2008, it is by itself even contrary to the medical ethos.

44 Schweizerische Akademie der Medizinischen Wissenschaften 2018, replacing guidelines from 2004 that had been adopted by the medical association *FMH*. The new guidelines have not been adopted by the FMH, however, firstly because they require intolerable suffering, a requirement that the FMH considers to be intolerably vague, secondly because the new guidelines no longer require that the patient must be approaching the end of his life, a requirement that, in the case of a psychiatric patient, had not been upheld by the Federal Court *(Schweizerische Bundesgericht*, BGE 133 I 58. 2006). In other respects the guidelines from 2004 have been enforced by several court decisions, resulting in the accused psychiatrists losing their licence to prescribe controlled substances, Black 2012. In *Gross* (footnote 7) the European Court, reiterating the position it took in *Haas*, added that these requirements, while justifiable in themselves, should be laid down by state law, not merely by professional regulations. In spite of some attempts the Swiss

Oregon requirements. (Historically Swiss law is of course completely independent.) In as far as they go beyond an assessment of competence and the absence of coercion, how are these requirements to be justified?

That was Mr. Haas' question when he brought his case to the European Court of Human Rights. The Swiss Federal Court (*Bundesgericht*) had judged that the legal requirement of a doctor's prescription for supplying lethal drugs was justified by the risks of uncontrolled dispersion, that it was also justified to give such a prescription only to competent people, and that in the case of a psychiatric patient like Mr. Haas the assessment of competency was of particular urgency, because it was necessary to distinguish between a death wish that could itself be considered the expression of an underlying mental illness and a death wish based on a reasonable assessment of the situation that has resulted from that illness. Having received this judgment Haas send letters to 170 psychiatrists in the neighbourhood of Basel, asking them to assess his competence and, arriving at a positive result, to give him a prescription for pentobarbital. All refused, most of them arguing that the professional guidelines required them to verify that his illness was untreatable.

In its verdict the European Court for the first time stated explicitly "that an individual's right to decide by what means and at what point his or her life will end, provided he or she is capable of freely reaching a decision on this question and acting in consequence, is one of the aspects of the right to respect for private life" *(European Convention on Human Rights,)* Article 8 (Section 2.5). The Court agreed with Mr. Haas that he had a legitimate interest in preventing the consequences of a failed attempt to end his life, and that his right therefore implied a right of access to some safe and effective means like pentobarbital. That right could only be limited for relevant reasons, as summed up in Article 8, in particular in order to protect the rights and freedoms of others. But the Court argued that the answers of the 170 psychiatrists did not show that collectively they blocked Mr. Haas' access to pentobarbital. They had only refused because he had shown himself merely to be prepared to have his competence examined, and not the treatability of his illness. That argument doesn't at all address Mr. Haas' question why the State had a legitimate interest in making such *additional* requirements. Perhaps we could understand these requirements as an indirect way to ensure the

---

government has not succeeded in satisfying this demand. Since 2019 a new organization, *Pegasos*, based in Basel, offering suicide assistance to older people (70+), only requires candidates to have decisional capacity. Whether even capacity is seriously examined is open to doubt. Because the Swiss Public Prosecutor's Office doesn't intervene, it is at present doubtful to what extent it still understands the Academy's guidelines to be legally binding. At present Swiss law therefore clearly doesn't meet the standards of the ECHR.

satisfaction of the basic requirement that the patient's request has to be voluntary and well-considered. If a person is suffering severely and his suffering cannot be alleviated, or only in ways that have disproportional burdens attached to them, the probability that his death wish is produced by coercion or manipulation will be relatively low.[45] We cannot always expect effective legal rules to be finely adjusted to their proper targets. But neither the Swiss state, nor the Swiss medical association, nor the European Court has advanced an argument of that kind.

Whatever the force of that argument, it is in any case much more problematic that so many other countries know a blanket ban on all kinds of suicide assistance, including deblocking the access to humane means. It can hardly be denied that in such countries the right to determine the time and manner of one's own death really is only 'theoretical' and 'illusory'. As we have seen, the reason why the European Court nevertheless allows such legal arrangements is that the weighing of the right to a private and family life against the protection of the right to life is a complex and morally sensitive matter that the court should leave within the margin of appreciation of individual states.[46] But, as I have argued in Section 5.2, that doesn't relieve the courts of those individual states from the duty to decide whether the limitations on the right to suicide introduced by the law really are necessary ones. This has been recognized by English and German courts.[47]

45 In Belgium this argument has occasionally been used, for example by the Court of Arbitration (*Arbitragehof*) in its decision of January 14 2004, Nys 2007, 199.

46 This argument has been repeated in *Koch* (footnotes 4, 7, cf. 50), *Gross* (footnotes 7, 44) and *Nicklinson and Lamb* (footnote 7).

47 Viz. the House of Lords in *R (Purdy) v Director of Public Prosecutions* [2009] UKHL 45, [2010]AC 345, discussed in Section 4.2, and its successor, the Supreme Court, in *Nicklinson v Ministry of Justice*, [2014] UKSC 38 [2014] 3 W.L.R. 200, mentioned in Section 2.5. In *R (on the application of Conway) v Secretary of State for Justice*, [2018] EWCA Civ 1431, however, the Court of Appeal judged that Parliament is in a better position than the courts to decide whether a blanket ban on suicide assistance is justifiable. On 27 November, 2018 the Supreme Court rejected an application for permission to appeal against that decision, although "not without some reluctance". In a remarkable final verdict of 2 March, 2017 concerning the appeal of Mr. Koch (see footnote 4), ECLI:DE:BVer wG:2017:020317U3C19.15.0, the German Federal Administrative Court (*Bundesverwaltungsgericht*) decided, appealing to Art. 8 *ECHR* and the corresponding article of the German constitution, that the acquisition of a drug with the aim of ending one's own life could be legal in circumstances of extreme urgency. (The federal minister of health care [*Bundesgesundheitsministerium*] responded by prohibiting the Federal Institute for Medicine and Medical Products to provide such drugs in any case, even when an appeal to the decision of the federal administrative court had been made.) On the recent decisions of the German and Austrian Constitutional Courts, see Section 16.1.

It could be objected that the right to end one's own life really *is* 'concrete and effective' after all. If we consider Mr. Haas' six years of legal battle against additional requirements, it is not without its surrealistic elements. He could easily have acquired pentobarbital, at that time by buying it without prescription in an animal shop in Mexico, by now by ordering it on the internet. Similarly, when the Swiss state defends the requirement of a prescription by pointing to the need to protect the vulnerable, the question arises how realistic this appeal still is in a world in which it is becoming increasingly easy to acquire these drugs without a prescription.

But this cannot be a reason for the state to hold on to additional requirements for providing people like Mr. Haas with a prescription, beyond a test of the voluntary and well-considered character of his request. Let alone to hold on to blanket prohibitions. The state can hardly say to the next Mr. Haas: we will not lift the barrier for you, for you are smart enough to know how to get around it.[48] These new developments should rather be an additional, pragmatic reason to subject people who make a request for a prescription to no other requirements than those implied by the justification of requiring a prescription in the first place: preventing error and abuse. If no other conditions are stated for granting the request, and some effort is made to enforce the requirement of a prescription to begin with, most people may still prefer to visit the doctor to ordering the drugs from abroad.

A possible objection to requiring a doctor's prescription is that it continues to medicalize a decision that should be a normal decision for autonomous people to make and carry out on their own. The presence of a doctor translates an intimate decision into a clinical event.[49] But in this case her task is merely the limited one of deblocking access to lethal drugs. It is true that there is no principled reason to entrust that task to doctors. The pragmatic reason is that it is already a normal part of her job to write prescriptions and to make estimations of patients' competence, either within or outside the context of health care. If the expertise that is needed for making such estimations is already available, it is natural to involve these experts in this case as well.[50]

In this chapter I have argued that the right to determine the time and manner of your own death should imply a special right to involve your family and friends in the preparation and carrying out of a decision to end your life, either by stopping eating and drinking or by ingesting

48 The editors of the journal *European Human Rights Cases* pointed out to me that the ECHR follows some such (rather perverse) argument in *ABC v. Ireland* (16 dec. 2010, nr. 25579/05): because Irish women can go to another country in order to get an abortion, the Irish prohibition of abortion creates a 'fair balance' between the right to self-determination of women and the protected right to life of the unborn.

49 Salem 1999.

50 For proposals to assign the task to the members of a new guild of licensed end of life facilitators, see Section 14.6.

lethal drugs. The right should also imply a special right to get access to those drugs. Because both these special rights are finally derived from the right to self-determinations, you can only properly exercise them by a voluntary and well-considered decision, and it is a proper task of the state to design a regulatory system that guarantees as well as possible that these conditions are satisfied. But this task cannot be discharged by issuing a blanket prohibition. The recognition of a right to suicide that is now legally binding on European states should be a reason for all states that still know a blanket ban on all kinds of assistance, to reconsider that part of the law, even though the European Court itself considers it to be within the margin of appreciation of member states to maintain such a ban. Perhaps states may decide to exclude categories of people from access to lethal drugs, if in the case of these people it is particularly difficult to verify the voluntary and well-considered nature of their decision. But this has to be argued for (Part IV, *Hard cases*).

I have also argued that providing access to lethal drugs should be distinguished from participating in a joint act of procuring death in a safe, effective and painless way. Whether legalization of this second procedure can be justified, and, if so, under which conditions, is still an open question. I will tackle that question in Chapter 9 and the following chapters. In the meantime I will consider some other ways in which people can determine the manner and time of their own death: by requesting palliative care (Chapter 6) or palliative sedation (Chapters 7 and 8). These chapters are related to the main argument in several ways, but in particular because the choices discussed in them are often supposed to make a choice for euthanasia redundant.

One consequence to be drawn from the argument of this chapter is that 'physician-assisted suicide' is not a helpful term at all. Not because it isn't suicide that is assisted with (Section 3.6), but because it is not really assisted with. Providing access to lethal drugs is less than assistance: it only implements a negative right.[51] Taking final responsibility for procuring an efficient, quick and safe death is more than assistance: it is a form of joint action. In the remainder of this book I will therefore avoid the term 'assisted suicide', except when referring to other people's views or existing documents. Instead, I will differentiate between two kinds of medical action: providing access to lethal drugs and participating in the joint action of ending a person's life. But in particular the second phrase is too cumbersome for regular use. Because in jurisdictions permitting both euthanasia and 'physician-assisted suicide' the large majority of joint actions are of the first kind,

51 Lindsay 2009. The Maine *Death with Dignity Act* (2019) states that it does not legalize 'assisted suicide'. The doctor's action must be referred to as 'obtaining and administering life-ending medication' in state reports.

from now on I will use the term 'euthanasia' as covering both kinds of joint actions. I make this stipulation only for convenience; I don't want to offer a new definition. That there is no basic moral difference between euthanasia proper and suicide assistance of the full-blooded kind is not a conceptual truth.

5.7 Postscript: should one always comply with the requirement of a prescription?

Pentobarbital and other barbiturates, as well as opiates – but not the antimalaria drug chloroquine that Albert Heringa gave his mother – fall under international drug control conventions. If your state is not prepared to lift the barrier in any way, by ordering pentobarbital from Mexico or Peru you will disobey the law that forbids you to acquire it without a prescription, and you will invite a more serious breach of the law by the person who sells them to you. Should that be a decisive reason not to order them? This is not the place to discuss our obligations to obey the law in any depth, but it is relevant to note that on all minimally plausible accounts of such obligations we have no obligation *always* to obey *every* law, not even every law that aims at protecting or producing important goods and satisfies other minimum requirements of moral acceptability. Every explanation of our obligations specifies the area of its application and thereby provides its own limits. If, for example, we have a natural duty not to be a threat to each other by our very existence,[52] that duty does not explain why we are obliged to abide by a legal prohibition of actions that cannot be considered threatening to others in any way. If we have duties of fairness to contribute to cooperative enterprises from which we benefit, they cannot imply duties to abstain from actions that do not transfer any costs to others. *Etcetera*, for each plausible account of (some of) our duties to obey the law.[53]

A clearly relevant question will always be whether our disobedience to any law detracts from the legitimate aim of that law. In this case, the legitimate aim of the law, as we have seen, is to prevent abuse and thereby to promote both safety and a sense of safety in society. Perhaps the law doesn't serve this aim in the best possible way. That doesn't justify disobedience, however, for, even if we have shared aims, we will often disagree about the best way to pursue them, and one of the aims of the law is to solve such disputes by authoritative arbitration. But there are limits to what can be claimed to be a *bona fide* attempt at arbitration, and they are particularly significant when human rights are at stake. Suppose that you make arrangements, as Mrs. Heringa did, for

52 The Kantian view, ably defended by Stilz 2011.

53 For some multiple principle theories of political obligation see den Hartogh 2002, ch. 4–5; Klosko 2005, ch. 5; Mokrosinska 2012.

making it fully transparent and checkable in your case that the decision to end your life is fully your own and the outcome of a serious weighing process. You also take due precautions that the drugs that you need cannot come into any unauthorized person's hands. In that case you could argue that ordering the drugs from abroad does not endanger anyone at all and could only have a negative impact on anyone's sense of safety if your actions are wilfully misrepresented by the media or others, who are then accountable for that effect.

On the other hand, you also contribute to keeping someone in business in Mexico or Peru, who may obtain the drugs in some illegal and uncheckable way and will not restrict himself to providing people with them who, like you, are (otherwise) irreproachable. Couldn't you say that for this state of affairs, deplorable as it may be, *you* are not to be held responsible, but only the state that refuses to you the access to the means that you need for implementing your legally recognized right to end your own life? The state could reply that you have legal means to try to redress that supposed wrong: you should go to the courts and require access to the drugs, as Mr. Haas, Noel Conway (UK 2017), Gloria Taylor (Canada 2015) and so many others did, rather than act unilaterally on your own sense of your rights. But one can hardly require someone like Mrs. Heringa to start fighting legal battles.

I have only indicated an area of moral problems that needs to be explored much more extensively. My provisional conclusion is that it can sometimes be a responsible decision to order lethal pharmaca from abroad, if you take all due precautions.

Part II

Palliative care and palliative sedation

6 Suffering and dying well

On the proper aim of palliative care[1]

6.1 Outline

Suffering is an all-too-common experience in human life, in all its phases. But it looms particularly large at the end of life, for patients dying from a lethal illness like cancer, in particular during the days, weeks or months that follow when every treatment with the exception of palliative care has been stopped. Though occasionally it is one particular symptom that causes severe, even extreme suffering, in most cases patients have to cope with the combined effects of multiple symptoms. Their suffering may also be aggravated by events in their own life, the loss of a partner, for example, or by the memory of traumatizing events or of personal failings during the course of their lives.

It is severe or extreme suffering that is normally seen as motivating death wishes, both in the terminal stage of a fatal illness and in other situations. (At the end of Section 6.2 I will consider to what extent that assumption is correct.) In many cases, however, such suffering can be alleviated by palliative care interventions. The question that this chapter addresses is how death wishes should be dealt with in the context of palliative care. But in order to consider that question properly (in Section 6.8) I will first extensively discuss the proper aims of palliative care in relation to suffering. That will also enable me to decide whether, as is often claimed, a practice of palliative care and a practice of euthanasia should be seen as mutually exclusive. Chapters 7 and 8 will continue the examination of this question by focusing on palliative sedation, in particular deep sedation that is meant to be sustained until death.

A second ambition of the discussion of the aims of palliative care in this chapter is to provide a richer phenomenology of suffering than I have offered in Chapter 2. We will need this richer phenomenology in discussing possible conditions for permissible euthanasia in Chapters 9–12. For in all jurisdictions that have legalized ending a person's life on

1 The larger part of this chapter (Sections 6.1–6.7) is an updated version of den Hartogh 2017c.

DOI: 10.4324/9781003281115-8

her request (euthanasia) the existence of unbearable and unremittable suffering is one of the conditions of due care, but misunderstandings about the nature of that condition will turn out to be widespread. (See, for example, Sections 12.2, 12.7, and 14.2.)

The alleviation of suffering is traditionally considered one of the main aims of medicine. But when Eric Cassell published his classical paper on the nature of suffering and the goals of medicine in 1982,[2] mainstream medical literature had for a long time been almost silent about the phenomenon. In the wake of the palliative care movement a substantial number of empirical studies of suffering, in particular of suffering at the end of life, have been published since then, the flow of such papers accelerating in recent years. This chapter is based on a sample of such studies that, because of their many similarities, may be considered representative of the literature. Almost all these studies refer to Cassell, and in particular to his 'definition' of suffering. It therefore seems fitting to start (Section 6.2) by considering Cassell's views in some detail. In this discussion I will make a number of conceptual points that I will rely on in later sections.

In a second step (Section 6.3) I will consider the new empirical work on suffering in the end-stage of life. All authors accept Cassell's point that suffering is not merely a matter of pain and other physical symptoms, but in addition, has psychological, existential and social dimensions. In other respects, however, as I will show, they only pay lip-service to Cassell's authority.

The main criticism that I will make of this literature (Section 6.4) goes beyond Cassell's own views, although it builds on them. Cassell conceives of suffering as "a specific state of severe distress related to the imminent, perceived or actual, threat to the integrity or existential continuity of the person".[3] This means that suffering is an attitude vis-à-vis a certain state of affairs, that is understood to endanger the person's life, his identity or his social role. If that person perceives her situation as threatening, it is always a relevant question whether she has understood that situation correctly. Suffering is therefore not a brute mental fact that can simply be established by silent introspection. Rather it is normally an occasion for reflection, for the person herself and her intimates. Is my situation really as threatening as I perceive it to be, and how can I best cope with that threat? I do not deny that professional caregivers could play a modest role in this dialogue, providing support and, sometimes, consolation. But they misinterpret that role if they understand it as consisting of 'spiritual interventions or therapies', exclusively aimed at the alleviation of the patient's suffering. The patient's actual situation can be such that he would have to live in a world of illusion in order

2 Cassell 1982. Included in Cassell 1991.
3 Cassell 1982, 640; 1991, 33; 1999, 531.

not to suffer. To the extent that grief, sadness, fear and other negative emotional states are appropriate responses to the actual circumstances in which the patient finds himself, they are not to be considered 'symptoms' of a pathology, to be fought at all costs. I will call this a functional approach to suffering, because it understands suffering as a signal to take medical action.

In Section 6.5 I will illustrate my criticism of the functional approach by discussing the famous 'dignity therapy', developed by Harvey Chochinov and his associates. In Section 6.6 I will offer another illustration of my criticism by considering the common view that a doctor should never rob a patient of his hope of recovery. In Section 6.7 I will consider a third important dimension of suffering at the end of life, loss of coping ability, not only in order to further specify that criticism, but also in order to nuance it. In considering the facts as they are we should consider them from the personal perspective of the patient, even when that perspective as such is vulnerable to criticism (Sections 2.4, 8.4, and 8.5). And when suffering reaches a peak where the patient is helpless in the face of an overwhelming force, we should no longer be scrupulous about selling him illusions.

In Section 6.8, finally, I will use a Position paper from the European Association for Palliative Care (2015) to show how the idea that the practice of palliative care is incompatible with euthanasia rests on a purely functional understanding of that practice. Although the EAPC recommends an 'open dialogue' with the patient about his death wish, the aim of that dialogue is only to identify the elements of the patient's suffering that cause his death wish, in order to make these elements amenable to therapy. This means that the death wish itself is only seen as a symptom to be treated. If, on the contrary, death wishes can often be understood as intelligible responses to a person's actual situation, the wish to eliminate both suicide and euthanasia from the context of palliative care is wrongheaded.

Suffering, I will conclude (Section 6.9), is sometimes and to some extent a condition that requires to be respected. I do not dispute that the alleviation of suffering is the main aim of palliative care for the dying. But pursuing that aim should remain within the boundaries of a constraint of realism.

The direct object of my criticism is a certain literature, the new empirical literature on the dimensions of suffering, not the general literature on palliative care, nor its practice. But although I am sure that many doctors and nurses try to find an equilibrium between relieving suffering and respecting it, I am also sure that the functional approach I am criticizing is fairly common in practice as well. We can only identify the proper place of palliative care for the dying in relation to other possible decisions at and about the end of life if we understand why that functional approach is in error.

6.2 Cassell on suffering

As we saw Cassell conceives of suffering as being distressed by circumstances understood as threats to one's person. The term 'distress' obviously refers to a state of consciousness. If something happens that you consider undesirable, you only suffer from the event if you experience its occurrence or its effects with grief and sorrow. These are negative emotions, but their negative character is not enough for recognizing you to suffer. You should understand the event or its effects as endangering the core of your personhood.

Threat and endangerment imply mere possibilities that need not be actualized and could, perhaps, still be staved off. But surely suffering doesn't stop when the threat has become the reality of an irremediable injury or an irreversible loss.[4] However, whether it is a response to a mere threat or to a real loss, suffering is always an intentional state, not merely a sensation with a certain tonality. In this respect it is similar to happiness.[5] All intentional states have two aspects: the state itself and its object. If you believe, hope, fear or desire, there has to be *something* that you believe, hope for, fear or desire. This something can be unpacked as a proposition: you believe that something is the case, or you hope, fear or desire that it will be. Many such states involve cognitive claims: if that 'something' is not really the case, your belief is false; and if there is no reason at all to expect it to happen, your hope and your fear are inappropriate. (But not your desire: if your desire doesn't fit the world, it is rather the world that is 'at fault'.[6]) Suffering may involve a whole range of negative emotions: in addition to grief and sorrow, anxious concern, fear, anger, rage, despair, boredom, frustration, bitterness, guilt, embarrassment, shame, even self-hatred and panic. These emotions all have their own cognitive element: you are angry because you think that people are unfair to you, or Fate is, you are desperate because something that is extremely dear to you is irrevocably escaping you. But suffering, according to Cassell, has a cognitive aspect of its own: it implies the belief that essential elements of your sense of self are threatened, or already injured.[7]

As Cassell explains in his topology of personhood, the threat or injury may be directed at different aspects of your person.[8] Most basically, you may consider your biological life to be at stake, and even

4 Tate, Pearlman 2019. But I see this as a natural extension, not as a fundamental criticism of Cassell's view.

5 On every understanding of happiness, including a hedonist one, cf. Feldman 2010, chs. 6 and 7.

6 Cf. Anscombe 1963, 56 on what has come to be called the direction-of-fit criterion for classifying intentional states (and speech acts).

7 For a similar approach to suffering, couched in a somewhat different language, see Svenaeus 2014.

8 In this paragraph I do not aim to summarize Cassell's topology but reorder it in anticipation of my own discussion.

if you don't attribute any inherent value to being barely alive, it is a necessary condition of everything else that is valuable to you about your life (Section 2.3). Your illness and its effects may also endanger you as the subject of the story of your life, by making it difficult or impossible for you to go on contributing to causes that gave meaning and coherence to that story. Perhaps even more fundamentally it may endanger you as a person having a life of her own to live at all, by invading your daily routines and corroding your intimate relationships. You may experience your body as an alien object disabling your normal functioning. You may also feel that you are no longer your normal self in social contacts, because you are losing the essential elements that determine your role and status in those contacts: the person you are, and the person you think you are, in the eyes of others. As a result your self-esteem may be endangered as well. In all these respects there is a growing disparity between what you are accustomed to do and to be and what you find yourself to be able to do and to be. You are disconnected from others, from the world as you know it, from your body and from your sense of self.[9]

Suffering never consists of pain, dyspnea, nausea, fatigue or other physical symptoms alone. Pain, for example, is an element of suffering, not merely a cause, but in order to know, when someone is in pain, whether she is also suffering, we have to understand what the pain means to her. The pain in childbirth, to cite the standard-example, may be severe, but it is rarely experienced as an element of suffering. Pain of the same severity would definitely be an element of suffering if it didn't announce a new life but death. Injury to oneself or to the child may turn childbirth into a case of suffering, and the same is true of continuing intense, overwhelming pain.[10] It is not only the case that the meaning of the pain determines to what extent you are suffering, it even determines the nature of the sensation itself: how painful the pain really is. If you learn that the pain you are feeling during an operation will be over in a minute, it is already less biting.[11] On the other hand, fear and anxiety can intensify restlessness, vomiting, sleep disturbance and other physical symptoms.

If we understand suffering in the way Cassell proposes, it can never be a good argument, in assessing someone's suffering from a certain disease, to say that other people who are in exactly the same physiological condition, do not suffer, or do not suffer severely. For whether this condition can intelligibly be perceived by someone as endangering her

9 Van Wijngaarden 2021.

10 Svenaeus 2014.

11 Wall, Melzack 1999, ch. 1, quoted by Wijsbek 2012b. Gupta et al. 2017 use this observation to criticize the Québec *Act Respecting End of Life Care* (2015) for categorizing unbearable suffering as either physical or psychological.

integrity as a person will depend on the person she is, her character, her life history, her roles and her values. An amputation may mean something completely different to you when you have been a dancer all your life than when you have been an arm-chair philosopher. In this sense suffering is a subjective matter.

Cassell, however, understands it as a subjective matter in a stronger sense. According to him a person has a privileged access to her own suffering: because she is the one who suffers, she alone knows she does, and to what extent, and she knows it with certainty. Even people who know her well, her personality, her biography, her relationships and her values, and who can take into account her behaviour and body language, have no independent access to her suffering but, at best, an empathic understanding of it by imagining what it would be like to be in her condition. But except for its phenomenology suffering also has a cognitive dimension, and on this dimension the suffering person is not in an absolutely authoritative position to interpret and assess her own suffering. You might think that you are suffering from the death of a pet, while you are actually suffering from social isolation. This is confirmed by the fact that people usually don't assess the severity of their suffering by silent introspection, but rather by talking with others, most often their friends and relatives, but sometimes also their doctors and nurses. Each partner in this conversation can be mistaken in his interpretation and be corrected by the other party. One relevant consideration always is whether other ways are still available to protect the valuable aspects of one's life which are being impaired or threatened.[12]

All laws that permit ending someone's life on his request, not only assisting him in ending it, require intolerable suffering as a condition of legitimate action, but most recent laws suggest that suffering is intolerable if the suffering person says it is (Section 12.7). This assignment of normative authority doesn't necessarily presuppose an assignment of epistemic authority, but I suspect that the first assignment usually is at least bolstered by the second.

Another problem with Cassell's 'definition' is that he presents it as a conceptual truth. In that case we could not say of newborn children or (most) animals that they suffer, even if they experience severe pain.[13] A patient in an advanced stage of Alzheimer may only dimly understand to be under attack, or not at all, but still suffer. But even if we accept that objection, the core of truth in Cassell's view that, in comparison with the suffering of cats and babies, the suffering of beings who understand themselves as living their own lives is qualitatively different because it

12 That suffering is intersubjectively accessible is forcefully argued for by Wijsbek 2012b. One could also appeal to Wittgenstein's private language argument in order to criticize the idea of exclusive private access to our own mental states.

13 Edwards 2003.

has the interpretative component (cf. Section 10.3). The condition which they experience with distress is understood by them as a threat or a loss of some highly valued aspect of the life they live.

Suffering is a mental state with a phenomenology and a cognitive aspect. For self-conscious beings both aspects are necessary elements. It is therefore a mistake to hold that a condition of the person (or a non-person) as such can be a state of suffering, independently of the person's awareness of that state.[14] Even if the object of suffering is the frustration of interests that are essential to a person's existence, the frustration of those interests by itself is not yet a form suffering. The subject must be aware of his condition with distress, even if he doesn't understand what exactly is troubling him (Section 15.5). Otherwise he is badly off but not suffering.

The dual nature of suffering is also relevant when we ask whether it is really extreme suffering that motivates death wishes. If we consider the reasons people mention themselves for requesting euthanasia (Section 2.2), these reasons include pain and similar physical symptoms that we can understand as elements of suffering, but for the most part they mention things like loss of meaning, independence, control, dignity and hope. It is plausible, however, that they suffer from these losses, and that the severity of that suffering is a fairly reliable index of the importance to them of the items they lose. That relation may be strong enough to justify the law fixing on 'unbearable suffering' as a criterion of permissible euthanasia. But the relation is not a conceptual one. It is, for example, possible for someone to consider a future loss, for example of his cognitive capacities, a reason for wanting to end his life, even though he doesn't anticipate any suffering from that loss and presently is not suffering severely from the anticipation either (Section 15.7). We should also keep in mind that suffering is not merely unbearable because of its felt quality, but because of the importance to us of its object – the loss of meaning *etcetera* – and is therefore accessible to others and a possible subject for discussion.

6.3 Empirical work on suffering

The new literature on suffering, mainly focusing on the end-stage of life, aims to provide us with an organized list of elements of suffering, informing us for each element about its incidence, and sometimes also giving us scores for the average severity of the suffering on that particular dimension. Such lists are only meant to offer a checklist for understanding the

14 *Contra* Van Hooft 1998. Tate, Pearlman 2019 suggest that you either have to accept such an 'objective' conception of suffering or to agree with Cassell that suffering is a mental state that is only accessible to the sufferer. That view overlooks the intentional structure of mental states.

specific nature of a person's suffering, they are not supposed to be usable for calculating an overall score of the severity of that suffering. Usually the elements are grouped into four classes: physical symptoms, psychological, existential and interpersonal or social dimensions of suffering.[15] This standard classification, however, is not very stable: the same or similar aspects are often differently classified.[16]

On closer look the so-called physical symptoms are all mental states. They are only different from other sensations and perceptions because of their relation to a more or less clear bodily location. If it itches, it itches somewhere. Coughing, vomiting and bodily disfigurements may be forms of suffering because of the way these physical states and events are experienced. Some symptoms mentioned on the lists, however, are clearly perceptions, for example smelling unpleasant. Others seem to be mere sensations, for example itching.[17]

When Cassell wrote his paper, it was common for doctors to understand the very term 'suffering' to refer to pain. Although this is no longer true, many doctors still have a narrow focus on physical symptoms.[18] Some studies have found that physical symptoms are the most important elements of suffering, in terms of incidence and of average severity.[19] But according to most studies the non-physiological elements are more important. The second conclusion seems to be confirmed by the findings of studies of the reasons people have for requesting physician assistance to end their lives. Existential and social concerns are often more prominent on these lists than physical symptoms[20] (Section 2.2).

The list of possible physical symptoms is very long,[21] but the most prominent seem to be: fatigue, pain, breathlessness and nausea. Fatigue (including weakness, exhaustion, cachexia) seems generally to be the

15 Cherny, Coyle, Foley 1994 seem to have introduced this fourfold classification.

16 For example, anxiety as a physical or as a psychological symptom. For other examples see footnotes 21, 27 and 28.

17 It is disputed whether pain is a mere sensation normally caused by tissue damage or a perception of injury, see the introduction to Aydede 2006, or the same author's entry 'Pain' in the *Stanford Encyclopedia of Philosophy*.

18 As a substantial number of Dutch doctors still have in assessing 'unbearable suffering' in the case of a request for euthanasia (Section 12.2).

19 Benedict 1989; Kuupelomäki, Lauri 1998; Wilson et al. 2004, 2007. Krikorian, Limonero, Maté 2012, p. 800, refer to a Spanish study by Maté, reporting that most caregivers attribute a peaceful death to symptomatic control, most family members to psychosocial matters.

20 Van der Wal et al. 2003, 51; Pearlman et al. 2005; Ganzini, Goy, Dobscha 2009; Pasman et al. 2009; Dees 2011; Oregon Health Authority, annually; Washington State Department of Health, annually; *Second Annual Report on MAID* in Canada 2020; cf. Dees 2010 for a review of relevant studies. For exceptions see Chapter 2, footnote 11.

21 The most detailed list, in Ruijs et al. 2009, contains 37 items, but some of these (feeling tense, depressed, anxious) are clearly misclassified.

most common.[22] An important finding is that even for patients who we may assume to receive the best possible palliative care, for example in a hospice, it is not uncommon that they rate the pain and other symptoms they experience as severe.[23] On the non-physiological dimensions the variation in the relevant aspects is much greater. Understanding oneself to be a burden for others, for example, is very prominent on some lists but absent on others.[24] But, if one goes through a substantial number of these research reports, a fairly coherent picture of the most important dimensions emerges (see Section 6.6). It is confirmed by the studies of the reasons for requesting physician-assisted death.

As I said, almost all these studies refer to Cassell, and one idea that they have all learned from him is that suffering cannot exhaustively be described in terms of physical symptoms. But in other respects they are not at all true to his insights. This is particularly true of the studies that do not only give lists of elements of suffering but try to measure their importance. If, for example, a person is extremely tired, it will be difficult for her to engage in meaningful activities, to take care of her own needs or even to find a way of coping mentally with her condition. Fatigue makes the hard work of dying even harder. Now, when we ask her to tell us how important fatigue is as an element of her suffering, do we mean: fatigue as such, abstracting from these further effects? If that is what we mean, we do not really accept Cassell's point that in order to determine the severity of a person's suffering from fatigue we have to consider to what extent this physical symptom is understood as threatening. But if we are prepared to take these further effects into account, we are already measuring a psychological or existential dimension of suffering, not a mere physical symptom.[25]

Making lists of elements can only be the first step in understanding suffering. In order to really understand it we have to consider the

22 Except for 'general malaise' or 'general discomfort' in a number of studies, e.g. Morita et al. 2004. Kwon et al. 2006 found that pain was the most common and severe symptom but fatigue the most interfering in patients' lives. According to Oi-Ling, Man-Wah, Kam-Hung 2005 caregivers and physicians agree with patients on the distress involved in most symptoms but underrate fatigue and cachexia.

23 According to Baines, Norlander 2000, for example, 26% of hospice patients reported moderate, 24% severe pain in the last 24 hours.

24 It is the most important non-physiological dimension of suffering according to Wilson et al. 2004, cf. Singer, Martin, Kelner 1999, but is not mentioned by Oi-Ling, Man-Wah, Kam-Hung 2005, or by Lloyd-Williams, Reeve, Kissane 2008. According to McPherson, Wilson, Murray 2007 it is an element of suffering that is systematically underrated, both by professional and informal caregivers.

25 Yun et al. 2006 differentiate between the incidence and severity of the symptom and its interference in the life of the patient (general activity, mood, work, relation, walking and enjoyment). The model of dignity developed by van Gennip et al. 2013 distinguishes between illness-related conditions (physical symptoms, functional/cognitive ability, appearance) and their effects on 'personal dignity'.

interplay of these elements. If your pain is rated as an important element of your suffering because it interferes with your activities, that effect may be reinforced by your sense that these activities have lost their point anyway. If you are already suffering from losses of meaning and of autonomy because of further losses of sight, hearing and mobility, that effect can be multiplied by fatigue or by fear. Hence we cannot assess the extent of a person's suffering by considering the elements of suffering one by one, let alone by scoring their severity one by one.[26] Holism is an essential characteristic of Cassell's conception of suffering.

An additional problem of using measuring scales is the problem of interpersonal comparability. Perhaps the person who gives his suffering the highest possible score today will discover tomorrow that it can still become much worse. So how do we know that the same score indicates a comparable level of suffering?

The most important common weakness of the existing studies, however, is that they do not recognize the dual nature of suffering as an intentional state. Some items on their lists only refer to the subjective side of the intentional state, others to such states identified by their object, or even only to the intentional objects as such. One study, for example, includes the following elements as 'personal aspects of suffering': feelings of guilt, of worthlessness, of loneliness, of hopelessness, feeling no longer the same person, feeling tired of life, feeling dependent on others, feeling loss of control, feeling being a nuisance, feeling not important to others.[27] All these 'feelings' are identified by their object. Another study lists the following emotions as 'psychological symptoms': being afraid,

26 In various studies, e.g. Benedict et al. 1989, Byock, Merriman 1998, Holland 1999/2014 (the 'distress thermometer'), Schulz et al. 2010, Ruijs et al. 2012, subjects have been asked to give a separate overall score of their suffering. It is then unclear how this overall score is supposed to be related to the scores on individual aspects. A mysterious finding of Ruijs et al. 2012, for example, is that the number of people with an overall score of 'serious or very serious suffering' was lower than the number with the same score on some specific aspects. A very different measure of suffering is provided by the Pictorial Representation of Illness and Self-Measure (PRISM), developed by Büchi et al. 2002. Subjects are asked to put a red disk, representing their illness, on a yellow disk, representing their 'Selves'. Suffering is measured by the distance between the centres of the disks: the Self-Illness Separation (SIS). As the authors observe, this measure can be understood to operationalize Cassell's conception of suffering.

27 Ruijs et al. 2009. Chochinov et al. 2009 mention the following 'feelings' among 25 aspects of distress in the terminally ill: feeling no longer who I was, feeling of not having control, feeling uncertain, feeling anxious, feeling of reduced privacy, feeling a burden to others, feeling how your look has changed, feeling depressed, feeling of unfinished business, feeling life no longer has meaning or purpose, bot feeling worthwhile or valued, feeling not have made meaningful contribution, not feeling able to mentally fight illness, not feeling supported by health-care providers or by friends and family. Ruijs 2014 observes the overlap between categories of suffering but fails to explain it.

worried or anxious, irritable, depressed, hopeless, sad, burden to others (sic), angry, lonely, embarrassed about oneself, guilty, abandoned, rejected.[28] Most of these 'feelings' are described in purely subjective terms, but if we ask, what makes these people afraid, worried, angry, *etc.* – referring by that question to the objects of those intentional states, not merely their causes – the answers obviously are such things as: present or future dependence on the care of others, loneliness, being a burden to others, abandonment, rejection. This means that basically the same items may occur on the list within several classes, in particular as psychological and as social or existential elements.[29]

But the real problem is not only a matter of double counting or of an inaccurate system of classification. It goes much deeper.

6.4 The constraint of realism

That basic problem is the following. If you focus on the subjective side of the intentional state and not on the intentional object, it becomes easy for you to treat all the elements of suffering in the same way as physical symptoms. The intentional objects are then only seen as accidental causes of suffering, the suffering itself is identified with the subjective state of distress which consists of all the physical and emotional 'symptoms' taken together. Some of the earlier studies of 'physical and psychological distress' used only this simple dual classification.[30] But even when 'feelings' are identified by their objects and classified as existential or social concerns, the understanding of suffering as a basically pathological state doesn't change. Loss of faith is then simply one other item to be taken into account in determining one's score on the 'distress thermometer', together with indigestion and constipation.[31] The obvious aim of palliative care remains to reduce all symptoms, from whatever category, as much as possible. The checklists are supposed to enable us to concentrate our efforts on the relevant elements. They are instruments for diagnosis, ideally to be followed by treatment. We could call this a purely functional approach to suffering: if we come across any case of suffering, we have a reason to do something about it.

28 Schulz et al. 2010. Cf. Kuupelomäki, Lauri 1998: anxiety, depression, feelings of anger and guilt, aggressiveness, irritability, nervousness, and various fears and worries; de Haes et al. 1990: irritability, worrying, depressed mood, nervousness, desperate feelings about the future, tension, anxiety and concentration problems.

29 Although Schulz et al. 2010 combined measuring instruments for the domains of physical symptoms, psychological distress and existential or spiritual suffering in order "to compile a comprehensive set of non-overlapping items".

30 E.g. the Symptom Assessment Scale, Bruera et al. 1991, that is still widely used, cf. Richardson, Jones 2009.

31 Holland 1999/2014. Cf. the measurement scales for spiritual suffering at the end of life, developed by Peterman et al. 2002, Steinhauser et al. 2006.

This approach fails to recognize the cognitive aspect of all emotions, including the negative ones: they are all more or less adequate responses to the situation the person finds herself in. The same is true of suffering as an overall response to that situation. To give one example: many studies seem to use the term 'depression', either as an equivalent of 'sadness', or as an indication of a high degree of sadness. This suggests that sadness as such is a pathological state that should always be attenuated as much as possible. But the essential characteristic of depression as a pathological state is being sad without loss, or, in case of a loss, out of proportion to it, and when you are acutely aware of, for example, losing all options for meaningful activities and self-care, it would rather be pathological for you not to be sad. Sadness is by itself a mood, not a mood disorder, and hence not necessarily something to be avoided or minimized.

Or consider fears for the future. Such fears may concern the further development of the illness with its accompanying symptoms, possible treatment outcomes, including side-effects, as well as death. Fears may also be directed to increasing social stigma or isolation. Such fears may be exaggerated, and they often are, but they may also be fully warranted. In that case they should not be treated as the expression of an 'anxiety adjustment disorder'. We should rather consider what we can still do to prevent them from being realized.[32] To recognize that negative emotions may be appropriate responses to reality could be called a realistic approach to suffering.

But why shouldn't we take a purely functional approach? Would that not be much better from the point of view of the patient? After all, if we would succeed in reducing his negative feelings, however appropriate, it would result in a higher level of happiness and well-being for him, a higher quality of life. Wouldn't it?

Whether it would, always or even normally, depends on another question: what is a good life, and hence a good death, for a person? Is it only determined by the way in which she experiences the world, disregarding whether this experience is consonant with reality (experientialism)? This is a fundamental philosophical question on which a large literature has appeared. Well-known is Robert Nozick's thought experiment of

32 Kissane 2012 uses the terms 'adaptive adjustment' and 'maladaptive response' themselves in a purely functional way, for positive, resp. negative feelings and social environments. 'Fear of being a burden', for example, is then always a 'maladaptive response', whether that fear is warranted or not. 'Fulfilled life, with accomplishments and legacy', is always an 'adaptive adjustment', even for someone like Ivan Ilyich, cf. footnote 34. Kissane et al. 2001 even argue for the recognition of a 'demoralization syndrome' as a new psychiatric diagnosis, characterized by loss of meaning, dysphoria, disheartenment, helplessness and a sense of failure, cf. Kissane et al. 2004; Chochinov et al. 2006. Slavney 1999 objected that this is not a psychiatric disorder at all, but a normal response to adversity, cf. Berghmans, Widdershoven, Widdershoven-Heerding 2013.

the experience machine: neurologists have figured out a way to stimulate your brain to induce whatever pleasurable experiences you program to have. Once in the program you cannot distinguish between these programmed experiences and those of real life. Would you prefer to be hooked on to the machine for the rest of your life, with only some interruptions giving you opportunities for reprogramming?[33]

I cannot enter into a full discussion of this large issue, but I will appeal to what seems to me one conclusive argument against experientialism. Imagine a man who believes that he has a very good life: he is successful in his professional activity and appreciated for his expertise by his colleagues, he has a loving partner, *etcetera*. But all this is untrue: his professional performance is bad, his colleagues ridicule him behind his back, his partner betrays him with a lover. Suppose that he continues in his false beliefs until his death. Has he had a good life?[34] Thomas Nagel's answer to the question is the following: we all agree that it would be very bad for this man to discover the truth. But how can it be bad for him to come to know the facts, if these facts are not bad for him in themselves?[35] Experientialism is basically inconsistent with the first person view of agents themselves: when they are afraid of losing their ability for self-care, they are concerned about that loss, not about their fear.

If well-being is primarily a matter of the state of the world and not of the state of our mind, we can only promote or maintain well-being by staying in contact with reality. Otherwise we will not be able to cope with the vicissitudes of life. By leaving Nagel's deceived man to live in his illusionary world, his colleagues and his partner also bereave him of any opportunity to try to improve things. Only the truth can liberate us. It is therefore usually better to recognize the facts as they are with sadness than to live in blissful denial of them. Bringing the patient in an artificially euphoric state may rob him of his sense of urgency for doing what his situation calls for: arranging his affairs, taking leave, transmitting family traditions, redressing past wrongs, seeking reconciliation, coming to terms with the nearing end of his life, making proper decisions about the manner and time of his death. To be sure, whether he

33 Nozick 1971, 1974, 42–45; 1989, 104–108. Although suggestive, the question is less than fully compelling as an argument against experientialism because answers are sensitive to framing effects, and positive answers are not unknown, Feldman 2011; Weijers, Schouten 2013; Lin 2016.

34 Would Ivan Ilyich have had a good life if he had suddenly died from a heart attack a day before the accident that led to his terrible death? If that would be true his very idea that he had spoiled his life would rest on a mistake.

35 Nagel (1970) 1979. Varelius 2019 objects that the experientialist can bite the bullet, as he would do in the case of Nozick's argument (footnote 33), and deny that the deceived man is faring badly. That objection misses the point of Nagel's argument: if the truth makes no difference to the deceived man's welfare, the discovery of the truth should not do so either.

really is missing something important in this way is a contingent matter, and even if he is, this may not always be a decisive consideration[36] (Sections 6.7 and 8.4). But it often is. People cannot even give meaningful consent to continuing a form of treatment if the treatment itself prevents them from being adequately informed.

This point also answers an objection that is often made by supporters of a purely functional approach: that what I call realism really is rationalism, betraying a typical Western overrating of cognitive abilities. But that suggestion on the one hand neglects the fact that emotional states are characterized by their cognitive content as much as by their felt quality ('what it is like to be' sad, angry, shameful etc.) On the other hand the suggestion doesn't take into account that our cognitive abilities, including the ability to respond with adequate emotions, are the main resources we have at our disposal for coping with the difficulties of life, including the consequences of illness. That is why a purely functionalist approach easily becomes counterproductive.

I do not deny that the alleviation of suffering is the most important aim of palliative care. It is far from me to claim that suffering is always to be welcomed, for example because of the opportunities it provides for personal growth and for focusing on the elements of life that are really important (cf. Section 8.5). It sometimes does, but most of the time as an essential by-product of a process that cannot be avoided. For what one may learn from suffering is primarily how to cope with bad luck, but it is impossible to seek suffering for that reason. Often suffering is merely or mainly destructive. There are many forms of suffering that we can quite happily give up without losing our ability to deal with adverse circumstances. Suffering itself often compromises that ability. A fatal illness is not the optimal condition for learning. If fatigue, pain, breathlessness, nausea can be reduced, that will by itself, abstracting from further side-effects, be only highly beneficial to a dying patient and, among other things, enable him to think more clearly. He is no longer in a state in which it matters that symptoms have a functional value of their own, that, for example, pain alerts to tissue damage and sickness helps to save energy.

But as regards the cognitive dimension of suffering, suffering as a response to a threatening situation, it should not be seen as merely

36 My argument in den Hartogh 2017c has been misunderstood as claiming that 'living in contact with reality' has an objective value, whether or not people value it themselves, Varelius 2019; Streeck 2019. The argument would then rely on an objective list or perfectionist theory of well-being. My actual claim, however, consists of two elements. (1) Well-being is primarily, though not exclusively, a matter of how things are. (2) Therefore, robbing people of their awareness of the world risks disabling them to promote their well-being, on any understanding of it that is compatible with (1), including, for example, a desire-fulfilment theory. In Section 8.5, I briefly consider what would follow from ascribing an objective value to awareness of the facts as such.

consisting of 'symptoms'. Rather the adequacy of the response should be an object of reflection and of dialogue, with family and friends and, maybe, spiritual counsellors. Nurses and doctors can to some extent participate in this dialogue, in particular when the patient's way of coping with his condition is relevant to medical decisions, perhaps occasionally also outside the context of medical decision-making altogether, if such contacts are welcomed by the patient and are not considered to intrude into his private life. But when we talk with a fellow human being about his hopes and fears, the meaning of his life, his difficulties to accept his mortality or to preserve his self-respect, we are no longer involved in therapy.[37]

6.5 An illustration: dignity therapy

Harvey Chochinov is one of the researchers of end-of-life suffering who is most true to the person-oriented and holistic character of Cassell's programme.[38] With his associates he has in particular done important research on the loss of dignity as a dimension of suffering. Using these findings, they have developed a 'psychotherapeutic intervention' that they call 'dignity therapy'.[39] It seems by now to be widely used in practice, and the available studies report overall beneficial effects, although not very consistently, in particular as regards the elements of suffering that are positively affected.[40]

Actually, the aim of the intervention is much broader than to restore a sense of dignity and self-worth, it is also concerned with losses of purpose and meaning, the loss of hope, and even with the loss of the ability to cope with the effects of illness. Patients who consent to participate are offered the opportunity to address issues that matter most to them. An edited transcript of these sessions is returned to the patients for them to share with individuals of their choosing. The discussion is structured by a series of interview questions, such as the following:

- Tell me a little about your life history; particularly the parts that you either remember most or think are the most important? When did you feel most alive?

37 For similarly motivated reservations about palliative sedation (taking away the patient's ability to deal practically and emotionally with his condition in an appropriate way) see Jansen, Sulmasy 2002a; Battin 2013; cf. my comments in Section 8.4. Similar objections have also been made to pharmacological mood enhancement. "Suffering from grief at the loss of a loved one is not the kind of … negative emotion one should want to 'get rid of' by means of a mood enhancer", Schermer 2014, cf. Olsen 2006. See also Chapter 13 at footnote 30.

38 See in particular Chochinov 2006; Chochinov et al. 2002; 2009.

39 Chochinov et al. 2005.

40 Martinez et al. 2017. Patients with high levels of distress seem to benefit most. Chochinov et al. 2011 report positive effects on quality of life, spiritual well-being and appreciation of the patient by his family, but no effects on desire for death or suicidality.

- What are your most important accomplishments, and what do you feel most proud of?
- What are your hopes and dreams for your loved ones?

My problems begin when an instrument like this is called a 'psychotherapy' or a 'non-pharmacological intervention'.[41] The very terminology shows that, although the suffering individual is supposedly addressed as a person, he really is only being treated as a patient, and his 'feeling undignified' as a symptom to be relieved. The method used to achieve this is to represent the patient's life in the rosiest light possible, by focussing on the positive aspects of that life, the aspects that he wants his family to remember him by. Surely, it may be nice for you to be enabled to pass on the resulting document to your loved ones. More than 90% of the patients who consent to being interviewed welcome the opportunity. But perhaps your children would have preferred to receive a more honest assessment of your merits instead of this piece of self-advertising, maybe even a request for forgiveness for the ways in which you have made life more difficult for them, by your indifference or your relentless ambition. An instrument to pretty up your self-image is not necessarily the best you could give your children to remember you by. (Of course it is also possible that you are unaware of your true achievements.)

It is important to strike the right balance here. I do not dispute that many people in the end stage of their illness are in a state of despondence that causes them to have an unduly negative image of their present and past selves. It will help them to be consoled and counting their blessings may be a proper form of consolation.[42] My point, however, is that not every negative assessment is an unduly negative one. This should be taken into account even in consoling patients. (Such realistic consolations may also be the more effective ones, but that is not my point.)

The 'dignity therapy' turns out to be a kind of experience machine *light*, you could indeed imagine the same result to be achievable by the administration of a drug. In many respects, it seems to me, opium is to be preferred.[43]

6.6 Loss of hope

Loss of hope is commonly recognized by the surveys as a major element of suffering, but a weakness of many discussions of this element is that the lost hope is not specified. The hidden presupposition seems to be that a person

41 Similarly, some of the procedures, recommended by Chochinov 2006, 95 ff. should be seen as requirements of humanity or professionality and not as 'therapeutic interventions' at all, for example 'ask permission to examine patients' or 'treat the patient as worthy of honour, esteem and respect'.

42 Cf. the story of Jacques in Chochinov 2003.

43 Similar comments could be made to Wendy Duggleby's Living With Hope Program, Duggleby et al. 2007.

needs some hope, it doesn't matter what for. Obviously, you can lose the hope of recovery from your illness but retain the hope to die in peace or to live eternally. Or only long enough to see your first great-grandchild.

We need hope because we are bad in fine-tuning our emotions to variations in probability. Hope is a mixture of belief and desire: the belief that there is a real possibility that something will occur and the desire that it will. Loss of hope of survival is clearly related to the fear of death (and, what is something different, the fear of dying). On their cognitive aspects they are fully compatible: you can recognize both the real possibility that something will occur and the real possibility that it will not occur. But on their affective and conative aspects these ideas are often rivals. If both are present, the patient will be said to be torn between hope and fear.[44] Because of the modulating role of hope it can already be a form of false hope to recognize a small but real welcome probability, if this is the only probability one really takes into account, mentally and in action. But on the other hand we should also take this modulating role into account in specifying a constraint of realism on hope. We should not require hope to be an unfailing reflection of the best possible estimation of the relevant probabilities. If the belief involved almost inevitably errs on one side or the other, there may indeed be such a thing as an 'optimal margin of illusions'.[45] What we need is not a superhuman requirement of realism, but a humanly achievable constraint. 'Optimal' in that case does not mean 'what causes the best results for the patient', but: what will best enable the patient to cope with her circumstances as they really are. It combines a functional with a realistic element. It will often be realized by a combination of hoping for the best and preparing for the worst.[46]

A purely functional treatment of the hope of survival is still quite common, even in countries in which the requirement of informed consent is legally entrenched and extends to palliative care.[47] If you do an internet search under the terms 'hope' and 'medicine', you will find an avalanche of statements like 'no person should ever leave a doctor's office without hope', and patients are often indignant when their doctor tells them, tactfully but clearly, that their diagnosis is fatal. As a result doctors often try to square the circle: not to deceive their patient but not to rob him of his hope either. In the first half of a sentence they inform the patient of his poor diagnosis, but in the second half they already start telling him what they can still do in order to, perhaps, postpone death for some time. Many patients conclude that there still is some hope of surviving. Willingness to participate in

44 Musschenga 2019.

45 Baumeister 1989; Snyder et al 2002; Musschenga 2019.

46 Truog et al. 2008.

47 For a recent purely functional approach to hope, see Olsman et al. 2014. Interesting attempts to balance functional and realistic concerns have been made by Ruddick 1999 and Musschenga 2019.

research is usually motivated by the hope for a therapeutical effect, even if it has been explained that this is not the aim of the research.[48]

It has also been found that many patients think in stages: as long as any treatments are available that can possibly prolong life, they refuse to seriously reflect on the unavoidability of death in the near future.[49] Living by the day is for them a form of coping. Some patients believe that as long as they are not actually dead, it is always possible for a miracle to occur, and some others believe that, as long as they succeed in maintaining hope, that will by itself help to delay Death. That is what they call 'fighting' their illness[50] (Section 2.1). If doctors only half-believe this, their reluctance to disillusion the patient and thereby to increase his suffering will be reinforced. The result is a collusion between doctor and patient: a secret alliance for avoiding the truth, even though it is formally acknowledged.[51] Collusion of this kind is probably one of the main factors causing overtreatment at the end of life.

One of the main driving forces of the functional approach to hope is the belief that the only alternative to it is despair. But of course a third alternative is available: acceptance, and at the moment of death many, perhaps most patients actually are at least resigned, if not reconciled to the ending of their lives.[52] However, reflection and dialogue are required in order to achieve that state, and when false hope is maintained too long, the remaining time to go through that process may become too short.[53] Hope may then turn into despair.

For these reasons the idea that hope should always be fostered, or at least maintained as much as possible is a dangerous mistake.

6.7 Loss of coping ability

I might go on discussing other major components of suffering at the end of life, described in terms of their intentional object, that on the evidence of the empirical studies seem to belong to the most important ones, both in terms of incidence and of severity. Loss of meaning and purpose, for example, or fear of future suffering.[54] In this section, however, I will focus on another dimension of suffering,

48 Cox 2002.

49 Buiting et al. 2011.

50 Martial metaphors are not only problematic from a realistic but also from a functional perspective, Reisfield, Wilson 2004; Berghmans 2012; Hendrickx et al. 2018 with further references. If you are losing the war, apparently you don't have the true fighting spirit.

51 The et al. 2001; Buiting et al. 2011.

52 Mack et al. 2008. Acceptance of one's fatal illness reduces distress, Secinti et al. 2019.

53 Cf. Snyder, Caulfield 2019 on the adverse impact of false hope inspiring crowdfunding campaigns.

54 One example of a purely functional approach to fear: Karlsson, Milberg, Strang 2012. I have discussed the belief that one is a burden to others in den Hartogh 2018.

because considering it will enable me to point to an important limitation of the realistic approach I have advocated in this chapter. This is the loss of coping resilience. It is often referred to by the name of 'loss of autonomy' or 'loss of control'. But these terms could also be interpreted as referring to the loss of the ability of self-care, and this should be seen as a different element of suffering (Section 2.2). That is shown by the fact that the loss of the ability of self-care is one of the conditions that some people succeed in coping with. Suffering occurs when we understand our condition as threatening or impairing core aspects of our sense of self, but in many cases people are able, with a lot of effort and almost always with a little help of their friends, to mentally cope with such threats and injuries, to keep standing on their legs and walking, however insecurely. You can come to accept the fact that you will die soon, that you will no longer be able to contribute to causes that are dear to you, that you can no longer take care of yourself, and even that you are in a pitiful condition to behold for others (Section 2.4). But in other cases people do not succeed in this task. They succumb to the attack on the integrity of their person. That shows that coping resilience is itself the most central aspect of personhood. There is an (inverse) conceptual relation between the perception of a threat to your personhood and your awareness of resources to cope with that threat, including hope, a sense of meaning, of self-worth and of connectedness.[55]

Coping resilience may itself be very much assailed by physical and mental symptoms such as fatigue or frailty, physical and mental exhaustion, nervousness, confusion, concentration problems. For such reasons the patient may not be able to think clearly. If your condition is one that you haven't been in before, if the task of handling it weighs heavily, and your coping abilities are curtailed, your autonomy will even more than usually be in need of being 'scaffolded' by the support of others.[56] But this support will not always be available and sufficient.

Some ways in which people try to adjust to their situation, sometimes resulting from obsessional personality traits, are inept, even counterproductive ones. This may be true of emotional states like frustration and anger, insistence on improper forms of care or phobic avoidance of other forms. In such cases the functional and the realistic approach point in the same direction. Denial is also a very common coping strategy that in the end may lead to more rather than less suffering.

Precisely because coping resilience is an essential element of intact personhood, it is the worst kind of suffering if you are overwhelmed by

55 Krikorian, Limonero, Maté 2012. The PRISM-measure of suffering (see footnote 26) was originally developed as a measure for coping ability.

56 Borrowing a concept from Joel Anderson, cf. Anderson, Honneth 2005; MacKenzie 2008.

grief, despair, anxiety, anger and guilt.[57] If that happens, it would be pointless to insist on realism, to go on requiring you to take an appropriate attitude even to that situation. If nothing else helps, mercy may require sedating you. Some guidelines for palliative sedation explicitly allow this, attributing to you (characteristically) a 'refractory existential symptom'[58] (Section 8.3). Yes, sedation for these reasons may be considered the use of an experience machine, at least as long as sedation is only mild. I don't deny it. But under these circumstances that use may be entirely warranted.[59]

6.8 Death wishes

How should palliative care professionals deal with death wishes of their patients? Although concern with suffering at the end of life no doubt was the major motivation of the pioneers of the palliative care movement, the hope to relieve the pressure for euthanasia was a secondary one. In the Benelux countries the availability of euthanasia as an option in some circumstances by now is embedded in mainstream palliative care,[60] but in other countries it is still usual for palliative care specialists to believe that palliative care and euthanasia are mutually exclusive practices.

In 2015 the European Association for Palliative Care, against the opposition of its member organizations from the Netherlands and, in particular, Belgium, adopted a position statement in which it declared that "the provision of euthanasia and physician-assisted suicide should not be included into the practice of palliative care".[61] It is not exactly clear what this means. Obviously palliative care specialists are called upon not to grant any request for euthanasia or suicide assistance themselves, even if they work in a country in which these practices have been legalized. But in the Netherlands and Belgium such specialists do not often receive such requests themselves. They are normally involved in advisory and supporting roles. Does the EAPC request them to stop providing advice to doctors and nurses and support to patients as soon as

57 See characteristic statements of people with a low SIS in Büchi et al. 2002: "My illness is always there, it will never go away...it's all my life, it's like the end of the world."

58 Including KNMG 2009 and Zorgnet Vlaanderen 2012.

59 Cf. Wijsbek 1999 about the circumstances in which it would be a good idea to hook on to Nozick's experience-machine.

60 Bernheim et al. 2008; Federatie Palliatieve Zorg Vlaanderen 2011; Van den Berghe et al. 2013.

61 Radbruch et al. 2016; cf. Nauck, Ostgathe, Radbruch 2014 (*Deutsche Gesellschaft für Palliativmedizin*); Australian and New Zealand Society of Palliative Medicine 2016.

these start on a course that will or might lead to euthanasia or some form of physician-assisted suicide?

The EAPC Position paper does not spend much time on arguing for its view. The main argument is the usual essentialist conception of medicine: the task of doctors *is* to cure and to alleviate suffering, not to end life (Section 9.6). Another essentialist argument is that euthanasia is incompatible with palliative care as it has been 'defined' by the WHO, for according to the WHO palliative care does neither hasten nor postpone death. Taken seriously that argument would also imply that palliative care cannot be combined either with any kind of treatment (usually called 'palliative treatment') that offers any hope of prolonging life. If such treatment isn't palliative care itself, that doesn't mean that it is incompatible with it.

But my present question is how, on the view of the EAPC, death wishes should be dealt with in the context of palliative care. According to the EAPC "requests for euthanasia and physician-assisted suicide require respect and careful attention, together with openness and sensitive communication in the clinical setting". Doctors and nurses should enter into an "open dialogue about the request" and an "exploration of the burdensome experiences underlying" it. The EAPC concedes that even the best possible palliative care will not prevent all such requests. "It is the responsibility of palliative care professionals to hear and explore the implicit or explicit requests for euthanasia and address the suffering underlying these requests".

Proponents of the legalization of euthanasia take the request of the patient as the point of reference of the patient's autonomy and try to comply with his personal preference. Palliative care experts should also acknowledge the requests for euthanasia in these patients who express them, but make this the starting point of holistic care, beginning with the comprehensive assessment and communication and trying to understand the motivation and attitude behind the patient's wish.

It is often not present suffering, but fear of further deterioration and future suffering that motivates a death wish, and what the patient needs in such situations is "information and reassurance and perception of staff competence in symptom control". According to the final sentence of the statement the aim should always be to bring the patient to the insight that her life is worth living.

I have quoted extensively from the EAPC statement because it is so revealing about its understanding of the proper aims of palliative care as regards patients with a death wish. An 'open dialogue' obviously doesn't mean that the doctor or nurse considers it conceivable that the patient, given his present and future condition and the values that have governed and still govern his life, can reasonably prefer death to survival. That patient errs: life is always worth living. His death wish has to be understood as an expression of underlying forms of suffering, and the real task of the palliative care professional is to 'address' these.

This is a purely functional approach. It necessarily implies a kind of make-believe because it suggests that the patient is 'respected' as a person, and his request is taken seriously, while in reality he is only being treated for his symptoms, including his death wish itself. 'Suicidal ideation' is always a pathological state. In the approach of the EAPC there is not even room for understanding a dying patient's (and his family's) hope for a quick redemption. Such a patient is 'demoralized', and the aim of therapy should be to restore his appreciation of life's value, by engendering hope and a sense of meaning.[62] That is a kind of care that is not only paternalistic, but also oppressive: it imposes the palliative care movement's values on patients who don't endorse them[63] (Section 2.4).

What would a realistic approach require? It will in no case mean that the professional should simply "try to comply with the preferences of the patient", as the EAPC caricatures the position it opposes. Rather the patient's request should be understood as allowing the professional to join in the patient's search for the best possible response to the situation as it really is. If necessary, she should explain to the patient that she will only be prepared to grant his request if she is convinced that there is no acceptable alternative.[64] Often it will be possible to find such alternatives, either in the form of symptom control, or of assistance in coming to terms with the facts. If the request is primarily motivated by fear of the future, it may often help to reassure the patient (honestly) that euthanasia will still be an option if those fears come true. If death wishes are dealt with in this way, the possibility of euthanasia is not only compatible with palliative care but integrated into it.[65]

This route is not open to a professional who is not prepared under any circumstances to grant a request for euthanasia, or to collaborate in that action in any way. For such a doctor or nurse a realistic approach will mean that she should be open about her position from the start. In a country in which euthanasia or writing a prescription for lethal drugs has been legalized that will imply that she offers to withdraw from the case and to refer the patient – who should not become a hostage to her personal convictions – to others. In a country in which euthanasia and giving access to lethal drugs have not been legalized it will at the very least mean that she explains her position to the patient. 'I can understand your attitude', she could say, 'but my personal view is that life is

62 Cf. footnote 32.
63 Ten Cate 2019, ch. 5.
64 Cf. the 'dual track' approach of psychiatric patients with a death wish, described in Section 13.8.
65 Bernhem et al. 2008; Bernheim, Raus 2017.

always worthwhile, or that the law of the land should be complied with'. Or whatever her true reasons are. That will be the only way to respect the patient as a person. She should not give the false impression that she is prepared to enter into an 'open dialogue' about the patient's request, if she already knows that she will refuse it.

Palliative care specialists are often more concerned about the guiding values of their specialism than medical professionals usually are. One of those leading values should be honesty.

6.9 Conclusion

What is basically at stake in this discussion is a normative conception of dying well. The functional approach rests on the ideal of a patient who is enabled to die in peace because both his physical symptoms and all other elements of his suffering are under full medical control. All deviations from this ideal are seen as defects, to be repaired as far as possible by therapy.[66] Family support and spiritual care are both fully in the service of this aim. Every practitioner knows of course that this ideal is not always attainable, that not all suffering can be taken away. My point is that, even if that end could be achieved, we shouldn't aim for it. Some aspects of suffering are beyond the legitimate scope of palliative care, even if such care is understood, as it should be, in a personalized, relational and holistic way.

For some patients, their main concern in this phase is to round off the story of their life in a fitting way[67] (Section 15.1). It can only be fitting if it continues to be sensitive to the world in which they live as it is, even if this means recognizing highly disquieting facts for what they are. It is true that there is often a spectrum of responses that can be seen as appropriate to adverse circumstances, and it is also often hard to know what *is* an appropriate response. Moreover, anxious concern, fear, despair, anger are often quite excessive and not amenable to reflection and discussion. Therefore in the search of an adequate response there is not only room for reflection and discussion but also for support and consolation, backed up, if necessary, by medication. But these ingredients of a functional approach should, with the exceptions that I pointed at in Section 6.7, be used within the constraints of realism. They should not destroy the patient's contact with reality.

At this stage it is almost always helpful to soothe persisting physical symptoms of the terminal illness because they can no longer serve any

66 See also the Missoula-VITAS Quality of life index for patients with terminal illness. (Byock, Merriman 1998, 243–244) The underlying *ars moriendi* is described in Byock 1996.

67 Morita et al. 2000; Duggleby 2000; Chochinov et al. 2002.

beneficial function. But we shouldn't conceive of all elements of suffering on the model of distressing physical symptoms, as phenomena that it is always in the interest of the patient to get rid of, whether by pills or by talk.[68] Paradoxical though it may sound, suffering is a condition that, to some extent, requires to be respected as an integral part of dying well.

The target of my criticism in this chapter is a certain kind of medicalization. The essence of living is coping with life's challenges and this is a task for each person who is living a life that he cannot properly transfer to a health-care worker. Few people will on reflection want to delegate that task. The pursuit of a good death is one of those challenges. Shouldn't we conclude that doctors and nurses should only address symptoms of physical and mental illness and the defects in functioning that such illnesses cause but shouldn't aim at relieving any kind of suffering that goes beyond those basic forms?[69] The problem of that view is that it is impossible to separate levels of suffering from each other in the way the view requires. If the doctor tries to alleviate suffering from physical symptoms by using opioids, she will also reduce the patient's capacity to think and talk about the good death. In such cases a choice has to be made, preferably by doctor and patient together. Moreover, if a patient suffers from loss of meaning, control and dignity and decides that it would be better for him to be fully sedated until his death, he will need a doctor to sedate him. Whether this is a proper medical task we will discuss in Chapter 8. And whether doctors should ever be allowed to participate in the joint action of ending a patient's life we will consider in Chapter 9.

68 Cf. the WHO definition of palliative care: "an approach that improves the quality of life of individuals and their families facing the problems associated with life-threatening illness, through the prevention and relief of suffering by means of early identification and impeccable assessment and treatment of pain and other problems, physical, psychosocial and spiritual" (WHO 2002).

69 Van Hooft 1998.

7 Continuous deep sedation and homicide

7.1 How should we call the procedure?

In a substantial number of cases dying patients are brought into a state of lowered consciousness and kept in it until they die in order to stop severe suffering. Many guidelines and position statements have been published in recent years on this procedure. Some have been published by professional organizations and are meant to be binding for their members, others are the work of task forces and merely aim at providing medical, moral and legal guidance.[1] In this chapter and the following one I will discuss some positions that are taken by all or almost all these guidelines. In Chapter 8 I will consider restrictions that the guidelines propose as regards the proper indications for the procedure. Another common requirement mentioned in at least all recent guidelines is that in order to be eligible for the procedure the patient should have a life expectancy of not more than 'hours or days'. That is the requirement to be discussed in this chapter. The question that I will take up in particular is how we should classify the procedure in cases in which the requirement is not satisfied. But in the remainder of this section I will first discuss how we should call it.

We are talking about a procedure of lowering the consciousness of a patient, either permanently or at least intermittently, which is meant to go on until the patient dies. 'Terminal sedation' would be a fully appropriate name for this policy.[2] However, this has become a taboo term, because it is felt to suggest that the sedation shortens the patient's life, just as a 'terminal illness' suggests a terminating illness. A more neutral term which has been proposed is 'sedation at the end of life'. But even a dying patient can be sedated for a relatively short time, in order "to break the cycle of fear, fatigue, and insomnia, thereby allowing patients the opportunity to regain psychological strength in order to face the existential issues that precipitated the

1 For surveys see Gurschick, Mayer, Hanson 2015; Schildmann, Schildmann 2014.
2 Introduced by Enck 1991.

DOI: 10.4324/9781003281115-9

sedation",[3] or to create time for deciding about the proper way to proceed in a crisis. Such episodic 'respite sedations' do not raise any of the ethical questions I will address.

In 2000 Bert Broeckaert proposed to speak of 'palliative sedation' instead, and by now this term has been widely accepted internationally.[4] But this term does not exclude episodic sedation either. We can of course identify specific kinds of palliative sedation, for example 'palliative sedation until death',[5] but in that case we do not really need the adjective. A more important drawback of the term is that it does not only identify the procedure but also the aim for which it should be used, which makes it impossible to discuss whether and why this is the only *proper* aim. You cannot even state that palliative sedation should not be used in order to shorten the life of a patient, because any sedation started with that aim in mind would simply not be *palliative* sedation. It is true that we cannot require all descriptive terms in medicine, beginning with the term 'medicine' itself, to avoid every reference to aims and values, but in all cases in which we want to discuss such aims and values, we should use terms that do not already presuppose them. For this reason we need a more neutral term and a more neutral definition of it than the guidelines almost invariably provide, to enable us to ask the normative questions that we want to ask. The term and its definition should leave open, in particular, the aim of the procedure (only relief of suffering?), its indications (only so-called refractory symptoms?), the drugs to be used (benzodiazepines, but what about opiates?) and any restrictions on the class of patients who are candidates for its application (only patients with a life expectancy of hours or days?), for the very reason that these are the substantial issues to be discussed and decided upon.[6]

A final drawback of the term 'palliative sedation' is that it is a euphemism, and not only because of the positive connotation of the

3 Schuman-Olivier et al. 2008, 344.

4 Broeckaert 2000. See also Rousseau 2000.

5 Hasselaar 2008, cf. American Academy of Hospice and Palliative Medecine 2006.

6 Almost all guidelines include one or more of these aspects in their definition, in particular the aim of the treatment. Zorgnet Vlaanderen 2012, for example, defines palliative sedation as "providing sedatives in dosages that are required to lower a terminal patient's consciousness to the extent necessary to adequately control one or more refractory symptoms", without noticing that as a result many of the requirements made by the guideline are mere tautologies. See for three even more extreme cases Massachusetts Protocol 2005; Bigorio Switzerland 2005; EAPC 2009, 581. "By definition, symptoms requiring PS should be refractory to other therapy", Cowan, Palmer 2002. De Graeff, Dean 2007 criticize terms and definitions which do not mention the proper aim of the practice; Hasselaar, Verhagen, Vissers 2009 praise a definition by Morita et al. 2001 for indicating that sedatives *should* be titrated. (My ital.) Only KNMG 2009 (2005) and Imai et al. 2020 are aware of this pitfall, but even these guidelines do not fully succeed in avoiding it. For overviews of definitions see Claessens et al. 2008, Tables 3 and 4; Hasselaar et al. 2009, Table 2.

adjective.[7] Palliative care is given to a patient in order to alleviate his severe suffering. Normally this is being done by freeing his experience from burdening aspects such as pain, lack of breath, nausea, panic or anxiety. But when a patient is deeply and permanently sedated until death, it is being done in a far more radical way, by freeing him from any experience at all.

Often the euphemism seems to be consciously chosen in order to accentuate as strongly as possible the difference between sedation of this type and euthanasia. For the same reason it is stressed that palliative sedation is a normal option in palliative care, even if only an option of last resort. It may be true that sedation by proper means in adequate dosages, usually midazolam or another drug from the family of benzodiazepines, is not likely by itself to hasten the death of the patient; by providing tranquillity it sometimes may even postpone it. (But see Section 7.2 for some doubts.) But as soon as the stage of permanent unconsciousness is reached, there is no difference from the subjective point of view of the patient between that state and death, not because the experience is the same, but because in both cases all experience has ended.[8] This does not mean that at the moment this stage is reached the person has died, or that her friends, her relatives, her nurses and doctors are free to act as if she had died. It only means that the difference between that state and death cannot be explained in experiential terms. Both death and deep sedation until death mean the end of a patient's biographical life, the life of which she is the conscious subject. By deep sedation she is left in the state of a living organism, a state she shares with an irreversibly comatose patient, even if in her case the coma is still technically reversible. To refer to this as 'palliative sedation' is similar to referring to euthanasia as 'palliative killing'.[9] It does not sufficiently recognize the qualitative difference between a state of relieved suffering and of coma. Sedation until death by itself causes serious harm, almost always. It can only be justified if it is nevertheless rightly considered to be in the patient's best overall interests.

Says a nurse: "I don't usually use the word 'sedation', I use the term 'make him more comfortable and settled'".[10] But unconsciousness is not a comfortable state. (Of course it is not an uncomfortable state either.)

7 Den Hartogh 2006; van Delden 2007; Battin 2008; Rady, Verheijde 2010; Raus, Sterckx, Mortier 2012.

8 Juth et al. 2010.

9 Hence when de Graeff, Dean 2007 state that palliative sedation provides no distinctive ethical problem as long as there is no intention to hasten death, this is completely beside the mark, as Janssens, van Delden, Widdershoven 2012 comment, cf. van Delden 2013. Rather, "(s)edation at the end of life is a serious concern. It is, in a way, a harm done at the end of life which produces social death. We should reluctantly embark upon palliative sedation; we should perform sedation within guidelines, but with a bit of regret and sadness" (Davis 2009).

10 Seymour et al. 2015.

7.2 'Hours or days'

Most guidelines stress that by itself deeply sedating a patient in the medically appropriate way probably does not shorten his life.[11] This is a fairly recent view and many physicians still continue to believe the contrary.[12] And recently the awareness has grown that the evidence for the view is not very strong.[13] It is mainly based on the observation that the time from admission into a palliative care unit until death is not significantly different in the case of sedated and non-sedated patients. But it is possible that patients who will develop refractory symptoms, or already exhibit them, enter the unit at a relatively earlier stage. A randomized clinical trial that would end the uncertainty is obviously out of the question. What we really want to know is whether from the moment of sedation on survival time changes, but we cannot identify any particular moment in the dying process of the non-sedated patients that would make a comparison possible. Some authors argue in addition that deep sedation, if continued for a longer time than two days, is likely to depress vital functions in the brainstem, with life-shortening effects.[14]

Let's nevertheless assume that the proper use of sedatives by itself has no life-shortening effects. But when a patient's consciousness is lowered, even moderately, to a level short of full unconsciousness, he will no longer be able to eat or drink. Hence a decision has to be made whether or not to start (or, occasionally, to continue) artificial nutrition and, in particular, hydration. In some cases the patient will already have died before it becomes necessssary to answer that question, but in other cases the question will eventually require an answer. In the case of deep sedation until death it will in some countries be decided almost routinely to abstain from the artificial provision of fluids, in other countries they will be provided in most cases.[15] If it is decided to withhold

11 Metareviews: Maltoni et al. 2012; Barathi, Chandra 2013; Beller et al. 2015.

12 In the Netherlands (2015) 40% of the doctors who decided to start continuous sedation until death considered a life-shortening effect possible, Onwuteaka-Philipsen et al. 2017, 129.

13 Beller et al. 2015; Riisfeldt 2019. An additional problem is that all available studies covered different types of sedation, including intermittent, mild and moderate sedation. We can therefore not conclude that continuous deep sedation doesn't cause death.

14 EAPC 2009 ('a small risk of hastened death'); Rady, Verheijde 2010; Leheup et al. 2012; Beller et al. 2015 (evaluating the available studies on the effects of sedation); Twycross 2019 (continuous deep sedation 'certainly' reduces mean survival).

15 According to Miccinesi et al. 2006 in 2001–2002 it was decided to abstain from artificial nutrition and hydration in the following percentages of cases of palliative sedation: 35% (Italy), 39% (Flanders), 56% (Sweden), 60% (German Switzerland), 64% (Denmark and the Netherlands). Later reports of similarly designed research concern the Netherlands 2005 (66%, Rietjens et al. 2008); 2010 (79%, van der Heide et al. 2012); 2015 (91%, Onwuteaka-Philipsen et al. 2017, 129); and Flanders 2007 (57.5%); 2013 (61.7%, Robijn et al. 2016). Both in the Netherlands and Flanders

fluids and the patient goes on to live for more than a week, chances are that he eventually dies from dehydration. (The immediate cause of the patient's death will in most cases be heart failure, caused by a lack of kalium and natrium that results from dehydration.[16]) Should we in these cases think of the doctor as ending the life of her patient, either with or without his request?[17]

If we consult the existing guidelines we will, remarkably, find no answer to that question. That doesn't mean that they are not concerned about the issue, on the contrary. Most guidelines state as a condition for starting deep and continuous sedation that a patient has a reduced life expectancy, often specified as 'hours or days',[18] sometimes as 'days or weeks'.[19] If a more precise upper limit is given, it is usually put at 14 days.[20] Because that is about the maximum time that people can live without fluids, one may guess that the reason for this restriction has something to do with a possible life-shortening effect, and this is confirmed in the few cases in which a reason is given.[21] So the guidelines are certainly concerned about

---

fluids are almost never provided by GPs (Papavasilious et al. 2014; Onwuteaka-Philipsen et al. 2017). We have no comparable data for non-European countries, but for some indicative data see Bruinsma, Rietjens, van der Heide 2013, 44.

16 KNMG/V&VN 2014, 25.

17 What do doctors think? According to Anquinet et al. 2011 6 out of 28 Flemish physicians classified the procedure as similar to euthanasia (2) or to ending of life without request (4). Van Delden et al 2011 asked doctors to evaluate a vignette case in which the life expectancy of the patient was a month, the patient was sedated and did not receive artificial hydration and died after a week. Some respondents observed that this was 'a kind of euthanasia', but only few of them considered this a reason for a negative assessment of the decision (cf. Section 10.8).

18 Braun, Hagen, Clark 2003; Morita et al. 2005a (but elsewhere: days or weeks); Hospice and Palliative Nurses Association 2008; EAPC 2009; Fraser Health 2011; National Comprehensive Cancer Network 2009, section Palliative Sedation. A guideline from the Svenska Läkaresällskapets Delegation for Medicinsk Etik (2003,) reported in: Førde, Materstvedt, Syse 2008, specified: one week.

19 Quill, Byock 2000; de Graeff, Dean 2007; Dean et al. 2012.

20 NMA 2001; KNMG 2009; National Hospice and Palliative Care Organization 2010; Zorgnet Vlaanderen 2012; Haute Autorité de Santé 2018. Cf. Morita et al 2005a: two to three weeks. According to the Collège des Médecins du Quebec 2016 "if a person at the end of life has refractory and intolerable symptoms, the option of palliative sedation should not be ruled out owing to prognostic uncertainty regarding the two-week timeframe".

21 NEC-VHA 2006; National Hospice and Palliative Care Organization 2010. According to the chairperson of KNMG 2009, Marian Verkerk, "(i)t is unprofessional to render a person with a longer life expectancy asleep and refrain from hydration and nutrition. That's just euthanasia with other means, because without food and fluid everyone dies after a week." *De Volkskrant* 23-5-2007. (My transl.) One other reason that is sometimes mentioned, is the prolonged distress of the family, NEC-VHA 2006; EAPC 2009; Collège des Médecins du Quebec 2016. Medical reasons include increasing risk of paradoxical agitation, but such reasons also apply to cases in which the provision of fluids is continued.

the *dual procedure*, as I will call it, of continuous sedation until death and withholding fluids, when the patient has a life expectancy beyond a certain number of days or weeks and that concern seems primarily to be motivated by the possibly life-shortening effect of that procedure. But the guidelines do not describe it as a form of killing.

Should they? From the beginning of the ethical and legal discussion about 'terminal sedation' (as it was then called), the suspicion has been voiced that this medical procedure sometimes amounts to 'slow euthanasia'.[22] It has been a primary concern of the guidelines to refute that accusation. That is why they stress that even deep continuous sedation, if done by using appropriate dosages of sedatives, by itself has no life-shortening effects. If that is true, such effects could only occur when the decision to start sedation is followed by the decision not to administer artificial nutrition and hydration. And for this dual procedure they have addressed the concern by setting upper limits to the life expectancy of the patient to be sedated.

How should the upper limit be specified for this strategy to succeed? As we have seen the guidelines give varying answers to this question, roughly in a range from 4 to 14 days. Even older people (60+) are supposed to be able to survive 10–14 days without the intake of any fluids. But in this case we are talking about people in the last stage of a fatal illness. Patients in that category may be expected to die from dehydration after a few days. Even within that time frame estimations of life expectancy are unreliable and the uncertainty increases when death is farther away. Hence the upper limit should be closer to 4 than to 14 days.[23]

Having stipulated an upper limit, the question remains how we should describe the dual procedure when the life expectancy of the patient exceeds that limit. Shouldn't we squarely face the fact that it is probably a form of homicide, and be consistent in drawing the legal and moral consequences of that insight?

7.3 Slow euthanasia?[24]

It is often unproblematic to start continuous deep sedation without administering any fluids. In each dying process there comes a point at which the patient spontaneously stops eating and drinking because he loses the craving for it. That is a normal part of dying, and the dominant view among physicians and ethicists is that it should always be respected.

22 Brody 1993; Craig 1994; Billings, Block 1996; Orentlicher 1998; Gauthier 2001; Battin 2008.

23 For a more detailed analysis see van Delden 2013; den Hartogh 2016a, Section 4; for a systematic review of relevant studies White et al. 2016.

24 This section is an updated version of den Hartogh 2016a, Section 2.

To start artificial hydration in such a case is an unnecessary prolonging of the dying process, and may induce additional forms of suffering, for example by causing incontinence, oedema, ascites or bronchial and gastrointestinal secretions.[25] Hence it may not only be futile but even cruel treatment. If sedation begins when this point has already been reached, it is still obvious that artificial hydration should not even be considered, even when we assume that, as a result of deep sedation, it will no longer cause suffering.

Some guidelines suggest that in the large majority of cases in which continuous deep sedation is decided upon, the patient has already spontaneously stopped taking fluids.[26] There seems to be an element of wishful thinking in that contention: surely refractory symptoms don't only occur in the final stage of the dying process, and this is all the more clear if we recognize that existential distress can be 'refractory'. But even if it would be true, the few cases left would be worth discussing.[27]

It is a constantly recurring theme in the guidelines that the decision to start or withhold the artificial provision of food and fluids has to be made on independent grounds. Neither decision should be automatically implied in the decision to start sedation.[28] This makes sense as long as the patient has not become fully unconscious. Even at moderate levels of unconsciousness she may still experience feelings of hunger and thirst, or suffer from a dry mouth on the one hand, whereas providing food and drink may cause its own forms of suffering (for example resulting from obstipation) on the other.[29] In such cases it is true

25 Sutcliffe, Holmes 1994; KNMG 2009, 36; Collège des Médecins du Quebec 2016. According to Suchner 2018, lack of hydration may also have harmful effects and the decision to provide or not to provide fluids should be made on an individual basis.

26 De Graeff, Dean 2007; KNMG 2009; Zorgnet Vlaanderen 2012; Collège des Médecins du Quebec 2016.

27 Maltoni, Scarpi, Rosati 2012 (meta-review) report a mean and median duration of the sedation of resp. 2 and 4 days, range 0–43 days. Barathi, Chandra 2013 found in nine studies a mean duration of 2.5–4.3 days. For other data about survival time see Onwuteaka-Philipsen et al. 2017, 129 (the Netherlands); Robijn et al. 2016 (Flanders); Seale 2010 (UK); Morita et al. 2002 (Japan); Schur et al. 2016 (Austria). Unfortunately, these data don't differentiate between cases in which artificial hydration has and has not been provided. If it has not been provided, as is common in the Netherlands and Belgium, survival time will automatically not exceed one to two weeks, even though the patient had an *ex ante* life expectancy of months or years. Hence the available data tell us next to nothing about the extent to which the requirements about life expectancy of the guidelines are being complied with.

28 Quill, Byock 2000; Cowan, Palmer 2002; Morita et al. 2005a; Massachusetts Protocol 2005; NEC-VHA 2006; de Graeff, Dean 2007; Hospice and Palliative Nurses Association 2008; EAPC 2009; National Hospice and Palliative Care Organization 2010; Cherny 2014 (ESMO); Irish Association for Palliative Care 2015. According to Dean et al. 2012 both decisions should be considered separately as well as together.

29 For extensive discussions of these effects see de Graeff, Dean 2007, 76–77; Gurschick, Mayer, Hanson 2015; Collège des Médecins du Quebec 2016. Cf. Suchner 2018.

that the benefits and burdens should be balanced against each other; the available evidence does not allow us to draw any general conclusion about that balance.[30] But as soon as the patient is in a state of coma, either as the final outcome of titration or as the result of a non-titrating policy, such balancing makes no sense anymore. The patient, we assume, does not experience anything at all and hence does not suffer, either from being provided or from not being provided fluids. The only possibly relevant effect of providing them is that death from dehydration is thereby prevented.

The Dutch and Flemish guidelines and a few others take the view that in such cases artificial hydration should be withheld or withdrawn because it is to be considered futile.[31] It is futile because for a patient who has permanently, if not irreversibly, lost consciousness, it doesn't matter in which condition she is, not even if she fully dries out.[32] But how can a treatment be futile that prolongs her life or at least prevents it from being shortened? In that judgement it is presupposed that merely being alive has no value of its own for the living person, if that life isn't the vehicle of other goods, a conscious and not too painful experience of the world to begin with. On this assumption mere biological life cannot be good *for you*, if you do not have and never again will have a point of view from which you can endorse (or, for that matter, deny) that evaluation. I have defended this view in Section 2.3 and shall assume that in secularized societies it can be acted upon, unless a patient indicates that in his view mere biological life is by itself a basic human good, and therefore always to be protected, at least by 'ordinary means'.[33]

If artificially administering fluids to a person who will be fully unconscious until her death is a futile procedure, it seems that we can argue as follows. There is no problem with sedation, even to full unconsciousness, because it has no life-shortening effects by itself. There is no problem with abstaining from artificial hydration either, because it is only a form of allowing to die, and the treatment may properly be considered futile. Neither of these decisions is a form of killing, both are justified on

30 Good et al. 2014.

31 KNMG 2009; Neitzke et al. 2010; Zorgnet Vlaanderen 2012; National Comprehensive Cancer Network 2009.

32 "One of the most difficult situations is where deep, permanent sedation is given to a patient who is expected to survive for more than one week. Some would argue that, in this situation, dehydration may hasten death. Others would argue that giving fluids would neither prevent death, nor make it more comfortable, but merely prolong the dying process. There is no evidence to support either view" De Graeff, Dean 2007, 76. But as regards their empirical content, both views are correct, and fully compatible.

33 NEC-VHA 2006; de Graeff, Dean 2007; EAPC 2009. Cf. the debate about ending artificial feeding of patients in a persistent vegetative state, as in the famous case *Airedale NHS Trust v. Bland* (1993) AC 789 HL. (Or, rather, an Unresponsive Wakefulness Syndrome, cf. von Wildt et al. 2012.)

their own grounds, independently of each other. And so the combination of the two cannot be a form of killing either.[34]

Is this a valid argument? If it is, the requirements made by the guidelines as regards the maximum life expectancy of the patient should be reconsidered. For even in cases in which we could expect the patient eventually to die from dehydration rather than from his illness, he would not be killed. Indeed, he would not be killed if he still had a life expectancy of several years.

But the argument is fallacious. If of two actions, for example both consisting of the injection of a certain amount of muscle relaxants, neither has a lethal effect by itself, but the combination has, knowingly following a procedure consisting of both actions surely amounts to killing. This much is obvious. As a matter of fact, doing the first action with the intention to do the second is already considered a crime by the law, whether or not the second action will actually be performed. But even when the first action has been done without this intention, clearly it is impermissible to go on and do the second.

Does it make a difference to the plausibility of the argument that in the sedation case we are talking about the combination of an action and an omission? Consider the following analogy. Someone wants to get rid of his enemy, but in order not to be liable to prosecution for murder, he first sedates his victim to unconsciousness and then sees to it that no food or drink is being provided to him. The victim dies after two weeks. Of course the scheme will be unsuccessful, and the criminal convicted of murder, for his two subplans (to sedate and to avoid the administering of food and drink) only make sense as constitutive elements of one plan: to bring about the death of the victim.

On being confronted with a similar counterexample Torbjörn Tännsjö suggests that even if the policy of our criminal is morally on a par with murder, *stricto sensu* it isn't a form of killing.[35] If the law considers it to be homicide, it is using a legal fiction. On his view the policy consists of an action of taking away someone's liberty and then allowing her to die from hunger and thirst. But if he is right, one doesn't kill a person either by throwing her into the sea from an aeroplane. That procedure also consists of an action: displacing the victim into the sea, and a failure to act: allowing her to drown, and neither the action nor the omission is a killing by itself. It could be objected that the combination of the two is

34 The argument has most explicitly been stated by Tännsjö 2004. It is implied by all authors who suggest that the decision to abstain from providing artificial fluids should be judged in the same way as other decisions to withhold or withdraw treatment, e.g., Williams 2001; Lewis 2008, 359; Gevers 2002, 365; Delbeke 2013, 144. Guidelines taking that position include AMA 2008; EAPC 2009; and the guidelines mentioned in footnote 28.

35 That counterexample came from Kuhse 2004, 61: Frieda putting her kitten into a box and deliberately leaving it there without food and water until it dies.

a killing in this case because the process which, if not interrupted, will end the victim's life, is initiated by the killer; it is only when one hasn't initiated the process which ends her life that one can be said to merely allow her to die. On that view a person who stops eating and drinking does not kill herself either, she only allows herself to die from an independent process, to which we are all subjected, of dying from lack of food and drink. We only don't notice that natural process because we routinely block it by our actions. That view I discussed and rejected in Section 4.3. But even if it would be correct, sedating a person is another matter, for it means actively *disabling* the person to block that 'natural' process herself. If you don't compensate for that by taking over the blocking, you are thereby killing her. Hence, by sedating a person with a more than minimal life expectancy you are killing that person, unless you artificially provide her with food and drink, just as you would kill her by throwing her into the sea, unless you took active steps to get her out. Such actions are incomplete killings which are completed by 'allowing nature to take its course'. The action and the abstaining are successive elements of a single plan which has someone's death as its foreseeable effect.[36]

It is true that in many cases the doctor would have decided to start continuous deep sedation even if in that case he had been obliged to start administering fluids as well. That first decision is in that case correctly understood to be independent of the second one, the decision to withhold hydration.[37] That second decision, however, certainly is not made independently of the first one, and it is this second decision which, therefore, should be seen as part of a single procedure which should be evaluated as a whole. Similarly, if we throw a person into the sea from an aeroplane for some independent reason, and only then decide not to take her out, we are still killing that person.

A standard reply to this line of reasoning is that artificial nutrition and hydration are medical actions that can only be started with the informed consent of the patient (or his representative), which he is fully authorized to refuse. According to this objection the argument about futility is a red herring; what we should say instead is that continuous deep sedation is justified by the consent of the patient (and a proper medical indication) and abstaining from artificial hydration by his refusal to have it administered.[38] This argument seems to have convinced even those authors who most prominently have suggested

36 Orentlicher 1998; Kuhse 2004; van Delden 2013, 218–227; Raus, Chambaere, Sterckx 2016.

37 Delbeke 2013.

38 Orentlicher 1998; Hallenbeck 2000; Cowan, Palmer 2002; McIntyre 2004; Cantor 2006; Quill et al. 2009; Olsen, Swetz, Mueller 2010; Cellarius 2011; Delbeke 2013; Holm 2013, 232; Raus, Chambaere, Sterckx 2016.

that the dual procedure sometimes constitutes slow euthanasia. Note again that, if the argument would be valid, it would justify the dual procedure, irrespective of the life expectancy of the patient.

Is it valid? It is true that if the patient is not prepared to consent to the provision of artificial hydration once sedation has started, it is not an option for the doctor to provide it, whether or not he considers it futile treatment. But this means that in deciding whether or not to start sedation, he has to take into account that he will have to abstain from artificial hydration. When he decides to go on, even though the patient has a life expectancy of more than, say, two weeks, he still knowingly initiates a course of events that will cause the death of the patient and at the same time disables her to prevent that effect from occurring. That analysis still applies, even though the patient doesn't want to prevent that effect from occurring. She is also disabled to change her mind. Hence the doctor knows that he will probably cause the patient to die by dehydration, and therefore, by following the dual procedure, will probably kill her, albeit with her consent. Similarly, if you throw someone into the sea with his consent, knowing that he will then refuse to be rescued, you are still causing his death by drowning, albeit on his request. It is still the same 'salami-slicing technique' to consider the two decisions independently of each other.[39] You are participating in the joint action of ending his life.

It has been suggested that the problem does not arise if someone first independently decides to stop eating and drinking, and the doctor then starts sedating her.[40] In that case the doctor doesn't facilitate the person's suicide by making it easier for her to make that decision. It regularly happens, however, that a person who has started acting on her plan to stop taking fluids, changes her mind after a few days.[41] By sedating her on her request a doctor makes this impossible. This means that, even if he had no influence on the person's decision, he played a major role in its implementation. He should therefore still be considered to have participated in the joint action of ending the person's life. It is, moreover, usually impossible for an outside observer to determine whether or not the decision to stop eating and drinking is really made independently of the prospect of sedation. It will often even be impossible for the person and the doctor involved to determine this themselves. It is therefore not an eventuality that professional guidelines or the law should take into account. If they did, they would create a loophole in the rules that would put their supposed protective function in jeopardy.

The analogies I have used in this section (incarceration, hurling a person into the sea) might suggest that I have argued for a strong normative conclusion. But that has not been my intention. My aim has only been to

39 van Delden 2007; 2013, 219.
40 KNMG 2009; Jackson 2012, 17.
41 Once in six times according to Harvath et al. 2006 (report from an American hospice).

show that the dual procedure should sometimes be recognized for what it is: a kind of homicide. It might nevertheless be impeccable, legally and morally. 'A justified killing' is not an oxymoron. My point is only that, if the killing is done with the person's request, it is a kind of euthanasia and should morally and legally be evaluated as such.[42] It cannot be seen as an alternative way to determine the time of one's own death.

It has been proposed by some authors that doctors should retain the option of choosing the dual procedure without any requirement as regards the life expectancy of the patient.[43] Why leave patients with refractory and intolerable symptoms to their fate when their life expectancy exceeds two weeks or any other arbitrary limit? But if the law is going to permit only one form of euthanasia, it is hard to see why it should be the slow one. The same reasons the patient may have for preferring sedation until death without hydration he may cite for preferring euthanasia in its standard form to any kind of sedation. Which reasons can be given for not allowing it? The patient has nothing to gain, and both the patient and his relatives have a lot to lose by this restriction. If the sanctity of life or the vocational integrity of the doctor is at stake in one practice, it is equally at stake in the other, and if the possibilities of abuse and error can be controlled in one case, they can equally be controlled in the other.[44]

Only when a patient has a life expectancy of no more than a few days, the dual procedure, if consented to by the patient, can be an alternative to euthanasia. In other cases it is a form of euthanasia. Even if one is not convinced by my argument and still prefers to consider it a different kind of medical practice, one should agree that is equally in need of regulation as euthanasia and for the same reasons. It is therefore not a good argument against legalizing euthanasia that we always have this alternative at our disposal.

42 In den Hartogh 2016a, Section 3, I have discussed the legal consequences of the view that I have argued for in this section.

43 Cellarius 2008; Orentlicher 2013; Lipuma, DeMarco 2015 (up to six months); cf. Collège des Médecins du Quebec 2016 (footnote 20).

44 For these reasons Kon 2011 calls euthanasia in comparison with sedation until death "medically indicated".

8 Sedation until death: indications[1]

8.1 Introduction

The existing guidelines on 'palliative sedation' all take the following positions: the patient's consciousness should not be lowered more than is necessary for preventing her from suffering; it must be impossible to alleviate the suffering in any alternative way; and the patient's mere preference for dying peacefully cannot justify the procedure. In addition, some guidelines stipulate that existential suffering cannot do so either. Most of these restrictions are merely asserted, or at best argued for in terms of principles of proportionality and subsidiarity which are mentioned but not articulated. My aim in this chapter is to evaluate the few arguments I have found in the guidelines themselves and in the literature, and in particular the argument that it is either a vital interest, or even a duty of the patient to preserve consciousness as long as possible at all times. In Chapter 6 I have argued that we should be cautious with forms of palliative care that disable patients to consider their circumstances as they are and to adjust their decisions to these circumstances. It may seem to follow that we should be most reluctant to compromise their consciousness.

Another requirement that is common to all the guidelines is that the patient should give her informed consent, if she is still capable of considering the matter and communicating about it. In the concluding section, it will turn out to be essential to my argument as a whole to take this demand into account. As regards the other requirements that I will discuss I will conclude that they can at best have a default status only; it should be permitted to deviate from them in the interest of the patient. But what we should consider to be in the interest of the patient largely depends on her personal values and priorities. This means that the physician should not postpone discussion of the issue until the moment that

1 This chapter is an updated version of den Hartogh 2016c. Copyright © 2016 Johns Hopkins University Press. The article appeared in *Kennedy Institute of Ethics Journal*, Volume 26, Issue 4, December 2016, pages 369–397. Published with permission by Johns Hopkins University Press. I had the good fortune of receiving extensive and incisive comments on a draft of that paper from Jos Welie.

DOI: 10.4324/9781003281115-10

the decision to start sedation has to be taken, for it will then often be too late for the patient to weigh the option of sedation against remaining alternatives in the light of her priorities.

In short, in this chapter I will argue for a twofold thesis. In some respects the guidelines are unnecessarily restrictive. But greater permissiveness is only justifiable in cases in which stricter conditions regarding consent have been satisfied than the conditions most guidelines insist on at the moment.

8.2 Two procedures

Suppose a dying patient has one or more refractory symptoms, symptoms which cause a great deal of suffering but cannot be alleviated by any standard treatment from the repertoire of palliative care, and therefore it is decided to sedate her. One could start by sedating her for a certain time only (respite sedation); some palliative care specialists suggest one always should. But suppose the symptoms recur when the original level of consciousness is re-established, and for that reason a policy of ongoing sedation is proposed. This proposal can be implemented in two ways.[2]

The first option is to lower the patient's consciousness just enough for her symptoms to disappear, and then to go on to monitor her condition regularly, only sedating her deeper when observable signs of suffering reoccur. One could even try to wake her up at regular intervals in order to enable her to communicate with her relatives and her doctor.[3] In some cases it will be possible to go on in this way until the death of the patient. In other cases it will turn out to be necessary to increase dosages until full unconsciousness has been achieved. Let us refer to this first policy as a policy of titration.

The second way of implementing non-episodic sedation is by bringing the patient into a state of coma from the start by rapidly increasing dosages of sedatives and maintaining that state until death. Monitoring is then still necessary, but only to make sure that no outward signs of a raised level of consciousness can be observed. If the patient unexpectedly returns to a calm state of consciousness, due to an at least partial recovery from the pathology that made her suffer, it could be decided to discontinue deep sedation. But that is a variant of the first procedure, a kind of backwards titration.

According to almost all guidelines, in particular the recent ones, only the policy of titration is an acceptable one.[4] The only exception they are

2 Imai et al. 2020.

3 Advised by de Graeff, Dean 2007.

4 An exception is Haute Authorité de Santé 2018, implementing the French *Claeys-Leonetti End-of-Life Law* (2016) that granted a right to continuous deep sedation to certain categories of patients (Chapter 4, footnote 51). According to Imai et al. 2020 it is occasionally clear at the start of the procedure that nothing less than complete unconsciousness will be sufficient to end the patient's suffering.

prepared to allow concerns emergency cases in the dying stage: uncontrollable bleeding or a sudden threat of suffocation. Indeed, they tend to use essentialist language to suggest their preference: palliative sedation 'is' following the titration policy. No explicit argument for the policy is then provided.

If any argument is offered or suggested it is the following: the proper aim of palliative sedation is to suppress refractory symptoms. Hence it is a requirement of proportionality that the dosage of sedatives given should be sufficient to achieve that aim, and no more should be given.[5] Quite often it is explained that the administration of higher dosages would be suggestive of aims other than palliation.[6] Which aims? Hastening death, even if it is known that the dosage given is not likely to have any effect of that kind? One gets the impression that the titrating policy is often meant to send a message: look, I am *not* engaged in euthanasia.

But the assumption that a non-titrating policy can have no legitimate aim is disputable, and hence this policy does not, by itself, reveal an intention to shorten life. Suppose that we give the patient the choice between the two options, at a time at which she is still able to consider the matter carefully. Some patients will opt for the titrating policy, because they want to preserve as much awareness of their surroundings as possible, as long as possible, and they want to be able to communicate with others, at least occasionally, as long as possible, even at the cost of severe suffering during those occasions. Other patients, however, will take into account that a titrating policy is inherently reactive: it responds to the recurrence of signs of suffering. They may prefer a proactive approach that prevents such suffering from reocccurring. In addition they may be aware of the fact that the ways in which doctors usually assess the level of consciousness, that is, clinical observation, in particular of facial expressions of discomfort, and (at best) the use of observational coma scales, are not very reliable.[7] It is therefore not uncommon even for patients who have been deeply sedated to wake up.[8] Occasionally patients do not respond

5 More frequently the argument is only offered implicitly by appealing to 'the' principle of proportionality. But what is proportional depends on one's justifiable purposes, as is recognized by the exception in emergency cases.

6 Hallenbeck 2000; NEC-VHA 2006; AMA 2008, commented upon by Battin 2008; Zorgnet Vlaanderen 2012; Sullivan, Heng (IACB) 2012. "Repeated doses, titrated to ease an individual's distress, are the mark of proportionate sedation. Single large doses are the mark of ignorance or intentional harm" (de Graeff, Dean 2007). Such a policy "betrays a different intention. This is *not* palliative sedation" (Claessens et al. 2008).

7 Raus et al. 2013. Assessing the depth of unconsciousness is difficult even for anaesthesiologists (Shafer and Stansky 2008; Mashour 2010), and the scales they use have, with one exception, not been validated for use in the setting of palliative sedation (Brinkkemper et al. 2013; Deschepper et al. 2013).

8 Eight out of 28 patients studied by Anquinet et al. 2011 woke up due to insufficient medication; similarly 3 out of 27 patients studied by Pype et al. 2018; cf. Morita et al. 2005b.

to midazolam at all, or in the wrong way, by showing aggravated symptoms, in particular agitation.[9] These risks cannot be fully eliminated, but they can be reduced by inducing deep sedation from the start.

We even have indications that patients may be unresponsive to stimuli and yet aware to some extent, and therefore capable of suffering.[10] Absence of suffering can therefore not be definitively proven by the use of coma scales.[11] Even when awareness can be reliably detected it may still be difficult to assess the level of distress of patients who are unable to communicate. And the very attempt to measure response to stimuli may even cause additional suffering. For all these reasons[12] it makes sense for some patients to prefer to have the maximum assurance that could be given – even if that is not equivalent to complete assurance – that, when sedation starts, this will really be the end of all suffering.[13] Whether this makes sense for any particular patient will depend on the values that guide her life and on her view of dying well. Even aesthetic aspects of this view (a peaceful appearance) may be relevant.[14] Unless we are given an additional argument to the contrary (see Sections 8.4 and 8.5), preferences for either procedure should be considered to be equally legitimate, and doctors should therefore be allowed to let the priorities of their patients settle the choice.[15] Insisting on a titration policy may be experienced by some patients as a kind of medical harassment. It imposes on them a conception of the good death that they do not share (Section 6.8, at footnote 63).

9 Cheng, Roemor-Becuwe, Pereira 2002; Morita et al. 2005b. In the study by Anquinet et al. 2011, 7 out of 28 patients did not die a gentle death according to the physicians involved. In the review of the literature by Claessens et al. 2008, 78% of families were satisfied with the decision afterwards, persistent distress in patients after sedation being one of the main determinants of dissatisfaction.

10 Noreika et al. 2011; Kon 2011; Rady, Verheijde 2010, 2012; Deschepper et al. 2013.

11 Alkire, Hudetz and Tunoni 2008. "Consequently, midazolam alone in patients with delirium and/or severe refractory pain could result in a drug-induced 'locked-in' syndrome, and the patient dying in great, but unrecognized, distress". Twycross 2019, with references.

12 Summarized by Deschepper et al. 2013.

13 For similar reasons some patients may have an understandable preference for physician-assisted death rather than relying on even deep continuous sedation. This justifies the view of the Dutch and Belgian review committees for euthanasia that when a patient refuses to be sedated, the legal requirement that there should be no reasonable alternative to euthanasia can still be satisfied, Griffiths, Weyers, Adams 2008, 92, footnote 179.

14 Swart et al. 2012.

15 Seymour et al. 2015 found that in the UK the usual practice is to titrate, but in Belgium sedation was often deep from the start, the Netherlands taking a middle position. The motive mentioned by Belgian and Dutch doctors was to make sure that the patient would not suffer anymore, what they presumed (but had not always verified) to be his first priority.

8.3 Indications

All guidelines and almost all authors who discuss sedation until death agree that it may only be a proper treatment for refractory, that is, otherwise untreatable, symptoms: pain, convulsions, nausea, shortness of breath, physical restlessness, insomnia and general malaise. Many cancer patients are being treated with high-dose opioids for pain or dyspnoea. Hence sedation is also often used for intractable suffering due to the side effects of such treatment: delirium, hyperalgesia and myoclonus. Delirium even seems to be the most common indication altogether.[16] In addition, it is now generally accepted, at least in theory,[17] that the class of refractory symptoms includes symptoms belonging to psychiatric conditions, in particular depression. But it is still controversial whether doctors should be allowed to sedate patients who are in a state of existential suffering that cannot be alleviated in other ways.[18] Existential suffering includes the loss of a sense of meaning and purpose, the loss of the ability to cope with one's circumstances, loss of dignity and self-esteem, dependence on the care of others, being a burden to others, hopelessness, loneliness (Section 2.2). Some guidelines, in particular American ones, prohibit sedation until death in order to end existential suffering.[19] Some guidelines permit it only in rare cases.[20] And in the task forces that developed some other guidelines no consensus on the issue could be achieved.[21]

16 Sykes 2013; Schur et al. 2016.

17 Overall 68% of the studies reviewed by Claessens et al. 2008 listed only physical symptoms as reasons for sedating a patient.

18 See Rodrigues, Crokaert, Gastmans 2018 for a survey of the arguments *pro* and *contra* this view, found in the literature. Overall 36% of respondents in Morita 2004 reported clinical experience in continuous deep sedation for psycho-existential suffering: feeling of meaninglessness/worthlessness (61%), burden on others/dependency/inability to take care of oneself (48%), death anxiety/fear/panic (33%), wish to control one's time of death oneself (24%), and isolation/lack of social support (22%). Two Dutch studies revealed that existential suffering was the indication in resp. 16% and 26.4% of cases in which palliative sedation was applied, van Deijck et al. 2010, 2015. In a nationwide Austrian study existential distress was the indication for sedation until death in 30% of the cases, Schur et al. 2016. See also Boston, Bruce, Schreiber 2011; Claessens et al. 2011.

19 NMA 2001; NEC-VHA 2006; AMA 2008. In a study of 2010 two of three American physicians opposed deep sedation for existential suffering, Putman et al. 2013.

20 Morita et al. 2005a; de Graeff, Dean 2007; Hauser, Walsh 2009; Dean et al. 2012, Imai et al. 2020. Some guidelines only permit respite sedation for existential refractory symptoms, e.g. Massachusetts Protocol 2005.

21 Braun, Hagen, Clark 2003; EAPC 2009; National Hospice and Palliative Care Organization 2010. In a worldwide Delphi study, 9% of participating physicians found sedation until death in the case of existential suffering acceptable in the first round, 19% in the second, Benitez-Rosario, Morita 2019.

Such hesitations show a reductionist conception of suffering.[22] As we learned from Cassell in Chapter 6, pain, lack of breath, nausea are only *elements* of suffering. In all cases involving patients of minimal competence another constitutive element of their suffering is the meaning that these symptoms and other aspects of their present condition have for their present and future functioning as persons. In the final analysis their suffering is always existential suffering. It is the burdened experience of a person who understands that her way of life and her integrity as a person are fundamentally threatened or impaired, whether it is by uncontrollable pain, by loss of functions, by loneliness, by the imminence of death or by a combination of such factors.[23] Sometimes either the 'existential' or the 'physical' elements of suffering cannot be considered unbearable on their own, but only in combination with each other.[24] When deciding about the appropriateness of sedation it would therefore be arbitrary or short-sighted to consider only 'symptoms' and not also the loss of meaning, of autonomy and of dignity, which are usually the most important dimensions of suffering, even for end-stage cancer patients.

One objection that is often made to this view appeals to 'what-doctors-are-for' (cf. Sections 9.6; 14.2). Their task is to combat illness, and, if that is impossible, to soften its consequences, not to solve people's existential problems.[25] But in the case of dying patients 'existential' suffering is, to a large extent, the consequence of illness and therefore squarely within the domain of physicians, even on a restricted conception of that domain. For example, a patient would not suffer from death anxiety if she did not know that she was going to die from her illness shortly. It is a mistake to think that different causes of suffering correspond to different kinds of suffering. For sure, there may be other causal factors involved, such as regret about some aspects of the patient's past life, that may also contribute to her burden. But the effects of those factors are indistinguishable from the effects of illness. Effects from various sources may reinforce each other; even physical pain itself may be greatly increased by the fear that the pain will not be controlled or by uncertainty about its source (cf. Chapter 6, footnote 11). The severity of a person's suffering can therefore only be assessed by considering it holistically, as a single condition. The suffering of dying patients is inevitably shaped by their physical condition and the knowledge of their impending death, even if this experience primarily results from events and circumstances in their life rather than from the illness that is about to end it. And, whatever the cause of a

22 Cf. van Delden et al. 2011, 98–99, 162, showing that many Dutch physicians and nurses, in assessing the severity of a terminal cancer patient's suffering, only or primarily take her physical symptoms into account (Section 12.2).

23 Cassell, Rich 2010; Juth et al. 2010; Rich 2012; ten Have, Welie 2014, 129.

24 KNMG 2009; Swart et al. 2014.

25 NEC-VHA 2006; Materstvedt, Bosshardt 2009a; Hauser, Walsh 2009.

patient's distress, if it is in her overall best interests to end it definitively by sedation, medical expertise is required to effectuate that decision.

Another objection to considering so-called existential suffering a possible indication for sedation until death is that it is much harder to decide, in an intersubjectively persuasive way, whether it still can be relieved in any other way, for example by any available treatment of depression.[26] But, if suffering can only be assessed holistically even if it is predominantly caused by physiological disturbances, whether any proposed relief will be adequate can also only be judged holistically. On the other hand, as regards a patient with a fatal illness and only a few days of life ahead, we may be quite certain that their experience of the loss of meaning ('I am only waiting for death'), of failing dignity and of lost control will continue as long as they will have any ability to interpret their experience at all. Within that timeframe the requirement that all other possible interventions to relieve the patient's suffering should be exhausted is puzzling.

Even if alternative ways of relieving the patient's suffering, whatever its cause, are available, why should we always require that the patient tries them out?[27] All ways of dealing with severe suffering, in particular when it has many dimensions, have their own drawbacks, and why should it be a matter of medical protocol, rather than of patients' values, to choose between them? The choice will often be similar to the choice between titrated and non-titrated sedation procedures. One patient will reasonably prefer to be fully conscious and able to communicate as long as possible, the other will be tired of all these ongoing new adjustments in her treatment and care, and, equally reasonably, prefer to be assured as much as possible that she will suffer no longer.[28] For the first patient sedation may be an improper option to choose, even if the alternative is a complex set of palliative measures which require the constant monitoring of their combined effects (and possibly therefore the attendance or support of palliative experts). But for the second patient it is equally unjustified for a guideline to require her symptoms to be strictly intractable, and sedation to be only an option of last resort. As I argued in Section 8.2, both preferences are reasonable ones, possibly fitting into a comprehensible pattern of personal value commitments.

Need the patient be in a state of severe suffering at all? As we have seen in Chapter 2, people's conceptions of a good death tend to converge in many respects: almost everyone prefers to die at home, peacefully, free from burdensome symptoms, surrounded by one's nearest and dearest, satisfied with one's life and reconciled with one's death. But in other respects people's conceptions diverge. Some people want to be in control

26 Hallenbeck 2000; AMA 2008; Schuman-Olivier et al. 2008; NEC-VHA 2006; EAPC 2009; Schur et al. 2016.

27 Den Hartogh 2006; Battin 2008; 2013; Berger 2010; 2011; van Delden 2013.

28 As described by Robijn et al. 2017.

to the last minute, and the prospect of lying in bed in a comatose state for an indeterminate number of 'hours or days' is fairly abhorrent to them. For other people this very indeterminacy is attractive: a good death for them consists in sliding down quietly into a deep sleep from which they will never awake. What is attractive to them is that the process is gradual and, once it has started, does not require any further decision-making on their part. It mimics a natural way of dying,[29] even if, strictly speaking, it isn't, and the patient may know that for his relatives this may make it somewhat easier to cope with the way he dies.

What is wrong with helping them to slide down?[30] It is a comprehensible conception of a (relatively) good death, not an idiosyncratic one. If someone holds that conception, strongly and stably, and dies in that way naturally, we will consider her fortunate in this respect. If this is true, we need additional arguments why doctors cannot be allowed to help patients to die in a similar way, at least when death is not hastened thereby.

In this section and the previous one I have considered whether the several requirements I have discussed can be justified by the appeal to a principle of proportionality. I have argued (1) that what is 'proportional' depends on the aims we should consider legitimate ones, (2) that the following are aims which we can intersubjectively understand and sympathize with (on the condition that these are the aims of a patient who has only 'hours or days' of remaining life): (a) being free from suffering, whether or not it is caused by physical or psychological illness; (b) not having to experience any further inadequate relief of such suffering during those last hours or days; (c) not having to experiment anymore with any alternative forms of relief that may still turn out to be inadequate or even to cause additional iatrogenic suffering; and, finally, (d) to 'go gently into that good night'. None of these aims require or imply life to be shortened. If these aims mean a lot to a patient, doctors can understandably consider sedation until death to be in that patient's best overall interest. In that case sedation is a proportional intervention, given its aims, even if it does not satisfy the requirements of the guidelines. That means that these requirements cannot be justified by appealing to 'the principle of proportionality'.

8.4 The patient's interest in retaining consciousness

Two related arguments for restricting the indications for sedation until death, in particular for continuous deep sedation, merit a more extensive discussion. They are only rarely mentioned in the guidelines, but

29 Seymour, Janssens, Broeckaert 2007; Battin 2008; Raus, Sterckx, Mortier 2012. In a number of cases in which Dutch patients had a choice between euthanasia and sedation, they chose sedation for this reason, Rietjens et al. 2004.

30 '(A) truly deplorable practice', according to Pope Pius XII in 1957, quoted by Raus, Sterckx, Mortier 2012, repeated by Pontifical Council for Health Pastoral Care 1995.

I suspect that they are the basis of many of their recommendations that I have suggested to be unduly restrictive.

Both arguments point to the importance of being conscious as a precondition of coping with one's circumstances. As Jansen and Sulmasy state in an influential essay,

> (A)s patients approach death they confront many important questions. How should they face death? Should they pray or not? How should they say good-bye to loved ones and family members? Do they have outstanding concerns that have not been addressed? ....(P) atients have an important interest in responding to these questions in a manner that is consistent with their character and considered values...[31]

And, so the argument goes, in order to be able to deal with these questions, to retain control over their situation and to participate in medical decision-making, they have to retain consciousness.[32] This is the first argument I will consider: sedation until death can, at best, only be a means of last resort, for it is almost always contrary to vital interests of the patient. It is therefore wrong for a physician to start continuous deep sedation simply because a dying patient wants to fade away into an eternal sleep, and in the rare cases in which sedation is justified, a titration policy is always to be preferred.

Jansen and Sulmasy's argument rightly points out that it may harm a patient to deprive her of the opportunity to go through this last phase of her life with full awareness. As I argued in Chapter 6, avoiding suffering is not the only and not necessarily the most important interest of a dying person. She may have concerns in dealing with her circumstances that require her to retain her ability to understand those circumstances as they are. That, indeed, is one of the reasons why the decision to start continuous deep sedation is normally such a momentous one, and why it is a fundamental mistake to regard it as only one instrument out of many from the standard repertoire of palliative care (Section 7.1).

But the argument cannot support the conclusion that continuous deep sedation can only be a measure of last resort. In the first place we have those exemplary deaths – Socrates, David Hume – where all questions that needed to be asked have been asked and answered. Not every death comes too early, at a time when the dying person is insufficiently prepared for it. Secondly, it will often, perhaps usually, be evident that it will not be possible for the patient in the time still left to her and in her present condition to become reconciled with estranged relatives, to forgive those who have wronged her, or to come significantly closer to the solution

31 Jansen, Sulmasy 2002a, 327; cf. Sulmasy 2018, 239.

32 Davis 2009; Sykes 2013.

of any of her other remaining existential problems. Thirdly, even when some of those interests in coping have not fully been fulfilled and can still possibly be addressed to some extent, the weight of these interests can vary from one patient to another. One cannot assume that pursuing those interests always prevails over the patient's interest in avoiding further suffering or dying peacefully, in accordance with his own views of a good death. Some questions can forgivably be left unanswered.

In all these cases it may still be true that the loss of consciousness is a cost by itself, whether or not we need to be fully conscious in order to dealing with the remaining challenges of life, even for a Socrates or a Hume. But even if consciousness is always a good thing, that goodness can still be outweighed by the badness of the contents of consciousness (Section 2.3). Coma, like death, could be a comparative good (Section 2.1).

The patient can be mistaken in her assessment of the relative weights of these interests, and her assessment can therefore be a matter of discussion with her friends and relatives, perhaps even occasionally with her doctor or nurse. But it is hard to see why the doctor or the nurse should have any epistemic authority to make that assessment for her and act on it. Normally the doctor and the nurse will not even have sufficient information about her person and her life to make that kind of judgment, even tentatively.

Suppose that a person's life could be a better life for her, a more successful and rewarding life, if her consciousness would not be lowered, either because living in full awareness of one's actual circumstances is good in itself, or because of the opportunities for closure it offers, or both. And suppose that medical staff could confidently make that judgment. It could be objected that even in that case the possibility of an improved life will not be realized if the person does not endorse the judgment that it will be improved. If she is an experientialist, she may prefer tranquility to awareness. It is often suggested that your life can go wrong in two ways: by failing to exemplify those characteristics that make it a good life, and by exemplifying those characteristics without your recognition of their value.[33] This general suggestion can be criticized.[34] What seems true in this particular case, however, is that, even if ongoing consciousness could have some intrinsic or instrumental value for a person who doesn't endorse that value, the value would substantially increase if she *did* endorse it. If she doesn't use her opportunities to look back on her life, to say good-bye or to ask for forgiveness, but merely lies in her bed hoping that it will all be over as soon as possible, there is not much point in keeping her awake.

33 Dworkin 1993, 206; 2000, 216–218, on the 'endorsement constraint'. I subscribed to the general suggestion in den Hartogh 2016c, but it is inconsistent with my argument in Chapter 6, in particular with the contention that a doctor who goes along with a patient's death-denying attitude normally harms him.

34 Wilkinson 2003, 175–181.

Even if endorsement is only "frosting on the cake",[35] this particular cake may be of limited interest without the frosting. This may give doctors and nurses an additional reason not to act on their own judgement of the person's basic interests.

8.5 The patient's duty to retain consciousness

But perhaps we should not focus on the dying person's remaining interests in answering specific question. Jansen and Sulmasy believe that their argument generally outlaws deep sedation as a response to existential suffering. Sedation for that reason would, they suggest, deprive you of an important opportunity of spiritual and emotional growth. The losses that you are confronted with as a result of your illness ask for reflection and communication, not for total forgetfulness. It is the last challenge of your life to find an appropriate attitude to what happens to you in this final stage. Sedation prevents you from meeting that challenge from your own resources. What is really at stake is the value of being a rational self-conscious agent and remaining to be one. (There is irony in the fact that it is the very recognition of the importance of this interest which tends to characterize people who prefer a physician-assisted death to continuous deep sedation.) The argument is clearly stated by the authors of a German guideline which in strong terms forbids physicians to sedate patients who do not exhibit 'refractory symptoms'.

> The option of sedation should be protected against claims to be saved any kind of suffering, and against the delegation to medicine of a person's own responsibility to get reconciled with the fact of his death.[36]

On this view a patient should not simply be allowed to die in accordance with her preferences, because she has not got her values right. She should adapt herself to her sufferings and see Death in the eye, for both suffering and dying are essential aspects of living a human life. (Obviously this view is also critical of any conception of the good death that values ignorance of one's own fatal condition. See Sections 2.2; 6.7.)

What the argument seems to postulate is a duty a person has to herself, a duty of self-improvement. This duty can be articulated in an Aristotelian way, by pointing out that rational agency, the conscious

35 Dworkin 2000, 217, on the 'additive view' that he rejects.

36 Neitzke et al. 2010, my transl.; cf. Eckerdal 2004; Sulmasy 2018. "However, painkillers that cause unconsciousness need special consideration. For a person not only has to be able to satisfy his or her moral duties and family obligations; he or she also has to prepare himself or herself with full consciousness for meeting Christ". Sacred Congregation 1980; cf. Pontifical Council for Health Pastoral Care 1995; Sullivan, Heng (IACB) 2012.

coping with the circumstances you find yourself in, is in itself a basic form of human flourishing, not merely an instrumental good. The argument can also be articulated in a (supposedly) Kantian way, by pointing out that the moral status of a person, which requires other people to respect your rights and fulfil their duties towards you (including the professional duties of a physician) depends on the exalted value of rational agency.[37] By deciding 'from self-love', for example in order to avoid suffering, to eliminate your capacity for rational agency or block its exercise forever, you would compromise that value. This duty of self-improvement requires that you cope with the problems of existence as long as you have the capacity to do so. The physician's task can only be to help restore that capacity. So the argument goes.

We will meet the (quasi-)Kantian argument again in Chapter 9, as an argument against euthanasia. In this chapter I will therefore focus primarily on the Aristotelian argument. The existence of a duty of self-improvement, and indeed of duties to oneself as such, is controversial, but I have no qualms about granting both. One could exchange the language of duty for the language of virtue, but what the notion of duty rightly stresses is that, if you fail, you fail someone. I have also agreed already with the view that the permanent loss of consciousness is almost always harmful to you, because it deprives you of your ability to promote your own good, on any non-experientialist conception of it (Section 6.4). Perhaps awareness of the world has an intrinsic value of its own, whether or not it enables us to promote other elements of our well-being (Section 2.3). But it is much less plausible that the interests people have in remaining conscious don't allow of any trade-offs. Is it categorically forbidden to sacrifice a few hours or days of conscious life in order to avoid severe suffering altogether or to die in the way one prefers? That is not evident at all.[38] On the 'Kantian' view the value of rational agency trumps all personal interests, it being the presupposition of the moral recognition of such interests.[39] This makes it understandable why a trade-off is regarded as generally impossible. But it also points to one exception. If you are irredeemably losing the capacity of rational agency, either because your cognitive faculties fail or because your coping capacities are overwhelmed by the sheer enormity of your suffering, you can be allowed to choose the alternative of self-effacement[40] (Section 6.7). The same exception seems to be compatible with, or even implied by the Aristotelian approach.[41]

37 Hasselaar 2008. The Vatican Pontifical Council for Health Pastoral Care 1995 also claims that the loss of a person's "highest faculties" induces a state "unworthy for human beings".

38 Arneson 2005, 281.

39 Whether this is Kant's own view is disputable (Chapter 9, footnote 29).

40 Velleman 1999, 2015, 34–35, referred to in Chapter 9, footnote 20.

41 Sulmasy 2018.

Setting this point aside the adherents of the Aristotelian approach owe us a separate argument why a trade-off of rational agency with other basic aspects of human flourishing is impossible. A possible argument of that kind we have already met in Section 2.3: the basic elements of human flourishing are incommensurable; therefore, it is impermissible to encroach on any one of them. If that is right, however, sedation until death could never be justified, not even by the aim of preventing intolerable suffering from refractory symptoms in the case of a complete loss of coping ability.

Could we not escape from that conclusion by appealing to the *Doctrine of Double Effect*?[42] (Sections 1.3; 2.3) One could try to invoke that doctrine in either of two ways. First one could try to describe the primary aim of the action that foreseeably results in the loss of consciousness in purely physiological terms, as a treatment of pathological states.[43] Both the relief of suffering and the loss of consciousness could then be portrayed as a mere side effect. However, if any of those states, myoclonus for example or any other neurological disorder, would not be accompanied by the experiential state of distress, no-one would feel the need to restore a dying patient's 'normal physiological state', and we would be equally concerned to reduce that patient's distress if we did not know its underlying pathology at all. In this respect continuous deep sedation resembles a nerve block: both interventions interrupt the process that causes suffering but do not restore normal functioning.

Secondly we could describe the primary aim of sedation as the relief of suffering, and the loss of consciousness as an unintended side effect.[44] If it is objected that the person's suffering *consists in* being painfully aware of her condition and prognosis, and that we can only reduce her suffering *by* reducing her awareness, the answer would be that it is only a certain range of aspects of her awareness that we want to get rid of. Being anxious or agitated, for example, might constitute her suffering, and it is only contingently true that we cannot eliminate those aspects without eliminating more.[45] But if that is enough to declare the total loss of consciousness a mere side effect, the Doctrine of Double Effect loses most of its bite. In most cases a person accused of violating the Doctrine could defend himself by pointing out that he could only secure an important good by using a blunt instrument. It would, for example, be no problem to justify euthanasia in this way. ('We only aim at eliminating

42 Jansen, Sulmasy 2002a; National Hospice and Palliative Care Organization 2010; Sullivan, Heng (IACB) 2012; Sykes 2013; most extensively: Sulmasy 2018. Overall 85% of physicians in an American study agreed that unconsciousness is an acceptable side effect of sedation but should not be directly intended, Putman et al. 2013.

43 Sulmasy 2018.

44 Imai et al. 2020.

45 For this reason it has been suggested that full unconsciousness is merely an unintended side effect if it is the end result of a policy of titration (e.g. Quill et al. 2009).

the suffering from this person's life. Unfortunately, this cannot be done without eliminating his life'.)[46]

Actually, the teaching of the Roman-Catholic church on the permissibility of sedation doesn't appeal to the incommensurable value of rational agency or the Doctrine of Double Effect (Chapter 2, footnote 25).[47] It stresses that loss of consciousness is always harmful but allows balancing that harm against the good of avoiding otherwise unavoidable physical suffering. It is consistent with that view to prefer reflection and communication to sedation as ways of coping with extreme suffering, whether it is suffering from physical symptoms or not. But if reflection and communication don't help the person to come to terms with her suffering, it would be inconsistent not to allow sedation, whatever the nature of her suffering.

How is the duty of self-improvement of the patient to be translated into duties of the physician? Suppose that a surgical intervention has been arranged for a certain day and the doctor accidentally discovers that this is the wedding day of the patient's daughter. Should he cancel the appointment, if the patient refuses to do so herself? Obviously not. The relation between doctor and patient must be seen in the context of a moral division of labour in which the doctor is responsible for recognizing and honouring his professional duties and the patient is responsible for recognizing and honouring her personal duties. This is all the more true if these personal duties are self-regarding ones.

This idea of a moral division of labour is central to every professional morality because it is essential for maintaining the client's trust.[48] Duties of professional secrecy provide a clear example. For the same reason a patient should be able to trust her doctor to act only in her interest, with her consent. She should not be afraid of the doctor trying to make her a better person, let alone treating her as the better person she isn't. For this reason, in considering the proper indications of sedation until death, we should not only be wary of doctors' paternalism but even more of their moralism.[49] Perhaps a person has a duty, either to others or to herself, to remain aware of her condition as long as this does not require heroic efforts. But even then it is only her own responsibility to recognize this duty and act on it.

Let me summarize. I have started my argument by observing that physicians need strong justifications for lowering a patient's consciousness. But, I have argued, patients have a legitimate interest in dying in a way that corresponds to their own stable, intelligible view of a good

46 See Section 4.1, at footnote 8 on the problem of the proper description of the intended effect.

47 For a summary see Davis 2008. This teaching is proportionalist rather than absolutist, cf. Sullivan, Heng (IACB) 2012. The same is true of Kant's personal view of the medical use of narcotics, see *The Metaphysics of Morals*, transl. Mary Gregor 1991, 223.

48 Jacobs 2005.

49 Using those terms as Feinberg 1984, 12, defined them.

death. That interest can prevail over the interest in retaining consciousness in a wider range of cases than the guidelines presently acknowledge (Section 8.3). It is too restrictive to allow sedation until death only as a response to refractory and intolerable symptoms or to insist on titration in all cases. Even in cases in which the doctor has personal doubts about the patient's priorities, he should exercise restraint in allowing his decisions to be dictated by these doubts. I have spelled out some of those reasons: lack of epistemic authority (Section 8.4), the (comparative) importance of endorsement (Section 8.4) and the moral division of labour (this section).

The upshot is, I submit, that when death is only a few hours or days away, deep sedation until death should normally be available to every patient who consistently requests it. If the patient rejects an alternative way of proceeding that seems preferable to the doctor, doctor and patient should discuss the issue. Occasionally the patient may be clearly mistaken about a matter of fact, but normally her preference will be understandable from her point of view.

8.6 The condition of consent

In most countries about which we have data, sedation until death is a frequently used procedure. A problem in interpreting these data is that the research that produced them used different terms and diverging definitions. The one series of studies of continuous deep sedation that, due to a similar study-design, gave us largely comparable data about the incidence of the practice, cover a range from 2.5 to 19.6% of all deaths, respectively in Denmark in 2001 and in Italy in 2007.[50] In almost all cases in which this research has been repeated, a substantial increase has been reported. These figures include a considerable number of cases in which only opioids have been used.[51] Opioids may indeed lower a patient's consciousness for some time, but they do not reliably induce

50 Resp. Miccinesi et al. 2006; Miccinesi, Puliti, Paci 2011 (8.5% in 2001). We also have data for Sweden: 3.2% in 2001, Miccinesi et al. 2006; Switzerland: 4.7% in 2001, 17.5% in 2013, Bosshard et al. 2016; the UK: 18.7% in 2007/2008, Seale 2010 (recalculated, cf. Seale 2009); Flanders: 8.2% in 2001, 14.5% in 2007, Chambaere et al. 2010a, 12.3% in 2013, Chambaere et al. 2015; Robijn et al. 2016; the Netherlands: 5.6% in 2001, 12.5% in 2010, 18% in 2015, van der Heide, van Delden, Onwuteaka-Philipsen 2017; and Austria (4.6%, Schur et al. 2016). We have no comparable data about North-America or Asia, but in palliative care settings incidence estimates range between 15 and 60%, Bruinsma, Rietjens, van der Heide 2013, with references (up to 2003). In another study 10% of the participating American physicians reported to have kept a patient sedated until his death in the previous 12 months, Putman et al. 2013.

51 The percentage was 22 in the UK 2007, Anquinet et al. 2012. In Flanders it fell from 30.7% in 2007 to 16.7% in 2013, Robijn et al. 2016; in the Netherlands from 16% in 2005 to 4% in 2015, Onwuteaka-Philipsen 2017.

a coma. If opioids have been used in dosages that are appropriate for relieving pain or dyspnoea, we should not classify these cases as cases of sedation, irrespective of the self-reported intention of the physician (Section 10.5).

Even disregarding such cases, and even taking account of the fact that the relevant concepts of 'refractory symptoms', 'available alternatives' and 'titration' all have blurred edges, these data suggest that the restrictions imposed by the guidelines are often not respected in practice.[52] If the procedure is used in 10–20% of all deaths, it is evidently not a mere 'choice of last resort'. As Johannes van Delden comments: "(m)odern palliative care is not omnipotent, but it can do better than that".[53] I have argued, however, that the justification provided for these restrictions is insufficient and even concluded that sedation until death should be available to dying patients who want it. Should we then be happy that medical practice obviously is so much more permissive than the guidelines?

Not really. My argument led to the conclusion that we should not insist on titration, on the absence of every alternative way of relieving suffering or even on the presence of refractory symptoms, if these requirements conflict with the stable priorities of the patient as regards her way of dying. But this requires that at some point these priorities have clearly and explicitly been stated, in full awareness of possible alternative ways of providing relief that might still be available. Often that is not the case.[54] In many cases sedation is started, not only without any consent of the patient, but also without any prior discussion of the option.

All guidelines require, of course, that the patient is actively involved in the decision-making process, if that is still possible. But the circumstances under which sedation is an option to be considered are usually such that it is no longer possible for her to consider that option freely and reflectively, or even at all. Even if it is still possible to communicate with her, extreme distress may sometimes be a reason not to start any discussion. In emergency cases not enough time may be left to do this. Family members or other designated surrogate decision makers often have only limited insight into the patient's priorities, simply because these have never been extensively discussed. It is often thought improper, both by relatives and by professionals, to discuss such matters until the very last moment, or, in some cases, at all (Section 2.2). Some relatives exert pressure on the medical team to start deep continuous sedation because they

52 In the study by Anquinet et al. 2011, in 23 of 28 cases one or more of five key recommendations had not been met.

53 Van Delden 2013, 220.

54 In Flanders continuous deep sedation was started without explicit request or consent of the patient in 70% of the cases in 2007, 65.2% in 2013, Robijn et al. 2016. These figures strongly contrast with the findings in a review of the academic literature by Claessens et al. 2008. But even they conclude that caregivers play a major role in the decision-making process and suspect that patients play a relatively minor role.

expect it to hasten death, others reject the option out of hand because they want to make use of every possible option to postpone it.[55]

Such circumstances, however, do not necessarily excuse the ignorance of the patient's priorities. The occurrence of refractory symptoms is rarely completely unexpected. In most cases patients have been suffering from the same symptoms for some time, before they worsen to such an extent that sedation has to be considered. In other cases the occurrence of these symptoms can be predicted on the basis of the diagnosis. Some guidelines therefore rightly recommend to take a pro-active stance.

> Physicians are strongly encouraged to address end-of-life care preferences with all patients at risk of dying, particularly those with progressive terminal illness or illness characterized by intermittent life-threatening exacerbations. The scope of these discussions should be predicated on the general goals and priorities of care.[56]

If such discussions, preferably involving non-medical staff and family members, clarify the patient's personal values in terms of which his legitimate interests have to be understood, this may also create the opportunity for more meaningful forms of informed consent at later stages, not only for forms of sedation but also for other forms of palliative care, and even for remaining treatment options aiming at the lengthening of the life of an incurable patient.[57] A welcome side effect is to relieve the relatives of the burdens of having to make decisions at moments of crisis.[58] In order to achieve these objectives it is necessary to consider in detail possible scenarios of the dying process and to make advance decisions about them.

Whether or not such anticipatory conversations have taken place, the basic point remains that for any of the deviations from the requirements of the guidelines that we have found to be acceptable under some circumstances, consonance with the patient's values is a necessary condition. Throughout this chapter I have stressed that from the perspective of the patient the preservation of consciousness is normally of the same order of importance as the preservation of life. For many patients the value of life will end if consciousness ends, even if life itself does not. This value can only be overruled by competing values, in particular the value of a good death, if these are the patient's values. Hence the restrictions that I have criticized should remain in place, unless it is clearly beyond doubt that deviating from them promotes the patient's interests, as defined by her own priorities. The overall outcome of these changes

55 Bruinsma, Rietjens, van der Heide 2013; Robijn et al. 2017.

56 EAPC 2009; similarly Morita et al. 2005a; de Graeff, Dean 2007; KNMG 2009; cf. van Delden 2013; van Deijck 2017, 102–103.

57 One obstacle to advance care planning may be patients' wish to narrow their horizon to the present stage, as long as treatment hasn't fully stopped, cf. Chapter 6, at footnote 49.

58 Blanker et al. 2012.

of the rules may well be a much lower incidence of sedation until death than is registered at present in many countries. The explosive growth of the incidence may not so much be a sign of improved recognition of patients' proper interests as a part of the refocusing of palliative care as a whole to intervention rather than "presence, listening and communication"[59] (Section 6.4). Insisting on prior conversations about people's priorities is essential for providing them the necessary protection against the risks involved in loosening the restrictions of the guidelines.

Actually, the decision to start sedation until death seems often to be more dependent on the priorities of physicians than on those of patients.[60] Symptoms are sometimes labelled refractory ones, because healthcare providers lack the palliative skills to manage them.[61] Sedation until death may in particular seem an easy way out in cases in which the occurrence of many persistent symptoms at the same time requires a complex set of palliative measures to be employed which should not interfere with each other. There is some evidence suggesting that fatigue and burnout of medical staff result in an increased use of sedation until death.[62] The decision to sedate may also basically be made to the benefit of the family rather than to the benefit of the patient. In pleading for a relaxation of the restrictions of the guidelines I do not mean to justify or excuse sedation until death under such circumstances.

In many countries the incidence of sedation until death is lowest in specialized palliative care units, highest in general care settings, particularly in home care.[63] To some extent this may reflect an understanding of the moral justification of the practice that is more open to the variety of people's conceptions of the good death. But it may also be a symptom of a practice that is suboptimal in many respects.[64] It seems advisable, therefore, outside the context of specialized palliative care to require consultation by an independent palliative care expert. At present most guidelines recommend, but only some require this.[65] The consultant

59 Sulmasy 2018, 255. Cf. ten Have, Welie 2014 on "the return to silence" in palliative care settings. "The wards are quiet, the patients alone in their rooms, and the staff is busy."

60 Morita 2004; Swart et al. 2012; Seymour et al. 2015.

61 Barclay et al. 2002; Fraser Health 2011; ten Have, Welie 2014.

62 Morita et al. 2002.

63 Claessens et al. 2011; Mercadante et al. 2012. In 47 out of 113 cases in which a Dutch palliative consultation team was consulted, a negative advice was given, almost always because the physical symptoms of the patients were not considered refractory, de Graeff et al. 2008. This is relevant information to the physician, even though she may have good reason not to follow the advice.

64 Ten Have, Welie 2014.

65 Braun, Hagen, Clark 2003; de Graeff, Dean 2007 ("advisable if not mandatory"); EAPC 2009; Quill et al. 2009; National Hospice and Palliative Care Organization 2010; Dean et al. 2012; Haute Autorité de Santé 2018. In the Netherlands the recommendation is rarely complied with, van Deijck et al. 2015.

should in particular give his advice about alternative options of providing relief, by pharmacological means and otherwise, as well as an assessment of the life expectancy of the patient.

Relaxing the indications for sedation until death (Sections 8.3–8.5) and tightening the requirement of consent are two sides of the same coin. The practice of sedation until death as it is presently regulated is based on a medical value system that is almost exclusively focused on the prevention of suffering rather than on the promotion of a good death in consonance with patients' values.[66] Of course, the alleviation of suffering is high on almost every patient's list of priorities, but many patients are willing to make trade-offs with other values: being in control, spending time with intimates. There is something wrong when most patients prefer to die at home and almost all actually die in a medical setting. On entering a world in which we can to some extent decide about the manner and time of our own death we should not allow one particular kind of death to be imposed on us.

Suppose that we allow, as we should, deep sedation until death in the case of refractory existential symptoms. Wouldn't that make the legalization of euthanasia redundant? Jurisdictions that at present permit euthanasia all require a voluntary and well-considered request, which is more than the guidelines for palliative sedation require. The guidelines also require 'refractory symptoms', but that is medicalese for the unbearable and unremittable suffering that the laws permitting euthanasia require. So if existential symptoms aren't excluded, why do we need euthanasia?

In this chapter I have pointed to two reasons why some dying patients might prefer euthanasia to sedation until death in similar conditions. The first reason is that it better corresponds to their conception of dying well: dying at home, being in control until the end and in contact with others rather than fading away. The second reason (Section 8.3) is that we are not as sure as we would wish to be that supposedly deep sedation completely removes all consciousness and hence all suffering. The most obvious reason, however, why sedation until death cannot take over from euthanasia is that the option of deep and continuous sedation is only supposed to be available when death is near. That means that the option is not or should not be available to all people who cannot procure their own death by stopping eating and drinking and have no access to lethal drugs, or who prefer to involve the doctor in a directive role in the process of ending their lives anyway.

Even in countries in which some kind of physician-assisted death – as it is usually called – is legally permitted under some conditions, doctors sometimes push dying patients in the direction of sedation until death.[67] The relative incidence of sedation and physician-assisted death

66 Battin 2013.
67 KNMG/V&VN 2014; Robijn et al. 2017.

in Belgium, the Netherlands and Switzerland suggests that this happens quite often. But even if a doctor is not prepared to provide assistance, she should at least provide information about the option (Section 16.5). Otherwise she interferes with the patient's right to choose the manner and time of his own death.

8.7 A note on sedation in the care for people who have stopped eating and drinking

The discussion of sedation until death in this and the foregoing chapter should enable us to solve a question that I left as a loose end in my examination of voluntary dehydration as a way of ending one's life (Sections 4.2–4.4). It is fairly common for a person in the end stage of that process to enter into a state of delirium, either as a result of fever or as a side effect of the use of morphine. In that case it is essential for a physician to step in in order to sedate that person. But some time may pass before the doctor is available and has made the correct diagnosis. Many people would prefer to arrange with their doctor that at the moment at which a delirium starts to be a real possibility he will sedate them anyway. A promise of that kind would also help them to overcome an understandable hesitation that they might have in deciding to start the process. Should it be permissible for a doctor to make such a promise?

At that particular moment they have not yet developed any 'refractory symptoms'. But I have argued in this chapter that this is not an absolute requirement to be insisted upon in all cases. Deep and permanent sedation would enable the person to die in peace, and this should be considered a proper justification of the procedure, at least when it has been agreed upon by doctor and patient together at a moment at which the patient is still able to make up her mind after due reflection.

In Chapter 7, however, I have contended that the dual procedure, deeply and permanently sedating the person and at the same time abstaining from providing fluids to her, amounts to killing her, in all cases in which death is still not to be expected in a few days if she is not sedated. We cannot argue that as a result of her decision to abstain from taking fluids her life expectancy is not much more than a few days anyway, because by sedating her we deprive her of the opportunity to reconsider her decision. We should therefore insist on the requirement that death should be near and unavoidable.

That may, however, well be the case before she arrives at the stage at which delirium is a real possibility. Many people who have stopped taking fluids altogether after six or seven days suddenly lose a surprising amount of urine, indicating an irreversible degree of organ damage.[68]

68 Chabot 2019, 66.

They may still be fully conscious at that stage. Hence the law and professional regulations should allow a doctor to start the dual procedure if the person who has stopped eating and drinking has arrived at a point at which recovery is no longer a real possibility and has properly consented to starting it. If that condition is not met, the procedure will be equivalent to a joint action of ending the person's life (Section 7.3) and should be evaluated as such.

Part III

Euthanasia

9 Euthanasia and the right to self-determination

9.1 Justifying the legalization of euthanasia

In Section 2.5, I argued that our right to self-determination implies, or should imply, a right to determine the manner and time of our own death, because our lives belong to the core of our personal domain. If we aren't living of our own free will, all our other decisions are only free in a limited sense. This right includes a right, by now recognized in many jurisdictions, to refuse any medical treatment, including a life-saving or life-prolonging treatment. It also implies a right to kill oneself, theoretically but not effectively recognized by the European Court of Human Rights. It might seem that it is only a short step from the recognition of a general right to end one's own life to the recognition of a right to permit someone else to end it. If we have the authority to decide to do something, correlated to other people's duty not to interfere, do we then not also have the authority to consent to someone else doing it, or cooperating with us in doing it? Generally speaking we do,[1] but there are exceptions. In some legal systems, for example, it is not forbidden to escape from prison, but it is of course forbidden to help someone else escaping. I am allowed to kill in self-defence someone who threatens my life but isn't aware of the fact or is unable to avoid threatening me, but it is not evident that someone else is also allowed to kill that other person on my request.[2] So we have to consider whether euthanasia is covered by the rule or by the exception.

I will use the term 'euthanasia' as I announced in Section 5.6. The term means: ending someone's life on his explicit request, but, as I use it, it will also cover assisting a person to end her own life, if that assistance implies taking the final responsibility for assuring that she dies swiftly, safely and without pain. For, as I argued in that chapter, there is no principled difference between this kind of action and euthanasia. Moreover,

1 Some legal systems, including the German one, recognize a general principle that you cannot criminalize the accessory if you don't criminalize the principal (Chapter 16, footnote 2).

2 McMahan 2002, 459.

DOI: 10.4324/9781003281115-12

the second agent involved in the joint action of ending the person's life will always be a doctor. I make these stipulations only because it would be cumbersome to repeat complete descriptions every time.

Someone's right to suicide justifies some actions and omissions of others, in particular of his relatives, as discussed in Chapter 5. The reason why it isn't evident that it also justifies euthanasia is that it is a universal and structural element of the law everywhere that consent isn't recognized as a defence in any case of homicide. The right to life is a member of a small set of basic human rights – also including the right to personal freedom and the right to bodily integrity[3] – that are traditionally held to be inalienable. It is hardly controversial that it is not possible either to relinquish any of those rights, or to transfer any of them to another person, but actually it is in all legal systems equally impossible to waive such a right.[4] Any attempt to waive it is not merely wrong, but null and void. No legal system accepts consent as a defence when people have been held captive or in slavery, when their limbs have been amputated without medical necessity, or when they have been killed. This is not only true in the majority of jurisdictions in which euthanasia is categorically forbidden, but also in the minority of states that allow it when a number of requirements of due care have been satisfied. (Chapter 1, footnote 1) For these requirements do not only concern the quality of the request – that it must be voluntary and made with sufficient competence – but also the condition of the requester. It can, for example, be a condition of eligibility for euthanasia that a person's fatal illness "is causing suffering to the person that cannot be relieved in a manner that the person considers tolerable".[5] Hence her consent is only a necessary, not a sufficient condition for the physician being permitted to grant her request.

That some rights are unwaivable is one of the two major objections to the so-called choice-theory of basic rights.[6] According to this theory a right is a power to determine the normative position of others, in particular whether or not they are under a particular obligation. The other

3 In the case of the right to bodily integrity every legal system makes a distinction between more and less grave infringements of that right, less grave infringements being justifiable by consent. Systems are widely divergent in the way they make that distinction. The way in which it is made is often heavily influenced by moralistic considerations. Physical harm incurred in the course of BDSM-play is often much more readily punishable than similar harms incurred by engaging in 'manly sports', Bergelson 2009. But the amputation of arms or legs is nowhere justifiable by mere consent.

4 For the distinction see Feinberg 1978, 114ff; cf. van der Wal 1987; Sumner 2011, 86–87. In addition to the traditional inalienable rights several other rights cannot be waived, e.g., rights to some basic conditions of employment or to mandatory education.

5 *Voluntary Assisted Dying Bill*, Victoria 2017. But see Section 12.7, on the question whether these legal conditions have any real bite.

6 Proposed by Hart 1982, 183–184, but revoked by him, at least as a general theory of rights, *ibid.*, 189ff.

major objection to this theory, at least as an account of all basic rights, is that every person has these inalienable rights, whether or not she is able to exercise a power to waive them.

Why is consent not sufficient to make euthanasia permissible? Loss of life, of personal freedom, and grave bodily injury normally belong to the greatest harms that a person can suffer. That the corresponding rights protect such important personal interests therefore seems to be the obvious explanation of the fact that they cannot be waived. This is a paternalistic rationale, but the paternalism is of a special kind: indirect paternalism. We owe the distinction between direct and indirect paternalism to Gerald Dworkin, the terminology to Joel Feinberg.[7] Direct paternalism is a two-place relation: A interferes in the execution of B's plans in order to prevent harm to B. Indirect paternalism is a three-place relation: A interferes in the execution of B's plans in order to prevent harm to C, even though C has consented to B's actions. According to Feinberg paternalistic considerations can never be a good reason for the state to criminalize any action, and on his view this is as true of indirect as of direct paternalism.[8]

This is explained, or at least asserted, by the *Volenti* principle: *Volenti non fit iniuria*, you cannot be wronged by an act to which you have consented. If you have consented, you can still be harmed by the action, but in that case you have nothing to complain about and no-one to blame but only yourself. (If anyone at all: you can of course quite properly accept some costs to yourself in order to advance another person's benefit or an impersonally good cause.) On Feinberg's view *Volenti* should apply without any exceptions, both in criminal law and in tort law.[9] If we have to decide that it should, that would be an important step in developing the right to determine the manner and time of one's own death into a justification of euthanasia.

However, even if *Volenti* applies, that doesn't mean that consent should be accepted as a defence in all cases of homicide, or even in any case. Even if you aren't wronged by an action that harms you, the action can be wrong because it threatens to harm other people, or because it is wrong for a reason that has nothing to do with harm to anyone. In Feinberg's classification of the possible reasons for criminalization, it could be 'harm to others' or 'harmless wrongdoing', rather than 'harm to self', that motivates the prohibition of euthanasia, or the restrictions on its permissibility. In many countries the most prominent argument against the legalization of euthanasia in any form is at present that this would create grave risks of abuse and error,

7 Dworkin 1972; Feinberg 1986, 9–10.

8 He accepts paternalistic reasons for public policy, e.g. taxes on the sale of cigarettes, Feinberg 1986, 23–24.

9 It is worth observing that J.S. Mill's position is different: "choices depending on the assistance of others are not strictly within the definition of individual liberty". Mill 1956, 120.

both to persons considered eligible for granting their request for euthanasia and others. I will consider these risks in the next chapters (Chapter 10–12). My conclusion will be that the risks are real enough, but to a large extent manageable by a well-designed system of substantial and procedural safeguards. They cannot motivate a blanket prohibition of euthanasia.

In this chapter, I will first consider (Sections 9.2–9.4) whether euthanasia is wrong even when it harms or threatens nobody. I will argue that it is wrong sometimes, but that arguments of this kind that purport to show that it is always wrong fail. I will also argue that there are reasons to believe that it is after all primarily for indirectly paternalistic reasons that consent is not accepted as a defence for homicide. This will bring me to the question whether Feinberg was right in believing that indirect paternalism is morally as problematic as the direct variety. This discussion will lead me to a justification of euthanasia that doesn't rely on the right to self-determination.

9.2 Thou shalt not kill

The topic of the possible wrongness of euthanasia is not exhausted by considering the rights and interests of its potential 'victims'. That there is another dimension to the prohibition of killing is brought out by the attitude of Dutch and Belgian physicians to euthanasia.[10] Even when a physician in a particular case has no doubt at all about the fact that someone's request to put an end to their life is voluntary and well-considered, nor has doubts about the severity of the suffering that motivates the request, it is commonly still difficult for that physician to grant the request and perform the euthanasia. Many of them report a sense of moral discomfort, some even of guilt, even when they have no doubts about having made the right decision.[11] The formula of a 'conflict of duties' fits their views: it is a duty not to abandon the patient, but at the same time it is a moral transgression to kill him. Some physicians are not able to do so at all, even though they do not oppose the idea as such on the basis of their personal moral views. If a physician is able to do so, this is largely because he can do it in close cooperation with a grateful patient, often surrounded by an equally grateful family.

That option is missing when the euthanasia has been requested in an advance directive and the patient is no longer able to confirm the request. Only a minority of Dutch physicians can imagine performing euthanasia under these conditions (Chapter 15, at footnote 66). Most physicians rationalize this, for example by claiming that people who draw up such an advance directive have no idea what it really means to live the life of an Alzheimer

10 Haverkate et al. 2001; van Marwijk et al. 2007; Snijdewind et al. 2016. For an international review including nine studies see Kelly et al. 2020.

11 Overall 52% report feelings of discomfort, only 5% doubts about having conducted the euthanasia, Haverkate et al. 2001.

patient. But even physicians, who fully understand why such a patient once wrote a document of that kind, often find themselves unable to act in the way requested in it. It is hardly thinkable for most physicians to sneak up on somebody quietly dozing off in the sunshine to attack her with a deadly needle just because she once asked for it and had very good reasons for asking it. In such a scenario not only the immediate and urgent claim to action that comes with very serious suffering is missing, but, worse, also the communication with the patient that normally turns the act of killing into a joint action. Killing an Alzheimer's patient, who no longer has an inkling of his own decision to request it, will be felt to be the work of an executioner, even though the physician knows that it would be a good thing for this person to be allowed to die now, in view of her attitude towards life and death throughout her entire life. The doctor would be relieved if the patient would die from a pneumonia. But killing her is something entirely different.

Where does this reluctance come from, if it is not derived from the interests or rights of the person involved? It seems to reflect the awareness of a basic moral boundary: *Thou shalt not kill.* There is the well-known pronouncement by the American Supreme Court Judge Antonin Scalia that the law protects the sanctity of life, even if it is "contrary to a person's interests, and opposed by his autonomous will".[12] But the European Court on Human Rights actually said the same thing in the Diane Pretty case, remarking that Article 2 of the European Convention on Human Rights, in which the right to life is laid down, is "unconcerned with issues to do with the quality of living or what a person chooses to do with his or her life".[13]

The question I want to ask is whether we can find a rationale for this taboo on killing. According to some people it is wrong to pose that question. They regard the taboo itself as an ultimate given in our moral experience that cannot and need not be justified.[14] As one doctor explains his reluctance to act on an advance directive requesting euthanasia: it is an 'ethical atom'.[15] If you ask for an explanation, to quote Aristotle, you thereby show that you need a whacking rather than an answer.[16] But I will take the risk of insisting on an answer.

12 In a concurrent opinion added to *Cruzan v. Director, Missouri Department of Health* 497 US 261 (1990).

13 *Pretty v the United Kingdom*, 2346/02, 29 April 2002. According to the court Art. 2, in securing the right to life, cannot without distortion be interpreted as conferring a diametrically opposed right to die. Apparently your right cannot, as the choice theory of rights would have it, be understood as the power to determine other people's obligations as regards your life.

14 "In crucial cases ... repugnance is the emotional expression of deep wisdom beyond reason's power fully to articulate it. Shallow are the souls that have forgotten how to shudder." Kass 1998; cf. Burms, de Dijn 2011.

15 Bert Keizer in an interview in *Relevant*, the journal of the Dutch right-to-die society, November 2012.

16 *Topics*, Book 1.9.

I don't deny that justification comes to an end somewhere, and that the point at which we reach bedrock and our spade is turned is determined by our elementary moral responses in paradigmatic situations (Section 1.3). Neither do I dispute that a deep reluctance to kill belongs to the core of the set of these elementary moral responses. But that basic fact about human morality cannot be caught in any principle that doesn't allow for exceptions. The standard proposal for such a principle is that one shouldn't kill the innocent. This formula is supposed to allow an exception in the case of individual and collective self-defence, even in the case of innocent (!) threats. And as we have seen before (Section 1.3; cf. Section 10.5) a doctor who foreseeably shortens a patient's life by administering a dosage of palliative medicine that is medically indicated for the relief of the patient's suffering, and proportional, is also considered to be off the hook. But the doctor who ends the life of his patient on her request in order to end her unrelievable suffering isn't. This is not explained by pointing out that one shouldn't 'kill the innocent', it is specifying the meaning of that formula by stipulation. The term 'innocent', as it is used in the formula, has a technical meaning that is not itself given in our moral experience. Sure enough, for some people the principle, as specified, fully corresponds to their moral convictions: that is the whole point of the specification. But for other people it doesn't. For the first category the prohibition of suicide and euthanasia is a moral atom. But in many countries the majority of the citizens can imagine situations in which they would consider both suicide and euthanasia justified. A whacking will not help to convince them.

I do not deny that we already know that killing someone is normally wrong. That is a moral 'fact' that is, indeed, not in need of further explanation; rather, any proposed explanation has to be judged by its power to explain it. My claim is that we need a further explanation of the prohibition of killing in order to determine in controversial cases the boundaries of the prohibition. For all I have said it may still be true that these boundaries can be fixed by some interpretation of the absolute prohibition of killing the innocent. But that is a claim that really *is* in need of a justification.

9.3 Two conceptions of human dignity[17]

In Section 2.3 I already considered one way of providing a rationale to an apparently absolute prohibition of killing the innocent that applies to both suicide and euthanasia. It appealed to the idea that human biological life is an ultimate, unconditional and incommensurable good. As I observed, the conception of the good used in that argument seemed to be a personal one: life is valuable to the person who lives it. But if we interpret it as an impersonal value, unrelated to the will or the interests

17 This section uses some text material from den Hartogh 2014a.

of anyone, the objections to that idea that I formulated in that section would have (at least) equal force.

At present probably the most common proposal for a rationale rather appeals to human dignity. To the extent that this concept, in addition to its rhetorical force, can be given any clear meaning,[18] it has been analysed in various ways.[19] On one analysis human dignity is equated with the ultimate and unconditional value of the human person. This idea has been used by David Velleman in an influential argument against the legalization of euthanasia. Morality requires us to take the interests and decisions of people into account in certain ways. Why should we heed the requirement? Because these people have a fundamental value themselves. As Velleman puts it, "what's good for you wouldn't matter if you didn't matter".[20] Having the capacities of a self-directing being isn't merely good for you or for anyone else, it's good *simpliciter*, an impersonal value. If that is true, Velleman argues, it cannot be right for anyone to willingly destroy you because it is better for you to die, for that personal value only counts for the agent because of the impersonal value of your person that he would thereby violate.

Velleman doesn't at all deny that it can be better for you to die, and therefore rational to want to die. But his argument is meant to apply to self-regarding reasons as well: what is good for you only matters because *you* matter, and to decide to end your own life on a balance of prudential reasons is therefore as impermissible as euthanasia. Velleman's objection even applies to sedation until death as much as to suicide and euthanasia. For that would also permanently end someone's existence as a self-directing being for the sake of his welfare interests.[21]

Velleman's view of human dignity is an example of a *foundational* view. A view of that kind is by now an integral element of human rights law. The German Constitution of 1949 opens in Article 1 with the arresting declaration: "human dignity is inviolable" and goes on in Art. 2 to state that the German people *therefore* acknowledge certain rights as inalienable. Other human rights instruments, for example the *International Covenant on Civil and Political Rights* (1966) and the *Helsinki Accords* (1975), even more explicitly claim that human rights derive from the inherent dignity of the human person. You have rights

18 Surveying the appeal to human dignity by the German Federal Constitutional Court, Suchomel 2010 observes a lack of consistency: the weighing of conflicting interests diverges between cases, and limits are seemingly arbitrarily drawn.

19 For a helpful survey see Zylberman 2016.

20 Velleman 1999, 2015, 26; cf. Velleman 2006, 40–44; 2008, 2015, ch. 3. The statement I quote is intended to summarize an argument presented by Anderson 1993, 26–30, see footnote 36. This argument is also subscribed to by Korsgaard 1996, ch. 4; 2004, 93; Wood 1999, 115, 132–139; McMahan 2002, 242; O'Neill 2002; Darwall 2002, ch. 1. For an earlier version of the argument, see Vlastos 1962, referred to by Velleman.

21 Kamm 1999. Cf. Jansen, Sulmasy 2002a, 327, quoted in Section 8.4.

because you have dignity. It should be noted that in Velleman's version a person has dignity on account of her own properties as an individual. In an alternative version she has it on account of the 'natural' properties of a member of the human species, whether or not these properties have been actually realized in her.[22] I will concentrate on Velleman's view because it isn't burdened with very specific and controversial metaphysical claims, but my comments will apply to any foundational view of the relation between human dignity and human rights.

I believe that foundational views are mistaken, for two related reasons. If your interests and your decisions only count because you have dignity, it should be possible for another being, an angel, alien or primate, to have the same kind of interests and make the same kind of decisions that, nevertheless, do *not* count, because that being has no dignity. That seems morally problematic. Rather, if a being is like you in having similar interests and similar decision-making capacities, the interests and the decisions of such a being, angel, alien or primate, *ipso facto* count. That does not depend on the additional contingent fact whether or not it also has dignity.

My second argument is a conceptual one: it cannot be true that such a being has no dignity. Suppose we identify the properties that you need in order to be ascribed basic rights, for example having interests and decision-making capacities. It cannot be the case that, before we finally allow you basic rights, we still have to decide whether you also have dignity. For we can only decide whether you have dignity by checking whether or not you have those very same properties. 'Dignity' cannot sort out the rights-bearers from a class of beings having the same relevant properties. It is not a filter or membrane.[23]

Human dignity belongs to a family of moral concepts that Thomas Scanlon has described as *buck-passing* ones.[24] "The badness of a toothache ... does not add a further reason to the reasons for going to the dentist that are already given by the nature of the toothache".[25] Similarly the fact that you have human dignity does not add a further reason to the reasons people have for taking your interests and decisions into account. That you have human dignity merely confirms that such reasons exist. It also merely asserts but does not explain why reasons that apply equally to all are more important than reasons that don't. If it is good for you that your life ends, or if you have freely decided to end it, that matters, and these considerations are not defeated by the fact that you matter.

It is interesting to consider the way in which the concepts of human dignity and human rights together entered human rights law in the

22 Lee, de George 2008; Sulmasy 2008, 2013.
23 For similar arguments see Feinberg 1973, 88–94; 1980, 151; Griffin 2008, 66.
24 Scanlon 1998, 95–98; cf. Kagan 1989, 60, on the 'placeholder view'.
25 Dancy 2005, 37.

preparatory phase of the *Universal Declaration of Human Rights* (1948). The aim of appealing to human dignity was not to single out any particular conception of the foundation of human rights, but rather to use the concept as a placeholder for whatever the real foundation was. The representatives of strongly opposed ideologies who participated in these discussions consented to agree about the rights, but on condition that no one asked them why.[26] Basically that constellation hasn't changed; the present idea of human dignity as a foundational value in its own right is an aberration. Human rights instruments should still not be considered to express an antecedent commitment to any particular view of the foundation of human rights.[27] Rival conceptions of that foundation should rather be primarily evaluated by the extent to which they match the undisputed core of existing human rights law, rather than any independent theoretical framework.

9.4 Does euthanasia violate human dignity?

However, this placeholder view of human dignity is not the whole truth of the matter either. If it were, human dignity would be a redundant concept in our thinking about rights and duties; we could dispense with it without any loss. But we cannot, for the following reason. An appeal to human dignity does not only point out that for some reasons you are required to treat people in certain ways, for example to honour their rights. For these same reasons you are also required to act in those ways with a certain emotional disposition, an attitude of respect. At this point we should again avoid cluttering the conceptual space, by saying that people deserve to be respected because they have dignity. Rather, because of your capacities for self-direction, or whatever properties deemed relevant, you deserve both: to have your rights recognized and to be treated with respect. Your dignity consists in your being deserving of both kinds of responses. Both requirements usually converge, but sometimes the second requirement adds something to the first. A certain action may not violate your rights, but nevertheless express a lack of respect, either of your person or, perhaps, of humankind as such.[28] I will call this the *qualification* view of human dignity.

26 As Jacques Maritain 1949 formulated it, quoted by McCrudden 2013, footnote 4. Cf. Glendon 2001 on the history of the Declaration.

27 Schultziner 2004; Luban 2009; Lukow 2018. Use of the concept then reveals an 'incompletely theorized agreement', as Sunstein 1996 calls it.

28 *Gattungswürde*, Habermas 2005, 56ff. When some behaviour is judged to be an affront to human dignity, one can often ask whether it is the affected person's individual dignity as a human person that has been violated, or the dignity of the human species. Take for example the French ban on dwarf-tossing in the famous case of *Manuel Wackenheim*, Conseil d'Etat ass., 27/10/1995, Recueil Dalloz 1966, Jur. P. 177, upheld by the ECHR, 16/7/1996 and by the UN Human Rights Committee 26/7/2002.

Dignity is not the foundation of human rights; it only qualifies the foundation, whatever it is, as a proper object of respect.

The foundational view of dignity is mostly held by Kantian authors, but to tell the truth it is not a Kantian view. As I understand Kant, he argues that, if you are an agent with practical rationality, you are necessarily bound to a moral law that requires you to treat other beings who, like you, have their own ends, in certain ways, and this amounts to recognizing their dignity.[29] In Kantian ethics self-legislation is the foundation, not the recognition of the impersonal value of rational beings. If Kant held the foundational view of dignity, he would be a moral realist of some kind. Perhaps he was,[30] but in that case he was not a Kantian.

One sign of a foundational view, and hence of realism, can perhaps be found in what I consider Kant's most interesting argument against the permissibility of prudentially motivated suicide. Here Kant claims that "to annihilate the subject of morality in one's own person is to root out the existence of morality itself in the world, as far as one can".[31] This seems to suggest that the existence of self-legislating beings in the world is impersonally valuable, and should therefore be protected, perhaps even promoted.[32]

In a similar vein it is often argued that it is contradictory to justify euthanasia in terms of respect for autonomy, because euthanasia doesn't maintain or promote the autonomy of the person who requests it, but rather destroys her existence as an autonomous being.[33] Intuitively this is unconvincing, most clearly so in the case of a person who prefers death to loss of freedom or dignity. And it is clear where the argument goes wrong: respecting someone's autonomy isn't at all the same thing as protecting, let alone promoting his existence as an autonomous being. Similarly, there is no contradiction in the idea of respecting – for the last time – the sovereignty of a state when it freely decides to end its own independent existence.

On the proper Kantian view dignity is not the impersonal value of a state of affairs to be protected or promoted but the status of a certain being to be respected.[34] This is in line with common usage: 'dignity'

29 Sensen 2009 shows that human dignity is not the foundation of the validity of the moral law, but its implication. In the *Metaphysik der Sitten* Kant uses the concept only in relation to duties to oneself.

30 As some authors have suggested, cf. critical discussion by Rauscher 2002.

31 *Metaphysik der Sitten* 6:423; cf. Mertens 2015.

32 Velleman 1999b, 357ff., correctly points out that Kant rejects this consequentialist view, but the question is whether this rejection is consistent with his own objection to suicide.

33 E.g. Doerflinger 1989; Gordijn, Janssens 2000; ten Have 2001; Materstvedt 2003; Materstvedt, Bosshardt 2009b. Cf. J.S. Mill on voluntary slavery: "The principle of freedom cannot require that he should be free not to be free." *Utilitarianism*, ch. V.

34 Waldron 2009. Waldron considers his own view of dignity to be a foundational one.

means a high place in a status-hierarchy. Hats off is the response that it calls for. If you have the dignity of a judge, that does not merely imply that you have the authority to make legally binding judgements, but also that people have to stand up when you enter the courtroom. Similarly, basic dignity is the status of human (and some non-human) beings, determined by their needs or their capacities or both, who deserve to have their interests and their decisions to be taken into account and also deserve to be treated with deference. This is at least part of the explanation why you owe some duties to yourself and cannot waive the corresponding rights.[35]

According to Velleman what is good for you matters because you matter. I have criticized the 'because' in this statement. But I have no objection to the statement that what is good for you can only matter *if* you matter, as long as this isn't understood to imply a foundational claim. If you ascribe any value to a state of affairs, including the existence of someone or something, there has to be someone or something *for the sake of* whom or which you value it. Valuing a state of affairs implies recognizing the normative relevance of a thing being what it is.[36]

Interestingly, at some places David Velleman clearly recognizes that human dignity is a status of human beings, not the value of their existence. "The value of persons does not oblige us to maximize the number of people in existence; it obliges us only to respect the people who do exist. And respecting these people is not necessarily a matter of keeping them in existence; it is rather a matter of treating them in the way that is required by their personhood-whatever way that is".[37] He even concedes that destroying a being with dignity isn't necessarily disrespectful. But he isn't consistent in recognizing this. When he objects to suicide that it is disrespectful to 'trade' your own person for the acquisition of benefits or the avoidance of harms, this still seems to prioritize the existence of one state of affairs to the existence of another. And when Velleman says that killing a person necessarily violates that person's autonomy, even if it is done on request,[38] the exercise of autonomy seems again to be treated as a valuable state of affairs to be maximized, or at least maintained, rather than respected.

On a qualification view, the way in which we derive reasons from a self-directing person's interests and decisions should be compatible with a general attitude of respect. If that is correct, it is still an open question

35 Van der Rijt 2016.

36 That is precisely what Anderson 1993 wanted to argue, cf. footnote 20. She didn't ascribe an impersonal value to the existence of any kind of being.

37 Velleman 2015, 33, cf. Velleman 2006, 41; fully endorsed and explained by Velleman 1999b in agreement with Anderson. In Velleman 2015, ch. 2, he also denies that respecting autonomy requires us to maximize options.

38 Velleman 2015, 41.

whether killing a person out of deference to his decisions or out of concern for his welfare, or both, is compatible with that respect.

The same question can be asked about the other inalienable rights. As Velleman observes, whatever a person's actual interests and decisions, it is always disrespectful to keep her as a slave, even if she has sold herself into slavery of her own free will. It is undeniable that the same holds for some instances of killing someone on his request or with his consent. Consider the hypothetical case described by Judith Thomson: "Suppose I am terminally ill, and want to be able to provide for my children. Here is a rich man, who likes to kill. I say 'for so and so much, to be given to my children, you may kill me now.' Suppose, then, that he accepts my offer, and kills me".[39] Or consider the actual case of Armin Meiwes, the Rotenburg cannibal, who was extremely scrupulous in establishing that his victim cooperated of his own free will, even with enthusiasm. A psychiatrist told me that a man with a personality disorder once came to him requesting euthanasia, saying "I am a plague to humanity, I am wrecking the lives of everyone around me". In a file concerning another psychiatric patient the following disturbing explanation of her request is given: "The patient indicated that she had had a life without love and therefore had no right to exist".[40] Such death wishes seem to result from a basic lack of self-respect, and the doctor who grants a request for euthanasia in such cases seems to confirm that attitude. (In the first case the request was refused, but in the second case granted.) Similarly, all violent suicides are obvious violations of human dignity, even if they are voluntarily committed. In such cases it makes sense to talk about 'duties to oneself' (Section 8.5).

As Velleman also recognizes, respect isn't the only moral emotion that is the proper response to the properties that give persons their moral status. Some human rights protect human interests that require to be responded to with care rather than with respect, even though that care should be given in a respectful way. On a correct understanding of the concept of dignity, the proper concern for a person's welfare should not be considered a response to her dignity but to her needs. That is another reason why it is mistaken to consider human dignity the single basis of human rights.[41]

In Section 2.2 I surveyed the actual reasons people have for requesting euthanasia. As I stressed in the same chapter (Section 2.3), these reasons have hardly anything to do with a cost/benefit calculation. What people talk about is the irretrievable loss of everything that gave meaning to their

39 Thomson 1986, 40. According to Thomson his act may be impermissible, but it doesn't infringe my rights. Whether that is right I consider in the next section. My present point is only that the act is impermissible because it violates human dignity.

40 Case 2012-46, quoted by Kim, de Vries, Peteet 2016, 365. Cf. Gupta et al. 2017, 10, for a similar case. And see Hill 1991, 87, on self-abasing suicides.

41 Den Hartogh 2014a.

lives, and the increasing difficulty to adequately cope with the burdens of illness. Most of these people are physically and emotionally exhausted to begin with. It is true that they also often talk about their aversion to being totally dependent on the care of others, and of being ashamed about certain conditions, like incontinence, that they are not responsible for. In Section 2.4 I expressed some reservations about such motives.[42] I also indicated, however, that the relevant preferences for independence and personal dignity can become integral elements of a person's coping style, and as such beyond reform. What Velleman finds repellent in people considering prudential suicide is that they ask themselves what they can get out of life, but most of these people rather ask themselves how they can live up to life's challenges, as they understand them.

A doctor who would grant a patient's request for euthanasia merely because it has been competently made would be lacking in proper concern for that patient. Perhaps he would even be lacking in proper respect. But a doctor, who grants the request because he reasonably considers it to be in the patient's true interest to do so, cannot be accused of violating that patient's dignity. In the presently existing laws that permit euthanasia under some conditions, this particular condition is usually expressed by requiring the patient to be in a condition of intolerable suffering without any prospect of relief. But suffering is not merely a negative hedonic state. As Eric Cassell described it, it is a state of severe distress responding to an imminent, perceived or actual, threat to the integrity of the person (Section 6.2). Even within Velleman's own terms that is close to a sufficient justification for granting a request for euthanasia.[43]

9.5 Why indirect paternalism is different[44]

As we saw in Section 9.1 consent is not accepted by any legal system as a defence in any case of killing, hence not in any case of euthanasia. (It may be relevant for the determination of the exact crime that a person is charged with, and of the penalty to be imposed on her.) Whether this can be justified by the risks involved in permitting euthanasia under any conditions I have left for discussion in the next chapters, but my conclusion in those chapters will be that this concern cannot justify a blanket ban

42 These reservations are shared by Velleman 2015, ch. 2.

43 In Velleman 1999 his view was that you could only consider ending the life of a person for her own sake if she had lost her rational powers and hence her claim to human dignity; cf. Rhodes 2007. Responding to a point made by Frances Kamm, Velleman 2015, 34, allows for cases in which a person is overwhelmed by pain and as a result "is disintegrating as an autonomous being". In both cases, however, the action would either amount to killing a person without her voluntarily and competently made request, or the request itself would show that she had not yet lost her rational powers, cf. Jongepier 2018.

44 This section contains some text material from den Hartogh 2013b.

on euthanasia. In the last section I have argued that considerations about human dignity cannot justify a blanket prohibition either.

This leaves the possibility of an indirectly paternalistic justification. To begin with, it seems likely that 'harm to self' actually plays a role in prohibiting euthanasia, or at least in limiting the scope of its permissibility.

When doctors cause bodily injury to patients in order to avert greater physical or psychological harm from them, this is generally recognized as an exception to the prohibition of infringements on people's bodily integrity. Only because of that recognition the doctor's action doesn't count as battery. An appeal to the *medical exception* requires consent of the patient, if it can be acquired. But that consent is not sufficient as a justification of the doctor's action. It is also required that the action is a professionally legitimate way of benefiting the patient.[45] This justification is even sufficient in all cases in which no consent can be obtained from either the patient or his surrogate.[46]

The medical exception extends to infringements on the right to life, in cases in which there is a medical indication for a form of palliative care, even though it possibly or probably has a life-shortening effect. The permissibility of euthanasia is not implied by this particular specification of the medical exception. But if acting in a way that foreseeably causes the shortening of a person's life with an above-threshold probability in the absence of any medical indication is permitted as a second exception to the prohibition of killing, it is plausible that at least the same conditions must be met: consent and benefit. The conclusion must be that, if euthanasia can at all be justified by an extension of the professional morality of doctors, this cannot be done by the application of the *Volenti* principle.

Requiring benefit in addition to consent is indirect paternalism. Isn't that a fatal objection? Shouldn't we be prepared to revise medical professional morality much more thoroughly, requiring for a justification of medical action only the consent of the competent patient? In order to answer that question we will have to consider whether the basic objections to paternalism apply to the indirect variety as well.

What is basically wrong with paternalism? Joel Feinberg is at his rhetorical best in replying to this question. If people are treated paternalistically, "their grievance is not simply that they have been unnecessarily inconvenienced or 'irked', but rather they have been violated, invaded, belittled. They have experienced something analogous to the invasion

45 Lewis 2012, in particular 357–359 on patient-focused public policy justifications.

46 It is often claimed that in that case the action should, if possible, be justified by an appeal to the patient's presumed consent, by considering what we know about his basic personal values. But on the proper view of 'consent' it has to be actually, although perhaps tacitly, given in order to have authority, and an appeal to a person's 'presumed consent' is merely a metaphor for an appeal to her interests, cf. Chapter 10, at footnote 7; den Hartogh 2011.

of their property or the violation of their privacy".[47] That paternalism is insulting is an important point, and certainly the point which people care most about, for few things are as important to people as their social status. But it must, as the analogy with property and privacy shows, be dependent on other points. For why should people believe that their status vis-à-vis each other depends on the extent to which it is left to them to govern their own actions, unless they would already attribute great value to this authority? And, indeed, elsewhere Feinberg gives a second reason to reject paternalism: "the life that a person threatens by his own rashness is after all his life; it belongs to him and to no one else".[48] As I have put the point in Section 9.1 (and in Section 2.5), your life belongs to the core of your personal domain.

If we want to get clear about the moral defensibility of indirect paternalism, including the indirect paternalism of the professional morality of physicians, we should ask: are these reasons for objecting to paternalism – the intrinsic value of self-governing authority and the status conferred to people by having this power – at stake with indirect paternalism as well?

First consider the value of self-governance. It is important to see that the question whether indirect and direct paternalism are different with respect to that value is not identical to the old question about negative and positive liberty. I fully agree with John Locke against many so-called Lockeans that to consciously let a person starve when you can feed him is equivalent to murder.[49] If you are motivated by the person's best interests, it is at least still homicide. So let us presuppose a tolerably just system of property rights and of claims on resources. With this background in place my claim is that the value of self-governance is given its full due when competent people are allowed to set their own aims and strive for their realization with their own resources, within the limits set by the harm and the offence principle and the requirement of respect for human dignity. The mere fact that a directly paternalistic and an indirectly paternalistic interference have the same effect on the amount of resources, capabilities, opportunities, 'real liberty' in your possession – or whatever coinage you want to count justice in – doesn't necessarily mean that the same objections apply to both interferences. It depends on your legitimate antecedent claims.[50]

47 Feinberg 1986, 27.

48 Feinberg 1986, 59.

49 Locke 1988 I, 42, cf. II, 6; II, 172. On this view the Harm Principle should be understood to presuppose a baseline of secured entitlements. It follows that a failure to rescue can be a violation of that principle, cf. Feinberg 1984, ch. 4; 1986, ch. 19, on the concept of a personal domain.

50 Overlooking this is the basic mistake of the few presently available discussions of the question of the possible moral difference between direct and indirect paternalism: Schramme 2013; Schramme 2015, 32ff; Von Hirsch, Neumann 2010; Simester, von Hirsch 2014, ch. 10.

If people are allowed to set and pursue their aims with the means at their disposal, it is by itself morally irrelevant whether or not they succeed in this enterprise. Whether such success is valuable is entirely a matter of the relevant values, including their own real interests: if the enterprise is misguided, we may *hope* that they will not succeed. Nothing is therefore wrong if other people refuse to help them because they believe that such help would only be harmful. On the contrary, if they provide such 'help' out of indifference for the other person's fate, they are morally criticisable, at least for lack of concern. When they are not allowed to provide such help, that doesn't compromise the value of self-governance either.

Suppose that you are a painter and at a certain moment you arrive at the conclusion that the paintings you have made until now are no good at all, but inauthentic caterings to popular taste. Being for the moment in hospital you ask your best friend to go to your studio and destroy all your work. But your friend disagrees with you, he believes that destroying your work would have a negative impact on the value of your life, meaning: its value for you. (I assume that the intrinsic value of your paintings as works of art does not weigh with him as an independent consideration.) He therefore says to you: 'Look, do it yourself when you have recovered, if you still think it is a good idea, but I will not do it'. I cannot see that in refusing to comply your friend fails to recognize that your life belongs to you. As I argued in the last section, respecting a person's autonomy isn't the same thing as maximizing her options. But in that case a third party who prevented your friend from helping you would also not fail to respect your autonomy. If your autonomy isn't infringed upon by a person's refusal to help you, it cannot be infringed upon either by the state obligating that person to refuse.

In Section 9.1 I defined indirect paternalism as a three-place relation: A interferes in the execution of B's plans in order to prevent harm to C. But it makes a difference whether A claims the authority to identify what is harmful to C or leaves this to B. Accordingly we could distinguish between a strong and a weak variety of indirect paternalism. My claim that indirect paternalism doesn't fail to respect autonomy only concerns the weak variety.

It may be the case that, in spite of the strong objections against it, even direct hard paternalism should not be ruled out in all cases.[51] However, it is always a risky business. If the paternalist doesn't get it right, his mistake is much weightier than a mistake about his own interests. But the person who refuses to help you because he thinks it would not be in your interest to do so, is not burdened by this special moral hazard, nor is the person who blocks the provision of such help.[52]

51 See, e.g., Dworkin 1988; Kleinig 1984; Loewy 2005; Arneson 2005; Husak 2009. In den Hartogh 2016b I have argued that the whole distinction between hard and soft paternalism is in need of reconsideration.

52 Athanassoulis 2002, glossing Mill.

I have insisted that this argument presupposes that the agent who is refused assistance has sufficient resources at his command to exercise his self-governing powers. Some persons are unable to end their own life in any humane way at all, for example because they are almost totally paralyzed as a result of a high spinal cord injury and are not old or ill enough to be able to achieve their aim in a humane way by stopping eating and drinking.[53] A corollary of my argument might be that such people should in principle have a right to assistance, if they request it in a fully voluntary and well-considered way, without having to meet any further requirement of unbearable and unremittable suffering.[54] It is an empirical question how often this condition applies. In any case, by itself the argument doesn't suffice to reject indirectly paternalistic considerations in the assessment of the legality of euthanasia in the large majority of cases.[55]

Secondly, there is the question of status. By refusing to destroy your paintings, it seems to me, your friend only shows concern for you, not any lack of respect. He leaves you full responsibility for your own actions, and only takes an equal responsibility for his own. Of course, his refusal means that he believes that your own beliefs about your true interests are false. That is not an insulting belief, however; in truth it may be entirely right. It might be the case that he has good reasons to think that you are better placed than he is to decide about your interests, but that need not be the case, and it is up to him to weigh those reasons. By refusing your request out of concern for your interests, he doesn't deny your dignity as a self-governing agent.

If that is true, how can a moral code or law that enjoins people to refuse a request that isn't in the interest of the requester, be interpreted as showing disrespect? If you are not allowed to take your own life for any reason you find compelling, you may well feel insulted because, as I argued (Section 2.5), all the decisions that you are then still allowed to make are necessarily, not merely contingently, second-best decisions only. But if other people are prohibited to end your life on your request, unless they are convinced on reasonable grounds that it is in your best interests to die, this isn't equally insulting. The basic difference is that direct paternalism by its very nature creates an asymmetry between the two people involved, A and B. A is prevented from acting on his own judgment about his interests, because B uses his power to act on his contrary judgment of those same interests. But in the case of indirect paternalism A and B are both allowed to use their own resources in symmetrical ways, they are

53 As in Brian Clark's play *Whose Life is it anyway?* (1978), commented upon by Feinberg 1986, 351–354.

54 Schramme 2013, 483–484; 2015, 33–34. It is only in this condition that the Victoria *Voluntary Assisted Dying Law* (2017) permits a patient's life to be ended on his request by a physician.

55 As Schramme 2015, 32 recognizes.

both fully allowed to cause harm to themselves, and both required to take responsibility for the harm they cause to the other.

Direct paternalism by means of criminal prohibitions is insulting in a particularly strong way, because it is not only belittling but censuring. Even if its final aim is to promote its addressee's own good, it also sends the message: you do not only deserve to be constrained but even to be punished. But if the law prohibits me to kill you on your request, that doesn't necessarily express any disapprobation of your death wish.[56]

Certainly, on many, probably most occasions indirect paternalism would show lack of proper respect. If we make an ordinary contract, and you are prevented from performing your part of the agreement by a third person who thinks you are harming me, that is equally insulting to me as it is to you. But that is, I suggest, because the contract is already to be considered a valid one on independent grounds. Consequently I already have a right to expect your performance. That right is already part of my moral assets, that is why the action of this third person is analogous to 'the invasion of my property or the violation of my privacy'. That doesn't rule out certain categories of harmful consequences to invalidate contracts to begin with.

What this example suggests is that the *Volenti* principle is related to the principle of respect for self-determination in an indirect way only. To begin with, *Volenti*'s aim is to protect legitimate expectations, arising from consenting acts. If a person in good faith performs his part of an agreement, he should not normally be held responsible for any harm befalling his partner to the agreement as a result. Similarly, the *Volenti* principle does not primarily aim at protecting the autonomy of the consenting party, but rather at shielding the other party from liability. Only if it is already established on independent grounds that my consent is sufficient for justifying your action, even if the action harms me, is the interference of a third person disrespectful to me. *Volenti* doesn't help us to define the boundaries of the domain of the agent's sovereignty, because its validity itself is limited to that domain.

The absolute rejection of indirect paternalism suggests that the consenting person lends his *persona* to the agent who now acts under the full responsibility of the other.[57] But consent should rather be seen as

56 Simester, von Hirsch 2014, 157–159, 172. For example, on the *Hemmschwellentheorie*, proposed by some German authors and discussed by Simester, von Hirsch 2014, 176–179, the aim of the prohibition may be to ensure that the choice for death is not made too easily, not that it isn't made at all. I don't agree with the authors that this amounts to intimidating the would-be suicide into continuing his life, at least not if humane means of suicide are accessible.

57 "Consensual acts originate with the consenting individual, and are merely carried out by another person." Athanassoulis 2002, 143; cf. Feinberg 1986, 100. This is particularly inappropriate when the consent is a response to a request and may signal mere indifference.

extending the sphere of responsibility to include the consenter. It initiates a form of cooperation in which responsibility is shared. If I consent to your action even though it will harm me, you are not merely reduced to an instrument of my will, you still have your own responsibility for your actions and can be called to account for what you do. It is not a conceptual impossibility that you can even be called to account by me.[58] It is not contradictory for the law to allow a patient to initiate disciplinary proceedings against a physician who has caused grave harm to him with his informed consent.

Two conclusions follow from this argument, a negative and a positive one. The negative conclusion is that euthanasia cannot be legitimized by appeal to the requirement of respect for self-determination. The positive conclusion is that ending a person's life on her explicit request can be justified if it is reasonable to agree with her that she has an overriding interest in discontinuing her life. At least as long as the risks of legalization are minimal or manageable. Whether they are we will consider in the next chapters.

If these conclusions are plausible, they commit us to a certain view of the wrongness of killing. The commonsense view is that killing is normally wrong because it deprives us of something that, whether or not it is an intrinsic good for us, at least is a vehicle of (almost) all other things that are intrinsically good for us (Section 2.3). Accordingly the right to life is seen as protecting our interest in survival. This harm account of the wrongness of killing is not very popular among philosophers these days. A major objection to it is that the extent of the deprivation that death causes us is very variable between people of different ages and different conditions. Hence the harm account seems to imply that the wrongness of killing is also very variable. But one of the fixed points of our moral convictions, endorsed by all legal systems, seems to be that killing people, if it is wrong, is always equally wrong.[59]

I believe that this objection can be met by focussing on the nature of rights rather than on the interest in survival. Briefly: rights protect our interests precisely by forbidding others to determine the weight of those interests in any particular case. However, I will not spell out that argument here. To that extent the argument of this chapter is incomplete. It is supposed, however, to contribute to the unresolved debate about the wrongness of killing by discrediting the main rivals of the harm account. In Section 2.3 I have argued that it is mistaken to claim that killing is wrong because it destroys the (personal or impersonal) value of the human person. In this section I hope to have shown that killing may

58 Kleinig 1979, 343–344; Kuflik 1986; Dworkin 2012.

59 Kamm 1993, 210–221; McMahan 2002, 189–265; cf. 2007; Luper 2009, 147–148. Discussion: Lippert-Rasmussen 2007; Hanser 2013; Soto 2013.

be wrong even if it is done on the request of the victim. It follows that killing cannot be wrong merely because it disregards the self-regarding authority of the victim.

But if it is a principle of compassion or care that provides the basic justification for ending someone's life on his request, why do we, at least normally if not always, need a request? That question will be one of the topics to be discussed in the next chapter.

9.6 'Doctors must not kill'

One of the most common objections to the legalization of euthanasia points out that performing euthanasia goes against a universally accepted norm that is integral to the professional morality of doctors.[60] This traditional norm, however, far from being a special norm of the profession, reflects an understanding of the general prohibition of killing as implying a prohibition of suicide that in the Western world has been almost undisputed since Augustine. Elsewhere it is also primarily a religious norm. In pluralistic societies it is no longer universally held. We should therefore ask whether there is a special reason that can be articulated in secular terms why doctors should cling to it.

One particularly influential suggestion is that killing is incompatible with the essential goal of medicine: healing.[61] As it is sometimes put more pompously, killing 'violates an aim that is internal to the practice of medicine'. But it is an odd form of essentialism to hold that medicine has one essential goal only. It has always been a second goal of medicine to alleviate suffering. 'Cure sometimes, relieve often, comfort always'. And just as the aim of healing does not only involve the promotion of health but also the prevention of illness, the aim of providing relief involves the prevention of suffering. In various medical specialties the protection of health is only one aim, in addition to (and sometimes in possible conflict with) other aims, for example the boosting of sportive achievement or the creation of an aesthetically more satisfactory appearance.

60 Many medical associations condemn the practice, even when legal, for this reason. The World Medical Association, for example, in 2013 reaffirmed "its strong belief that euthanasia is in conflict with basic ethical principles of medical practice", 194th WMA Council Session, Bali, Indonesia; cf. British Medical Association 2017 (changed to a neutral position in 2021). According to the *Code of Medical Ethics* of the *American Medical Association* (reaffirmed in 2018), "physician-assisted suicide is fundamentally incompatible with the physician's role of healer".

61 Gaylin et al. 1988; Orentlicher 1989; Kass 1989; Pellegrino 1992, 1998, 2001; Garcia 2007; Boudreau, Somerville 2013. Garcia is more consistent than the others because she denies that the alleviation of suffering is fundamental to medicine in the way that healing and the conservation of life are. But consistency comes at the price of implausibility, Seay 2011.

Moreover, it is doubtful whether the aims of medicine are internal to it in the way in which the aims of soccer seem to be internal to it. (And in the end even soccer has to be evaluated in terms of its contribution to external values.) Suppose that some action, for example medical examination for eligibility for a job or an insurance deal, requires medical expertise, is of great benefit to the people involved or to third parties, for example employers or insurance companies, and of manageable risk to society. Then, if medical tradition forbids that action because it cannot be understood to be a form of 'healing', surely doctors should collectively decide to change their traditional norm, and the law should abstain from enforcing it. Medicine isn't there for its own aims, but to serve people and society. No tradition, however venerable, is immune to critical reflection, even if it may be worthwhile to consider carefully whether it may have a justification that is not obvious on first inspection. If, however, the action doesn't require medical expertise, is not of substantial benefit to anyone and generates unacceptably grave risks to society, the tradition is vindicated, but the appeal to it is redundant.

Another common way to elaborate the appeal to tradition is by pointing out that, if doctors do not respect the traditional norm, the public will start mistrusting them. It is true that if patients, rightly or wrongly, believe doctors to respect the norm, they will not fear that doctors will kill them.[62] They may still fear that doctors will, criminally or by mistake, end their lives prematurely by withholding 'futile' treatment or by forms of palliative care with a life-shortening effect (Section 11.2). Moreover, they may fear that they will not be relieved from intolerable suffering. It is an empirical question which of these fears actually is the greater one in any society.[63] It is rather paradoxical for doctors to use the argument from public trust in a society in which the larger part of the population would welcome legalization of euthanasia because the fear of intolerable and unrelievable suffering looms larger for them than the fear of being abandoned[64] (Section 12.9).

In this chapter I have offered a *minimally revisionist* justification for the legalization of euthanasia (including assisting suicide as an alternative

62 According to Brock 1992 this fear would be mistaken anyway, because no person's life will be ended except on her explicit request. But the fear might be that doctors, either by deceit or by mistake, will suggest that there is a voluntary and well-considered request where there is none. And patients might even trust doctors to protect them against their own wishes, as Ulysses trusted his comrades, Snyder, Sulmasy 2001; cf. the quotation from Baroness Campbell of Surbiton, Chapter 11, footnote 45.

63 See Cohen et al. 2014 about the opinions in 47 European countries. The authors find a clear and widening West-East division in euthanasia acceptance, corresponding to the development of general trust in existing institutions. In the USA at least a small majority of the population has been in favour of some form of physician-assisted death since 50 years, Emanuel et al. 2016.

64 See e.g. Snyder, Sulmasy 2001 (ACP-ASCM position paper).

way of participation in the ending of another person's life) (Section 1.3). It is revisionist because it rejects the view, almost universally accepted not too long ago, that euthanasia contravenes some principle of the inviolability of human life. The justification is minimally revisionist because it is in line with the medical exception, requiring both consent and benefit for medical actions that (seemingly) infringe on inalienable rights. It is also minimally revisionist because it doesn't require us to deny the moral relevance of the distinction between killing and letting die, or of the distinction between palliative action with a foreseeable life-shortening effect and euthanasia.

The justification is not complete, because I have not discussed the risks of legalization, in particular the risks of abuse and error. This will be my subject in the following chapters (10–12).

10 Ending lives with and without request

10.1 Committed to permit killing without request?

Since Yale Kamisar's seminal paper from 1958 one of the most common objections to the legalization of euthanasia has always been that permitting the ending of a patient's life at his explicit request will necessarily lead to permitting it without request.[1] The basic claim is a logical one: having permitted one practice, a society would be committed to permitting the other. Usually, this is explained as follows: the only reason that can justify euthanasia in the eyes of its supporters is that it ends a patient's unbearable suffering by ending his life. But a patient can suffer to the same extent, whether or not he is able to express a voluntary and well-considered, hence valid request for having his life ended. The justification therefore applies to both cases. In the last chapter I have endorsed the premise of this argument. It is therefore an urgent matter for me to consider whether the conclusion follows.

If permitting one practice commits a society to permitting the other, we may expect the legal introduction of the first practice to cause the spreading and eventually the legalization of the other. The logical connection will be reflected by a law-like causal relation. This argument seemed too many to receive empirical confirmation long ago, in 1991, when the results of the first national survey of medical decisions at the end of life were published in the Netherlands.[2] Termination of life without explicit request occurred in 0.8% of all deaths: the notorious *Remmelink 1000*. Although that percentage has only decreased in later surveys, ending the life of patients without their request is still reported to occur in the Netherlands, and, much more often, in Flanders, the Dutch-speaking part of Belgium. Understandably, a recent attempt to

1 Kamisar 1958; Kass 1989; Doerflinger 1989; Callahan 1992; Capron 1992, 31; New York State Taskforce 1994; Callahan, White 1996; Keown 2002, ch. 11; Keown 2018, ch. 10; 2012; Gorsuch 2006, 103–115; Jones 2011; Spaemann et al. 2015; and many others, including Brock 1992 (not an opponent of legalization). From 1992 on all these authors appeal to the evidence from the Netherlands for confirmation.

2 English transl.: van der Maas, van Delden, Pijnenborg 1992.

DOI: 10.4324/9781003281115-13

revitalize the argument focusses on the evidence from Flanders.[3] The combination of the logical argument with the empirical evidence that is supposed to confirm it is therefore still often presented as one of the most convincing arguments against the legalization of euthanasia. It has even been reported that people who are in favour of legalization tend to reconsider their views when they are "informed about the Dutch data".[4]

In Sections 10.2 and 10.3 I will discuss the logical argument, in Section 10.4 I will consider whether the available evidence really supports it. In Section 10.5 I will discuss that evidence from a legal point of view. I will conclude that in many cases in which the doctor reports to have ended the life of a patient without his request, he actually administered opioids in a dosage that is indicated for symptom management. Such a dosage is not likely to hasten death, and even if it would be likely to do so, would be considered normal medical action by the law. So why do doctors report an intention to shorten life? That is the question I will discuss in Sections 10.7–10.9. An excursion in Section 10.6 considers the seemingly low reporting rate of euthanasia in the Netherlands and Flanders.

10.2 The logical argument

Kamisar's argument that accepting the ending of lives on request commits one to accept the ending of lives without request, is surprising at first sight, because the practices seem so very different. The argument looks like the claim that you cannot permit buying without being committed to the condonation of stealing. Isn't consent the obvious and essential difference?

The reason why opponents of legalization don't buy this quick reply is that they believe that consent isn't really essential to the justification of euthanasia. The reasons that are standardly offered for considering euthanasia morally acceptable under some circumstances are, they suggest, equally good reasons for ending someone's life without his request under similar circumstances. It is obvious that the cogency of this argument depends on the actual reasons offered. If it is true, as most supporters of the legalization of euthanasia seem to think, that an appeal to the principle of respect for autonomy is both necessary and sufficient to justify euthanasia, the argument clearly is a non-starter. If the right to life implies the power to waive other people's duty not to take your life, it is obvious that no-one can legitimately consider taking it without your consent.

But this line of reasoning is rarely followed with full consistency, as John Keown in particular has correctly pointed out. For most authors

3 Jones 2017.
4 Cohn, Lynn 2002, 240.

who offer a justification in terms of respect for self-determination, only want to legalize a doctor's assistance in ending the life of a patient who is terminally ill or severely suffering, or both. Indeed, these are the only practices that have actually been legalized until now. Some authors address the question whether it can ever be permissible to end the life of a patient who is severely suffering in the end stage of his illness, and then derive an affirmative answer from that person's right to self-determination. But if that right implies the right to kill oneself, and *that* right implies the right to being helped by others, it seems inconsistent to restrict the exercise of that right to severely suffering patients in the end-stage of their illness. So the right of self-determination apparently isn't doing all the work.

Some authors argue that purely autonomy-based justifications are incompatible with the role morality of doctors.[5] That is right and relevant, but it invites the question how this role morality itself can be justified. That is the question I discussed in Section 9.5. I concluded that the common view of the law that the right to life cannot be waived is defensible. Hence a doctor has to make sure, not only that a request for euthanasia is voluntary and well-considered, but also that, in granting it, he will act in the best interests of that person, for example, because she is in a state of unbearable suffering that cannot be ended in any other way.

'So the principle that you appeal to isn't a principle of respect for self-determination, but a principle of compassion or beneficence? But in that case you really *are* committed to justify the ending of any patient's life who is in a similar state of unbearable suffering without prospect of relief'. Again, it may seem that this argument can be quickly disposed of. Why should the justification we propose consist of only one principle that gives us both the necessary and sufficient condition for the permissibility of legalization? Why shouldn't it identify two conditions that are individually necessary and only jointly sufficient: consent and net-benefit?[6] That is in line with the general role morality of doctors: without consent even a clearly beneficial action would be battery, a violation of the patient's rights. But benefit is equally necessary.

That observation points to the real difficulty that Keown *cum suis* are after. For consider a categorically non-competent person who never has been and never will be in a position to give or withhold consent to any form of treatment. If a medical treatment is clearly identified as beneficial to that patient, we normally consider that a sufficient justification for providing it. It is true that in many countries the consent of a surrogate is required, but the legal authority of the surrogate is more limited than the authority of a competent patient, and if the surrogate

5 De Haan 2002; Miller, Truog 2012; Birnbacher 2017, ch. 4.

6 Lillehammer 2002; de Haan 2002; Smith 2005; Griffiths, Weyers, Adams 2008, 514. For authors defending a justification in terms of both consent and benefit see Chapter 1, footnote 6.

isn't available and the treatment cannot be postponed, the doctor is justified in proceeding. It is also true that in such cases we often talk about the consent that the patient would have given if he had been able to give it, but, most clearly in the case of a person who has lacked all capacity from her birth on, this 'presumed consent' seems a mere re-description of her benefit.[7] Hence in such cases the principle of beneficence is really doing all the work.

Similarly, it seems, in deciding about the ending of a person's life, we require consent in the case of people with sufficient decision-making capacity, but that is only because we owe this to them as self-governing agents. The interest of the patient is a contributing factor to the justification of euthanasia, his consent only an enabling factor.[8] The requirement of a voluntary and well-considered request has to be understood as a side-constraint that only applies in the case of competent individuals.

Keown brings the point home in the following way:

> Imagine two patients of Dr A: X and his brother Y. They are identical twins, with an identically painful terminal illness and suffering to an identical degree. They lie, side by side, in hospital. X, who is competent, pleads with Dr A for a lethal injection of potassium chloride because 'suffering is unbearable'. Dr A agrees that death would indeed be a benefit for X and agrees to administer the injection to give him a 'merciful release'. X requests the same for his brother Y, who is incompetent, on the ground that he, too, must be experiencing 'unbearable and useless' suffering. Is Dr A to deny Y the same benefit he has agreed to confer on X? If so, what has become of the doctor's duty to act in the best interests of his patient?[9]

10.3 Evaluating the logical argument

It is a challenging argument, but I believe that the challenge can be met. To begin with, Keown seems to assume that the risks involved in permitting the doctor to end her patient's life will be the same in the two cases. But that is improbable, even when we only take possible harms to the patient's interests into account, and not the effects on the feelings of safety in the population at large. For if you think that a competent patient because of his intolerable and irrelievable suffering would be better off dead, the first thing you should do, obviously, is to ask him. Wouldn't a negative reply be a decisive reason for doubt? Ending his life

7 See Chapter 9, footnote 46.

8 Using the helpful terminology of de Haan 2002.

9 Keown 2002, 78; Keown 2018, 84. Varelius 2015 argues similarly that, if mercy-killing of a competent person on her request is permitted, it is a matter of justice also to permit mercy-killing of an incompetent patient in the same condition.

is, after all, an irreversible decision. And wouldn't a positive reply be a strong, even if not by itself a decisive indication that, indeed, he is suffering to an extent that makes it understandable for him to want to discontinue living? On the other hand, even if it is not impossible to attribute 'unbearable suffering' to a person who cannot report and explain it, it is much harder. Hence the possibility of error is much greater, at least great enough to counsel additional caution.

My second point concerns the benefits rather than the risks involved in ending the lives of Keown's two brothers. Keown stipulates that the brothers are suffering to the same degree, but that stipulation is vacuous. For if two patients are physically in exactly the same condition, the answer to the question whether they are suffering to the same extent, will depend on the meaning they attribute to being in that condition[10] (Section 6.2). As we have seen in Section 2.2, suffering from untreatable physical symptoms is only one possible motive for requesting euthanasia, and not the most prominent one. It is, however, the only relevant interest in dying that is shared by both brothers. But categorically non-competent patients who are unable to make a request at all, will not be able to appraise their present, let alone their future discomfort in terms of their personal values. Hence, even if the two brothers both have the same physical symptoms, they will not suffer in the same way or to the same extent. The first brother possibly has, in addition, relevant interests in meaning, independence, personal dignity and, incorporating these interests, a general interest in having a life of a certain shape. He may, for example, have reasons to prefer suicide to deep continuous sedation that the second brother cannot have. It may be the kind of death that best fits his life. The possible benefits of euthanasia are therefore necessarily different and possibly much larger in his case than in the case of his brother. And for establishing the meaning that the first brother's condition has for him, communicating with him will normally be essential.

I don't deny that it is possible for a categorically incompetent person, for example a newborn baby with severe *epidermolysis bullosa* (a condition that makes every touching of the skin excruciatingly painful), to be in a state of intolerable suffering that justifies the judgement that it would be best for that person to die. Indeed, this seems obviously true (Section 2.3). But by itself that view doesn't commit me to advocate the legalization of the ending of lives by doctors (or by anyone else) without

10 Stingl (2010) even suggests that a categorically incompetent patient like Tracy Latimer can be in a state of severe pain, but cannot really suffer, let alone suffer unbearably, because she cannot evaluate the painful state in terms of her personal values. (Cf. van Delden 2004 for a similar view.) But as I argued in Section 6.2, criticizing Cassell, from the fact that in order to assess a competent person's suffering we have to take into account the meaning that her present and future condition have for her, we cannot conclude that cats and newborns cannot suffer.

request for all incompetent people in a state of unbearable and intractable suffering.[11] In order to decide whether this is a good idea, we would have to consider severely handicapped newborns,[12] severely mentally handicapped people like Tracy Latimer, or other particular classes of cases, each class on its own merits, taking into account the frequency of such cases, possible alternative forms of relief, and in particular the special risks and benefits involved. It is quite possible that this will lead to the conclusion that for some or the other well-defined class of patients we should create a legal option of ending their lives without request.[13] It is also quite possible that for another class of patients the law should not create such options or only much more restricted ones than it allows in the case of competent patients. Because this book is about determining the manner and time of your own death, I will not consider that issue here (Section 1.1). For now I am satisfied that an argument for the legalization of euthanasia under some conditions does not by itself commit one to consider the practice of the ending of lives without request permissible under any conditions. That conclusion needs additional argument.

10.4 Empirical confirmation?[14]

As I pointed out in Section 10.1, the *Remmelink 1000* and the corresponding figures from later surveys, both from the Netherlands and Flanders, have often been quoted as corroborating the argument that by legalizing euthanasia a society starts an unstoppable movement downwards on a slippery slope. A practice of ending lives without request will be introduced or at least expand, and in the end consistency will require the lawgiver to legalize it. The slippery metaphor of a slippery slope, however, at least implies a causal direction. Originally it was contended that the recognition of the legal permissibility of euthanasia by the Dutch Supreme Court in 1984 explained the number of cases of killing without request in 1990. The problem with that contention was, of course, that no one had any idea of the corresponding number before 1984.[15] Later surveys, in Flanders from 1998 on, provided new figures

11 As Jones 2011 assumes.

12 See den Hartogh 2014b.

13 For the ending of the life of a severely handicapped and suffering newborn, a reporting and review procedure has been introduced in the Netherland in 2006, that at the time was the focus of much, largely critical, international attention, Griffiths, Weyers, Adams 2008, ch. 6. But only two cases have ever been reported to the Committee of Experts. Van de Vathorst et al. 2013 explain this by new developments in prenatal screening and in palliative care for newborns.

14 In Sections 10.4–10.6 I use text-material from den Hartogh 2020a, a comment on Jones 2017.

15 Griffiths, Bood, Weyers 1998, 300–303; Otlowski 1997, 438–441.

that fuelled the argument, but the causal link was still always merely postulated.[16] This is not merely like thinking that the consumption of ice cream causes an increase in drownings, for there is not even a *correlation* to begin with. Data from countries that had not legalized euthanasia at the time gave us sometimes lower, sometimes comparable and sometimes higher percentages. Available percentages range from 0.06% (Italy 2000–2001) to 3.5% (Australia 1996).[17] We have a series of sequential data for three countries, showing increase in Switzerland, decrease in Flanders and the Netherlands.[18] In the Netherlands and Belgium euthanasia has been legalized by statute in 2002, but in the Netherlands it had already been legal since 1984 on account of judge-made law. It is therefore only for Flanders that we have pre- and post-legalization data, showing substantial decrease, in combination with an increase in the incidence of euthanasia cases. It is a plausible explanation of this development that legalization promoted more open communication between doctor and patient. Taken together, these data in any case do not confirm the hypothesis of a causal link.[19]

But there is more to be said.[20] These cases have been classified under the category 'termination of life without request' because the doctor who gave information about them reported (1) that death had occurred as a result of a drug that he had administered with the explicit intention of hastening the death of the patient, and (2) the patient had not made an

16 For a comprehensive and even-handed discussion of the relevant data up to 2007 see Lewis 2007.

17 Sweden 2000–2001: 0.23%; the UK 2007–2008: 0.3% (Seale 2009); France 2009: 0.6% (Pennec et al. 2012, using a somewhat adapted questionnaire; 0.5% according to Riou et al. 2015); Denmark 2000–2001: 0.67%; Belgium 2005–2006 (the whole country): 1.3% (Meeussen et al. 2010). All data regarding 2000–2001 come from van der Heide et al. 2003. The Australian results (Kuhse et al. 1997) have been contested because of the small size of the sample studied and of alleged methodological flaws, but they are in line with other Australian results at the time, see footnote 77; cf. Neil et al. 2007. Recent research in Victoria (2018–2019, i.e. after the passing but before the coming into effect of the *Voluntary Aid-in-Dying Law* 2017) gave much lower data, Willmott et al. 2021.

18 Switzerland (German-speaking part): from 0.5 (2000–2001) to 0.8% (2013, Bosshard et al. 2016), cf. Hurst et al. 2018: resp. 1.1, 1.9 and 1.4% for the German-, French- and Italian-speaking parts (2013); Flanders: from 3.2% (1998, Deliëns et al. 2000) to 1.7% (2013, Chambaere et al. 2015; cf. Verkissen et al. 2018: 1.8% of cancer patients); the Netherlands: from 0.8% in 1990 to 0.3% in 2015 (Onwuteaka-Philipsen et al 2017, 119).

19 In the second edition of Keown 2002, from 2018, the author almost entirely disregards the steady decline of this percentage in the Netherlands, only observing (p. 318) that these latter surveys prove that legalization has not prevented the ending of life without request. That is indisputably true, but of course a much weaker claim than the original one.

20 The following analysis updates den Hartogh 2012. I presented the core of the argument for the first time in den Hartogh 2003.

explicit request for the ending of his life.[21] But if we look at the cases more closely, it turns out that only in a minority of them barbiturates or neuromuscular relaxants were used, the drugs that are recommended by the relevant pharmacological guidelines for the safe and effective procurement of death.[22] In most cases opioids were used, either as the only drug, or in combination with sedatives (mostly benzodiazepines).[23] Opioids are of course standardly used as the primary means for alleviating pain and shortness of breath. Three surveys also provide us with some information about the dosages of opioids and sedatives used. About the Flemish cases of ending a patient's life without request from 2007 (1.8% of all deaths), we are informed that in 93.8% of those cases (61 cases of 66), no regular euthanatics had been administered, but opioids, with or without sedatives. In 22.7% of these cases (15 of 66) the dosage of opioids administered to the patient was reported to be higher than necessary for symptom control. But in 43.9% of the cases (29 of 66) the dosages had not been higher, and only low-dose benzodiazepines or none at all had been administered.[24] As for the Netherlands, in 2010 only in 1 case of the 13 classified as termination of life without request (in a sample of 6861 deaths studied), regular euthanatics had been used, in 4 of these 13 cases an overdosage of morphine.[25] About two cases no data about dosages were available. In 2015 muscular relaxants had been used in 2 of 18 cases in a sample of 7661 deaths, an overdosage of morphine only in one case. In one other case it was unknown which drugs had been used.[26] We can conclude that in 2010

21 For the full Dutch questionnaire used in 2015 see Onwuteaka-Philipsen et al. 2017, 293–300. On the methodology of the research see Deliëns et al. 2011, 22–24, cf. Mortier et al. 2000. When on account of the answers to these questions a case is classified as a termination of life without request and the doctor involved, replying to a later question, reports about the same case that he had sedated the patient with the explicit intention or co-intention to hasten his death, Jones 2017 registers a second case of termination of life without request: a clear case of double-counting. You cannot get two killings out of the report of one case. Keown 2018, 188–190, repeats the mistake.

22 KNMP 2012, and a similar guideline from the Belgian Professional Association for Pharmacologists. The use of benzodiazepines and opioids is advised against in these guidelines because of the uncertainty of a lethal effect and because of the possibility of adverse side effects.

23 In 1990 morphine had been used in 62% of the cases, van der Maas, van Delden, Pijnenborg 1992, 52. In 12 out of 13 cases reported by Meeussen et al. 2010 and in all 26 cases reported by Riou et al. 2015 opioids and benzodiazepines had been used. None of these sources provide any information about dosages.

24 Chambaere et al. 2014. About 2 cases no information was available, in the remaining 20 cases (30.3%) strong sedatives (barbiturates, propofol or high-dose benzodiazepines) had been administered, in unknown dosages.

25 van der Heide et al. 2012, 23, 37.

26 Onwuteaka-Philipsen et al. 2017, 119, 132. (These passages report different numbers of cases but Dr. A. van der Heide informed me that the correct number is 18.) In 5 of the 18 cases the doctors themselves thought (inconsistently) that probably no life shortening had occurred after all, *ibid.*, 120–121.

at least in 6 of 13 cases, in 2015 in at least 14 of 18 cases opioids have been administered in normal dosages.

However, it is now generally believed by experts that patients will not die from opioids, if these are given in the (regularly increasing) dosages, necessary for providing symptom relief, or even somewhat larger ones.[27] As we have seen before most experts also believe that patients will not die from sedatives, administered in the proper dosages for lowering their consciousness, even deeply (Section 7.2). Doctors are generally slow in absorbing this message,[28] perhaps because they often witness patients dying quickly after the first use of morphine or midazolam, or the raising of the dosage, and are prone to *a post hoc propter hoc* illusion. But if that view is mistaken, this means that at least a substantial minority of the Flemish cases in 2007, and a large majority of the Dutch cases in 2015, have been misclassified as termination of life without request. It is highly improbable that the drugs administered in those cases actually caused the death of the patient, whatever the doctor believed or intended. And if an action doesn't cause a death, it can't be a killing.

Two cases in which muscular relaxants, one case in which an overdose of morphine has been used, in a sample of 5% of all deaths: the common belief that the legalization of euthanasia in the Netherlands has led to the widescale killing of incompetent people now rests on the slender shoulders of these three physicians. We cannot conclude that in the Netherlands only about $20 \times 3 = 60$ cases of the ending of life without request occurred in 2015 (0.04% of all deaths), because these figures are too small to allow extrapolation to population level.[29] But as regards the Netherlands we can safely conclude that the common belief has been disproven. The number of cases in Flanders, though not known exactly either, is clearly higher. But there is still no shred of proof that the number is causally linked to the legalization of euthanasia. The hypothesis of a general law-like connection has been falsified by the Dutch case; this makes the existence of such a connection in Flanders improbable. Perhaps the remaining Dutch and Flemish cases of termination of life without request have rather to be understood as atavistic remnants of an older practice, by now largely supplanted by termination of life on request with proper means. If that is true, we should expect this older practice still to exist elsewhere (see Section 10.9).

10.5 The legal status of these cases

Even if a life-shortening effect would have been plausible, as many doctors and some experts still believe (Section 8.2), all cases in which morphine or midazolam have been used in dosages indicated for the alleviation of symptoms or for sedation would still have been misclassified

27 Sykes, Thorns 2003; Dahani, Aarts, Smith 2010.
28 Vander Stichele et al. 2004. Cf. footnote 61.
29 Onwuteaka-Philipsen et al. 2017, 119; Chambaere et al. 2014.

by reckoning them to be cases of the termination of life without request. Even if death occurred as the result of the drug that the doctor administered, that action would still be justified by the medical exception to the prohibition of killing that I discussed in Section 9.5. As we saw already in Section 1.3, that exception can be interpreted in two ways. According to the first way, enshrined in the *Doctrine of Double Effect*, the doctor would be justified if he didn't intend the life-shortening effect, but only took it into account as a probable side effect, and satisfied conditions of proportionality and subsidiarity. According to the second understanding of the medical exception the doctor would be legally in the clear, if the condition of the patient justified the use of drugs for the relief of the patient's suffering, if that use conformed to professional standards. Although I have occasionally pointed at some problems in the application of the *Doctrine of Double Effect*,[30] in this book I have not committed myself to any of these two interpretations. But neither the Dutch nor the Belgian criminal law takes that neutral position. Both systems have a doctrine of the criminal mind that is incompatible with Double Effect.

The Dutch legal conception of 'opzet' (*dolus*, intent), for example, lays down two conditions, one regarding belief and one regarding volition.[31] Regarding belief, the agent has to be aware in advance that the action he plans has a significant probability of causing a harmful effect or effects. No special mental act of recognition of this prospect is required, only awareness in the dispositional sense. As regards volition, it is enough that, being aware of this significant probability, the agent nevertheless decides to execute his plan. He doesn't take the harmful effect as a reason to discard the plan, and in this sense willingly allows or 'endorses' the effect to occur. He may intend it as his end or as a means to his end, or he may only take it into the bargain; that doesn't matter. Nevertheless, in Dutch and Belgian law a medical action that foreseeably hastens death is legally permitted when hastening death is only "a subsidiary effect of a treatment that is necessary for the alleviation of suffering and adjusted to that end".[32] What justifies the action in that case is the availability of a proper medical justification, irrespective of the role that justification played in the actual deliberations of the doctor.

This means that, legally, cases in which the doctor acted with the explicit intention or the co-intention to hasten death, but a medical indication was available for the use of midazolam or morphine in the dosage she actually used, her action would legally count as leading to a 'natural

30 Sections 4.1; 8.5. For an extended discussion of these problems see den Hartogh 2019a.

31 Dupont 2004; van Dijk 2008; or any introduction to Belgian or Dutch penal law. For the history of the doctrine from Roman law on see Monballyu 2014, 70–72.

32 Staatscommissie 1985; cf. Griffiths, Bood, Weyers 1998, 69–72. For Belgian law see VanSweevelt 2008.

death', even if the probability of a life-shortening effect would be much greater than most experts now believe it could possibly be. Her action should be classified as the medically indicated and proportional use of palliative medicine, irrespective of her intentions.[33]

Of course, the opponents of the legalization of euthanasia under any conditions may also be critical of the understanding of 'intent' in Dutch and Belgian criminal law, and in many other jurisdictions. As a matter of fact such opponents have occasionally applauded the Dutch and Flemish researchers for using a methodology that enabled them to appraise their results in terms of the *Doctrine of Double Effect.*[34] But even if the definition of 'intent' in the Dutch and Belgian law would be criticizable from a moral point of view, it is obvious that it should be the one to adopt in research that is meant to evaluate the effectiveness of the law. It is an inconsistency in such studies, when its legal and epidemiological chapters rely on different definitions of the same basic concepts, as has been the case in the Dutch evaluations of the euthanasia law, reporting the situation in 2005, 2010 and 2015, all commissioned by the government, and the Flemish survey of the situation in 2007.

Even more importantly, even in jurisdictions in which the criminal law takes the intention of the agent into account to some extent, a medical action that is indicated and proportional will never be considered an offence because of the intention of the physician. Intention to cause harm may magnify a more basic wrong, making a minor wrong punishable or a manslaughter a murder. But whether the medical exception is understood as a species of a more general genus, for example necessity, or as being *sui generis*, it cannot be understood as the mere absence of an aggravating circumstance. This is as true of the medical exception to the prohibition of killing as of the exception to the prohibition of battery.

10.6 The reporting rate

The points I have made in Sections 10.4 and 10.5 are also relevant for evaluating the second common criticism that is made of the Dutch and Belgian regulatory system for euthanasia on the basis of the results of the surveys. The first Dutch survey of medical decisions at the end of life found that in 1990 only 19% of the cases of euthanasia had been reported, at that time to the Public Prosecution Office. Since 1998 the reports have to be sent to a Regional Euthanasia Review Committee, and since the introduction of the euthanasia law in 2002 the judgements

33 Cf. the decision of the disciplinary board Zwolle in the Vencken case, 10-3-2005, *Medisch Contact* 60 (2005): 499–501; and the Belgian decision in KI Gent, 9 December 2004, *Tijdschrift voor Gezondheidsrecht/Revue de Droit de la Santé* 2007, 39, with note E. Delbeke.

34 Keown 2002, 100; Keown 2018, 108.

of these committees are only forwarded to the Public Prosecutor (and the Inspectorate for Health Care) if the committees conclude that the doctor has not met all legal requirements of due care. From 19% in 1990 the reporting rate increased to 82% in 2015.[35] But the critics are still not satisfied.[36] For this figure still means that of 18% of the cases (by now amounting to some 1000 cases a year) we would have reason to suspect that the requirements of due care have not been met. For why would the doctors involved not report their actions if they had nothing to hide? And because the reporting rate in Flanders is so much lower (63.5% in 2013),[37] our suspicions should accordingly be higher.

A first point to be made about this criticism is that a reporting rate of 82% would still compare rather favourably with the reporting rate of zero we find in all prohibitive jurisdictions.[38] But consider again the denominator in the determination of the Dutch and Belgian rates: the number of cases of euthanasia. In most of the reported cases the doctor had used proper euthanatics: barbiturates and muscle relaxants. As regards these cases the reporting rate is close to 100% in the Netherlands, ca. 92% in Flanders.[39] In a steadily decreasing percentage of cases, however, the doctor used opioids, occasionally in combination with sedatives, or in rare cases sedatives only.[40] Such cases are never reported in the Netherlands and rarely in Flanders.[41] Even though the doctors involved told the researchers that they had acted with an explicit intention to shorten the patient's life, they had administered a larger dosage than necessary for symptom relief in only a small part of those cases, at least in the Netherlands. In 2015 morphine had been administered in 14% of all cases classified by the Dutch researchers as cases of euthanasia, but a higher dosage than necessary for symptom relief only in 1.1% of all cases.[42] We should again conclude that the large majority of these

35 Onwuteaka-Philipsen et al. 2017, 32.

36 E.g, Keown 2012, 125–128; Justice Smith in *Carter v Canada* (Attorney General) [2015] 1 SCR 646–685.

37 Dierickx et al. 2018.

38 Magnusson 2004.

39 The Netherlands: 100% in 2005 and 2010; 97% in 2015, Onwuteaka-Philipsen et al. 2017, 186. Flanders 92% in 2007; 92.3% in 2013, Dierickx et al. 2018.

40 Onwuteake-Philipsen et al. 2017, 108: morphine, with or without benzodiazepines in 14%, benzodiazepines in 2% of the cases. The number of Flemish euthanasia cases in which non-recommended drugs had been used was 88.1% in 1998, 44.7% in 2007 and 33.2% in 2013, Dierickx et al. 2018.

41 In 2007 and 2013 resp. 4, 5 and 3.8%.

42 Onwuteaka-Philipsen et al. 2017, 108, 132; cf. van der Heide et al. 2012, 38, about the corresponding figures for 2010 (resp. 17 and 3%). In 1995 the median dosage of morphine used in all cases in which a physician reported an explicit intention to hasten death was identical to the median dosage used for all dying patients in a German palliative institution, Groenewoud 2002, 97, 158. Except for Bilsen et al. 2006, see footnote 44, no research about dosages used in Belgium have been published until now.

cases have been misclassified, because it is highly improbable that death has actually been hastened in these cases. And even if the action did cause death, it would not legally count as ending a person's life on his request, but, for the reasons discussed in Section 10.5, as the medically indicated and proportional use of palliative medicine.

In addition, however, about 2% of the Dutch doctors who reported to have administered morphine for symptom relief and only took the possibility of a life-shortening effect into account, confess, oddly enough, to have used a higher dosage than necessary for that aim.[43] By itself this is a mysterious result. Why use an overdose if your intention is only to relieve pain and shortness of breath? (I hope to shed some light on this mystery in my discussion of the 'grey area' in Sections 10.7 and 10.8) In order to decide whether any of these actions should be classified as euthanasia in spite of the reported intention, we would need to know more about the actual dosages used. What we do know, however, is only that the dosage that is considered necessary for symptom relief in the last 24 hours before death is somewhat lower in the Netherlands than it is in other European countries.[44] Anyway, it is implausible that the overdosage in these cases will often be large enough to be likely to cause death. Taking these data into account we should conclude that the actual reporting rate for the Netherlands is higher than the surveys tell us, probably much higher.

As regards Flanders, we can only say that at present we have no accurate picture of the prevalence of euthanasia, and hence no accurate picture of the reporting rate either.[45] By now it is common in the literature to make a number of criticisms of the Flemish euthanasia practice, and therefore of the effectiveness of the Belgian regulatory system.[46] In a substantial number of cases the request for euthanasia had only been expressed orally, not in writing,[47] no colleague had been consulted, at least no sufficiently independent one, and the drugs had been administered by a nurse, sometimes not even in the presence of a physician.

43 Overall 1% in 2005, Rurup et al. 2009; 2% in 2010, van der Heide et al. 2012, 38; 1.9% in 2015, Onwuteake-Philipsen et al. 2017, 132, cf. 124.

44 Bilsen et al. 2006 listing the dosages of opioids given during the last 24 hours before death in six European countries (data from 2001 to 2002). A dosage beyond 599 mg was given in 6.5% of the cases in Belgium, 2.7% in the Netherlands and 3.8% in the six countries on average. For comparable information about the Netherlands (2005) see Rurup et al. 2009.

45 FCECE 2018, criticized for disregarding the available research by Raus, Vanderhaegen, Sterckx 2021, 95.

46 Chambaere et al. 2010b, Table 4; Smets, Bilsen 2011, 290–291; Cohen-Almagor 2013; Cohen et al. 2014; Montero 2017; Dierickx et al. 2018; Raus, VanderHaegen, Sterckx 2021. In 12 cases of the ending of life with, and 43 of cases of the ending of life without request, nurses had administered the supposedly lethal drug, opioids in resp. 9 and 34 cases, Inghelbrecht et al. 2010.

47 This is a legal requirement in Belgium but not in the Netherlands.

As far as we know, however, most of these alleged violations of the requirements of due care may have occurred in cases which the doctors involved did not classify as cases of euthanasia at all. And in many of these cases their classification may be the right one.

By now the researchers are aware that cases in which morphine or midazolam have been used in normal dosages, should not be classified as cases of the ending of life with or without request.[48] That is why they have started to acquire information about these dosages. But they have not integrated this insight into their methodology. They still classify on the basis of the doctor's intention and use these classifications for calculating numbers of cases of termination of life without request and reporting rates. These figures are used in debates about legalization all over the world. The researchers also have not acknowledged that it is at least a legal mistake to classify medical actions at the end of life by reference to the intention of the doctor. Adapting their questionnaires to these insights would of course disrupt an impressive series of results since 1990 that enables comparisons over time and between a sizable number of countries. It is also difficult to study the use of disproportionate dosages because in individual cases you have to know the development of the dosage during a longer time and other individual characteristics in order to be able to identify disproportionality. But in order to get correct data, it would nevertheless be necessary to change, or at least to supplement those questionnaires, focusing on drugs and dosages, rather than on intentions.

10.7 How doctors classify

Why do Dutch and Flemish doctors fail to report cases in which they executed an intention to hasten death by administering morphine or midazolam? It used to be thought that they wanted to avoid the administrative burdens involved in following the procedural requirements of due care, in particular the requirements to record their actions, to consult an independent colleague and to report to a review committee. Or they were aware that their actions did not satisfy the requirements and wanted to avoid the judicial consequences.[49] In the Netherlands one of those requirements is that the euthanasia has been performed in a medically careful way, and using morphine or midazolam isn't considered a careful way. (In Belgium this is only a professional rule, not a legal requirement.)

48 Rurup et al. 2008; van der Heide et al. 2012, ch. 4; Chambaere et al. 2010b, 2014.

49 Oddly, Dierickx et al. 2018 still suggest these explanations, though their own results (about Flanders, 2013) show that they apply to very few cases, many less than even in 2007. For example, the percentage of doctors who say not to have reported a case of euthanasia with non-recommended drugs because they knew the case didn't meet the legal requirements, or because they considered it a matter between doctor and patient, is resp. 0 and 2.1 (6.2 and 7.1 in 2007).

But since the pioneering work of Donald van Tol we know that physicians themselves almost never classify cases in which they administer morphine or midazolam as the ending of the patient's life, with or without explicit request, irrespective of the dosages they have used, and irrespective of their intentions. They normally choose the pigeonholes of pain and symptom relief or – by now in the large majority of cases – of palliative sedation.[50] Obviously doctors classify by reference to the standard aim of the drugs they use, not to their personal intentions or expectations in the individual case. The researchers standardly deplore their lack of knowledge of the law, and invariably advise to educate them better. But as a matter of fact they may often classify more correctly than the researchers do. Legally they will only be mistaken when they use the kind of substantial overdose that has a significant probability, according to expert consensus, of really hastening death.[51]

Nevertheless, it is difficult to understand their classification in the other cases. How is it possible that they use these drugs with the explicit intention to hasten death, believe that it actually has that effect, and still deny that they are ending a life, on request or without? Who are they fooling?

Retrospective self-ascriptions of intentions are often highly unreliable. The intention reported is not a mental state found by introspection or memory, but rather a far from infallible reconstruction of one's own reasons. The reconstruction of the agent may not be superior to the reconstruction of others. The fact that his intentions may be multiple and ambiguous may in particular confound the agent, but it also creates some room for more or less intentional manoeuvring.[52] When administering drugs the physicians involved in these cases expected two effects: an almost certain and immediate effect of alleviated suffering, and a less certain and perhaps somewhat later occurring life-shortening effect. They welcomed both effects. How should we, how should they establish which of these effects they intended?

50 Van Tol 2005. See further Onwuteaka-Philipsen et al. 2007, ch. 4; Griffiths, Weyers, Adams 2008, 199–204; Buiting et al. 2010; Smets, Bilsen 2011; Smets, Cohen, Bilsen 2011; Deyaert et al. 2014; Chambaere et al. 2014; Dierickx et al. 2018; cf. Riou et al. 2015 on France.

51 As in the tragic Tuitjenhorn case, 2013. In spite of the enormous dosages of morphine and midazolam he administered the physician involved described his action as 'palliative sedation', insisting that his intention had not been to shorten the life of his patient.

52 Quill 1993; Pool 1996, 225; van Tol 2005, 104 (on 'negotiating' a classification); Douglas, Kerridge, Ankeny 2008 (on 'managing' intentions); Neil et al. 2007; Syme 2008, 13–17, 25–29, cf. comments Magnusson 2009; Willmott et al. 2021. In 1995 interviews were held with a number of physicians after they had completed a questionnaire. Of the 46 physicians who on that occasion had reported an 'explicit intention to hasten death' 6 withdrew that description during the interviews, van der Wal et al. 1996, 303. For a similar revocation see Emanuel et al. 1998, 508–509.

Supporters of the *Doctrine of Double Effect* propose to use the so-called Failure Test.[53] Suppose that you somehow learn that the life-shortening effect will not occur after all, would that be a reason for you to change your plan and, for example, not to administer the drug or administer it in a lower dosage? In many cases the doctor involved may simply not know the answer.[54] If you consider an action with two welcome effects, you usually need not ask yourself whether you would act in the same way if the action would have had only one of those effects, in order to decide to act in that way. Sometimes you can reconstruct the answer afterwards from your past actions and your general way of thinking. But at other times you cannot.

In this particular case there might be a special reason why some doctors would be able to sort out their intentions. For if their action could not be justified by a palliative aim, it would always be medically improper and, if a life-shortening effect would really be plausible, illegal. It is therefore probable that some doctors would not act with the aim of hastening death if that action could not also be justified by the aim to alleviate suffering, even when they report 'the explicit intention to hasten death'.[55] If forms of palliative treatment are medically indicated, it is plausible that in the large majority of these cases, including many 'explicit intention' cases, doctors would also provide them if they did not believe them to have any life-shortening effects. In that case they would not satisfy the Failure Test. However, an unknown percentage of them would use lower dosages.

These are murky waters. The problem of knowing what doctors mean when they report intentions also casts doubt on the significance of the research in other ways. Of two doctors acting in the same way in similar situations that evoke in them comparable hopes and feelings, one may ascribe to herself an intention to hasten death, the other may not. One of them may believe to use an overdosage and the other not; there is no full consensus on proper dosages, even within, let alone between countries. Most importantly, not every doctor has a clear grasp of the distinction between intention and foresight to begin with.[56]

10.8 Why do doctors classify this way?

Why do doctors use morphine in the first place if they 'intend' to hasten death? Donald van Tol has suggested that it is precisely the lack of certainty about the consequences of their actions that makes doctors sometimes prefer such procedures to straightforward euthanasia. It enables

53 Duff 1980, 150; Jansen 2010.

54 This is even more clearly true in the cases in which a doctor reports to have had the 'co-intention' to hasten death, den Hartogh 2020a.

55 Cf. Syme 2008, 14.

56 Douglas, Kerridge, Ankeny 2008.

them to harbour the somewhat contradictory thoughts: yes, I am helping this suffering patient, I am not leaving him to his fate, but, no, I am not killing him 'on the needle', I do what doctors always do in such cases. Perhaps I use a little more morphine than I do in other cases, but not really a dosage outside the normal range.[57] To a considerable extent these doctors may be aware that they are "playing tricks with themselves".[58] It is also relevant for them that a life-shortening effect, even if it occurs, will occur at an unpredictable moment. As they perceive it, that further weakens the causal link with their own action. And death will, at most, only occur at a slightly earlier moment than it would have come anyway. Some doctors will then claim that it is still caused by the underlying illness, even if the causal process is somewhat speeded up.[59] For all these reasons acting in this way may seem acceptable to doctors who shy away from 'euthanasia'.[60]

These thoughts are probably shared by many doctors involved in providing symptom relief and sedation to dying patients. This may help to explain the surprisingly large numbers of doctors who at least *ex ante* think, notwithstanding the recent consensus among experts, that these actions may have life-shortening effects.[61] In many cases the doctor herself believed afterwards that no such effect had occurred.[62] The standard research design since the first Dutch survey of 1991 aims at subdividing this class into groups of doctors having the 'explicit intention', the 'co-intention' or no intention to hasten death. But, if my argument in this section is valid, these self-descriptions may not correspond to any real difference in thinking and motivation between the doctors involved.[63]

These insights suggest that a substantial part of the medical actions that are standardly classified as endings of life with or without request do not differ from normal palliative actions.[64] The doctors involved don't act differently and don't even think differently. This is perhaps confirmed by the fact that, although the use of opioids with the 'explicit intention' to hasten death decreased in the Netherlands from 2.4 to 0.8% of all

57 Van Tol 2005, 208.

58 To quote one of them, from Douglas, Kerridge, Ankeny 2008. Other statements quoted in this study refer to "well-intentioned self-deception" and "kidding yourself".

59 Van Tol 2005, 203; Neil et al. 2007.

60 Douglas, Kerridge, Ankeny 2008.

61 From 19% of the cases in 1990 to 36% in 2010 and 2015, Onwuteaka-Philipsen et al. 2017, 122. According to Clive Seale the high percentage is to some extent an artefact of the wording of the questionnaire, Seale 2009. Repeating in 2007 a study from 2004 with a reworded questionnaire he found 17.1 instead of 32.8% cases of the alleviation of symptoms with a probability of hastening the end of life.

62 Overall 63% in 2005, Rurup et al. 2009. In 2015 48% of GPs had not consulted with the patient, the most common explanation being that probably no life-shortening effect had occurred, Onwuteaka-Philipsen et al. 2017, 123–124.

63 Cf. Douglas, Kerridge, Ankeny 2008, criticizing Forbes, Huxtable 2006.

64 Meeussen et al. 2010; Chambaere et al. 2014; Riou et al. 2015.

cases of such use from 1995 to 2005, there was no change in dosages used.[65] These doctors had not changed their behaviour, only their way of describing it, in particular their use of the term 'intention'. When doctors administer morphine to dying patients or sedate them, they will, as we have seen, often hope that the drugs will not only relieve the patient's suffering but also hasten his death. Because of this dual hope they may use dosages at the upper end of the normal range and occasionally go beyond that range. The range will not be exactly delineated to begin with, and these doctors will often overrate the life-shortening effect of their actions. Is such an action the ending of a life with or without request? That may be indeterminable. Even if we knew the dosages used in those cases, experts might disagree about the probability of a life-shortening effect. It is a grey area, and that is precisely what attracts some doctors to it. They try to ensure at the same time that the dying phase is not too long and their own responsibility for any shortening of life is minimal.

In many of these cases doctors will act without prior discussion with their patients. Part of the reason may be that they know they are moving around in a legally dangerous area. But the main reason will be that in most cases the patients will already be in a stage of the dying process in which communication is difficult or impossible. These reasons are related to each other. If doctors in permissive countries use proper euthanatics they will often have discussed this as a possible option for the future at an earlier time, when the patient was still approachable, but when acting within the grey zone they will tend to avoid such discussions. This explains why such actions, whether or not they are actually likely to hasten the death of the patient, will often be done without his explicit request.[66]

Cases of this kind have to be distinguished from cases in which the doctor starts using morphine in large overdosages (above 100–200 mg), or suddenly raises the dosage dramatically, with death as the immediate and foreseeable result. At present we do not know whether cases of both kinds are at the ends of a continuous spectrum or tend to cluster. Perhaps they cluster: a relevant result of the Dutch survey of 2005 is that, when doctors used morphine with the explicit intention or co-intention to hasten death, the mean dosage given during the last 24 hours of life was much higher than the median dosage (resp. 285 and 180 mg),[67] suggesting a small group of extremely high dosages.

We have some indications suggesting that such cases mainly concern severely suffering patients in the last hours of their lives. The initiative for the first Dutch research was taken by the *Remmelink commission* that had been commissioned to study the incidence of all medical actions

65 Rurup et al. 2009.
66 Out of 36 cases 26 reported in Riou et al. 2015.
67 Rurup et al. 2009.

at the end of life and to make recommendations about possible legal responses to the findings. That commission commented on the finding of the *Remmelink 1000* that a short shortening of life at its very end, when an irreversible process of failing of the vital functions has started, should not be classified as homicide, but as 'aid-in-dying' (*stervenshulp*) and should be considered normal medical action, leading to a natural death.[68] If a patient is in great pain, why should we make a fuss when he dies within five minutes from an overdosage of morphine rather than five hours later 'naturally'? This proposal met with general criticism, except from some physicians, and it may have expressed a not uncommon view among doctors at the time, before even the term 'terminal sedation' was widely known. That view may not have died out completely, and the corresponding practice may not have been replaced completely by deep sedation until death either.[69] The same idea of the legitimacy of a 'little push at the very end' is also still alive in Belgium; it can be found in a statement of the Belgian Society of Intensive Care Medicine from 2014.[70] Probably such cases still occur, although we know next to nothing about them. But we *do* know that their number can only be small.

10.9 What do we know about the practice elsewhere?

Both procedures, the use of opioids and sedatives in more or less normal and in extremely high dosages, seem to be used more frequently in Wallonia, the French-speaking part of Belgium, than in Flanders, the Dutch-speaking part. This difference seems to be related to somewhat different attitudes doctors in these regions have to the euthanasia law of their country.[71] When the law was discussed in the Belgian parliament, many Belgian doctors opposed it, not because they believed that doctors should never kill, but because they believed that compassionate doctors sometimes should hasten death, but that this is only 'a matter for doctor and patient' to decide (in practice mostly for the doctor alone), not a proper concern of the state.[72] Because the Public Prosecutor left them alone, they were entirely comfortable with the *status quo*.[73] In Belgium

68 Commissie Onderzoek Medische Praktijk inzake Euthanasie 1991, summarized by Weyers 2004, 317ff.

69 This may explain the indignant reactions of many physicians to the conviction of doctor van Oyen 2003, Weyers 2004, 380–382, and to the prosecution of the doctor involved in the Tuitjenhorn case, footnote 51.

70 Vincent et al. 2014, commented upon by Cohen-Almagor 2015; Montero 2017.

71 Cohen et al. 2012.

72 Overall 38% of Walloon and 20% of Flemish doctors still agreed with that view in 2009; 55% of Walloon and 71% of Flemish physicians found it useful to consult a second physician, Cohen et al. 2012.

73 Adams in Griffiths, Weyers, Adams 2008, 293, 329; Griffiths *ibid.*, 511–512.

the euthanasia law therefore created more rather than less legal pressure on doctors. When the euthanasia law was adopted by parliament, this attitude could be found at both sides of the language border. This may explain the relatively high number of cases of the termination of life without request in Flanders before the introduction of the law. But the attitude was more often found in Wallonia than in Flanders, and, although such attitudes don't immediately change when the law changes, that process is more advanced in Flanders than in Wallonia.[74] This may partly explain the relatively low number of reported cases of euthanasia from Wallonia, in addition to a greater reluctance to grant requests.[75] Walloon doctors tend to prefer sedation until death to euthanasia. If all this is true, we should expect the percentage of cases of the ending of life without request to be higher in Wallonia, but at present we have no data confirming this.[76]

We have much anecdotal evidence confirming that the practice also exists elsewhere, in jurisdictions that prohibit ending a person's life with or without her request. Unfortunately, we have very little relevant information from research. What we need in particular are robust data about drugs and dosages. In Section 10.4 I mentioned the extremely low percentage of cases of the termination of life without request in Italy in 2000. But a more recent study found that in 19.1% of the patients who died in a deeply sedated state (41 patients out of 246) opioids had been used in a higher dosage than necessary for symptom relief.[77] Such data make us wonder to what extent the differences in self-ascription of 'intentions to hasten death' between, let's say, Italy and New Zealand,[78]

74 See footnote 49.

75 According to FCECE 2020 23.3% of the reports received in 2017 came from French-speaking physicians, even though 38% of the population speaks French.

76 Cf. the percentage of cases of termination of life without request found by Meeussen et al 2010 for home and hospice care in the whole of Belgium, 2005/2006 (1.3%), and by Chambaere et al. 2015 for Flanders 2013 (1.7%), reported in footnote 18. But these percentages are not fully comparable.

77 Miccinesi et al. 2015: stable administration in the last three days (7), gradual increase in the last three days (17), abrupt increase in the last day (17). According to Folker et al. 1996 12% of Danish physicians had at least once doubled morphine dosages with fixed intervals, thus providing doses substantially higher than necessary for pain control. According to Mitchell, Owens 2004, 5.6% of GPs in New Zealand (1999–2000) reported to have supplied or administered a lethal drug to a patient, administered explicitly for the purpose of hastening death; in 43.6% of those cases (2.4% of all deaths) the action had not been discussed with the patient. In 2013 the percentage found was 4.5%, Malpas, Mitchell, Koschwanez 2015. According to Douglas, Kerridge, Rainbird 2001 36.2% of Australian surgeons had given drugs at dosages greater than necessary to relieve symptoms, with the intention to hasten death, most of them (at least 20.4%) without an explicit request. Out of 38 American oncologists who had participated in euthanasia or physician-assisted suicide, 8 had not received any request from the patient, Emanuel et al. 1998, Table 2.

78 See footnotes 17, 77.

correspond to any reality. They might largely depend on local conventions of self-ascription of intention. Doctors may also differ in the extent to which they conceal their intentions, even in anonymous interviews, perhaps even to themselves, in particular in non-permissive jurisdictions.[79] Our ignorance about these matters is deep.

It has been one of the main aims of the Dutch euthanasia law to displace this practice by a transparent and controllable one, in which termination of life would only occur on the voluntary request of the patient, after independent consultation, by the use of proper drugs, and subject to review.[80] The Dutch legal arrangement has largely succeeded in creating such a practice (Chapter 12), with a reporting rate close to 100%. It has not succeeded and may never succeed in fully weeding out the older practice.

Some authors sympathize with the traditional view of the Walloon doctors: maintain the blanket prohibition of euthanasia, but do not harass doctors who raise dosages of morphine to levels that somewhat exceed what is necessary for pain relief but don't certainly and promptly kill the patient. Or allow them to deeply sedate patients until their death and withhold fluid, even when their life expectancy exceeds a few weeks. The norm will help to keep the practice small but suffering patients will be helped out in the most urgent cases.[81]

But we already know that the norm would not everywhere succeed to keep the practice small.[82] In addition the policy of tolerating an underground practice has some significant disadvantages. Perhaps the most important drawback is that in many cases no open discussion with the patient about the procedure to be followed will take place. In that secretive environment it will often be unclear whether the patient has expressed a well-informed and well-considered request. Moreover, the doctor will only rarely discuss his plan with a colleague, let alone an independent consultant. As a result, the doctor will not be sufficiently able to check his diagnosis and prognosis, his assessment of the suffering of the patient, its cause (depression?), and of alternative ways to alleviate it.[83] Because there will not be any guidelines, we may also expect medical mistakes and complications to occur regularly: difficulties with

79 Draper et al. 2009. Merry et al. 2013 found 80% of New Zealand doctors (2006) prepared to give honest answers about prescribing drugs with intention to hasten death, 60% about alleviating pain and suffering with the intention of hastening death. (One wonders whether we can trust those replies.) Cf. Chambaere et al. 2014.

80 A major theme in Kennedy 2002.

81 New York State Taskforce 1994, ch. 6 (reporting the view of 'some members'); Douglas, Kerridge, Ankeny 2008; Velleman 2015, 19–20 ('the best policy is no policy at all').

82 Consider the percentage of cases of the ending of life with and without request reported for Flanders 1998 (resp.1.2, 3.2%, Deliëns et al. 2000); Australia 1996 (resp. 1.8, 3.5%, Kuhse et al. 1997); France 2009 (resp. 0.2, 0.5%, Riou et al. 2015), cf. footnotes 17, 18; and the data for New Zealand, reported in footnote 77.

83 Quill, Cassel, Meier 1992.

intravenous injections, regurgitation of orally taken drugs, mistaken dosages, resulting in extended time until death and sometimes failure, leading to panicky reactions ('pillow jobs').[84] A culture of deception in which doctors may even fabricate symptoms in order to explain their use of overdosages, may also be an undesirable by-product.[85] And it will be impossible for patients and their families to determine or even to know in advance the manner and time of the patient's death.

84 See the graphic description of an underground practice (20% botched attempts) in Magnusson 2002, summarized in Magnusson 2004.

85 Magnusson 2004.

11 The risks of legalization

11.1 Risks of abuse and error

In Chapter 9 I revisited the principled arguments for and against the legalization of euthanasia; on the one hand the appeal to principles of respect for autonomy and beneficence and their relation, and on the other hand, in addition to the idea that the continuation of life is always a benefit to the living person (Section 2.3), several conceptions of the impersonal value and inviolability of human life, as well as the appeal to the proper aims of medicine. If one considers recent debates about legalization proposals, however, another argument appears to be much more effective in blocking such proposals: that legalization of both euthanasia and the providing of access to lethal drugs involves grave risks to patients and third parties, which cannot be contained within acceptable limits by legal safeguards. Whether this is true I want to discuss in this chapter, having started that discussion already in the last one. I will continue that discussion in Chapter 12, considering the possible efficacy of safeguards in more detail.

In discussing the risks of legalization I will avoid talk about 'slippery slopes'. The term is used for some forms of argument that have little in common and that can better be identified by descriptively more precise terms. In addition, it is the essence of the metaphor of a slippery slope to suggest a downward slide along several stations on the slope, but some of the most prominent arguments usually referred to by that name, only suggests that if you accept the legalization of the kind of physician assistance that is presently under discussion, you are committed to accept another form that is supposed to be obviously unacceptable. There is no further downhill movement involved. I have already discussed an argument of this type in the last chapter.

The metaphor is most at home when it points out that, for every set of cases between which we would want to draw a line, a series of intermediate cases can be identified that are too close to each other to allow

DOI: 10.4324/9781003281115-14

drawing that line.[1] But even in such cases an additional weakness of the metaphor is that it looks in one direction only: the natural movement along a slope is downwards. We should, however, not only look at the risks implied in legalization but also consider the risks involved in failing to legalize. A balance sheet is incomplete if it only registers costs. That legalization involves risks is a truism: every option that people acquire creates its own opportunities for abuse and mistake.[2] We have to estimate these costs, preferably on the basis of empirical evidence, not mere speculation, and to weigh them against the costs of foreclosing that option altogether, or restricting it, including the risks involved in the existence of an underground practice, as I described these risks at the end of the last chapter.

In Chapter 5 I made a distinction between cases in which a doctor participates in the joint action of ending a patient's life and cases in which a doctor merely provides a patient with access to lethal drugs. Cases of the first kind include euthanasia – ending someone's life on his explicit request – and the kind of assisted suicide in which the doctor takes final responsibility for the effective, painless and safe character of the joint action. For the purposes of this chapter, however, these distinctions are largely irrelevant: regimes that legalize any of these kinds of cases may all run the risks of abuse and error that I discuss, although they may imply somewhat different means to address these risks. Because there is no term covering all kinds of cases that is nearly precise enough and 'euthanasia' covers the kind of cases that is supposed to exemplify the risks most clearly, I will in this chapter continue to use that term. But the issues that I will discuss also concern regulatory regimes of the Oregon type that merely provide access to lethal drugs.

A final remark before we start. Every legal option creates its own possibilities of error and abuse, and no system of safeguards can guarantee that these will always be discovered and properly dealt with. As I said, that is a truism. A substantial part of the literature discusses individual cases,[3] but I will not do so, because even if it would be undisputable that a case exemplifies abuse or error of some kind – it seldom is – that only confirms the truism. Discussion of cases can be interesting as a way to sharpen our understanding of the meaning of a rule, but it is next to irrelevant in assessing the implementation of the rule.

1 See den Hartogh 2009 for an evaluation of arguments of that type, concluding that determinacy may have a value in law, even though requiring it in ethics would be fallacious.

2 This insight is essential to one type of theodicy, perhaps first proposed by Irenaeus, that appeals to human free will in order to explain evil.

3 See for example footnote 49.

11.2 Abuse

One of the most important concerns that we have to consider is that if we legalize euthanasia under any conditions, we necessarily open the door to killings that we don't want to allow. This is sometimes argued to be the unavoidable consequence of legalization in any jurisdiction.[4] But it is also often argued that a permissive law will be more susceptible to abuse in some countries than in others.[5] The USA is often mentioned as the prime example. In this section and the next one I will focus on such countries because they present us with the hardest case.

Abuse is often predicted with respect to one particular group of people considered to be vulnerable: women, Afro-Americans, the disabled, the poor, the elderly.[6] But the general form of the objection holds across the board: it is argued that legalization will inevitably create unacceptable risks to vulnerable people. Members of these groups already receive less treatment than indicated for their medical condition, as well as less sophisticated kinds of treatment (but more amputations). They also receive less adequate pain relief. If euthanasia is legalized, so the objection continues, the law may state conditions of due care, but that will be empty talk: we cannot trust doctors and hospitals to respect them any more than we can at present trust them to give vulnerable patients the treatment and palliative care that they are already entitled to.

In order to evaluate this claim we have to distinguish between several possible scenarios. In the first scenario, to be discussed in this section, the risk is that patients are 'euthanized' who have not made a request for euthanasia at all, or not a truly voluntary one. The idea is that, if doctors or hospitals have to care for dying patients knowing that they will not be able to recover the costs of that care, either from the patients, their insurance schemes, Medicare or Medicaid, or any special fund for uninsured cases, they will be tempted to get rid of the burden by getting rid of the patient. They may even be tempted to make that decision in cases in which the patient can still be cured, but only by expensive forms of treatment. Now it is obvious that if patients are killed on purpose, that will always legally count as murder, and if the patients take their own lives having been coerced or manipulated to ask for 'assistance',

4 Kamisar 1958; Callahan, White 1996; Keown 2002; 2018; Gorsuch 2006.

5 Singer, Siegler 1990; Capron 1992; Arras 1997; Bok 1998, ch. 7; Emanuel 1999; Caplan et al. 2000; cf. Battin 1994, ch. 6.

6 Wolf 1996; Tong 2000; George 2007; Tomsons, Sherwin 2010 (women); King, Wolf 1998 (Afro-Americans); Bickenbach 1998; Siegel 1998; Coleman 2002; Golden, Zoanni 2010; Krahn 2010 (the disabled); Doerflinger 1989; Tuffrey-Wijne et al. 2018 (the elderly). The classical exposition of the general argument is New York State Taskforce 1994, ch. 6; cf. Cohn, Lynn 2002; Gorsuch 2006, 125ff; and the position statements of medical organisations quoted in Battin et al. 2007.

that will equally be conceived as a crime against life by the penal law in every jurisdiction.

So what is the problem? It is often suggested that any system of procedural safeguards a permissive law might institute will be a lame tiger, unable to prevent abuse, because it necessarily has to rely on self-reporting. And doctors who kill their patients for the reasons I mentioned cannot be expected to report their actions. But that, of course, is already true everywhere: it is true for any action that the agent himself understands to be a crime. No system of criminal justice relies on the criminals confessing their sins spontaneously. It follows that no procedures of prospective or retrospective review that would be instituted by any euthanasia law can be expected to catch the Harold Shipmans and Niels Högels, but only to promote a more careful practice among doctors who are already committed to minimum standards of professionalism. It cannot deal with intentional abuse, only with good faith error and, to some extent, negligence. That cannot be considered a weakness of the system.[7]

A remarkable characteristic of the fear of murderous doctors is its selectivity. This has often been observed.[8] Consider the decision to abstain from treatment. It is true that if we want to dispose of some person, we will often, with the necessary effort, be able to get into a position to kill him, but only rarely into a position to let him die. That may be one reason for the law to be more concerned about the first possibility than about the second one. But this general rule doesn't apply to doctors, and in particular not to doctors who care for dying patients. They will often be in a position to dispose of these patients by withholding or withdrawing life-sustaining treatment. It is a decision they already make in about 15–25% of all deaths.[9] Of course, when they have no good reason for this decision – the refusal of the patient, the disproportionate burdens of treatment, the futility of prolonging the patient's life in his present condition or the disproportionate costs of the treatment – that is criminal behaviour no less than killing the patient. It will, however, hardly ever be

7 As many critics suggest, e.g. Callahan, White 1996; Spaemann et al. 2015, 134; Montero 2017, 28; Keown 2018, ch. 21, quoting Griffiths 1998, 274–275 (and disputing Griffiths' retractation, Griffiths, Weyers, Adams 2008, 49, 209ff); Miller, Kim 2017. Doctors who either publicly violate the requirements of due care by way of protest, or want to test the readiness of a review committee to relax the rules, will also come within the purview of such committees.

8 Brock 1992; Orentlicher 1998, 306–307; Dworkin 1998, 66–70; Mayo, Gunderson 2002; Jackson 2004; Downie 2004, ch. 9; Battin 2005, 58–59; Young 2007, 187; Sumner 2011, 203–204; Canadian Supreme Court in *Carter v Canada*, 2015, SCC 5, [114]–[115]. Cantor 2004, 1812, rightly comments that 'manipulation of vulnerable patients is a potential problem accompanying any serious medical intervention for which informed consent is required', e.g. cessation of dialysis.

9 Van der Heide et al. 2003 (six European countries); Seale 2009 (England).

considered murder or manslaughter or even life-endangering negligence. Moreover, it will normally be easier for a doctor to appeal, lyingly, to any acceptable reason for abstainment than it is for him to claim, equally lyingly, that the patient has voluntarily requested euthanasia. That the suggested reason for abstainment does not really apply may be much less clear, even to members of the same medical team. And hardly anywhere in the world are there any procedural safeguards in place as regards withholding and withdrawing treatment.[10]

So we should expect people who fear that as a result of the legalization of euthanasia doctors will more easily kill their patients, to be genuinely alarmed by the possibilities these same doctors already have of letting them die.[11] And some of them, not many, are. But the remarkable fact is that they don't use these concerns as arguments for restricting people's powers to refuse life-saving treatment or to sign Do Not Resuscitate orders, or even for introducing procedural safeguards to protect patients from improper abstainment decisions. They only quote the possibility of such illegal decisions in order to underline the risks involved in the legalization of euthanasia.[12]

This is remarkable indeed, but what can we conclude from it? If opponents of the legalization of euthanasia aren't alarmed, perhaps they should be. Or perhaps they realize that, even though a threat of this kind to vulnerable people already exists, the greater danger is not that doctors wrongly stop treating patients, but rather that they don't stop when they should, thereby excessively prolonging the dying process. Similarly they may fear that aggressive policing of sedation practices would have a disastrous effect on palliative care. The selectivity of their fears may relativize their view of the possible risks of the legalization of euthanasia to some extent, but it does not refute it.

So let us confront their view head-on. If there is a danger of doctors killing non-paying patients, the danger already exists, and doctors can pursue their criminal aims in other, less risky ways. The danger can only be aggravated by a law permitting euthanasia, if such a law makes it easier for the killers to get away with their crimes, pretending their victims to have made voluntary requests.

It seems, however, that this particular risk can be contained by procedural safeguards, in particular by a requirement of independent consultation. If the patient hasn't made a choice for death or isn't really committed to that choice, it will be difficult to deceive an impartial and skilled observer, who is required to interview the patient extensively and in private and to report her findings. If the patient has decided on the

10 In Denmark an ethics panel is required to survey decisions to withdraw treatment.

11 Cook et al. 1995 report that the major determinants of decisions to withdraw care are highly idiosyncratic to the healthcare worker concerned.

12 See for example footnote 47.

basis of insufficient or biased information about his condition and prospects, the consultant will also be in a position to identify such defects.

The independency of the consultant is essential: she should not have any business, family or friendship relation with the doctor who asks for the consultation. It is a major weakness of many existing regulatory models that they don't require the consultant to be independent.[13] The ideal way to guarantee independence would be to institute a scheme like the Dutch SCEN-system: doctors who volunteer to be available for consultation for some period according to a fixed schedule.[14] In that case no doctor has any influence on the selection of the consultant. The guarantee can be strengthened by incorporating the system into the regulatory structure prescribed by the law. This has recently been done in New Zealand.[15]

Isn't this simply another lame tiger? Any doctor who wants to go ahead without consultation can do so. Actually, however, we have to distinguish between two procedures. The doctor may decide to end the patient's life by using an overdose of opioids or benzodiazepines. The risk of abuse of this procedure is substantial, but this is what some doctors already do in prohibiting jurisdictions.[16] Even in permissive countries they will not be tempted to pretend to be involved in euthanasia, because it will be less risky to pretend to be involved in symptom management. Hence legalizing euthanasia would not create any new risks. The doctor

13 Rightly criticized by Keown 2002, 172; 2018, 353; Gorsuch 2006, 117. Of the North American laws only the Californian and the Canadian law require independence. The Canadian law clearly states what 'independence' means. Colorado's End-of-Life Options Act doesn't require the consultant to check the voluntariness of the request; New Mexico's Act requires him only to report on the existence of terminal illness, the patient's capacity and his ability to self-administer drugs. Of the Australasian laws only the laws of New Zealand and Tasmania require and define independence, but in New Zealand the consultant need not confirm the voluntariness of the request. The Belgian euthanasia law doesn't normally require the consultant to assess the voluntary and well-considered character of the patient's request, only in cases in which a second consultation is required, Adams 2008, 321; cf. Keown 2018, 293. According to Montana's judge-made law consultation is not mandatory; in Switzerland it is not a legal requirement. The rules of the Swiss Academy of Medical Sciences require the doctor's judgement to be verified by 'an independent third party who need not be a physician'.

14 SCEN (Support and Consultation on Euthanasia in the Netherlands) is an initiative of the Royal Dutch Society of Medicine (KNMG), and almost all consultants are by now provided by the network, but doctors are legally free to invite others. The Flemish LEIF and its Wallonian counterpart Médecins EOL are societies with broader aims and a more pronounced, autonomy-oriented ideology. Consultants from these societies are invited in about 25% of all cases.

15 According to the *End of Life Choice Act* 2019, article 25, a SCENZ-group (Support and Consultation for End of Life in New Zealand) is established that maintains a list of medical practititioners willing to act as independent consultants. The attending medical practitioner must ask the SCENZ-group for the name of a consultant from this list. Some of the Australian laws have similar arrangements.

16 See Chapter 10, at footnote 77.

may also decide to use barbiturates or muscle relaxants, although in that case it is evident that she isn't involved in symptom management. But the risk of abuse of this kind can be minimized, on the example of the Oregon law, requiring pharmacists to report all prescriptions of this kind that they receive to a reviewing body. If this requirement is made, it will be too risky for doctors to go ahead without consultation.[17]

These days doctors rarely work fully independently of other healthcare providers. That fact will also limit their options to skip the consultation and nevertheless pretend to act on the patient's voluntary request. Blanket prohibitions of euthanasia are at present already mainly maintained by mechanisms of informal control, often with harmful effects on palliative care,[18] rather than by active investigation by policemen or inspectors.[19]

The requirement of independent consultation will only serve its aim if the consultants don't do sloppy work. In Section 12.4, I will discuss whether there is anything we can do to promote the quality of their work. At the very least that quality has to be monitored and evaluated.

In this section I have argued that legalizing euthanasia under some conditions neither excludes nor increases the already existing risks of criminal violations of the law, provided the conditions include a requirement of independent consultation that is properly implemented in practice. By creating a more open climate of communication about end-of-life decisions, both within medical teams and between doctors, nurses, patients and families, legalization may even decrease those risks.

11.3 The grey zone between abuse and error

But perhaps undue influence will be exerted on patients from vulnerable groups in more subtle ways. The doctor may sincerely or half-sincerely believe that euthanasia is the best option for her patient, even though she wouldn't have thought that in the case of a better-educated middle-class patient in the same condition, and that opinion may colour the way in which she informs the patient, even though that information is accurate as regards the facts. And the consultant may not be able to identify that kind of bias, or even share the underlying discriminatory attitude. The doctor may in that case even recommend a choice for death, and many patients are still in the habit of doing what the doctor

17 Lewy 2011, 141.

18 According to Goldstein et al. 2012 over half of their respondent American physicians had had an experience in the last five years in which a patient's family or another healthcare professional had characterised palliative treatments as being euthanasia or murder.

19 The doctor's action in the Tuitjenhorn case (Chapter 10, footnote 51) was reported by a student assistant.

recommends.[20] It will be hard to determine in particular cases whether influence of that kind really undermines the voluntary character of the request, but it is to be deplored anyway.[21]

If such effects were fairly widespread, you would expect the fact to show up in a disproportionate representation of the victims in the number of deaths from euthanasia. But that is not what the available data tell us. Men are slightly overrepresented,[22] the better-educated, well-housed and well-to-do more clearly are. Afro-Americans, immigrants and members of other minority-groups, residents of institutions, the poor and even the elderly are underrepresented. So, if there is any bias, it 'favours' the privileged.[23]

That is not really surprising. Requests for euthanasia are mostly motivated by losses of meaning, autonomy, independence and dignity: the typical concerns of the higher educated. Members of underprivileged groups on the other hand often deeply distrust all offers of palliative care and demand aggressive treatment until the very end. In order to convince your doctor and her consultant that your choice is voluntary and well considered, and your suffering is unbearable and without prospect of improvement, you'd better be fairly articulate.[24] The less educated often know so little about the legal options that they will not take the initiative of even asking for information, and many hospices don't allow doctors to offer information on their own initiative.[25] A final obstacle for the poor in the USA is the extremely high cost of the drug most often used for suicide-on-prescription, Secobarbital. The fact that the underprivileged are less, rather than more, likely to make a request for euthanasia or get it granted surely is a matter of grave concern.[26] (If only for that reason prohibiting doctors to broach the subject is unfortunate because it buttresses inequality.[27]) But unless the correct theory of justice justifies levelling down, it is hardly an argument against legalization.

20 New York State Taskforce 1994, 122.
21 New York State Taskforce 1994, ch. 6.
22 In Switzerland women are, Steck et al. 2014, 2018.
23 Battin et al., 2007 (Oregon, Belgium and the Netherlands); Chambaere et al. 2013; Dierickx et al. 2015 (Flanders); Loggers et al. 2013 (Washington); Steck et al. 2014; 2018 (Switzerland); Hedberg, New 2017 (Oregon); Buchbinder 2018 (Vermont); Downar et al. 2020 (Ontario); Emanuel et al. 2016. The *Annual Reports* about the American *Death with Dignity* and *End-of-Life Choice* acts give information about sex, age, race, marital status, education and type of insurance of requesters, e.g. Oregon Health Authority 2020, Table I. I agree with Lemmens 2018, 514, that special studies about psychiatric and demented patients and patients suffering from a cumulation of old-age ailments would be welcome.
24 86.3% of the requests for euthanasia from patients with a college or university education had been granted in Flanders 2013, 69.5% of patients with only primary education. Dierickx et al. 2015.
25 Buchbinder 2018.
26 Sumner 2011, 183; Buchbinder 2018.
27 *End-of-Life Choice Act* New Zealand, Art. 10. Cf. Chapter 16 at footnote 75.

It could be objected that the available evidence doesn't prove much, for both under- and overrepresentation of vulnerable groups could be due to other factors. Patterns of morbidity and mortality could be different in those groups, leading to lower or greater incidence of extreme suffering.[28] People from these groups could subscribe to different values, they might not mind being dependent on the care of others, be less concerned about being a burden, or have different conceptions of dignity. Hence, if the percentage of people from some group asking for and receiving euthanasia would not deviate from the average, that could still tend to confirm, rather than disconfirm, the existence of undue pressure on that group, if we took all relevant facts into account.[29] This is true, and an invitation for further research. But it is equally true that the available data already could easily have suggested undue pressure but don't. The least we can say, therefore, is that the prediction that the legalization of euthanasia would necessarily put vulnerable groups at risk has until now not been confirmed by any evidence.

The relevance of the available evidence has also been challenged by the suggestion that we should not identify the 'vulnerable' by reference to sex, age, race, education or socio-economic status.[30] Other characteristics such as emotional state, response to loss, personality type and the sense of being a burden to others, would be more relevant. This argument is puzzling. The personal characteristics that are mentioned are the characteristics that we already know to dispose people to develop death wishes. Death wishes derive from people's stable conceptions of a (relatively) good death (Sections 2.1 and 2.2), in combination with unfavourable conditions. The claim that the availability of (legal or illegal) euthanasia 'threatens' people who have such conceptions and live in such conditions doesn't add anything to that factual insight except a negative valuation. That people who by their conception of a good death are predisposed to develop a death wish under certain conditions are more exposed to undue pressure for requesting euthanasia when these conditions (seem to) arise is also a truism.

For the same reasons it is problematic when people are considered 'vulnerable' for living alone, being divorced or having no children.[31] Clearly these circumstances may be relevant from the point of view of their own conception of a good life and hence of a good death.

28 Chambaere et al. 2013 found that the initially strong correlation between the prevalence of euthanasia and higher education largely disappeared when their data were adjusted for cause of death. But that result doesn't confirm the hypothesis of undue influence on the lower educated either.

29 Materstvedt 2003.

30 Finlay, George 2011, approvingly quoted by the Irish High Court in *Fleming v Ireland* (2013), IEHC 2 [61]: suffering and illness are 'vulnerabilities'.

31 Steck et al. 2014, 2018.

Perhaps, however, we should understand vulnerability in a different way. Perhaps the vulnerable are driven to a choice for death, not by misinformation and undue pressure from physicians and others, but because of their own attitudes. The problem may arise, or at least be exacerbated, because they tend to internalize a negative image of themselves that is dominant in society and, as a result, to make a mistakenly negative assessment of the value of their own lives.[32] Yes, death wishes derive from stable personal values, but these values are themselves the product of the internalization of malicious social influences.

Some of the strongest opposition against legalization proposals comes from *Not Dead Yet* (founded 1996) and other disability rights groups, both in the USA and elsewhere. They point out, correctly, that the main motives for requesting euthanasia are not pain and other physical symptoms but losses of meaning, autonomy, independence and dignity, all caused by the loss of physical and mental capacities, hence by disabilities (Section 2.2). They suggest that the negative evaluation of these losses is the result of 'fear, bias and prejudice against disability',[33] and that these same attitudes will be expressed and reinforced by legalizing euthanasia. The really vulnerable are the disabled, and it is because of widespread discriminatory attitudes to them that their lives are threatened by offering them the legal option of euthanasia, for their own conceptions of the good death derive from these attitudes and therefore ultimately also from 'fear, bias and prejudice'. And these conceptions will predispose them to make use of the new option of having their lives ended, if that option is offered to them.

As we know from other contexts in the twentieth century, we should be wary of such appeals to the false consciousness of the supposedly oppressed. The assumption is hard to falsify, may be used to justify extremely paternalistic measures or abuse of power, may perpetuate a stereotype and can even become self-fulfilling.[34] For such reasons 'force them to be free' is not an attractive model of emancipation.

But couldn't the assumption be true, or true enough? It seems plausible that almost every person with a death wish will be substantially limited in his activities because of physical or mental impairments (Section 14.2). But if you have a death wish because you are disabled in this sense, that doesn't mean that you claim every disabled person to be better off dead.[35] Suppose

32 Doerflinger 1989; Wolf 1996; King and Wolf 1998; Bickenbach 1998; Bok 1998, ch. 7; Tong 2000. Bickenbach is right in identifying this as a distinct sub-type of the argument that legalization threatens the vulnerable.

33 Golden, Zoanni 2010. It is, by the way, arbitrary not to consider being prone to physical discomfort a 'disability' in this sense.

34 Batavia 1997; Silvers 1998; Sumner 2011, 184.

35 Sumner 2011, 184. "If society endorses the right of a person to seek physician assistance to end his or her life because of increasing loss of functional autonomy, what does that say about how our society values the lives of people who live with comparable limitations every day of their lives for years on end?", Krahn 2010. The answer is: nothing.

you lose your eyesight at the age of 95, when you are bedridden and have no other way to spend your days than by reading, looking at the television and at your garden. If you believe that the loss is a catastrophe for you, you don't thereby imply that the philosopher Brentano was wrong when he thanked God for his blindness because that enabled him to concentrate on his inner life. Such losses have a different meaning and (personal) value for people, depending on their own basic values and the history of their life. Some people with high spinal cord injury persistently want to end their lives, others don't. A person from the first group doesn't necessarily think that the people from the second group are mistaken in valuing their own lives. It would not even be inconsistent for him to envy them.

In a powerful blog 'Bad Cripple' Bill Peace lists the reasons why people in Washington ask to be assisted in ending their lives: loss of the ability to engage in enjoyable activities, lack of autonomy and of control over bodily functions, being a burden to others, a history of gut-wrenching pain. He comments that all these reasons apply to him. "Yet here I sit at my desk and cannot help but be perplexed. Why does my crippled body command so little respect? Why is my existence so easily called into question?"[36] If you are able to cope with such adverse circumstances, that is to be admired rather than pitied (Section 2.4). But why should I be committed to deny this if, as a result of my personality, my biography and my personal values, I prefer to be dead rather than to live in such circumstances? I don't have to believe that this must be true for everyone. And I most certainly don't have to believe that people in my condition are somehow inferior, not entitled to equal concern and respect. People who explain why they are suffering to such an extent that they want to end their lives don't sit in judgement about anyone else.

It is true, as we have seen in Sections 2.1 and 2.2, that their motivations mostly derive from conceptions of the good death that are widely shared and perfectly intelligible. These death wishes are not simply the product of malign social influences (Section 14.4). But that doesn't mean that such death wishes imply general value judgements about particular conditions, let alone about some people's existence. It is not even to say that these death wishes, however intelligible, are beyond criticism (Section 2.4). But such criticism is a matter of personal morality: it isn't the proper business of either the state or the medical profession to give patients points for correct valuations and to draw paternalistic or moralistic conclusions from the score. A doctor should not say to a patient who asks for euthanasia because he is completely dependent on the care of strangers, even for going to the toilet, that this is an unacceptable motive that disqualifies his request. Valuing independence, even if it amounts to overrating it, may be a commitment that has shaped his life (Sections 8.4 and 8.5).

36 Quoted from Behuniak 2011.

Even if death wishes that are motivated by the loss of meaning, of independence, of 'dignity' and of autonomy are a universal human phenomenon, the actual wishes are also determined by a social context that is itself the cumulative outcome of a multitude of individual decisions made in similar circumstances[37] (Section 16.6). I don't deny that. When is suffering unbearable, when does your appearance lack dignity? Views about these matters change, and the process of change is unavoidably influenced by stereotype and prejudice. We should counteract these influences as best we can. But we shouldn't counteract them by using state power to block personal choices that people could also make for entirely respectable reasons.

11.4 The real threat to the vulnerable

Many arguments against the legalization of euthanasia that start from a concern for vulnerable groups suffer from another defect. Consider the case of a doctor who has no criminal intent or discriminatory attitude herself. However, she really has no choice but to inform you that, yes, there is a form of palliative care that might relieve your suffering (or even a form of treatment that might cure you), but it is unavailable to you for reasons of cost. There is no place for you in the nursing home or the hospice that you can pay for or that will be paid for you from public pockets. And, yes, the doctor understands that, as a result, you hardly have any option but to choose death, and she is willing to help you, provided an independent consultant will agree with that decision. Let us suppose that this doctor is not only honest but also right: the care or the treatment that you need is really beyond your means. And let us suppose, what is not necessarily the case, that this is the result of unjust social arrangements.[38]

But how exactly is this supposed to be a reason against the legalization of euthanasia? That is rarely spelled out. The claim is that the vulnerable group is 'threatened', not only by the unjust arrangements but, in addition, by the availability of euthanasia as a legal option. But if the members of that group still have a preferable alternative, the mere availability of that option is not a threat to them, and if they really have no such alternative, the availability of the option is a blessing rather than a threat. By taking away that option we do not help them to escape their miserable condition but only deny them the one way out they still have.

Or suppose that most death wishes really are the product of the internalization of discriminatory values. In that case the argument against legalization of euthanasia still needs to be completed. Is it

37 De Dijn 2016.
38 New York State Taskforce 1994, 83–84; Singer, Siegler 1990; Caplan et al. 2000.

enough to force an alternative that is objectively preferable to euthanasia on the victims of oppression, even if, as a result of that oppression, they are presently unable to endorse it as a better alternative? If not, will we be able in the remaining time of their lives to re-educate them about the true value of their lives? Are we sure enough that at least most of them will then opt for continuing life? Leaving people to a fate that they, however mistakenly, consider being worse than death, may not lead them to re-evaluate that fate. In that case trying to undo the effects of false consciousness is not even paternalistic but cruel, because it only creates additional burdens for the people suffering from that condition.

The argument could also be completed in a different way, also well known from marxist ideology. Even if it would be best for the victims of an unjust social arrangement individually to receive the option to end their lives, a law that gives them that option will lessen the urgency of doing what is needed to eliminate the injustice. It creates disincentives for addressing the injustice directly, counteracting discriminatory attitudes or providing adequate treatment and palliative care for everyone.

It is doubtful whether this could be a significant effect, if only because the number of people who make use of an exit-option will probably always be relatively small, far below the number of people involved in decisions to abstain from treatment.[39] The most plausible suggestion of this kind is that a euthanasia law may reduce the political will to spend money on the development of palliative care, but there is no evidence confirming that suggestion as regards the existing permissive jurisdictions.[40] But even if it would be plausible that a significant effect of this kind exists in some country or state, the question remains whether we should counteract it by denying people the option of choosing death. Even if the vulnerable group they belong to might profit in the end, would it be fair to let them pay the price? Doing so would, like any other strategy of *Verelendung*, amount to using them as a mere means for dealing with a social problem.

On the evidence we have at present, in the jurisdictions that have by now for some time legalized euthanasia (or giving access to lethal drugs), members of vulnerable groups – properly so-called – do not appear to use that option more often than others. If they did, that might point to some very fundamental forms of injustice in existing social arrangements that would need to be addressed. But even then it would be doubtful whether maintaining or reintroducing a legal prohibition of euthanasia would be a proper way of addressing it.

39 Brock 1992.

40 On the Netherlands, Belgium, Luxembourg and Switzerland see Chambaere et al. 2011. On Oregon and Washington Emanuel et al. 2016.

11.5 Is the request really voluntary?

Requests for euthanasia should at least be truly voluntary and well-considered. That much is common ground. Are doctors always able reliably to ascertain whether they are? One possible reason for doubt is that 'voluntary' and 'well-considered' are open concepts that aren't precise enough to exclude problematic decisions.[41] It is true that such concepts cannot be mechanically applied and that there will always be borderline cases. That is one good reason to involve more than one person in decision-making. That there is a grey area, however, doesn't mean that in that area there is a hidden truth that we are prone to miss. Rather the application of the concepts in that area is indeterminate. If competent judges cannot arrive at a reasonable agreement, probably we don't err in deciding either way. This is a common situation. We have to assess the quality of consent in all areas of medicine, and, indeed, in many other areas of social interaction, including market transactions. There is nothing exceptional about this particular assessment.[42] Many of the decisions for which consent is required are as momentous and irreversible as the decision to end a patient's life or give him access to means to end it himself.

However, it is far from inconceivable, if euthanasia is legalized, that a doctor thinks he can proceed because the patient's request is voluntary, whereas as a matter of fact, it isn't. This may occur because the doctor has been negligent in forming his judgement, giving the matter insufficient time and thought, or because he is lacking in certain relevant competences, being, for example, too credulous. But it may also occur, even though the doctor has been maximally diligent and competent.

If the request is insufficiently voluntary, it will usually be the family, close friends or some non-professional caretaker whom we have to blame. Occasionally the request may be the outcome of a mutually recognized open process of coercion, but it is much more probable that it is the outcome of some more or less subtle form of manipulation, of which either the manipulator or the manipulated patient, or both, may only be dimly aware, or not at all. The manipulator may, for example, make the patient feel that he stands in the way of other people's happiness.[43]

This is an example of the more general phenomenon that by adding a new option to a person's menu of choices you can actually decrease rather

41 E.g., Keown 2018, 166–168. For further comments see Section 12.9.

42 According to Callahan, White 1996, 42, "the nature of the physician-patient relationship itself militates against voluntariness and may inherently involve undue influence even in the best of circumstances". If this would be true, it could hardly be a specific argument against allowing any particular medical decision.

43 Kamisar 1958, 1991; Marquis 1998; Bickenbach 1998; Spaemann et al. 2015, 70, 130–134, and many others.

than increase her freedom.[44] This includes cases in which the person is challenged to defend herself for not taking the option. Blocking an option might also increase a person's freedom because it protects her against her own weakness of will.[45] A blanket prohibition should then be interpreted as a form of collective self-binding. But this presupposes that the option opened by permissive legislation is a bad one for everyone or at least the majority, otherwise the prohibition protects you against one danger but exposes others (or in other circumstances perhaps even you) to another one. So let us focus on the possibility of coercion and manipulation.

That the coercing or manipulating party knows what she is doing is most probable in a case in which it is the inheritance of the patient that she is after. It is only under extremely rare circumstances that this will be the case when the patient is in the last stage of the dying process. Usually even the most greedy heir will be able to wait some more days or weeks. It is most probable when the patient is not suffering from a lethal illness at all, or even if he will die of his present illness in the end, that end may still be years ahead. The cases that, in the absence of more specific evidence, we have the most reason to worry about are cases in which the burdens of care – either the financial burdens or the direct burdens of caregiving – weigh heavily on the caretaking person but still are such that she may reasonably be expected to go on bearing them.[46] She may then hope for her task coming to an end, and more or less consciously, be motivated by that hope to hint at the possibility of a choice for death.[47] "The most successful form of manipulation is to lead a person to think that someone else's idea is actually his or her own, or to nudge that person's already existing ambivalence one way or the other".[48]

Although there is a grey zone between influencing and manipulating someone, we should be clear that there is a distinction. Almost all decisions people make are the outcome of interaction with others and there is nothing

44 Kamisar 1991; New York State Taskforce 1994, 69; Marquis 1998; Bickenbach 1998; Velleman 1992, 2015, ch. 2. For the general point see Schelling 1960, 22ff.

45 "The Bill offers no comfort to me. It frightens me because, in periods of greatest difficulty, I know that I might be tempted to use it. It only adds to the burdens and challenges which life holds for me". Baroness Campbell of Surbiton, opposing Lord Falconer's Bill in the House of Lord, 18 July 2014, quoted from *The Independent.*

46 GPs judged family carers of 28% (Belgium), 30% (the Netherlands), 35% (Spain) and 71% (Italy) of patients at the end of life to be physically or emotionally overburdenend. For 8% (Spain), 14% (Belgium), 36% (the Netherlands) and 43% (Italy) of such patients, GPs reported difficulties in covering care-related costs, Pivodic et al. 2014. Cf. Hardwig 2013, 115, for some details about the burdens involved in family caregiving in the USA.

47 New York State Taskforce 1994, 125. Covinsky et al. 1996 show that burdened family members are more ready to refuse life-sustaining treatment for their dying relatives. Quoted by Emanuel 1999, 637, who, characteristically, concludes that euthanasia should be forbidden, not that abstainment decisions should be better controlled.

48 Callahan, White 1996, 7.

wrong with that. As long as the resulting decision is such that the deciding person can consider it as her own after due reflection, that will normally, disregarding cases of deception about the relevant facts and brainwashing, be enough to exclude the possibility of manipulation. This may be true even if the person with whom he has been interacting has a somewhat overbearing personality.[49] It is not falsified either by the fact that people's motives are very often mixed ones, for example consisting of a blend of compassion and self-interest, and not fully transparent, even to themselves.

Although we should recognize that a well-considered choice for death will hardly ever be made without any trace of ambivalence, a problematic and therefore suspect lack of identification with that choice should be detectable, both by a doctor, who spends sufficient time interviewing the patient in private about her motives, and by an experienced consultant, required to speak with the patient under four eyes.[50] This will in particular be true if the doctor already knows the patient and his family fairly well before being confronted with a request for euthanasia, and if the consultant, on the other hand, has sufficient emotional distance from the patient and her family to avoid the risk of collusion. That is the case in the Netherlands and Flanders where family doctors are involved in most euthanasia cases, and many consultants are selected by the random mechanism of SCEN and LEIF.[51] Many other healthcare systems don't have family doctors in this particular role, but they could at least require extensive and repeated interviewing and independent consultation. In addition they might consider giving a legal role to social workers who would have to talk with both the patients and their families.

Still it is hard to estimate the probability of error in this area, and to calibrate one's estimation. We have no data that are of any help from the countries in which worries about this possibility seem to be the main reason for turning down legalization proposals, and only some data from the countries in which legal options exist and substantial numbers of people make use of them. Doctors occasionally refuse a request because they are not convinced that it has been voluntarily made, and consultants occasionally advice to refuse it for that reason, but this happens only rarely.[52] It may,

49 As the daughter of Kate Cheney had, a much discussed case from Oregon, see Foley, Hendin 2002, 156–158; Goodwin 2004, 187–188; Steinbock 2005; Lindsay 2009.

50 See for missing or defective requirements about consultation footnote 13.

51 Although there is some evidence of doctors handpicking consultants in Flanders, see Section 12.4.

52 In the Netherlands doctors reported to have refused a patient's request for this reason in 5% of the cases in 2005, in 0% (GPs 1%) in 2010, van der Heide et al. 2012, 18. During the period 2012–2017 SCEN-consultants annually found a lack of voluntariness in 1.6–16.7% of the last cases in which they concluded that not all requirements of due care had been satisfied, SCEN 2017, table 4.5. In Flanders 1.3% of all requests had been refused in 2007 because the doctor didn't consider the request to be sufficiently voluntary, 0% in 2013, Dierickx et al. 2015.

however, be that doctors sometimes don't register an explicit request as such if they have any doubt about its voluntary character.

It is of course possible that Dutch and Flemish doctors are generally too naïve, but it strains credulity to suggest that they miss the large number of cases of undue pressure that, for example, the opponents of legalization proposals in the UK predict.[53] If pressure from relatives and caregivers would be a phenomenon that occurred far more often than it is observed by doctors and consultants, one would also expect this to become a scandal in the press or the social media every now and then, or at least to cause some unrest in a limited circle of people that might then spread in the way of circles in a pond. In recent years that has regularly happened in euthanasia cases involving psychiatric patients or patients in an advanced stage of dementia who have requested euthanasia in an advance directive.[54] This strongly contrasts with the large majority of euthanasia cases that involve patients in the end stage of a lethal illness. None of these cases draw out any concerns in the media. As a result there seems to be virtually no fear of undue pressure under the general population in either Belgium or the Netherlands.[55] Old ladies carrying tattoos saying 'don't euthanize me' only walk around in the American press. A further sign of trust is that even the 5% of Dutch people who are still categorically opposed to legalization tend to believe that the euthanasia law does a good job in regulating the practice they disapprove of.[56] Overall 98% of people who had experience with euthanasia in their surroundings have a favourable attitude towards the practice.

Trust is a precious social capital. It would be quite mistaken to suggest that, because there is so little evidence of undue pressure, we could relax procedural requirements aiming at preventing it. There is a global movement to identify lethal drugs or other means of ending one's life in a humane way that would, as so many violent means of ending one's life already are, become universally available to everyone beyond the power of the state to regulate that availability.[57] I am inclined to believe,

53 See e.g. Butler-Sloss et al. 2010.

54 Cf. the three Belgian cases reported in Chapter 12, at footnotes 99 and 100.

55 Montero 2017 suggests the contrary as regards Belgium, but without citing any evidence.

56 Van Delden et al. 2011, 54. Cf. Moonen, Kloosterman 2019: 8% opposed under all circumstances, almost all for religious reasons (42% of Muslims).

57 See the website of Exit International. A Dutch initiative to make sodium azide available to members of the Cooperative Last Will was stopped in 2019 when the Public Prosecution Office announced a criminal investigation of the activities of the Cooperative's board. In 2021 the Office started investigating activities of the president of the board and several other members of the Cooperative suspected of having assisted people in acquiring the drug or of selling it to them. By now the drug is already regularly used for committing suicide, even though it has turned out in some reported cases not to provide a humane death. Several cases have also been reported of use by people with probably impaired decisional capacity.

admittedly on mere speculative grounds, that such initiatives seriously underrate the possibilities of abuse of such means, in particular by overburdened care-providers. But the main point is that trying this out means gambling with people's lives and public trust. At the same time we have at present no reason to believe that the regulatory systems in permissive jurisdictions miss out on large numbers of cases of abuse. People who claim that they do owe us more than mere speculation to substantiate that claim, for some of these systems have functioned for several decades by now and, for all we know, functioned well, at least in this respect.

We should keep in mind that, if euthanasia is forbidden, that doesn't mean that doctors will not use procedures aimed at hastening death, for example by providing large overdoses of morphine or sedatives or by sedating the patient and withholding fluids (Section 7.3). Nor does it mean that patients will not end their own lives by using lethal drugs they have somehow collected or procured from abroad. By legalizing some kind of involvement of physicians and requiring independent consultation, at least for a part of these practices, a check on the voluntariness of the decision is introduced that is now missing in prohibitive jurisdictions.[58] If there is a legal option, most doctors and most patients will prefer to make use of it. That is why John Griffiths claimed that we should understand the Dutch legal regime to be a way of climbing up, rather than sliding down the slippery slope.[59]

11.6 Is the request really well-considered?[60]

Oregon's *Death with Dignity Act* requires the patient to be 'able to make and communicate healthcare decisions', as do other similar North American laws.[61] (Is it really a 'healthcare decision' to request lethal drugs?) The Dutch and Belgian euthanasia laws require the doctor to verify that the patient's decision is well-considered. These requirements are not identical. Decision-making capacity or competence is a set of abilities needed for making decisions regarding one's own life: the ability to distinguish between the alternatives at hand, to understand the major relevant consequences of each of those choices, to take the probability of their occurrence into account in some rough-and-ready way, to evaluate those consequences in view of one's own values and to actually make the decision recommended by this

58 It is therefore remarkable that many opponents of legalization in the UK (e.g. Butler-Sloss et al. 2010) support the present prosecution policy as regards suicide assistance (Chapter 5, footnote 12). That policy doesn't require any independent professional check of voluntariness.

59 Griffiths 2001; cf. Griffiths, Weyers, Adams 2008, 514–520.

60 This section relies for parts of the argument and some formulations on den Hartogh 2016b, Section 1.

61 In addition the DWDA requires that the patient's decision should be based on an appreciation of the relevant facts.

evaluation. People have the required cognitive and affective capacities to a greater or lesser degree. Capacity is therefore a concept that allows for degrees; the level of someone's capacity can be marked on a scale.

The decision that the Oregon act requires a doctor to make, however, is a binary one: whether the patient has the relevant capacities to a sufficient degree to confer authority to his decision, yes or no. It is generally agreed that capacity is a task-related concept. The question is whether the patient has sufficient capacity (in the scalar sense) to make decisions of a certain kind: 'healthcare decisions'. But why should it be decisive that you have sufficient abilities to perform a task of a certain standard type, if the particular (token) task you have to execute differs from others of that type in precisely the one respect which explains why you bungle the task?[62] For this reason it seems preferable to require, with the Benelux laws, that the patient exercises his relevant capacities to a satisfactory degree in the present case. That the request is well-considered can only be established in a series of conversations, in which the doctor verifies whether the patient takes the relevant information about his present and future condition into account, and the patient explains, in terms of his own conception of a good death, why that information motivates him to want his life to end. It is not enough to follow a standard procedure for establishing informed consent.

If the doctor's judgement as regards this particular requirement has been checked by an independent colleague, are there still reasons to suspect that the judgement is often incorrect? The main reason for doubt is the following. Any decision to end one's own life, and hence any request for being assisted in enacting that decision, can be the product of depression. GPs and other doctors who have not specialized in psychiatry have little expertise in recognizing depression. Even psychiatrists who are of all physicians best trained in capacity assessment consider their ability to do so mediocre.[63] We should therefore not leave capacity assessments to anyone less qualified.[64]

62 Wijsbek 2000. Instruments for measuring decision-making capacity like the MacCAT therefore rightly focus on the particular decision to be made.

63 Ganzini et al. 2000.

64 Quill, Cassel, Meier 1992; Breitbart et al. 2000; Ganzini et al. 2000; Chochinov, Schwartz 2002; Lewy 2011, 144–145. Psychiatric assessment of competence was mandatory in the *Rights of the Terminally Ill Act* that legalized euthanasia in the Australian Northwestern Territories in 1996. Some medical centres in Washington and California have made a mental health assessment by a psychiatrist mandatory, Bourgeois et al. 2018. Studies of the prevalence of depression in patients requesting or receiving euthanasia include Chochinov et al. 1995 (59% of patients with a strong death wish); Meier et al. 1998 (19% of patients who received a prescription for a lethal dose and 39% of patients who received a lethal injection); van der Lee 2005; Ganzini, Goy, Dobscha 2008b (26% of requests). Levene, Parker 2011 provide an excellent survey, reporting an 8–47% prevalence of depressive symptoms among patients requesting, 2–17% prevalence among patients receiving euthanasia. Underdiagnosis of depression is a well-known phenomenon, Passik et al. 1998; but overdiagnosis is also common, Aragonès, Piñol, Labad 2006 (26.5%).

How should we evaluate this argument? It is common to consider depression an illness that causes people to be unduly pessimistic, as cancer may cause them pain, cachexia or dyspnoea, and thereby possibly to undermine their decisional capacity. But to call someone 'depressed' is a description on the level of symptoms, not of causes. As the concept is now standardly being used, in particular in the *DSM*, it identifies a family of 'symptoms' (a 'syndrome') that invites a limited set of medical interventions. A patient doesn't need to have all the symptoms; two patients can even both be diagnosed as having a 'major depressive disorder' who have only one symptom in common. It isn't claimed that depressive states all have the same, unknown, biological causes or that they correspond to a limited set of identical anatomical states, in particular of the brain. Indeed, we have strong reasons to believe that they don't.[65] Hence the diagnosis by itself doesn't provide us with any causal information.

It has, moreover, an irreducibly normative aspect. Though people often use 'depressive' carelessly as a synonym of 'desolate' – basically suggesting that the world can never be such that it entitles you to be gloomy – the term, properly used, implicates both that the depressive person's emotions are inappropriately negative (or flat), and that this is part of a general disposition of responding to states of the world in an unduly negative (or uninterested) way. People suffering from bipolar disorder may be in an elated mood that is similarly out of contact with reality.

Because 'depression' is a container-concept and the decision to classify someone as depressed is a normative one, we should sometimes be cautious about diagnostic claims identifying depression. As we have seen in Section 3.2, suicidality is itself usually taken to be one major 'symptom' of depression, reflecting the belief that, whatever your actual situation and future prospects, it can never be rational for you to prefer death. For that reason we should not take supposed findings about a strong correlation between requests for euthanasia and depression for granted uncritically: they may to a considerable extent be tautological. Of course there will be some correlation: if you are not concerned, you cannot be overconcerned either. But that is no reason to suspect every concern to be an overconcern.

An assessment of a person's capacity in the binary sense is also a normative judgement. It is by now commonly recognized that decisions are at least as much based on emotions as on reasoning, and assessments of decision-making capacity should therefore also consider whether a person's emotions are an appropriate response to her circumstances. Hence it doesn't come as a surprise that a psychiatrist's moral views about euthanasia influence her evaluation of the decisional capacity of

65 Kupfer 2002; Hyman 2007.

patients requesting it. For these reasons, as Linda Ganzini expressed the point, a psychiatric consultation is in danger of becoming a *de facto* ethics consultation.[66]

Which role, then, should the possibility of depression play in the assessment of the well-considered nature of a request for euthanasia? We should, as always, start from a presumption of competence: we assume that a person's decision-making capacity is sufficient for granting authority to the decision unless we have reason to suspect the contrary. This means that the very fact that someone wants to end his life is by itself not a reason to distrust his decisional capacities. Rather we should inspect the reasons for his death wish. Perhaps the losses of his physical and mental capacities as a result of his illness isn't nearly so catastrophic as he thinks it is. Perhaps his prognosis isn't nearly as bleak as he describes it. In such cases we may suspect depression, and we may also conclude that we have to suspend a judgement about the well-considered character of the request. But we don't derive the conclusion from the suspicion. Rather, both the conclusion and the suspicion express the judgement that is hard for us to understand why he wants to end his life. It follows that, when he is able to explain his death wish to us in terms of his actual and future condition, his personality, biography and basic values in such a way that the wish makes sense, there is no need to subject his competence to a psychiatric examination, in particular not when our findings are corroborated by an independent and experienced consultant. A psychiatrist will normally be more experienced than a GP, but basically he will decide in the same way. A GP may compensate his lesser experience with a more intimate knowledge of the patient. A hospice social worker in Oregon may even have both specialized expertise in assessing competence in this context and a long-standing relationship with the patient and his family.[67]

In cases of doubt, either about the patient's capacity or about a causal link between mental illness and his death wish, consulting a psychiatrist may be indicated. Such doubts can be reinforced by external considerations, in particular a history of chronic or returning treatment-resistant depression, which, on the understanding of the nature of that diagnosis that I have suggested, implies a long-standing tendency to unwarranted pessimism. Other psychiatric conditions (psychotic or personality disorders) also increase the possibility of defects in capacity. Past suicide attempts of the lonely, quasi-impulsive and violent kind clearly are a red flag. A general decline of the patient's mental capacities may also be an indication. The psychiatrist could also provide expert advice about remaining possibilities of treating the patient's mental illness or

66 Ganzini 2014, referring to Ganzini et al. 2000.
67 Ganzini 2014.

alleviating his suffering from it. A regulatory system could formalize these considerations by requiring a psychiatric examination in the case of all patients suffering from a psychiatric illness or dementia.[68] But even an actual diagnosis of treatment-resistant depression doesn't automatically mean that the request for euthanasia cannot be well-considered (Section 3.5). It is merely a reason for special caution. It seems also advisable to require expert examination of capacity in all cases in which the independent consultant has doubts about it.[69]

There is, however, no justification for a general rule requiring a psychiatric assessment of competence in all cases. In most cases the requirement would only create an unnecessary burden to the patient.

68 In the *Euthanasia Code 2018* the Dutch Regional Review Committees have confirmed that an expert in psychiatry has to be consulted in all cases involving a psychiatric illness, but not in all cases of early stage dementia. On my view there are equally good reasons for the requirement in both cases, den Hartogh 2015b.

69 The number of cases in which patients in Oregon are actually referred to psychiatrists is remarkably low, Lewy 2011, 143. According to Lee 2014 this is to be explained by the fact that physicians in relevant cases don't refer but deny the patient's request.

12 The Dutch and Belgian euthanasia laws: Potemkin villages?[1]

12.1 Can legal safeguards be effective?

In Chapter 9 I proposed a minimally revisionist justification of the legalization of euthanasia, appealing to considerations developed in earlier chapters. This justification, however, did not take into account the risks of harm to patients and third parties that would be involved in legalization. In Chapters 10 and 11 I therefore considered those risks as they could arise from either abuse or error. I argued that they are real enough, but that they can be managed to a considerable extent by an effective system of legal safeguards, consisting of substantial and procedural requirements of due care, prominently including a requirement of independent consultation.

Predictably, opponents of legalization reject this defence. On the one hand they argue that the actual safeguards that have been introduced so far are inadequate to contain the risks sufficiently. Patients may be considered eligible for euthanasia, even though their requests are not voluntary or not well-considered. That part of the critical argument, I concluded in Chapter 11, is not very persuasive, in particular not because there is so little empirical evidence supporting it. But in addition the opponents claim that these laws are not and never will be adequately implemented. Doctors will have incomplete knowledge and understanding of the legal conditions, and they will often fail to take the time needed for seriously considering whether they have been fulfilled. They will interpret these conditions in terms of their own views, or simply ignore them. They will be unable to resist pressure from patients and family. Consultants will rubber-stamp the decisions of their colleagues, as members of the medical guild always do. And review committees will almost never have the courage to judge that a doctor hasn't satisfied the requirements of due care. If they had, the only effect would be that doctors who are not sure that their behaviour is impeccable will stop reporting it. Hence, systems of legal safeguards will be mere Potemkin villages.

1 This chapter is an update of den Hartogh 2017b, to which Sections 12.6–12.9 have been added.

DOI: 10.4324/9781003281115-15

This criticism has already forcefully been made at a time when the various systems of legal safeguards had not even begun to function, in particular by Daniel Callahan and Margot White, who started talking about Potemkin villages in 1996.[2] The weaker form of the criticism is that actual systems of safeguards fail, the stronger form that all such systems are bound to fail. By now, some systems have operated long enough to enable us to evaluate these charges by reference to a body of evidence, in particular from the jurisdictions in which the largest numbers of requests have been handled and the largest collection of relevant data has been assembled, the Netherlands and Belgium, in particular Flanders.

The criticism that the Dutch and Belgian regulation systems are mere façades behind which doctors do what they want, misfires at least in one respect, as we already have seen in Chapter 10. These systems have succeeded in creating a new practice in which doctors who decide to hasten the death of a patient on his request use proper euthanatics, barbiturates and muscle relaxants, for realizing that aim. Only these cases doctors will classify as cases of euthanasia or physician-assisted suicide. In these cases they will almost always invite consultation, and they will almost always report these cases to the review committees (Chapter 10, footnote 39). I have argued that the supposedly low reporting rate is largely an artefact of the way in which the Dutch and Flemish researchers classify medical end-of-life decisions (Section 10.6). By themselves, however, these facts don't show that the substantial and procedural requirements of the Dutch and Belgian euthanasia laws make any further difference to the choices of doctors, for example for their decision to grant or to refuse a request for euthanasia. In order to get an idea of the real impact of these laws we will have to consider additional evidence. I will focus on recent Dutch data because we have more of them, but compare them with Belgian, mostly Flemish data wherever this is possible.[3]

In the first sections of this chapter I consider what we know about physicians' knowledge of the law (Section 12.2) and the impact that the legal requirements have on their decisions (Section 12.3). They are legally obligated to consult at least one independent colleague. Is it true that these consultants only give the doctors the advice that they want to hear (Section 12.4)? In both countries both doctors and consultants are required to report to a review committee, but these committees only rarely conclude that the reporting doctor hasn't satisfied the legal requirements of due care. Doesn't this show that such committees are mere paper tigers? In order to assess this criticism, I consider the ways in which the committees communicate with the medical community (Section 12.5) and the nature

2 Callahan, White 1996. See also New York State Taskforce 1994, ch. 6; Coleman, Fleischman 1996; Caplan et al. 2000; Cohn, Lynn 2002, Section 9.

3 For comparable older data see Griffiths, Weyers in Griffiths, Weyers, Adams 2008, 188–216, 331–344; Lewis, Black 2012.

of their assessments (Section 12.6). In Section 12.7 I discuss two crucial aspects of their interpretation of the law. The final link in the regulation chain concerns legal enforcement. Even in the rare cases of a negative judgement by the review committees, legal authorities nearly always abstain from prosecution. Doesn't this show that the whole system in the end is all bark and no bite[4] (Section 12.8)? Looking back I consider what we can expect any regulatory system to accomplish (Section 12.9). I make up the balance in Section 12.10.

The Netherlands and Belgium are countries that have legalized *euthanasia* under some conditions, not only giving access to lethal drugs. This group of countries presently also includes Luxemburg, Colombia, Canada, Spain, New Zealand and most Australian states (Chapter 1, footnote 1). In almost all of these countries it is permitted for doctors to participate in a joint action of ending the patient's life by either performing the last action – mostly injecting a muscle relaxant – or by assisting the patient to perform it – usually swallowing a barbiturate. Patients are only eligible for having a request for euthanasia granted under the law of these countries if they satisfy a number of requirements that do not only concern their request – it should be voluntary and well-considered – but also their condition – they should be in a state of unbearable suffering that cannot be ended in any other way. In Chapter 11 I looked at requirements of the first kind only, but in this chapter I will take requirements of both kinds into account.

12.2 Knowledge

Dutch doctors are far more pleased with their own knowledge level than their Belgian colleagues.[5] With reason? When barbiturates and muscular relaxants have been used, they almost always classify cases of euthanasia and assisted suicide correctly.[6] They are able to reproduce the requirements of due care, although mostly in their own words. They know that they have to consult an independent colleague and almost invariably contact the SCEN-network of (by now 650) trained volunteers that send the person who happens to be on duty (Chapter 11, footnotes 14–15). They don't always know that it is a separate legal requirement of due care to carry out the euthanasia in a medically competent way, but they know what competent action amounts to or at least how to find out what it is. They know that

4 As John Griffiths predicted in 1998, Griffiths, Bood, Weyers 1998, ch. 6.2. But see footnote 107.

5 Overall 92% of them consider themselves to be sufficiently informed, Onwuteaka-Philipsen 2007, 48. Only 48.9% of Flemish and 37.6% of Walloon doctors share this self-confidence, Cohen et al. 2012.

6 Only 1% of Dutch doctors labels such cases incorrectly, Buiting et al. 2010, compared to 19% of Flemish doctors, Smets et al. 2010. Resp. 50 and 57% of Flemish geriatricians and GP's correctly recognized the legal basis for euthanasia in a vignet case presented by van Humbeeck et al. 2022.

they are supposed to report to a review committee and how to do this. Most importantly: when they tell about their own experience the legal requirements are often recognizable as structuring elements in their narratives.[7]

Accustomed as they are to focus on physical symptoms for diagnosis and treatment, some physicians incorrectly believe that the patient's suffering should mainly consist of physical complaints.[8] Others mistakenly think that the suffering should be caused by a fatal illness, and that the patient should be in the terminal stage of that illness.[9] Even if a doctor knows that the law doesn't make these requirements, she may nevertheless make them herself.

Many doctors are not prepared to grant a euthanasia request from a still competent patient in an early stage of dementia, from a psychiatric patient or from a very old person suffering from an accumulation of old-age ailments.[10] Although we have no recent data showing this, some of them may still mistakenly believe that these categories of patients are ineligible for euthanasia under the law. Doctors often say that 'merely existential suffering' cannot be unbearable suffering as it is understood in the euthanasia law. These doctors probably fail to distinguish between the cause and the nature of a patient's suffering (Section 14.2). They may not be aware that even in the case of terminal cancer the most prominent elements of that suffering are loss of meaning, loss of control, loss of dignity and loss of hope (Section 1.2).

All-in-all the level of knowledge of Dutch doctors seems higher than you might expect, although not quite as high as you would hope for. The main concern is the degree of divergence in their understanding of the legal norms. In addition to these norms many doctors apply their own standards.[11] They are legally allowed to do that: there is no 'right to

7 Van Delden et al. 2011, ch. 7.

8 Overall 17% according to van Tol, Rietjens, van der Heide 2010; cf. Pasman 2012. Noteworthy in this respect is the observation that reporting physicians tend to describe the patient's suffering in terms of physical symptoms to a much larger extent than consultants and patients, Rietjens et al. 2009. Flemish physicians also tend to assess the severity of a patient's suffering by considering her physical symptoms, van Humbeeck et al. 2022. Studying reasons for a request for physician-assistance in suicide Fischer et al. 2009 found that Swiss physicians mention physical symptoms to the same extent as patients do, existential reasons far less (loss of control resp. 12 and 39, loss of dignity resp. 6 and 38%).

9 14%, Van Delden et al. 2011, 132, 162.

10 Resp. 52, 47 and 37% of physicians can imagine themselves ever granting such requests, Onwuteaka-Philipsen et al. 2017, 103. Bolt et al. 2015a found substantially lower percentages, resp. 40, 37 and 27%.

11 For example the patient must have reflected on life and death and be at peace with his situation; there should not be unsolved conflicts within the patient's family, ten Cate, van Tol, van de Vathorst 2017. The authors show that these norms reflect the physician's own conception of a 'good death'. See also van Delden et al. 2011, 132 ("loss of control is a normal occurrence in human life"), 178–179; Dees et al. 2012.

euthanasia' in the Netherlands (or Belgium).[12] But if the aim of the law is to enable patients to have a (relatively) good death in accordance with their own values, it is improper for a physician to assess the patient's request in terms of her own concept of a good death, and hence a failure of the system if this happens (Sections 8.4 and 8.5; Section 11.3). Occasionally doctors seem to project their own standards into their understanding of the law.[13]

We have not many relevant data as regards Belgium, but the data we have suggest a substantially lower level of knowledge.[14]

12.3 Decision-making

In both countries the number of reported cases of euthanasia (including a small and decreasing number of cases of physician-assisted suicide) has spectacularly risen in recent years, in the Netherlands from 1815 in 2003 to 6938 in 2020, in Belgium from 235 in 2003 to 2656 in 2019. Callahan and White would not have been surprised. They would have considered this development to confirm their prediction that in the long run doctors will not be able to withstand the pressure exerted on them by patients and relatives.

In both countries part of the growth can be explained by the extension of euthanasia to new categories of patients, characterized by an indeterminate life expectancy: patients suffering from a psychiatric illness, dementia, and old-age ailments.[15] These categories had never been excluded by the euthanasia laws. Hence, we can understand this part of the growth as the result of the occupation of an already available legal space. The same process may explain some other significant data: the percentage of cancer patients within the group of people who die as a result of euthanasia has decreased, the percentage of patients older than 80 has increased.[16] In Flanders the percentage of requests from seniors, women and people with a lower education that has been

12 15% of Dutch doctors, however, believe that patients who satisfy the legal conditions have some such right, van Delden et al. 2011, 161–162.

13 As they used to do as regards the legal status of advance directives requesting euthanasia in an advanced state of dementia, Onwuteaka-Philipsen et al. 2010, 41–43; van Delden et al. 2011, 152–155. This may have changed recently as a result of a Supreme Court decision (Chapter 15, footnote 59).

14 See footnotes 5 and 6.

15 Resp. 88, 170 and 235 patients in 2020, a total of 493 cases, RTE Annual Report 2020. For Belgium (2019) 26 cases involving beginning dementia and 26 cases involving psychiatric ailments have been reported, FCECE 2020.

16 The percentage of cancer patients dropped from 86% in 2006 to 65% in 2020, RTE Annual Reports 2006; 2020. The percentage of 80+ patients grew from 20% in 1995 to 35% in 2015, Onwuteaka-Philipsen et al. 2017, 101.

granted has spectacularly grown.[17] Ten years ago euthanasia was in practice almost only available for cancer patients and patients suffering from neurological diseases in the final stage of the dying process. For many older patients it was not an option to be considered at all, even if they had no religious objections. It has now become normal for a larger group of people to seriously start thinking and talking about euthanasia, at an earlier stage of their illness[18] (Section 16.6). This development, however, is characterized by large differences between geographical areas and social groups.[19]

But there is more to be said. In all categories the number of requests grows, and the percentage of cases in which these requests are refused drops. That these trends go together is by itself remarkable at first sight: if the number of requests increases you would expect it to contain rather more requests that do not satisfy the legal criteria. However, if requests are more easily granted, you can expect patients to make requests more easily as well.[20] If the increased awareness among the public of the option of euthanasia leads to earlier deliberation, this may also create more opportunities for consistent repetition of the request.

In the Netherlands the percentage of requests for euthanasia that were granted was 37 in 2005, 45 in 2010 and 55 in 2015.[21] In about one third of the cases in which the request had not been granted, the doctor thought that the requirements of due care had not been met.[22] In the remaining cases the request had been withdrawn by the patient, or the patient had died from his illness before the doctor had come to a final decision. (In both categories implicit refusals may occur because the doctor prevaricated hoping to avoid an explicit refusal.) In Flanders the percentage of requests that had been granted rose from 55.4% in 2007 to 76.7% in 2013. In about one of five cases the reason for not granting the request was that the legal criteria had not been met.[23] In both the

17 From 2007 to 2013 the percentage of requests granted grew from 55.4 to 76.7%, but in the category 80+ from 38.1 to 75.4%, of women from 45.7 to 76.4% (now equalling the percentage of men), of people with a lower education from 35.1 to 69.5% and with very large numbers in all non-cancer cases, Dierickx et al. 2015. The percentage of cases in which the requesting patient was expected to die in the near future decreased from 93.9% in 2003 to 84.1% in 2013, Dierickx et al. 2016.

18 Dees et al. 2012.

19 Groenewoud et al. 2021, see Chapter 16, footnote 16.

20 Cf. Cohen et al. 2012 explaining why the number of euthanasia requests is so much lower in Wallonia than it is in Flanders.

21 Onwuteaka-Philipsen et al. 2017, 108, for general practitioners only resp. 33, 49 and 61%.

22 Resp. 38, 35 and 30% of all requests that had not been granted in 2005, 2010 and 2015, Onwuteaka-Philipsen et al. 2017, 109.

23 Overall 21.1% in 2007, 19.6% in 2013, Dierickx et al. 2015. On the basis of a survey in 2009 among Belgian physicians (including physicians from Wallonia and Bruxelles) Van Wesemael et al. 2011 reported that 5% of the requests doctors received had been rejected by them.

Netherlands and Flanders two requirements were most often mentioned in this respect: that the patient's suffering should be unbearable and that his request be well-considered.[24] We can conclude that in the last year that we have data about (resp. 2015 and 2013) 13.5% of the Dutch requests have been refused with reference to the legal requirements, and 4.6% of the Flemish ones.

The decrease of the percentage of refusals motivated by the legal requirements is striking, but it is hard to evaluate. Was 27.7% (2005) too high or is 13.5% (2015) too low? Or even still too high? We would need more data to enable us to calibrate these figures. We have seen (Section 12.2) that some refusals are motivated by an unduly restrictive interpretation of the law, or by constraints imposed by the individual doctor without reference to the law. We have also seen that part of the already available legal space has been occupied in recent years. Occupying it has been the explicit aim of the Expertise Centre Euthanasia that started to work on the initiative of the Dutch right-to-die society NVVE in 2012, and offers euthanasia, within the limits of the law, to patients whose treating physician is unwilling to grant a request. The work is done by ambulant teams of doctors and nurses.[25] The influence of the Centre is not restricted to the requests for euthanasia it considers itself. Doctors may transfer their patients to the Centre, but also decide to grant their requests when the Centre has judged them to meet the criteria or ask the Centre for support.

What we also know from recent research is that a substantial and probably growing number of physicians, in particular of general practitioners, feel themselves pressurized by patients and families to grant requests for euthanasia or to carry out positive decisions as soon as possible.[26] Patients announce their decisions ('I have told my family that it will be done next Thursday') or remind the doctor of actual or imaginary promises. Emotional blackmail occurs ('if you don't help me this week, I will jump').[27] Several factors explain this development. Patients and relatives don't properly appreciate what they ask of a doctor: a

24 See also Jansen-van der Weide, Onwuteaka-Philipsen, van der Wal 2005 (results of 2002); Dees et al. 2012.

25 According to the director 16–17% of the requests that the Centre receives don't meet the legal criteria, *Relevant,* November 2018. The Centre grants about 30% of the requests it receives, 899 in 2020, Expertisecentrum Euthanasie, *Jaarverslag 2020* (Annual report).

26 Pressure to grant a request is reported by 29 (patients) to 34 (relatives), pressure to act more quickly by 44% of doctors in the past five years, among GP's resp. 37–39 and 56%, Onwuteaka-Philipsen et al. 2017, 107. According to van Delden et al. 2011, 12–17% of doctors report feeling pressured, mostly by relatives; according to van Wylick, van Dijk 2015 (study with low response rate) 70%. 64% felt an increase of pressure over the years.

27 De Boer et al. 2019.

difficult decision to make, and a burdensome one to carry out. They often believe that they have a legal right to euthanasia on demand. And some relatives think that they can make the request as the patient's stand-in.[28] According to many doctors, patients are insufficiently aware of the actual requirements of the euthanasia law.[29] If they are informed about them, they often find them unacceptably paternalistic.

That response may be a sign of a changing public attitude. If asked for their views of the justifying grounds for euthanasia Dutch citizens always referred primarily to the right of self-determination, but, inconsistently, they also used to think that this justifying ground only applied to dying patients suffering from extreme pain, breathlessness and similar physical symptoms.[30] That seems to change at present.[31]

Doctors also perceive a process of shifting standards, 'stretching the boundaries of the law'.[32] As I said before, this is largely a misperception: the legal space was always there, but doctors only realize this now because the space is actually getting occupied. But the general public seems to welcome this development to a larger degree than the medical community.[33] There seems to be a growing discrepancy between the expectations of the public and the willingness of physicians to deliver.[34] That the personal and moral boundaries of doctors don't always coincide with the legal ones may contribute to their sense of overstretch.

Doctors will of course agree that it is their professional duty to withstand undue pressure, but it is not a wild hypothesis to suppose that growing pressure is part of the explanation of the decreasing percentage of refused requests for euthanasia.[35] Callahan and White had a point here.

In assessing that percentage we should keep in mind that the actual number of refusals will be significantly higher than doctors report them to be, because we know that doctors often don't consider the expression of a patient's death wish as a request for euthanasia, though it is intended

28 Snijdewind et al. 2018.

29 Overall 60% of doctors believe this, FMS 2014. The percentage of Dutch people who hold that euthanasia should be a right has increased from 51% in 2010 to 67% in 2015, Onwuteaka-Philipsen et al. 2017, 85.

30 Van Holsteyn, Trappenburg 1995, 194ff.

31 Onwuteaka-Philipsen et al. 2017, 254–255; cf. Kouwenhoven 2019. Dierickx et al. 2015; Montero 2017, 37, describe a similar development in Belgium.

32 Snijdewind et al. 2018.

33 Although the approval rate among the general public as regards euthanasia in the case of patients suffering from dementia, mental illness and old-age ailments is only slightly higher than among doctors, Onwuteaka-Philipsen et al. 2017, 85–91, but cf. footnote 10 on deviating findings by Bolt et al. 2015a.

34 Snijdewind et al. 2018.

35 24% of doctors find it hard to say 'no' to the patient, but only 6.7% at any time has regretted granting a request, 11% to have refused it, FMS 2014.

as such by the patient.[36] Hence in some cases in which the patient dies before his doctor has communicated a final decision that patient will believe to have received a refusal. The final decision is normally the outcome of a deliberation and negotiation process between doctor and patient in which it is somewhat arbitrary to identify the moment at which there is an explicit request that requires to be granted or refused. As a result of these considerations, we should understand the percentage of refusals as a lower limit.

It should also be noted that it is a requirement of the Belgian, but not of the Dutch law, that the patient should present the doctor a request in writing. This may to some extent explain why the rate of refusals in Flanders is so much lower than in the Netherlands: the patient may not bother to produce a document if he already knows from his conversations with the doctor that she will not be prepared to go along with him, and the doctor may in such cases not acknowledge the existence of a valid request. A remarkable finding about Flanders is that doctors in many cases ask for expert consultation in addition to the mandatory one, and more often consult at least one palliative care team.[37] This is a sign of serious decision-making.

When a doctor appeals to the law for justifying her refusal we cannot know whether the appeal reveals her real motivation. But we cannot maintain that the law is only a puppet show that has no impact at all on reality. This is confirmed by the few ethnographic studies that have described the interaction between doctors, patients and families that (sometimes) leads to a decision to grant or not to grant a request.[38] It is normally a conversation that goes on for days, weeks or even months, in which the patient has to convince the doctor that his request is well-considered and his suffering truly intolerable. Although in the case of a refusal the doctor is expected to inform the patient about her reasons, throughout the process the burden of proof is on the patient.

12.4 Consultation

According to the Potemkin-script of Callahan and White consultants will eventually always comply with the wishes of the doctors who request a consultation. In order to evaluate this prediction, as regards the Netherlands we only have data from SCEN, but by now almost all consultations are SCEN-consultations. In 2008 SCEN-consultants

36 Van Delden et al. 2011, 175; Meeussen et al. 2011; Pasman 2012; Tolle et al. 2004 reports about Oregon that according to the relatives only 4% of requests for lethal drugs are granted, according to the doctors 18%.

37 Resp. in 25 and 42.6% of reported euthanasia cases in 2013, Dierickx et al. 2016.

38 In particular Norwood 2009, summarized Norwood, Kimsma, Battin 2009. Older studies (in Dutch) include Pool 1996 and The 1997. See also Dees et al. 2012.

concluded in 19% of the cases that not all requirements had (yet) been met.[39] That number dropped to 13% in 2018 and to 7% in 2020.[40] The requirement that motivated the largest number of negative judgements by far concerned the unbearable suffering of the patient.[41] In 5% of the cases consultants report to have experienced some pressure from the requesting doctor to take a specific decision. For consultations in Flanders we have similar percentages.[42]

Before we draw any conclusions from these data we should take into account that in some cases a negative judgement is precisely what the doctor who has solicited the consultation hoped for, because it enables her to refuse the request without having to face a conflict with the patient or his family. But the number of such cases seems limited, and in such a case the doctor may also, in spite of her own intention, receive a positive judgement.[43]

In many cases in which the consultant judges that not all requirements have (yet) been met, she will be invited to come back at a later stage.[44] Often she then reverses her judgement. In the meantime the doctor has often followed some specific advice the consultant gave the first time, for example to try out a new palliative treatment or to invite a psychiatrist in order to assess the patient's competence. The law requires an independent consultation, but it doesn't require that the consultant agrees with the doctor that the legal conditions have been satisfied. A negative advice therefore does not necessarily prevent the doctor from going on and explaining to the review committee why he believes the judgement of the consultant to be mistaken. This happens only rarely.[45] In a larger number of cases the doctor will ask a second consultant to give her opinion. He could go on shopping for the result he wants, and although the Royal Dutch Society for Medicine KNMG and the review committees have made it

39 Onwuteaka-Philipsen et al. 2010. For older data see Griffiths, Weyers in Griffiths, Weyers, Adams 2008, 195–196.

40 Spiegelinformatie SCEN 2011, 2020 (3% in Amsterdam, 2020). In 35.9% of the cases that a consultant considered the most difficult one to assess in 2015 she decided that the legal requirements had not (15%) or not yet (20.9%) all been met, Spiegelinformatie SCEN 2015.

41 Overall 70% of the cases in 2008, 61.2% of 'most recent cases' in 2017, Spiegelinformatie SCEN 2017. In 30, resp. 28.2% of those cases the request was not well-considered, in 19, resp. 7.5% of the cases not all reasonable treatment options had been tried.

42 Overall 80.5% of positive judgements in 2009, 90.2% if the consultant comes from LEIF, Cohen et al. 2014.

43 In 3.3% of the requests for consultation the consultant thought that the requesting doctor probably intended to refuse the request, and in 3.3% of all cases the request was refused in spite of a positive advice from the consultant. Spiegelinformatie SCEN 2015; cf. Van Wesemael et al. 2010.

44 In 5.1% of the consultations performed by SCEN-consultants in 2017, another consultation had already taken place before, Spiegelinformatie 2017.

45 Van Wesemael et al. 2010.

clear that he is only allowed to do this when the patient's situation clearly worsens, to an unknown extent the practice still exists.

In Belgium a similar network exists that enables physicians to invite an independent and experienced consultant,[46] but most of them still prefer to invite a colleague of their own choice, often from the circle of their near colleagues who cannot always be considered to be properly independent. Often the consultant is even already involved in the treatment of the patient. The reports about this practice seem fairly disturbing.[47] But we should remember that for a substantial part it concerns cases in which the doctor reports to have acted on an explicit intention to hasten the death of the patient, but actually used opiates or benzodiazepines in dosages, indicated for symptom relief, that could hardly have had the intended effect (Chapter 10, at footnote 46). Therefore the actual number of cases of euthanasia that deviate from the legal criteria in this particular way is unknown.[48] But that the practice exists is beyond doubt.

One could speculate that many doctors who are involved in the Belgian regulatory system, either in a consulting or in a reviewing role, still understand themselves to be part of an emancipatory movement. As Callahan and White acutely observe, this may result in the understandable, although mistaken idea that one should not be too critical about any case of proposed or performed euthanasia. Disapproval would only be scaremongering, wouldn't it? [49]

As in the Netherlands the advice of the consultant isn't binding. The attending physicians only have to report the advice to the Federal Control and Evaluation Commission (see next section) without attaching the advice itself. The Commission cannot even check whether the

46 See Chapter 11, footnotes 14–15.

47 In Flanders and Bruxelles in 2009 only in 41.8% of the cases the consultant was not a direct colleague of the doctor requesting consultation, and only in 65.7% not co-attending the patient, Cohen et al. 2014; cf. Van Wesemael et al. 2010. Cf. the views of Belgian doctors about the usefulness of independent consultation, reported in Chapter 10, footnote 72.

48 FCECE 2020, 28, refers to "some rare cases" of procedural failures. But in all cases in which the file of the anonymously reporting physician is not opened the independence of the consultant cannot be checked, Raus, VanderHaegen, Sterckx 2021.

49 Callahan, White 1996; cf. Montero 2017, 29. As Montero notes LEIF and EOL are both initiatives of right-to-die societies. The co-president of the Federal Commission, the oncologist Wim Distelmans, is also the founder of LEIF, one of the most prominent contributors to the public debate about euthanasia in Belgium and responsible for some highly controversial euthanasia cases, including the case of the mother of Tom Mortier that is now being considered by the European Court of Human Rights (footnote 100). When a new selection procedure for independent consultants had been set up in 2013, giving a prominent role to LEIF and EoL, four physicians lodged a formal complaint with the Council of State because in their eyes the procedure was ideologically biased, but the Council rejected the complaint, explaining that respect for the will of the patient was at the heart of the euthanasia law (Arrest *Raad van State* 229461, 2014).

advice is accurately represented. We don't know what role a negative advice plays in the deliberations of the Commission.[50]

In spite of the problems I have mentioned, however, I am inclined to conclude that the implementation of the consultation requirement is one of the more robust links in the regulation chain in both countries, most clearly in the Netherlands.

12.5 Review

Having performed a euthanasia a Dutch doctor is required to report a non-natural death to the coroner and to fill out a model form in which he describes the medical history of the patient and explains, for every requirement of due care, why he believes that it has been satisfied. Usually he adds medical correspondence, extracts of his journal and the patient's written request, if this exists. He is also required to send the report of the independent colleague he has consulted. The report of the consultant is often more informative than that of the doctor, because the consultant doesn't use a model form, and because SCEN-consultants in particular know better what kind of information the review committees are interested in. Not uncommonly the physician describes the patient's suffering primarily in physical, the consultant in existential terms. The coroner sends the whole file to one of the five regional review committees, consisting of a lawyer, a doctor and an ethicist or their deputies. The review committee judges, within a period of six weeks, whether or not the doctor has satisfied the legal requirements of due care. The doctor then receives an explanation of the judgement. Except for the part that summarizes the relevant facts of the case, this explanation is by now standardized in most cases, but it may be quite extensive in more complicated ones.

The Belgian system differs in some important respects: there is only one Federal Control and Evaluation Commission for Euthanasia, consisting of sixteen members, nine of them physicians,[51] the form that the attending physician has to fill up is considerably shorter,[52] and he is not required to attach the consultant's written report, only to summarize her advice in his own words. His report to the commission doesn't itself contain his name; the commission will only open the sealed envelope containing that name if it wants to obtain additional information from him or to make some comments. This happens in one out of four cases.[53] The doctor doesn't receive an explanation of the commission's judgement.

50 Raus, Verhaegen, Sterckx 2021. Van Wesemael et al. 2011 found that in 4 of 363 cases euthanasia was performed in spite of a negative advice from the consultant.

51 All files are submitted to all 16 members. The commission has to deal with ca. 240 cases in each of its meetings, 11 each year.

52 Raus, VanderHaegen, Sterckx, referring to some examples in FCECE 2016, 25.

53 24.8%, FCECE 2020.

These review systems require some modest expenditure: the budget of the Dutch committees amounted to 3.7 million euro's in 2020, paying for a staff of 25 members, the Belgian commission has only two staff members and a mere 160,000 euro's to spend. Many observers are not very impressed by the results. In the Netherlands from 1998 up to 2020, the committees have concluded in 114 cases that the doctor had not satisfied all due care requirements. Most of these judgements concerned either the requirement of independent consultation or the requirement of medically careful performance. The reporting doctor had hierarchical or financial connections with the consultant, or the consultant had been involved with the patient's treatment. Or the reporting doctor had not given the patient an effective coma-inducing drug before administering muscular relaxants. The number of such medical failings has decreased significantly since the publication of a new edition of an authoritative guideline in 2012.[54]

Only in 24 of the 114 cases the doctor was judged to have failed to meet one or several of the substantial due care requirements. He could not reasonably have concluded the patient's request to be voluntary and well-considered (five cases), the patient's suffering to be unbearable and beyond any prospect of improvement (twelve cases) or no alternative solution to be available (eight cases). All these cases concerned patients from special categories: psychiatric patients, patients suffering from a chronic illeness, from old-age ailments or from dementia, or patients in an irreversible comatose state. That is remarkable because by far the largest category of patients receiving euthanasia consists of patients in the end stage of a lethal illness.[55]

In Belgium the Federal Commission has only once, in 2014, judged a doctor not to have met the legal requirements.[56] The difference between the Dutch and the Belgian record is striking, all the more so because the Belgian law is more detailed in its requirements than the Dutch one. It should be observed that the Belgian law doesn't contain the requirement of medically appropriate action, hence medical mistakes are signalized

54 KNMP 2012.

55 97% of all patients in 2010, 92% in 2015, Onwuteaka-Philipsen et al. 2017, 104.

56 The case was only referred to the Public Prosecutor, not to the Order of Physicians that has disciplinary powers. It concerned a GP, the president of a right-to-die society, who assisted a woman to end her life who suffered from a 'reactive depression' after the death of her daughter, three months before her own death. The doctor had consulted two colleagues but no psychiatrist, as the law in such cases requires. The case was dismissed by an Antwerp court in 2019 because the doctor had not administered a lethal injection to the patient but given her a 'glass of poison' to drink. Assisted suicide is not expressly forbidden in Belgian law and not explicitly regulated by the euthanasia law, but the FCECE in its first biennial report (2004) stated that it considered assisted suicide to fall under the definition of euthanasia, Nys 2017, 10. The Commission repeated its position in FCECE 2020.

by the committee but never lead to a negative judgement. But the main difference between the two systems is the following one. Even if the Federal Commission establishes that a doctor clearly has failed to satisfy one or several of the requirements of due care, it claims the authority to determine whether or not the case should be referred to the Public Prosecutor. In the case of a procedural failure (for example lack of independence of the consultant) the committee judges whether that failure raises doubts about the extent to which the substantial requirements have been met. The Dutch committees leave this assessment to the prosecutorial authorities.

It is hardly believable that the substantial requirements have been violated only once in 20 years. Even in such cases, however, the Commission claims the authority to decide whether the violation concerns an 'essential' condition of the law and should, therefore, be a reason for prosecution.[57] That decision requires, moreover, a two-thirds majority of the votes, hence the consent of at least some of those members of the Commission who are physicians. As Kasper Raus and associates conclude, the commission operates as a protecting shield for possibly misbehaving doctors.[58] That is precisely as Callahan and White predicted it would function.

Even the Dutch figures invite the question whether they justify all the bureaucracy of the system. But that question presupposes that the impact of the system on the behaviour of doctors is restricted to those negative judgements. In reality the operation of the system has other relevant effects. To begin with it simply provides an address for reporting. In Oregon and the other American states that have legalized access to lethal drugs, and now also in Canada, doctors are legally required to file a report, but these documents are almost exclusively used for administrative purposes (cf. Chapter 16, footnote 42). It stands to reason that the mere fact that the reports will be read during a review process will induce doctors to write them more carefully.[59]

The committees have other means to influence doctors' behaviour. If a committee suspects either major or minor defects, it will start asking questions of the reporting doctor, the consultant or both.[60] If necessary, it will invite either of them or both to an interview.[61] If the suspicion of a minor defect is corroborated the committee may comment on this, either

57 FCECE 2018, 26.

58 Raus, VanderHaegen, Sterckx 2021, 99–100.

59 Griffihts, Weyers, Adams 2008, 209.

60 In 1999 and 2005 the doctor has been asked for additional information in 6% of the cases, the consultant in 2.5%. In 2015 4% of reporting doctors reported to have been asked for additional information, Onwuteaka-Philipsen et al. 2017, 209. In 70% of these cases doctors appreciated this contact with the committees, *ibid.*, 199.

61 In 2005 en 2015 in resp. 0.5 en 1% of reported cases, Onwuteaka-Philipsen et al. 2007, 196; Onwuteaka-Philipsen et al. 2017, 197. In 2020 14 physicians and one consultant have been invited for an interview, RTE Annual Report 2020.

in communication by telephone, in a letter accompanying the committee's judgement, or in the judgement itself.

The committee may also follow this procedure when the doctor and the consultant turn out to have acted correctly, but reported their actions too summarily, or left out important relevant information from their reports. Insisting on adequate reporting may seem formalistic. But the best way to assure that the legal requirements, as they are interpreted by the committees, are really internalized by doctors and consultants is to require them to argue for each requirement why they think that it has been satisfied. These activities can be seen as contributions to a learning process that aims to promote careful action by providing doctors with feedback.[62] Activities of the SCEN-network also contribute to that process, including regional meetings discussing problems of interpreting the legal requirements and reports on hard cases.[63] It has been commented that this system only teaches doctors how to report, not how to act. That comment presupposes a general unwillingness to learn that is not confirmed by any evidence.[64] A real flaw of the system is the use of a model report form that, even though it mainly consists of open questions, tends to limit the amount of information provided by reporting doctors.

The Belgian Federal Control and Evaluation Commission uses some of the same methods. In 2016–2017 it requested additional information in 16.8% and added comments to its judgements in 6.9% of the reported cases. Most of the questions concerned lacking administrative data and minor procedural inaccuracies.[65] Half of the comments concerned violations of the anonymity requirement in the doctor's report. A total of 179 comments were made in a 'didactic letter', for example reminding the doctor about the mandatory waiting time in cases in which the death of the patient isn't foreseeable.[66] However, the Federal Commission doesn't publish its judgements or summaries of them in its biennial reports, and has only once, as an appendix to its first report, published some short remarks about its understanding of the law, in later reports only followed by comments on single issues. The Dutch committees, on the other hand, publish a substantial number of their decisions, in particular in more complex cases, on their website, and summaries of the most important

62 This corresponds to the self-image of the committees, Onwuteaka-Philipsen et al. 2017, 208–209.

63 Onwuteaka-Philipsen et al. 2010, 62–66.

64 Overall 67% of reporting doctors considered the committee's judgement to provide support for future decisions, Onwuteake-Philipsen et al. 2017, 198.

65 FCECE 2018, 26ff. The number of questions is decreasing, the number of comments is increasing in recent years. In 2017 29 questions were asked about the request, 13 about the nature of the suffering and 10 about the impossibility to alleviate the suffering.

66 At least two cases in 2018, (not 42, as Raus, VanderHaegen, Sterckx 2021, report), FCECE 2018, 18.

decisions in their annual reports. In 2015 they issued a *Code of Practice*, in 2018 updated as the *Euthanasia Code*, in which they give a detailed exposé of the way they interpret each legal requirement.

This points to an important difference between the two systems. The Dutch legislator has consciously used open norms, leaving the specification of those norms to the case law of the review committees. The committees can of course only fulfil that task by publicizing their judgements. That process implies both an element of specification and adaptation to changing social conditions. In particular it results in quite a number of lower order auxiliary norms that a doctor has to comply with unless he is able to convince the committee that he had compelling reasons not to comply. Examples include the requirement that a request for euthanasia laid down in an advance directive has to be confirmed by the patient during the time that he is still sufficiently competent, that in the case of a request of a psychiatric patient consultation of a psychiatrist is always required, that after a second negative advice by a consultant the doctor should not go on shopping for a positive advice. These auxiliary norms can be found in their annual reports and the *Euthanasia Code*. This is a characteristic element of the Dutch review system that is almost completely lacking in the Belgian one. As I already observed, the biennial reports of the Federal Commission only occasionally contain a short remark on the interpretation of the law.

Because of its almost total lack of transparency it is hard to assess the impact of the Belgian review system. In particular we would have to know more about the comments the Federal Commission makes in its didactic letters. What we do know is that the system doesn't give any feedback to others than the reporting physicians, not even to consultants.

12.6 What kind of review?

In order to get a better idea of the nature of the assessment that the Dutch review committees make, I have studied the non-standardized judgements that have been published on the website of the committees between 2012 and 2017, in particular the (167) judgements that give special attention to the suffering of the patient.[67]

A total of 89 of those judgements discuss the requirement that the doctor should be convinced that the patient's suffering was unbearable. This requirement is always considered in two special kinds of cases: those in which the consciousness of the patient unexpectedly has been lowered after the doctor has promised to end the patient's life (22)[68]; and cases

67 This section summarizes den Hartogh 2019c and uses some formulations from that paper.

68 According to the 'auxiliary norms' of the Committees euthanasia is then only possible if either there are still clear signs of suffering, or if the state of lowered consciousness is the result of medical action and hence reversible.

of presently incompetent patients who have requested euthanasia in an advance directive (12). The question is hardly ever raised in cases of patients in the end stage of a lethal illness. In two of those cases the committee describes how its initial doubts about the unbearable character of the suffering had been abated when information about the personality, the biography and the value system of the patient had fully been taken into account.[69] Considerations of that kind are also put forward in 25 other cases, mostly concerning patients suffering from old-age ailments. In six cases the committee considers whether it is understandable that a patient's suffering became unbearable at the death of a care-providing partner. In eight cases concerning patients suffering from either a chronic illness or a combination of a psychiatric and a somatic illness the committee considers whether unbearable suffering was plausible, given the nature of the illness.[70]

The other requirements about the patient's suffering are usually discussed together: that the doctor could reasonably conclude that the suffering was beyond hope of improvement, and that doctor and patient together could reasonably conclude that there was no acceptable alternative way out. Attention is given to these requirements in 78 cases. The majority (44) of them concern psychiatric patients, and in most (30) of these cases the question is whether the doctor has satisfied the requirement to consult a psychiatrist. In most of the other cases the evaluation is also procedural: did the doctor consult the right experts, for example in palliative care, was she sufficiently informed about the medical facts and was her contact with the patient sufficiently intensive to arrive at a judgement? Such questions are often asked in cases in which the doctor has decided to go on with the euthanasia in spite of a negative advice from the consultant. In five cases only the committee considered itself whether alternative procedures had been sufficiently tried out.[71]

Appraising this evidence we can conclude that in assessing cases of patients in the end stage of a lethal illness – up to 80% of the total number of euthanasia cases – the committees only rarely examine the doctor's claims about the suffering of the patient, mostly when the initial information of the doctor or the consultant was insufficient. A study of the work of the committees quotes one member explaining: "if the reporting doctor and the consultant judge the patient's suffering to have been unbearable, who are we to contradict them?"[72] This seems largely in accordance with the practice of the committees. In the case of patients suffering from a chronic or psychiatric illness, dementia or old-age ailments closer attention is paid to the patient's suffering, in particular by

69 E.g., 2016-74: facial mutilation of a patient who highly valued her looks.

70 E.g., 2014-03: 'light' dementia of a professor.

71 E.g., 2017-31: was COPD really the cause of the patient's shortness of breath?

72 Van der Heide et al. 2012, p. 191; cf. Kim, de Vries, Peteet 2016.

considering it in relation to the patient's personality, biography and value system. Whether there really is no alternative way out of the patient's suffering is most often explicitly considered in the judgements concerning patients suffering from a psychiatric or chronic illness. The comments are almost always merely procedural.

A study by Miller and Kim of the cases in which the committees judged that the requirements of due care had not been satisfied arrives at similar conclusions.[73] The authors find them disappointing. In their view these conclusions prove that the review committees don't really try to decide whether euthanasia was an appropriate decision for the doctor to make, only whether he arrived at the decision in a careful manner. This evaluation presupposes that it is the aim of the review system to check the correctness of the doctor's decision. But this cannot be done on the basis of the testimony of witnesses and written documents. On Cassell's understanding of suffering there cannot be any metric of suffering (Section 6.2). Because suffering is a matter of the meaning that a person's condition, including her medical condition, has for her, it normally depends on many disparate dimensions that are only partially commensurable. An assessment of the severity of someone's suffering is therefore necessarily a holistic judgement that requires personal knowledge.[74] For this very reason the law requires consultants to speak with the requesters in person. For the same reason it is not a good idea to require *ex ante* committee approval, as Miller and Kim advocate.[75]

In that case doctors would transfer their accountability for the decision to end a person's life to a committee that is simply not in a position to make that kind of decision. Contrary to the assumptions of Miller and Kim the legal task of the review committees is not, and cannot be, to decide whether the patient's suffering was really unbearable beyond improvement, but only whether the doctor could reasonably come to the conclusion that it was. The basic aim of a review system can only be to improve decision-making by doctors and consultants by the means I described in Section 12.5. It cannot be to authorize their decisions.

But even such a 'marginal' or 'limited review', as the committees themselves call it,[76] should not be restricted to procedural matters and should not attribute final authority to a consensus between doctor and consultant. The data I have presented in this section suggest that the

73 Miller, Kim 2017; see also Tuffrey-Wijne et al. 2018.

74 Magnusson 2004; Norwood, Kimsma, Battin 2009; Wijsbek 2012b.

75 Cf. VandenBerghe 2017, 166–167 for a similar proposal in the case of a request for euthanasia from psychiatric patients (Section 13.8). *Ex ante* authorization is required by the Colombian and Spanish euthanasia laws, Benavides 2018, Sanz et al. 2021 (Section 16.4.2).

76 RTE Annual Report 2016, 24; *Euthanasia Code 2018*, 10–11; cf. Openbaar Ministerie, *Aanwijzing vervolgingsbeslissing* (full reference in footnote 97).

present Dutch review practice, with the exception of some special categories of hard cases, has become somewhat *too* marginal. This will be checked in the next section.

12.7 Two crucial issues

It is a commonplace about the requirement of intractable and unbearable suffering to say that 'intractable' refers to an objective, 'unbearable' to a subjective criterion. Whether the underlying medical condition that causes the patient's suffering can be improved is a matter of medical judgement that other doctors will supposedly agree with. But it is only the patient who experiences his suffering; hence, he is also the only one who can judge whether it is bearable or not.[77] If this is true, both the doctor and the consultant could only come to the reasonable belief that the patient's suffering is unbearable by asking him.[78] But even if you are the only one who experiences your suffering, it is not a mental state that is directly accessible to introspection and can be determined infallibly[79] (Section 6.2). It is your response to a state of the world that is dependent on your perception and interpretation of that state, and you can discuss with others whether your perception and interpretation are correct. That is what suffering people do all the time.

Even if it is common for Dutch doctors to agree that judgements about the severity of suffering are 'subjective', they also commonly hold that the patient's belief that his suffering is unbearable should at least be understandable to them. As a result they still seem to take the requirement of unbearable suffering seriously (cf. Section 12.3 at footnote 26). It is the legal requirement that they commonly report to be the most difficult one to apply.[80]

But in one of their first annual reports (2002) the review committees have rejected this idea of the subjectivity of 'unbearable suffering' altogether. They agree that suffering is subjective in one sense: it is person-related, because it depends on the personality, biography and value system of the suffering person. In order to assess the severity of her suffering, her doctor and the colleagues he consults therefore have empathically to assume her perspective, as determined by those factors. But it doesn't follow that they cannot challenge her judgement. Psychologists and behavioural economists have shown that people's ability to make important

77 Sumner 2011, 171; Schuklenk, van Delden, Downie 2011, 35–36; Downie, Chandler 2018, Section 3.2.

78 As Cassell thought, Chapter 6 at footnote 12. See also Brock 1992; Weir 1992; Sumner 2011, 171. Some guidelines for palliative sedation, including Morita et al. 2005a; EAPC 2009; National Hospice and Palliative Care Organization 2010 also consider 'intolerable suffering' a state defined by the patient, Schildmann, Schildmann 2014.

79 Wijsbek 2012b; 2016.

80 Buiting et al. 2008.

decisions in their own interests, as defined by their own priorities, is mediocre at best.[81] There is no reason to assume that choices for death are an exception.

In Section 12.6 we have seen that the review committees sometimes consider whether an assessment of unbearable suffering was understandable in these person-relative terms. What we presently don't know is to what extent committee members, but also doctors who perform euthanasia and SCEN-consultants agree with this alternative conception of the subjectivity of assessments of unbearable suffering and are aware of the fact that it conflicts with the common idea that it is fully up to the patient to decide whether his suffering is unbearable. What doctors tend to say, somewhat inconsistently, is: yes, it is only up to the patient, but she has also to convince *me*.[82] That is why they find it difficult to apply the requirement of unbearable suffering.

As the cliché has it, it is an 'objective' judgement whether the patient's suffering is beyond hope of improvement. But as we already saw in the last section, the authority of the patient may be relevant in making this judgement as well. Patients have the right to refuse any treatment proposal, even if it concerns life-sustaining treatment. It is often thought that the recognition of this right logically implies that a treatment that has been refused by the patient cannot be considered a 'reasonable alternative' to euthanasia.[83] Actually there is no such implication. In 1994 the Dutch Supreme Court stated that suffering was not beyond hope of improvement if a viable alternative for alleviating that suffering had been freely rejected by the patient.[84] This has also been stressed by the ministers who defended the Euthanasia law in parliament.[85] On the whole the review committees still formally subscribe to that view.[86] An alternative is considered a reasonable one if it opens a real possibility of improvement within a foreseeable time span, and without creating disproportionate additional burdens. If this is the case, the consequence of a refusal can be that the patient's request cannot be granted, at least not at that moment.

But only in two cases of the 167 that I reviewed in the last section a committee actually considered an alternative that had been rejected by the

81 Tiemeijer, Prast 2009.

82 LEIFdraad 2015, an information leaflet for physicians.

83 Sumner 2011, 171; Schuklenk, van Delden, Downie 2011, 35–36; Downie, Chandler 2018, Section 3.2.

84 *Chabot* case, HR 21-6-1994, NJ 1994.656, ECLI:NL:PHR:1994:AD2122, translated by J. Griffiths, *Modern Law Review* 58 (1995): 232–248.

85 They added that as a result of the refusal the patient could get into a condition in which the reasonable alternative no longer existed, Pans 2006, 94, with reference to the sources.

86 In spite of an incidental *lapsus*, e.g., case 2015-107; cf. RTE Annual Report 2009, casus 10. See also the *Euthanasia Code 2018*, 25: the effect of a refusal of treatment can sometimes be that the patient's request cannot be granted.

patient to be a reasonable one.[87] In all other cases the committees accepted the doctor's estimation, supported by experts, of possible benefits and burdens that led him to accede to the patient's refusal. Sometimes that refusal was seen to reveal a lack of motivation that substantially decreased the probability of a possible treatment to succeed.[88] Clearly the committees are wary of considering an alternative a reasonable one that the patient has freely rejected.[89] This may also explain why they rarely ask doctors to substantiate their claim that no reasonable alternative existed.[90]

The view that it is fully up to the patient to decide whether his suffering is unbearable, because it is a subjective concept, was subscribed to in the parliamentary debates about the Belgian euthanasia law. In its first biennial report the Federal Commission (2004) observed that, although certain objective factors could indicate unbearable suffering, it was largely subjective and dependent on the personality, views and values of the patient. In judging whether the patient's suffering can still be alleviated one should take into account the patient's right to refuse treatment, including palliative care.[91] These statements are repeated in later reports.[92] We don't know how the Commission applies these norms in its judgements.[93]

These two issues are crucial for deciding whether a law that permits euthanasia under certain conditions is in accordance with its professed moral foundations. As we have seen in Chapter 9 for such a law respect for individual autonomy is an enabling, the doctor's duty of beneficence, a justifying ground. That is why that law contains requirements regarding the patient's request *and* regarding his condition. The question is whether the requirements about the patient's condition are really enforced. Consider the following analogy. According to Dutch law a woman has no *right* to terminate her pregnancy; her request for an abortion can only be granted if she is in a state of extreme need. But whether she is in such a state is up to her, and only to her, to decide. This means that it is in the end only her voluntary request that matters, as long as she formulates that request in

87 2015-01: a patient with serious intestinal complaints who refused to reconsider a diagnosis, even though the diet prescribed to her on the basis of that diagnosis could possibly be the cause of her complaints; 2017-79. On the view of the committees, see also Griffiths, Weyers, Adams 2008, 79, 91–93, cf. Chapter 8, footnote 13.

88 E.g., 2015-24, discussed by Tuffrey-Wijne et al. 2018 (Tinnitus).

89 "In the end, however, the autonomous right to refuse treatment has to be respected". Boer 2018, claiming to describe the common view of committee members.

90 Buiting et al. 2009. The Belgian Commission asked this 15 times in 2018–2019, FCECE 2020.

91 "Regarding the persistent and unbearable physical or mental suffering it is the patient, and the patient alone, who determines whether he or she is suffering from it. The physician's task is simply to be certain that *the patient finds him-or herself* in such a situation." Nys 2017, 17; cf. Montero 2017, 32–33.

92 E.g., FCECE 2020, 20.

93 Raus, VanderHaegen, Sterckx 2021 suspect that the Commission even considers an illness incurable if the patient has refused a promising curative treatment.

the proper way.[94] Similarly, the requirement of unbearable and intractable suffering is actually vacuous if only the patient can decide whether his suffering is unbearable and no alternative can be a reasonable one if he rejects it. A legal regime of that kind only pays lip service to the doctor's duty to relieve suffering. We cannot say at present that the Dutch regulatory regime for euthanasia is a regime of that kind, but it clearly is in danger of becoming one. The Belgian situation is at least as worrisome.

What about the other jurisdictions that have legalized euthanasia? No legal regime that at present permits euthanasia under certain conditions claims that respect for the right to self-determination is its sole justifying ground, because all these regimes restrict the exercise of that right to persons in a certain condition. The Canadian *Bill C-7* (2021) requires persons who wish to receive MAID to "have enduring and intolerable physical or psychological suffering that cannot be alleviated under conditions the person considers acceptable".[95] Western Australia's *Voluntary Assisted Dying Act* (2019) merely requires that in order to be eligible for access to VAD a person should be diagnosed with a medical condition that "is causing suffering to the person that cannot be relieved in a manner that the person considers tolerable".[96] In none of these jurisdictions doctors' judgements about the applicability of the eligibility criteria are systematically reviewed. Whether doctors in performing euthanasia do not only consciously act out of respect for the patient's will but also out of concern for his interest seems therefore everywhere largely a matter of their own discretion.

12.8 Prosecutorial policy

The judgement of any of the Dutch committees that a doctor has not satisfied all legal requirements will be sent on to the Public Prosecutor's Office and to the Inspectorate of Health Care. The Office has issued a procedural guideline for dealing with such reports.[97] If the doctor has failed to perform the euthanasia in a medically appropriate way, this is

94 This has been acknowledged by the Dutch Supreme Court when, in a wrongful life case, it recognized a right to abortion deriving from the right to self-determination, HR 18-3-2005, ECLI:NL:HR:2005:ARS213 (*Baby Kelly*). On my view the Dutch abortion law should be revised accordingly.

95 Of the 9375 written requests for MAID (2020) 21.2% did not result in a MAID death, including 6% of patients deemed ineligible. 15.2% of those ineligible patients did not experience suffering that was intolerable to them, Health Canada 2020.

96 New Zealand's *End of Life Choice Act* (2019) stipulates that the patient "experiences unbearable suffering that cannnot be relieved in a manner that the person considers tolerable". Spain's recent euthanasia law (2021) requires a "serious, chronic and incapacitating illness or serious and incurable disease" and "constant and intolerable physical or psychological suffering", but doesn't mention alternative ways of relieving that suffering, Sanz 2021.

97 Openbaar Ministerie, *Aanwijzing vervolgingsbeslissing inzake levensbeëindiging op verzoek (euthanasie en hulp bij zelfdoding)*, 2003, most recent edition 2017.

not considered a matter to be dealt with by a criminal proceeding, and therefore left to the Inspectorate. If a procedural mistake has been made, in particular in the consultation process, the Public Prosecutor will consider whether the failure leads to the suspicion of a failing on one of the substantial requirements. This has never been the case.

Finally, in those few cases in which the review committee has concluded that one of the substantial requirements has not been met, the Public Prosecutor's Office reconsiders the case on its merits, sometimes using its own methods of acquiring additional evidence, or findings of the Inspectorate. Even in those cases the Public Prosecutor has, until recently, never found a failure that was serious enough to warrant prosecution. The case will then be dismissed. Only in a few cases the dismissal has been a conditional one, which means that a second similar failure within a probation time will lead to prosecution. More often the Prosecutor's Office or the Inspectorate will be satisfied if the physician acknowledges that she has made a mistake.

That none of these cases has led the Public Prosecutor to request criminal sanctions is by itself not problematic. As I argued in Section 11.2, it cannot be the aim of a system of legal safeguards to track down cases of criminal abuse, because the system has to rely on self-reporting. In at least one important case, however, the decision of the Public Prosecutor, as reported back to the review committees and summarized in one of their annual reports, appears to have been motivated by several interpretations of the provisions of the euthanasia law that fundamentally diverged from the interpretation of the committees as published in their annual reports and (more recently) in the *Euthanasia Code*.[98] According to the Public Prosecutor, for example, admission to a nursing home could not be considered a 'reasonable alternative' for the patient because she had rejected that option in her advance directive. Such a dispute about the basic meaning of the law is highly undesirable; it should be settled by a court. This happened in 2020 when the Dutch Supreme Court arbitrated a long-standing dispute about the permissibility of euthanasia on the basis of an advance directive in the case of patients in an advanced state of dementia (Section 15.7). In its verdict the court confirmed a ruling of a lower court and overturned rulings by a review committee and two disciplinary courts.

In Belgium the one case in which the Federal Commission had given a negative judgement, has been dismissed by a court because it didn't consider it a case of 'ending a person's life on his explicit request' (Section 12.5, footnote 56). Prosecution started in another case on the request of relatives of the deceased, in spite of a positive judgement of the Commission. The doctor who had performed the euthanasia and two consultants were acquitted by a grand jury in a procedure that seemed,

98 Case 2012-03, cf. Chapter 15, footnote 53. For the decision of the Public Prosecutor see RTE Annual Report 2014, 73–75.

on both sides, mainly to aim at arousing the sentiments of the public.[99] In a third case that is now considered by the European Court of Human Rights, the patient's son accuses the Belgian state of having failed to protect his mother's right to life by granting her request for euthanasia without a proper examination of possible alternatives.[100] All these cases concerned psychiatric patients. Taken together these three cases clearly show that the law in this area is in need of clarification.

I don't deny of course that criminal procedures should be started and sanctions imposed when, however accidentally, gross violations of the law come to light. But the primary aim of legal proceedings in this area should be to obtain authoritative decisions on the interpretation of the law.[101] This instrument should be used with restraint. If the Public Prosecutor is too trigger-happy, this can have negative consequences: loss of trust within the medical community, and suffering patients who are unnecessarily let down.[102] In both countries the law has, in this respect, functioned to some extent, but hardly optimally.

12.9 'Precise' and 'strict'

I have stressed that in order to evaluate the success of any regulatory system we have to be clear what we can properly and realistically expect it to accomplish. John Keown recently published 400 pages of relentless criticism of all existing regulatory systems that can be summarized in five words: These people trust their doctors![103] One part of his argument is that the requirements of due care these systems prescribe are too indeterminate to be useful because their central concepts, 'unbearable suffering', 'impaired judgment' and so on, are imprecise.[104] However, as Aristotle taught us, it is the mark of an educated person to look for precision in each class of things just so far as the nature of the subject

99 Case of *Tine Nys*, Court of Assizes Oost-Vlaanderen, Ghent 30-1-2020.

100 Tom Mortier petitioned the ECHR for violation of *ECHR*, Art. 2 & 8.

101 Griffiths, Weyers, Adams 2008, 209; cf. Callahan, White 1996, 6, discussing the view that a regulated legalization of euthanasia is to be preferred to an absolute prohibition that is not enforced.

102 Following the appointment of a new Procureur-General the Dutch Public Prosecution Office in 2018 suddenly announced to start criminal investigations in five cases in which the doctor according to the review committees had not satisfied all legal requirements. All these cases were very special and complicated ones, but the result was a sudden drop in the total number of euthanasia cases, from 6585 cases in 2017 to 6126 in 2018. In the end only one doctor was prosecuted (and finally acquitted) (Section 15.7).

103 Keown 2018.

104 "Euthanasia opponents sometimes try to goad advocates of legalisation to put forward a 'safe' proposal, which can then be gleefully shot down. The underlying problem is that the process of assessing patients, and interpreting safeguards, calls for judgments, and judgments can be value-laden, difficult, and uncertain." Magnusson 2004.

admits.[105] Requirements that are as precise as those regulating the permissible measures of luggage to be taken aboard of an aeroplane would necessarily fail to do justice to the nature of this particular subject. The legal criteria have to reflect the actual reasons why people all over the world sometimes decide to end their lives, and these reasons constitute a complex whole.

But can we really trust doctors to make such complex judgements, even if they are indispensable? The answer is that we have no alternative because such judgements are equally indispensable in many other areas of medicine, and in particular in the larger area of end-of-life decisions.[106] This is as true of prohibitive as of permissive regimes. When can a treatment option rightly be abstained from because it is 'futile', when is a dosage of opioids used for palliative aims 'proportional' and when do 'refractory symptoms' justify starting palliative sedation? There are also large indeterminacies in the law of homicide, for example as regards stopping eating and drinking – is it a form of suicide (Section 4.3)? – and as regards the combined policy of sedation until death and abstaining from artificial hydration (Section 7.3).

The second part of Keown's argument is that the rules of the existing regulatory system are not strictly enforced. Apparently, he means by 'strict enforcement' that every application of the rules by a doctor or a consultant is or at least can be checked for correctness by a controlling body. As I have argued in Section 12.6 as regards the concept of 'unbearable suffering', given the fact that the application of such concepts requires complex holistic judgements of the actual case, strict enforcement in this sense is impossible. Moreover, the requirement itself leads to an infinite regress: if we don't trust the doctors, why should we trust the enforcers? Who is to control the controllers? And again, the question arises why this requirement should be made for decisions to grant a request for euthanasia or access to lethal drugs, but not for the decision to abstain from treatment, to use palliative drugs that will shorten life when used in sufficiently high dosages, to start continuous deep sedation, to amputate a leg, or, in a case of ovarian cancer, to remove the uterus of an otherwise healthy young woman (Chapter 2, footnote 58). Courts that have to decide about the involuntary confinement of patients who pose a risk for themselves or others also have to rely on medical judgements that they can only marginally evaluate. In the case of the medical profession generally we have no alternative but to trust the professionals, if not unconditionally, at least to a large extent. (We pay them accordingly.) A regulatory system can only work if most doctors can be trusted to have some commitment to its rules beyond their (usually excessive) fear of sanctions.

105 *Nicomachean Ethics* I, 1094b.24.
106 Magnusson 2004.

12.10 Conclusion

It is false that regulatory systems are necessarily Potemkin villages, mere façades covering a medical reality in which anything goes: at least one existing system is not.[107] In the large majority of the reported Dutch cases the reporting doctor has in good faith and with a reasonable degree of knowledge of the law assessed the case in terms of the legal requirements, and the doctor she has consulted has in equally good faith and with a pretty good knowledge of the law confirmed her assessment. The review system contributes to the stability of the system, mainly by providing feedback to doctors and consultants about the meaning of the legal requirements. The work of John Griffiths on the social working of law may explain the success of the Dutch regulatory system: a practice of the ongoing interpretation and implementation of relatively open norms through procedures that aim at minimizing bureaucracy and maximizing transparency and accountability.[108]

This is not to deny that some elements of the evidence we have considered about the Dutch system are worrisome. These elements include:

- divergences in the understanding of the law by doctors, and the imposition of personal moral views by some of them on patients;
- indications of the fairly common and probably increasing occurrence of pressure on doctors, both by patients and their families, to grant requests for euthanasia or speeding up its performance; and
- signs of the erosion of the requirement of intolerable and intractable suffering, which may be part of a development to a predominantly autonomy-driven system.

My findings as regards Flanders suggest the same problems, but also additional ones. This is true, even though many of the standard criticisms of the Belgian system cannot be substantiated because they rely on mistaken criteria for the identification of cases of euthanasia (Section 12.4). The knowledge of Belgian doctors of the legal requirements seems rather defective. The percentage of requests that are refused by reference to these requirements is much lower than in the Netherlands, although this may partially be explainable by the fact that the Belgian law requires a request in writing. Hand-picking of the 'independent' consultant seems to occur regularly, although we have no precise picture of the practice as regards genuine cases of euthanasia. The reporting doctor has no obligation to add

107 See Griffiths, Weyers in Griffihts, Weyers, Adams 2008, 137, explaining why their low expectations of the functioning of the Dutch review committees of ten years before (footnote 4) had been "quite wrong"; cf. pp. 49, 209–212. See also chapter 11, foonote 7.

108 Griffiths 2003. The paper provides the theoretical foundation of his work on the regulation of euthanasia. Cf. Kiewiet 2018.

the consultant's report to his own, hence we know nothing about the quality of these reports. The review system is an inscrutable black box. If that system provides doctors with any feedback, this is limited to the didactic letters that are sent to reporting doctors, of which we know almost nothing. Finally, in cases in which the doctor's behaviour showed shortcomings, the Commission has too much discretion to conclude, nevertheless, that she had satisfied the legal requirements.

These problematic features of the Belgian system are to a large extent to be explained by the process of legal change.[109] The euthanasia law introduced legal pressure on physicians who were accustomed to an almost unlimited extent of *de factor* freedom to do as they thought best. The system as it functions still holds back on making inroads on that *de facto* freedom (Chapter 10 at footnote 75).

Many of the defects of these systems could possibly be addressed by legal reform. That observation confirms the conclusion that the risks of legalization can largely be managed by a system of legal safeguards that turns out to be an appropriate one, not only on the drawing board but also in practice. I don't deny, however, that success also depends on social and cultural factors, in particular ideas and perceptions in the population at large and the medical community (cf. Chapter 9, at footnote 63; Section 16.1). It may be impossible at this stage for any review system to exercise a significant degree of scrutiny of the judgements of doctors and consultants about the legal requirement of intolerable suffering that cannot be alleviated. Anyway, this requirement is at present everywhere mainly left in the hands of doctors and consultants.

In the next chapters I will discuss whether legalization could and should be extended to people who want to end their lives but do not suffer from a lethal illness that will cause them to die within a few months anyway. In particular I will focus on patients suffering from mental illness or from an accumulation of ailments that are characteristic of old age. Is there any system of legal safeguards that we could trust to protect these patients to a sufficient extent against the risks of abuse and error? The results of the discussion in these chapters will be used in the final chapter to design, at least in outline, a relatively satisfactory legal framework.

109 As described by Adams in Griffiths, Weyers, Adams 2008, ch. 8.

Part IV

Hard cases

13 Mental illness

13.1 The urgency of the question

Until recently the question whether psychiatric patients could be eligible for being assisted in ending their lives was a question of almost purely academic interest. Debates about legalizing assisted suicide in American states invariably focused on patients with a fatal illness and a life expectancy of no more than half a year. Only in Belgium, the Netherlands, Luxembourg and Switzerland both the law and professional regulations for doctors already for some time permit euthanasia in some psychiatric cases, but even in these countries the actual number of such cases was until recently extremely small. In recent years, however, the topic has become the subject of an urgent, indeed heated debate. One reason for this is that, first in Belgium and now also in the Netherlands, a growing number of psychiatric patients actually receive medical assistance in ending their lives.[1] But it is still true that only a small minority of psychiatrists is willing to make such use of the legal options; many of their colleagues are quite critical of the practice. In both countries published cases have sparked an impassionate debate among psychiatrists and in

1 In the Netherlands the number of reported cases of euthanasia (including physician-assisted suicide) involving psychiatric patients rose from 2 in 2008 to 88 in 2020, RTE Annual report 2020. A total of 35 cases had been reported by psychiatrists, 14 by GPs and most of the others presumably by specialists in geriatric medicine. In a survey from 2016 60 psychiatrists reported to have granted a request for euthanasia in the past year (having received 1100 requests), Onwuteaka-Philipsen et al. 2017, 137. The number of cases of euthanasia involving psychiatric disorders reported to the Belgian Federal Comission for Euthanasia Control and Evaluation in 2019 was 34, FCECE 2020. For earlier data see Dierickx et al. 2017, Table 1. As regards Switzerland Steck, Junker, Zwahlen 2018 studied 3941 assisted suicides reported between 2003 and 2014. The underlying illness was reported to be mental or behavioural illness in 5.8% of the cases in the age group 25–64, and in 4.2% in the age group 65–94 (2.9% mood disorder, 0.8% dementia). Bruns et al. 2016 counted 17 cases of mental illness in a total number of 117 cases of assisted suicide performed by *Sterbehilfe Deutschland* (Assistance in Dying Germany) between 2010 and 2013, when medical assistance was permitted in parts of Germany.

DOI: 10.4324/9781003281115-17

the media. The three Belgian cases in which doctors had or have to face criminal proceedings all concerned psychiatric patients.[2] In that country a number of professional organizations have recently proposed adding some new, much more exacting requirements of due care to the ones already provided for by the euthanasia law.[3]

The second development that gave a new urgency to the topic occurred in Canada. Only at the last moment the text of the Canadian *Bill C-14* (2016) that allowed for 'medical assistance in dying' was amended by adding the requirements that eligible patients should be 'in an advanced state of irreversible decline in capabilities' and that for them natural death should have become 'reasonably foreseeable'. These requirements effectively excluded psychiatric patients. The change, however, was highly controversial. Both camps in this controversy appealed to the Dutch and Belgian experience to bolster their view, thereby connecting the European and Canadian discussions.[4] On 27 March 2021 the Canadian parliament passed *Bill C-7* that deleted the life-expectancy restrictions on eligibility. This opened the way for euthanasia in the case of psychiatric patients, but the Bill introduced a *sunset clause*, giving the government two years for designing a system of protocols, guidance and safeguards.[5] Clearly the parliamentarian majority felt already sure enough that a satisfactory system can be found, even though it was not yet able to identify it.

Three positions are basically defended in this debate.[6] On the one hand there are people who believe that the law should categorically forbid euthanasia in the case of psychiatric patients. This group includes, of course, people who are unhappy with any legal space for euthanasia; they will typically argue that the Dutch and Belgian developments give evidence of an unavoidable downwards movement on the slippery slope that, apparently, is still waiting to start in Oregon and the other American states that have legalized assisted suicide.[7] In this chapter I will concentrate, however, on the reasons for a special prohibition in the case of psychiatric patients.

On the other side we find people who argue that euthanasia should be available to psychiatric patients on the same conditions as to patients suffering from a lethal illness.[8] In-between there are people who believe

2 See Chapter 12, footnotes 56, 99, 100.

3 Belgisch Raadgevend Comité voor Bioethiek (Belgian Advisory Committee on Bioethics) 2017; Vlaamse Vereniging voor Psychiatrie (Flemish Psychiatry Association) 2017; Gastmans, Denier 2018 (Zorgnet-Icuro); Orde der Artsen/Ordre des Médecins 2019. The first three are analyzed by Verhofstadt et al. 2019.

4 See Council of Canadian Academies 2018a; 2018b. See also the use of (largely false) information about the Dutch and Belgian practice in American Psychiatric Association 2016.

5 Okninski, Grieger 2021.

6 Nicolini et al. 2020 offer a helpful survey of arguments on the subject of this chapter.

7 E.g., Jones, Gastmans, MacKellar 2017, 282.

8 E.g., Shuklenk et al. 2011; Schuklenk, Van de Vathorst 2015a; Downie 2016; Rooney, Shuklenk, Van de Vathorst 2018.

that euthanasia should be accessible to psychiatric patients, but on more strict conditions than in the case of patients in the last stage of a physical illness. The arguments they use for additional caution tend to be the same arguments that motivate proponents of a categorical prohibition, but they also recognize arguments for the other side, or make a different weighing. My aim in this chapter will be to evaluate these arguments. Psychiatric disorders are widespread, often chronic and fairly often associated with a desire to die. Although at present euthanasia in cases of mental illness is still infrequent in permissive jurisdictions, the legal regulation of this issue therefore has a considerable impact on the way in which psychiatric patients think about their prospects and discuss them with their intimates and doctors.

In this section I have already used the term 'euthanasia' even though in many actual cases the patient performed the last action in the series of actions necessary for ending his life. I have announced this use of the term in Section 5.6, arguing that in the case of any joint action it doesn't matter who completes it. What *does* matter is whether the physician who is involved takes final responsibility for a quick, safe and painless death. In Section 13.9 I will address the question whether it wouldn't be enough to allow doctors to provide a psychiatric patient access to lethal drugs, as they are legally permitted to do in Switzerland.

I will avoid the term 'treatment-resistant depression', because, even if we could score a depressive condition on a scale indicating the probability of treatment failure (see Section 13.4), it would still be undecided at which point on the scale we should call the patient's condition 'treatment-resistant'. And actually there is no consensus about the required number of trials and the evaluation of the patient's response to them.[9] It is a substantive normative question when it is legitimate to stop trying additional treatments.[10] We should not conceal that question by using quasi-diagnostic labels.

13.2 An undisputed starting point

Is there any common ground between the three positions that I have identified in Section 13.1? Almost no-one will deny, I suppose, that when a psychiatric patient dies, we will sometimes be able to judge that it would have been better for him to have died months or years earlier. Life has been extremely hard for such a patient, usually for a much longer time than for patients suffering from a fatal illness. The very fact that a natural death was not in sight may have added to her misery.

9 Trachsel et al. 2016.

10 An important issue that I will not discuss in this chapter is whether the law should require, not only recommend, the patient's family to be informed or consulted. Cf. the cases of Tine Nys and Tom Mortier's mother, Chapter 12, footnotes 99–100.

In some cases the suffering of such patients will consist of symptoms of their illness. Think of hallucinations, paranoia, feelings of guilt or anxiety and mood disturbances.[11] Other elements of suffering are the effects of behaviour that expresses the illness. Eating disorders provide an obvious example, as do forms of self-injury involved in other disorders. Psychosomatic symptoms – chronic fatigue, general malaise, headache, nausea and of course stress – are common elements in most cases of mental illness, often resulting from or aggravated by one or more additional physical or psychiatric conditions, including pain and injuries produced by suicide attempts.[12] In addition much suffering results from the impact of the illness on the patients' capacity to cope with problems in life, and therefore their capacity to engage in meaningful pursuits, in intimate relations or even to be open to matters of interest in the surrounding world. Mental illness can lead to poverty, homelessness and inability to use educational and employment opportunities, and lack of self-care. Some of these elements of suffering are the side-effects of treatment, including forms of coercion involved in treatment. Many of these patients will have long-standing death wishes, often leading to suicide attempts.

In some of these cases in which we judge, in retrospect, that it would have been better for the patient to have died earlier, the patient has at some time made a request for euthanasia. And so we can conclude that it would have been better for him if that request had been granted. But can we ever anticipate on this conclusion at the moment that the request is being made? There are three problems that, although not unknown in the case of somatic patients, are more pressing in the case of psychiatric ones.[13]

13.3 The first problem: multiple meanings and ambivalence

The first problem concerns the meaning of the patient's death wish. What exactly is it about death that makes it attractive to him? In the case of somatic patients we may normally assume that death represents to them the only way out of their suffering that is still available. But sometimes it may simply be an expression of burnout, of extreme fatigue. 'Let me sleep and never wake up again'. And of course, in some cases patients suffering from a physical illness may express a death wish because they

11 Strangely these elements of suffering are not mentioned by Verhofstadt, Thienpont 2017, a paper that otherwise offers an extensive description. See also Verhofstadt et al. 2021.

12 Kim, de Vries, Peteet 2016 reported 58% somatic comorbidity (from reports of euthanasia cases to a Dutch review committee); Evenblij et al. 2019 (from answers of psychiatrists to a questionnaire) 19% only.

13 All three already mentioned by Nederlandse Vereniging voor Psychiatrie 2009 (Dutch Psychiatry Association). This guideline (first edition 1998) has been replaced in 2018 by a more bureaucratic document that offers much less argumentation for the requirements it makes.

believe that their suffering is not taken seriously enough and not sufficiently addressed, by their families or by their doctors or both. In such cases the death wish is primarily a cry for (more) help, or at least for recognition. In the case of psychiatric patients this is more often the meaning, or one of the meanings, of the death wish, and it may be more difficult to understand it as such.[14] The patient may even want to end his life in order to punish his partner or children for the lack of attention he believes they give to his predicament.

Death can have other meanings as well. As we saw already a tendency to cause self-injury may be one of the symptoms of the illness, and the death wish may be an extreme expression of that tendency (Section 3.3). The physical harm the patient causes to himself may itself have multiple meanings. It may, for example, be the result of his belief that he deserves to be punished for his sins.[15] He may also want to escape from perceived threats that are exaggerated or completely illusory.

Because the understanding of the death wish is an important element in the therapeutic relationship, its development may also to some extent be a function of that relationship. The patient may use it as a negotiation asset and focussing on it may have – but need not have – a self-fulfilling effect.

On some of these understandings of the meaning of death, the death wish is an expression of the patient's illness, on others an appreciation of his present and future life as conditioned by his illness.[16] This is obviously relevant both for estimating the possibility of identifying an alternative to death as a 'solution' to the patient's problem (Section 13.4), and of his competence (Section 13.5). But the problem to identify the proper meaning or meanings of the death wish is also relevant by itself, independently of these further problems. In order to consider a request you have to know what it means.

That the death wish of a psychiatric patient can have multiple meanings that are open to the influence of the dynamics of the therapeutic relationship may also help to explain another characteristic of such wishes. Most death wishes are ambivalent to some extent, because death is not what the patient basically wants, he wants to escape from present and future misery (Chapter 3, footnote 33). Even some minor changes in his condition – or a firm commitment of his doctor to honour a

14 One patient tried for years to have her request for euthanasia granted in order to obtain recognition for her suffering as 'unbearable', and when the request had finally been granted felt unable to withdraw. Case as described by her friend, Boer, Groenewoud, de Jonge 2021, 70–77. Cf. Pesut et al. 2021b on people entering the assessment procedure for MAID in order to obtain support, social connection or even housing.

15 "The patient said she had had a life without love and therefore had no right to exist", quoted in Chapter 9 at footnote 40.

16 Berghmans, Widdershoven, Widdershoven-Heerding 2013.

future request for euthanasia – may therefore motivate him to postpone his appointment with death. This ambivalence, however, is more pronounced in the case of mental illness.[17] It is also more prominent in some conditions, e.g., a bipolar or a personality disorder, than in others.[18] Ambivalence also explains why after a failed attempt to kill themselves people frequently feel grateful for having been rescued.[19]

A certain degree of ambivalence in holding a death wish does not discredit it. It may even show that it is really the result of a serious weighing process in which alternative ways of dealing with the patient's situation are considered on their merits.[20] But a request for euthanasia that expresses a death wish that is extremely urgent one day but vanishes the next day cannot be called well-considered.

In order to be sure of both the meaning and the stability of a patient's death wish it often seems necessary to consider the development of that wish as an element of the evolution of the illness during a substantial stretch of time, in relation to attempts to deal with the patient's illness and to relieve his suffering. That is one good reason for believing that a request for death can best be considered by a therapist who for a long time has been involved with the patient's treatment[21] (see Section 13.7–13.8).

13.4 The second problem: uncertain prognosis[22]

Another reason why it is difficult in advance to be sufficiently sure that the patient's life will be characterized by severe suffering that cannot be relieved derives from our limited understanding of psychiatric disorders. Consider the way we classify them (Section 11.6). If the presence of a certain number of symptoms on a list can be established, we diagnose the patient, for example, as having a depressive disorder. The overlap of present symptoms between any two patients diagnosed as having a depressive disorder may be small, and the diagnosis tells us little about the aetiology of the illness. It is therefore no wonder that we are not very good at predicting the spontaneous development of the illness,

17 According to Emanuel et al. 2000 terminally ill patients with depression are more likely to change their minds about physician-assisted suicide than patients without depression.

18 Applebaum 2016.

19 Blaustein, Fleming 2009, cf. Chapter 3, footnote 33.

20 Nederlandse Vereniging voor Psychiatrie 2009, 31. Cf. Rössler 2017, ch. 1, arguing that in general ambivalence need not undermine autonomy.

21 Chabot 2017. According to VandenBerghe 2017 "one year with ten consultations is an absolute minimum to guide the patient through (the relevant) themes in a thorough and careful way".

22 Van Veen, Ruissen, Widdershoven 2020 provide a short but helpful survey of the arguments given in the literature about this subject.

nor – with some remarkable, largely unexplained exceptions – of the effects of any attempted form of treatment.[23] Often external events or social interventions, for example the development of a friendship or the assignment of a new apartment, can make the patient's condition tolerable without necessarily 'curing' his illness in any sense. Such events can also lead to the disappearance of his death wish.[24] It is therefore understandable that it is by far the most common reason why Dutch psychiatrists decline a patient's request for assisting him in ending his life that treatment-options have not yet been exhausted.[25] Although in the case of physical illness the prognosis and even the diagnosis may also be uncertain, in the case of mental illness uncertainty of that kind is much more widespread.

On the other hand, even if spontaneous remission, or, more often, partial recovery occurs, sometimes after decennia of illness, the probability of that event is growing smaller over time, and generally speaking the probability of success is also growing smaller for each new unsuccessful attempt to treat the illness.[26] This tendency is often reinforced by the experience of inadequate treatment and care or coercion. Often the prospects of positive treatment effects are also worsened by comorbidity. And, as the eventual outcome at the 'natural' death of the patient reminds us (Section 13.2), in deciding whether or not to grant his request for euthanasia there is no safe side to err on. It is true that the decision to grant the request is irreversible and the decision not to grant it reversible, but if that is a reason for never granting a request, the difference disappears.

One common criticism of the Dutch and Belgian practice is that the review committees in both countries sometimes approve of euthanasia in a case in which some standard treatment for the condition of the patient has not been attempted.[27] It is then suggested that for each condition there should be a list of treatments, regularly to be updated,

23 Kelly, McLoughlin 2002.

24 The palliative care or recovery movement in psychiatry aims, in the case of therapy-resistant depression or schizophrenia, at the management of symptoms that cause the patient's low quality of life and the provision of an environment that best enables him to cope with the resulting problems, without any ambition of cure, Berk et al. 2012; Trachsel et al. 2016; Gastmans, Denier 2018, Section 1.4. Actually this is what many psychiatrists always did.

25 Overall 53% of 66 refusals, Onwuteaka-Philipsen et al. 2017, 147; Evenblij et al. 2019. Of Belgian psychiatrists who had performed euthanasia only 70% considered the patient's disorder incurable, Verhofstadt et al. 2021.

26 This is the empirical basis of attempts to measure treatment-resistance on the basis of past antidepressant treatment failures, Fekadu, Donocik, Cleare 2018. The authors recognize that, until the pathophysiology of depression is better understood, such methods can only be tentative approximations.

27 Kim, De Vries, Peteet 2016; Lemmens, Kim, Kurz 2018. On similar concerns among Belgian and Dutch psychiatrists see Lemmens 2018, 486ff.

that should have been attempted before a request for euthanasia can be considered.[28]

The underlying principle of this suggestion is correct: every evidence-based treatment option that has a substantial chance of success within a reasonable time frame and that does not involve burdens to the patient that are disproportional to that chance should be tried out.[29] Otherwise we cannot be sure enough that there is insufficient hope for improvement. The question is whether we should implement that principle by ticking off a standardized list. The effects of some treatment options, e.g., electroconvulsive therapy (ECT), other brain stimulation therapies with less risk of creating cognitive impairments, or some kinds of medication, may be so clear and pervasive that we should insist on trying them out in all cases for which they are indicated. In the case of other treatments, however, the effectiveness of a treatment may be disputable in particular circumstances, for example as a result of social problems or because of a history of non-responsiveness to related treatments. Comorbidity adds new dimensions to a kind of suffering that is already multidimensional. If any alternative treatment promises to decrease the level of suffering in one dimension, what about the other dimensions?

The unclarities surrounding psychiatric diagnosis and prognosis exacerbate this problem. If in going through the list of prescribed treatments we register only failures, we may start to doubt whether we work with the correct list. This point also applies to social interventions, community-based treatments, outpatient care, protected living *etcetera*. Sometimes we may be able to specify the prognosis for a subgroup with a particular constellation of symptoms. In such cases a psychiatrist who knows the patient's history could be justified in judging that the possible burdens of a try-out do not weigh up against its promise, in particular when an independent colleague confirms his view. In such cases insisting on ticking off a standard list is a clear example of therapeutic obstinacy.[30] In the end it can only be a matter of judgement in the individual case whether any proposed alternative has any realistic promise of success.[31] Machine learning algorithms based on clinical information and biomarkers may increasingly support us in making such judgements, but they cannot replace it.

28 See, e.g., the Maudsley Treatment Inventory discussed by Fekadu, Donocik, Cleare 2018. Nederlandse Vereniging voor Psychiatrie 2009, 38 offers a list of indicated biological and psychotherapeutic treatments that should have been attempted in the case of a depressive disorder. Vlaamse Vereniging voor Psychiatrie 2017, 17 specifies the medically indicated regular biological treatments that should have been tried.

29 Nederlandse Vereniging voor Psychiatrie 2009, 37–39; cf. Regionale Toetsingscommissies Euthanasie, *Euthananasia Code* 2018, 26.

30 Warned against in the recent deontological guideline of the Orde der Artsen 2019.

31 Steinbock 2017; Verhofstadt et al. 2021.

Both sides to this dispute appeal to their own sources, occasionally even to the same source,[32] in order to argue that the effects of many treatments are either substantial or unimpressive. What we can say in any case is that the effectiveness of many psychiatric treatments is not well known or disputed. In most psychiatric environments some patients are no longer offered any new treatment at all because the chances of success are considered too low. When such patients request euthanasia, the argument that no psychiatric illness can ever be judged untreatable,[33] is not particularly convincing. For such patients it means that they have to wait for spontaneous improvement or a new form of treatment.

In many cases a treatment option, including electroconvulsive therapy (ECT), cannot be attempted because the patient refuses to cooperate. It is often supposed that such a refusal cannot rule out the patient's eligibility for euthanasia because he has the right to refuse.[34] If he refuses, and is sufficiently competent to do so, he cannot be subjected to the treatment, but that doesn't imply that his normative position does not change in other respects, in particular that his request for euthanasia can still be considered (Section 12.7). Refusal of treatment by a patient who is considered to have capacity may nevertheless be influenced by distorted perceptions that reflect either the patient's illness or a history of incompetent treatment.[35] Perhaps such perceptions could be corrected by the very treatment that he refuses.[36] It doesn't follow, however, that a treatment-refusal is always irrelevant for assessing alternatives.[37] Not every such refusal is a use of negotiation power. When a Dutch review committee judges that a doctor could judge a treatment option not to be a 'reasonable alternative' because it had been refused by the patient, the committee usually argues that this particular option has little promise if the patient has no confidence in trying it out, and that the patient's lack of confidence is understandable after a long history of unsuccessful treatment attempts. A psychotherapeutic approach in

32 Fekadu et al. 2012, appealed to by Kim, Lemmens 2016, and by Rooney, Schuklenk, van de Vathorst 2018.

33 Kelly, McLoughlin 2002.

34 Dembo, Schuklenk, Reggler 2018, but cf. Rooney, Schuklenk, van de Vathorst 2018. According to Nederlandse Vereniging voor Psychiatrie 2009, 21, 39, a request for euthanasia cannot be granted if the patient refuses a treatment that could alleviate his suffering without creating disproportional burdens. Similarly, Nederlandse Vereniging voor Psychiatrie 2018, 69; Belgisch Raadgevend Comité voor Bioethiek 2017, criticizing the view of the Federal Control and Evaluation Commission for Euthanasia (FCECE); Vlaamse Vereniging voor Psychiatrie 2017; Orde der Artsen 2019.

35 Council of Canadian Academies 2018b, 78–79.

36 Rudnick 2002.

37 Kim, De Vries, Peteet 2016 seem to draw this conclusion when they point out that 37 of the 66 Dutch psychiatric patients they studied had refused at least one proposed treatment. Cf. Tuffrey-Wijne et al. 2018.

particular normally requires a genuine willingness to cooperate at the side of the patient. This is not by itself an illegitimate consideration, though the Dutch committees may appeal to it too easily (Section 12.7). But the point remains that the evaluation of patients' refusals further complicates the assessment of the possible success of remaining options for treatment and care.

In some cases a person's reasons for refusing treatment options have to do with the core of her personal identity. She may consider the very idea of relieving her suffering by refocusing her mind a betrayal of persons who have been central figures in the history of her life. Take for example the case of a very old Jewish lady, diagnosed with Post Traumatic Stress Disorder, who not only suffers from memories from the Second World War but also considers these memories, however painful, a way of honouring her loved ones "who haven't made it".[38] In such cases the basic question isn't merely how effective a proposed treatment would be. By insisting on trying it out as a condition of eligibility we might show lack of respect for the person she is.

The Canadian law differs from the Dutch and Belgian laws by not requiring a professional judgement of the availability of possibly effective treatment options but only a subjective judgement by the patient that he doesn't consider such options promising and acceptable (Section 12.7). This seems particularly problematic in the case of mental illness. Even psychiatrists who are prepared to consider the patient's request seriously will sometimes correctly believe that she has neither the ability nor the motivation to properly evaluate possible alternatives in terms of her own values. In such cases the patient's refusal may also complicate, perhaps even compromise, the assessment of her decisional capacity.

13.5 The third problem: assessing competence and authority

The third factor that complicates the evaluation of a request of a psychiatric patient for euthanasia is a fairly obvious one: how to decide whether the request is made with sufficient competence to be taken as an authoritative representation of the patient's will. In earlier chapters I have argued that a death wish as such is not a reason to suspect lack of competence; it only is when, under the circumstances, it is insufficiently intelligible (Section 11.6). Hence there is no general reason to require each person who requests euthanasia to be examined by a psychiatrist. A request from a psychiatric patient is not necessarily a symptom of his

38 Case 2021-137; cf. Wijsbek 2012a on Mrs. Bosscher, the patient in the *Chabot* case 1994. Since then Chabot's view is that such patients should preferably be informed about ways to end their own lives in a humane way, *Trouw* 26-6-1996, cf. Section 13.9.

illness either, but possibly reflects an understandable evaluation of his present and future condition as it results from his illness. Even most chronically depressed patients go through intermediate periods in-between episodes of deep depression, and during these periods may be capable of a sober assessment of their situation.[39] The same is true in the case of other disorders, including bipolar disorder and schizophrenia. Even in the case of a permanent death wish, for example of patients suffering from mood or personality disorder the wish need not be a mere product of distorted valuation.

But this is difficult to make out. "How can one be sure that one is not unwittingly colluding with a person's pathology rather than respecting a persons' well-considered judgment?"[40] At the least, therefore, there are, in the case of a request from a psychiatric patient, reasons always to require expert examination of his competence[41] (Sections 3.5; 11.6). One reason is that some categories of mental illness – neurocognitive disorders and intellectual disabilities – involve a clear diminishing of the relevant cognitive abilities, and other categories – e.g., major depressive, bipolar and anxiety disorders – a risk of impaired capacity due to the impact of the disorder on the patient's mood and emotions. In some conditions, in particular in psychotic and bipolar disorders, the patient is often unaware of his own mental illness,[42] in other conditions, depressive disorders in particular, he is aware of the medical facts, but often fails to appreciate their significance[43] (Section 3.3). The reason may be that he can only imagine one possible future, a very bleak one, and is unable to think through alternative possibilities.[44] Another reason may be that the meaning of the death wish needs to be clarified. And even in cases in which it would be understandable as a response to the actual condition of the patient and his circumstances that need not be his real or primary motive.

39 Nederlandse Vereniging voor Psychiatrie 2009, 32.

40 Gupta, Desmarais 2016, quoted by Kious, Battin 2019.

41 The Belgian euthanasia law requires the consultation of at least one psychiatrist, but this requirement is not always satisfied, perhaps because of comorbidity, Dierickx et al. 2017. The guideline of the Nederlandse Vereniging voor Psychiatrie 2009 required the consultation of one psychiatrist, but this guideline applied only to psychiatrists. This largely explains why in 9 of 55 reported cases no psychiatrist had been consulted, den Hartogh 2015b, cf. Kim, de Vries, Peteet 2016 for a similar finding. In five cases in which the consulting psychiatrist gave a negative advice, the deciding doctor (in all cases a psychiatrist) invited a GP as consultant. In 2015 the Regional Review Committees confirmed the requirement of the guideline and extended it to all physicians, cf. *Euthanasia Code* 2018, 41. In cases 2014-01 and 2018-42 the committee decided that the doctor had not met the legal requirements of due care because of his failure to consult a psychiatrist.

42 Cairns et al. 2005; Owen at al. 2008.

43 Hindmarch, Hotopf, Owen 2013 with further references.

44 Meynen 2011; Halpern 2012.

I do not dispute that in some cases no special psychiatric expertise is needed to establish the well-considered character of a psychiatric patient's request for euthanasia. Even if that is true, however, it is questionable whether a doctor who hasn't such expertise can identify such cases with sufficient confidence. If only for that reason a regulatory framework for decision-making in this area should require psychiatrists to be involved in determining whether the patient's request reflects a stable death wish, competently made, and caused by conditions that cannot realistically be expected to improve. The problem is not that we don't know that such cases exist – we do know – but to design institutional arrangements capable of identifying them.[45]

Critics, however, argue that this is not enough. One reason they advance is that, even among psychiatrists, there seems to be a substantial lack of consensus in assessing competence in this case.[46] Whether this is generally true is disputed.[47] But assessing competence is a normative judgement and psychiatrists have fundamentally different attitudes towards requests for euthanasia. It is therefore no wonder that they also disagree in judging the capacity of the requesters.[48] Some of them still believe that they are always a sign of lack of competence (Section 3.2). The Flemish doctor Lieve Thienpont, on the other hand, has been consulted in 100 cases between 2008 and 2011 and judged the patient to be sufficiently competent in all those cases.[49]

Another criticism of Dutch and Belgian practice is that even a psychiatrist who considers granting a request, let alone a consultant, rarely uses available instruments for the measurement of competence, as for example the MacCAT (MacArthur Competence Assessment Tool). Most of the time they only make a global clinical judgement.[50] The MacCAT judges whether the patient understands the information that is relevant to the decision that he has to make and uses it correctly in his practical reasoning. But the unavoidable consequence is that the instrument to some extent assesses the appropriateness of the decision in the eyes of the doctors who use the instrument, and therefore already relies on their normative judgement.[51] In any case it is unavoidable to inquire into the meaning or meanings for this patient of his death wish, and to consider its development over time in relation

45 Steinbock 2017.
46 Evidence is scarce. Doernberg, Peteet, Kim 2016 found that in 8 of the 66 Dutch cases (12%) they studied the physicians involved in the case (including GP's) disagreed about the patient's competence. That doesn't seem an exceptionally high percentage.
47 Cairns et al. 2005; Kim et al. 2006; Okai et al. 2007.
48 Ganzini 2014, quoted Chapter 11 at footnote 66; Ganzini et al. 2000.
49 Thienpont et al. 2015.
50 Doernberg, Peteet, Kim 2016.
51 Jongsma 2016, 13, with further references. Note also that the instrument is validated by the correspondence of its results to the clinical judgements of physicians.

to the development of his illness and the dynamics of his relation to his treating doctors. Finally, people's decisions are to a large extent actually determined by their affective states, and although these can be evaluated as more or less rational, that evaluation cannot be made by the MacCAT or similar tools.[52] For these reasons the use of such instruments, while generally helpful, is not equally helpful in all cases and it never makes a global clinical judgement dispensable.

These tools only measure a patient's relevant capacities on a scale. The instrument doesn't help us to determine the point on that scale where we should judge the patient to be sufficiently competent to recognize the authority of his self-regarding decisions (Section 11.6). And this binary judgement of authority doesn't depend on his decision-making competence in the scalar sense only, but also on other factors, prominently including what is at stake in making the decision, the risks and benefits involved.[53] It is also relevant how important the decision that the patient has to make is in terms of his own values, and how invasive interference with the execution of his decision would be.[54] An attribution or denial of authority can only rest on a holistic judgement concerning the case at hand, taking many disparate factors into account.[55] In the case of a request for assistance by a psychiatric patient who intends to end his life that judgement is even more complex than in other cases.

One of the factors that often has to be taken into account is the following. In the case of some mental illnesses the patient's cognitive abilities may be generally unimpaired, even excellent. Patients suffering from anorexia nervosa often belong to this category. But it is still problematic that they give such an inordinate priority to the value of being thin.[56] Similarly, a depressed patient can very well understand that the choice he is about to make will cause considerable harm to him or even endanger his life, but he just may not care.[57] It is often said that these warped valuations express underlying pathological conditions, but that explanation doesn't help us when it turns out that the condition is considered a pathological one precisely because it expresses itself in such non-standard valuations. (If you think that being thin is the most important thing in life you must be mad.) In many cases these valuations conflict with other basic values that these people are committed to, and in these

52 Welie 2001; Berghmans, Dickenson, Ter Meulen 2004; Breden, Vollmann 2004; Charland, Lemmens, Wada 2016.

53 Den Hartogh 2016b.

54 For that reason we may be more prepared to recognize the authority of a non-treatment decision than of a request for euthanasia, even if these decisions are made for the same motives and with the same level of (scalar) competence.

55 Den Hartogh 2016b; cf. den Hartogh 2019d. responding to Kious, Battin 2019.

56 Tan et al. 2006. For the general problem see Charland 2001; Winburn, Mullen 2008 (case study); Charland et al. 2013.

57 Elliott 1997; Rudnick 2002; cf. Buchanan, Brock 1990, 392.

cases we may diagnose the problem as a lack of authenticity. However the problem is to be explained, we should not see it as compromising the person's decision-making capacity in the scalar sense.[58] But it certainly is another element that complicates the attribution of decision-making authority in the case of psychiatric patients.

13.6 Should we always require competence?

There is an obvious tension between the requirement that there should be no 'reasonable' alternative for ending the patient's suffering and the requirement that he should be sufficiently competent to assess his condition. The more severe and chronic his suffering is, the more probable it will be that there is no reasonable alternative, but the less probable that his request will be sufficiently competent, and *vice versa*.[59] It seems to follow that the patients who are most in need of help in order to escape from their misery, are actually beyond help.

Take for example the case of two chronically depressed patients who are suffering from their condition to the same extent. One of them intermittently has periods of normal functioning, and in these periods is able to make the well-considered decision that, given the predictable return of periods of deep depression, it will be better for him that his life ends. The other patient lives more or less permanently on the same level of gloom and sadness, and we cannot deny that this condition to some extent taints his assessment of his own future. In both cases the patient's judgement that it would be better for him that his life ends is, given his condition and his prospects, fully understandable. It has been proposed that in these circumstances it is acceptable to lower the threshold of competence for the second person in order to make it possible for his request for euthanasia to be granted.[60] Otherwise it is the same condition that causes the patient's suffering that stands in his way of getting out of it.[61]

The proposal might seem preposterous, a step on the slippery slope from 'voluntary' to 'nonvoluntary euthanasia'.[62] Actually, it doesn't deviate from the usual ways in which judgements of (scalar) competence are being handled in medical practice. The basic issue is whether we should allow a person's decision to represent his interests authoritatively. In considering that issue we take several factors into account: his relevant

58 As Charland, Lemmens, Wada 2016 do. It is therefore not a defect in the MacCAT that it doesn't take this problem into account, as these authors suggest, den Hartogh 2016b.

59 Broome, de Cates 2017.

60 Nederlandse Vereniging voor Psychiatrie 2009, 51; Thienpont et al. 2015, 133. 82% of Dutch psychiatrists reject this proposal, Onwuteaka-Philipsen et al. 2017, 175.

61 As one psychiatrist observes regarding patients with personality disorders, Onwuteaka-Philipsen et al. 2017, 164.

62 Lemmens 2016, 303.

cognitive and affective abilities, the coherence of his valuations, but also, prominently, his interests. As a result, if a patient consents to a treatment proposal that seems an obviously prudent one to accept, our requirements on his decision-making capacities are allowed to be lower than when he rejects the proposal.[63]

In other cases, however, we can only conclude that the death wish of a patient is fully determined by his illness, for example by false beliefs of being persecuted by people who want to torture him.[64] Such cases belong to the class of psychiatric conditions that are least accessible to treatment, for the patient will believe that a treatment proposal is a denial of the obvious truth, and suspect the proposing psychiatrist to be involved in the persecution. Nevertheless, the permanent misery in which he lives as a result may fully justify the belief that it will be best for him to have his life ended. Should a psychiatrist be allowed to grant his request for euthanasia, even if this request is motivated by the wrong reasons? In that case the request wouldn't really matter, only the patient's suffering.

It is possible, indeed easy, to construct a clear case of this kind, but as a matter of fact such cases seem to be extremely rare. At the same time making legal space for euthanasia in such cases infringes on requirements of due care that are essential for the general protection of patients against risks of error, and of the public against fears of such risks. Even if we stipulate strict conditions for allowing an exception to these requirements, there will be a new problem of monitoring the practice and assessing appeals to these conditions. Regulatory frameworks cannot be fully adjusted to all individual problem cases (Section 10.3). I therefore suggest that a system that under some conditions permits euthanasia in the case of a psychiatric patient, should insist on a well-considered request of that patient as one of those conditions. If that policy has its casualties in very rare cases, that outcome is unavoidable.

13.7 How to implement additional caution

In this chapter I address two questions: should we make any legal space at all for assisting psychiatric patients in ending their lives, and, if so, should the conditions for doing this legitimately, be the same as the conditions we lay down in the case of patients suffering from a lethal somatic illness, or should we make additional requirements? I have identified three reasons why it is often particularly difficult to assess whether the request of

63 Kim et al. 2006; Akerboom et al. 2011. Perhaps we should interpret the response that the Swiss psychiatrists gave to Mr. Haas (Section 5.6) in this way: we cannot properly assess your competence without considering the reasons for your death wish and your refusal to consider alternatives.

64 Varelius 2015.

a psychiatric patient meets conditions that we consider essential in other cases: multiple meanings and pervasive ambivalence, uncertainty about the possibilities of spontaneous remission and effective treatment, and the possibility of the competence of the patient being compromised by his illness. These reasons don't apply to all cases, and no doubt to some cases none of them applies at all. But requirements of due care and the institutional arrangements for verifying that they apply cannot simply leave it to doctors to determine in individual cases to what extent these problems arise. The whole point of introducing such requirements and arrangements is to increase social confidence in the making of such judgements. We should therefore conclude that these complicating factors, even in systems that do not rule out euthanasia in all cases of mental illness, require additional caution in comparison to standard euthanasia requests. A further reason for additional caution is the fact that in Belgium and the Netherlands euthanasia cases almost never raise any public concern, but cases involving psychiatric patients regularly do.

Some of these reasons for additional caution may be more prominent in the case of some psychiatric disorders than of other ones. The problem of ambivalence is particularly characteristic of the desire to die of patients suffering from personality or bipolar disorders, the problem of warped values that I discussed at the end of Section 13.5 of depressive and eating disorders. The ability to understand relevant information will most commonly be defective in the case of psychotic and neurocognitive disorders, and, of course, mental retardation. It could therefore be asked for any particular psychiatric diagnosis whether it requires additional regulations, or even a categorical prohibition of euthanasia. But I will confine myself to a general discussion.

If we consider stipulating additional requirements which ones should we decide upon? [65] It seems plausible to require a waiting period between the first request and the actual life-ending act of more than the one month presently demanded by the Belgian law.[66] It seems also plausible that both the doctor who has to decide about the request and at least one of the legally required consultants should be a psychiatrist.[67] Mandatory consultation

65 For the requirements presently laid down by Dutch and Belgian law see footnote 41.

66 Vlaamse Vereniging voor Psychiatrie 2017 proposes six months, Gastmans, Denier 2018 one year. In 23 Belgian cases, discussed by Verhofstadt et al. 2021, the mean and median length of time of the assessment procedure was 13.5 and 6 months resp. In nine Dutch cases from 2016 the procedure took from 2 months to 2.5 years, Evenblij et al. 2019.

67 Vlaamse Vereniging voor Psychiatrie 2017, followed by Gastmans, Denier 2018 and Orde der Artsen 2019, requires the deciding psychiatrist and two consulting psychiatrists to physically meet each other in order to discuss the case and come to a unanimous decision. Actually, in the case of psychiatric patients euthanasia is sometimes performed by GP's without any involvement of a psychiatrist, possibly because in a case of comorbidity the underlying illness can be classified as 'polypathology', Dierickx et al. 2017, cf. footnote 41.

of a social worker could be considered in order to ascertain that there are no promising social interventions still worth trying.

In Sections 13.3–13.5 I have already indicated that each of the complicating factors I discussed in those sections provides us with a reason to require a long-standing therapeutic relationship between doctor and patient. Such a relationship best enables the psychiatrist to understand the meaning or meanings of the patient's death wish, verify its stability, assess the reasons for resisting treatment proposals and make an appropriately holistic judgement of competence. Are there any reasons not to insist on a long-standing relationship? In the first place such a relationship doesn't necessarily function optimally, in particular due to the psychological dynamic involved, what psychiatrists call transference and countertransference. Of course, psychiatrists are trained to deal with these phenomena in a professional way, not allowing themselves to get angry or irritated or frustrated or emotionally too much involved in the patient's suffering.[68] Peer consultation, intervision and supervision may help, and the adoption of these procedures as an integral part of the decision-making process should therefore at least be recommended, perhaps required. But no procedural requirement can guarantee a satisfactory result.[69] A patient's death wish may remind the doctor of the limitations of his healing powers and his own mortality.[70] (That may also explain the exaggerated claim that 'every possible treatment should first have been tried'.)

The main problem with the requirement of a long-standing therapeutic relationship, however, is that in all countries, including the Netherlands and Belgium, the number of psychiatrists who cannot only imagine themselves ever to consider a request for euthanasia, but are really disposed to consider an actual request seriously, is small.[71] The requirement would therefore exclude most patients from having their request properly considered. There even is a real chance that the patient at first finds his doctor willing to discuss his request for euthanasia,

68 Onwuteake-Philipsen et al. 2017, 162.

69 VandenBerghe 2017.

70 Chabot 2000.

71 In 2016 37% of Dutch psychiatrists could imagine themselves ever to grant a request for euthanasia in a case of mental illness (in 1995 47%), Onwuteaka-Philipsen et al. 2017, 139, as well as 47% of GP's, *ibid.*, 102–103, cf. Evenblij et al. 2019. 54% had at least once received a request for euthanasia, 4% at least granted one, *ibid.*, Evenblij et al. 2019. Although 74.5% of Flemish psychiatrists accept euthanasia as a legal option for psychiatric patients, only 8% of them would be willing to perform euthanasia in the case of their own patients, 4.5% in other cases. 54% would be prepared to act in a consulting role, Verhofstadt et al. 2020. Of Canadian psychiatrists only 29.4% support Medical Aid in Dying on the basis of mental illness, Rousseau et al. 2017; of Swiss psychiatrists only 29.3%, although up to 35.4% in the case of some vignettes, Hodel et al. 2019. 55.4% would not be prepared to write a psychiatric report in the context of a request for euthanasia.

but in the end discovers that this discussion is supposed to have only one possible outcome: dropping the request (see the next section). For this reason in the Netherlands such requests are sometimes dealt with by general practitioners who take over from treating psychiatrists, and often by the Euthanasia Expertise Centre, a network of ambulant teams, each consisting of a doctor and a nurse, that considers requests for euthanasia throughout the country (Section 12.3). A growing number of psychiatrists – presently seven – participate in the work of the Centre. It is by now responsible for the larger part of the cases of euthanasia involving psychiatric patients.[72]

One advantage of the operation of the Centre is that the participating doctors are trained by experience to deal with such requests. An important disadvantage is that their contact with the patient is focussed on one decision only: to grant or not to grant the request for euthanasia. Granting it is not merely one option from a larger range to be considered, and hence the exploration of the death wish is not integrated into the treatment process as a whole. Another possible disadvantage I have already considered in the context of evaluating a general criticism of permissive regimes suggested by Daniel Callahan and Margot White (Section 12.4). According to them doctors who are prepared to consider a request or be consulted about it usually belong to an ideologically motivated vanguard, and this self-understanding doesn't dispose them to take the requirements of due care as seriously as they should, with erosion of these requirements as a result.[73] This suggestion may to some extent apply to the present situation in the Netherlands and Belgium as regards requests for euthanasia from psychiatric patients. On the one hand the number of cases is still small, and most psychiatrists are extremely reluctant to seriously consider a request. On the other hand, some psychiatrists who are willing to do so seem to have a special sense of vocation. I already referred to the Flemish doctor Lieve Thienpont who has been asked as a consultant in 100 cases between 2007 and 2011, and concluded that all requests had been made with sufficient competence, and that in no case a treatment option was still available that could be considered a reasonable one.[74]

72 See footnote 77.

73 A Canadian MAID-coordinator confesses in screening potential assessors to be "kind of protective of the patients and (to) try not to expose them to people that are going to say no", Pesut et al. 2021a.

74 Thienpont et al. 2015. In 52 cases the request has nevertheless not been granted, in 38 cases because the patient withdrew it, presumably seeing some reasonable alternative. In 35 cases the patient's life has been ended by euthanasia, in 4 cases by unassisted suicide. During those years Thienpont may have approved as a consultant close to 50% of all cases of euthanasia for psychiatric patients in Belgium, Claes et al. 2015. Thienpont was also one of the three psychiatrists involved in the case of Tine Nys, Chapter 12, footnote 99.

The Euthanasia Expertise Centre usually makes a much more serious assessment of the extent to which the requirements of due care have been met, and, partially as a result of that assessment, accepts less than 10% of the requests it receives in cases of mental illness.[75] Only incidentally cases in which the Centre granted a request have not been approved by the review committees.[76] Nevertheless, it is undesirable that decision-making and consultation in this area are mostly in the hands of a very small group of specially motivated professionals. The very availability of the Centre's service apparently tempts psychiatrists who have no general objections against assisting suicide to refer patients actually requesting it to the Centre.[77]

13.8 A categorical prohibition?

If it is that difficult to design and implement an adequate regulatory regime, wouldn't it be better to forbid physicians altogether to give psychiatric patients who want to end their lives a helping hand? One objection to that proposal that has often been made is that it will lead to a number of 'quasi-impulsive' and violent suicides that could have been avoided by a more permissive regime. That would not only be a worse way of ending one's life, it would also be much worse for one's relatives, and harm bystanders.[78] But if a person is able to take his own life in a violent way, she will rarely have what it takes to make a sufficiently competent request for euthanasia. She will normally also miss the patience to go through the whole procedure of checking the extent to which the requirements of due care have been satisfied, including the waiting time and, perhaps, the try-out of additional therapeutic options. Although there will be individual exceptions to this rule,

75 62 out of 717 requests, Expertisecentrum Euthanasie, *Feiten en cijfers patiëntenzorg 2019*. In 264 cases not all due care requirements were considered to have been met.

76 In the cases 2014-01 (see footnote 41) and 2017-24 the review committee judged that not all requirements of due care had been met, in 2013-27 the committee formulated equally strong criticism without drawing the same conclusion.

77 Until 2019 the percentage of cases of euthanasia involving psychiatric patients handled by the Centre rose each year, from 9 on a total of 42 cases in 2013 to 56 on a total of 67 cases in 2018, RTE Annual Reports 2013; 2019. The practice is criticized by Nederlandse Vereniging voor Psychiatrie 2018, 91 and deplored by the Centre itself. In 2020, however, the number of other psychiatrists involved in such cases rose to 20 out of 88 cases, RTE Annual Report 2020, and the number of psychiatrists asking staff members of the Centre for consultation rose from 5 to 30, Expertisecentrum Euthanasie, *Feiten en Cijfers 2020*.

78 E.g., *Carter v Canada* (AG), 2015 SCC, [1], [12, statement Gloria Taylor], [15]. When their request for euthanasia has been declined, 16% of Dutch psychiatric patients kill themselves, Groenewoud et al. 1997 (1996); Onwuteaka-Philipsen 2017, 150; Evenblij et al. 2019. But we have no information about the means they use.

generally speaking suicides of the two types seem to be mutually exclusive classes[79] (Section 3.5).

In evaluating a categorical prohibition a more weighty consideration is the following. As I observed in Section 6.8, according to the first recommendation that all guidelines for palliative care make as regards death wishes, doctors and nurses should take them seriously, even though all these guidelines, except the Dutch and Belgian ones, consider it the sole aim of doctors and nurses in those cases to create a situation in which the wish disappears. I commented that these two recommendations are incompatible. The same point applies to death wishes of psychiatric patients. It is quickly said that they should be taken seriously.[80] But in practice that would mean an extensive exploration of the meaning of the wish and the condition of the patient that motivates it. You can hardly expect the patient to cooperate wholeheartedly in that endeavour if it is clear to him from the outset that your only aim is to prevent his wish to be fulfilled. That attitude will taboo a substantial part of the patient's concerns.

Interestingly, a prohibitive regime may make it easier to keep contact with your patient in spite of your unwillingness to 'help' him. For it makes it possible for you not to foreclose the conclusion that you understand his wish, or even agree with him that the ending of his life would be a blessing for him. It is simply not your fault that you are unable to be of any assistance. But in that case you should make it clear from the beginning that you will be legally disabled, and that information may still to some extent constrain your attempts to explore the patient's wishes and condition. If you inform the patient that this is a form of aid that you are prepared to consider, but only if all other reasonably promising options have been ruled out, that may allow you to go much deeper into the matter. And that may have the effect that the patient really feels being taken seriously, and it may even enable him to go on with his life, knowing that an 'emergency exit' will be available if necessary.[81] In this way doctor and patient enter into a kind of contract, in which possible ways of recovery and the way of death are both explored with a shared commitment. That the doctor makes this double commitment is of course rather tricky. In the insightful paper in which Joris VandenBerghe

79 Of 66 cases in which a Dutch psychiatrist refused a request for euthanasia from a psychiatric patient, 28% had been refused because the request was not seen as voluntary and well considered, Evenblij et al. 2019. In 16% of those 66 cases the patient went on to commit suicide. Unfortunately we don't know the overlap between the two groups. Of 1308 psychiatric patients on the waiting list of the Euthanasia Expertise Centre for the evaluation of a euthanasia request only 10 committed suicide, in spite of a 1–2 year waiting time and a less than 10% chance of success, Kammeraat, Kölling 2020.

80 Sulmasy 2018; Gastmans, Denier 2018.

81 Steinbock 2017. Of the 48 patients accepted for euthanasia after consultation by Thienpont (footnotes 49, 74) 11 cancelled the procedure, 8 because the approval gave them the peace of mind they needed to continue their lives, Thienpont et al. 2015.

describes this 'dual track' approach, he comes perilously close to saying that it is a life-saving strategy that will fail if the doctor, in the end, cannot avoid endorsing the patient's death wish.[82] You can only start on the dual track if you are really prepared to accept that it can have two outcomes: an improved situation in which life is at least bearable or an unimproved situation in which death is welcome. Paradoxically, the chance of the patient choosing for life may improve if the doctor is really prepared to accept him choosing for death, if the alternative roads turn out to be dead alleys.[83]

One objection that has been made to this approach is that the very fact that the doctor does not categorically exclude going along with the patient's request will tend to undermine the patient's hope.[84] That objection is an example of the purely functionalist approach to hope that I criticized in Section 6.6. The whole idea of the dual track is that doctor and patient make a combined effort to explore the patient's real prospects, in order to decide what the proper object of the patient's hope should be: life or death. The paradox is that this may actually increase his hope to be able to continue living, and hence may be the superior policy in purely functionalist terms as well. The wish to maintain hope at all costs may motivate invasive and useless treatments and it may also be harmful by deepening the patient's despair. But if these considerations are, secretly, the leading ones, that would be dishonest as well as probably counterproductive.

In Section 13.7 I argued that the special problems involved in permitting euthanasia in cases of mental illness might be manageable within the framework of a long-standing therapeutic relationship. In this section I added that the chance of providing real help to the patient is improved if the doctor is prepared to explore and eventually grant the patient's request, if that is the outcome of the exploration. That is an additional reason for legally permitting psychiatrists to start such an exploration.

82 "Irremediability is very hard to establish and luckily so". VandenBerghe 2017. His second motive for the approach is to prevent the patient from falling into the hands of colleagues who, because of a strong commitment to patient autonomy, are too trigger-happy. Gastmans, Denier 2018 recommend "the greatest possible restraint", but that is of course full abstinence.

83 The dual-track approach has been adopted by the Vlaamse Vereniging voor Psychiatrie 2017 (Flemish Psychiatry Society). But the VVvP proposes to entrust different psychiatrists with the 'life' and the 'death track', which seems to defeat the point of the procedure. See on the basic idea also Chabot 2000.

84 Kissane, Kelly 2000; Kissane 2004; Appelbaum 2016; Blikshavn, Husum, Magelssen 2017. See Berghmans, Widdershoven, Widdershoven-Heerding 2013 for an extensive discussion. Dazzi et al. 2014 show that discussing suicide doesn't induce suicidal ideation. Resp. 59 and 37% of Belgian psychiatrists who had been involved in an assessment procedure of a euthanasia request reported that the procedure led to a lower suicide risk and the reestablishment of relationships between patient and significant others, Verhofstadt et al. 2021.

13.9 Why should the doctor be responsible?

Suppose that a psychiatrist arrives at the conclusion that the patient's wish to end his life is, all things considered, perfectly understandable. Why, in that case, should the doctor be responsible for procuring the patient's death? This is a question that until now has hardly received any attention in the literature.[85] Actually, at least many of these patients do not only have the physical capacity, but, if the death wish is really a well-considered one, also the mental capacity to carefully plan and execute their own decision. If they do, they will act within their right and need no assistance.

The standard response to this suggestion is that acting on it would amount to abandoning the patient. As VandenBerghe explains, the patient's request:

> is also a social interaction, a way of reaching out, of getting in touch, of sharing thoughts and feelings, of connecting with the outside world. It is fundamentally different in many ways from a person isolating himself or herself and preparing to committing suicide on his or her own.[86]

In a similar vein the Dutch 2009 guideline doesn't consider it good professional care to offer the patient the opportunity for 'solitary suicide'.[87] But why should a suicide that is not under the final direction of a doctor necessarily be a solitary one? If the objection was correct, an Oregon doctor who writes a prescription for a lethal drug would also 'abandon' his patient. Actually, a person who prepares to commit suicide on her own can and should do so in intensive communication with her intimates and, if possible, her doctor. These people can also offer some kinds of support without taking over the final responsibility for an effective, quick and humane procedure. For example, many psychiatric patients are old or physically ill enough to end their own lives in a relatively humane way by stopping eating and drinking. Any patient who decides to act that way will need intimates to prevent his mouth from drying out and will need a doctor to monitor the process and take palliative steps if necessary, for example when a delirium develops (Section 8.7).

If a psychiatric patient is able to make that decision and follow this road to the end, that will silence all possible doubts about the stability of his wish, and many (but not all) doubts about his reasons for welcoming

85 When I raised the question in den Hartogh 2015a (comment), this met with indignation from Schuklenk, van de Vathorst 2015b (reply), see also Dembo, Schuklenk, Reggler 2018. These authors seem to be unaware of the *de facto* universal availability of humane means of committing suicide, including stopping eating and drinking, Jansen, Wall, Miller 2019.

86 VandenBerghe 2017, 154.

87 Nederlandse Vereniging voor Psychiatrie 2009, 18.

death. Some of the other problems that I identified in Sections 13.3–13.5 will also be solved. The doctor would not need to be convinced that no alternative treatment or other way of providing relief still held any real promise. For it is up to a sufficiently competent agent to weigh his own alternatives and act on the outcome of his weighing. That weighing should, it is true, at least be understandable; if a patient rejects a standard treatment without any good reason that would be a reason to suspect a lack of competence. And if the patient doesn't involve his friends and relatives – if he has any – in his deliberations, that could be a reason for similar suspicions. But in the end he has the authority to make his own decision. No-one is in a position to veto it, although others are permitted, and, if they have special responsibilities of care for his well-being, perhaps even required, to put his decision into question if they disagree with it. Finally, some possible doubts about such a patient's competence will also be silenced. Most severely depressed patients in a suicidal mood will only be able to kill themselves in what I have called a quasi-impulsive way, by violent means. In some other conditions (anorexia, delusion) patients may, however, be able to act on their distorted priorities in a well-organized manner.

But not all psychiatric patients are old and ill enough to be able to make this choice. Should it be possible for them to legally acquire humane means to end their own lives, with only the voluntary and well-considered character of their decisions being subjected to examination? This question I will take up in the final chapter of this book.

13.10 Conclusion

There are three reasons why it is particularly difficult to evaluate a psychiatric patient's request for euthanasia: multiple meanings and ambivalence, uncertain prognosis and the problem of establishing a sufficient level of competence. I have argued that, because of these problems, any legal system that would allow a doctor to perform euthanasia in such a case should introduce some substantial and procedural requirements of due care in addition to the requirements that apply to patients suffering from a lethal illness. Some of these requirements will concern treatment options that should have been attempted, waiting periods and expert consultation. But the most important of the possible requirements to be considered is that the decision to grant the patient's request can only be made in the context of a long-standing therapeutic relationship.

Wouldn't the special problems involved in cases of mental illness justify a categorical prohibition of euthanasia in those cases? I have argued that these problems are manageable in the context of a well-functioning therapeutic relationship. That would be a reason to permit a psychiatrist to grant a request for euthanasia as the outcome of a 'dual-track' procedure. Such a procedure also has an important therapeutic value of its own.

But if we require a long-standing therapeutic relationship, we seem to leave all those patients who haven't found a psychiatrist willing to seriously start a dual-track procedure to their own wits. Wouldn't that be a reason to permit volunteering psychiatrists to fill the gap? The experience of the Dutch Euthanasia Expertise Centre teaches us that what we intend to be a complementary option may become a substitute one. This means that the second-best procedure will tend to crowd out the best one. That could be a good reason not to open the second-best option. If we permit VandenBerghe to proceed, but not Thienpont, it is more probable that the psychiatric community will develop a more open attitude to the death wishes of its clients.

I am therefore inclined to favour a legal regime that allows euthanasia in cases of mental illness, but only within the framework of a long-standing therapeutic relationship. But I am not suggesting this as the generally best policy for all countries. Too much depends on local circumstances, the general attitudes of the population and psychiatrists to begin with. A dual-track approach can only be implemented in healthcare systems that allow long-standing psycho-therapeutic relations between doctor and patient to develop. Such relationships are increasingly rare, in the Netherlands and Belgium no less than elsewhere.

14 Death wishes of the very old[1]

14.1 Introduction

Mr. Kalisvaart is almost 90 years old. He has been a very independent and active man all his life. Since 15 years he suffers from glaucoma in both his eyes, and by now, he is almost completely blind. His hearing has also much declined in recent years. He is therefore unable to listen to classical music which used to be his passion. Moreover, as a result of disc degeneration, he has serious back pain. 'I'm sitting in my chair all day, waiting for nothing'. Only with the assistance of staff members of the nursing home where he lives, he is able to move a bit around with a walker. In doing so he has fallen down a few times. Being dependent on others, knowing that his situation will only deteriorate further increases his suffering. For these reasons he has asked his physician to provide him with the means for committing suicide, and he repeats this request every time the physician visits him.[2]

This is not an uncommon situation for people of very high age. Nor is it a recent phenomenon, the product of growing prosperity, medical progress and the resulting lengthening of the average lifespan, or of the growing power of physicians to keep people alive in conditions of bad health, although these factors help to explain the growth of the phenomenon. Here is a voice from the second century BC:

> O death, how welcome is your sentence
> to one who is in need and is failing in strength,
> very old and distracted over everything;
> to one who is contrary, and has lost his patience![3]

1 In this chapter, I use some text material from den Hartogh 2013c and den Hartogh 2017d.

2 RTE Annual Report 2008, case 9. Cf. the case of Mrs. Heringa, described at the beginning of Chapter 4.

3 *Ecclesiasticus (Wisdom of Sirach)* 41: 3, King James' translation, one of Brahms' *Vier ernste Lieder.*

DOI: 10.4324/9781003281115-18

We are talking about persistent death wishes of old people who don't have any life-threatening illness and do not suffer severely from pain, breathlessness or similar physical symptoms. The death wish of an old person may also be the result of a mental disorder that she may already have had for a longer time, or of earlier traumatic experiences, sometimes even dating from childhood. Such death wishes do not belong to the subject of this chapter either. I want to focus on death wishes of old people that are somehow related to their age. Suicide rates are highest in the age cohort of 75+, and the lethality of suicide attempts also increases with age.[4]

How often do old people long for death? Because researchers use very different questionnaires and time frames, it is hard to find consistent percentages, but most results are in the range of 5–10%.[5] But this percentage concerns people who occasionally have death wishes; they need not be persistent ones. According to one study 3.4% of the Dutch population beyond the age of 58 reported to have had death wishes during the last week before being interviewed and to have no wish or only a weak wish to live, 0.7% reported to have a strong desire to be dead at the moment of the interview.[6] (This group included people with mental disorders.) We do not really know how many of these people plan to end their lives, or start acting on those plans, although one Italian study gives a percentage of 0.14%.[7]

If these people ask a doctor to assist them in ending their lives, should doctors, under any conditions, be allowed to grant such requests?[8] It has often been argued that it is a mistake to burden the doctor with such a request because the problem that the patient wants to address is not really a medical one. In Sections 14.2 and 14.3 I will consider different versions of this argument. According to still another version of it the basic problem is a social one: death wishes of old people are the result of their exclusion from society. In much of the socio-gerontological literature there is a tendency to deny the negative aspects of becoming (very) old,[9] because it

4 Conejero et al. 2018, with further references.

5 Bonnewyn 2009 (survey); cf. van Wijngaarden, Leget, Goossensen 2014 (10–20%); Cheung 2017 (9.5%).

6 Rurup et al. 2011, reporting a study from 2005/2006; cf. Scocco, de Leo 2002.

7 Scocco, de Leo 2002.

8 In 2017, 2018, 2019 and 2020 resp. 293, 205, 172 and 235 patients suffering from a cumulation of old-age ailments had their request granted, RTE Annual Reports 2017–2020. Studying 49 cases reported by the Dutch review committees from 2013 to 2019, Buijsen 2020 found 38 patients to be women and also 38 to be older than 90. In Belgium the number of patients suffering from polypathology rose from 3 in 2004 to 461 in 2019, FCECE 2020, but 54–65% of these patients were considered terminal, *ibid.*, 36.

9 According to Gilleard 2018 "the possibility that ageing might be inherently deleterious and that old age, *qua* old age, is an undesirable state is virtually excluded from the discipline's collective consciousness". That it could be rational to want to die for age-related reasons is sometimes already seen as an ageist view, cf. O'Connell et al. 2004.

would be discriminatory and stigmatizing to acknowledge these aspects, and therefore amount to a self-fulfilling prophecy. In Section 14.4 I will argue that, on the contrary, this very denial harms old people by failing to take their own concerns seriously. Until this point in the chapter I will find no reason to take the problem out of the hand of doctors. In Section 14.5, however, I will argue, that, even if they find an old person's decision to end his life fully understandable, they may have good reasons not to take co-responsibility for implementing that decision. Instead their default response might be to leave it to the patient's own responsibility to implement it. Section 14.6 will then consider the options that the patient has in this respect.

The chapter presupposes some by themselves contentious views that I have defended in earlier chapters. Most basically I assume that a person's desire to die can derive from a realistic and understandable assessment of her own present and future condition (Section 2.2). This is as true of very old people as it is of anyone else. The chapter also implies that we should not consider death wishes of old people, any more than of anyone else, to constitute by themselves reasons for suspecting a mental disorder or decisional incompetence (Sections 3.3; 11.6). We should therefore also be somewhat sceptical about the extent of the association between death wishes of the elderly and depressive disorders or depressive symptoms, as it is reported in the literature.[10] To a considerable extent the correlations 'found' may be tautological. It should also be kept in mind that a relatively large percentage of old-age suicides may belong to the 'invisible' category of well-planned actions, performed in interaction with relatives and in a non-violent way (Section 3.4).[11] It is because of its focus on the association with mental illness and the correlated loss of social connections, that the existing mainly quantitative research has underrated the vital significance of the loss of functional abilities, considering it a mere risk factor among others for suicidality (footnote 22). Finally I will assume that a competent person has the right to end his own life, but that the mere request for euthanasia by such a person is not sufficient for a doctor to be justified in performing it. She should also be reasonably convinced that she is doing the right thing. This is the indirect paternalism that I argued for in Section 9.5.

10 Barnow, Linden, Freyberger 2004; Rurup et al. 2011 (20% disorders, 67% symptoms, with further references); van Wijngaarden, Leget, Goossensen 2014 (survey: 5–30% not associated with psychiatric disorders); Appel, van Wijngaarden 2021 (survey). In the Canadian sample studied by Corna, Cairney, Streiner 2010, more than 2/3 of respondents with suicidal ideation did not meet the criteria for clinical depression.

11 Spittler 2017.

14.2 Outside the doctor's area of competence?

Should doctors be allowed to grant a request for euthanasia from a very old person who wants to end her life but is not suffering from a lethal disease or a major psychiatric disturbance? When the Dutch euthanasia law was discussed in parliament, this was an important subject of debate. The Minister of Justice declared: "Suffering that doesn't derive from a medical context should not be assessed by a physician". He described that kind of suffering as follows: "the condition of people who are mostly at an advanced age and who, even though they don't suffer from an illness and ailment that is untreatable and accompanied by serious suffering, have decided that the value of their life has decreased to such an extent that they prefer death to continued living".[12] Shortly afterwards the Dutch Supreme Court decided in the *Brongersma* case that a request for euthanasia could only be considered by a doctor if the suffering of the patient that motivated his request was at least predominantly caused by a medically classifiable disease or ailment.[13] As a result, in addition to the six requirements of due care laid down by the euthanasia law, Dutch law actually recognizes a seventh requirement: that the patient's suffering should have a 'medical foundation'.[14]

The Court insisted on this requirement because it held that, if a healthy person has existential problems that motivate him to long for death, it is not a proper medical task to address those problems.[15] This justification can be questioned. If I am suffering from insomnia because of stress caused by an overload of work or a conflict with my partner, my doctor will first discuss with me possible ways of reducing the stress or coping with it in other ways, but eventually be prepared to give me a receipt for sleeping pills. What matters is that I can be effectively helped by medical means, whatever the cause of my need for them (cf. Section 9.6).

The main question, however, raised by the *Brongersma* decision is to what extent it excludes any actual requests for euthanasia from old people from being considered. For a long time the Dutch medical community interpreted the verdict to require the patient's suffering to be

12 *Kamerstukken* II, 2000/2001, 26 691, nr. 22.

13 HR 24/12/2002, ECLI;NL:PHR:2002:AE8772; cf. Griffiths, Weyers, Adams 2008, 35–39. The Belgian euthanasia law (2002) requires "a serious and incurable ailment caused by accident or illness". Canada's *Bill C-14* (2016) required "a grievous and irremediable medical condition", explained as "a serious and incurable illness, disease or disability". In 2020, when the law still required natural death to be foreseeable, the underlying medical condition of the patient could be classified as "multiple comorbidities"; this category "encompassed a wide range of conditions, including diabetes, osteoporosis, osteoarthritis and fractures. Frailty was also commonly cited (near 3% of all MAID cases)". Health Canada 2020, 18.

14 KNMG 2011.

15 Similarly, Sumner 2011, 171.

the result of a 'serious' illness. Cancer and ALS were considered serious illnesses, and so was therapy-resistant depression, but Mr. Kalisvaart's ailments, blindness, deafness and loss of mobility were not. When Mr. Kalisvaart's doctor, however, went along with his request for euthanasia, the Regional Review Committee to which he reported judged this decision to meet all requirements of due care, including the additional one of the *Brongersma* verdict, because his suffering was the result of a cumulation of old-age ailments, and these certainly belong to the class of medically classifiable diseases or ailments.[16]

According to recent insights ageing is a process of accumulated random damage to a complex physical system, which as a result gradually loses its reserve capacity, hence its ability to compensate for harm and loss and to recover from stress. Physical changes include loss of muscle mass, slowed down activity, decrease of weight and permanent fatigue. As a result there is an increase and accumulation of diseases and ailments, and an acceleration of both the increase and the accumulation.[17] The process can be described as a cascade.[18] These afflictions include arthritis, Parkinson's disease, decompensatio cordis, glaucoma, macular degeneration, diabetes, diabetic retinopathy, stomach problems, respiratory problems, heart attack, stroke, hypertension, flu, osteoporosis, broken hip, broken bones, spinal fractures, decubitus, prostate disorders, infections of the urinary tract, angina, incontinence, impotence, loss of sensory abilities, speech impairments, problems with teeth and feet, with vision and hearing, neurocognitive impairments, including dementia, as well as depressive symptoms. The loss of one's reserve capacity increases one's vulnerability to bacteria and viruses.

The process can result in pain, lack of breath, fatigue and other physical symptoms, but in particular in an increase of functional disabilities which has the same cascading characteristics of accelerated increase and accumulation. These not only include difficulties in eating, dressing, walking around, climbing stairs, getting in and out of bed, bathing, toileting, using the telephone, going out, shopping, cooking, cleaning, housekeeping, gardening, reading, looking television, taking medicine and managing money but also include sleeplessness, daytime drowsiness, loss of energy, loss of appetite, anxiety, anhedonia and other negative affective states.

It is sometimes suggested that such disabilities do not belong to the medical domain, because they are the result of a statistically normal

16 My description of the suffering of old people in this section relies on Crocker, Clare, Evans 2006; Kjölseth, Ekeberg, Steihaug 2009, 2010; Rurup et al. 2011; Defesche 2011; van Wijngaarden, Leget, Goossensen 2014 (survey); Bonnewyn et al. 2014; van Wijngaarden 2016, 2021; Conejero et al. 2018 (survey of recent studies).

17 Izaks, Westendorp 2003; Fishman et al. 2008; Boenink 2010; Schermer 2013.

18 Boenink 2010.

process of physiological ageing.[19] But each of the diseases which cause them may occur at any age, although as a result of 'cascading' they are most characteristic of old age. It makes no sense to count them as medically classified diseases at other ages, but not at old age, because at that time they occur more often and in combination. All these conditions invite and direct medical attention at any age.[20]

Not only the individual conditions by themselves are to be considered medically classifiable diseases or ailments. What as a result of the process of ageing understood in the way I described is most characteristic of old age is the plurality of health deficits, interacting with each other, and creating a decreased resistance to environmental stressors. This condition is by now known as 'frailty' or the 'frailty syndrome' and it is increasingly measured by means of a 'frailty index'.[21] The concept of frailty presents itself as an important new medical classification, because at the dawn of the 'fourth age' it has both predictive value for incomplete recovery from acute ailments, falling down, loss of control, hospitalization and death, as well as a guiding value for medical efforts, e.g. as regards nutrition and physical activity, and in particular for adapted treatment of the component diseases.

This process of ageing is the causal background of the emergence of the characteristic death wishes of the elderly.[22] The most prominent factors seem to be, as in the case of Mr. Kalisvaart, declined eyesight, hearing and mobility. Chronic pain is also fairly common. The effect of these factors is reinforced by other losses, of energy, memory, concentration and other cognitive abilities, as well as by fear of further physical decay and loss of independence.

It is clear that doctors are professionally equipped to deal with suffering that consists of pain, lack of breath, nausea, exhaustion and similar physical symptoms, or with losses of sight, of hearing, of mobility and similar functional disabilities. But the suffering of very old people that leads them to welcome death mainly consists of loss of meaning, loss of control, loss of dignity and loss of coping resilience. It is sometimes suggested that doctors have no special competence to deal with these

19 This is the view of a minority of the members of the Belgian Federal Commission, as reported in its reports since 2010, Montero 2017, 31.

20 Izaks 2001. This is a major objection to an analysis of the concept of 'health' (e.g. Boorse 1977) that relies on statistical information.

21 Some descriptions of the syndrome focus on functional disabilities (Rockwood et al. 2000), others include diseases. Some descriptions are restricted to physiological conditions (Fried et al. 2001), but there is no reason not to include psychological ones as for example mood disorders or loss of cognitive abilities, Gobbens et al. 2010; Hertogh 2013.

22 Functional disabilities due to old-age ailments have for the most part been described as merely correlated to suicidality in older people in the literature, as 'risk factors' enabling us to recognize suicidal tendencies, Kjölseth, Ekeberg, Steihaug 2010. Qualitative studies, however, tend to confirm their etiological importance. Interestingly, these studies also find less depressive symptoms than quantitative ones.

kinds of existential suffering. But if we consider the main reasons why patients in a terminal stage of cancer request euthanasia, we get exactly the same list (Section 2.2). This is even true when physical symptoms are prominent, which they only are in a minority of cases. Take for example cachexia. Surely it is a very unpleasant experience by itself to feel completely exhausted, but the consequences of that condition are even more important: that you are unable to do anything, and even hardly to observe what happens in your immediate surroundings. You can only understand the suffering of terminal cancer patients if you do not only take their physical symptoms and functional disabilities into account but also consider the meaning which those symptoms and disabilities have for them, and the emotions which they evoke because of this meaning: sorrow, anguish, despair and sometimes regret or anger (Section 6.2).

In some cases this meaning is evident. If a person has a strong and continuous sense of suffocation because of lack of breath, you need not to know anything else about her to understand that she is in a state of extreme suffering. But in the majority of cases you can only understand the nature and severity of the suffering against the background of the patient's personality, biography and values. That is the basic task which the Dutch euthanasia law requires to be performed in all cases of euthanasia, both by the doctors involved and the colleagues they consult. Doctors should be equipped to perform that task, and many of them are.[23] The very distinction between 'somatic' and 'existential' suffering is misleading because it doesn't distinguish between the cause and the nature of the suffering.[24] In the case of old people with death wishes that are related to their age, the cause will often be physical illness, but suffering, by its nature, is always existential.

If we understand the suffering of very old people with death wishes in this way – a cascade of health defects, resulting in functional disabilities, leading to losses of meaning, independence, dignity and coping resilience – we can make the following observation: many very old people live with these conditions and go on living with them. For many of them the idea of dying in the near future is no longer frightening, they may even long for death (Section 14.1). But only some of the people living with those conditions have explicit and permanent wishes to die and even of those people only some are prepared to take active steps in order to realize that wish. The research results that we presently have at our disposal seem to indicate that, generally speaking, the condition of the people with persistent and active plans for ending their lives is not systematically worse than the condition of many others (Chapter 2 at footnote 17). If that is true, it must be their personality, biography and values that differentiate them.

23 But cf. Chapter 12, footnote 8.

24 The *Brongersma* verdict itself shows traces of this confusion.

Meaning, control, dignity and autonomy may be (even) more important to them than to the others. But even if people have the same priorities, their coping style may be different, more or less action-oriented and more or less adaptable to changing circumstances.[25] And some people are simply too frightened of death to consider killing themselves. That this analysis applies to the very old at least as well as to others seems to be confirmed by the growth of the percentage of euthanasia requests from their age category. It cannot fully be explained by demography. The most plausible explanation is that it signals a change to a more autonomous coping style in the oldest generation.

14.3 The myth of the completed life

If we accept that old people suffering from functional disabilities as the result of old-age ailments are not excluded by the requirement of a 'medical foundation', does that mean that the requirement doesn't really exclude any request for euthanasia from being granted at all? Remember that the Dutch Minister of Justice wanted to exclude requests from people who, "even though they don't suffer from an illness and ailment that is untreatable and accompanied by serious suffering, have decided that the value of their life has decreased to such an extent that they prefer death to continued living". In the Dutch debate these people are standardly described as 'considering their life to be completed'.[26] The media call them 'healthy seniors with death wishes'. Who are they?

The term 'completed life' conjures up the image of a person who thinks that he has enjoyed everything that life can offer and therefore can round off that life with a peaceful mind. Life is then seen as a project that can be considered completed at a certain moment. Although it is a philosophical myth that every person has a 'life plan', many people have, probably in particular in the richer part of the world. They want 'to make something out of their life', and at the end to look back with some satisfaction if they have succeeded in this ambition to some extent. We should, however, distinguish between two kinds of projects. Examples of the first kind are the plan to write a book or to build a house: at a certain moment the book has been written and the house has been built. Examples of the second kind of project are the plan to preserve a wilderness area or to acquire philosophical insight. Such projects are never completed; you can only

25 Ruijs et al. 2014; Kjölseth, Ekeberg, Steihaug 2010; Rurup et al. 2011; Defesche 2011; van Wijngaarden et al. 2014, 209. This view is confirmed by the similarities between the experience of frail old age as such, as described by Nicholson et al. 2012, and the experience of old people with suicidal tendencies.

26 Elsewhere the common term, in particular in the debate about the eligibility criteria for euthanasia, is 'being tired of life', Appel, van Wijngaarden 2021; van den Noortgate 2016; van Humbeeck et al. 2020.

be compelled by external circumstances to give them up or lose your interest in pursuing them. It may not be impossible to conceive of your life as a project of the first kind, but surely this is rare and not a little bit weird.[27] Imagine yourself explaining to your partner, your children and your friends that, as far as you are concerned, they belong to that kind of life plan. But, anyway, even if your life is completed in this sense, that is no reason at all to end it. You can go home and quietly wait for death, with a mixture of afterglow and some saudade, reading good books and drinking an occasional glass of port wine.

Surely it is not uncommon for people to have death wishes that they don't consider themselves to be caused by a disease or ailment. Even people with severe functional impairments may not describe themselves as being in bad health. People may have depressive symptoms and occasional death wishes all their lives, but nevertheless succeed in building a normal life without medical help. When their wish to be dead intensifies in old age, they may still not conceive of themselves as psychiatric patients. That people don't recognize a causal link between their medical condition and their death wish doesn't prove, however, that such a link doesn't exist.[28]

In Chapter 13 I have used the terms 'psychiatric patients' and 'patients suffering from mental illness' interchangeably. Actually psychiatrists sometimes treat people for a condition that one might hesitate to call a mental illness or disorder, for example prolonged grief after a traumatic loss. Perhaps such grief should rather be seen as an appropriate or at least intelligible response to the loss, given its meaning in the person's life.[29] The psychiatrist Andries van Dantzig declared as a witness in the famous *Chabot*-case (1994): "I would find it decidedly odd if pills would help against grief. As a matter of fact I would deplore it".[30]

27 Karl Jaspers 1970, 200, even denies that it is possible. The empirical hypothesis that in any case of supposed 'rounding off' loose ends will remain, seems highly plausible, but Jaspers' conceptual arguments are less so, as Scarre 2007, 40–44 shows.

28 Van der Heide et al. 2012, 149: in almost all cases in which there was no 'serious' ailment, there were ailments, cf. van Wijngaarden et al. 2020a, 78. The Dutch Regional Review Committees have only once judged that in a certain case the requirement of a 'medical foundation' had not been satisfied, Annual Report 2012, case 6.

29 Chabot 1996, ch. 7; Wijsbek 2012a, both discussing the case of Mrs. Bosscher (Chapter 13, footnote 38). The Dutch Supreme Court and a disciplinary court considered it a case of mental illness, but Chabot and Wijsbek dispute that understanding. Prolonged or complicated grief used to be considered a depressive condition, but the *DSM-V* (2013) introduced, in the chapter on areas for further study, persistent complex bereavement disorder as a separate category. See also RTE Annual Report 2011, case 13, concerning an otherwise healthy woman who received euthanasia one year after her husband's death. Interestingly a similar case was used by van Wijngaarden et al. 2020 in their questionnaire (footnote 34) in order to identify death wishes of people who considered themselves to have no serious illness.

30 Chabot 1996, 168.

That doesn't mean, however, that it didn't make sense for Chabot to treat Mrs. Bosscher, in particular to try to find an alternative for her choice of death. Such cases are not 'outside the medical domain'.

As such cases illustrate, biographical factors are often involved in the aetiology of the death wishes of the elderly: occasionally financial or legal problems, more often the loss of a partner, of children, of peers, of a job or of other meaningful occupations, of social status, all of which may result in a sense of emptiness, loneliness, even worthlessness, often made worse by disappointment about the perceived lack of attention and care from significant others. An important additional factor is forced relocation, often to a nursing home.[31] Some people accuse themselves because of missed chances, lost opportunities and unfulfilled aspirations during their lives. You can consider your life completed because you have wrecked it irreparably. In the case of very old people, however, the final effect of such biographical factors will normally still be dependent on functional disabilities. When you lose your comrades when you are 30, you may be able to build a new social network, but probably not when you are 90. People need to cope with losses and failures at every age, but frailty usually also implies a loss of coping resilience. In its turn this causes increased dependency on the care of others and loss of privacy and 'dignity'. If ageing and biography are both relevant, it makes no sense to attribute to both parts of the causal responsibility, adding up to 100%. These factors may both be necessary conditions.

I don't deny, of course, that health deficits may sometimes be of minor importance or of no importance at all in explaining a persistent death wish, for example when someone plans to end his life in order to avoid bankruptcy or imprisonment. Some predicaments of that kind may emerge more frequently in old age, for example when old people for financial reasons have to move in with their children, with conflicts and a sense of dependency as a result.[32] In general, however, the less a death wish has a medical foundation, the less it will tend to be age-related at all.[33]

In order to decide whether in addition to the euthanasia law a special regulatory framework was needed for old people who didn't satisfy the *Brongersma* criterion, the Dutch government recently commissioned Els van Wijngaarden and Ghislaine van Thiel to estimate the number of such people.[34] This was a difficult task because most people reporting any kind of death wish suffer from some ailment (footnote 28), and you can only exclude a causal relation between the ailment and the death

31 Moss et al. 2005.

32 A fairly common motive of suicidal thoughts and actions in Brazil, da Silva et al. 2018.

33 Refreshed memories of earlier traumatic experiences may be age-related, van Wijngaarden, Leget, Goossensen 2014, 204.

34 Van Wijngaarden et al. 2020a summarized in Hartog et al. 2020.

wish in the individual case, not by a large survey. The researchers therefore asked people of 55+ whether they had a severe illness. The group as a whole nevertheless reported a considerable burden of health problems (median 7 on a 1–10 scale), and, as the researchers recognize, it is possible for a death wish to be caused by an illness that is not a severe one in the person's own eyes.[35] Anyway, they found 0.17% of 55+ people (corresponding to a total of 10,000 people) to have no self-ascribed severe illness but, nevertheless, an active death wish for more than a year that they described as a wish to end their lives, not merely as a wish not to awaken tomorrow. But 79% of this group was younger than 75, and only 8% of them reported this wish always to outweigh the wish to go on living. These results confirm that the number of people who do not meet the *Brongersma* criterion but durably want to end their lives for age-related reasons is very small.

14.4 A social problem?

When an elderly person has an explicit and stable death wish that is causally related to her age, her suffering will normally be due to a cumulation of old-age ailments. One could, however, still deny that the problem is a medical one by pointing out that it should not be addressed by medical means, let alone by helping that person to end her life. For even if the person's suffering finally derives from old-age ailments, for the most part it doesn't consist of untreatable physical symptoms. Rather it consists in the experience of lost abilities, and those losses could substantially be compensated for by social interventions. The old person could be allowed and stimulated to participate in social activities, giving her a sense of purpose and a sense of belonging, restoring her self-image, and her connections to the world and to other people. In the final analysis her suffering should, on this view, be seen as deriving from social expectations that she is no longer able to satisfy. Hence the problem would disappear if those expectations disappeared. Old age by itself is simply a variety of human existence, a stage of life that is as unproblematic in its own right as any other stage, only made problematic by negative social reactions and the lack of adequate support. We should change our attitudes and perceptions, rather than help old people to kill themselves. Offering old people the option of euthanasia is stigmatizing, and if these people protest that they still prefer the option with the supposed stigma to the withdrawal of both, they show 'internalized ageism' (Section 11.3 at footnote 32). This is a common view, in particular in (socio-) gerontology.

Fighting ageism is a worthwhile aim. But it is not a matter of a few policy measures or volunteer initiatives, but of a change in social

35 Van Wijngaarden et al. 2020a, 164; Hartog et al. 2020.

sensibilities and behaviour that will be as radical as the emancipation of women, homosexuals or transgenders. You can hardly ask a 90-year-old person to wait for it. Even less can you tell him that assisting him in ending his life would decrease the pressure for the social change that we need.[36] That would be another example of a strategy of *Verelendung* that uses individual people as a means for achieving social ends (Section 11.4).

We should also keep in mind that we are not talking about the general category of people who live on a retirement pension, people in the 'third age', but about the much more restricted category of people in the 'fourth age', who are in the process of losing important functional abilities as the result of a cumulation of old-age ailments. Can we really compensate for those losses in all or at least in most cases? Let me consider those elements in the condition of old people with death wishes that seem most susceptible to improvement by social intervention. I derive these elements from the pioneering work of Els van Wijngaarden.[37]

1 Loneliness. Very old people almost always have lost several and, sometimes, all people who played a significant role in their lives, siblings, partners and close friends. They may still have children, but these may live far away, and sometimes the relation is under strain. This is probably the single most prominent cause of suffering that elicits persistent death wishes,[38] and it seems a factor that society can really do something about.[39] A relevant finding of research, however, is that old people who suffer from loneliness at the same time have the tendency to withdraw themselves from existing social contacts and not to be open to new ones.[40] They find it more and more difficult to communicate spontaneously with others; every social activity is an effort, even the more, of course, if they have impaired eyesight or hearing. Decreasing mobility also makes social relations hard to sustain.[41] An additional reason for disconnecting from social life is the feeling that existing contacts are lacking in

36 See for example American Geriatric Society 1995.

37 Van Wijngaarden 2016, summarized by van Wijngaarden, Leget, Goossensen 2015. Van Wijngaarden interviewed 26 people who considered their own lives to be 'completed'. She is largely sympathetic to the view that the suffering of the elderly that motivates death wishes is primarily a social problem, but I will argue that her own findings do not support that view.

38 According to Conejero et al. 2018 bereavement and social isolation are the main 'risk factors' for death by suicide of older adults, cf. Joiner 2005, as quoted in Section 3.2.

39 American Medical Association 2008.

40 Van Wijngaarden, Leget, Goossensen 2015; Hartog et al. 2020; Gaignard, Hurst 2019 ('chosen loneliness'); van Wijngaarden 2021.

41 Nicholson et al. 2012. Crocker, Clare, Evans 2006 report that old people see that connection themselves.

reciprocity: you are the object of benevolence and can do nothing in return. It is always more blessed to give than to receive.[42]

Moreover, the significant people these people have lost are often irreplaceable. If you lose your partner after having lived 60 or 70 years together, the loss cannot be compensated for by buddies or bingo evenings. The mere suggestion is insulting.[43]

2 Loss of meaning and purpose. Many old people feel themselves socially down and out, useless. The failure to contribute to society also implies a loss of social status. That may seem another element of suffering that society can do something about. And, indeed, it will sometimes be possible to give even the very old a serious social role. But we should stress the 'serious'. Sometimes old people are given some odd job to do but are fully aware that their performance is not really appreciated.[44] And it will not do either merely to feign appreciation: the old person will see through it and feel being treated like a child. The basic problem remains that for most socially useful activities the very old have lost the necessary abilities, both as a result of physical, often also of cognitive impairments and of loss of energy. 'After half an hour I am totally exhausted'. If you are sitting in a wheelchair, you will not be able to do any gardening or to provide any care to your grand grandchild, however much you would like to do so.

But shouldn't we consider the very desire to be useful a mere internalized norm of a meritocratically organized society that makes the unproductive feel themselves to be parasites?[45] It may be true that there is a tendency in our society to understand 'contributing to society' in narrow economic terms.[46] But the general ideal doesn't seem to be specific to a particular type of culture. Moreover, it is also a widespread ideal in our society to retire from labour as early as possible and spend the 'third age' on full-time leisure, fishing and going to the beach. The need to contribute to society doesn't therefore seem to be a mere inauthentic product of social pressure. Whatever its genealogy, that need apparently is by now an integral part of some old people's identity.

3 Loss of self. One of the most common elements in the suffering of old people with suicidal thoughts is a low perceived level of mastery, an increasing incapacity to cope with the problems of living in one's own characteristic way and a corresponding loss of self-respect, as well as feelings of confusion, anxiety and despair. They feel overwhelmed

42 *Acts 20:35*. According to Nicholson et al. 2012 the elderly generally dislike the professional care they receive for this reason.
43 As van Wijngaarden 2016, 40, recognizes.
44 Van Wijngaarden 2016, ch. 3, gives some poignant examples.
45 Van Wijngaarden 2016, 65ff.
46 A stark example is the classic paper by Rowe, Kahn 1987.

by the task of living. In some cases society can do something about this, for example by helping people to stay as long as possible in their own familiar environment, or to offer them a kind of nursing home care that is attentive to their own lifestyle. But for the larger part this is also a loss that is inherent to the loss of functional abilities and therefore irreversible.

All these disabilities can also be found in younger people who have to live with them all their lives. This fact may confirm the suspicion that death wishes of the elderly are the result of the internalization of a general depreciation of the lives of people with disabilities.[47] The elderly are different, however, first because their functioning deficits tend to accumulate, but mainly because they only crop up at the end of their lives. If you are born blind or become blind as a young adult, you will normally be able to adapt to the condition and to integrate it in your personal identity. But when you lose your eyesight at 90 – possibly in addition to your hearing and mobility – it will often be impossible to learn to cope with the condition.

4 Loss of control. As a result of your increasing physical and perhaps cognitive disabilities, you can no longer rely on your own body in order to do what you want or even need to do. You may be painfully aware of your incapacity and resent to be dependent on the care of others, as a result, fearing increased incapacity and dependency in the near future. The worst of this may be that you feel yourself increasingly to become a burden on others. Again, society can do something about this, by providing you with a wheelchair and other compensating technology, and by giving you the assurance of an adequate level of care that doesn't make extremely large demands on the informal care of relatives and friends. But if you lose the ability to take care of yourself even in regard to the most elementary daily needs, that loss cannot be remedied or compensated for by social interventions. Many old people are ashamed of their physical appearance. That is clearly to a large extent dependent on social attitudes (that are hard to change). 'Old people smell badly'. But there are circumstances about which almost anybody would feel ashamed.[48]

So, yes, we can and should do more than we presently do to compensate for the negative effects of ageing. But for the most part the irreversible functional disabilities that old age brings along and,

47 Tuffrey-Wijne et al. 2018.

48 The fifth dimension in the suffering of very old people that van Wijngaarden 2016 identifies is a permanent feeling of physical and mental exhaustion. This is an element of suffering that increases the effects of the other elements and is itself hardly amenable to social intervention.

in particular the sum of those disabilities, cannot be compensated for. Whatever society does, at 80, 90, 100, the moment arrives at which you become unable to drive a car, to cook a meal, to play the piano, to repair your own clothes, to shop, to provide care to others, to read the newspaper and to learn braille. You may even lose your interest in doing these things. "My life shrinks".[49] It is precisely for these reasons that, as Jesus Sirach reminded us, death wishes of the elderly are not a specific phenomenon of our time and culture.[50]

14.5 The role of doctors

Should doctors be allowed to help very old people who want to end their lives even though they do not suffer from a lethal or a psychiatric illness? I have argued that it is a mistake to hold that the requests for euthanasia of these people are 'outside the medical domain', because they are almost always largely caused by a cumulation of old-age ailments. It is certainly true that society can and should do more to compensate for the effects of this ageing process, but it would be an illusion to expect that this will eliminate all reasons for preferring death to continued life. It is also true that this preference doesn't only derive from ageing but also from a characteristic set of personal values and attitudes, prominently including a desire of being useful and of being in control, which is not shared by everyone. But that is not different in the case of the euthanasia requests of patients dying from cancer. At this stage of our argument the conclusion seems therefore to be that, if we permit doctors to grant a request for euthanasia to dying patients, we should also permit them to grant it to the oldest old, under similar conditions.

As a matter of fact, Dutch doctors are more reluctant to grant such requests from very old people who are not suffering from a terminal illness than requests from dying patients.[51] Some of them may still have mistaken ideas about the requirement of a 'medical foundation' as demanding a 'serious illness' (Section 14.2). Others may believe that, even if there is unbearable suffering in some sense in the case of a very old person, it is not of the right kind, being merely existential suffering (Section 14.3). Research has shown that a substantial number of doctors still interpret 'unbearable suffering' to require serious physical

49 Gaignard, Hurst 2019.

50 Van der Geest 2012 describes the perception of old age of the Aku people in Southern Ghana as a positive phase of life. But he recognizes that this perception reflects an ideal, not the actual facts of old age among the Aku.

51 In 2015 14% of granted euthanasia requests came from patients with an accumulation of old-age ailments, 22% of non-granted requests, Onwuteaka-Philipsen et al. 2017, 100.

symptoms.[52] Some doctors fail to take the patient's perspective, considering his suffering only to be unbearable if they themselves would regard it unbearable if they were in the same conditions.[53] Perhaps many doctors share the view that the problem is mainly a social one and should be solved by social interventions (Section 14.4). And some will believe that perseverance is always the best response to the problem. In Section 8.5, I have argued, however, that doctors should not impose their own view of a good death on patients, whether or not their view is the morally superior one (see also Section 2.4). For one thing, it is now simply too late to re-educate these patients in the art of dying.

Some reasons for restraint are better ones than these. It may sometimes be difficult for a doctor to empathize with the patient, for example because he seems not to be prepared to accept *any* decline of abilities he once had, or because he insists on the authority of his own personal view without being ready to discuss or even explain it. These people are often cared for by overburdened informal caregivers, and because they still may survive for an indeterminate time, the possibility of undue pressure on them is greater than in the case of dying patients. Ambivalence is characteristic for all kinds of death wishes, but particularly prominent in this category. They may either at the same time have a strong wish to die and an equally strong wish to live or have the first wish on one day and the second one on the next[54] (cf. Section 13.3). It is therefore often difficult to make sure that the patient's death wish is ascendant and stable. Even though the psychopathological perspective on this kind of 'suicidal ideation' that still dominates the literature (footnote 10) is largely of the tautological kind and the extent to which a person's decisional capacity is compromised may therefore be overrated, in some cases it will really be hard to assess that capacity.

But perhaps the most important consideration is that in the case of old-age afflictions that are not life-threatening, it is much more difficult than in most cancer cases to establish that there is no alternative way to protect or to strengthen the valuable elements of the patient's life which are threatened by these afflictions and by the loss of functional abilities resulting from them. It may be true that very old people have less

52 Chapter 12, footnote 8. In 2016 27% of Dutch doctors could imagine themselves ever to grant a request for euthanasia of a patient who suffered as a result of weariness of life, his suffering having a 'medical foundation', but not being caused by a 'severe' physical or psychiatric illness, Onwuteaka-Philipsen et al. 2017, 102. In a 'fulfilled life' case presented in a vignette only 27.5% of Flemish GPs and 5.1% of geriatricians would be prepared to perform euthanasia, van Humbeeck et al. 2022.

53 Van Tol, Rietjens, van der Heide 2012.

54 Van Wijngaarden 2016, ch. 7; van Wijngaarden et al. 2020, ch. 6, 10; cf. Hartog et al. 2020.

time left for unexpected twists and turns in their biography to occur,[55] but often changes in perspective are still quite possible. The old woman who is utterly lonely in her apartment can get an equally lonely new neighbour tomorrow with whom she communicates easily and is able to start a close companionship. Their relation will then be characterized by reciprocity; hence she need not say 'thanks' for each visit. Even if social intervention cannot be considered a panacea, in individual cases we may not be sure about its possibility and its possible effects. And even if external circumstances do not change, people's attitudes can change. Death wishes of the oldest old are a response to a series of experienced losses. You need not have a moralizing judgement about the way a person is coping with these losses to realize that as regards that way of coping developments may still be possible.[56]

The mere fact that in such cases you may shorten the person's life by years rather than days may strengthen an attitude of caution. Much can happen in those years, and the decision to help the patient end his life is irreversible.

14.6 Taking responsibility for ending one's own life

If doubts of that nature arise the doctor could reasonably ask the patient why he thinks he needs help. Precisely the oldest old who are suffering from an accumulation of old-age ailments belong to the category of people, old and ill, who can end their own lives in a humane manner by stopping eating and drinking.[57] As we have seen (Section 4.4), if a patient decides to go that way, the doctor should consider it her professional task to monitor the process, make sure that the patient's mouth is kept moist by his relatives or other caregivers and sedate him if he gets into a state of delirium. As I argued in my discussion of this option, these actions should not be considered a form of assisting suicide in the legal sense, but rather of palliative care. If a doctor fulfils his professional duty of relieving his patient's suffering, that doesn't make him an accessory to the bringing about of the patient's plan. The legal status of the aid provided by relatives is sometimes less clear, but in practice they will hardly anywhere be liable to be prosecuted.

55 Dijkstra in the explanatory statement to her law proposal, Tweede Kamer 2019–2020, 35 534, nr 3.

56 Of eighteen 70+ persons with a persistent and active death wish, interviewed by van Wijngaarden in 2013 (footnote 37), nine had ended their lives by 2019, three had an intensified death wish, three a diminished one and three no desire to end their lives anymore at all, because of a newly found volunteer job, a new partner and/or a changed attitude to life, van Wijngaarden et al. 2020b.

57 Jansen, Wall, Miller 2019.

Even if this is a humane way of dying, it requires some effort and determination to go through with it. In order to do that your decision has to be consistent and durable. If you reject the option and insist on euthanasia because you enjoy good food too much, one may wonder whether your death wish isn't still too ambivalent to be considered a well-considered one. It is still possible to make that decision in an impulsive way, for example when a doctor refuses to grant you a request for euthanasia, but you cannot implement it in an impulsive way, for you need to make good preparations and arrangements in order to prevent suffering from feelings of thirst, delirium and other complications. You need to involve relatives or friends, and this means that you will have to explain your decision to them. It will also be next to impossible for informal caregivers or heirs to coerce or manipulate you to go through the process. For these reasons the very fact that a person ends his own life in this way will be the best possible guarantee that his decision is both voluntary and well-considered (Section 4.2). And if it is, he has the right to make that decision and execute it (Section 2.5).

The availability of this option is also important in another respect. Many older, but not yet that old, people, still living in the 'third age', have concerns about the future. They anticipate that at a certain moment they may want to end their lives but will not be able to find a doctor prepared to help them, even in jurisdictions in which such help is legally permitted under some conditions. For that reason they want to have access to lethal drugs, but not in order to use them now.[58] Rather, the mere possession of them would give those people the assurance they desire that they can use them at the moment they choose. But if at that stage they will have the option to stop eating and drinking, with the help of relatives and friends and monitoring from a physician, they need not be concerned. Of course, at the present time they also have the option of (mostly illegally) ordering lethal drugs on the internet.[59]

In most cases a doctor who has doubts about granting a request for euthanasia can reasonably say to the patient: 'you need no doctor to carry out your plan. If you have no reasonable hope of things changing for the better, you have some options of ending your own life. If you decide to stop eating and drinking, I will not abandon you: I promise to keep an eye on the process and to provide advice and palliative care at the moment you need them. But this is a decision you have to make in line with the story of your life and your personal values. You should take your own responsibility for implementing it as much as possible'.

58 The former Dutch Supreme Court judge Huib Drion proposed in 1991 to make such drugs available to people of 75+, Drion 1992. The proposal is therefore known as 'Drion's pill'.

59 Of some lethal drugs, e.g. chloroquine, possession may be legal because they are not covered by international drug conventions, Chabot 2014, 52.

Unfortunately, it cannot be claimed that this option is available to every old person. You need to have relatives or friends, or nurses, prepared to provide you the necessary care, for example by keeping your mouth moist. You also need some residual mental vigour to take and implement the decision. If a very frail old person lacks that strength, she will need another person who is authorized by the law to end her life on her request. Such patients are probably the patients whom Dutch physicians are most readily prepared to help. They also have the best chance of being considered to satisfy the requirements regarding life expectancy of the American and Australasian laws.[60]

But some very old people who have decided to bring their life to an end will not satisfy the legal requirements or, even if they actually do, be unable to find a doctor prepared to recognize the fact and to act on that recognition. Or they would prefer not to involve a physician in a directive role at all. It may or may not be an option for them to stop eating and drinking, but even if it is they could protest that they have the right to decide about the manner as well as the time of their own death, and that they prefer to die by using lethal drugs. Many more people will want to be assured that they get access to such drugs if they request it in the future. In the final chapter I will discuss whether legal arrangements should be made to meet their wishes.

Should we make special arrangements of this kind for old people? In 2016 an MP of a Dutch liberal party, Pia Dijkstra, proposed a member's bill that aimed to provide access to lethal drugs to persons beyond the age of 75 who 'considered their life completed'.[61] They would only have to satisfy the requirement that their request is voluntary and well-considered. Whether they did would have to be assessed by a member of a new professional guild of end-of-life facilitators, doctors being supposed to be unavailable for that assessment because the relevant death wishes had no 'medical foundation'. When research showed that the target group of her bill was very small,[62] Dijkstra replied that her law would also meet the needs of people who want to be assured of the possibility of access to lethal drugs independently of a physician's judgement of the intolerability of their suffering and the absence of alternative ways of relieving it. But if that is its real aim, the law should have been designed

60 Overall 74% of people who died by stopping eating and drinking have a life expectancy of less than one year, Bolt et al. 2015b (Chapter 4, footnote 29).

61 Footnote 55. A similar system had been proposed by *Uit Vrije Wil*, a Dutch citizen's initiative from 2010, rejected by the Dutch parliament in 2012, Peters, Sutorius et al. 2011. The *Assisted Suicide Bill* rejected by the Scottish parliament in 2015 would also have introduced a similar system. But in that system a doctor would still have been needed to write a prescription.

62 Overall 20% of 8% of 10,000 = 160 persons according to van Wijngaarden et al. 2020a, see Section 14.3 at footnote 35.

to meet it, and the problems of that design should have been discussed on their own merits, as I will do in Chapter 16.

The 'completed life' bill has substantial support, both in the Dutch population and in parliament.[63] But because it is designed to meet the wrong problem, it has some special problems of its own. If it is only the voluntary and well-considered nature of the request for access to lethal drugs that has to be assessed, there is no reason at all not to outsource this assessment to physicians. They are already standardly asked to make that kind of assessment outside a medical context, for example on the request of notaries in cases of disputed wills. That practice isn't forbidden by the *Brongersma* verdict. (Even if it was, the lawgiver could of course overrule that decision.) The most important objection, however, is that, as we have seen in this chapter, death wishes that have no medical foundation are in no way characteristic of advanced age. Any age limit is therefore arbitrary.

63 Overall 58% of the population agrees that old people who are tired of life should be eligible for euthanasia, Onwuteaka-Philipsen et al. 2017, 90. But only 38% considered the doctor's action in a representative vignette case to be acceptable.

15 The authority of advance directives[1]

15.1 The problem

In my wallet I always keep my membership card of a road service company, my organ donor card, a blood group card and a ragged piece of paper stating my living will.

> I consider it of vital interest to me to be at any time in possession of the mental capacities needed for understanding the situation in which I am living and for taking responsibility for my own responses to that situation. If because of a CVS, brain tumor, postoperative complications, trauma, dementia, or by whatever other cause, I get into a condition in which I irreversibly lose the ability to understand the consequences of my own decisions, and to take those decisions in a well-considered way, being in that condition will detract from the value (for me) of my life as a whole, whether or not I would feel unhappy or discontented in that condition.

I go on to mention some signals of the arrival of that phase (not being able to read or write a coherent piece of text) and make stipulations about reanimation and life-prolonging treatment, including not only artificial respiration, nutrition and hydration, but also handfeeding (see Section 15.8 at the end). And if I would not die shortly in a humane manner as a result of abstention from medical treatment, I urgently request the doctor attending me to fulfil my wish to die by administering medication that will ensure a humane death.[2]

1 This chapter uses substantial parts from den Hartogh 2013a. That paper had been translated from the Dutch by Michiel Wielema.

2 For a similar advance directive see Cantor 2018. As far as I know no research has been done on the reasons people have for drawing up an advance directive. But in my experience my reasons are fairly common ones. Another important reason is the wish to relieve one's relatives from the burdens of care, Davis 2014, cf. den Hartogh 2018.

DOI: 10.4324/9781003281115-19

Do I honestly think that both these stipulations, the prohibition and the request, will be honoured when the moment arrives? Yes and no. I do believe there is a real chance that the negative directive (refusal of reanimation and life-prolonging treatment) will indeed be observed when they apply.[3] Although Dutch intensive care specialists still routinely brush aside such clauses when they have to decide about re-animation after an accident or stroke,[4] nursing home doctors appear to take them more seriously.[5] My confidence is greatly increased by the fact that my living will also identifies legal representatives whom I can trust to know my interests well and to actively promote them.

As regards the positive provision (request for the termination of my life), however, I have hardly any illusions. Although the Dutch euthanasia law has created the possibility for doctors to treat an advance directive as a 'voluntary and well-considered' request, most of the other requirements of due care must also be met. It used to be the general view of the Dutch medical community, that the suffering that results from dementia cannot by itself be considered unbearable, as the law requires.[6] That view is still widespread among doctors. It is one of the reasons why for a long time no cases of euthanasia on patients in an advanced state of dementia were reported to any of the euthanasia review committees. From 2011 on a number of such cases have been reported, adding up to 27 cases by the end of 2021.[7] In four of those cases the review committee concluded that not all requirements of due care had been satisfied. Two of the doctors involved had to stand trial in criminal or disciplinary proceedings or both.[8]

So why have I put both provisions in my advance directive? What am I so afraid of? Do I have exaggerated ideas of the suffering that awaits an

3 All states in the USA have legislation governing advance directives, as do most of the Canadian provinces, a number of Australian states, New Zealand and a number of European countries. Only the Netherlands, Belgium and Luxemburg give some legal status to advance requests for euthanasia, but in Belgium and Luxumburg this is restricted to an irreversible state of unconsciouness. *Bill* C-7 (Canada, 2021) enables patients whose natural death is reasonably foreseeable to write a waiver of final consent when they are at risk of losing decision-making capacity before the arranged date for receiving MAID.

4 Kleijer 2005, 100ff. Family doctors have similar attitudes, Vezzoni 2005, ch. 8.

5 Vezzoni 2005, ch. 7; The et al. 2002. It may be that the availability of a non-treatment directive doesn't make much of a difference for them because they are already inclined to act as these directives demand anyway, even without being directed (Teno et al. 1994).

6 KNMG 1997; NVVA 1997; Gezondheidsraad 2002.

7 This number includes all cases in which cognitive impairments of the patient would have made it impossible for the doctor to claim the existence of a voluntary and well-considered request if the advance request had not existed. It doesn't include cases of patients in a state of lowered consciousness, in which the review committee considered it necessary to take the advance request into account, den Hartogh 2017e.

8 Case 2016-85 (footnote 59) and case 2017-103.

Alzheimer patient? One of the most common criticisms of the authority of advance directives is that the people who sign them do not, perhaps cannot really know what it is like to be in an advanced state of dementia, and hence act on unfounded fears, possibly resulting from prejudice and stigma.[9] However, when I started to carry an advance directive, more than 30 years ago, the thought of future suffering was hardly on my mind at all. In the meantime, it is true, I have begun to appreciate that it may indeed be a horrible thing to become aware that you have entered upon an irreversible process that will end in the complete loss of your mental faculties and hence of your independence and your coping abilities. By now I also believe that the permanent confusion and disorientation to which you may fall prey in the subsequent stages of that process, your inability to put on your shoes, the fear and paranoia, may constitute very severe forms of suffering. I well remember my mother-in-law being restless all the time, looking for her coat and the front door key for hours on end, because she wanted to go 'home', by which she meant the home of her parents who had been dead for 50 years. I now believe that the view that a demented person cannot be considered to be suffering unbearably, at least not as a result of the dementia, is dead wrong (see Section 15.5). But, as I make clear in my advance directive, the fear of suffering is still not my main motive for carrying it with me. My dread of losing decorum is certainly relevant as well. But even if I would do nothing *then* of which I would *now* feel ashamed, I still would not like that final stage of my life to be a part of my biography. What scares me is the peeling away of my self- and personhood, the gradual loss of everything that was important in my life. I would not want my grandchildren to remember me in the way in which my own children remember my mother-in-law. Both to be in that state and to be perceived to be in it would, I believe, taint my life.[10] Because it is mainly the state of dementia itself, not any kind of distress involved in it, that I want to avoid, the criticism that I don't know what it is like to be in that state fails.

The usual reaction to these motives is that my attitude may be understandable in a professor who thinks that life has no value if you are no longer capable of writing fat books that nobody reads. But what typifies the whole process of getting demented is precisely the fact that this peculiar system of values will irretrievably get lost itself, and my self-conception be completely effaced. Even when I will initially go through a stage of suffering, that stage will eventually pass. A moment will come when I sit in the sunshine and doze off and not even remember what a book is.

9 Dresser, Robertson 1989; Buchanan, Brock 1990, 153; Hope 1992; Dresser 1995, 34; Dresser 2002–2003, 1834; Fagerlin et al. 2004; Fried et al. 2007; Miller, Dresser, Kim 2019; Walsh 2020; and other authors referred to by Levi, Green 2010. Berghmans 1998 calls epistemic failure inevitable.

10 On the importance of the perception of others see Nys 2013; Cantor 2018.

In a column in a medical journal Frans Meulenberg relates the story of Iris Murdoch watching Teletubbies, and a number of similar dramatic tales of loss. He comments: becoming older is attended by much loneliness and sorrow, but the shrinking of the brain prevents us from experiencing all of it. No process of de-humanization, then, rather a protective mechanism to secure our happiness. "Horrible? Grotesque? Tragic? Degrading? It depends on how you look at it. The Teletubbies, after all, doubtless bring joy to the demented. What's wrong with that? Man is just a happiness-seeking animal".[11]

Why should we treat people according to the conceptions of their past self? That would mean allowing the earlier self to tyrannize the later one. An advance directive would have the effect of tying oneself to the mast like Ulysses. But why should we regard the sweet call of life in the case of the elderly suffering from Alzheimer a Siren's song?

This is how the problem of the authority of advance directives has often been posed in the literature: as the question of who has the final say on the matter, the earlier or the later self. Although some of the authors who formulate the problem in this way make courageous attempts to save the authority of the advance directive, I fear they are waging a losing battle. After all, the person doctors are confronted with and often the only one they have ever known is the Alzheimer patient, and it seems unthinkable to disregard his present will and his present interests on the authority of a piece of paper representing a will and interests he no longer shares. I will argue, however, that the problem is wrongly posed in this way. In my view there is no conflict of will or interests between different stages of the self, although there may be a conflict between different sets of present interests (Section 15.5).[12]

I have, for once, given the problem I want to discuss a first-person formulation. One of my aims was to declare an interest. My main aim, however, was to neutralize from the very start a standard objection against recognizing the authority of an advance directive: that this reveals a depreciation of the life of the mentally less gifted[13] (Section 11.3). I'm not talking about the personal value of other people's lives – the value it holds to them – but about the value, to myself, of a possible stage in my own life. Such personal interests cannot be determined independently of

11 *Medisch Contact* 61 (2006): 515.

12 When Davis 1999 advocates pre-emptive suicide for people who expect their advance directive to be disregarded, Boetzkes Gedge 2004 even interprets this as an act of agression of the former against the later self, as do Hertogh et al. 2008, in their reply to critics. This view presupposes that the later self may be expected to have an overriding interest in survival. Davis' worry, however, concerns people who are prepared to overrule *her* authority because *they* have such beliefs about later selves in general. See also Davis 2014.

13 As Rhoden 1990 commented, this view doesn't distinguish between the severely demented person and a person who never has had any decisional capacity.

a person's own priorities. My priorities are different from Meulenberg's. For me the prospect of being happy with the Teletubbies would not detract from the horror; it would rather be its culmination.[14]

But could I not be mistaken in my priorities? Or, for that matter, could Meulenberg not be mistaken in his? I do not deny that, even if personal interests are to a large extent dependent on personal values, personal values can be open to criticism themselves. But even so, I will argue, both Meulenberg and I have the right to be treated in accordance with our own mistaken views (Section 15.6, cf. Sections 2.4; 8.5).

The larger part of my discussion will apply to my advance directive as a whole, both its negative and its positive parts. Many of the arguments put forward in the literature against the authority of a request for euthanasia actually apply with equal force to the prohibition of life-prolonging treatment which is far less controversial. Only in the last sections (15.7 and 15.8) I will focus on the authority of advance requests for euthanasia, discussing both the limits of that authority and the extent to which we can rely on it. The topic of this chapter differs in many ways from the other topics discussed in this book, although I will often appeal to considerations advanced elsewhere. But at this point (Section 15.8) the reasoning of the chapter will be integrated into the main line of argument of the book.

15.2 The structure of my argument

The discussion about the authority of advance directives has been dominated during the past 30 years by an impressive chapter that Ronald Dworkin dedicated to it in his book *Life's Dominion*.[15] There Dworkin makes a distinction between critical interests and experiential interests. Experiential interests are interests you have in the quality of your experience, from moment to moment. Do you on the whole feel good or bad? Critical interests are interests in how your life is going. Is or isn't it unfolding in accordance with your basic values? In order to decide this, you have to make a value judgment about your life as a whole or at least a significant stretch of it. My advance directive, says Dworkin, must be regarded as an authoritative representation of my critical interests. What I value is ending my life in a way which is consonant with the character of my life as a whole, just as one might want a play to end with a scene that fits the play as a whole, or a poem with a stanza that brings the work to an appropriate climax. On the other side of the balance we only find the frail happiness of some pleasant moments the Alzheimer patient

14 De Beaufort, van de Vathorst 2016. Cf. the case of Margo, discussed by Dworkin 1993, 220–2021.

15 Dworkin 1993, ch. 8; cf. McMahan 2002, 493–503. An important predecessor is Rhoden 1990.

may still experience, looking at the Teletubbies. According to Dworkin critical interests carry more weight than experiential ones, and therefore my advance directive has authority.

Dworkin's argument can be countered in two ways. The first option is to deny that experiential interests must always give way to critical interests. The second option is to argue that the patient suffering from advanced dementia still *has* critical interests of his own, even after having lost his competence as regards his decision to go on with his life. Actually, these objections do not really exclude each other because they seem roughly to apply to succeeding stages of the disease. In relatively earlier stages it is most plausible to ascribe critical interests to the person, in relatively later ones they may seem to fade away and give away to experiential interests. We have therefore to consider the authority of advance directives in both stages. I will do this in Sections 15.3 and 15.4 (later stage) and Section 15.5 (earlier stage), respectively.

People like me who want to uphold the authority of advance directives are often accused of an inflated respect for personal autonomy, as the one and only relevant moral concern in this area.[16] It is true, of course, that if my advance directive has any authority, that is because in signing it I exercised my right to self-government that implies the right to determine the manner and time of my own death (Section 2.5). But the objections to be discussed in Sections 15.3–15.5 can only be countered by showing that the directive should be understood as an authoritative representation of my contemporaneous interests. For that reason my argument in those sections will focus on considerations of well-being. Basically my argument will be that, given the values to which my life as a whole has been oriented, I will benefit from having my living will executed. That benefit should not be conceived of as merely deriving from the interests of a past self, standing opposed to the interests of my present self. It is only to those who protest that I am mistaken in my view of my own interests that I will reply (Section 15.6) that ultimately it doesn't matter whether I am mistaken or not. It is at that point, and only at that point, that, properly speaking, I will argue for the *authority* of my advance directive. For by allowing someone authority you recognize that his decision stands, even if it is mistaken.[17]

As regards the authority of a positive advance directive there is an additional reason to focus primarily on the demented patient's interests. As I have argued in Section 9.5 the right to self-government doesn't provide a full justification for the doctor to grant a request for euthanasia in any case. For a full justification the doctor should also be reasonably

16 Dresser, Whitehouse 1994; Widdershoven, Berghmans 2001; Dawson, Wrigley 2010.
17 On content-independence as the essence of authority see Section 2.5, at footnote 54, with references.

convinced to act in the patient's best interests, as co-determined by her own basic values. Even if my advance directive should be seen as an authoritative representation of my interests, it doesn't follow that doctors are morally required, or even permitted to comply with it. Other relevant values may be at stake. I discuss this possibility in Section 15.8.

I will argue that it is a mistake to believe that in deciding whether or not to comply with an advance directive we have to take sides in a conflict between two stages of the self. One radical way to deny that there may be such a conflict is to deny that there is one self. Relatives of a patient in an advanced stage of Alzheimer sometimes say: 'That is no longer my mother'. They mean to say this metaphorically, but couldn't they be right literally? Isn't there a point in the demolition of the self at which the connection between the present individual and the former person has become too thin to maintain that they are stages of the same being? In that event the advance directive would have no authority whatsoever.[18] It seems preposterous to claim the final say about someone else's life.[19]

When do 'I' start to exist, when do 'I' cease to exist? What are the criteria for the numerical identity of people? That is a fascinating topic, but it deserves a separate treatment. Let me only observe that many people are deeply concerned about a future state of advanced dementia. It has replaced cancer as the most feared illness.[20] If an account of personal identity leads to the conclusion that their concern is mistaken, that is a reason to doubt that account. In that future state I will be a mere ruin of my present self. Comforting me by saying that the ruin is merely a remnant of me, not really me, presents the reason for my concern as a reason for comfort. Even if my physical, psychological and social state will then be very different from what it is now, the change will take place day by day by very small steps, and perhaps that historical continuity is enough to establish identity across those steps.[21] Anyhow, in this chapter I will just assume that I am the same person, or at least the same being, as the future Alzheimer patient carrying my name, that my relatives will make no mistake in (modestly) celebrating my birthday, calling me by my name and considering themselves my legal representatives, that they will also be right in not-starting to apportion my estate, and that my present concern about getting into that stage is entirely warranted.

18 Dresser, Robertson 1989; Dresser 1995, 32–38; Shiffrin 2004; Wrigley 2007; cf. Furberg 2012.

19 Some authors suggest that a person may have authority about the fate of his post-person successor, his 'living remains', just like he has authority about what happens to his estate and his mortal remains, Buchanan, Brock 1990, ch. 3, Section 5; Kuhse 1999; Persad 2019. But we do not normally consider even radically incompetent people to be at the disposal of others in this way; they have interests of their own and therefore moral status, whether they are persons or non-persons.

20 Dementia YouGov Survey 2015.

21 Buchanan, Brock 1990, ch. 3.

Anyway, as Wayne Sumner comments, "it would seem foolhardy to let the fate of advance directives for dementia turn on the outcome of a contest between rival metaphysical theories".[22]

I will also spend little time on some pragmatic objections commonly made to the authority of advance directives. One of those objections is that such directives do not really help a doctor to decide because they always require interpretation.[23] Of course I do not dispute that advance directives may be so inadequately formulated that they are of no use at all.[24] However, every law requires interpretation, but that doesn't mean that judicial decisions are unconstrained by law. In general doctors are able to recognize the conditions for which the living will has been written[25]; their claims to the contrary may primarily reflect a reluctance to comply with it. Because of this common reluctance, it is essential to give the durable power of attorney to a trusted friend or relative, and to discuss future decisions extensively with that person, as well as with your doctor.

Many people who write an advance directive, including an advance request for euthanasia, primarily try to be as specific as possible about the exact moment at which the condition for implementing the directive will be realized. On my view it is more important to explain what it is about the state of advanced dementia that makes you to prefer death to it. For example, if you forbid every life-prolonging treatment because you don't want to get into a state of severe suffering and believe that Alzheimer always is such a state, but you are in fact as happy as Iris Murdoch was looking at the Teletubbies, it can be argued that your prohibition has no authority.

15.3 The experiential interest in survival

When I drew up that advance directive, I thought of the implications which a period of increasing dementia at the end of my life would have for my life as a whole: a gradual disintegration of my person leaving me a mere ruin of my former self. One could look at it as a way of slowly dying. But once I arrive in an advanced phase of dementia I will not be able to think in that way anymore. When that happens, the quality of my experiences from day to day will be the only thing that counts for me: the days will be bad when I suffer and relatively good when I feel well.

Suppose I am on the whole pleasantly demented. Should my critical interests still take precedence as a matter of general principle? Should

22 Sumner 2021, 25.

23 E.g. Widdershoven, Berghmans 2001; van Delden 2004; Gastmans, Denier 2010. According to de Boer et al. 2010 76% of the nursing home doctors interviewed considered it impossible to decide at which moment the euthanasia had to be performed. For slightly lower percentages see van der Heide et al. 2012, 145.

24 For an example see Crippen et al. 2000, and commentary by Truog.

25 Rurup et al. 2005.

I always be treated in accordance with the basic values that have governed my life? Maartje Schermer discusses the not uncommon case of a woman who has throughout her life put great value on good appearances, but who in the nursing home opposes all attempts to make her look a bit decent.[26] For Schermer it is of major importance that the attempts to force her into the system of her own previous values not only withhold something good from her, but also positively cause her anguish. It also seems relevant that her looks used to be for her a source of self-respect and self-confidence. But that is no longer the case because she can no longer see herself through the eyes of others.

I agree that critical interests do not necessarily prevail over experiential ones. For that reason we should, as Dworkin admits, disregard an advance directive instructing us not to provide palliative care to a severely suffering Alzheimer patient, even if we could understand the directive as deriving from the fundamental martial values he has subscribed to during his life. However, the question now is about the interests one can have in continuing one's life. Is a positive hedonic balance sufficient to conclude that an Alzheimer patient has an interest in survival?

This question could be rephrased in terms of the famous Epicurean challenge that I already referred to in Section 2.3. This time, let me quote Epicurus himself from his letter to Menoeceus:

> Death is nothing to us. For all good and bad consists in sense-experience, and death is the privation of sense-experience. That knowledge makes the mortality of life a matter for contentment, not by adding a limitless time to life but by removing the longing for immortality. For there is nothing fearful in life for one who has grasped that there is nothing fearful in the absence of life. ... So death is nothing to us; since when we exist, death is not yet present, and when death is present, then we do not exist. Therefore, it is relevant neither to the living nor to the dead, since it does not affect the former, and the latter do not exist.

According to Epicurus the fear of death is irrational, and in this brief passage he gives various reasons for thinking so. One reason is: what you do not experience as good or bad cannot be good or bad for you. There are no interests but experiential ones. But once you are dead, you do not experience anything anymore, so it cannot be good or bad for you to be dead. A second reason is the following: *for whom* would it be an evil to be dead? It cannot be an evil for you while you live, and once you are dead you do not exist any longer, so then it cannot bother you either. Therefore, there is never a subject that actually has the bad luck.

26 Schermer 2009. Cf. the example of Mrs. S who agrees to cohabit with Mr. R, falsely believing him to be her husband of 40 years marriage, Post 1995.

However strong these arguments seem, the conclusion cannot be true. If it were true, you would not harm anyone by killing him, as long as you do so unexpectedly and without causing pain. *Of course* death is an evil for most of us. But Epicurus does force us to wonder *why* exactly this is the case.

Already in Antiquity the following objection was raised against Epicurus. He is right to say that death is not a positive evil, it is not a terrible state to be in, because it is not a state in which *you* can be at all. But that does not mean that death may not be a negative evil, an evil that consists of what you are deprived of. This *pure deprivation account*, by now the standard refutation of the Epicurean argument,[27] claims to be correct irrespective of the conception that one has of the value of life, so even if one grants Epicurus (or rather modern Epicureans) that life has only experiential value, that value consists of the sum total of the positive and negative experiences one gradually gathers during one's life. As long as that sum total can be predicted to be positive, it is in your interest to go on living.

But Epicurus could still ask: *who* is really affected by being deprived of that surplus of positive experiences? Suppose you compare two possible lives: a shorter life which leads to death in 2025 and a longer life which ends in 2050. It is only a bookkeeping truth that the longer life will probably consist of a greater sum total of positive rather than negative experiences than the shorter one. Both lives are completely identical until 2025, hence up to 2025 the deficit cannot make any difference to the value of your life. But after 2025 there are no longer two lives that can be compared with each other. You simply cannot be worse off for no longer existing, as you cannot be worse off for never having existed.

How then can the evil of death be explained? Let me give an example of a person who is deprived of something when she dies and is thereby really made worse off. It concerns a woman who is seriously ill during her youth, and long after that is still affected by her illness. Moreover, she grows up in a situation of social-economic deprivation. During her study she has to take care of a disabled parent, even while not completely cured herself yet, and she has to accept a boring job to provide for her cost of living. She succeeds in finishing medical school only with the help of enormous will power and extraordinary talent, but the day before she will receive her master's degree in medicine she dies as the result of a traffic accident. So her life consists of a period with a lot of sadness which seems to usher in a period that is happy and successful. That this development is interrupted retrospectively deprives that first period of its positive meaning: this preparatory stage has led to nothing.[28]

27 Apparently subscribed to by Dworkin 1993, 229–231. A canonical exposition is Feldman 1992, chs. 8–9.

28 Pitcher 1984; Feinberg 1984, 89–91.

From an Epicurean (or rather a modern-Epicurean) point of view the value of each moment of life is independent of the value of each other moment, and the value of life as a whole is the sum of those discrete units. That is why it does not really matter that you are deprived of some experiences when you are no longer there to experience them. In my example it is the other way around: the value of each moment or period depends on the value of a whole life or of a certain stage of that life, and that value is conditional on the structure or pattern that is being realized in that life. That structure may take on the shape of the execution of a plan, as in my example: the meaning of each step is then based on the attainment of the final result. When the building collapses, its construction has made no sense. In other cases the structure of a life may be more like a plot than a plan, for example when it concentrates on the development of an intimate relation. Most lives will be woven from several of such threads.

A plan presupposes a planner, someone who can place his present actions into a continuous line of actions and events from yesterday to tomorrow. A plot presupposes a main character who goes through a series of interconnected actions and events. We must therefore object as follows to Epicurus' first argument: good and bad not only consist of single experiences, but also in the achievement of a certain life structure, of which death may be a radical interruption. We must answer the question which he formulates in his second objection as follows: the subject of the evil, the one suffering the evil, is the main character of the life story which has thus been interrupted, the person who lived to 2025 but might have lived to 2050.

My explanation of why death is an evil could be objected to by saying that it seems to imply a form of backward causation that is usually held to be impossible. The key to a clear understanding here lies in the theory of action. Actions have a teleological structure, an action is designed to bring about a situation which only obtains as a result of the action. Therefore, the success of that action can only be judged afterwards. No reverse causation is involved: the facts themselves are not determined retroactively, only the meaning and the value of those facts. An action may of course be valuable as such, even if it is not successful. But it is also possible that only needless expenses have been incurred when it fails to achieve its object.

But Alzheimer patients in the penultimate stage of their illness no longer carry out any plans and do not live a life story anymore. They can no longer align their present actions and experiences with those of the previous and next years, not even with yesterday's and tomorrow's actions and experiences. They cannot engage in meaningful relations with others, because these presuppose a sense of continuity and of reciprocity.[29] They can only have pleasant and unpleasant experiences which

29 Harvey 2006.

do not add up in any meaningful way.[30] So the point Epicurus made *does* apply to such patients. For them death is no longer an evil. Only suffering is. If the evil of death consists in the rupture of the threads that hold a life together, they have been hit by that evil already before they die.[31]

Suppose that during that last stage the unrest and confusion are gone and I just doze off in the sunshine and watch the Teletubbies. Is it, then, really not in my interest to have a few more of those peaceful days? It seems counterintuitive to deny it. But following Bernard Williams we should make a distinction between conditional and categorical interests.[32] If I do get these extra days, then I would prefer them to be calm and pleasant: that is a conditional interest. It is no reason for wanting more extra days. But the main character in my example had an interest in the success of her enterprise, and that interest could only have been realized if she had been given time to live on. That is a categorical interest. The personal value or disvalue of the life of the Alzheimer patient has to be decided in terms of his categorical interests, and these can only be determined from the views about his life as a whole which he had when he was still capable of having them.[33]

If we reject the pure deprivation account of the value of survival, we must conclude that one cannot have a purely experiential interest in survival because such an interest can only be a conditional one. If it can be concluded from my living will that it is in my critical interest to avoid that final stage of decay and devastation, that critical interest is therefore unopposed.

15.4 On changing one's mind

But can we really conclude from my living will that, even when I end up in a state of deep dementia, it will still be in my critical interest to end my life? It may be clear that this was in my interest when I composed that document. But that interest derived from my values at the time, and these have been lost by now. Compare the situation of cancer patients. It quite often happens that in advance they draw a line identifying a moment in the future at which they don't want to go on: if I lose my dignity, if am fully dependent on the care of strangers. But when that

30 McMahan 2002, 503.

31 As Henri Wijsbek suggested to me.

32 Williams 1973. He distinguishes between conditional and categorical desires, but the distinction can easily be extended to interests.

33 "... to affirm that severely demented patients retain an interest in experiencing simple pleasures while alive is quite different from saying that these patients retain an interest in being kept alive, so as to experience whatever pleasures are available to them." Brock 1988, p. 90. Kuhse 1999 makes the same point. But most of the literature simply presupposes that it is a matter of showing compassion to the pleasantly demented to allow her to live on. See, e.g., Kadish 1992; Post 1995.

situation arrives, they find it not so bad after all, or their will to live still prevails. They are pushing back their frontiers. Experiencing the situation that they anticipated with horror leads them to change their appreciation of that situation, as well as the priorities that inspired the horror. And, of course, they have the right to change their mind. No one will be tempted to kill them 'because that is in their critical interest'. Why should we react differently when an Alzheimer patient goes through a similar 'response shift'?[34]

Of course, people change their view of what matters in life, sometimes dramatically, while they live and it would be ridiculous to put claims on Paul's life deriving from Saul's values. That would really be the earlier self tyrannizing the later one.[35] Saul's values are no longer relevant for determining Paul's interests, because they have been *revoked*. But the development of dementia is not a process of conversion. If I find myself in the situation that I describe in my advance directive and give no signs of wanting to end my life, I have not revoked the values expressed in that directive, they have simply evaporated.[36] The advanced Alzheimer patient doesn't change her mind, because, as Ron Berghmans pithily expressed it, she hasn't enough of a mind left to change.[37] She doesn't rearrange her priorities in the light of new experience, because she is unable to re-evaluate or even to recollect those priorities and is equally unable to appreciate the relevance of any new information.[38] She doesn't exchange her former preferences for preferences she considers to be more appropriate ones in the situation.[39]

It is often said that 'she no longer wants to die'. But that phrase is ambiguous. It suggests that something is present: the will not to die, though it only asserts that something is absent: the will to die. But isn't the absence of a will to die relevant by itself? Should we not say that, in whatever way,

34 Dresser 2002–2003; Hertogh et al. 2007; de Boer et al. 2007; Hertogh 2008; Cohen-Almagor 2016; Miller, Dresser, Kim 2019; Walsh 2020.

35 My view is that not only do the interests of a past self count for less than the interests of the present self, as Jaworska 2007 suggests. Rather, as such they count for nothing. In Parfit's famous example of the Russian count, Parfit 1984, 327, the dilemma for the count's wife is only created by her promise to disregard his present preferences, not by his former preferences as such.

36 Jongsma, Sprangers, Van de Vathorst 2016; Sumner 2021, Section 7.

37 Berghmans 2000, 107.

38 Walsh 2020 argues that we cannot know whether the change in appreciation of her condition by the demented person results from a failure to use new information due to loss of capacity or from recent 'transformative' experiences. But if you lose your capacity to process new information, of course your response to new experiences will change, Jox 2020.

39 Hertogh et al. 2007 deduce the will not to die from the fact that patients accept the care offered to them. But if patients have the conditional wish to be well taken care of while they live, it does not follow that they also have the categorical wish to continue to live.

she has lost these priorities and therefore also the corresponding critical interests? As my example of the medical student shows, later events can retroactively determine the meaning and value of parts of your life. That is why those values are still in place for the evaluation of what my life means to me, even though I can no longer perform that evaluation myself. Otherwise, you could have no reason either to honour my wishes concerning my estate, my body, my sperm or my organs after my death. It isn't required that I still hold my values at that time, as long as I haven't revoked them. It would, as Wayne Sumner says, "be perverse to disregard my earlier directive simply because I am now in the very condition of incapacity I anticipated in executing it in the first place".[40]

I have carried that advance directive or a similar one with me half my life, and everyone who knows me can witness that my views never have changed during that time. As I said, it is of vital interest to me that I need not go through that last stage, that I do not have to live on like that in the memories of my grandchildren. That is not the interest of my earlier self, myself in 1989 or in 2022, it is the interest of myself as such, as the main character of my life story from the beginning to the end, or at least through half of that story, whether or not I am presently still aware of it.[41] And during that last stage I will not have any conflicting interest.

15.5 The threatened self

But this conclusion only applies to a late stage in the development of Alzheimer. Before that stage has been reached, the patient still has traces of critical interests on which he presently acts. He may be involved in some elementary project which he is able at least intermittently to recognize as such. Or, more probable, he may interact with other people in ways which justify us to conclude that he cares for those people in a special way and therefore is aware of the fact that he has a special relationship with them.[42] Even people who don't recognize their relatives by name sometimes still show signs of such a special attachment. In such cases, we should ascribe to the person a categorical interest in survival, because it is a precondition for going on with her project or her relationships.

Until that late stage Alzheimer patients still have a sense of self and concerns for that self, or concerns for other things that matter to them. But you can only have a sense of self if you have some conception of that self as existing through time. That is even shown when a patient like my mother-in-law wants to return to her familial home: she still identifies herself as the child of her parents. It is also shown when a patient

40 Sumner 2021, Section 7; cf. Dworkin 1993, 226–227.
41 Dworkin 1993, 230.
42 Taylor 2008.

expresses her resentment for being treated in a humiliating way and thereby exhibits that basic human concern for being properly respected. She wants to be treated as the person she thinks she is.[43] Hence it is still true of her that the value of each moment of her life depends on some rudimentary structure exhibited by that life over time. She may have lost the grasp on her life as a whole, or perhaps even of any significant stretch of it which includes the present. But she still has a conception of herself, and that may be enough to ascribe to her some interest in survival. Relatives may, for example, be touched by some characteristic way of responding to circumstances, a trace of humour, an act of gentleness. Another structural element which binds the stages of our life together, in addition to our projects and ongoing intimate relations, is our characteristic way of coping with the vicissitudes of life. It could therefore be suggested that it adds to the value of her life if that character is still expressed in some recognizable form under such adverse conditions.

In such cases there may be a conflict of critical interests: an interest in survival and an interest in preventing a further loss of self. But these should not be conceived as the interests of a past and a present self, but as colliding interests of the present self. They depend on elements that structure a person's life during a stretch of time; the more structure they provide, the more important they are. If this is correct we can order a person's relevant critical interests to some extent. A stable long-standing interest in avoiding the loss of responsible agency has a good claim to a high place in that hierarchy.[44]

Since the 1990s laudable efforts have been made to get access to the inner life of Alzheimer patients.[45] But what this new psychology of dementia has revealed to us is often alarming. Yes, there is a remaining sense of self, but it is not an intact sense of an intact self, and it is precisely for that reason that the descent into the abyss often involves severe suffering. Being to some extent aware of the loss of one's powers, not being able to take care of oneself, feeling frightened because of events one cannot understand, judging social situations incorrectly and then interpreting other people's responses as disrespectful, panicking about events which don't happen, embarrassment, sadness and paranoia, all these states of consciousness reflect a sense of self indeed, but a sense of a progressively threatened and disintegrating self. The increasing losses of cognitive ability leave a self which is confused and disoriented in the world, unable to execute any effective control, and to the extent that it is aware of its condition, feeling uprooted and insecure, lacking basic trust.

43 Sabat, Harré 1992; Sabat 1998; Jaworska 1999; 2007; Shriffin 2004.

44 Cf. Menzel, Steinbock 2013, arguing that, if there is little anticipation or memory, a demented patient has little stake in survival.

45 Post 1995, 2000; Kitwood 1997; Sabat 1998; Cheston, Bender 1999; Nolan et al. 2002; MacQuarrie 2005; Hertogh et al. 2007.

It is therefore a mistake to suggest that an advance directive expresses an overrating of rationality and other cognitive performances at the expense of the affective dimensions of human life, which may be sufficient to make it worthwhile. Basic cognitive abilities are our primary instruments of coping with the normal tasks of life, and therefore losing them can hardly fail to be experienced with extreme distress and alarm, even if it happens with only some dim awareness of the fact. It is also a mistake that the condition of dementia by itself doesn't cause extreme suffering. The physical symptoms may be relatively mild (although physicians often fail to recognize them because of communication problems). But, as we have learned from Eric Cassell, pain, breathlessness, cramps, contractures, ulcers, malnutrition only constitute suffering because of the attack on the self that they imply (Section 6.2). To the extent that the demented patient has a sense of self that is still in some contact with reality, that self is often under attack. Contrary to received opinion,[46] agitation, confusion, delusion and anxiety are therefore to be understood as essentially resulting from the dementia itself, and not from concomitant disorders.[47]

It is true, I conclude, that the demented self still has critical interests in a later stage than Dworkin may have assumed. Her lifestory may retain structural elements that could sustain an interest in survival. But that story is often a tragedy. Precisely the appeal to take the patient's perspective seriously should make us sensitive to the extent to which the deteriorating condition of the Alzheimer patient may involve severe suffering.[48] It is then a blessing when eventually "all the confusion, embarrassment and agony of self-observation are forfeited in favour of grateful amnesia".[49] To that extent Meulenberg's comment on Iris Murdoch that I quoted in Section 15.1 was to the point. But if it is in the person's overall interest to avoid that stage as well, the better way for the patient is to quit life at an earlier moment.

It is true that many other demented patients cope or seem to cope with their alarming condition. What often enables them to do so is *anosognosia*, unawareness of their illness. This is particularly characteristic of patients suffering from Alzheimer's disease.[50] 'Everyone at my age is somewhat forgetful', they might say. Perhaps it is only to be expected that the self defends itself by destroying its sense of the world as it is, even beyond the extent to which this has already been done by its

46 As represented by the three Dutch documents referred to in footnote 6. But by now most nursing home doctors believe that the suffering of demented patients can be unbearable, even in the absence of a concomitant illness, Rurup et al. 2005.

47 Post 1995.

48 Goering 2007. Hertogh et al. 2008 concede in their reply that 'he has a point', but then go on to ask whether it is not too much to ask of a doctor to kill such a patient. Perhaps it is, but then the reason cannot be provided by the interests of the patient. See Section 15.7.

49 Post 1995.

50 Hertogh 2009.

cognitive losses. Cees Hertogh has stated this well: the patient "has to find a way of shutting out what happens to him, even if this means losing contact with reality, or he has to face the changes which occur, but this amounts to an apprehension, probably too painful to bear, that one is on the brink of losing oneself".[51] But then Hertogh cannot be right when he also holds that advance directives lose their authority because Alzheimer patients, like patients suffering from other fatal illnesses like cancer, adapt their preferences to their conditions. As we have seen in Section 15.4, Alzheimer patients do not, as cancer patients do, arrive at a new assessment of their condition, taking into account new experiences. Rather they progressively lose their capacity to assess. In addition, whatever assessment they still make may itself be an expression of a fear too large to be faced, in particular with the coping resources still at their disposal. The only possible way of coping left may be denial.[52]

But shouldn't we take them seriously even in this state of denial? A critical interest, as Dworkin rightly stresses, is an interest in things happening, not only in experiencing them to happen (Section 6.4). Your critical interests are not fulfilled when you are only given the impression of being respected or of being praised for doing something worthwhile. Any interests satisfied in that way are only experiential ones. Similarly, your 'critical interest' in safely returning to the home of your parents cannot be fulfilled when they have been dead for many years. A demented person's wish to continue living cannot automatically itself be seen as an expression of her critical interests, because it may result from losing contact with reality.

As long as the demented patient still has a sense of self, and therefore a life which possibly might be sufficiently structured to sustain some interest in survival, that self will often be threatened to such an extent that its life will be characterized by continuous severe suffering. If the patient succeeds in avoiding this suffering, he can often only do so by retreating into an illusionary world. In the first case he still has critical interests, but on balance these can, after all, hardly be interests in survival.

15.6 The limits of the authority

Up to now I have appealed to a person's advance directive as a source of information that enables us to identify her critical interests. It can only function as such a source if it represents the person's stable views, held over a long period, and never revoked on reflection during the time that

51 Hertogh, Droës, de Boer 2006, cf. Hertogh et al. 2007, 53.

52 The analysis is also inconsistent with the view that the suffering of Alzheimer patients is largely the result of 'malignant social psychology': stigma, prejudice and lack of understanding (Kitwood 1997, ch. 3; Patterson et al. 2007). On such views see Sections 11.4; 14.4.

she was still able to properly reconsider them. It is therefore necessary to periodically renew one's signature, to confirm the directive orally and to continue end-of-life conversations with one's care-givers and family-members.[53] According to the case law of the Dutch Regional Review Committees this is indeed required for an advance request for euthanasia to retain its evidentiary value. In the happy phrase of Paul Mevis, the advance directive is not a 'locker-document', not a document to be merely kept in a safe.[54]

The document, however, is not only a source of evidence. When it is sufficiently confirmed, it is also an *authoritative* representation of the person's priorities. Making it up is a public act by which she determines the normative position of others, in particular of the doctor who is responsible for her treatment. It will obligate her to abstain from the treatments the document forbids and, under the appropriate circumstances, permit her to end the person's life. That the document is authoritative means that its validity does not depend on an assessment of its content. This content-independence also covers the philosophical issues that I have discussed. Even if I am mistaken in my view that one cannot have a merely experiential interest in survival, that doesn't justify a doctor to put my living will aside in order to give me some additional happy days.[55] If, on the other hand, Frans Meulenberg draws up an advance directive requiring all life-prolonging measures in the case he is pleasantly demented, it is equally irrelevant whether the pure deprivation account of the evil of death is right or wrong. It is up to each person to determine which view matters. This authority is derived from her right to sovereignty within her personal domain (Section 2.5). An additional consideration is that physicians are only on the scene because of their medical expertise, not because they have any special competence in determining people's basic interests as regards life and death,

53 *Euthanasia Code* 2018, 38–39; cf. judgments 2012-3 and 2017-103 (footnote 8), both finding fault with a doctor who disregarded the requirement. Cf. Menzel, Steinbock 2013, 494.

54 Mevis et al. 2014, 51. A corollary of this view is that it should be permitted in interpreting the document to appeal to other statements that the person has made, both to relatives and to care-providers. This has explicitly been permitted by the Dutch Supreme Court in its verdict in the *Arends*-case, footnote 59. Considering the document in this context would also, at least partially, overcome the criticism that the law doesn't require the patient's competence at the time of writing of the request to be assessed by an expert, Miller, Dresser, Kim 2019. When that happens after the patient has been informed of her diagnosis, the criticism may be on target (but cf. footnote 68).

55 Blustein 1999; Koppelman 2002; Nys 2013 advocate leaving the decision to arbitrate between the former and the later self to surrogates, significant others who have co-authored and therefore are still able to continue co-authoring the story of my life. That may be wise counsel, but, as Nys recognizes, that doesn't mean that these surrogates have any *authority* to decide unless I have given it to them.

let alone the truth of their philosophical views. In regard to these issues they have no epistemic authority (Section 8.5).

15.7 Two controversial issues about advance requests for euthanasia

The Dutch euthanasia law of 2002 was largely a codification of pre-existing judge-made law. But one entirely new article (2.2) was added: "If a patient of sixteen years or older is no longer able to express his will, but before he entered into that state was deemed to have the capacity of reasonably taking care of his interests and had made a written statement containing a request for the termination of his life, the doctor can grant that request". The requirements of due care apply in such cases to the extent that they can possibly apply. It is for example impossible that doctor and patient together arrive at the conclusion that no alternative way is available to relieve the patient's suffering. Only in 2011 the article was for the first time appealed to in a case of advanced dementia.[56] This created an uproar among doctors and in the media, and a heated debate about the precise meaning of the article and about the ethical acceptability of its application in dementia cases. The legal, although not the ethical dispute was finally decided by two decisions of the Dutch Supreme Court of 2020.[57]

These decisions concerned a case involving the geriatrician Marinou Arends.[58] Her patient was a woman of 73 who lived in a nursing home in spite of the fact that she had declared in an advance directive that she wanted euthanasia when admission to such a home would otherwise become unavoidable. At the time of her admission her GP had attempted to discuss her advance directive with her, and so did doctor Arends at two later occasions. When it had been explained to her what euthanasia meant she had declared that she didn't want to die. But at other moments a conversation with her about that subject had been impossible and she expressed a death wish to the SCEN-consultant who doctor Arends invited to see her. During her daily outburst of anger and frustration she could shout up to 20 times a day that she wanted to be dead.

Doctor Arends had the bad luck that this case was ideally suited for evoking contrary responses to the main issue in the ongoing debate: the legal relevance of a patient's expressions of a wish to live. The legal agencies that made statements about the case – the regional review committee, two disciplinary courts, the Public Prosecutor, a district court,

56 RTE Annual Report 2012, case 7. See footnote 7 on the present number of cases.
57 ECLI:NL:HR:2020:712; 713.
58 The case and the legal procedure are described in Arends 2020.

the Attorney General and finally the Supreme Court – all agreed that the patient had no decisional capacity as regards the decision to perform euthanasia, that she was in a state of unbearable and unrelievable suffering, and that doctor Arends had amply complied with all consultation requirements.[59] The review committee, the disciplinary courts and the Public Prosecutor, however, thought that, given the statements made by the patient, doctor Arends could not have concluded that her advance directive could be taken to fulfil the requirements of a voluntary and well-considered request. The district court and the Attorney-General on the other hand concluded that the directive could be taken to fulfil that requirement because the statements of the patient had not been clear and consistent.

The Supreme Court annulled the verdicts of the disciplinary courts and sided with the district court. But the Supreme Court took the matter one step further. On its view even clear and consistent statements of the patient that would have been at right angles with her request for euthanasia could not have revoked her request. The court agreed with a statement made by the district court that a valid request has authority if it has been competently made and that this authority cannot be annulled by any declaration that has not been competently made. But it explained the meaning of competence in the standard way as implying the capacity to understand relevant information and make use of it in decision-making.[60] Besides fitting in with Dutch law,[61] this argument can be understood as a conceptual one. As I stated in the last section (Section 15.6) the authority of any declaration should be understood as being content-independent. A patient's statement about the continuation of his treatment has legal effect whether it is positive or negative. Therefore, it cannot be the case that the patient's consent has no effect, but his failure to consent has.[62]

59 Review committee: 2016-85, RTE Annual Report 2016, 54–58, commented upon by Miller, Dresser, Kim 2019; Menzel 2019. Disciplinary courts: C 2018.033; C 2018.352. District Court The Hague 11-09-2019: ECLI:NL:RBDHA:2019:9506. Attorney General: ECLI:NL:PHR:2019:1338. For the initial proceedings see Asscher, van de Vathorst 2019; for the later ones Sumner 2021, Sections 8–11; Buijsen 2022.

60 It therefore should be understood to interpret Art. 2.2 as referring to the *competent* expression of a will. The district court seems to have understood 'competence' to be the mere ability to express one's will clearly and consistently. But my mother-in-law clearly and consistently expressed her will to go home; nevertheless she made that statement without having decisional capacity.

61 BW (Civil Code) Art. 3. 34: if a person doesn't have decisional capacity, a will to realize a legal consequence is supposed to be lacking.

62 Wicclair 1991; den Hartogh 2016b. When the regional disciplinary court stated in the *Arends*-case that a person lacking competence still has the right to self-determination and can exercise it by revoking her advance directive, this was a contradiction in terms: being incompetent (in the relevant binary sense, Sections 11.6; 13.5) *means* lacking authority.

The Supreme Court's argument can be seen as applying this *symmetry requirement* on the authority of valid declarations to the case.

This view doesn't imply that statements made by the patient after she has lost decisional capacity count for nothing. The Supreme Court, on the contrary, required the doctor to attempt to communicate with the patient about her present desires about life and death, albeit not necessarily after having decided to perform the euthanasia.[63] If the patient states, and in particular if she states clearly and consistently, that she doesn't want to die, the doctor cannot conclude that she has not made a voluntary and well-considered request, but she may have to conclude that one of the other legal requirements that still apply to the case have not been satisfied, for example the requirement that the patient should be in a state of unbearable suffering.

That very requirement was at stake in a second dispute about the authority of advance directives that the Supreme Court ruled on. According to some authors we should, at least in cases of late dementia, understand 'unbearable suffering' to exist as soon as the situation arises that the patient has indicated in his advance directive as the condition for his request for euthanasia to become actual.[64] That would mean that the requirement of unbearable suffering would become redundant: it would be automatically met in any case in which the request laid down in the living will would apply (Section 12.7). The Supreme Court ruled that the requirement could only be satisfied by a demented person experiencing actual severe distress. This interpretation means that the request that I have made in my own advance directive (Section 15.1) could, contrary to my intentions, only be granted if I would be in an extremely unhappy and discontented state.

In Chapter 9 I have argued that it should not be sufficient for granting a request for euthanasia that it has been properly requested: the request should not only express the requester's competent will but also represent his overall interests. Eliminating unbearable suffering is not by itself the only relevant interest of the person who wants to end her life. Her primary interest is rather to avoid conditions that are the object of her suffering: loss of meaning, of independence, of dignity, of coping resilience. But if she doesn't severely suffer from these losses, we would doubt

63 As the review committee and the disciplinary courts (footnote 59) had required.

64 Matthijssen 2019, Section 7; Sumner 2021, Sections 10–11. On a related view suffering requires experience, but it should be considered 'unbearable' if its object is the condition described in the directive, see the advice of the Attorney General in the *Arends*-case (footnote 59) and the explanation of the Public Prosecutor on its decision not to prosecute the doctor in case 2012-03, RTE Annual Report 2014, 73–74. Sumner, 42ff, refers to 2014-02, *ibid*, 31–35, in which the reporting doctor explicitly denied that the patient was in an experiential state of distress. Interviewed by the Inspectorate, however, he retracted that denial, Annual Report 2015, 68–69.

whether these were her real reasons to want to end her life. The desire to avoid unbearable and unrelievable suffering is therefore a proper proxy indication of her interests (Section 6.2).

But that is not true in this particular case. As a result of progressing dementia facts and experience of the facts can come apart, and that is precisely the reason why people like me want to make sure in advance that a proper response will be made. For that reason a legal instrument like article 2.2 should provide another description of the possible interests of people who want to avail themselves of that instrument.

15.8 Can we rely on an advance request for euthanasia?

I have argued that a patient in an advanced stage of dementia (severe dementia) has no interest in survival that conflicts with the critical interest that she may have, as the protagonist of the story of her life, in ending that life at a stage that can still be integrated into that story. At an earlier stage (moderate dementia) she may still have some critical interest in survival, but it is ephemeral in comparison with her interest in dying as she lived. An advance directive has to be understood as an authoritative representation of that interest. In many cases, moreover, she will also have an important experiential interest in avoiding the characteristic kinds of suffering that dementia may imply.

Advance prohibitions of life-prolonging treatment are by now legally binding in many countries and many doctors are prepared to respect them. But even in the Netherlands the large majority of doctors are opposed, often vehemently, to complying with advance requests for euthanasia.[65] Many of the arguments that they appeal to would equally apply to prohibitions of treatment. The ‘response shift’ argument (Section 15.4) is a clear example. But, at least in the Netherlands, these arguments are rarely used to question the authority of such prohibitions. This seems to show that they are a mere rationalization of a basic reluctance against ending a person’s life on the basis of an advance request. What is so special about this particular kind of euthanasia?

Almost all Dutch doctors share that reluctance, even if a few of them are prepared to overcome it in the interest of the patient. It is a strong form of the general reluctance to kill that I have described before (Section 9.2). It will be even stronger in cases in which the patient makes statements expressing a wish to live. Because of that reluctance most doctors who believe that euthanasia is sometimes justifiable consider it only a possibly acceptable choice in a conflict of duties. They are conscious of a duty not to kill which may not be a duty that is owed to the patient.

65 In 2016 78% of Dutch doctors (71% in 2011), as compared to 16% of the general public, Onwuteaka-Philipsen et al. 2017, 102, 89.

If compassion prevails that may only be possible because severe suffering evokes that response directly and urgently, and it is only possible when they can share responsibility for ending someone's life with that person herself, not only with a piece of paper. To sneak up with a deadly needle on that Govert den Hartogh who is dozing off in the sunshine, or to stir dormicum through his coffee in order to kill him without any fuss is a different matter altogether.[66] Even if you agree that he has an interest in the integrity of his life story, that is a fairly abstract interest.

Are the psychological obstacles to killing which doctors experience just that, perhaps atavistic remainders of an old taboo, or do they have moral meaning? In Section 9.2 I have suggested that, on the one hand, prohibitions on killing belong to the core of every morality that every serious articulation of the ethics of killing has to account for. *Thou shalt not kill.* On the other hand, however, the boundaries of that prohibition require an explanation; they should not be postulated as 'ethical atoms'. But it is also true that such fundamental norms need to be internalized, and we cannot expect everyone to fine-tune his moral sentiments to complex moral reasoning, as I have presented it in this chapter. It would be fortunate for me if at the appropriate time I could find a courageous doctor like Ms Arends willing to grant my advance request but I don't reckon on it. When the time comes that I have indicated in my living will, I may not be suffering at all, let alone 'unbearably', and I may, perhaps even explicitly and consistently, deny any wish to die. It is quite understandable for doctors to hold back in such situations.

So I'm aware that I cannot really rely on doctors to fulfil my wish. But they should not say that they refuse to do so because of *me,* in my interest, out of respect and consideration for the person that I am or have become. Such doctors claim an authority to define my interests that they do not have. According to Cees Hertogh even in the most severe cases of suffering "what holds us back is the defenceless power of human need and vulnerability".[67] That is extremely paradoxical: is it my very vulnerability to severe suffering that will prevent him from showing mercy? If doctors say that they hold back because they care for me, they deceive themselves and show lack of respect to me as the human being that I have been and still am.

66 This prepratory use of a sedative was objected to by the review committee in the *Arends*-case (footnote 59) because the committee held, implausibly, that a fearful reaction of the patient to a syringe could be understood as resistance to the euthanasia. I have explicitly permitted the use of a sedative in my living will, cf. Menzel 2019.

67 Hertogh, Droës, de Boer 2006; cf. views of doctors reported in The et al. 2002; de Boer et al. 2010; and cf. Boudewijn Chabot, Never kill a defenceless person who is unaware of what you are doing, *De Volkskrant* 21-1-2017, a proclamation eventually signed by ca 450 physicians.

Nevertheless, for the time being, an advance euthanasia request is a highly problematic way of securing euthanasia at the 'proper' time. The request saddles doctors with an onerous burden that most of them consider morally unacceptable. At the moment at which the conditions stipulated in the request have been met the patient may not be in a recognizable state of severe suffering that could evoke compassion. For these reasons, the Dutch experiment of giving legal status to advance euthanasia requests cannot be considered successful, in spite of its ethical justifiability, as I have defended it in this chapter. For me the only real alternative will be to end my own life, with or without some help from a doctor, when I still have the decisional capacity to do so in a well-considered way, hence at the latest at an early stage of the development of the dementia. Better too early than too late. That will also prevent me from being supposed to revoke my decision when in the mild stage of dementia I am still considered competent to do so, but am really already losing the sense of my illness (see Section 15.3 at footnote 50).[68] If advance requests for euthanasia had a better chance of being acted upon, preventing such untimely suicides would be one additional reason for recognizing the authority of such requests.[69] As things stand, however, this recognition will hardly succeed in providing peace of mind to people who fear the consequences of Alzheimer.

On the argument that I have made in this book euthanasia – the participation by a doctor in the join action of ending a person's life, whether this is classified as euthanasia or as physician-assistance – is not the only or necessarily the prioritized way of carrying out a decision to end one's life. If a person with a dementia diagnosis acts on that decision herself at a moment that she is still capable of doing so, either by stopping eating and drinking or by taking lethal drugs, she may lose a stretch of life-time that could possibly still be valuable to her. But if her first priority is to avoid the loss of self involved in the unstoppable progress of her illness, it may be the best choice to make.[70]

An alternative option that I have made use of in my living will, but that will also be legally available in many countries that forbid euthanasia, is to indicate conditions at which you refuse to be administered

68 Estimations of the degree to which decision-making capacity is retained during the stage of mild dementia, or even the foregoing stage of mild cognitive impairment, differ, Marson et al. 1997 (56% agreement); Kim, Caine, Currier 2001; Vollmann et al. 2003; Moye, Karel, Azar 2004; Okonkwo et al. 2007. The divergence is understandable because of the irreducibly normative character of such judgments (Section 13.5). Cf. case 2020-16, in which the review committee agrees with the physician against the consultant that the patient could be considered competent as regards his request.

69 Sumner 2021, Section 5, referring to *Carter v Canada* at Sections 57, 58.

70 Cf. Davis 2014 on new developments in the diagnosis and prognosis of dementia that make it less precarious to determine the right moment.

food and drink. Ignoring that refusal may legally count as a violation of your right to bodily integrity. You should make it the responsibility of your legal representative to pinpoint the exact moment. If you are in residential care, it may be necessary for you to request to be send home to begin with. You should of course be sure in advance of the willing and informed cooperation of the people who will have to care for you, either your family and friends or nurses. A doctor should be prepared to monitor the process and intervene in the case of complications.[71]

71 Cf. Quill et al. 2021, part 2. The book came too late to my attention to be taken account of.

16 Designing a regulatory system

16.1 The task ahead

If a country or state has decided to legalize euthanasia or some kind of physician-assisted suicide, what would be the best system of substantial and procedural requirements for guaranteeing people's rights and promoting as well as protecting their interests, individually and collectively? What is the system that promises maximum benefit and minimum risk? In this abstract form the question hardly makes sense: we cannot expect any particular legal system to be ideally suited to all cases. 'One size fits all' is an impossible idea: such choices are necessarily path dependent.[1]

To give one example: in Germany legalizing euthanasia will be out of the question for evident historical reasons, but since Frederick the Great suicide has not been a crime and German law recognizes the principle that if an act is permitted to some-one, the act of assisting that person cannot be forbidden either.[2] Whereas in the neighbouring Netherlands suicide assistance by relatives and other laypersons is forbidden, in Germany it is allowed[3] (Section 5.1). In recent years the main obstacle for doctors to make use of this legal option consisted in professional regulations. As a result many Germans had to travel to Switzerland to obtain lethal drugs with the aid of organizations like *Dignitas*. More recently similar organizations started to operate in Germany itself. This development led parliament in 2015 to adopt a law (Section 217 of the Criminal Code) that prohibited the provision of assisted suicide services. Although the aim of the law was not to criminalize all suicide assistance by physicians, the concept of 'assisted suicide services' was not well defined; hence few doctors had sufficient confidence of escaping criminal liability to provide any such assistance. When the German Constitutional Court

1 For lists of the jurisdictions that at present have decriminalized either euthanasia or assisted suicide, see Chapter 1, footnote 1; Chapter 5, footnote 28 resp.

2 *Grundsatz der Akzessorietät*, StGB Sections 28, 29. (17).

3 In its decision of 26 February 2020, 2 BvR 2347/15, the German Constitutional Court (*Bundesverfassungsgericht*) at some point remarks that some kind of legal protection against abuse of this freedom would be desirable.

DOI: 10.4324/9781003281115-20

struck down Section 217 in its landmark decision of 26 February 2020, it left it to the lawgiver to design a full regulatory framework for the protection of the possibly affected rights, but it made it clear that the purpose of this framework could only be to guarantee the voluntariness of the act and the competence of the agent. The decision fits with a legal tradition that is characterized by the rejection of paternalism of any kind and therefore tends to recognize consent as justifying any act, even an act that seemingly violates a right that is traditionally held to be inalienable (Section 9.1). Apparently the Court mainly thought of the provision of access to lethal drugs,[4] but it did not distinguish this kind of suicide assistance from participation in the joint act of ending a person's life, as I have done in Chapter 5.[5] Since 2020 the prohibitions of suicide assistance in the professional codes, both of the *Bund* and the *Länder*, have gradually been lifted, but claims of patients to get access to lethal drugs have even recently been denied by lower courts. And parliament has until now been unable to reach consensus about a regulatory framework. Several proposals have been presented by groups of MP's. The most promising of these proposals would still forbid commercial suicide assistance services, and 'normally' require two psychiatric examinations of the requester's competence with an interval of three months.[6]

As this example illustrates any proposal will have to fit into the existing legal system and to reflect salient experiences in recent history that have structured the public debate. It is also relevant how health care is organized and financed. Do general practitioners have an essential role, is there a national health insurance? And so on.[7]

Because the decisions legislators have to make are to such a large extent dependent on a pre-existing legal and political fabric and on the local history of the debate, it is difficult to make comparative judgements, and, considering the extent to which the Dutch experience has been misunderstood by commenters from abroad over the years, I am writing this chapter with some trepidation. Nevertheless, if we are to learn from the experience in other jurisdictions, such comparative evaluations have to be made. The American laws, for example, all follow the Oregon model of 1994 with only the smallest variations, but that also

4 2BvR 2347/15, Section 284.

5 See my commentary on the decision, den Hartogh 2020b.

6 According to the Austrian law that, following the decision of its Constitutional Court (*Verfassungsgerichtshof*) of 11 December 2020, G 139/2019-71, came into effect on 1 January 2022, only patients with a severe chronic or a fatal disease are eligible. After a notary or lawyer has provided a death writ (*Sterbeverfügung*) on the basis of the declarations of at least two physicians, the patient has to wait 12 weeks before receiving a prescription for lethal drugs, or 2 weeks, if he will die within 6 months.

7 Cf. Battin 1994, ch. 6 ('A dozen caveats concerning the discussion of euthanasia in the Netherlands'); Trappenburg 2012 on the social determinants of the Dutch euthanasia regime.

means that they may copy the limitations of the original model.[8] This procedure is therefore somewhat myopic.

Some generally valid starting points can be argued for. I hope to have shown in this book that people have, or should have, a right to determine the manner and time of their own death, within the closed circle of their intimates. That right can be limited if this is 'necessary in a democratic society' in the interests of public safety and for the protection of the rights and freedoms of others, but a blanket prohibition of providing access to lethal drugs under any conditions will be too broad to be justifiable in that way. If the law opens such access, it only 'stands out of the way' and therefore can only require requests for access to be made in a fully voluntary and well-considered way (Sections 5.4 and 5.5). But if the law allows doctors to take final responsibility for the effective, safe and painless implementation of the decision of a patient to end his life, they should make sure that they not only act in accordance with the will of the patient, but also in his best interests (Section 9.5). That is, for example, the rationale of a requirement that the patient should be in a state of unbearable suffering beyond hope of improvement, that is until now common to jurisdictions that permit euthanasia,[9] even though the robustness of that particular requirement is everywhere under threat (Section 12.7).

Starting from these principles I have considered general problems of designing an adequate regulatory system in earlier chapters, in particular from Chapter 10 onward. In bringing those lines together in this final chapter I will start by asking a comparative question about the two systems with the longest history. In the Netherlands euthanasia and physician-assisted suicide have been legalized in 1984 by a decision of the Supreme Court and by statute since 2002. Oregon's *Death with Dignity Act* became effective in 1997. If we consider the actual practices that these laws have enabled to develop, there is one difference that leaps to the eye. In 2020 6938 cases of euthanasia or assisted suicide have been reported to the Dutch Regional Review Committees, 4.1% of a total of 168,566 deaths in that year. In the same year 370 people received prescriptions for lethal drugs under the DWDA, and 245 people died from digesting them, 0.66% of 40,226 Oregon deaths.

Why are the legal opportunities used seven times as often in the Netherlands as in Oregon? Clearly contextual factors constitute a large part of the explanation. In the Netherlands 88% of the population appreciate the existence of the euthanasia law, and 76% can imagine making use of it at some future time. Overall 57% of the physicians (78% of GP's)

8 Pope 2018.

9 In Section 15.7, I have identified one situation in which that requirement doesn't cover the relevant interests of all patients.

ever have ended someone's life on his request, and an additional 24% (13% of GP's) can imagine doing so.[10] Public support for the Oregon law seems by now to be on a comparable level.[11] But among physicians support and in particular participation are not. In 1999 34% of all physicians were willing to write a prescription; at present 51% of GP's support the law.[12] In 2020 all prescriptions have been written by 142 physicians (1–31 per physician), out of more than 6000 licensed physicians in the state.[13] In the Netherlands 55% of requests, identified as such by doctors, are approved by them (Chapter 12, footnote 21), in Oregon only 18%, and only 59% of those requests resulted in death.[14] Under such conditions patients in Oregon – many of them confined to bed, in the final stage of a fatal illness – will sometimes have to be fairly tenacious to find a willing physician, and it is only to be expected that they often need to shop around before actually finding one.[15] Although the geographical variation of the incidence of euthanasia in the Netherlands is also remarkably large,[16] in Oregon 'assisted dying' is largely confined to urban areas in the Northwest of the state.[17]

These differences result in a different environment for decision-making, and that is, moreover, a self-reinforcing effect. Most patients who receive a diagnosis of incurable cancer in the Netherlands will start thinking and talking about the possibility of euthanasia in the future, in particular when all life-prolonging treatments have been stopped, but in the same circumstances only 17% of Oregonians consider physician-assisted suicide

10 Onwuteaka-Philipsen et al. 2017, 83, 98–99. Cf. Chapter 11, footnote 56, for even higher figures for support.

11 Overall 80% in 2012 according to Sandeen 2013 (doctoral dissertation).

12 Resp. Ganzini et al. 2000; Ganzini 2017.

13 Oregon Health Authority 2020. Only one of those physicians came from Eastern Oregon. From 2000 to 2016 374 physicians have written prescriptions under the DWDA, 10 wrote more than 20 prescriptions, up to 85, Hedberg, New 2017.

14 Ganzini et al. 2000. As reported by family only 4% of requests are approved, Tolle et al. 2004 (Chapter 12, footnote 36). The most common reason for declining a request is the suspicion of impairment of judgement by mental disorder, Lee 2014.

15 Of patients dying by prescribed drugs in the first year after adoption of the law, 69% changed doctors to find a willing physician, Chin et al. 1999; cf. Ganzini et al. 2000 for other relevant data. The median duration of patient-physician relationship was eight weeks in 2020 (range 0–1020). The high number of cases dealt with by a few physicians (footnote 13) is also indicative.

16 Groenewoud et al. 2021. The authors propose to attribute these differences to either 'demand' or 'supply' factors and, as regards supply, to identify cases of 'overuse', 'underuse' and 'misuse'. They seem to believe that there is a measure of 'proper supply' that only depends on medical facts, excluding the influence of patterns of social interaction.

17 Almost 50% of cases come from Portland Metropolitan area and almost 30% from other Northwestern counties. From 189 persons who died from medication received from doctors in Colorado 66.7% came from Denver Metropolitan area, *Colorado End-of-Life Option Act 2021 Data Summary.*

an option.[18] According to Frances Norwood these differences also reflect different attitudes to the place of death in our life, the Americans excluding death from consideration as much and as long as possible, the Dutch commonly valuing a sense of closure.[19] There may be such a difference, even though her picture of Dutch attitudes seems somewhat too rosy.

But these are not the only factors that explain the difference in numbers between the Netherlands and Oregon. Another part of the explanation can be found in the actual provisions of the Dutch and Oregon laws. (Of course, the legal options can also co-determine the attitudes of doctors.) In the next two sections I will focus on these legal provisions. In the first place it is of intrinsic interest to understand the divergence between the Netherlands and Oregon. But it will also turn out that the relevant dissimilarities between the two legal systems reflect some of the basic choices that any regulatory system will have to make: whether or not to introduce a waiting time for all cases, whether to restrict the role of the doctor to writing prescriptions for lethal drugs or extend it to taking final responsibility for the implementation of the patient's decision, and whether or not to allow either kind of action in the case of people who do not suffer from a lethal illness and have an indeterminate life expectancy. I will discuss these three choices in Sections 16.2 and 16.3. In Section 16.4 I will consider some of the most important procedural requirements that some but not all permissive regimes have introduced or that have been proposed in the literature. In Section 16.5 I will make a few pragmatic observations about the question whether the law should accommodate conscientious objections from doctors who don't want to participate in the practice it legalizes. Section 16.6, finally, offers some thoughts on the larger social consequences of legalization.

16.2 Comparing Dutch and Oregon law

The *Death with Dignity Act* required the patient to make a request for assistance, both orally and in writing, to the physician who has the primary responsibility for his care. The oral request had to be repeated not less than 15 days after the initial request. Of course, this doesn't mean that a patient with a life expectancy of less than 15 days had no access to lethal drugs, because he could make a request for access in advance, anticipating a deterioration of his condition. Presumably this was what most patient who requested access actually did: the average time between making the first request and death in Oregon used to be 43 days.[20] But only a minority of patients apparently thought ahead in this

18 Tolle et al. 2004. In the Netherlands the number of 'in due course' requests for euthanasia rose from 33,900 to 67,700 from 2011 to 2016, Onwuteaka-Philipsen et al. 2017, 96.

19 Norwood 2018.

20 Oregon Health Authority 2019.

way, confirming the difference in social attitudes between Oregon and the Netherlands that I speculated about in Section 16.1. A substantial number of patients only started considering assisted suicide when it was too late, either because they did not live through the waiting time or lost the capacity to make the second oral request.[21]

Since 1 January 2020 the DWDA gives physicians the ability to waive the waiting period for patients who are imminently dying. In 2020, 75 patients were given exemptions. In that year the number of prescriptions increased from 290 to 370 and the median duration of the period between first request and death fell from 43 to 32. But the other permissive American jurisdictions except New Mexico still have waiting times of at least 15 days.[22]

The Dutch law, on the other hand, doesn't stipulate a waiting time at all. Although this occurs very rarely, it is not impossible for a patient, for example in a case of severe lack of breath or sudden pain that is not responsive to any treatment, to request euthanasia, be visited by a consultant, and receive euthanasia all on the same day. (We may hope that euthanasia had been a subject of conversation long before.) It is only the mandatory consultation that always creates a time buffer between request and final decision. It is also possible that the patient has lost the capacity for reconfirming his request when the doctor arrives for performing the euthanasia, but is still suffering. If all other requirements of due care have also been met the doctor is then allowed to go on. In the most recent national survey the physicians who granted a patient a request for euthanasia estimated the resulting shortening of the patient's life as less than 24 hours in 10%, 1–7 days in 26% and 1–4 weeks in 36% of the cases.[23] Hence about half of the patients dying from euthanasia in the Netherlands could only have profited from a law of the original Oregon-type by planning ahead. That may be a substantial part of the explanation of the long-standing difference in numbers between the two countries.

What would have happened to such patients in Oregon before 2020, if they had not made a timely request for a barbiturate? Probably some of them would merely have received analgesics and some would have been deeply sedated. To the second practice, sedation until death, two problems are attached that I have extensively discussed in Chapters 7 and 8. In the absence of refractory symptoms, often in the absence of refractory *physical* symptoms, sedation until death is not allowed by presently applicable guidelines. As a result some patients will have to go through a dying stage

21 Ganzini, Dobscha 2004; Tolle et al. 2004; Ganzini 2017.

22 Hawaii, New Jersey and Maine of 17–20 days. Victoria and Western Australia have waiting times of nine days; in Victoria this waiting time can be waived if the person is expected to die or lose capacity within nine days.

23 Onwuteaka-Philipsen et al. 2017, 104. In Belgium resp. 41 and 22%, Dierickx et al. 2020.

in which forms of suffering that are either considered to be 'existential' or 'non-refractory' are not relieved. Because predictions of life expectancy are very uncertain, that period may be even longer than the mandatory waiting time of 15–20 days. Even if the patient is deeply sedated, on indications that are presently either permitted or not, this situation may not be in accordance with his preferences as regards the manner and time of his death. It may, for example, wear out his relatives or prevent him from saying goodbye to them in the way he wants. Moreover, if a dying comatose patient, who is not artificially hydrated, actually dies after more than a few days, he probably dies from dehydration.[24] Even if he has either requested lethal drugs in advance or consented to being sedated, that procedure will then amount to 'slow euthanasia' (Section 7.3).

The conclusion should be that as regards patients in the final stage of dying a legal arrangement of the Dutch type is to be preferred to the Oregon model. Another argument for this conclusion is the following. Laws of the Oregon type don't require the doctor or any other healthcare professional to be present when the patient actually ends his life with the drugs provided.[25] But at the end stage of a terminal illness many patients are no longer in a physical and mental condition that enables them to act in a way that guarantees a quick and safe death without complications and unwanted side effects, and not all of them can enlist support from their own social network. Hence there is good reason standardly to give a doctor the task to direct and control the whole process. In most cases she will already be intensely involved in providing palliative care. It would then be incongruous to send the patient home with a prescription to take care of himself.[26]

This brings me to a second difference between the Dutch and the Oregon system: the different roles of the doctor. In Oregon she only de-blocks the access to lethal drugs, in the Netherlands she directs and controls the whole process, whether or not it is the patient who performs the last act: ingesting the drugs or opening the syringe (Section 5.4). It is this divergence in roles that explains why the Oregon law only requires the patient to make his request voluntarily and competently, but the Dutch law also requires him to be in a state of unbearable suffering beyond hope of improvement, by either medical or non-medical means. Because of this raised burden of proof one might expect the hurdle of access to physician assistance to be higher in the Netherlands than in Oregon. But the difference in numbers that we are trying to explain suggests that the opposite may be true. If you are planning to end your life,

24 Den Hartogh 2016a.

25 In Oregon, 2020, the prescribing physician was present (sometimes by Zoom) in 12%, another healthcare provider in 22% and volunteers in 24% of the cases, Oregon Health Authority 2020.

26 Campbell, Cox 2010.

it may be easier to let a doctor implement the plan than to do it yourself. This is confirmed by the fact that even within the Dutch legal regime patients strongly prefer to have their life ended by the doctor than to do it themselves with his assistance, even when the assistance amounts to full direction and control.[27] The data from Canada since the enactment of *Bill C-14* in June 2016 also confirm this pattern: patients prefer their lives to be ended by the doctor, and when this option is available, the numbers quickly raise beyond the level of Oregon. In 2020 7384 residents of Canada died by MAID, on a population of 38 million. Only in seven of those cases the drugs were self-administered.[28]

Why do people prefer to have the doctor on the scene in a leading role? It might be suggested that the connotation of terms is a relevant element: to die by suicide is supposed to be abhorrent ('self-murder'), but euthanasia in Dutch ears suggests, indeed, a good death. That suicide has such a bad name clearly is an atavistic remainder of the history of its moral condemnation, reinforced by the relative invisibility of the non-violent, interactive and well-considered variant (Section 3.6). Even that variant may run counter to a deeply rooted inhibition to causing self-injury. But that euthanasia is not merely considered the implementation of a suicide plan by delegating it to a doctor is something that has to be explained itself. Perhaps it has something to do with the authority of the medicine man: having a death wish is a sign of mental disturbance, unless you receive the blessing of a substitute-priest.[29] Part of the explanation may also be that people don't trust themselves to be able to act effectively.[30]

16.3 An indeterminate life expectancy

In Section 16.2 I have argued that there are good reasons to involve doctors in a directing and controlling role in the case of patients in the last stage of a terminal illness. But which of the two models should we prefer in other cases?

27 Buiting et al. 2012. "(I)t is indisputable that, where physician-administered euthanasia is legalized alongside physician-assisted suicide, it has the effect of driving out the latter, and of driving up the number of hastened deaths dramatically". Preston 2018.

28 Health Canada 2020. In Switzerland, on the other hand, providing access to lethal drugs has never been a crime, but the number of cases in which the option is used, is still relatively low: resp. 1.6 (1.1 according to Bosshard et al. 2016) and 1.2% of deaths in the German- and French-speaking parts (2013), Hurst et al. 2018.

29 "Historically, in the United States suicide has carried a strong negative stigma ... Seeking a physician's assistance, or what can almost seem a physician's blessing, may be a way of trying to remove that stigma and show others that the decision for suicide was made with due seriousness and was justified under the circumstances". Brock 1992.

30 Although Oregon patients standardly start by drinking an anti-emetic, regurgitation still occasionally occurs (33 times of 1905 deaths since 1998), Oregon Health Authority 2020; cf. Lewy 2011, 134. Such complications can only be reported when a healthcare provider was present at the time of death. See also Chapter 5, footnote 24.

In order to address that question let me first consider the third important difference between the Dutch and the Oregon model. In Oregon the doctor has to determine that the patient has an incurable terminal disease that will produce death within six months. The Dutch law doesn't know any such requirement. It has often been pointed out that doctors are unable to estimate a life expectancy in the order of six months with any confidence. This is confirmed by the fact that under the Oregon law the time between the first request and the time of death can be more than 1000 days.[31] But that doesn't mean that there are no clear cases that are accepted under Dutch law but would not be acceptable in Oregon. In 2020 these cases included: accumulation of old-age ailments (235 cases), early stage dementia (168 cases), mental illness (88 cases), together 491 cases on a total of 6938, or 7%. An unknown number of patients with a chronic non-terminal illness or a degenerative illness and a relatively long life expectancy (multiple sclerosis, Parkinson) should be added.[32] In 2015 8% of Dutch euthanasia cases concerned a patient with a life expectancy of more than six months.[33]

This third difference between the Dutch and the Oregon legal regime explains only a relatively small part of the difference in total numbers between the two countries. But the difference is interesting because it largely concerns the category of hard cases that by now for some years has been at the centre of the controversy in permissive countries and states, most of all in Canada, Belgium and the Netherlands, and that I have discussed in the final part of this book. I have argued that in these cases for every substantial requirement of due care that has been laid down in the laws of these countries and states, it tends to be more difficult to make sure, or sure enough, that it has been met. Voluntariness is more under pressure when the person is expected to live longer. Ambivalence grows when you cannot be sure that every next day will be as bad as the present one, or worse. Suffering is even more multidimensional than in the case of people in the final stage of a terminal illness, and some elements of it may be too idiosyncratic to be understood and assessed by others. In the mental illness and old-age cases it is often hard to be sure that no alternative ways of alleviating the suffering exist: treatment or palliative care options or social interventions or personal growth. On the other hand, these are also the cases in which people tend to be most able, physically and mentally, to end their own lives. It would therefore be understandable if the law made this the default option in these cases.

31 Maximum: 1503 days, Oregon Health Authority 2020.

32 The Australian laws require death to be expected within 6 months, or 12 months in the case of neurodegenerative diseases. But Queensland stipulates a single 12-month time frame in all cases.

33 Onwuteaka-Philipsen et al. 2017, 104. (0% in 2005, 3% in 2010.) In Belgium 16.7% of patients death was not reasonably foreseeable, FCECE 2020.

As I have argued in Chapters 13 and 14, all very old people, almost all patients suffering from dementia in a stage in which they haven't lost decision-making competence in matters of life and death, and many psychiatric patients have the option of stopping eating and drinking, provided only that they have an appropriate network of informal care-providers and a doctor who is prepared to monitor the process and provide palliative care when needed.[34] Medical organizations and governments should make it a policy aim that the public is much better informed about this option than it is now, and in particular learns that when adequate precautionary measures are taken, it is a humane way of dying. Medical organizations should also make it clear that it is a normal part of a doctor's job, not a form of assisting suicide, to provide the necessary care (Section 4.4). It would be helpful if they produced guidelines. If all this is better known than it is today, many people will be more assured than they are today that they need not die a bad death.[35] It would help if they could be assured of being sedated when delirium starts to be a real possibility (Section 8.8).

As I have also pointed out more than once (Sections 4.2; 14.5) this is an option that has many advantages from a regulatory point of view: it is almost unthinkable that you go through the process if you start under pressure from others or impulsively. It is understandable, however, that people will not be happy if it turns out that their right to determine the manner and time of their own death comes to this. Even if it results in a humane death, it requires not only a social network and a willing doctor but also a lot of preparation and determination to implement the plan. Many people with a mental illness are too young and too healthy to be able to end their lives in this way. And as I have indicated in Chapter 5, it is arguable that governments are not justified in blocking access to lethal drugs, in particular barbiturates, altogether. Moreover, by allowing limited access, they may prevent to some extent that people get access illegally, by ordering these drugs from abroad or by using publicly available but unsafe drugs.[36]

What would it mean to allow limited access? To fix ideas, consider the following proposal. At least two doctors have to ascertain, by talking with the person and his relatives separately, that his request for access is voluntary, well-informed, well-considered and stable. If any suspicion arises that the person's decision-making authority is compromised by mental illness, at least one psychiatrist will have to determine whether or not the suspicion is founded. In order to establish stability, the request must be repeated no less than x (3?) months after the initial request.

34 In Oregon hospices three times as many patients die from stopping eating and drinking than from physician-assisted suicide, Sumner 2011, 203, footnote 149.

35 They are already in possession of *Drion's pill* (Chapter 14, footnote 52).

36 Cf. Chapter 11, footnote 57.

Isn't it too risky to make this option available to everyone? Will we not invite a death rush, a stampede of lemmings? I doubt it. As we already saw in Section 16.2 people apparently are much more reluctant to end their own lives than to have it ended by doctors. This is confirmed by the substantial number of cases in jurisdictions of the Oregon-type in which individuals have been issued prescriptions for lethal medication but don't use them.[37] In the Netherlands, on the contrary, it almost never happens, when a date for euthanasia has been set, that the patient withdraws at the last moment.

If the option is offered to everyone, that will include patients with a terminal illness and a relatively short life expectancy. If a person has decided to end his life in a voluntary and well-considered way, but his doctor isn't sure enough that his suffering is unbearable and beyond hope of improvement, or if that person doesn't want to burden his doctor with a request for euthanasia, he still has the right to determine the manner and time of his own death. As we have seen in Chapter 12, Dutch doctors who are willing to seriously engage with a patient's request for euthanasia tend to feel overloaded because of increasing pressure by patients who believe that they have a right to euthanasia on demand, and their families. Doctors are often unsure about the legitimacy of their own resistance to this pressure. Doesn't the patient really have a right to euthanasia on demand, derived from his right to self-determination? We free these doctors from their moral overload if we give them the alternative option of advising the patient about *his* alternative options.[38] This will also promote clarity about the differences between the two routes to the self-chosen death.

It cannot be denied that the assessment of voluntariness and competence in these cases is often more difficult than in the case of patients with a terminal illness and a short life expectancy. It is also not fully clear at present, in spite of the Canadian parliament's confidence about the matter (Chapter 13 at footnote 5), whether or not psychiatrists with different convictions about the acceptability of providing access to lethal drugs to psychiatric patients, could agree in their assessment of candidate-patients decisional capacity (Chapter 13 at footnote 48). Suppose they couldn't. We could then consider limiting the resulting risks by restricting the option of acquiring access to special categories of people, and in particular to exclude patients with mental illness. But for reasons that I have discussed in Section 13.8, it would be unacceptable to block the way to a self-chosen death to psychiatric patients altogether. As a minimum the 'dual-track' system that I described there would deserve serious consideration.

37 From 1998 until 2020 2895 prescriptions have been granted in Oregon, but only 1905 persons have died from the medication they received, Oregon Health Authority 2020.

38 In Section 14.6, I argued that there is no reason why we shouldn't entrust doctors, or a category of specialized doctors, with the task of assessing decisional capacity, rather than a new guild of end-of-life facilitators, as had been proposed by MP Pia Dijkstra.

I have argued that we should prefer a 'Dutch' arrangement for patients in the final stage of a fatal illness, and an 'Oregon' arrangement for people with an indeterminate life expectancy.[39]At which point should we draw the line between these regimes? It has been suggested that people should prefer to be autonomous, not only in deciding about the manner and time of their death but also in implementing their decisions. Hence, they should only appeal to doctors for assistance, if for some reason – perhaps because they are unable to swallow – they cannot do without help.[40] This ideal of personal autonomy has its attractions, but it cannot be imposed on individuals, either by the state or by doctors. The right to self-determination includes the right not to be autonomous in this sense. Hence it is up to people, within the area outlined by the law for other reasons, to decide whether or not to involve doctors in a directing and controlling role.

I have no further principled considerations to offer on the question of the borderline between the two tiers of the system that I proposed. Any line will to some extent be arbitrary. That isn't an objection: an intrinsically vague line can only be made somewhat more determinate in an arbitrary way. That natural death should be reasonably foreseeable may still seem too indeterminate, but that it should be foreseeable within a certain time frame, for example of six months, doesn't really help because of the lack of reliability of such predictions. Perhaps we should therefore settle for 'reasonably foreseeable'.

16.4 Procedural requirements

Are there any general points we can make about proper procedural requirements?

Some recent laws stack formal and procedural requirements on each other. The idea seems to be that the protecting force of the law depends on the quantity of formal law it contains. All that bureaucracy will certainly be burdensome to severely suffering and often dying patients and may deter willing practitioners from participating. It may also decrease rather than increase the extent to which the substantive due care requirements of the law will be internalized by those practitioners and thereby be integrated into medical practice.[41]

39 *Bill C-7* (2021) introduced a two-track system in Canada, but both tracks are medicalized to the same extent. If natural death is not reasonably foreseeable some special requirements have to be met: the person should be informed of available means to relieve her suffering, including counselling services and palliative care, and the person and the health practitioners involved must agree that the person has seriously considered those means.

40 Ost 2010; Vink 2016b.

41 See the work of John Griffiths, referred to in Chapter 12 at footnote 108.

16.4.1 *Consultation and review*

There is no doubt that the requirement of independent consultation will be the most important procedural safeguard in every permissive legal system. Independence can be guaranteed by requiring the doctor to invite a consultant who is randomly selected from a register of physicians willing to act as such (Chapter 11, footnote 15). As I stated already, it is a major criticism of some of the existing laws that they don't require the consultant to be independent, and it is almost equally problematic that according to some laws the consultant need not check whether all the substantive requirements of due care have been met (Chapter 11, footnote 13). All laws in addition rightly require a psychiatric assessment in all cases in which the doctor or the consultant suspects that the patient's decision-making capacity is impaired by a mental disorder.

It is also of some importance that the consultants, as well as the attending doctors, are obliged to account for their decisions and actions, and this obligation can only make sense if their reports are read and checked by someone.[42] Reporting your actions in terms of an explicit set of standards is an effective way of internalizing the standards.[43] As we saw in Section 12.5, it makes sense to extend the reporting requirement to a proper review procedure, but only if that procedure provides feedback to the reporting doctor, the consultant and, by the publication of the most significant judgements in an anonymized form, to other doctors and the general public.[44] In the same chapter we have seen that the present Dutch review system by now only has a marginal effect of that kind in the case of patients with a terminal illness and a limited life expectancy, the large majority of cases (Section 12.6). In some respects that effect could be improved, in particular by a more active policy of correcting common misunderstandings about the 'subjectivity' of suffering and the possible reasonableness of alternatives that have been refused by the patient (Section 12.7). All things considered a review procedure

42 In Oregon the prescribing and the consulting doctor, the mental health consultant and the dispensing pharmacist all have to report to the Oregon Health Authority, but this is not a proper review body, its main task being to assemble data for statistical purposes. Nevertheless, if it discovers irregularities in the doctor's report, it will report these to the appropriate agency, as it did twice in 2018.

43 In the large majority of the cases in which a Dutch SCEN-consultant thought that the requirements of due care have not been satisfied, she anticipated the review committee to agree with her judgement. Only in 8% of cases she didn't believe this, Onwuteaka-Philipsen et al. 2010.

44 New Zealand's *End of Life Choice Act* (2019) requires physicians who have provided voluntary assistance in dying to report to a committee consisting of one ethicist and two health practitioners. On their turn they have to report to the Registrar, an employee of the Ministry of Health Care, whether or not the practitioner has complied with the act's requirements, and, if not, to direct the Registrar to follow up on this information. No further feedback seems to be given, except in an annual report with statistical data.

seems an important link in the chain of safeguards, but only if it doesn't merely check on formalities and procedures. And it may not be necessary to subject all reported cases to the same kind of scrutiny.

16.4.2 Ex ante review

The Colombian and Spanish euthanasia laws require a committee of experts to approve the euthanasia in advance.[45] In both cases it may have been believed that such a committee would guarantee a more thorough and impartial kind of assessment of the extent to which the requirements of due care are satisfied in a particular case than the individual judgements of the attending and consulting physician could provide. In, Section 12.6 I have already commented that this system will as a matter of fact transfer the final responsibility for a complex decision from people who have the personal knowledge required to make it to a bureaucratic agency that hasn't. A second objection to the system is that the procedure necessarily involves a waiting time that excludes patients in the last weeks of their illness, even long before sedation until death could be considered an alternative way to prevent extreme suffering.[46]

16.4.3 Doctor-patient relationship

In the first years after the passing of the Dutch euthanasia law the regional review committees held that a doctor could only grant a patient's request for euthanasia if at that time she was responsible for that patient's treatment. For that reason the doctor was in one case judged not to have acted carefully because he had ended the life of a person who had approached him with the mere aim of getting euthanasia.[47] But after it had been pointed out that this requirement could not be found either

45 In Colombia the committee consists of a doctor with specialty in the relevant pathology, a lawyer and a psychiatrist, Benavides 2018; in Spain a lawyer and a physician, both members of one of the Commissions of Guarantee and Evaluation, composed of minimally seven members. If the two experts don't agree the whole commission has to decide, Sanz et al. 2021.

46 The Spanish law provides for a waiting time of at least 40 days that in a situation in which loss of competence is feared can be reduced to 28 days by skipping the normally obligatory waiting time of 15 days between two written requests, Sanz et al. 2021. If we are afraid that the patient may lose competence within a time frame of 40 days, we will rarely be assured by a reduction of that frame to 28 days, even if it would be possible for physicians to determine life expectancy with that kind of precision.

47 RTE Annual Report 2005, case 9. Quill, Cassel, Meier 1992 already proposed to require a 'meaningful doctor-patient relationship'; cf. New York State Taskforce 1994, 129; Kimsma 2010. In Oregon it is required that the physician who writes a prescription has a treatment relation with the patient. The median duration of that relation is eight weeks, range 1–1020, Oregon Health Authority 2020. In many cases the doctor is actually approached by the patient with the mere aim of getting assistance in ending his life.

in the law or other authoritative sources,[48] the requirement was dropped. Too quickly perhaps: it had been open to argue that the norm provided a safeguard for the serious consideration of some of the essential legal conditions, in particular the requirement that the patient's suffering could not be alleviated or ended in any other way. Other auxiliary norms have been introduced in a similar way (Section 12.5). A long-standing doctor-patient relation as it is (or used to be) characteristic of the role of GP's in the Netherlands, might also bring the doctor in a better position to understand the nature of the patient's suffering and to assess his decision-making capacity.[49] On the other hand, even if we could require a treatment relation, we can hardly require it to be long standing, and even a long-standing relation need not be a good relation. And if it is, that may increase the risks of transfer and countertransfer.[50]

This is a general form of the dilemma that we met in its most acute form in Chapter 13, as regards psychiatric patients. The two-tier system that I propose in this chapter offers a solution. Yes, we should require that doctors can only decide about a request for euthanasia if they have a treatment relation that enables them to propose and provide alternative treatments and interventions or to monitor their use. But we should make that requirement only in cases in which the doctor considers taking on a directing and controlling role; we shouldn't make it when he is only asked to de-block access to lethal drugs.

16.4.4 Mandatory palliative care advice

In order to decide whether any alternative way out of the patient's suffering is still available, it may help to ask palliative experts for advice. In Flanders this is often done, apparently more often than in the Netherlands.[51] During the debate about the Belgian euthanasia law it was proposed to make this obligatory. The proposal used to be referred to by the name of a 'palliative filter', a name that, unfortunately, suggested that the palliative experts could intervene in the doctor's decision to grant a request for euthanasia.[52] At the time the advocates of legalization considered the professionals involved in palliative care as opponents, as they still tend to be in many other countries,[53] and therefore the proposal as an attempt at obstruction. Many hospitals and nursing homes, however,

48 Legemaate 2005, 49.
49 Levene, Parker 2011.
50 The lifting of that particular norm made it possible, a few years later, to start the Euthanasia Expertise Centre (Sections 12.3; 13.7).
51 Dierickx et al. 2018.
52 Broeckaert 2001.
53 Cf. Young et al. 2019: on average 68% of the general population in New Zealand is in favour of legalizing some form of physician-assisted death, but only ca. 8% of Australasian palliative care specialists and GP's involved in palliative care.

made such an advice obligatory. By now the Belgian palliative care movement has recognized euthanasia to be one alternative way for the patient to end his suffering that supplements the other options available within palliative care (Chapter 6, footnote 60). Surely an expert advice about these other options should then be welcome, provided it doesn't create disproportional additional burdens to the patient.[54] Hence the advice should be provided within the available time span for consultation and decision-making, and it should be left to the doctor to decide whether it would be helpful for the palliative care team to visit the patient.[55]

16.4.5 Data collection

From Oregon and the other American states that allow doctors to write prescriptions for lethal drugs, we have data from the reports doctors are required to send to the Oregon Health Department and similar boards. In most states these are collected in annual reports. In addition studies have been done by dedicated independent research groups in Oregon and Washington, and recently in Vermont, but the information that we have about the actual practice is still very incomplete.[56] This makes the statement that non-compliance with the rules hardly occurs gratuitous.[57] Reported non-compliance is, unsurprisingly, "almost exclusively of a clerical nature"[58]: incomplete forms, missing signatures and the like. The functioning of the Dutch regulatory regime, on the other hand, has been evaluated every five years since 1990, resulting in a series of comprehensive surveys, commissioned by the government. These exercises have provided us with a multitude of the data we need for evaluating the system, even if these surveys did not really come up with a thorough evaluation themselves. It is desirable not to leave the collection of such data by independent research to private initiative alone.[59]

This, however, is not a problem of permissive jurisdictions only. Of what actually happens on the ground, or rather underground, in prohibiting jurisdictions we know much less than we even know of Oregon. Our most recent information about illegal physician-assisted suicide and euthanasia in the USA, Australia and New Zealand dates from 1995, 1998 and 2002, respectively; about Germany or Spain we have no such

54 Orentlicher, Pope, Rich 2016.

55 In 2020 95% of patients who received prescriptions for lethal drugs in Oregon were hospice enrolled, cf. Campbell, Cox 2010.

56 Keown 2018, 417. Because in Oregon pharmacists are legally obligated to report every prescription for barbiturates that they have dealt with, it is improbable that these drugs are often administered illegally. But we know nothing about dosages of morphine and midazolam that are administered.

57 For such a statement see, e.g., Leven, Quill 2018.

58 Lewis, Black 2012.

59 Cain 2016.

information at all. From all these countries we also have only the slightest information about stopping with eating and drinking, or about sedation until death, in particular about the extent to which it is combined with abstaining from hydration, and about the life expectancy of the patients involved.[60] It almost seems that people don't want to know.

16.5 A right to accommodation of conscientious objections?

Most presently existing permissive laws have an explicit 'conscience' clause for doctors who are unwilling to provide assistance of any kind to a patient with a persistent and active death wish. Many of these clauses are redundant, because the laws in which they occur don't obligate a doctor to grant any request for assistance, whatever his reasons for declining, moral conviction or squeamishness or fatigue after too many cases, or a private weighing of costs and benefits. In addition, there may be informal norms requiring a doctor at least to reveal the reasons why she declined a request,[61] but the possible reasons are not limited to the failure to meet legal requirements. In these cases conscientious objection clauses are not only redundant but also confusing, because they suggest that in order to decline a request that meets the legal criteria a doctor has to appeal to her conscience.

According to some recent euthanasia laws doctors have to report written requests that they have received and their decisions as regards these requests. If they reject a request they also have to report their reasons. If a doctor registers his conscientious objection, the administration must ensure replacement. The Spanish law, for example, intends in this way to ensure that the service is provided to every person who meets the requirements.[62] Such a law comes close to according a right to euthanasia to people who meet its eligibility criteria. Should this right be recognized explicitly?

It is arguable that people's interest in dying in a way that is consonant with their conception of a good death normally will be of such importance to them that, in addition to the right of access to lethal drugs, the state should recognize a right to euthanasia, at least in some cases, for example in the case of patients in the final stage of a terminal illness, and most clearly in the case of patients who are unable to self-administer lethal drugs. It is, however, less clear than in the case of a right to access to lethal drugs, what a right to euthanasia should imply. As I have insisted throughout, to decide whether a person's suffering is unbearable

60 Bruinsma, Rietjens, van der Heide 2013, 32.

61 Snijdewind 2019.

62 Sanz et al. 2021. The Australian laws contain similar requirements. If in New Zealand your doctor rejects your request, or you do not feel comfortable discussing it with her, she must inform you that you have the right to ask the Registrar (see footnote 44) for the name and contact details of a replacement.

and beyond hope of relief is a complex decision that requires a large set of heterogeneous facts to be taken into account. Speaking in terms of rights about such a sensitive decision may only buttress the common idea that euthanasia is available on demand and increase the pressure on doctors to accede to every request. The best one can do may be to ask the doctor to explain his decision if it is a negative one and to enable the requester to approach another doctor, possibly from the pool of doctors who have registered their willingness to act as consultants.

If a right to euthanasia would be recognized, it would not necessarily imply valid claims on every individual doctor. The service could be available to every eligible person, occasionally perhaps requiring some additional but not unreasonable effort, even when doctors would be allowed to quit. But this could be seen as unfairly shifting the burdens that are implied by the recognition of the right on to colleagues. The fall-back position of unwilling doctors would then be an appeal to their conscience. Should such an appeal be recognized?[63]

It is obvious that we cannot grant an unlimited right to the members of any profession to have their moral convictions accommodated, whatever the impact on clients and colleagues. You can have no right to enter the army if your moral beliefs forbid you to wear arms. You can have no right to become a doctor if you are opposed to blood transfusions or vaccinations. Whether there is a limited moral right of conscientious objection, and whether it would apply to a law that gives patients a right to euthanasia is a question too large to be taken up at the end of a long book. Providing a full discussion would require me to consider some basic questions of political philosophy. I will therefore only make a few observations that, independently of the outcome of that discussion, suggest that there are good reasons for the law not to obligate doctors to perform euthanasia if they, for whatever reason, are unwilling to do so.

First, what could be the point of obligating them? It seems that 70% of Italian gynaecologists refuse to perform an abortion, with predictable detrimental consequences for women's health and well-being.[64] But precisely this large number makes it infeasible to solve the problem by obligating these gynaecologists to perform abortions on pain of losing their licence. That, on the other hand, Dutch doctors aren't obligated to grant a request for euthanasia in standard cases when all requirements of due care have clearly been satisfied, no longer has any great impact on patients, because of the large numbers of willing doctors. It is much better to enable unwilling doctors to be open about their position without having to fear unwelcome consequences than to induce them to sabotage the law, for example

63 The question has recently been put on the bioethical agenda by Udo Schuklenk and Julian Savulescu, see, e.g., Schuklenk, Smalling 2016. There is already a substantial literature, including Giubilini, Savulescu 2017.

64 Savulescu, Schuklenk 2016.

by falsely declaring requesting patients not to be in a state of intolerable and unrelievable suffering. The best we can do is to enable patients to avoid such doctors. So this is the paradox: the more we have reasons to ban the option of conscientious refusal, the less we will be able to do so.

In most countries the opposition to legalization of euthanasia from the ranks of the medical profession and (usually even more) their leaders is still very strong. In that situation tolerance is required. As both Chapter 12 and the present chapter illustrate, introducing a regulatory regime for any kind of physician-assisted suicide or euthanasia is a delicate matter. To quote Roger Magnusson again:

> Since prohibition has failed to prevent covert euthanasia, any statutory regime must—if it is to do any better—attract some measure of support and voluntary compliance from doctors. If the law is too bureaucratic, too intrusive, or gives insufficient legal shelter to doctors acting in good faith, it will be ignored in practice and will fail in its objective of re-regulating physician-assisted suicide and active euthanasia. The challenge for those interested in minimizing harm is to design a regime that is robust, but which is also more attractive than the stresses and risks of illicit action.[65]

Such laws are in need of the moral commitment of a substantial segment of the medical profession, not only of an ideologically driven avant-garde. We would jeopardize this commitment by not allowing doctors to choose their position freely. But if the support for the law in the medical community is large, there is no need to compel the last objectors. A liberal regime should be more averse to coercion than an illiberal one.

Should a doctor who declines a request that he believes possibly to meet the legal criteria be obligated to refer the patient to a willing colleague? Some doctors refuse to do this because they consider it cooperating in a homicide.[66] What they actually do is to abuse their privileged position in an asymmetrical professional-client relation to make the client a captive of their own world view. Within the division of moral labour that is implied by such a relation, responsibilities are different than they are between private persons. A doctor has to inform a patient that he can refuse any treatment offered; this doesn't make him responsible for the patient's choice to make use of that option, anymore than a lawyer is responsible for the decision of his client not to confess his crimes. In a permissive regime requesting euthanasia is also a legally protected option. Hence if the professional agent enables the principal to use that option, the agent is not responsible for the principal's choice.

65 Magnusson 2004.

66 In the Netherlands (2005) 7% of the 15% of doctors who are unwilling to perform euthanasia, 1% of all doctors, Onwuteaka-Philipsen et al. 2007.

The law should therefore make referral mandatory, at least referral to an agency that can contact a willing doctor.[67]

16.6 Social effects

Providing legal access to lethal drugs and permitting doctors to participate with a patient in a joint action of ending the patient's life open new options for individuals, but the choices they then make cumulatively also have larger effects. They co-determine the social environment within which other people make these and similar choices.[68] No-one is an island. In considering these effects we should, however, be aware that these choices are only a small part of a wider range of possible decisions regarding the manner and time of one's own death, including stopping eating and drinking, other kinds of suicide, withholding or withdrawing consent to treatment, enrolling in palliative care programmes and agreeing to sedation until death. Social attitudes are expressed and determined by decisions from the whole range. Still, providing access to lethal drugs and permitting euthanasia will make a difference.

It has been suggested that as a result doctors and others will kill more easily. "If the practices become a standard part of the arsenal of medical treatments, it would profoundly affect our response to those cases that are sanctioned and to those that are not. The momentous nature of the actions, and the sense of caution or gravity with which they are pursued, would naturally lessen for both health care professionals and for the public. By legalizing the practices, we will blunt our moral sensibilities and perceptions".[69] If a doctor performs euthanasia rather often, he may perhaps start doing it in a more routinely way, without the caution that is required. That may be one reason not to entrust this task to physicians (or end-of-life facilitators) who specialize in it. But the idea that in a permissive jurisdiction people's respect for life will weaken is not only purely speculative. It presupposes that this respect is a mere taboo that cannot integrate a sense of the value of her life for the person who lives it (Section 9.2).

It has also been suggested that the quest for legalization is a symptom of a general decline in the level of tolerance people have for pain and suffering, and that legalization will reinforce that tendency.[70] Not only at the end of life but also in every other situation people will be less prepared to accept that suffering is an inescapable part of life, a proper response to

67 Cf. footnote 62.

68 De Dijn 2016 (deploring the fact).

69 New York State Taskforce 1994, 132.

70 E.g., Montero 2017, 48. According to Montero, 44, "the law carries a specific anthropological vision and imposes it on one and all". But if that vision gains ground, that is only because of the cumulative effect of people freely adopting it. All such laws carry an anthropological vision; only forbidding and obligating laws impose it.

circumstances that life confronts us with. But even in the Netherlands and Belgium euthanasia is only one of many ways in which suffering at the end of life can be reduced, and the numbers involved in the other ways are much larger. If there is such a causal relation as this argument suggests, we will primarily have to attribute it to the development of palliative care which everyone applauds, and only marginally to the legal performance of euthanasia. The main point, however, is that it is a perverse suggestion that we should prevent people from averting avoidable suffering in order to improve their attitude in cases in which it is unavoidable.

Legalization doesn't freeze the legal situation, but it changes the environment within which legal options are discussed, both the presently available and possible further ones. One remarkable aspect of the history of legalization is that until now legalization has never been reversed.[71] In the USA support for legalization and opposition against it have plateaued since the 1990s,[72] and most of the innumerable initiatives for legal change have failed. But legalization everywhere increases the level of support, in spite of continuous monitoring of the practice by opponents. Because the fear of abuse and error is by now the main argument against legalization, this seems to show that the antecedent fears tend to be falsified by experience (Section 11.5). As for further developments, the "inexorable logic of the slippery slope" (John Keown) hasn't really materialized until now, although the option of euthanasia has been extended to (at least some) minors deemed competent in the Netherlands and Belgium,[73] and the Dutch euthanasia law of 2002 created the option of euthanasia on the basis of an advance directive. But it is true that the number of people who make use of the existing legal options is presently growing everywhere. One reason might be that criteria of eligibility get eroded, but another reason surely is that available legal space gets occupied.[74] (I have discussed both possibilities as regards the Dutch and Belgian cases in Chapter 12.)

Although there is nothing inevitable about the process, it is quite possible, even probable, that legal initiatives for further liberalization will succeed in the future, in the Netherlands, Oregon and elsewhere. And the discussion about such proposals will necessarily appeal to the experience of the new legal situation and to attitudes that have been shaped by that experience. That will be equally true for arguments *pro*

71 The one exception is the Northern Territory of Australia in 1997, but in this case the law has been overturned by federal law. In New Mexico and South Africa legalization by lower courts have been struck down by higher ones.

72 Emanuel et al. 2016.

73 Resp. in the euthanasia law of 2002 and by an amendment to the law in 2014.

74 But sometimes legal space gets evacuated, for example in the case of severely handicapped newborns in the Netherlands, cf. Chapter 10, footnote 13. Having failed to operate on a newborn child with Down's syndrome and duodenal atresia doctor Jan Molenaar was acquitted for withholding a life-saving treatment, HR 28-4-1989, TvGR 1989/51, but his example has never been followed.

and *contra* further change. That is the way in which moral sensibilities change over time, for the larger part incrementally. The question is not what would have been acceptable *ex ante*, before the introduction of legal change, but what can be justified at the present time.

One important social effect is the following. Although the number of deaths by lethal drugs provided by a physician is only 0.66% of deaths in Oregon, 17% of dying patients discuss the possibility (Section 16.1). Because the number of patients dying from euthanasia in the Netherlands and Belgium is almost seven times as high, the option is much more prominent in those countries in reflection and conversation. Observers sometimes criticize the fact that it is not forbidden in those countries for a doctor to broach the subject of euthanasia,[75] but that criticism overlooks the fact that the subject will already be in every patient's mind. In mentioning it the typical aim of the doctor will be to increase the patient's trust that the option will be given proper consideration, and precisely thereby enable the patient to enter into a free discussion of the available options, including symptom management and comfort care. It is not only the conversation about access to lethal drugs and euthanasia that is more open than in prohibitive countries, but 'euthanasia-talk' also changes the nature of thought and discussion, with relatives, friends and doctors, about other end-of-life options, and even about the dying process as such.[76] Permitting laws initiate a process of 'social calibration': doctors, nurses, patients and families adjust themselves to new experiences, new discussions and new procedures.[77]

One further effect of this change is the emergence of a new culture of dying. Doctors who have agreed to perform euthanasia are sometimes surprized, or shocked, to find on arrival a room filled with people in a somewhat festive mood, sipping wine, reciting poetry or even dividing jewellery among themselves.[78] This is of course only made possible by the fact that the time of death has been planned, but it is nevertheless an element in a larger change of the nature of dying. It becomes a more personalized experience, in which the dying person's life is celebrated and family bonds are confirmed and strengthened.[79]

Euthanasia is an essentially social procedure and the same is true about stopping with eating and drinking and suicide by using lethal drugs that have been acquired by prescription. The nature of health care at the end of life is changed by this fact. Traditionally, the palliative

75 E.g., Cohen-Almagor 2004, ch. 8. Broaching the subject is legally forbidden in New Zealand and labelled unprofessional conduct in Victoria.

76 Quill 2007; Norwood 2009.

77 Pesut et al. 2021a.

78 De Boer et al. 2019.

79 As in Eddy Terstall's 2004 film *Simon*, referred to by Raz 2013. "A gathering of family and friends can be a rich experience for all". Orentlicher, Pope, Rich 2016.

care movement has focussed on family relations and spiritual needs. If we consider the actual range of people's concerns about the manner and time of their death, part of that range tended to be overlooked or even disapproved of (Chapter 2 at footnote 37). This includes wishes to stay in control, to be independent of the care of others and not to be a burden on them. The legalization of euthanasia could trigger a correction of that one-sidedness.[80] But this should be a two-way street: family relations and the search for closure are much more important in the way in which people in permissive societies actually determine the manner and time of their own death than is suggested by the laws that regulate this practice. These laws focus on the relation between the individual patient and his healthcare provider, neglecting the relation between the individual person and her intimates.[81] This second relation will be prominent in both tiers of the system I proposed, but it will be paramount in the second one. The law should take this fact into account (Sections 5.1, 5.2).

The basic meaning of these social changes is that the place of death in our lives is transformed, or at least modified. Death is no longer the outer boundary of our lifetime that we can anticipate on – to some extent – but cannot influence. We can – again, to some extent – implement a conception of death that fits into the conception we have of our life, thereby, as Joseph Raz says, "integrating our dying into our life".[82] This happens when a psychiatric patient and his doctor at the end of a 'dual-track' procedure as described in Chapter 13 together conclude that it is preferable for the patient to die. It happens in early dementia when you would forget your death wish as a result of the illness unless you consciously decide to keep the idea alive, in conversation with others, that the end of your life should be in accordance with the nature of that life. It happens when, for the same reason, you request euthanasia in an advance directive. It also happens when you decide to accept the losses that old age brings with it, and to persevere even in the face of extreme suffering. In that case that suffering is not a mere trick that Fortune plays on you but a challenge that you have decided to meet.

Determining the manner and time of your own death, to the extent that this is possible, is part of shaping your life. Some people don't want to acquire that option,[83] but the fact is that they already have it. Legalizing the access to lethal drugs and euthanasia not only extends the option but also increases the social awareness of its existence. Some people don't like to live in that kind of society either. Others welcome the opportunity. But these social consequences are neither an argument for nor against legalization. In a free society the general moral climate of that society is not a proper object of social design.

80 Ganzini 2017.
81 Roest, Trappenburg, Leget 2019.
82 Raz 2013.
83 Cf. quote from Baroness Campbell of Surbiton, Chapter 11, footnote 45.

Works cited

Ach, JS 2011. *Autonomer Suizid?* Preprints of the Centre for Advanced Study in Bioethics. Münster 2011/20.

Ackerman, F 1998. Assisted suicide, terminal illness, severe disability, and the double standard. In: Battin, Rhodes, Silvers eds.

Adams, M 2008. Belgium. In: Griffiths, Weyers, Adams.

Ahronheim, JC, MR Gasner 1990. The sloganism of starvation. *Lancet* 335: 278–279.

Akerboom, CPM, JCJ Dute, JKM Gevers et al. 2011. *Thematische Wetsevaluatie Wilsonbekwaamheid en Vertegenwoordiging.* Den Haag: ZonMw.

Alkire, MT, AG Hudetz, G Tononi 2008. Consciousness and anesthesia. *Science* 322(5903): 876–880.

Alt-Epping, B 2018. Con: Der freiwillige Verzicht auf. Nahrung und Flüssigkeit ist kein Suizid. *Zeitschrift für Palliativmedizin* 19: 12–15.

AMA 2008. Sedation to Unconsciousness in End-of-Life Care. American Medical Association, Council on Ethical and Judicial Affairs, *CEJA Report* 5-A-08.

American Academy of Hospice and Palliative Medicine 2006. *Statement on Palliative Sedation, Approved by the Board of Directors of the AAHPM.* Replaced by a revised statement 2014.

American Association of Suicidology 2017. *Statement: "Suicide" Is Not the Same as "Physician Aid in Dying"*, https://suicidology.org/wp-content/uploads/2019/07/AAS-PAD-Statement-Approved-10.30.17-ed-10-30-17.pdf.

American Geriatric Society 1995. The care of dying patients: a position statement from the AGS Ethics Committee. *Journal of the American Geriatric Society* 43(5): 577–578.

American Nurses Association, Center for Ethics and Human Rights 2017. *Nutrition and Hydration at the End of Life. Revised Position Statement*, https://www.nursingworld.org/~4af0ed/globalassets/docs/ana/ethics/ps_nutrition-and-hydration-at-the-end-of-life_2017june7.pdf.

American Public Health Association 2008. *Patients' Rights to Self-Determination at the End of Life*, Policy Statement. Replaced by a revised statement 2014.

Anderson, E 1993. *Value in Ethics and Economics.* Cambridge, MA: Harvard UP.

Anderson, J, A Honneth 2005. Autonomy, vulnerability, recognition, and justice. In: J Christman, J Anderson eds. *Autonomy and the Challenges to Liberalism: New Essays.* Cambridge UP.

Andriessen, K 2006. On "intention" in the definition of suicide. *Suicide and Life-Threatening Behavior* 36: 533–538.

Anestis, MD, LR Khazam, KC Law 2015. How many times and how many ways: the impact of number of nonsuicidal self-injury methods on the relationship between nonsuicidal self-injury frequency and suicidal behavior. *Suicide and Life-Threatening Behavior* 45(2): 164–177.

Anquinet, L, JAC Rietjens, L van den Block et al. 2011. General practitioners' report of continuous deep sedation until death for patients dying at home: a descriptive study from Belgium. *European Journal of General Practice* 17: 5–13.

Anquinet, L, JAC Rietjens, C Seale et al. 2012. The practice of continuous deep sedation until death in Flanders (Belgium), the Netherlands and the U.K.: a comparative study. *Journal of Pain and Symptom Management* 44(1): 33–43.

Anscombe, GEM 1963. *Intention*, second edition. Oxford: Basil Blackwell. (First edition 1957).

Appel, JE, EJ van Wijngaarden 2021. Older adults who experience their lives to be completed and no longer worth living: a systematic mini-review into used terminology, definitions, and interpretations. *Frontiers in Psychology* 12: 734049.

Appelbaum, PS 2016. Physician-assisted death for patients with mental disorders: reasons for concern. *JAMA Psychiatry* 73(4): 325–326.

Aragonès, E, JL Pinol, A Labad 2006. The overdiagnosis of depression in non-depressed patients in primary care. *Family Practice* 23: 363–368.

Arends, M 2020. *Aangeklaagd voor euthanasie*. Oisterwijk: Wolf Legal Publishers.

Arneson, RJ 2005. Joel Feinberg and the justification of hard paternalism. *Legal Theory* 11(3): 259–284.

Arras, JD 1997. Physician-assisted suicide: a tragic view. *Journal Contemporary Health Law Policy* 13(2): 361–389.

Asscher, ECA, S van de Vathorst 2019. First prosecution of a Dutch doctor since the Euthanasia Act of 2002: what does the verdict mean? *Journal of Medical Ethics* 46(2): 71–75.

Athanassoulis, N 2002. The role of consent in sado-masochistic practices. *Res Publica* 8: 141–152.

Atkinson, JM 1978. *Discovering Suicide: Studies in the Social Organization of Sudden Death*. Houndmills: Macmillan.

Aydede, M ed. 2006. *Pain: New Essays on Its Nature and the Methodology of Its Study*. Cambridge, MA: MIT Press.

Baechler, J 1981. *Suicides*. New York: Basic Books.

Baines, BK, I Norlander 2000. The relationship of pain and suffering in a hospice population. *American Journal of Hospice and Palliative Care* 17(5): 319–326.

Barathi, B, PS Chandra 2013. Palliative sedation in advanced cancer patients: does it shorten life? A systematic review. *Indian Journal of Palliative Care* 19(1): 40–47.

Barclay, S, C Todd, G Grande, J Lipscombe 2002. Controlling cancer pain in primary care: the prescribing habits and knowledge base of general practitioners. *Journal of Pain and Symptom Management* 23(5): 383–392.

Barkhuysen T 2013. De rechter en het Europese maaiveld. *Nederlands Juristenblad* 33: 2243.

Barnes, J 2008. *Nothing to Be Frightened of*. London: Jonathan Cape.

Barnow, S, M Linden, M Lucht, HJ Freyberger 2004. Influence of age of patients who wish to die on treatment decisions by physicians and nurses. *American Journal of Geriatric Psychiatry* 12(3): 258–264.

Barraclough, B, T Holding, P Fayers 1976. Influence of coroners' officers and pathologists on suicide verdicts. *British Journal of Psychiatry* 128: 471–474.

Bartsch C, K Landolt, A Ristic et al. 2019. Assisted suicide in Switzerland: an analysis of death records from Swiss institutes of forensic medicine. *Deutsches Ärzteblatt International* 116: 545–552.

Batavia, AI 1997. Disability and physician-assisted suicide. *New England Journal of Medicine* 336(23): 1671–1673.

Battin, MP 1982. *Ethical Issues in Suicide*. Englewood Cliffs, NJ: Prentice Hall.

Battin, MP 1994. *The Least Worst Death: Essays in Bioethics on the End of Life*. Oxford UP.

Battin, MP 2005. *Ending Life: Ethics and the Way We Die*. Oxford UP.

Battin, MP 2008. Terminal sedation: pulling the sheet over our eyes. *Hastings Center Report* 38(5): 27–30.

Battin, MP 2013. Recasting a metaphor as the ars moriendi changes. In: Sterckx, Raus, Mortier eds.

Battin, MP 2016. Goodbye, Thomas: the case for physician-assisted dying. *The Oxford Handbook of Ethics at the End of Life*. Oxford UP: 383–388.

Battin, M, A van der Heide, L Ganzini et al. 2007. Legal physician-assisted dying in Oregon and the Netherlands: evidence concerning the impact on patients in 'vulnerable' groups. *Journal of Medical Ethics* 33: 591–597.

Battin, MP, R Rhodes, A Silver eds. 1998. *Physician-Assisted Suicide: Expanding the Debate*. New York, NY/London: Routledge.

Baumann, U 2001, *Vom Recht auf den eigenen Tod: Die Geschichte des Suizids*. Weimar: Verlag Hermann Böhlau Nachfolger.

Baumeister, R 1990. Suicide as escape from self. *Psychological Review* 97: 90–113.

Baumeister, RF 1989. The optimal margin of illusion. *Journal of Social and Clinical Psychology* 8:176–189.

Beard, RL 2016. *Living with Alzheimer's: Managing Memory Loss, Identity, and Illness*. Cambridge UP.

Beauchamp, TL 1978. What is suicide? In: TL Beauchamp, S Pepline eds. *Ethical Issues in Death and Dying*. Englewood Cliffs, NJ: Prentice-Hall.

Beauchamp TL 1980. Suicide. In: Regan ed.

de Beaufort, ID, S van de Vathorst 2016. Dementia and assisted suicide and euthanasia. *Journal of Neurology* 263: 1463–1467.

de Beauvoir, S 1972. *Old Age* (*La Vieillesse*, transl. PO Brien). London: André Deutsch/Weidenfeld & Nicholson.

Beck, AT, M Kovacs, A Weissman 1979. Assessment of suicidal ideation: the scale for suicidal ideation. *Journal of Consulting and Clinical Psychology* 47(2): 343–352.

Behuniak SM 2011. Death with 'dignity': the wedge that divides the disability rights movement from the right to die movement. *Politics and the Life Sciences* 30: 17–32.

Beitz, C 2009. *The Idea of Human Rights*. Oxford UP.

Belgisch Raadgevend Comité voor Bioethiek (Belgian Advisory Committee on Bioethics) 2017. *Advies nr. 73 betreffende euthanasie in geval van niet-terminale patiënten, psychisch lijden en psychiatrische aandoeningen.*

Beller, EM, ML van Driel, L McGregoir et al. 2015. Palliative pharmacological sedation for terminally ill adults. *Cochrane Database of Systematic Reviews* 1: CD010206.

Benatar, D 2013. Suicide: a qualified defense. In: JS Taylor ed. *The Metaphysics and Ethics of Death: New Essyas*. Oxford UP.

Benavides, LLL 2018. The right to die with dignity in Colombia. *Forensic Research and Criminology International Journal* 6: 426–429.

Benedict, S 1989. The suffering associated with lung cancer. *Cancer Nursing* 12(1): 34–40.

Benitez-Rosario, MA, T Morita 2019. Palliative sedation in clinical scenario's: results of a modified Delphi-study. *Supportive Care in Cancer* 27: 1647–1654.

Bennett, J 1995. *The Act Itself*. Oxford: Clarendon Press.

Bergelson, V 2009. *Victims' Rights and Victims' Wrongs: Comparative Liability in Criminal Law*. Palo Alto, CA: Stanford UP.

Berger, JT 2010. Rethinking guidelines for the use of palliative sedation. *Hastings Center Report* 40(3): 32–38.

Berger, JT 2011. Pre-emptive use of palliative sedation and amyotrophic lateral sclerosis. *Journal of Pain and Symptom Management* 43(4): 802–805.

van den Berghe, P, A Mullie, M Desmet, G. Huysmans 2013. Assisted Dying – the current situation in Flanders: euthanasia embedded in palliative care. *European Journal of Palliative Care* 20 (6): 266–272.

Berghmans, R 2012. It's like...kankermetaforen en de evaring van de kankerpatiënt. *Tijdschrift voor Gezondheidszorg en Ethiek* 22: 106–111.

Berghmans, R, D Dickenson, R ter Meulen 2004. Mental capacity: in search of alternative perspectives (editorial). *Health Care Analysis* 13: 251–263.

Berghmans, R, G Widdershoven, I Widdershoven-Heerding 2013. Physician-assisted suicide in psychiatry and loss of hope. *International Journal of Law and Psychiatry* 36: 436–443.

Berghmans, RLP 1998. Advance directives for non-therapeutic dementia research: some ethical and policy considerations. *Journal of Medical Ethics* 24: 32–37.

Berghmans, RLP 2000. *Bekwaam genoeg? Wils(on)bekwaamheid in geneeskunde, gezondheidsrecht en gezondheidsethiek*. Utrecht: Nederlandse Vereniging voor Bio-ethiek.

Berk, M, L Berk, M Udina et al. 2012. Palliative models of care for later stages of mental disorder: maximizing recovery, maintaining hope, and building morale. *Australian & New Zealand Journal of Psychiatry* 46: 92–99.

Bernat, BL, B Gert, RP Mogielnicki 1993. Patient refusal of hydration and nutrition. An alternative to physician-assisted suicide or active euthanasia. *Archives of Internal Medicine* 153: 2723–2728.

Bernheim, JL, R Deschepper, W Distelmans et al. 2008. Development of palliative care and legalisation of euthanasia: antagonism or synergy? *British Medical Journal* 336: 864–867.

Bernheim, JL, K Raus 2017. Euthanasia embedded in palliative case. Response to essentialistic criticisms of the Belgian model of integral end-of-life care. *Journal of Medical Ethics* 43: 489–494.

Bickenbach, J 1998. Disability and life-ending decisions. In: Battin, Rhodes, Silver eds.

Bickhardt, J, RM Hanke 2014. Freiwilliger Verzicht auf Nahrhung und Flüssigkeit: Eine ganz eigene Handlungsweise. *Deutsches Ärzteblatt* 111(14): A590–A592.

Bigorio Switzerland 2005. *Recommandations Sédation Palliative: Consensus sur la Meilleure Pratique en Soins Palliative en Suisse*, https://www.soins-palliatifs-vaud.ch/sites/default/files/documentation/E_12_4_bigorio_2005_Sedation_fr._pdf.pdf.

Billings, JA, SD Block 1996. Slow euthanasia. *Journal of Palliative Care* 12(4): 21–30.

Bilsen, J, M Norup, K Deliëns et al. 2006. Drugs used to alleviate symptoms with life shortening as a possible side effect: end-of-life care in six European countries. *Journal of Pain and Symptom Management* 31: 111–121.

Birnbacher, D 1995. *Tun und Unterlassen*. Stuttgart: Philipp Reclam.

Birnbacher, D 2015. Ist Sterbefasten eine Form von Suizid? *Ethik in der Medizin* 27: 315–324.

Birnbacher, D 2017. *Tod*. Berlin: Walter de Gruyter.

Black I 2012. Suicide assistance for mentally disordered individuals in Switzerland and the state's positive obligation to facilitate dignified suicide: Haas c. Suisse. *Medical Law Review* 20: 157–166.

Blanker, MH, M Koerhuis-Roessink, SJ Swart et al. 2012. Pressure during decision making of continuous sedation in end-of-life situations in Dutch general practice. *BMC Family Practice* 13: 68.

Blaustein, M, A Fleming 2009. Suicide from the golden gate bridge. *American Journal of Psychiatry* 166: 1111–1116.

Blikshavn, T, TL Husum, M Magelssen 2017. Four reasons why assisted suicide should not be offered for depression. *Bioethical Inquiry* 14: 151–157.

Blustein, J 1999. Choosing for others as continuing a life story: the problem of personal identity revisited. *Journal of Law, Medicine and Ethics* 27: 20–31.

Boenink, M 2010. Molecular medicine and concepts of disease: the ethical value of a conceptual analysis of merging biomedical technologies. *Medicine, Health Care and Philosophy* 13: 11–23.

de Boer, ME, MFIA Depla, M den Breejen et al. 2019. Pressure in dealing with requests for euthanasia-capturing the experience of people with dementia in nursing homes: a conceptual mapping study. *Aging and Mental Health* 23: 4498–4506.

de Boer, ME, CMPM Hertogh, R-M Droës et al. 2007. Suffering from dementia-the patient's perspective: a review of the literature. *International Psychogeriatrics* 19: 1021–1039.

de Boer, ME, CMPM Hertogh, RM Droës et al. 2010. Advance directives in dementia: issues of validity and effectiveness. *International Psychiatrics* 22: 201–208.

Boer, T, S Groenewoud, W de Jonge eds. 2021. *Leven met euthanasie: Geliefden vertellen over hun ervaringen*. Utrecht: Kokboekcentrum.

Boer, TA 2012. Euthanasia in a welfare state: experiences from the review procedure in the Netherlands. *Philosophy Study* 2: 51–63.

Boer, TA 2018. Dialectics of lead: fifty years of Dutch euthanasia and its lessons. *International Journal of Environmental Studies* 78(2): 239–250.

Bok, S 1998. In: Dworkin, Frey, Bok.

Bolt, EE, MC Snijdewind, DL Willems et al. 2015a. Can physicians conceive of performing euthanasia in case of psychiatric disease, dementia and being tired of living? *Journal of Medical Ethics* 41(8): 592–598.

Bolt, EE, M Hagens, D Willems, BD Onwuteaka-Philipsen 2015b. Primary care patients hastening death by voluntarily stopping eating and drinking. *Annals of Family Medicine* 13.5: 421–428.

Bonnewyn, A, A Shah, K Demyttenaere 2009. Suicidality and suicide in older people. *Reviews in Clinical Gerontology* 19: 271–294.

Bonnewyn, A, A Shah, R Bruffaerts et al. 2014. Reflections of older adults on the process preceding their suicide attempt: a qualitative approach. *Death Studies* 38: 612–618.

Boorse, C 1977. Health as a theoretical concept. *Philosophy of Science* 44: 542–573.

Borst-Eilers, E 2013. Inleiding in: Hans Smit, Henri van Gelder, *Wils verklaring: De Alzheimerepidemie en het Recht op Zelfbeschikking*, Uitgeverij aquaZZ.

Bosshard, G, U Zellweger, M Bopp et al. 2016. Medical end-of-life practices in Switzerland: a comparison of 2001 and 2013. *JAMA Internal Medicine* 176(4): 555–556.

Boston, P, A Bruce, R Schreiber 2011. Existential suffering in the palliative care setting: an integrated literature review. *Journal of Pain and Symptom Management* 41: 604–618

Boudreau, JD, MA Somerville 2013. Euthanasia is not medical treatment. *British Medical Bulletin* 106: 45–66.

Bourgeois, JA, MT Mariano, J Wilkins et al. 2018. Physician-assisted death psychiatric assessment: a standardized protocol to conform to the California end of life option act. *Psychosomatics* 59: 441–451.

Brandt, R 1975. The morality and rationality of suicide. In: S Perlin ed. *A Handbook for the Study of Suicide*. Oxford UP.

Braun, TC, NA Hagen, T Clark 2003. Development of a clinical practice guideline for palliative sedation. *Journal of Palliative Medicine* 6: 345–350.

Breden, TM, J Vollmann 2004. The cognitive based approach of capacity assessment in psychiatry: a philosophical critique of the MacCAT-T. *Health Care Analysis* 12: 273–283.

Breitbart, W, B Rosenfeld, H Pessin et al. 2000. Depression, hopelessness, and desire for hastened death in terminally ill patients with cancer. *JAMA* 284: 2907–2911.

Brinkkemper, T, AM van Norel, KM Szadek et al 2013. The use of observational scales to monitor symptom control and depth of sedation in patients requiring palliative sedation: a systematic review. *Palliative Medicine* 27: 54–67.

Brinkman-Stoppelenburg, A, Y Vergouwe, A van der Heide, BD Onweteaka-Philipsen 2014. Obligatory consultation of an independent physician on euthanasia requests in the Netherlands: what influences the SCEN physicians judgment of the legal requirements of due care? *Health Policy* 115: 75–81.

British Medical Association 2017. *Physician-Assisted Dying*. Replaced by a new statement 2021.

Brock, D 1988. Justice and the severely demented elderly. *Journal of Medicine and Philosophy* 13: 73–99.

Brock, DW 1992. Voluntary active euthanasia. *Hastings Center Report* 22: 10–22.

Brody, H 1993. Causing, intending and assisting death. *Journal of Clinical Ethics* 4: 112–117.

Broeckaert, B 2000. Palliative sedation defined or why and when sedation is not euthanasia. *Journal of Pain and Symptom Management* 20(6): S58.

Broeckaert, B 2001. Een palliatieve filter in de euthanasieprocedure. *Palliatieve zorg* 8: 4–7.

Broome, MR, A de Cates 2017. Choosing death in depression: a comment on 'Treatment-resistant major depressive disorder and assisted dying'. *Journal of Medical Ethics* 41: 586–587.

Bruera, E, N Kueh, MJ Miller et al. 1991. The Edmonton Symptom Assessment System (ESAS): a simple method for the assessment of palliative care patients. *Journal of Palliative Care* 7(2): 6–9.

Bruinsma, SM, JAC Rietjens, A van der Heide, 2013. Continuous sedation until death: state of the art. In: Sterckx, Raus, Mortier eds.

Bruns, F, S Blumenthal, G Hohendorf 2016. Organisierte Suizidbeihilfe in Deutschland. *Deutsche Medizinische Wochenschrift* 141: e32–e37.

Buchanan, A, D Brock 1990. *Deciding for Others: The Ethics of Surrogate Decision Making*. Cambridge UP.

Buchbinder, M, E Ojo, L Knio, ER Brassfield 2018. Caregivers' experiences with medical aid-in-dying in Vermont. *Journal of Pain and Symptom Management* 56(6): 936–943.

Büchi, S, C Buddeberg, R Klaghofer et al. 2002. Preliminary validation of PRISM (pictorial representation of illness and self measure)—a brief method to assess suffering. *Psychotherapy and Psychosomatics* 71(6): 333–341.

Buijsen, M 2020. Uitzichtloos en ondraaglijk lijden? Over voltooide levens en gestapelde ouderdomsaandoeningen. *Tijdschrift voor Geneeskunde en Ethiek* 30: 84–89.

Buijsen, M 2022. Mutatis mutandis... On euthanasia and advanced dementia in the Netherlands. *Cambridge Quarterly of Health Care Ethics* 31: 40–53.

Buiting, HM, DJ Deeg, DL Knol et al. 2012. Older peoples' attitudes towards euthanasia and an end-of-life pill in the Netherlands: 2001–2009. *Journal of Medical Ethics*, *38*(5), 267–273.

Buiting, HM, J van Delden, B Onwuteaka-Philipsen et al. 2009. Reporting of euthanasia and physician-assisted suicide in the Netherlands: descriptive study. *BMC Medical Ethics* 10: 18.

Buiting, HM, JK Gevers, J Rietjens et al. 2008. Dutch criteria of due care for physician-assisted dying in medical practice: a physician perspective. *Journal of Medical Ethics* 34(9): e12.

Buiting, HM, A van der Heide, BD Onwuteaka-Philipsen et al. 2010. Physicians' labelling of end-of-life practices: a hypothetical case study. *Journal of Medical Ethics* 36: 24–29.

Buiting, HM, ML Rurup, H Wijsbek et al. 2011. Understanding provision of chemotherapy to patients with end stage cancer: qualitative interview study. *British Medical Journal* 342: d1933.

Burge, F 1993. Dehydration symptoms of palliative care cancer patients. *Journal of Pain and Symptom Management* 8(7): 454–464.

Burms, A, H de Dijn, 2011. *De sacraliteit van leven en dood*. Leuven: Pelckmans Klement.

Butler-Sloss, B et al. 2010. *Another 'Assisted Dying' Bill: Does It Pass the Public Safety Test?* https://livinganddyingwell.org.uk/another-assisted-dying-bill-does-it-pass-the-public-safety-test/.

Byock, I, M Merriman 1998. Measuring quality of life for patient with terminal illness: the Missoula quality of life index (MVQOLI). *Palliative Medicine* 12: 231–244.

Byock, IR 1996. The nature of suffering and the nature of opportunity at the end of life. *Clinics in Geriatric Medicine* 12: 237–252.

Cain, CL 2016. *Implementing Aid in Dying in California: Experiences from Other States Indicates the Need for Strong Implementation Guidance*. Policy Brief UCLA Center Health Policy Research.

Cairns, R, C Maddock, A Buchanan et al. 2005. Reliability of mental capacity assessments in psychiatric in-patients. *British Journal of Psychiatry* 187: 372–378.

Callahan, D, M White 1996. The legalization of physician-assisted suicide: creating a regulatory Potemkin village. *University of Richmond Law Review* 30(1): 1–83.

Callahan, D 1987. *Setting Limits: Medical Goals in an Aging Society*. Washington, DC: Georgetown UP.

Callahan, D 1990. *What Kind of Life: The Limits of Medical Progress*. New York, NY: Simon & Schuster.

Callahan, D 1992. When self-determination runs amok. *Hastings Center Report* 22 (2): 52–55.

Campbell, CS, JC Cox 2010. Hospice and physician-assisted death. *Hastings Center Report* 40(5): 26–35.

Cantor, NL 2004. On Kamisar, killing, and the future of PAD. *Michigan Law Review* 102: 1793–1842.

Cantor, NL 2006. On hastening death without violating legal and moral prohibitions. *Loyola University Chicago Law Journal* 37: 101–125.

Cantor, NL 2018. On avoiding deep dementia. *Hastings Center Report* 48(4): 15–24.

Caplan, A, L Snyder, K Faber-Langendoen 2000. The role of guidelines in the practice of physician-assisted suicide. *Annals of Internal Medicine* 132(6): 476–481.

Capron, A 1992. Euthanasia in the Netherlands: American observations. *Hastings Center Report* 22(2): 30–33.

Cassell, EJ 1982. The nature of suffering and the goals of medicine. *New England Journal of Medicine* 306: 639–645. Reprinted in Cassell 1991.

Cassell, EJ 1991. *The Nature of Suffering and the Goals of Medicine*. Oxford UP.

Cassell, EJ 1999. Diagnosing suffering: a perspective. *Annals of Internal Medicine* 131: 531–534.

Cassell, EJ, BA Rich 2010. Intractable end-of-life suffering and the ethics of palliative sedation. *Pain Medicine* 11: 435–438.

ten Cate, K 2019. *Dutch Doctors and Dying: Do Doctors' Personal Views Influence Their Professional Care at the End of Life- and Should They?* Thesis, University of Amsterdam.

ten Cate, K, DG van Tol, S van de Vathorst 2017. Considerations on requests for euthanasia or assisted suicide: a qualitative study with Dutch general practitioners. *Family Practice* 34(6): 723–729.

Cavanagh, JTO, AJ Carson, M Sharpe, SM Lawrie, 2003. Psychological autopsy studies of suicide: a systematic review. *Psychological Medicine* 33: 395–405.

Cellarius, V 2008. Terminal sedation and the 'imminence condition'. *Journal of Medical Ethics* 34: 69–72.

Cellarius, V 2011. 'Early terminal sedation' is a distinct entity. *Bioethics* 25(1): 46–54.

Chabot, B 2014. *Dignified Dying: A Guide*. E-book.
Chabot, B 2017. De weg kwijt: de zorgelijke staat van de euthanasiewet. Amsterdam: Nijgh & Van Ditmar.
Chabot, B 2019. *Uitweg: Een waardig levenseinde in eigen hand*. Amsterdam: Nijgh & Van Ditmar, 14th ed.
Chabot, BE 1996. *Sterven op Drift*. Nijmegen: SUN.
Chabot, BE 2000. De vraag om hulp bij zelfdoding. *Tijdschrift voor Psychiatrie* 42: 759–766.
Chabot, BE 2007. *Auto-Euthanasie. Verborgen Stervenswegen in Gesprek Met Naasten*. Amsterdam: Uitgeverij Bert Bakker.
Chabot, BE, A Goedhart 2009. A survey of self-directed dying attended by proxies in the Dutch population. *Social Science & Medicine* 68: 1745–1751.
Chambaere, K, JL Bernheim, J Downar, L Deliëns 2014. Characteristics of Belgian "life-ending acts without explicit patient request": a large-scale death certificate survey revisited. *Canadian Medical Association Journal Open* 2(4): E262–E267.
Chambaere, K, J Bilsen, J Cohen et al. 2010a. Continuous deep sedation until death in Belgium: a nationwide survey. *Archives of Internal Medicine* 170(5): 490–493.
Chambaere, K, J Bilsen, J Cohen et al. 2010b. Physician-assisted deaths under the euthanasia law in Belgium: a population-based survey. *Canadian Medical Association Journal* 182: 895–901.
Chambaere, K, C Centeno, EA Hernández et al. 2011. *Palliative Care Development in Countries with a Euthanasia Law: Briefing Paper for the Commission on Assisted Dying of the European Association for Palliative Care*, https://researchportal.vub.be/en/publications/palliative-care-development-in-countries-with-a-euthanasia-law-re.
Chambaere, K, JA Rietjens, J Cohen et al. 2013. Is educational attainment related to end-of-life decision-making? A large post-mortem survey in Belgium. *BMC Public Health* 13: 1055.
Chambaere, K, R VanderStichele, F Mortier et al. 2015. Recent trends in euthanasia and other end-of-life practices in Belgium. *New England Journal of Medicine* 372: 1179–1181.
Charland, L 2001. Mental competence and value: the problem of normativity in the assessment of decisional capacity. *Psychiatry, Psychology, and Law* 8 (2): 135–145.
Charland, L, C Hope, T Stewart, J Tan 2013. Anorexia nervosa as a passion. *Philosophy, Psychiatry, & Psychology*, 20: 353–365.
Charland, L, T Lemmens, K Wada 2016. Decision-making capacity to consent to medical assistance in dying for persons with mental disorders. *Journal of Ethics in Mental Health*.
Cheng, C, C Roemor-Becuwe, J Pereira 2002. When midazolam fails. *Journal of Pain and Symptom Management* 23: 256–265.
Cherny, NI 2014. ESMO clinical practice guideline for the management of refractory symptoms at the end of life and the use of palliative sedation. *Annals of Oncology* 25(Suppl. 3): iii143–iii152.
Cherny, NI, NM Coyle, KM Foley 1994. Suffering in the advanced cancer patient: a definition and taxonomy. *Journal of Palliative Care* 10: 57–70.
Cheston, R, MP Bender. 1999. *Understanding Dementia*. London: Jessica Kingsley Publishers.

Cheung, G, S Edwards, F Sundram 2017. Death wishes among older people assessed for home support and long-term aged residential care. *International Journal of Geriatric Psychiatry* 32: 1371–1380.

Chin, AE, K Hedberg, G Higginson et al. 1999. *Oregon's Death with Dignity Act: The First Year's Experience*. Oregon Health Division, https://www.oregon.gov/oha/PH/PROVIDERPARTNERRESOURCES/EVALUATIONRESEARCH/DEATHWITHDIGNITYACT/Documents/year1.pdf.

Chochinov, HM 2003. Thinking outside the box: depression, hope, and meaning at the end of life. *Journal of Palliative Care* 6: 973–977.

Chochinov, HM 2006. Dying, dignity, and new horizons in palliative end-of-life care. *CA: A Cancer Journal for Clinicians* 56: 84–103.

Chochinov, HM, TF Hack, S McClement et al. 2002. Dignity in the terminally ill: a developing empirical model. *Social Science & Medicine* 54: 433–443.

Chochinov, HM, TF Hack, T Hassard et al. 2005. Dignity therapy: a novel psychotherapeutic intervention for patients near the end of life. *Journal of Clinical Oncology* 23: 5520–5525.

Chochinov, HM, T Hassard, S McClement et al. 2009. The landscape of distress in the terminally ill. *Journal of Pain and Symptom Management* 38: 641–649.

Chochinov, HM, LJ Kristjanson, W Breitbart et al. 2011. The effect of dignity therapy on distress and end-of-life experience in terminally ill patients: a randomized controlled trial. *Lancet Oncology* 12(8): 753–762.

Chochinov, HM, L Schwartz 2002. Depression and the will to live in the psychological landscape of terminally ill patients. In: Foley, Hendin eds.

Chochinov, HM, KG Wilson, M Enns et al. 1995. Desire for death in the terminally ill. *American Journal of Psychiatry* 152: 1185–1192.

Cholbi, M 2011. *Suicide: The Philosophical Dimensions*. Peterborough: Broadview.

Claessens, P, J Menten, P Schotsmans, B Broeckaert 2008. Palliative sedation: a review of the research literature. *Journal of Pain and Symptom Management* 36: 310–333.

Claessens, P, J Menten, P Schotsmans, B Broeckaert 2011. Palliative sedation, not slow euthanasia: a prospective, longitudinal study of sedation in Flemish palliative care units. *Journal of Pain and Symptom Management* 41: 14–24.

Cohen, J, P van Landeghem, N Carpentier, L Deliëns 2014. Public acceptance of euthanasia in Europe: a survey study in 47 countries. *International Journal of Public Health* 59(1): 143–156.

Cohen, J, Y van Wesenmael, T Smets et al. 2012. Cultural differences affecting euthanasia practice in Belgium: one law but different attitudes and practices in Flanders and Wallonia. *Social Science & Medicine* 75: 845–853.

Cohen-Almagor, R 2004. *Euthanasia in the Netherlands: The Policy and Practice of Mercy Killing*. Dordrecht: Springer/Kluwer.

Cohen-Almagor, R 2013. First do no harm: pressing concerns regarding euthanasia in Belgium. *International Journal of Law and Psychiatry* 36: 515–521.

Cohen-Almagor, R 2015. First do no harm: intentionally shortening lives of patients without their explicit request in Belgium. *Journal of Medical Ethics* 41: 625–629.

Cohen-Almagor, R 2016. First do no harm: euthanasia of patients with dementia in Belgium. *Journal of Medicine and Philosophy* 41: 74–89.

Cohn, F, J Lynn 2002. Vulnerable people: practical rejoinders to claims in favor of assisted suicide. In: Foley, Hendin eds.

Coleman, CH, AR Fleischman 1996. Guidelines for physician-assisted suicide: can the challenge be met? *Journal of Law, Medicine and Ethics* 24: 217–224.

Coleman, D 2002. Not dead yet. In: Foley, Hendin eds.

Collège des Médecins du Quebec 2016. *Palliative Sedation at the End of Life: Practice Guideline*, http://www.cmq.org/publications-pdf/p-1-2016-08-29-en-sedation-palliative-fin-de-vie.pdf.

Commissie Onderzoek Medische Praktijk inzake Euthanasie 1991. *Rapport*. 's Gravenhage: SDU.

Conejero, I, E Olié, P Courtet et al. 2018. Suicide in older adults: current perspectives. *Clinical Interventions in Aging* 13: 691–699.

Cook, DJ, G Guyatt, R Jaeschke et al. 1995. Determinants in Canadian health care workers of the decision to withdraw life support from the critically ill. *JAMA* 273: 703–708.

Corna, LM, J Cairney, DL Streiner 2010. Suicide ideation in older adults: relationship to mental health problems and service use. *Gerontologist* 50(6): 785–797.

Cottrell, L, W Duggleby 2016. The 'good death': an integrative literature review. *Palliative and Support Care* 14: 686–712.

Council of Canadian Academies 2018a. *The State of Knowledge on Advance Requests for Medical Assistance in Dying*, https://cca-reports.ca/wp-content/uploads/2019/02/The-State-of-Knowledge-on-Advance-Requests-for-Medical-Assistance-in-Dying.pdf.

Council of Canadian Academies 2018b. *The State of Knowledge on Medical Assistance in Dying Where a Mental Disorder Is the Sole Underlying Condition*, https://cca-reports.ca/wp-content/uploads/2018/12/The-State-of-Knowledge-on-Medical-Assistance-in-Dying-Where-a-Mental-Disorder-is-the-Sole-Underlying-Medical-Condition.pdf.

Coventry, PA, GE Grande, DA Richards, CJ Todd 2005. Prediction of appropriate timing of palliative care for older adults with non-malignant life-threatening disease: a systematic review. *Age and Ageing* 34(3): 218–227.

Covinsky, KE, L Goldman, EF Cook et al. 1994. The impact of serious illness on patients' families (SUPPORT study). *JAMA* 272(23): 1839–1844.

Covinsky, KE, CS Landefeld, J Teno et al. 1996. Is economic hardship on the families of the seriously ill associated with patient and surrogate care preferences? *Archives of Internal Medicine* 156(1996): 1737–1741.

Cowan, JD, TW Palmer 2002. Practical guide to palliative sedation. *Current Oncology Reports* 4: 242–249.

Cox, K 2002. Informed consent and decision-making: patients' experiences of the process of recruitment to phases I and II anti-cancer drug trials. *Patient Education and Counseling* 46: 31–38.

Craig, G 1994. On withholding nutrition and hydration in the terminally ill: has palliative medicine gone too far? *Journal of Medical Ethics* 20: 139–143.

Crippen, D, M Levy, R Truog et al. 2000. Debate: what constitutes 'terminality' and how does it relate to a living will? *Critical Care* 4: 333–338.

Crocker, L, L Clare, K Evans 2006. Giving up on finding a solution? The experience of attempted suicide in later life. *Aging Mental Health* 22: 289–298.

Dahani, A, I Aarts, TW Smith 2010. Incidence, reversal, and prevention of opioid-induced respiratory depression, *Anesthesiology* 112 (1): 226–238.

Dancy, J 2005. Should we pass the buck? In: T Rønnow-Tasmussen, MK Zimmerman eds. *Recent Work on Intrinsic Value*. Dordrecht: Springer.

van Dantzig, A 1999. Doodgaan is doodgewoon: een pleidooi voor de medische exceptie. *Medisch Contact* 53: 633–634.

Darwall, S 2002. *Welfare and Rational Care*. Princeton: Princeton UP.

Das, C 2004. *Overlijdensverklaringen en artsen: wet en praktijk*. Thesis, Vrije Universiteit Amsterdam.

Daube, D 1972. The linguistics of suicide. *Philosophy and Public Affairs* 1(4): 387–437.

Davis, DS 1999. Rational suicide and predictive genetic testing. *Journal of Clinical Ethics* 10: 316–323.

Davis, DS 2014. Alzheimer disease and pre-emptive suicide. *Journal of Medical Ethics* 40: 543–549.

Davis, J 2004. Precedent autonomy and subsequent consent. *Ethical Theory and Moral Practice* 7: 267–291.

Davis, M 2008. Understanding terminal sedation. *Bioethics Matters (Canadian Catholic Bioethics Institute)* 6(3): 1–4.

Davis, MS 2009. Palliative sedation: four questions. *Progress in Palliative Care* 17(4): 203–204.

Dawson, A, A Wrigley 2010. A dead proposal: Levi and Green on advance directives. *American Journal of Bioethics* 10(4): 23–24.

Dazzi, T, R Gribble, S Wessely, NT Fear 2014. Does asking about suicide and related behaviours induce suicidal ideation? What is the evidence? *Psychological Medicine* 44: 3361–3363.

Dean, MM, V Cellarius, B Henry 2012. Framework for continuous palliative sedation therapy in Canada. *Journal of Palliative Medicine* 15(8): 870–879.

Dees, M, M Vernooij-Dassen, W Dekkers, C van Weel 2010. Unbearable suffering of patients with a request for euthanasia or physician-assisted suicide: an integrative review. *Psycho-Oncology* 19: 339–352.

Dees, MK, MJ Vernooij-Dassen, WJ Dekkers et al. 2011. 'Unbearable suffering': a qualitative study on the perspectives of patients who request assistance in dying. *Journal of Medical Ethics* 37: 727–734.

Dees, MK, M Vernooij-Dassen, WJ Dekkers et al. 2012. Perspectives of decision-making in requests for euthanasia: a qualitative research among patients, relatives and treating physicians in the Netherlands. *Clinical Medicine and Surgery* 27(1): 27–37.

Defesche, F 2011. *Voltooid leven in Nederland: wat ouderen ervaren, willen en doen als zij het leven voltooid vinden*. Assen: van Gorcum.

van Deijck, R 2017. *Continuous Palliative Sedation: Determinants, Practice and Outcome*. Thesis, Radboud UMC Nijmegen.

van Deijck, RH, JG Hasselaar, JPJ Krijnsen et al. 2015. The practice of continuous palliative sedation in long-term care for frail patients with existential suffering. *Journal of Palliative Care* 31(3): 141–149.

van Deijck, RH, PJ Krijnsen, JG Hasselaar et al. 2010. The practice of continuous palliative sedation in elderly patients: a nationwide explorative study among Dutch nursing home physicians. *Journal of the American Geriatric Society* 58(9): 1671–1678.

Delbeke, E. The legal permissibility of continuous deep sedation at the end of life: a comparison of laws and a proposal. In: Sterckx S, Raus K, Mortier F, editors. Continuous Sedation at the End of Life. Cambridge: Cambridge University Press; 2013. pp. 132–48.

van Delden, JJ 2004. The unfeasibility of requests for euthanasia in advance directives. *Journal of Medical Ethics* 30: 447–451.

van Delden, JJM 2007. Terminal sedation: source of a restless ethical debate. *Journal of Medical Ethics* 33: 187–188.

van Delden, JJM 2013. The ethical evaluation of continuous sedation at the end of life. In: S Sterckx, K Raus and F Mortier eds.

van Delden, JJM, A van der Heide, S van de Vathorst et al. 2011. *Kennis en Opvattingen van Publiek en Professionals over Medische Besluitvorming en Behandeling rond het Einde van het Leven: het KOPPEL-Onderzoek*. Den Haag: ZonMw.

Deliëns, L, J Cohen, I François, J Bilsen eds. 2011. *Palliatieve Zorg en Euthanasie in België: Evaluatie van de Praktijk en de Wetten*. Brussel: Uitgeverij ASP.

Deliëns, L, F Mortier, J Bilsen et al. 2000. *End-of-life decisions in medical practice in Flanders, Belgium: a nationwide survey. Lancet* 356: 1806–1811.

Denier, Y, C Gastmans, A Vandevelde eds. 2013. *Justice, Luck and Responsibility in Health Care*. Dordrecht: Springer.

Deschepper, R, S Laureys, S Hachimi Idrissi et al. 2013. Palliative sedation: why we should be more concerned that patients experience an uncomfortable death. *Pain* 154(9): 1505–1508.

Deyaert, J, K Chambaere, J Cohen et al. 2014. Labelling of end-of-life decisions by physicians. *Journal of Medical Ethics* 30: 505–507.

Dierickx, S, L Deliëns, J Cohen, K Chambaere 2015. Comparison of the expression and granting of requests for euthanasia in Belgium in 2007 vs 2013. *JAMA Internal Medicine* 175(10): 1703–1706.

Dierickx, S, L Deliëns, J Cohen, K Chambaere 2016. Euthanasia in Belgium: trends in reported cases between 2003 and 2013. *Canadian Medical Association Journal* 188(16): E407–E414.

Dierickx, S, L Deliëns, J Cohen, K Chambaere 2017. Euthanasia for people with psychiatric disorders or dementia in Belgium: analysis of officially reported cases. *BMC Psychiatry* 17: 203.

Dierickx, S, L Deliëns, J Cohen, K Chambaere 2018. Involvement of palliative care in euthanasia practice in a context of legalized euthanasia: a population-based mortality follow-back study. *Palliative Medicine* 32: 114–122.

Dierickx, S, B Onwuteaka-Philipsen, Y Penders et al. 2020. Commonalities and differences in legal euthanasia and physician-assisted suicide in three countries: a population-level comparison. *International Journal of Public Health* 65: 65–73.

van Dijk, AA 2008. *Strafrechtelijke Aansprakelijkheid Heroverwogen: Over Opzet, Schuld, Schulduitsluitingsgronden en Straf*. Thesis, Rijksuniversiteit Groningen.

de Dijn, H 2016. *Gangbare motieven voor euthanasie: maatschappelijke bepaaldheid en maatschappelijk impact. Ethische Perspectieven* 26(3): 246–261.

Doerflinger, R 1989. Assisted suicide: pro-choice or anti-life? *Hastings Center Report* 19(1): 16–19.

Doernberg, SN, JR Peteet, SYH Kim 2016. Capacity evaluations of psychiatric patients requesting assisted death in the Netherlands. *Psychosomatics* 57: 556–565.

Donnelly, J ed. 1998. *Suicide: Right or Wrong?* Amherst, NY: Prometheus.

Douglas, C, I Kerridge, R Ankeny 2008. Managing intentions: the end-of-life administration of analgesics and sedatives, and the possibility of slow euthanasia. *Bioethics* 22: 388–396.

Douglas, CD, IH Kerridge, KL Rainbird et al. 2001. The intention to hasten death: a survey of the attitudes and practices of surgeons in Australia. *Medical Journal Australia* 175: 511–515.

Downar, J, RA Fowler, R Halko et al. 2020. Early experience with medical assistance in dying in Ontario, Canada: a cohort study. *Canadian Medical Association Journal* 192: E173–E181.

Downie, J 2004. *Dying Justice: A Case for Decriminalizing Euthanasia and Assisted Suicide in Canada*. Toronto: University of Toronto Press.

Downie, J, J Chandler 2018. *Interpreting Canada's Medical Assistance in Dying Legislation*. IRPP Report, https://irpp.org/research-studies/interpreting-canadas-medical-assistance-in-dying-maid-legislation/.

Draper, H, J Ives, H Pall et al. 2009. Reporting end-of-life practices: can we trust doctors to be honest? *Palliative Medicine* 23: 673–674.

Dresser, RS 1995. Dworkin on dementia: elegant theory, questionable policy. *Hastings Center Report* 25(6): 32–38.

Dresser, RS 2002–2003. Precommitment: a misguided strategy for securing death with dignity. *Texas Law Review* 81: 1823–1848.

Dresser, RS, JA Robertson 1989. Quality of life and non-treatment decisions for incompetent patients: a critique of the orthodox approach. *Law, Medicine and Health Care* 17: 23–44.

Dresser, RS, PJ Whitehouse 1994. The incompetent patient on the slippery slope. *Hastings Center Report* 24(4): 6–12.

Drion, H 1992. *Het zelfgewilde einde van oude mensen, met reacties van Ch. J. Enschedé, H.M. Kuitert e.a.* Amsterdam: Balans.

DSM-V 2013. *The Diagnostic and Statistical Manual of Mental Disorders*, Edition 5.

Duff, RA 1980. Intention, mens rea and the Law Commission Report. *Criminal Law Review* 27: 147.

Duggleby, W 2000. Enduring suffering: a grounded theory analysis of the pain experience of elderly hospice patients with cancer. *Oncology Nursing Forum* 27(5): 825–830.

Duggleby, W, L Degner, A Williams et al. 2007. Living with hope: initial evaluation of a psychosocial hope intervention for older palliative home care patients. *Journal of Pain and Symptom Management* 33(3): 247–257.

Dupont, L 2004. *Beginselen van Strafrecht deel 1*. Leuven: ACCO.

Durkheim, E 1897. *Le Suicide: Étude de Sociologie*. Paris: Felix Alcain.

Dworkin, G, RG Frey, S Bok 1998. *Euthananasia and Physician-Assisted Suicide: For and Against*. Cambridge UP.

Dworkin, G 1972. Paternalism. *The Monist* 56: 64–84.

Dworkin, G 1988. Paternalism: some second thoughts. In: G Dworkin ed. *The Theory and Practice of Autonomy*. Cambridge UP. First publ. 1983.

Dworkin, G 2012. Harm and the Volenti principle. *Social Philosophy and Policy* 29: 309–321.

Dworkin, R 1993. *Life's Dominion: An Argument about Abortion and Euthanasia*. Hammersmith, London: Harper Collins.

Dworkin, R 2000. *Sovereign Virtue*. Cambridge, MA: Harvard UP.

Dworkin, R 2004. Ronald Dworkin replies. In: J Burley ed. *Dworkin and His Critics, with Replies by Dworkin*. Malden/Oxford: Blackwell.

EAPC (European Association for Palliative Care) 2009. Recommended framework for the use of sedation in palliative care. *Journal of Palliative Medicine* 23: 581–593.
Ebenau, A, J Hasselaar, J van Gurp 2017. Life values of elderly people suffering from incurable cancer: a literature review. *Patient Education and Counseling* 100: 1778–1786.
Echénique, J 2016. Human life as a basic good: a dialectical critique. *Ideas y Valores* 65(161): 61–87.
Eckerdal, G 2004. Sedation in palliative care: the doctor's perspective. In: Tännsjö ed.
Eddy, D 1994. A conversation with my mother. *JAMA* 272: 179–181.
Edwards, SD 2003. Three concepts of suffering. *Medicine, Health Care and Philosophy* 6(1): 59–66.
Egel, L 1999. On the need for a new term for suicide. *Suicide and Life-Threatening Behavior* 29: 393–394.
Elliott, C 1997. Caring about risks: are severely depressed patients competent to consent to research? *Archives of General Psychiatry* 54(22): 113–116.
Elzenga, D 2016. Stoppen met eten en drinken: sterven in eigen regie? In: M. Vink e.a. red. *Klaar met leven?* Bohn Stafleu, van Loghum.
Emanuel, EJ 1997. Whose right to die? *The Atlantic*: March.
Emanuel, EJ 1999. What is the great benefit of legalizing euthanasia or physician-assisted suicide? *Ethics* 109: 629–642.
Emanuel, EJ, ER Daniels, DL Fairclough, BR Clarridge 1998. The practice of euthanasia and physician-assisted suicide in the United States: adherence to proposed safeguards and effects on physicians. *JAMA* 280: 507–513.
Emanuel, EJ, DL Fairclough, ER Daniels, BR Clarridge 1996. Euthanasia and physician-assisted suicide: attitudes and experiences of oncology patients, oncologists, and the public. *Lancet* 347: 1805–1810.
Emanuel, EJ, DL Fairclough, J Slutsman, LL Emanuel 2000. Understanding economic and other burdens of terminal illness: the experience of patients. *Archives Internal Medicine* 132(6): 451–459.
Emanuel, EJ, BD Onwuteaka-Philipsen, JW Urwin, J Cohen 2016. Attitudes and practices of euthanasia and physician-assisted suicide in the United States, Canada, and Europe. *JAMA* 316: 79–90.
Enck, RE 1991. Drug-induced terminal sedation for symptom control. *American Journal of Hospice and Palliative Care* 8: 3–5.
Evenblij, K, HRW Pasman, R Pronk, BD Onwuteaka-Philipsen 2019. Euthanasia and physician-assisted suicide in patients suffering from psychiatric disorders: a cross-sectional study exploring the experiences of Dutch psychiatrists. *BMC Psychiatry* 19: 74.
Fagerlin, A, CE Schneider 2004. Enough: the failure of the living will. *Hastings Center Report* 34(2): 30–42.
FCECE (Federale Controle- en Evaluatiecommissie Euthanasie) 2004ff. *Biennial Reports*.
Federatie Palliatieve Zorg Vlaanderen 2011. *Visie: over Palliatieve Zorg en Euthanasie*, https://palliatievezorgvlaanderen.be/wp-content/uploads/2021/06/Over-palliatieve-zorg-en-euthanasie.pdf.
Feichtner, A, D Weixler, A Birklbauer 2018. Freiwilliger Verzicht auf Nahrung und Flüssigkeit um das Sterben zu beschleunigen. *Wiener Medizinische Wochenschrift* 168: 168–176.

Feinberg, J 1973. *Social Philosophy*. Englewood Cliffs, NJ: Prentice Hall.
Feinberg, J 1978. Voluntary euthanasia and the inalienable right to life. *Philosophy and Public Affairs* 7: 93–123.
Feinberg, J 1980. Legal moralism and freefloating evil. *Pacific Philosophical Quarterly* 61(1/2): 122.
Feinberg, J 1984–1990. *The Moral Limits of the Criminal Law*, vol. 1–4. Oxford UP.
Feinberg, J 1984. *Harm to Others*. Oxford UP.
Feinberg, J 1986. *Harm to Self*. Oxford UP.
Fekadu, A, JG Donocik, AJ Cleare 2018. Standardisation framework for the Maudsley staging method for treatment resistance in depression. *BMC Psychiatry* 18: 100.
Fekadu, A, LJ Rane, SC Wooderson et al. 2012. Prediction of longer-term outcome of treatment-resistant depression in tertiary care. *British Journal of Psychiatry* 201: 369–375.
Feldman, F 1992. *Confrontations with the Reaper*. Oxford UP.
Feldman, F 2010. *What Is This Thing Called Happiness*. Oxford UP.
Feldman, F 2011. What we learn from the experience machine. In: J Meadowcroft, R Bader eds. *The Cambridge Companion to Robert Nozick's Anarchy, State, and Utopia*. Cambridge UP.
Ferngren, GB 1989. The ethics of suicide in the renaissance and reformation. In: BA Brody ed. *Suicide and Euthanasia: Historical and Contemporary Themes*. Dordrecht: Kluwer.
Finlay, IG, R George 2011. Legal physician-assisted suicide in Oregon and the Netherlands: evidence concerning the impact on patients in vulnerable groups; another perspective on Oregon's data. *Journal of Medical Ethics* 37(3): 171–174.
Finnis, J 1980. *Natural Law and Natural Rights*. Oxford UP.
Finnis, J, J Boyle, G Grisez 1987. *Nuclear Deterrence, Morality, and Realism*. Oxford UP.
Fischer, JM ed. 1993. *The Metaphysics of Death*. Palo Alto, CA: Stanford UP.
Fischer, S, M Furter, R Mahrer-Imhof et al 2009. Reasons why people in Switzerland seek assisted suicide: the view of patients and physicians. *Swiss Medical Weekly* 139: 333–338.
Fischer, S, CA Huber, L Imhof et al. 2008. Suicide assisted by two Swiss right-to-die organisations. *Journal of Medical Ethics* 34: 810–814.
Fishman, JR, RH Binstock, MA Lambrix 2008. Anti-aging science: the emergence, maintenance, and enhancement of a discipline. *Journal of Aging Studies* 22: 295–303.
FMS, KNMG, LHV, NHG, Verenso 2014. *Helder Communiceren over euthanasie: belevingsonderzoek arts en euthanasie*.
Foley, K, H Hendin eds. 2002. *The Case against Assisted Suicide*. Baltimore, MD/London: Johns Hopkins UP.
Folker, AP, N Holtug, B Jensen et al. 1996. Experiences and attitudes towards end of life decisions amongst Danish physicians. *Bioethics* 10: 233–249.
Foot, P 1979. *Virtues and Vices and Other Essays in Moral Philosophy*. Berkeley, CA: University of California Press.
Forbes, K, R Huxtable 2006. Clarifying the data on double effect. *Palliative Medicine* 20: 395–396.
Førde, R, LJ Materstvedt, A Syse 2008. Scandinavia. In: Griffiths, Weyers, Adams eds.
Frankfurt, H 2004. *The Reasons of Love*. Princeton UP.

Fraser Health 2011. *Refractory Symptoms and Palliative Sedation: Therapy Guideline*, https://www.fraserhealth.ca/-/media/Project/FraserHealth/FraserHealth/Health-Professionals/Professionals-Resources/Hospice-palliative-care/Sections-PDFs-for-FH-Aug31/9524-28-FH---Sym_Guide-RefractoryPalliativeSedation.pdf.

Frey, RG 1978. Did Socrates commit suicide? *Philosophy* 53: 106–108.

Fried, LP, CM Tangen, J Walston et al. 2001. Frailty in older adults: evidence for a phenotype. *Journal of Gerontology Series A: Biological Sciences and Medical Sciences* 56: M146–M156.

Fried, TR, J O'Leary, PH von Ness et al. 2007. Inconsistency over time in the preferences of older persons with advanced illness for life-sustaining treatment. *Journal of the American Geriatrics Society* 55: 1007–1014.

Fumagalli, R 2018. Eliminating 'life worth living'. *Philosophical Studies* 175: 769–791.

Furberg, E 2012. Advance directives and personal identity: what is the problem? *Journal of Medicine and Philosophy* 37: 60–73.

Gaignard, M-E, S Hurst 2019. A qualitative study on existential suffering and assisted suicide in Switzerland. *BMC Medical Ethics* 20(1): 1–8.

Ganzini, L 2014. Psychiatric evaluations for individuals requesting assisted death in Washington and Oregon should not be mandatory. *General Hospital Psychiatry* 36: 10–12.

Ganzini, L 2017. Legalizing assisted death in Oregon: eighteen years of experience. In: GD Borassio, RJ Jox, J Taupitz, U Wiesing eds. *Assistierter Suizid: der Stand der Wissenschaft*. Berlin: Springer.

Ganzini, L, SK Dobscha 2004. Clarifying distinctions between contemplating and completing physician-assisted suicide. *Journal of Clinical Ethics* 15(2): 119.

Ganzini, L, ER Goy, SK Dobscha 2008a. Why Oregon patients request assisted death: family members' views. *Journal of General Internal Medicine* 23(2): 154–157.

Ganzini, L, ER Goy, SK Dobscha 2008b. Prevalence of depression and anxiety in patients requesting physicians' aid in dying: cross sectional survey. *British Medical Journal* 337: a1682.

Ganzini, L, ER Goy, SK Dobscha 2009. Oregonians' reasons for requesting physician aid in dying. *Archives of Internal Medicine* 169: 489–492.

Ganzini, L, ER Goy, LL Miller LL et al. 2003. Nurses' experiences with hospice patients who refuse food and fluids to hasten death. *New England Journal of Medicine* 349: 359–365.

Ganzini, L, GB Leong, DS Fenn et al. 2000. Evaluation of competence to consent to assisted suicide: views of forensic psychiatrists. *American Journal of Psychiatry* 157: 505–600.

Garcia, J 2007. Health versus harm: euthanasia and physicians' duties. *Journal of Medicine and Philosophy* 32: 7–24.

Gastmans, C, Y Denier 2010. What if patients with dementia use decision aids to make an advance euthanasia request? *American Journal of Bioethics* 10(4): 25–26.

Gastmans, C, Y Denier 2018. *Ethisch Advies 20: Levenseindezorg voor Niet-terminale Patienten met Ernstige Psychische Aandoeningen*. Brussel: Zorgnet Icuro.

Gastmans, C, J de Lepeleire 2010. Living to the bitter end? A personalist approach to euthanasia in persons with severe dementia. *Bioethics* 24: 78–86.

Gauthier, CC 2001. Active voluntary euthanasia, terminal sedation and assisted suicide. *Journal of Clinical Ethics* 12(1): 43–50.

Gaylin, W, LR Kass, ED Pellegrino et al. 1988. Doctors must not kill. *Journal of American Medical Association* 259: 2139–2140.

Gedge, EB 2004. Collective moral imagination: making decision for persons with dementia. *Journal of Medicine and Philosophy* 29: 435–450.

van der Geest, S 2012. Graceful and successful ageing: observations from Ghana and the Netherlands. In: B Röder, W de Jong, KW Alt eds. *Alter(n) anders denken: Kulturelle und Biologische Perspektiven*. Wien, Köln, Weimar: Böhlau Verlag: 227–238.

van Gennip, IE, HRW Pasman, MG Oosterveld-Vlug et al. 2013. The development of a model of dignity in illness based on qualitative interviews with seriously ill patients. *International Journal of Nursing Studies* 50(8): 1080–1089.

George, K 2007. A woman's choice? The gendered risks of voluntary euthanasia and physician-assisted suicide. *Medical Law Review* 15: 1–33.

Georges, JJ, BD Onwuteaka-Philipsen, MT Muller et al. 2007 Relatives' perspective on the terminally ill patients who died after euthanasia or physician-assisted suicide: a retrospective cross-sectional interview study in the Netherlands. *Death Studies* 31(1): 1–15.

Gert, B, CM Culver, KD Clouser 1998. An alternative to physician-assisted suicide: conceptual and moral analysis. In: Battin, Rhodes, Silver eds.

Gevers, S 2002. Terminal sedation: a legal approach. *European Journal of Health Law* 10: 359.

Gezondheidsraad (Dutch Health Council) 2002. *Dementie*. Den Haag: Gezondheidsraad.

Gilleard, C 2018. Suffering: the darker side of ageing. *Journal of Aging Studies* 44: 28–33.

Giubilini, A, J Savulescu eds. 2017. Conscientious objection in healthcare. *Cambridge Quarterly of Health Care Ethics* 26(1).

Glaser, BG, A Strauss 1965. Awareness of Dying. A Sociological Study of Attitudes towards the Patients Dying in Hospital. London: Weidenfeld & Nicolson.

Glendon, MA 2001. *A World Made New: Eleanor Roosevelt and the Universal Declaration of Human Rights*. New York, NY: Random House.

Glover, J 1977. *Causing Death and Saving Lives*. Penguin Books.

Gobbens, R, MLAM van Assen, KG Luijkx et al. 2010. Determinants of frailty. *Journal of the American Medical Directors Association* 11(5): 356–364.

Goering, S 2007. What makes suffering "unbearable and hopeless"? Advance directives, dementia and disability. *American Journal of Bioethics* 7: 62–63.

Golden, M, T Zoanni 2010. Killing us softly: the dangers of legalized assisted suicide. *Disability and Health Journal* 3(1): 16–30.

Goldney, YR 2009. A note on the reliability and validity of suicide statistics. *Psychiatry, Psychology and Law* 17: 52–56.

Goldstein, NE, LM Cohen, RM Arnold et al. 2012. Prevalence of formal accusation of murder and euthanasia against physicians. *Journal of Palliative Medicine* 15(3): 334–339.

Good, P, R.Richard, W.Syrmis et al. 2014. Medically assisted hydration for adult palliative care patients. *Cochrane Database of Systematic Reviews* (4).

Goodfellow, B, K Kolves, D de Leo 2018. Contemporary nomenclatures of suicidal behaviors: a systematic literature review. *Suicide and Life-Threatening Behavior* 48(3): 353–366.

Goodwin, P 2004. The distortion of cases in Oregon. In: Quill, Battin eds.

Gordijn, B, R Janssens 2000. The prevention of euthanasia through palliative care: new developments in the Netherlands. *Patient Education and Counselling* 41: 35–46.

Gorsuch, NM 2006. *The Future of Assisted Suicide and Euthanasia*. Princeton: Princeton UP.

Graber, GC 1981. The rationality of suicide. In: S Wallace, A Eser eds. *Suicide and Euthanasia: The Rights of Personhood*. Knoxville: University of Tennessee Press.

de Graeff, A, M Dean 2007. Palliative sedation therapy in the last weeks of life: a literature review and recommendations for standards. *Journal of Palliative Medicine* 10: 67–85.

de Graeff, A, AP Jobse, EH Verhagen, AAJ Moonen 2008. De rol van consultatie bij palliatieve sedatie in de regio Midden-Nederland. *Nederlands Tijdschrift voor Geneeskunde* 152: 2346–2350.

Griffin, J 1986. *Well-Being: Its Meaning, Measurement, and Moral Importance*. Oxford UP.

Griffin, J 2008. *On Human Rights*. Oxford UP.

Griffiths, J 2001. Comparative reflections: is the Dutch case unique? In: A Klijn ed. Regulating physician-negotiated death. *Recht der Werkelijkheid 22:* 197–205.

Griffiths, J 2003. The social working of legal rules. *The Journal of Legal Pluralism and Unofficial Law* 35: 1–84.

Griffiths, J, A Bood, H Weyers 1998. *Euthanasia and Law in the Netherlands*. Amsterdam: Amsterdam UP.

Griffiths, J, H Weyers, M Adams 2008. *Euthanasia and Law in Europe*. Oxford and Portland: Hart Publ.

Grisez, GG 1970. Toward a consistent natural law ethics of killing. *American Journal of Jurisprudence* 15: 64–97.

Grisez, GG 1978. Against consequentialism. *American Journal of Jurisprudence* 23: 21–72.

Groenewoud, AS, F Atsma, M Arvin et al. 2021. Euthanasia in the Netherlands: a claims data cross-sectional study of geographical variation. *BMJ Supportive & Palliative Care*. Available online (open access).

Groenewoud, JH 2002. *End-of-Life Decisions in Medicine: Empirical Studies on Practices and Attitudes in the Netherlands*. Enschede: Printpartners Ipskamp.

Groenewoud, JH, A van der Heide, BD Onwuteaka-Philipsen et al. 2000. Clinical problems with the performance of euthanasia and physician-assisted suicide in the Netherlands. *New England Journal of Medicine* 342: 551–556.

Gupta, M, J Rivest, S Leclair et al. 2017. *Exploring the Psychological Suffering of a Person Requesting Medical Assistance in Dying*. Preprint, http://www.cmq.org/pdf/outils-fin-de-vie/exploring-psychological-suffering.pdf?t=1535846400024.

Gurschick, L, DK Mayer, LC Hanson 2015. Palliative sedation: an analysis of international guidelines and position statements. *American Journal of Hospice and Palliative Medicine* 32: 660–671.

Gvion, Y, A Apter 2011. Aggression, impulsivity, and suicide behavior: a review of the literature. *Archives of Suicide Research* 15(2): 93–112.

Haan, J de 2002. The ethics of euthanasia: advocates' perspectives. *Bioethics* 16: 154–172.

Habermas, J 2005. *Die Zukunft der menschlichen Natur: auf dem Weg zu einer liberalen Eugenik?* Frankfurt: Suhrkamp.

de Haes, JC, FC van Knippenberg, JP Neijt 1990. Measuring psychological and physical distress in cancer patients: structure and application of the Rotterdam Symptom Checklist. *British Journal Cancer* 62: 1034–1038.

Hagens, M, HRW Pasman, A van der Heide, B Onwuteaka-Philipsen 2021. Intentionally ending one's own life in the presence or absence of a medical condition: a nationwide mortality follow-back study. *SSM-Population Health* 15: 100871.

Haishan, H, L Hongjuan, Z Tieying, P Xumei 2015. Preference of Chinese general public and health care providers for a good death. *Nursing Ethics* 2(2): 217–227.

Hallenbeck, JL 2000. Terminal sedation: ethical implications in different situations. *Journal of Palliative Medicine* 3(3): 313–320.

Halpern, J 2012. When concretized emotion-belief complexes derail decision-making capacity. *Bioethics* 26: 108–116.

Hanratty, B, P Holland, A Jacoby, M Whitehead 2007. Financial stress and strain associated with terminal cancer: a review of evidence. *Palliative Medicine* 21: 595–608.

Hanser, M 2013. The wrongness of killing and the badness of death. In: B Bradley, F Feldman, J Johansson eds. *The Oxford Handbook of Philosophy of Death*. Oxford UP.

Happé, RH 2014. Fiscale discriminatie in 26 jaar rechtspraak van de Hoge Raad: een fiscaal en rechtsstatelijk debat. *Weekblad Fiscaal Recht* 7060: 7 augustus.

Hardwig, J 2013. Is there a duty to die in Europe? If not now, when? In: Denier, Gastmans, Vandevelde eds.

Harris, J 1985. *The Value of Life: An Introduction to Medical Ethics*. London and New York, NY: Routledge.

Hart, B, P Sainsbury, S Short 1998. Promoting the interdisciplinary study of death and dying. *Mortality* 3(1): 65–77.

Hart, HL 1958. Legal and moral obligation. In: AI Melden ed. *Essays in Moral Philosophy*. Seattle, WA: University of Washington Press.

Hart, HLA 1982. *Essays on Bentham: Jurisprudence and Political Theory*. Oxford: Clarendon Press.

Hart, HL 1994. *The Concept of Law*, second edition. Oxford: Clarendon Press.

Hartog, ID, ML Zomers, GJMW van Thiel et al. 2020. Prevalence and characteristics of older adults with a persistent death wish without severe illness: a large cross-sectional survey. *BMC Geriatrics* 20: 342–355.

den Hartogh, GA 2002. *Mutual Expectations: A Conventionalist Theory of Law*. The Hague: Kluwer.

den Hartogh, GA 2003. Mysterieuze cijfers: meldingspercentage van euthanasie kan niet meer stijgen. *Medisch Contact* 58: 1063–1066.

den Hartogh, GA 2006. Palliatieve sedatie en euthanasie: commentaar op een richtlijn. *Tijdschrift voor Gezondheidsrecht* 30(2): 109–119.

den Hartogh, GA 2009. The slippery slope argument. In: P Singer, H Kuhse eds. *Companion to Bioethics*, second edition. Hoboken NJ: Wiley-Blackwell.

den Hartogh, GA 2011. Can consent be presumed? *Journal of Applied Philosophy* 28: 295–307.

den Hartogh, GA 2012. The regulation of euthanasia: how successful is the Dutch system? In: SJ Youngner, GK Kimsma eds.

den Hartogh, GA 2013a. The authority of advance directives. In: Denier, Gastmans, Vandevelde eds.

den Hartogh, GA 2013b. Is consent of the donor enough to justify the removal of living organs? *Cambridge Quarterly of Health Care Ethics* 22(1): 45–54.

den Hartogh, GA 2013c. Death wishes of the elderly. In: Schermer, Pinxten eds.

den Hartogh, GA 2014a. Is human dignity the ground of human rights? In: M Düwell, J Braarvig, R Brownsword, D Mieth eds. *The Cambridge Handbook of Human Dignity: Interdisciplinary Perspectives*. Cambridge UP.

den Hartogh, GA 2014b. Comforting the parents by administering neuromuscular blockers to the dying child. A conflict between ethics and law? *Journal of Applied Philosophy* 31(2014): 91–103.

den Hartogh, GA 2015a. Why extra caution is needed in the case of depressed patients. *Journal of Medical Ethics* 41: 588–589.

den Hartogh, GA 2015b. De beoordeling van euthanasie en hulp bij zelfdoding bij psychiatrische en demente patiënten. Wat houdt 'extra behoedzaamheid' in? *Nederlands Juristenblad* 90(21): 1406–1414.

den Hartogh, GA 2016a. Continuous deep sedation and homicide: an unsolved question in ethics and law. *Medicine, Health Care and Philosophy* 19: 285–297.

den Hartogh, GA 2016b. Do we need a threshold conception of competence? *Medicine, Health Care and Philosophy* 19: 71–83.

den Hartogh, GA 2016c. Sedation until death: are the requirements laid down in the guidelines too restrictive? *Kennedy Institute of Ethics Journal* 26: 369–397.

den Hartogh, GA 2016d. Two kinds of suicide. *Bioethics* 30: 672–680.

den Hartogh, GA 2017a. Two kinds of physician-assisted death. *Bioethics* 31: 666–673.

den Hartogh, GA 2017b. De WTL: een potemkindorp? In: Laura De Vito red. *15 Jaar Euthanasiewet*. Amsterdam: NVVE.

den Hartogh, GA 2017c. Suffering and dying well. The aim of palliative care. *Medicine, Health Care and Philosophy* 20(3): 413–424.

den Hartogh, GA 2017d. Doodswensen van hoogbejaarden: een probleem voor de maatschappij, voor de dokter, of alleen voor de ouderen zelf? *Filosofie & Praktijk* 38: 39–57.

den Hartogh, GA 2017e. Euthanasie bij een verlaagd bewustzijn: de richtlijn en de praktijk. *Tijdschrift voor Gezondheidsrecht* 41(7): 492–524.

den Hartogh, GA 2018. Relieving one's relatives from the burdens of care. *Medicine, Health Care and Philosophy* 21: 403–410.

den Hartogh, GA 2019a. The medical exception to the prohibition of killing: a matter of the right intention? *Ratio Juris* 32(2019): 157–176.

den Hartogh, GA 2019b. When are you dead enough to be a donor? *Theoretical Medicine and Bioethics* 40: 299–319.

den Hartogh, GA 2019c. De rol van de zorgvuldigheidseisen betreffende het lijden in de toetsing van euthanasie. *Nederlands Juristen Blad* 94(11): 739–743.

den Hartogh, GA 2019d. Why normative judgment is inescapable. Comment on: Kious, Battin 2019. *American Journal of Bioethics* 19(10): 48–50.

den Hartogh, GA 2020a. Counting cases of termination of life without request: new dances with data. *Cambridge Quarterly of Health Care Ethics* 29: 395–402.

den Hartogh, GA 2020b. Decriminalizing assisted suicide services: a comment on the decision of the German Federal Constitutional Court (*Bundesverfassungsgericht*) of 26 February 2020. *European Constitutional Law Review* 16: 713–732.

Harvath, TA, LA Miller, KA Smith et al. 2006. Dilemma's encountered by hospice workers when patients wish to hasten death. *Journal of Hospice and Palliative Nursing* 8: 200–209.

Harvey, M 2006. Advance directives and the severely demented. *Journal of Medicine and Philosophy* 31: 47–64.

Hasselaar, JG 2008. Palliative sedation until death: an approach from Kant's ethics of virtue. *Theoretical Medicine and Bioethics* 29(6): 387–396.

Hasselaar, JGJ, SCA Verhagen, KCP Vissers 2009. When cancer symptoms cannot be controlled: the role of palliative sedation. *Current Opinion in Supportive and Palliative Care* 3: 14–23.

Hauser, K, D Walsh 2009. Palliative sedation: welcome guidance on a controversial issue. *Palliative Medicine* 23: 577–579.

Haute Authorité de Santé 2018. *Comment mettre en oeuvre une sédation profonde et continue maintenue jusqu'au décès? Guide du Parcours des Soins*, https://www.has-sante.fr/upload/docs/application/pdf/2018-03/app_164_guide_pds_sedation_web.pdf.

ten Have, HAMJ 2001. Euthanasia: moral paradoxes. *Palliative Medicine* 15: 505–511.

ten Have, HAMJ, JVM Welie 2014. Palliative sedation versus euthanasia: an ethical assessment. *Journal of Pain and Symptom Management* 47(1): 123–136.

Haverkate, I, A van der Heide, BD Onwuteaka-Philipsen et al. 2001. The emotional impact on physicians of hastening the death of a patient. *Medical Journal of Australia* 175: 519–522.

Health Canada 2020. *Second Annual Report on Medical Assistance in Dying in Canada.*

Hedberg, K, C New 2017. Oregon's Death With Dignity Act: 20 years of experience to inform the debate. *Annals of Internal Medicine* 167(8): 579–583.

van der Heide, A, A Brinkman-Stoppelenburg, J van Delden, B Onwuteaka-Philipsen 2010. *Euthanasie en Andere Medische Beslissingen rond het Levenseinde: Sterfgevallenonderzoek 2010*. Den Haag: ZonMw.

van der Heide, A, JJM van Delden, B Onwuteaka-Philipsen 2017. End-of-life decisions in the Netherlands over 25 years. *New England Journal of Medicine* 377(5): 492–494.

van der Heide, A, L Deliëns, K Faisst et al. 2003. End-of-life decision-making in six European countries: descriptive study. *Lancet* 362: 345–350.

van der Heide, A, J Legemaate, B Onwuteaka-Philipsen et al. 2012. *Tweede Evaluatie Wet Toetsing Levensbeëindiging op Verzoek en Hulp bij Zelfdoding.* Den Haag: ZonMw.

Hendricks, RK, Z Demjén, E Semino, L Boroditsky 2018. Emotional implications of metahor: consequences of metaphor framing for mindset about cancer. *Metaphor and Symbol* 33: 267–279.

Hendry, M, D Pasterfield, R Lewis et al. 2012. Why do we want the right to die? A systematic review of the international literature on the views of patients, carers and the public on assisted dying. *Palliative Medicine* 27(1): 13–26.

Hertogh, C 2013. Aging beyond frailty: the future of old age. In: Schermer, Pinxten eds.

Hertogh, CMPM 2009. The role of advance euthanasia directives as an aid to communication and shared decision-making in dementia. *Journal of Medical Ethics* 35: 100–103.

Hertogh, CMPM, ME de Boer, RM Droës et al. 2007. Would we rather lose our life than lose our self? Lessons from the Dutch debate on euthanasia for patients with dementia. *American Journal of Bioethics* 7(4): 48–56.

Hertogh, CMPM, ME de Boer, RM Droës et al. 2008. Beyond a Dworkinian view of autonomy and advance directives in dementia. Response to open peer commentaries. *American Journal of Bioethics* 8(4): 4–6.

Hertogh, CMPM, RM Dröes, ME de Boer 2006. Dementie sluit praten over euthanasie niet uit. *Medisch Contact* 61: 15–17.

Hill, TE 1991. Self-regarding suicide: a modified Kantian view. In: *Autonomy and Self-Respect*. Cambridge UP.

Hindmarch, T, M Hotopf, GS Owen. 2013. Depression and decision-making capacity for treatment or research: a systematic review. *BMC Medical Ethics* 14: 54.

von Hirsch, A, U Neumann 2010. 'Indirekter Paternalismus' im Strafrecht – am Beispiel der Tötung auf Verlangen (§ 216 StGB). In: A von Hirsch, U Neumann, K Sellmann eds. *Paternalismus im Strafrecht: Die Kriminalisierung von selbstschädigendem Verhalten*. NOMOS.

Hodel, MA, P Hoff, SA Irwin et al. 2019. Attitudes toward assisted suicide requests in the context of severe and persistent mental illness: a survey of psychiatrists in Switzerland. *Palliative and Supportive Care* 17: 621–627.

Hoekstra, N, M Strack, A Simon 2015. Bewertung des freiwilligen Verzichts auf Nahrung und Flüssigkeit durch palliativmedizinisch und hausärztlich tätige Ärztinnen und Ärzte. *Zeitschrift für Palliativmedizin* 16: 68–73.

Holland, J 1999. NCCN practical guidelines for the management of psychosocial distress. *Oncology* 13(5A): 113–147, https://pubmed.ncbi.nlm.nih.gov/10370925/. Revised as: National Comprehensive Cancer Network. 2014.

Holm, S 2013. Terminal sedation and euthanasia: the virtue in calling a spade what it is. In: Sterckx, Raus, F Mortier eds.

van Holsteyn, J, M Trappenburg 1995. *Het laatste oordeel: meningen over nieuwe vormen van euthanasie*. Baarn: Ambo.

van Hooff, AJT 1990. A longer life for 'suicide': when was the Latin word for 'self-murderer' invented? *Romanische Forschungen* 102 (2/3): 255–259.

van Hooft, S 1998. Suffering and the goals of medicine. *Medicine, Health Care and Philosophy* 1: 125–131.

Hope, T 1992. Advance directives about medical treatment. *British Medical Journal* 304: 398.

Hospice and Palliative Care Federation of Massachusetts 2004. *Palliative Sedation Protocol*, https://cdn.ymaws.com/www.hospicefed.org/resource/resmgr/hpcfm_pdf_doc/pal_sed_protocol_2004.pdf.

Hospice and Palliative Nurses Association 2008. *Position Statement: Palliative Sedation*. Updated 2011.

Hospice and Palliative Nurses Association 2011. *Position Statement: Role of the Nurse When Hastened Death Is Requested.* https://www.ons.org/sites/default/files/Role%20of%20Nurse%20Hastening%20Death.pdf.

de Hullu, J 2009. *Materiëel Strafrecht.* Deventer: Kluwer.

van Humbeeck, L, M Driedijk, S de Mey et al. 2020. *Tiredness of Life in Older Persons: An Evolutionary Concept Analysis.* Preprint, https://assets.researchsquare.com/files/rs-120466/v1/a934beab-472d-4bdb-a826-b982f7c42598.pdf?c=1631863171.

van Humbeeck, L, R Piers, R de Bock, N van den Noortgate 2022. Flemish healthcare providers' attitudes towards tiredness of life and euthanasia: a survey study. *Aging & Mental Health* 26: 205–211.

Hurst, SA, U Zellweger, G Bosshard et al. 2018. Medical end-of-life practices in Swiss cultural regions: a death certificate study. *BMC Medicine* 16: 54.

Husak, D 2009. Legal paternalism. In: H LaFollette ed. *The Oxford Handbook of Practical Ethics.* Oxford UP.

Hyman, SE 2007. Can neuroscience be integrated into the DSM-V? *Nature Reviews, Neuroscience* 8: 725–732.

Imai, K, T Morita, T Akechi et al. 2020. The principles of revised clinical guidelines about palliative sedation therapy of the Japanese Society for Palliative Medicine. *Journal of Palliative Medicine* 23: 1184–1190.

Inghelbrecht, E, J Bilsen, F Mortier, L Deliëns 2010. The role of nurses in physician-assisted deaths in Belgium. *Canadian Medical Association Journal* 182: 905–910.

Institut für Demoskopie Allensbach 2010. *Ärztlich begleiteter Suizid und aktive Sterbehilfe aus Sicht der deutschen Ärtzteschaft: Ergebnisse einer Repräsentativbefragung von Krankenhaus und niedergelassenen Ärzten.* https://www.bundesaerztekammer.de/fileadmin/user_upload/_old-files/downloads/Sterbehilfe1.pdf.

Irish Association for Palliative Care 2015. *Palliative sedation: discussion paper. https://iapc1.wpengine.com/wp-content/uploads/downloads/2017/09/IAPC-Palliative-Sedation-Discussion-Paper.pdf.*

Ivanovic, N, D Büche, A Fringe 2014. Voluntary stopping of eating and drinking at the end of life – a 'systematic search and review' giving insight into an option of hastening death in capacitated adults at the end of life. *BMC Palliative Care* 13(1): 1–8.

Izaks, GJ 2001. *Determinants of Mortality in Old Age.* Thesis, University of Leiden.

Izaks, GJ, RGJ Westendorp 2003. Ill or just old? Toward a conceptual framework of the relation between aging and disease. *BMC Geriatrics* 3(1): 1–6.

Jackson, E 2004. Whose death is it anyway? Euthanasia and the medical professions. *Current Legal Problems* 57: 415–442.

Jackson, E 2012. In favor of the legalisation of assisted dying. In: E Jackson, J Keown eds. *Debating Euthanasia.* Oxford, Portland: Hart Publ.

Jacobs, F 2005. Reasonable partiality in professional ethics: the moral division of labour. *Ethical Theory and Moral Practice* 8: 141–154.

Jamison, KR 1999. *Nights Falls Fast: Understanding Suicide.* New York, NY: Knopf.

Jansen, LA 2004. No safe harbor: the principle of complicity and the practice of voluntary stopping of eating and drinking. *Journal of Medicine and Philosophy* 29: 61–74.

Jansen, LA 2010. Disambiguating clinical intentions: the ethics of palliative sedation. *Journal of Medicine and Philosophy* 35: 19–31.

Jansen, LA, DP Sulmasy 2002a. Proportionality, terminal suffering and the restorative goals of medicine. *Theoretical Medicine and Bioethics* 23: 321–337.

Jansen, LA, DP Sulmasy 2002b. Sedation, alimentation, hydration, and equivocation: careful conversation about care at the end of life. *Annals of Internal Medicine* 136: 845–849.

Jansen, LA, S Wall, FG Miller 2019. Drawing the line on physician-assisted death. *Journal of Medical Ethics* 45: 190–197.

Jansen-van der Weide, MC, BD Onwuteaka-Philipsen, G van der Wal 2005. Granted, undecided, withdrawn, and refused requests for euthanasia and physician-assisted suicide. *Archives Internal Medicine* 165(15): 1698–1704.

Janssens, R, JJM van Delden, GAM Widdershoven 2012. Palliative sedation: not just normal medical practice: ethical reflections on the Royal Dutch Medical Association's guidelines on palliative sedation. *Journal of Medical Ethics* 38: 664–668.

Jarvis, GK, M Boldt, J Butt 1991. Medical examiners and manner of death. *Suicide and Life-Threatening Behavior* 2: 115–133.

Jaspers, K 1970, *Philosophy*, vol. 2, transl. EB Ashton. Chicago IL: University of Chicago Press.

Jaworska, A 1999. Respecting the margins of agency: Alzheimer's patients and the capacity to value. *Philosophy and Public Affairs* 28: 105–138.

Jaworska, A 2007. Caring and full moral standing. *Ethics* 117: 460–497.

Joiner, T 2005. *Why People Die by Suicide*. Cambridge, MA: Harvard UP.

Joiner, T 2011. *Myths about Suicide*. Cambridge, MA: Harvard UP.

Jones, DA 2011. Is there a logical slippery slope from voluntary to non-voluntary euthanasia? *Kennedy Institute of Ethics Journal* 21: 379–404.

Jones, DA 2017. Euthanasia and assisted suicide in Belgium: bringing an end to interminable discussion. In: Jones, Gastmans, MacKellar eds.

Jones, DA, C Gastmans, C MacKellar eds. 2017. *Euthanasia and Assisted Suicide: Lessons from Belgium*. Cambridge UP.

Jongepier, F 2018. Zelfdoding en de waarde van een rationeel leven. *Algemeen Nederlands Tijdschrift voor Wijsbegeerte* 110(4): 453–472.

Jongsma, KR, MAG Sprangers, S van de Vathorst 2016. The implausibility of response shifts in dementia patients. *Journal of Medical Ethics* 42(9): 597–600.

Jox, RJ 2020. Living will versus will to live? How to navigate through complex decisions for persons with dementia. *American Journal of Bioethics* 20(8): 85–87.

Jox, RJ, I Black, GD Borassio et al. 2017. Voluntary stopping of eating and drinking: is medical support ethically justified? *BMC Medicine* 15(1): 186.

Juth, N, A Lindblad, N Lynöe et al. 2010. EAPC framework for palliative sedation: an ethical discussion. *BMC Palliative Care* 9(1): 1–5.

Kadish, SH 1992. Letting patients die: legal and moral reflections. *California Law Review* 80: 857–888.

Kagan, S 1989. *The Limits of Morality*. Oxford UP.

Kagan, S 2012. *Death*. New Haven, CT/London: Yale UP.

Kamisar, Y 1958. Some non-religious views against proposed 'mercy-killing' legislation. *Minnesota Law Review* 42: 969–1042.

Kamisar, Y 1991. When is there a constitutional 'right to die'? When is there no 'constitutional right to live'? *Georgia Law Review* 25: 1203–1242.

Kamm, FM 1993. *Morality, Mortality, Vol 1: Death and Whom to Save from It.* Oxford UP.

Kamm, FM 1999. Physician-assisted suicide, the doctrine of double effect, and the ground of value. *Ethics* 109: 586–605.

Kammeraat, M, P Kölling 2020. *Psychiatrische patiënten bij Expertisecentrum Euthanasie.* Den Haag: Expertisecentrum Euthanasie.

Kant, I 1991 (1797). *The Metaphysics of Morals*, ed. and transl. M Gregor. Cambridge UP.

Karlsson, M, A Milberg, P Strang 2012. Suffering and euthanasia: a qualitative study of dying cancer patients' perspectives. *Supportive Care in Cancer* 20: 1065–1071.

Kass, LR 1989. Neither for love nor money: why doctors must not kill. *Public Interest* 94: 25–46.

Kass, LR 1993. Is there a right to die? *Hastings Center Report* 1993: 34–43. Reprinted in Donnelly ed.

Kass, LR 1998. The wisdom of repugnance. In: GE Pence, *Flesh of my Flesh, The Ethics of Cloning Humans.* Oxford: Rowman & Littlefield.

Kaufmann, F 2016. Lucretius and the fear of death. In: M Cholbi ed. *Immortality and the Philosophy of Death.* London: Rowman & Littlefield.

Kehl, KA 2006. Moving toward peace: an analysis of the concept of a good death. *American Journal of Hospice & Palliative Medicine* 23(4): 277–286.

Kelly, B, P Burnett, D Pelusi et al. 2002. Terminally ill cancer patients' wish to hasten death. *Palliative Medicine* 16: 339–345.

Kelly, B, T Handley, D Kissane et al. 2020. "An indelible mark". The response to participation in euthanasia and physician-assisted suicide among doctors: a review of research findings. *Palliative and Supportive Care* 18(1): 82–88.

Kennedy, I, A Grubb 2000. *Principles of Medical Law.* Oxford UP.

Kennedy, J 2002. *Een Weloverwogen Dood: Euthanasie in Nederland.* Amsterdam: Prometheus.

Keown, J 2002. *Euthnasia, Ethics and Public Policy: An Argument against Legalisation*, first ed. Cambridge UP.

Keown, J 2012. Against decriminalising euthanasia; for improving care. In: E. Jackson, J. Keown, Debating Euthanasia. Oxford, Portland: Hart Publishing.

Keown, J 2018. *Euthanasia, Ethics and Public Policy: An Argument against Legalisation*, second ed. Cambridge UP.

Kiewiet, J 2018. De rechtsfilosofische grondslagen van John Griffiths' rechtssociologie. *Recht der werkelijkheid* 39(2): 18–34.

Kim, SYH, ED Caine, GW Currier et al. 2001. Assessing the competence of persons with Alzheimer's disease in providing informed consent for participation in research. *American Journal of Psychology* 158: 712–717.

Kim, SYH, ED Caine, JG Swan, PS Appelbaum 2006. Do clinicians follow a risk-sensitive model of capacity determination? An experimental video survey. *Psychosomatics* 47: 325–329.

Kim, SYH, T Lemmens 2016. Should assisted dying for psychiatric disorder be legalized in Canada? *Canadian Medical Association Journal* 188(14): E337–E339.

Kim, SYH, RG de Vries, JR Peteet 2016. Euthanasia and assisted suicide of patients with psychiatric disorders in the Netherlands 2011 to 2014. *JAMA Psychiatry* 73(4): 362–368.

Kimsma, GK 2010. Death by request in the Netherlands: facts, the legal context and effects on physicians, patients and families. *Medicine, Health Care and Philosophy* 13(4): 355–361.

King, PA, LA Wolf 1998. Lessons for physician-assisted suicide from the Afro-American experience. In: Battin, Rhodes, Silver eds.

Kious, BM, M Battin 2019. Physician aid-in-dying and suicide prevention in psychiatry: a moral crisis? *American Journal of Bioethics* 19: 29–39.

Kissane, D, DM Clarke, AF Street 2001. Demoralization syndrome—a relevant psychiatric diagnosis for palliative care. *Journal of Palliative Care* 17(1): 12–21.

Kissane, DW 2000. The contribution of demoralization to end of life decision-making. *Hastings Center Report* 34(4): 21–31.

Kissane, DW 2012. The relief of existential suffering. *Archives of Internal Medicine* 172: 1501–1505.

Kissane, DW, S Wein, A Love et al. 2004. The demoralization scale: a report of its development and preliminary validation. *Journal of Palliative Care* 20(4): 269–276.

Kitwood, T 1997. *Dementia Reconsidered: The Person Comes First*. Buckingham/Philadelphia, PA: Open UP.

Kjölseth, I, O Ekeberg, S Steihaug 2009. Why do they become vulnerable when faced with the challenges of old age? Elderly people who committed suicide, described by those who knew them. *International Psychogeriatrics* 21(05): 903–912.

Kjölseth, I, O Ekeberg, S Steihaug 2010. Why suicide? Elderly people who committed suicide and their experience of life in the period before their death. *International Psychogeriatrics* 22(2): 209–218.

Kleijer DJ 2005. *"Het wordt geregeld…", Een onderzoek naar (zelf)regulering bij het staken of onthouden van een levensverlengende behandeling op Intensive Cares in Nederland*. Thesis, Rijksuniversiteit Groningen.

Kleinig, J 1979. Consent as a defence in criminal law. *Archiv für Rechts- und Sozialphilosophie* 65(3): 329–345.

Kleinig, J 1984. *Paternalism*. Totowa, NJ: Rowman and Littlefield.

Klosko, G 2005. *Political Obligations*. Oxford UP.

KNMG. 1997. (Koninklijke Nederlandsche Maatschappij tot bevordering der Geneeskunst, Commissie Aanvaardbaarheid Levensbeëindigend handelen.) *Medisch Handelen rond het Levenseinde bij Wilsonbekwame Patiënten*. Houten: Bohn Stafleu Van Loghum.

KNMG 2009. *Guideline Palliative Sedation, revised edition* (first edition 2005), https://www.palliativedrugs.com/download/091110_KNMG_Guideline_for_Palliative_sedation_2009__2_%5B1%5D.pdf.

KNMG 2011. *Standpunt: de rol van de arts bij het zelfgekozen levenseinde*. Replaced by new edition 2021.

KNMG/V&VN 2014. *Caring for people who consciously choose not to eat and drink so as to hasten the end of life*. www.knmg.nl: Publications in English.

KNMP (Royal Dutch Society for Pharmacy) 2012. *Richtlijn voor de uitvoering van euthanasie en hulp bij zelfdoding*, https://www.knmp.nl/richtlijnen/uitvoering-euthanasie-en-hulp-bij-zelfdoding.

Koerselman, GF 1998. *Biologische Psychotherapie*. (Inaugural Address). Amsterdam: van Oorschot.

Kon, AA 2011. Palliative sedation: it's not a panacea. *American Journal of Bioethics* 11(6): 41–42.

Koppelman, E 2002. Dementia and dignity: towards a new method of surrogate decision-making. *Journal of Medicine and Philosophy* 27: 65–85.

Korsgaard, C 1996. *The Sources of Normativity*. Cambridge UP.

Korsgaard, CM 2004. Fellow creatures: Kantian ethics and our duties to animals. In: GB Peterson ed, *The Tanner Lectures on Human Values*, vol. 25/26. Salt Lake City, UT: The University of Utah Press.

Kouwenhoven, PS, GJMW van Thiel, NJH Raymaker et al. 2014. Euthanasia or physician-assisted suicide? *European Journal of General Practice* 20: 25–31.

Krahn, G 2010. Reflections on the debate on disability and aid in dying. *Disability and Health Journal* 3(1): 51–55.

Krikorian, A, TJ Limonero, J Maté 2012. Suffering and distress at the end of life. *Psycho-Oncology* 21: 799–808.

Krikorian, A, C Maldonado, T Pastrana 2020. Patient's perspectives on the notion of a good death: A systematic review of the literature. *Journal of Pain and Symptom Management* 59: 152–164.

Kuflik, A 1986. The utilitarian logic of inalienable rights. *Ethics* 97: 75–87.

Kuhse, H 1999. Some reflections on the problem of advance directives, personhood, and personal identity. *Kennedy Institute of Ethics Journal* 9: 347–364.

Kuhse, H 2004. Why terminal sedation is no solution to the voluntary euthanasia debate. In: Tännsjö ed.

Kuhse, H, P Singer, M Clark, M Rickard 1997. End-of-life decisions in Australian medical practice. *Medical Journal of Australia* 166: 191–196.

Kupfer, DJ, MB First, DA Regier 2002. *A Research Agenda for DSM-V*. Washington, DC: American Psychiatric Association.

Kupfer, J 1990. Suicide: its nature and moral evaluation. *Journal of Value Inquiry* 24: 67–81. Reprinted in Donnelly ed.

Kuuppelomaki, M, S Lauri 1998. Cancer patients' reported experiences of suffering. *Cancer Nursing* 21(5): 364–369.

Kwon, YC, YH Yun, KH Lee et al. 2006. Symptoms in the lives of terminal cancer patients: which is the most important? *Oncology* 71(1–2): 69–76.

Lavery, JV, J Boyle, BM Dickens et al. 2001. Origins of the desire for euthanasia and assisted suicide in people with HIV-1 or AIDS: a qualitative study. *The Lancet* 358: 362–367.

van der Lee, ML, JG van der Bom, NB Swarteet 2005. Euthanasia and depression: a prospective cohort study among terminally ill cancer patients *Journal of Clinical Oncology* 23(27): 6607–6612.

Lee, BC 2014. Oregon's experience with aid in dying: findings from, the death with dignity laboratory. *Annals of the New York Academy of Science* 1330(1): 94–100.

Lee, P, RP de George 2008. The nature and basis of human dignity. *Ratio Juris* 21: 173–193.

Legemaate, J 2005. *De zorgverlening rond het levenseinde. Een literatuurstudie naar begripsomschrijvingen en zorgvuldigheidseisen*. Utrecht: KNMG.

Leheup, BF, E Piot, X Ducrocq, B Wary 2012. Théorie du double effet et sédation pour détresse en phase terminale: réflexion autour de la survie des patients sédatés. *Presse Medicale* 41: 927–932.

Lemmens, T 2016. The conflict between open-ended access to physician-assisted dying and the protection of the vulnerable: lessons from Belgium's euthanasia-regime for the Canadian post-Carter era. *Les Grandes Conflits en Droit de la Santé*. Cowensvillen: Yvon Blais: 261–317.

Lemmens, T 2018. Charter scrutiny of Canada's medical assistance in dying law and the shifting landscape of Belgian and Dutch euthanasia practice. *Supreme Court Law Review* 85: 459–544.

Lemmens, T, H Kim, E Kurz 2018. Why Canada's medical assistance in dying legislation should be c(h)arter compliant and what it may help to avoid. *McGill Journal of Law and Health* 11(1): S61–S146.

de Leo, D, S Burgis, JM Bertolotto et al. 2006. Definitions of suicide: lessons learned from the WHO/EURO multicentre study. *Crisis* 27(1): 4–15.

de Leo, D 2022. Late-life suicide in an aging world. *Nature Aging* 2: 7–12.

Lester, D 2006. Can suicide be a good death? *Death Studies* 30(6): 511–527.

Leven, DC, TE Quill 2017. The clinical, ethical and legislative case for medical aid in dying in New York. *New York State Bar Association Health Law Journal* 22: 27–29.

Levene, I, M Parker 2011. Prevalence of depression in granted and refused requests for euthanasia and assisted suicide: a systematic review. *Journal of Medical Ethics* 37: 205–211.

Levi, BH, MJ Green 2010. Too soon to give up: re-examining the value of advance directives. *American Journal of Bioethics* 10(4): 3–22.

Lewis, P 2007. The empirical slippery slope from voluntary to non-voluntary euthanasia. *Journal of Law and Medical Ethics* 35: 197–210.

Lewis, P 2008. England and Wales. In: Griffiths, Weyers, Adams eds.

Lewis, P 2011. Informal legal change on assisted suicide: the policy for prosecutors. *Legal Studies* 31.1: 119–134.

Lewis, P 2012. *Assisted Dying and Legal Change*. Oxford UP.

Lewis, P, I Black 2012. *The Effectiveness of Legal Safeguards in Jurisdictions that Allow Assisted Dying*. Briefing Paper for the Commission on Assisted Dying. London: Demos.

Lewis, P, I Black 2013. Reporting and scrutiny of reported cases in four jurisdictions where assisted dying is lawful: a review of the evidence in the Netherlands, Belgium, Oregon and Switzerland. *Medical Law International* 13(4): 221–239.

Lewy, G 2011. *Assisted Death in Europe and America: Four Regimes and Their Lessons*. Oxford UP.

Lillehammer, H. Voluntary euthanasia and the logical slippery slope argument. *Cambridge Law Journal* 61: 545–550.

Lin, E 2016. How to use the experience machine. *Utilitas* 28(3): 314–332.

Lindsay, R 2009. Oregon's experience: evaluating the record. *American Journal of Bioethics* 9(3): 19–27.

Lippert-Rasmussen, K 2007. Why killing some people is more seriously wrong than killing others. *Ethics* 117: 716–738.

Lipuma, SH, JP DeMarco 2015. Expanding the use of continuous sedation until death: moving beyond the last resort for the terminally ill. *Journal of Clinical Ethics* 26(2): 121–131.

Lloyd-Williams, M, J Reeve, D Kissane 2008. Distress in palliative care patients: developing patient-centred approaches to clinical management. *European Journal of Cancer* 44(8): 1133–1138.

Locke, J 1988. *Two Treatises of Government*. P Laslett ed. Cambridge UP.

Loewy, EH 2001. Terminal sedation, self-starvation, and orchestrating the end of life. *Archives Internal Medicine* 161: 329–332.

Loggers, ET, H Starks, M Shannon-Dudly et al. 2013. Implementing a death with dignity program at a comprehensive cancer center. *New England Journal of Medicine* 368: 417–424.

Lonnqvist, JK 2009. Epidemiology and causes of suicide. In: MG Gelder, NC Andreasen, JJ Lopez-Ibor Jr., JR Geddes eds. *New Oxford Textbook of Psychiatry*, vol. 1. Oxford UP: 951–957.

Luban, D 2009. Human dignity, humiliation and torture. *Kennedy Institute of Ethics Journal* 19: 211–230.

Lukow, P 2018. A difficult legacy: human dignity and the founding value of human rights. *Human Rights Review* 19: 313–329.

Luper, S 2009. *The Philosophy of Death*. Cambridge UP.

Maas, PJ van der, JJM van Delden, L Pijnenborg, Euthanasia and other medical decisions concerning end of life. *Health Policy* 1992; 22(special issue:1–2):3–262.

Mack, JW, M Nilsson, T Balboni et al. 2008. Peace, equanimity, and acceptance in the cancer experience (PEACE): validation of a scale to assess acceptance and struggle with terminal illness. *Cancer* 112(11): 2509–2517.

Mackenzie, C, N Stoljar 2000. *Relational Autonomy: Feminist Perspectives on Autonomy, Agency and the Social Self*. Oxford UP.

Mackenzie, C 2008. Relational autonomy, normative authority and perfectionism. *Journal of Social Philosophy* 39: 512–553.

MacQuarrie, CR 2005. Experiences in early stage Alzheimer's disease: Understanding the paradox of acceptance and denial. *Aging & Mental Health*, 9: 430–441.

Magnusson, RS 2002. *Angels of Death: Exploring the Euthanasia Underground*. New Haven, CT: Yale UP.

Magnusson, RS 2004. Euthanasia: above ground, below ground. *Journal of Medical Ethics* 30: 441–446.

Magnusson, RS 2009. The traditional account of ethics at the end of life – and its discontents. *Bioethical Inquiry* 6: 307–324.

Mak, YY, G Elwyn 2005. Voices of the terminally ill: uncovering the meaning of desire for euthanasia. *Palliative Medicine* 19(4): 343–350.

Malpas, PJ, K Mitchell, H Koschwanez 2015. End-of-life medical decision making in general practice in New Zealand: 13 years on. *New Zealand Medical Journal* 128: 1418–1427.

Maltoni, M, E Scarpi, M Rosati et al. 2012. Palliative sedation in end-of-life care and survival: a systematic review. *Journal of Clinical Oncology* 30(12): 1378–1383.

Mann, JJ 2002. A current perspective of suicide and attempted suicide. *Annals of Internal Medicine* 136: 302–311.

Marquis, D 1998. The weakness of the case for legalizing physician-assisted suicide. In: Battin, Rhodes, Silver eds.

Marson, DC, B McInturff, L Hawkins et al. 1997. Consistency of physician judgments of capacity to consent in mild Alzheimer's disease. *American Geriatrics Society* 45: 453–457.

Martinez, M, M Arantzamendi, A Belar et al. 2017. 'Dignity therapy': a promising intervention in palliative care: a comprehensive systematic literature review. *Palliative Medicine* 31: 492–509.

van Marwijk, H, I Haverkate, P van Royen, AM The 2007. Impact of euthanasia on primary care physicians in the Netherlands. *Palliative Medicine* 21(7): 609–614.

Marzuk, PM et al. 1993. Increase in suicide by asphyxation *New England Journal of Medicine* 329: 1508–1510.

Mashour, GA ed. 2010. *Consciousness, Awareness and Anesthesia.* Cambridge UP.

Massachusetts Protocol 2005. *Hospice and Palliative Care Federation of Massachusetts: Palliative Sedation Protocol: A Report of the Standards and Best Practices Committee*, https://cdn.ymaws.com/www.hospicefed.org/resource/resmgr/hpcfm_pdf_doc/pal_sed_protocol_2004.pdf.

Materstvedt, LJ 2003. Palliative care on the 'slippery slope' towards euthanasia? *Palliative Medicine* 17: 387–392.

Materstvedt, LJ, G Bosshardt 2009a. Deep and continuous palliative sedation (terminal sedation): clinical-ethical and philosophical aspects. *Lancet* 10(9): 622–627.

Materstvedt, LJ, G Bosshardt. 2009b. Euthanasia and physician-assisted suicide. In: G Hanks, N Cherny, N Christakis et al. eds. *Oxford Textbook of Palliative Medicine*, fourth edition. Oxford UP.

Matthijssen, TJ 2019. Euthanasie bij gevorderde dementie: een belangrijke uitspraak. *Tijdschrift voor Gezondheidsrecht* 43: 46–58.

May, SC 2015. Directed duties. *Philosophy Compass* 10: 523–532.

Mayo, DJ 1986. The concept of rational suicide. *Journal of Medicine and Philosophy* 11: 143–155.

Mayo, DJ, M Gunderson 2002. Vitalism revitalized: vulnerable populations, prejudices, and physician-assisted death. *Hastings Center Report* 32(4): 14–21.

McCann, RM, WJ Hall, A Groth-Juncker 1994. Comfort care for terminally ill patients: the appropriate use of nutrition and hydration. *JAMA* 272(16): 1263–1266.

McCormick, RA 1977. *Ambiguity in Moral Choice.* Milwaukee: Marquette UP.

McCrudden, C 2013. In pursuit of human dignity: an introduction to current debates. In: C McCrudden ed. *Understanding Human Dignity.* Oxford UP.

McGee, A, FG Miller 2017. Advice and care for patients who die by voluntarily stopping eating and drinking is not assisted suicide. *BMC Medicine* 15: 222.

McInerney, F 1992. Provision of food and fluids in terminal care: a sociological analysis. *Social Science and Medicine* 34(11): 1271–1276.

McIntyre, A 2004. The double life of double effect. *Theoretical Medicine and Bioethics* 25: 61–74.

McIntyre, A 2014. Doctrine of double effect. In: *Stanford Encyclopedia of Philosophy.*

McMahan, J 2002. *The Ethics of Killing: Problems at the Margins of Life.* Oxford UP.

McMahan, J 2007. Challenges to human equality. *The Journal of Ethics* 12: 81–104.

McPherson, CJ, KG Wilson, MA Murray 2007. Feeling like a burden to others: a systematic review focusing on the end of life. *Palliative Medicine* 21: 115–128.

van der Meer, S 2011. Rol SCEN-arts te ruim opgevat. *Medisch Contact* 66: 939–942.

Meeussen, K, L van den Block, N Bossuyt et al. 2010. Physician reports of medication use with explicit intention of hastening the end of life in the absence of explicit patient request in general practice in Belgium. *BMC Public Health* 10: 186–198.

Meeussen, K, L van den Block, N Bossuyt et al. 2011. Dealing with requests for euthanasia: interview study among general practitioners in Belgium. *Journal of Pain and Symptom Management* 41: 1060–1071.

Meier, DE, CA Emmons, A Litke et al. 2003. Characteristics of patients requesting and receiving physician-assisted death. *Archives of Internal Medicine* 163(13): 1537–1542.

Meier, DE, CA Emmons, S Wallenstein et al. 1998. A national survey of physician-assisted suicide and euthanasia in the United States. *New England Journal of Medicine* 338(17): 1193–1201.

Meier, EA, J Gallegos, LP Montross-Thomas et al. 2016. Defining a good death (successful dying): literature review and a call for research and public dialogue. *American Journal of Geriatric Psychiatry* 24(4): 261–271.

Menzel, P, B Steinbock 2013. Advance directives, dementia, and physician-assisted death. *Journal of Law, Medicine and Ethics* 41(2): 484–500.

Menzel, PT 2017. Voluntarily stopping eating and drinking: a normative comparison with refusing life-saving treatment and advance directives. *Journal of Law, Medicine and Ethics* 45: 634–646.

Menzel, PT 2019. AEDs are problematic, but Mrs A is a misleading case. *Journal of Medical Ethics* 45(2): 90–91.

Mercadante, S, G Porzio, A Valle et al. 2012. Palliative sedation in advanced cancer patients followed at home: a retrospective analysis. *Journal of Pain and Symptom Management* 43(6): 1126–1130.

Merry, AF, M Moharib, DA Devcich et al. 2013. Doctors' willingness to give honest answers about end-of-life practices: a cross-sectional study. *BMJ Open* 3(5): e2002598.

Mertens, T 2015. Kant and the ends of life. In: D Dall'Agnol, MC Tonetto eds. *Morality and Life, Kantian Perspectives in Bioethics*. Pisa: Edizione ETS.

Mevis, PAM, SR Bakker, L Postma, JHJ Verbaan 2014. *Schriftelijke wilsverklaring euthanasie bij wilsonbekwame patiënten: een jurisprudentieonderzoek*. WODC, Ministerie van Veiligheid en Justitie.

Meynen, G 2011. Depression, possibilities and competence: a phenomenological perspective. *Theoretical Medicine and Bioethics* 32: 181–193.

Miccinesi, G, A Caraceni, JA Raho et al. 2015. Careful monitoring of the use of sedative drugs at the end of life: the role of epidemiology. The ITAELD study. *Minerva Anestesiologica* 81: 968–979.

Miccinesi, G, D Puliti, E Paci 2011. Cura di fine vita e decisioni medicali: lo studio ITAELD (end-of-life care and end-of-life decisions: the ITAELD study). *Epidemiologica & Prevenzione* 35(3–4): 178–187, with English abstract.

Miccinesi, G, JAC Rietjens, L Deliëns et al. 2006. Continuous deep sedation: physicians' experiences in six European countries. *Journal of Pain and Symptom Management* 31(2): 122–129.

Mill, JS 1956. *On Liberty*. Indianapolis, IN: Bobbs-Merrill. (1859).

Miller, DG, R Dresser, SYH Kim 2019. Advance euthanasia directives: a controversial case and its ethical implications. *Journal of Medical Ethics* 45: 84–89.

Miller, DG, SYH Kim 2017. Euthanasia and physician-assisted suicide not meeting due care criteria in the Netherlands: a qualitative review of review committee judgements. *BMJ Open* 7(10): e017628.

Miller, FG, DE Meier 1998. Voluntary death: a comparison of terminal dehydration and physician-assisted suicide. *Annals Internal Medicine* 128: 559–562.

Miller FG, RD Truog 2012. *Death, Dying, and Organ Transplantation: Reconstructing Medical Ethics at the End of Life*. Oxford UP.

Minois, G 1999. *History of Suicide: Voluntary Death in Western Culture*. Baltimore, MD: Johns Hopkins UP.

Mishara, BL, DN Weinstein 2016. The legal status of suicide: a global review. *International Journal of Law and Psychiatry* 44: 54–74.

Mitchell, K, G Owens 2004. End of life decision-making by New Zealand general practitioners: a national survey. *New Zealand Medical Journal*. 117.1196. (Available online)

Mitchell, S 2007. A 93-year-old man with advanced dementia and eating problems. *JAMA* 298: 2527–2536.

Miyashita, M, S Kawakami, D Kato et al. 2015. The importance of good death components among cancer patients, the general population, oncologists, and oncology nurses in Japan: patients prefer 'fighting against cancer'. *Support Care Cancer* 23: 103–110.

Miyashita, M, M Sanjo, T Morita et al. 2007. Good death in cancer care: a nationwide quantitative study. *Annals of Oncology* 18: 1090–1097.

Mokrosinska, D 2012. *Rethinking Political Obligation: Moral Principles, Communal Ties, Citizenship*. London: Palgrave Macmillan.

Monballyu, J 2014. *Six Centuries of Criminal Law: History of Criminal Law in the Southern Netherlands and Belgium (1400–2000)*. Leiden: Brill.

Monforte-Royo, C, V Villavicencio-Chávez, J Tomás-Sábado et al. 2012. What lies behind the wish to hasten death? A systematic review and meta-ethnography from the perspective of patients. *PLoS One* 7(5): e37117.

Montero, E 2017. The Belgian experience of euthanasia since its legal implementation in 2002. In: Jones, Gastmans, MacKellar eds.

Moonen, L, R Kloosterman 2019. *Opvattingen over Euthanasie*. CBS.

Morita, T 2004. Palliative sedation to relieve psycho-existential suffering of terminally ill cancer patients. *Journal of Pain and Symptom Management* 28: 445–450.

Morita, T, T Akechi, Y Sugawara et al. 2002. Practices and attitudes of Japanese oncologists and palliative care physicians concerning terminal sedation: a nationwide survey. *Journal of Clinical Oncology* 20(3): 758–764.

Morita, T, S Bito, Y Kurihara, Y Uchitomi 2005a. Development of a clinical guideline for palliative sedation therapy using the Delphi method. *Journal of Palliative Medicine* 8: 716–729.

Morita, T, Y Chinone, M Ikenaga et al. 2005b. Efficacy and safety of palliative sedation therapy: a multicenter, prospective, observational study conducted on specialized palliative care units in Japan. *Journal of Pain and Symptom Management* 30: 320–328.

Morita, T, Y Sakaguchi, K Hirai et al. 2004. Desire for death and requests to hasten death of Japanese terminally ill cancer patients receiving specialized inpatient palliative care. *Journal of Pain and Symptom Management* 27: 44–52.

Morita, T, Y Tei, S Inoue 2003. Ethical validity of palliative sedation therapy. *Journal of Pain and Symptom Management* 25: 103–105.

Morita, T, S Tsuneto, Y Shima 2001. Proposed definitions for terminal sedation. *The Lancet* 358: 335–336.

Morita, T, J Tsunoda, S Inoue, S Chihara 2000. An exploratory factor analysis of existential suffering in Japanese terminally ill cancer patients. *Psycho-Oncology* 9: 164–168.

Mortier, F, L Deliëns, J Bilsen et al. 2000. *End-of-life decisions of physicians in the City of Hasselt* (Flanders, Belgium). *Bioethics* 14: 254–267.

Moskop, JC 2021. Voluntarily stopping eating and drinking: conceptual, personal, and policy questions. *Journal of Medicine and Philosophy* 46: 805–826.

Moss, SZ, MS Moss, HK Black, RL Rubenstein 2005. How family members respond to residents' wish to die. *Omega: Journal of Death & Dying* 51(4): 301–321.

Moye, J, MJ Karel, AR Azar, RJ Gurrera 2004. Capacity to consent to treatment: empirical comparison of three instruments in older adults with and without dementia. *Gerontologist* 44(2): 166–175.

Musschenga, B 2019. Is there a problem with false hope? *Journal of Medicine and Philosophy* 44: 423–441.

Nagel, T 1970. Death. *Noûs* 4(1): 73–80, reprinted in: T Nagel, *Mortal Questions*. Cambridge UP 1979; and in: Fischer ed. 1993.

Nagel, T 1986. *The View from Nowhere*. Oxford UP.

National Comprehensive Cancer Network 2013. *Clinical Practice Guidelines in Oncology: Palliative Care Journal of the National Comprehensive Cancer Network* 2009(7.4): 436–473.

National Hospice and Palliative Care Organization 2010. NHPCO position statement and commentary on the use of palliative sedation in imminently dying terminally ill patients. *Journal of Pain and Symptom Management* 39: 914–923.

Nauck, F, C Ostgathe, L Radbruch 2014. Hilfe beim Sterben- keine Hilfe zum Sterben. *Deutsches Ärzteblatt* 111(3): A67–A71.

NEC-VHA 2006. The Ethics Palliative Sedation: A Report by the National Ethics Committee of the Veterans Health Administration. American *Journal of Hospice and Palliative Care* 23 (6): 483–491.

Nederlandse Vereniging van Verpleeghuisartsen (NVVA) 1997. *Medische zorg met beleid. Handreiking voor de besluitvorming over verpleeghuisgeneeskundig handelen bij dementerende patiënten.* Utrecht: NVVA.

Nederlandse Vereniging voor Psychiatrie 2009. *Richtlijn verzoek om hulp bij zelfdoding door patiënten met een psychiatrischa aandoening.* Second ed. (first edition 1998). Utrecht: de Tijdstroom.

Nederlandse Vereniging voor Psychiatrie 2018. *Richtlijn Levensbeëindiging op verzoek bij patiënten met een psychistrische stoornis*, https://richtlijnendatabase.nl/richtlijn/levensbeeindiging_op_verzoek_psychiatrie/startpagina_-_levensbe_indiging_op_verzoek.html.

Neil, DA, CAJ Coady, J Thompson, H Kuhse 2007. End-of-life decisions in medical practice: a survey of doctors in Victoria (Australia). *Journal of Medical Ethics* 33(12): 721–725.

Neitzke, G, M Coors, W Diemer et al. 2013. Empfehlungen zum Umgang mit dem Wunsch nach Suizidhilfe Arbeitsgruppe "Ethik am Lebensende" in der Akademie für Ethik in der Medizin e.V. (AEM). *Ethik in der Medizin* 25: 349–365.

Neitzke, G, F Oehmichen, HJ Schliep, D Wördehoff 2010. Sedierung am Lebensende: Empfehlungen der AG Ethik am Lebensende in der Akademie für Ethik in der Medizin (AEM). *Ethik in Der Medizin* 22: 139–147.

New Tork State Taskforce on Life and the Law. 1994. *When Death Is Sought: Assisted Suicide and Euthanasia in the Medical Context.* New York Department of Health.

Nicholson, C, J Meyer, M Flatley et al. 2012. Living on the margin: understanding the experience of living and dying with frailty in old age. *Social Science and Medicine* 75: 426–432.

Nicolini, M, JR Peteet, G Donovan et al. 2020. Euthanasia and assisted suicide of persons with psychiatric disorders: the challenge of personality disorders. *Psychological Medicine* 50(4): 575–582.

Nissim, R, L Gagliese, G Rodin 2009. The desire for hastened death in individuals with advanced cancer: a longitudinal qualitative study. *Social Science and Medicine* 69: 165–171.

NMA (Norwegian Medical Association) 2001. Medical Ethics Council: guidelines for palliative sedation of the dying. Reprinted in: Tännsjö ed., Appendix.

Nolan, M, T Ryan, P Enderby et al. 2002. Towards a more inclusive vision of dementia care practice and research. *Dementia* 1: 193–212.

van der Noortgate, N, P vanden Berghe, J de Leipeleire 2016. Oud en moe van dagen: levensmoeheid bij ouderen. *Tijdschrift voor Geneeskunde* 72(3): 145–157.

Noreika, V, L Jylhuankangas, L Móró et al. 2011. Consciousness lost and found: subjective experiences in an unresponsive state. *Brain and Cognition* 77(3): 327–334.

Norwood, F 2009. *The Maintenance of Life: Preventing Social Death Through Euthanasia Talk and End-of-Life Care – Lessons from the Netherlands.* Durham: Carolina Academia Press.

Norwood, F 2018. The new normal: mediated death and assisted dying in the United States. In: ACGM Robben ed. *A Companion to the Anthropology of Death*. Hoboken, NJ: John Wiley & Sons, ch. 32.

Norwood, F, G Kimsma, MP Battin 2009. Vulnerability and the 'slippery slope' at the end-of-life: a qualitative study of euthanasia, general practice and home death in the Netherlands. *Family Practice* 26: 472–480.

Nozick, R 1971. On the Randian Argument. In: *The Personalist*, reprinted in J Paul ed., *Reading Nozick*. Totowa, NJ: Rowman & Littlefield, 1981.

Nozick, R 1974. *Anarchy, State, and Utopia*. New York, NY: Basic Books.

Nozick, R 1989. *The Examined Life*. New York, NY: Simon & Schuster.

Nuhn, A, S Holmes, M Kelly et al. 2018. Experiences and perspectives of people who pursued medical assistance in dying. *Canadian Family Physician* 64: e380–e386.

Nys, H 2017. A discussion of the legal rules on euthanasia in Belgium briefly compared with the rules in Luxemburg and the Netherlands. In: Jones, Gastmans, MacKellar eds.

Nys, HFL 2007. Euthanasie: de toekomst van het Belgische model, *Tijdschrift voor Gezondheidsrecht* 31: 149–152.

Nys, TRV 2013. The wreckage of our flesh: dementia, autonomy, and personhood. In: Y Denier, C Gastmans, A Vandevelde eds.

Nys, TRV 2016. Autonomy, trust, and respect. *Journal of Medicine and Philosophy* 41: 10–24.

O'Neill, O 1996. *Towards Justice and Virtue: A Constructive Account of Practical Reason*. Cambridge UP.

O'Neill, O 2002. *Autonomy and Trust in Bioethics*. Cambridge UP.

O'Connell, H, A-V Chin, C Cunningham, BA Lawlor 2004. Recent developments: suicide in older people. *BMJ* 329(7471): 895–899.

O'Keeffe, TM 1998. Suicide and self-starvation. (First publ. 1981) In: Donnelly ed.

Oi-Ling, K, D Man-Wah, D Kam-Hung 2005. Symptom distress as rated by advanced cancer patients, caregivers and physicians in the last week of life. *Palliative Medicine* 19(3): 228–233.

Okai, D, G Owen, H McGuire et al. 2007. Mental capacity in psychiatric patients: systematic review. *British Journal of Psychiatry* 191: 291–297.

Okninski, ME, J Grieger 2021. Evolving law: further developments concerning MAID in Canada. *Bioethical Inquiry* 18: 371–376.

Okonkwo, O, HR Griffiths, K Belue et al. 2007. Medical decision-making capacity in patients with mild cognitive impairment. *Neurology* 69: 1528–1535.

Olsen, ML, KM Swetz, PS Mueller 2010. Ethical decision making with end-of-life care: palliative sedation and withholding or withdrawing life-sustaining treatments. *Mayo Clinic Proceedings* 85: 949–954.

Olsen, JM 2006. Depression, SSRIs, and the supposed obligation to suffer mentally. *Kennedy Institute of Ethics Journal* 16: 283–303.

Olsman, E, C Leget, B Onwuteaka-Philipsen, D Willems 2014. Should palliative care patients' hope be truthful, helpful or valuable? An interpretative synthesis of literature describing healthcare professionals' perspectives on hope of palliative care patients. *Palliative Medicine* 28(1): 59–70.

Onwuteaka-Philipsen, B, J Legemaate, A van der Heide et al 2017. *Derde Evaluatie Wet Toetsing Levensbeëindiging op Verzoek en Hulp bij Zelfdoding.* Den Haag: ZonMw.

Onwuteaka-Philipsen, BD, HM Buiting, HRW Pasman et al. 2010. *Evaluatie van SCEN: Wat is goede steun en consultatie?*

Onwuteaka-Philipsen, BD, JKM Gevers, A van der Heide et al. 2007. *Evaluatie Wet Toetsing Levensbeëindiging op Verzoek en Hulp bij Zelfdoding.* Den Haag: ZonMw.

Orde der Artsen 2019. *Deontologische richtlijnen voor de toepassing van euthanasie bij patiënten die psychisch lijden ten gevolge van een psychiatrische aandoening*,https://ordomedic.be/nl/adviezen/ethiek/euthanasie/deontologische-richtlijnen-voor-de-toepassing-van-euthanasie-bij-patiënten-die-psychisch-lijden-ten-gevolge-van-een-psychiatrische-aandoening.

van Orden, KA, TK Witte, KC Cukrowicz et al. 2010. The interpersonal theory of suicide. *Psychological Review* 117(2): 575–600.

Oregon Health Authority. 1998 ff. *Oregon Death with Dignity Act Data Summary* (Annual reports).

Orentlichter, D 1989. Physician participation in assisted suicide. *Journal of the American Medical Association* 262: 1844–1845.

Orentlicher, D 1998. The Supreme Court and terminal sedation: rejecting assisted suicide, embracing euthanasia. *Hastings Constitutional Law Quarterly* 24: 947–968.

Orentlicher, D 2013. Principles and practice for palliative sedation: gaps between the two. In: Sterckx, Raus, F Mortier eds.

Orentlicher, D, TM Pope, BA Rich 2016. Clinical criteria for physician aid in dying. *Journal of Palliative Medicine* 19: 259–262.

Ost, S 2010. The de-medicalisation of assisted suicide: is a less medicalised model the way forward? *Medical Law Review* 18(4): 4497–4540.

Otlowski, MFA 1997. *Voluntary Euthanasia and the Common Law.* Oxford: Clarendon Press.

Owen, GS, G Richardson, AS David et al. 2008. Mental capacity to make decisions on treatment in people admitted to psychiatric hospitals: cross-sectional study. *BMJ* 337: a448.

Pans, E 2006. *De Normatieve Grondslagen van het Nederlandse Euthanasierecht*. Tilburg: Wolf Legal Publishing.
Papavasiliou, E, K Chambaere, L Deliëns et al. 2014. Physician-reported practices on continuous deep sedation until death: a descriptive and comparative study. *Palliative Medicine* 28(6): 491–500.
Parfit, D 1984. *Reasons and Persons*. Oxford UP.
Pasman, HR, MJ Rurup, DL Willems, BD Onwuteaka-Philipsen 2009. Concept of unbearable suffering in context with patients and physicians. *BMJ* 339: b4362.
Pasman, HRW 2012. When requests do not result in euthanasia or assisted suicide. In: Youngner, Kimsma eds.
Passik, SD, W Dugan, MV McDonald et al. 1998. Oncologists' recognition of depression in their patients with cancer. *Journal of Clinical Oncology* 16: 1594–1600.
Patrick, DL, RA Engelberg, JR Curtis 2001. Evaluating the quality of dying and death. *Journal of Pain and Symptom Management* 22: 717–726.
Patterson, KM., C Clarke, EL Wolverson, ED Moniz-Cook 2018. Through the eyes of others–the social experiences of people with dementia: a systematic literature review and synthesis. *International Psychogeriatrics* 30: 791–805.
Pearlman, RA, C Hsu, H Starks et al. 2005. Motivations for physician-assisted suicide. *Journal of General Internal Medicine* 20: 234–239.
Pellegrino, ED 1992. Doctors must not kill. *Journal of Clinical Ethics* 3(2): 95–102.
Pellegrino, ED 1998. The false promise of beneficent killing. In: L Emanuel ed. *Regulating How We Die*. Cambridge: Harvard UP.
Pellegrino, ED 2001. Physician-assisted suicide and euthanasia: rebuttals of rebuttals. *Journal of Medicine and Philosophy* 26: 93–100.
Pennec, S, A Monnier, S Pontone, R Aubry 2012. End-of-life medical decisions in France: a death certificate follow-up survey 5 years after the 2005 Act of parliament on patients' rights and end of life. *BMC Palliative Care* 11(1): 1–13.
Pesut, B, S Thorne, DK Wright et al. 2021a. Navigating medical assistance in dying from Bill C-14 to Bill C-7: a qualitative study. *BMC Health Services Research* 21: 1195.
Pesut, B, DK Wright, S Thorne et al. 2021b. What's suffering got to do with it? A qualitative study of suffering in the context of MAID. *BMC Palliative Care* 20: 174.
Peterman, AH, G Fitchett, MJ Brady et al. 2002. Measuring Spiritual well-being in people with cancer: the functional assessment of chronic illness therapy. Spiritual Wellbeing Scale (FACIT-Sp). *Annals of Behavioral Medicine* 24: 49–58.
Peters, J, E Sutorius et al. 2011. *Uit Vrije Wil: Waardig Sterven op Hoge Leeftijd*. Amsterdam: Boom.
Phillips, PA, BJ Rolls, JGG Ledingham et al. 1984. Reducing thirst after water deprivation in healthy elderly men. *New England Journal of Medicine* 311(12): 753–759.
Pitcher, G 1984. The misfortunes of the dead. *American Philosophical Quarterly* 21: 183–188. Reprinted in: Fischer ed.
Pivodic, L, L van den Block, K Pardon et al. 2014. Burden on family carers and care-related financial strain at the end of life: a cross-national population-based study. *European Journal of Public Health* 24(5): 819–826.

Pontifical Council for Health Pastoral Care 1995. *Charter for Health Care Workers*, https://www.academyforlife.va/content/dam/pav/documents/papi/documentisantasede/ENGLISH/charter_for_health_care_workers_ENG.pdf.

Pool, R 1996. *Vragen om te sterven: euthanasie in een Nederlands ziekenhuis*. Rotterdam: WYT Uitgeefgroep.

Pope, T 2018. Legal history of medical aid in dying: physician-assisted death in US courts and legislature. *New Mexico Law Review* 48: 267.

Pope, TM, LE Anderson 2011. Voluntarily stopping eating and drinking: a legal treatment option at the end of life. *Widener Law Review* 17: 363.

Post, S 1995. Alzheimer disease and the "then" self. *Kennedy Institute of Ethics Journal* 5: 307–321.

Post, S 2000. Key issues in the ethics of dementia care. *Neurologic Clinics* 18: 1011–1022.

Preston, R 2018. Death on demand? An analysis of physicians-administered euthanasia in the Netherlands. *British Medical Bulletin* 125: 145–155.

Putman, MS, JD Yoon, KA Rasinski, FA Curlin 2013. Intentional sedation to unconsciousness at the end of life: findings from a national physician survey. *Journal of Pain and Symptom Management* 46(3): 326–334.

Putz, W, B Stelldinger 2012. *Patientenrechte am Ende des Lebens*, 4te Auflage. München: Deutscher Taschenbuch Verlag.

Pype, P, I Teuwen, F Mertens et al. 2018. Suboptimal palliative sedation in primary care: an exploration. *Acta Clinica Belgica* 73: 21–28.

Quill, TE 1993. The ambiguity of clinical intentions. *New England Journal of Medicine* 329(14): 1039–1040.

Quill, TE 2007. Physician-assisted death in vulnerable populations. *BMJ* 335(7621): 65–66.

Quill, TE 2015. Voluntary Stopping Eating and Drinking (VSED): physician-assisted death (PAD), or neither in the last stage of life? *Annals of Family Medicine* 13(5): 408–409.

Quill, TE, IR Byock 2000. Responding to intractable terminal suffering: the role of terminal sedation and voluntary refusal of food and fluids. ACP-ASIM End-of-Life Care Consensus Panel, American College of Physicians-American Society of Internal Medicine. *Annals of Internal Medicine* 132(5): 408–414.

Quill, TE, CK Cassel, DE Meier 1992. Care of the hopelessly ill: proposed clinical criteria for physician-assisted suicide. *New England Journal of Medicine* 327(19): 1380–1384.

Quill, TE, L Ganzini, RD Truog et al. 2018. Voluntarily stopping eating and drinking among patients with serious advanced illness-clinical, ethical, and legal aspects. *JAMA Internal Medicine* 178(1): 123–127.

Quill, TE, BC Lee, S Nunn 2000. Palliative treatments of last resort: choosing the least harmful alternative. University of Pennsylvania Center for Bioethics Assisted Suicide Consensus Panel. *Annals of Internal Medicine* 132: 488–493.

Quill, TE, B Lo, DW Brock, A Meisel 2009. Last-resort options for palliative sedation. *Annals of Internal Medicine* 151: 421–424.

Quill, TE, B Lo, DW Brock 1997. Palliative options of last resort: a comparison of voluntarily stopping eating and drinking, terminal sedation, physician-assisted suicide and voluntary active euthanasia. *JAMA* 278(23): 2099–2104.

Rachels, J 1980. Euthanasia. In: Regan ed.

Radbruch, L, C Leget, P Bahr et al. 2016. Euthanasia and physician-assisted suicide: a white paper from the European Association for Palliative Care. *Palliative Medicine* 30(2): 104–116.

Radbruch, L, L de Lima 2017. International Association for Hospice and Palliative Care Response regarding voluntary cessation of food and water. *Journal of Palliative Medicine* 20(6): 578–579.

Rady, MY, JL Verheijde 2010. Continuous deep sedation until death: palliation or physician-assisted death? *American Journal of Hospice and Palliative Medicine* 27(3): 205–214.

Rady, MY, JL Verheijde 2011. Distress from voluntary refusal of food and fluids to hasten death: what is the role of continuous deep sedation? *Journal of Medical Ethics* 38(8): 510–512.

Ramsey, P 1978. Incommensurability and indeterminacy in choice. In: R MacCormick, P Ramsey eds. *Doing Evil to Achieve Good*. Chicago, IL: Loyola UP.

Raus, K, K Chambaere, S Sterckx 2016. Controversies surrounding deep sedation at the end of life: the parliamentary and social debates in France. *BMC Medical Ethics* 17(1): 36.

Raus, K, M de Laat, F Mortier, S Sterckx, 2013. The clinical and ethical importance of measuring consciousness: the case of sedation at the end of life. In: K Raus ed. *Continuous Sedation at the End of Life: Practice, Perspectives and Ethical Analyses*. Thesis, University of Ghent, ch. 7.

Raus, K, S Sterckx, F Mortier 2012. Continuous deep sedation at the end of life and the 'natural death' hypothesis. *Bioethics* 26(6): 329–336.

Raus, K, B Vanderhaegen, S Sterckx 2021. Euthanasia in Belgium: shortcomings of the law and it application and of the monitoring of practice. *Journal of Medicine and Philosophy* 46: 80–107.

Rauscher, F 2002. Kant's moral anti-realism. *Journal of the History of Ideas* 4440(4): 477–499.

Rawls, J 1951. Outline of a decision method for ethics. *Philosophical Review* 60(2): 177–197.

Raz, J 1972. Normative powers and voluntary obligations. *Proceedings of the Aristotelian Society Supplementary Volume* 46: 79–102.

Raz, J 1997. Incommensurability and agency. In R Chang ed. *Incommensurability, Incomparability, and Practical Reason*. Cambridge: Harvard UP.

Raz, J 2001. *Value, Respect and Attachment*. Cambridge UP.

Raz, J 2013. Death in our life. *Journal of Applied Philosophy* 30(1): 1–11.

Regan, T ed. 1980. *Matters of Life and Death: New Introductory Essays in Moral Philosophy*. New York: Random House, 2nd ed.

Reisfield, GM, GR Wilson 2004. Use of metaphors in the discourse on cancer. *Journal of Clinical Oncology* 22(19): 4024–4027.

Rhoden, NK 1990. The limits of legal objectivity. *North Carolina Law Review* 68: 845–865.

Rhodes, R 2007. A Kantian duty to commit suicide and its implications for bioethics. *American Journal of Bioethics* 7: 45–47.

Rich, BA 2012. Terminal suffering and the ethics of palliative sedation. *Cambridge Quarterly of Healthcare Ethics* 21: 30–39.

Richardson, LA, GW Jones 2009. A review of the reliability and validity of the Edmonton Symptom Assessment System. *Current Oncology* 16: 53–64.

Rietjens, JA, J van Delden, B Onwuteaka-Philipsen et al. 2008. Continuous deep sedation for patients nearing death in the Netherlands: descriptive study. *British Medical Journal* 336(7648): 810–813.

Rietjens, J, A van der Heide, B Onwuteaka-Philipsen et al. 2006. Preferences of the Dutch general public for a good death and associations with attitudes toward end-of-life decision-making. *Palliative Medicine* 20: 685–692.

Rietjens, JA, A van der Heide, AM Vrakking, BD Onwuteaka-Philipsen et al. 2004. Physician reports of terminal sedation without hydration or nutrition for patients nearing death in the Netherlands. *Annals of Internal Medicine* 141: 178–185.

Rietjens, JA, DG van Tol, M Schermer, A van der Heide 2009. Judgement of suffering in the case of a euthanasia request in the Netherlands. *Journal of Medical Ethics* 35(8): 502–507.

Riisfeldt, TD 2019. Weakening the ethical distinction between euthanasia, palliative opioid use and palliative sedation. *Journal of Medical Ethics* 45: 125–130.

van der Rijt, JW 2016. Inherent dignity, contingent dignity and human rights: solving the puzzle of the protection of dignity. *Erkenntnis* 82: 1321–1338.

Riou, F, A Régis, S Pontone, S Pennec 2015. When physicians report having used medical drugs to deliberately end a patient's life: findings of the 'End-of-life in France' survey. *Journal of Pain and Symptom Management* 50: 208–215.

Robijn, L, K Chambaere, K Raus et al. 2017. Reasons for continuous sedation until death in cancer patients: a qualitative interview study. *European Journal of Cancer Care* 26(1): e12405.

Robijn, L, J Cohen, J Rietjens et al. 2016. Trends in continuous deep sedation until death between 2007 and 2013: a repeated nationwide survey. *PLoS One* 11(6): e0158188.

Robins, E 1981. *The Final Months: A Study of the Lives of 134 Persons Who Committed Suicide*. Oxford UP.

Rockwood, K, DB Hogan, C MacKnight 2000. Conceptualisation and measurement of frailty in elderly people. *Drugs Aging* 17: 295–302.

Rodrigues, P, J Crokaert, C Gastmans 2018. Palliative sedation for existential suffering: a systematic review of argument-based ethics literature. *Journal of Pain and Symptom Management* 55: 1577–1590.

Rodriguez-Pratt, A, A Balaguer, A Booth, C Monforte-Roya 2017. Understanding patient's experiences of the wish to hasten death: an undated and expanded systematic review and meta-ethnography. *BMJ Open* 7(9): e016659.

Roest, B, M Trappenburg, C Leget 2019. The involvement of family in the Dutch practice of euthanasia and physician-assisted suicide: a systematic mixed studies review. *BMC Medical Ethics* 20(1): 1–21.

Rooney, W, U Schuklenk, S van de Vathorst 2018. Are concerns about irremediability, vulnerability, or competence sufficient to justify excluding all psychiatric patients from medical aid in dying? *Health Care Analysis* 26: 326–343.

Rössler, B 2017. *Autonomie: Ein Versuch über das gelungene Leben*. Berlin: Suhrkamp.

Rousseau, S, S Turner, HM Chochinov et al. 2017. A national survey of Canadian psychiatrists' attitudes towards medical assistance in death. *Canadian Journal of Psychiatry* 62: 787–794.

Rousseau, PS 2000. The ethical validity and clinical experience of palliative sedation. *Mayo Clinical Proceedings* 75: 1064–1069.

Rowe, JW, RL Kahn 1987. Human aging: usual and successful. *Science* 237: 143–149.

RTE (Regional Euthanasia Review Commissions) 1999ff. *Annual Reports*.

Ruddick, W 1999. Hope and deception. *Bioethics* 13(3–4): 343–357.

Rudnick, A 2002. Depression and competence to refuse psychiatric treatment. *Journal of Medical Ethics* 28: 151–155.

Ruijs, CDM, AJFM Kerkhof, G van der Wal, BD Onwuteaka-Philipsen 2012. The broad spectrum of unbearable suffering in end-of-life cancer studied in Dutch primary care. *BMC Palliative Care* 11(1): 1–10.

Ruijs, CDM, BD Onwuteaka-Philipsen, G van der Wal, AJFM Kerkhof 2009. Unbearability of suffering at the end-of-life: the development of a new measuring device, the SOS-V. *BMC Palliative Care* 8(1): 1–10.

Ruijs, CDM, G van der Wal, AJFM Kerkhof, BD Onwuteaka-Philipsen 2014. Unbearable suffering and requests for euthanasia prospectively studied in end-of-life cancer patients in primary care. *BMC Palliative Care* 13(1): 1–11.

Rurup, M, S Borgsteede, A van der Heide et al. 2009. Trends in the use of opioids at the end of life and the expected effects on hastening death. *Journal of Pain and Symptom Management* 37(2): 144–155.

Rurup, ML, H Buiting, HRW Pasman et al. 2008. The reporting rate of euthanasia and physician-assisted suicide: a study of the trends. *Medical Care* 46: 1198–1202.

Rurup, ML, BD Onwuteaka-Philipsen, A van der Heide et al. 2005. Physicians' experiences with demented patients with advance euthanasia directives in the Netherlands. *Journal of the American Geriatric Society* 53: 1138–1144.

Rurup, ML, HWR Pasman, J Goedhart et al. 2011. Understanding why older people develop a wish to die. *Crisis: The Journal of Crisis Intervention and Suicide Prevention* 32(4): 204–216.

Rurup, M, CA Rhodius, SD Borgsteede et al. 2010. The use of opioids at the end of life: the knowledge level of Dutch physicians as a potential barrier to effective pain management. *BMC Palliative Care* 12: 9–23.

Sabat, SR 1998. Voices of Alzheimer's disease sufferers: a call for treatment based on personhood. *Journal of Clinical Ethics* 9: 38–51.

Sabat, SR, R Harré 1992. The construction and deconstruction of the self in Alzheimer's disease. *Aging and Society* 12: 443–461.

Sacred Congregation for the Doctrine of the Faith 1980. Declaration on euthanasia. In: Tännsjö ed., Appendix.

Sainsbury, PBM, B Barraclough 1968. Differences between suicide rates. *Nature* 220: 1252.

Salem, T 1999, Physician-assisted suicide: promoting autonomy or medicalizing suicide? *Hastings Center Report* 29.3: 30–36.

Sandeen, PJA 2013. *Public Opinion and the Oregon Death with Dignity Act*. Dissertations and Theses, Paper 1015.

Sanz, TRV, PP Pastor, B Moreno-Milán et al. 2021. Spanish regulation of euthanasia and physician-assisted suicide. *Journal of Medical Ethics*. Publ. online 30/7/2021.

Satalkar, P, S van der Geest 2020. Escaping the 'unprepared generation' trap: discussions about euthanasia after a 'completed life' in the Netherlands. *Mortality* 25(3): 282–296.

Savulescu, J, U Schuklenk 2016. Doctors have no right to refuse medical assistance in dying, abortion and contraception. *Bioethics* 31(3): 162–170.

Scanlon, T 1998. *What We Owe to Each Other*. Belknap Press of Harvard UP.
Scarre, G 2007. Death. Montreal/Kingston: McGill-Queen's UP.
Scarre, G 2012. Can there be a good death? *Journal of Evaluation in Clinical Practice* 18(5): 1082–1086.
Scheffler, S 2013. *Death and the Afterlife*. Oxford UP.
Schelling, T 1960. *The Strategy of Conflict*. Cambridge, MA: Harvard UP.
Schermer, M 2009. Over dementie, wilsverklaringen en het leven-als-geheel. Wiens leven, welke belangen? In: P Rijpkema, G van Donselaar, B Verbeek, H Wijsbek eds. *Als vuur, Opstellen voor Govert den Hartogh ter gelegenheid van zijn emeritaat*. Den Haag: Boom: 109–126.
Schermer, M 2013. Old age is an incurable disease-or is it? In: Schermer, Pinxten eds.
Schermer, M, W Pinxten eds. 2013. *Ethics, Health Policy and (Anti-) Aging: Mixed Blessings*. Dordrecht: Springer.
Schermer, M 2014. Ethics of pharmacological mood enhancement. In: J Clausen, N Levy eds. *Handbook of Neuroethics*. Dordrecht: Springer.
Schildmann, E, J Schildmann 2014. Palliative sedation: a systematic review and critical appraisal of available guidance on indication and decision-making. *Journal of Palliative Medicine* 17: 601–611.
Schramme, T 2013. Rational suicide, assisted suicide, and indirect legal paternalism. *International Journal of Law and Psychiatry* 36: 477–484.
Schramme, T 2015. Introduction to: T Schramme ed., *New Perspectives on Paternalism and Health Care*. Berlin: Springer.
Schuklenk, U, JJM Van Delden, J Downie et al. 2011. End-of-life decision-making in Canada: the report by the Royal Society of Canada Expert Panel on end-of-life decision-making. *Bioethics* 25: 1–73.
Schuklenk, U, R Smalling 2016. Why medical professionals have no moral claim to conscientious objection accommodation in liberal democracies. *Journal of Medical Ethics* 43: 234–240.
Schuklenk, U, S van de Vathorst 2015a. Treatment-resistant major depressive disorder and assisted dying. *Journal of Medical Ethics* 41: 577–583.
Schuklenk, U, S van de Vathorst 2015b. Treatment-resistant major depressive disorder and assisted dying: response to comments. *Journal of Medical Ethics* 41: 589–591.
Schultziner, D 2004. Human dignity – functions and meanings. *Global Jurist Topics* 3(3).
Schulz, R, JK Monin, SJ Czaja et al. 2010. Measuring the experience and perception of suffering. *The Gerontologist* 50(6): 774–784.
Schuman-Olivier, Z, DH Brendel, M Forstein, BH Price 2008. The use of palliative sedation for existential distress: a psychiatric perspective. *Harvard Review of Psychiatry* 16: 339–351.
Schur, S, D Weixler, C Gabl et al. 2016. Sedation at the end of life-a nation-wide study in palliative care units in Austria. *BMC Palliative Care* 15: 50–57.
Schwartz, JK 2014. Hospice care for patients who choose to hasten death by voluntarily stopping eating and drinking. *Journal of Hospice and Palliative Nursing* 16(3): 126–131.
Scocco, P, D de Leo 2002. One-year prevalence of death thoughts, suicide ideation and behaviours in an elderly population. *International Journal of Geriatric Psychiatry* 17: 842–846.

Seale, C 2009. End-of-life decisions in the UK involving medical practitioners. *Palliative Medicine* 23(3): 198–204.

Seale, C 2010. Continuous deep sedation in medical practice: a descriptive study. *Journal of Pain and Symptom Management* 39(1): 44–53.

Seay, G 2011. Euthanasia and common sense: a reply to Garcia. *Journal of Medicine and Philosophy* 36: 321–327.

Secinti, E, DB Tometich, SA Johns, CE Mosher 2019. The relationship between acceptance of cancer and distress: a meta-analytic review. *Clinical Psychology Review* 71: 27–38.

Seidel, RH 1978. Where are they now? A follow-up study of suicide attempts from the Golden Gate Bridge. *Suicide and Life Threatening Behavior* 8: 203–216.

Sensen, O 2009. Kant's conception of human dignity. *Kant-Studien* 100: 309–331.

Seymour, J, J Rietjens, S Bruinsma et al. 2015. Using continuous sedation until death for cancer patients: a qualitative interview study of physicians' and nurses' practice in three European countries. *Palliative Medicine* 29: 48–59.

Seymour, JE, R Janssens, B Broeckaert 2007. Relieving suffering at the end of life: practitioners' perspectives on palliative sedation from three European countries. *Social Science and Medicine* 64: 1679–1691.

Shafer, K, DR Stansky 2008. Defining depth of anesthesia. In: J Schüttler, H Schwilden eds. *Modern Anesthetics, Handbook of Experimental Pharmacology*. Berlin-Heidelberg: Springer Verlag: 409–423.

Shewmon, A 2001. The brain and somatic integration: insights into the standard biological rationale for equating 'brain death' with death. *Journal of Medicine and Philosophy* 26: 457–478.

Shiffrin, SV 2004. Autonomy, beneficence, and the permanently demented. In: J Burley ed. *Dworkin and His Critics, with Replies by Dworkin*. Malden/Oxford: Blackwell.

Shneidman, ES 1981. A psychological theory of suicide. *Suicide and Life Threatening Behavior* 11: 221–231.

Shneidman, ES 1996. *The Suicidal Mind*. Oxford UP.

Siegel, MC 1998. Lethal pity: the Oregon death with dignity act, its implications for the disabled, and the struggle for equality in an able-bodied world. *Law and Inequality* 16: 259–288.

da Silva, RM, GS Sousa, LJE Vieira et al. 2018. Suicidal ideation and attempt of older women in Northeastern Brazil. *Revista Brasileira de Enfermagem* 71: 755–762.

Silvers, A 1998. Protecting the innocents from physician-assisted suicide. In: Battin, Rhodes, Silvers eds.

Simester, AP, A von Hirsch 2014. *Crimes, Harms, and Wrongs: On the Principles of Criminalisation*. Oxford: Hart Publ.

Simon, OR, AC Swann, KE Powell et al. 2001. Characteristics of impulsive suicide attempts and attempters. *Suicide and Life Threatening Behavior* 32: 49–59.

Singer, PA, DK Martin, M Kelner 1999. Quality end-of-life care: patients' perspectives. *JAMA* 281: 163–168.

Singer, PA, M Siegler 1990. Euthanasia: a critique. *New England Journal of Medicine* 322(16): 1881–1883.

Slavney, PR 1999. Diagnosing demoralization in consultation psychiatry. *Psychosomatics* 40: 325–329.

Smets, T, J Bilsen 2011. Toepassing van de zorgvuldigheidscriteria. In: Deliëns et al., Ch. 19.

Smets, T, J Cohen, J Bilsen et al. 2011. The labelling and reporting of euthanasia by Belgian physicians: a study of hypothetical cases. *European Journal of Public Health* 22: 19–26.

Smith, M 1980. Did Socrates kill himself intentionally? *Philosophy* 55: 253–254.

Smith, SW 2005. Evidence for the practical slippery slope in the debate on physician-assisted suicide and euthanasia. *Medical Law Review* 13: 17–44.

Smith, SW 2012. *End-of-Life Decisions in Medical Care*. Cambridge UP.

Snijdewind, M 2019. Dying to be normal: an exploration of normalization in the practice of physician-assosted dying. Thesis, Free University Amsterdam: Conclusion.

Snijdewind, MC, DG van Tol, BD Onwuteaka-Philipsen, DL Willems 2014. Complexities in euthanasia or physician-assisted suicide as perceived by Dutch physicians and patients' relatives. *Journal of Pain and Symptom Management* 48: 1125–1133.

Snijdewind, MC, DG van Tol, BD Onwuteaka-Philipsen, DL Willems 2016. Developments in the practice of physician-assisted dying: perceptions of physicians who had experience with complex cases. *Journal of Medical Ethics* 44: 292–296.

Snyder, CR, KL Rand, EA King et al. 2002. "False" hope. *Journal of Clinical Psychology* 58: 1003–1022.

Snyder, J, T Caulfield 2019. Patients' crowdfunding campaigns for alternative cancer treatments. *The Lancet Oncology* 20: 28–29.

Snyder, L, DP Sulmasy 2001. Physician-assisted suicide. *Annals of Internal Medicine* 135: 209–216.

Soto, C 2013. Killing, wrongness, and equality. *Philosophical Studies* 164: 543–559.

Spaemann, R, G Hohendorf, FS Oduncu 2015. *Vom guten Sterben: warum es keinen assistierten Tod geben darf*. Freiburg: Herder.

Spiegelinformatie SCEN 2011ff. Steun en Consultatie bij Euthanasie in Nederland, KNMG. *Annual reports*.

Spittler, JF 2017. Suizidverhütung und Suizidbeihilfe: Unterschiedliche Erfahrungsbereiche. *Nervenheilkunde* 36: 416–422.

Staatscommissie 1985. *Euthanasie: Rapport van de Staatscommissie Euthanasie*. Den Haag: Staatsuitgeverij.

Stängle, S, D Büche, C Häuptle, A Fringer 2021. Experiences, personal attitudes, and professional stances of Swiss health care professionals toward voluntary stopping of eating and drinking to hasten death: a cross-sectional study. *Journal of Pain and Symptom Management* 61: 270–278.

Stängle, S, W Schnepp, D Büche 2020. Family physicians' perspectives on voluntary stopping eating and drinking: a cross-sectional study. *Journal of International Medical Research* 48(8): 0300060520936069.

Stallen JM, M. Marlet 2018. Voorkeur voor hulp bij zelfdoding: observaties en overwegingen. *Nederlands Tijdschrift voor Geneeskunde* 162: D303

Steck, N, C Junker, M Maessen et al. 2014. Suicide assisted by right-to-die associations: a population based cohort study. *International Journal of Epidemiology* 43: 614–622.

Steck, N, C Junker, M Zwahlen et al. 2018. Increase in assisted suicide in Switzerland: did the socioeconomic predictors change? Results from the Swiss national cohorts. *BMJ Open* 8: e020992.

Steinbock, B 2005. The case for assisted suicide, not (yet) proven. *Journal of Medical Ethics* 31: 235–241.

Steinbock, B 2017. Physician-assisted death and severe, treatment-resistant depression. *Hastings Center Report* 47(5): 30–42.

Steinhauser, KE, EC Clipp, M McNeilly et al. 2000. In search of a good death: observations of patients, family and providers. *Annals of Internal Medicine* 132: 825–832.

Steinhauser, KE, CI Voils, EC Clipp et al. 2006. 'Are you at peace?': one item to probe spiritual concerns at the end of life. *Archives of Internal Medicine* 166(1): 101–105.

Stengel, E 1964. *Suicide and Attempted Suicide*. London: Penguin Books.

Sterckx, S, K Raus, F Mortier eds. 2013. *Continuous Sedation at the End of Life: Ethical, Clinical and Legal Perspectives*. Cambridge UP.

Stilz, A 2011. *Liberal Loyalty: Freedom, Obligation & the State*. Princeton: Princeton UP.

Stingl, M 2010. Voluntary and nonvoluntary euthanasia: is there really a slippery slope? In: M. Stingl ed. *The Price of Compassion: Assisted Suicide and Euthanasia*. Peterborough: Broadview Press.

Streeck, N 2019. Death without distress? The taboo of suffering in palliative care. *Medicine, Health Care and Philosophy* 23: 343–351.

Strunk, DR, H Lopez, RJ DeRubeis 2006. Depressive symptoms are associated with unrealistic negative predictions of future life events. *Behaviour Research and Therapy* 44: 861–882.

Suchner, U, C Reudelsterz, C Gog 2018. 'Terminale' Dehydration Teil 1: Differetialdiagnose und Evidenzlage. *Der Anästhesist* 67: 709–722.

Suchomel, J-U 2010. *Partielle Disponibilität der Würde des Menschen*. Berlin: Duncker & Humblot.

Sullivan, WF, J Heng 2012. The use of sedatives in the care of persons who are seriously ill or dying: ethical distinctions and practical recommendations. International Association of Catholic Bioethicists. *National Catholic Bioethics Quarterly* 12: 494–501.

Sullivan, RJ 1993. Accepting death without artificial nutrition or hydration. *Journal of General Internal Medicine* 8: 220–224.

Sulmasy, DP 2008. Dignity and bioethics: history, theory, and selected applications. In: A Schulman ed. *Human Dignity and Bioethics: Essays Commissioned by the President's Council on Bioethics*. Government Printing Office.

Sulmasy, DP 2013. The varieties of human dignity: a logical and conceptual analysis. *Medical Health Care and Philosophy* 17: 937–944.

Sulmasy, DP 2018. The last low whispers of our dead: when is it ethically justified to render a patient unconscious until death? *Theoretical Medicine and Bioethics* 39(3): 233–263.

Sumner, LW 2011. *Assisted Death: A Study in Ethics and Law*. Oxford UP.

Sumner, LW 2021. *Advance Requests for Medically Assisted Dying* (Revised). Preprint.

Sunstein, CR 1996. *Legal Reasoning and Political Conflict*. Oxford UP.

Sutcliffe, J, S Holmes 1994. Dehydration: burden or benefit to the dying patient? *Journal of Advanced Nursing* 50: 71–76.

Svenaeus, F 2014. The phenomenology of suffering in medicine and bioethics. *Theoretical Medicine and Bioethics* 35: 407–420.

Swart, SJ, A van der Heide, L van Zuylen 2012. Considerations of physicians about the depth of palliative sedation at the end of life. *Canadian Medical Association Journal* 184(7): E360–E366.

Swart, SJ, A van der Heide, L van Zuylen et al. 2014 Continuous palliative sedation: not only a response to physical suffering. *Journal of Palliative Medicine* 17: 27–36.

Swerissen, H, S Duckett 2014. *Dying Well.* Carlton, Victoria: Grattan Institute.

Sykes, NP 2013. Clinical aspects of palliative sedation. In: Sterckx, Raus, Mortier eds.

Sykes, N, A Thorns 2003. The use of opioids and sedatives at the end of life. *The Lancet Oncology*, 4(5): 312–318.

Syme, R 2008. *A Good Death: An Argument for Voluntary Euthanasia.* Melbourne UP.

Szasz, TS 1971. The ethics of suicide. *Antioch Review* 31(1971): 7–17, reprinted in Donnelly ed.

Tait, G, B Carpenter, D de Leo et al. 2015. Problems with the coronial determination of 'suicide'. *Mortality* 20: 233–247.

Tan, JOA, T Hope, A Stewart, R Fitzpatrick 2006. Competence to make treatment decisions in anorexia nervosa: thinking processes and values. *Philosophy, Psychiatry and Psychology* 13: 267–282.

Tännsjö, T 2004. Terminal sedation: a substitute for euthanasia? In: Tännsjö ed.

Tännsjö, T ed. 2004. *Terminal Sedation: Euthanasia in Disguise?* Dordrecht: Kluwer.

Tate, T, R Pearlman 2019. What we mean when we talk about suffering – and why Eric Cassell should not have the last word. *Perspectives in Biology and Medicine* 62(1): 95–110.

Tayeb, MA, E Al-Zamel, MM Fareedet, HE Abouellail 2010. A 'good death': perspectives of Muslim patients and health care providers. *Annals Saudi Medicine* 30(3): 215–221.

Taylor, JS 2008. On recognition, caring, and dementia. *Medical Anthropology Quarterly* 22: 313–335.

Taylor, S 1982. *Durkheim and the Study of Suicide.* London: MacMillan.

Teno, JM, J Lynn, RS Phillips et al. 1994. Do formal advance directives affect resuscitation decisions and the use of resources for seriously ill patients? *Journal of Clinical Ethics* 5: 23–30.

Terman, SA 2006. *The Best Way to Say Goodbye. A Legal Peaceful Choice at the End of Life.* Carlsbad: Life Transitions Publications.

The A-M 1997. Vanavond om 8 uur…. In: *Verpleegkundige Dilemma's bij Euthanasie en andere Beslissingen bij het Levenseinde.* Houten/Diegem: Bohn, Stafleu, van Loghum.

The, A-M, T Hak, G Koëter, G van der Wal 2001. Collusion in doctor-patient communication about imminent death; an ethnographic study. *Western Journal of Medicine* 174: 247–253.

The, BAM, HRW Pasman, BD Onwuteaka-Philipsen et al. 2002. Withholding the artificial administration of fluids and food from elderly patients with dementia: ethnographic study. *British Medical Journal* 325: 1–5.

Thienpont, L, M Verhofstadt, T van Loon et al. 2015. Euthanasia requests, procedures and outcomes for 100 Belgian patients suffering from psychiatric disorders: a retrospective, descriptive study. *BMJ Open*, *5*(7): e007454.

Thomson, J 1986. *Rights, Restitution, and Risk*. Cambridge, MA: Harvard UP.

Tiemeijer, WL, C Thomas, H Prast 2009. *The Human Decision-Maker: About the Psychology of Choice and Behavior*. Amsterdam: Amsterdam UP.

van Tol, D 2005. *Grensgeschillen: een Rechtssociologisch Onderzoek naar het Classificeren van Euthanasie en ander Medisch Handelen rond het Levenseinde*. Thesis, Rijksuniversiteit Groningen.

van Tol, D, J Rietjens, A van der Heide 2010. Judgment of unbearable suffering and willingness to grant a euthanasia request by Dutch general practitioners. *Health Policy* 97: 166–172.

van Tol, D, JAC Rietjens, A van der Heide 2012. Empathy and the application of the 'unbearable suffering' criterion in Dutch euthanasia practice. *Health Policy* 105: 296–302.

van Tol, DG, B van der Vegt, P Kouwenhoven et al. 2011. Interviewonderzoek onder artsen. In: van Delden, van der Heide, van de Vathorst et al.

Tolhurst, WE 1983. Suicide, self-sacrifice, and coercion. *Southern Journal of Philosophy* 21: 109–121. Reprinted in Donnelly ed.

Tolle, SW, VP Tilden, LL Drach et al. 2004. Characteristics and proportion of dying Oregonians who personally consider physician-assisted suicide. *Journal of Clinical Ethics* 15(2): 111–121.

Tomsons, K, S Sherwin 2010. Feminist reflections on Tracy Latimer and Sue Rodriguez. In: M Stingl ed. *The Price of Compassion*. Petersburg: Broadview Press.

Tong, R 2000. Duty to die. In: J Humber, R Almeder eds. *Is There a Duty to Die?* Totowa, NJ: Humana Press.

Trachsel, M, SA Irwin, N Biller-Andorno et al. 2016. Palliative psychiatry for severe persistent mental illness as a new approach to psychiatry? Definition, scope, benefits, and risks. *BMC Psychiatry*, *16*(1), 1–6.

Trappenburg, M 2012. The Dutch social fabric: health care, trust, and solidarity. In: Youngner, Kimsma eds.

Truog, RD, ML Campbell, JR Curtis et al. 2008. Recommendations for end-of-life care in the intensive care unit: a consensus statement by the American College of Critical Care Medicine. *Critical Care Medicine* 36: 953–963.

Tuffrey-Wijne, I, L Curfs, I Finlay, S Hollins 2018. Euthanasia and assisted suicide for people with an intellectual disability and/or autism spectrum disorder: an examination of nine relevant euthanasia cases in the Netherlands 2012–2016. *BMC Medical Ethics* 19: 17.

Tugendhat, E 2006. *Über den Tod*. Frankfurt: Suhrkamp.

Twycross, R 2019. Reflections on palliative sedation. *Palliative Care Research and Treatment* 12: 1178224218824188 23511.

VandenBerghe, J 2017. Euthanasia in patients with intolerable suffering due to an irremediable psychiatric illness: a psychiatric perspective. In: Jones, Gastmans, MacKellar eds.

VanSweevelt, T 2008. Comparative legal aspects of pain management. *Medicine and Law* 27: 899–912.

Varelius, J 2015. On the moral acceptability of physician-assisted dying for non-autonomous psychiatric patients. *Bioethics* 30: 227–233.

Varelius, J 2019. Suffering at the end of life. *Bioethics* 33: 95–100.

Varlet, V, S Iwersen-Bergmann, M Alexandre et al. 2019. Helium poisoning: new procedures for sampling and analysis. *International Journal of Legal Medicine* 133: 1809–1818.

van de Vathorst, S, JKM Gevers, A van der Heide et al. 2013. *Evaluatie Centrale Deskundigencommissie Late Zwangerschapsafbreking in een Categorie-2 Geval en Levensbeëindiging bij Pasgeborenen*. ZonMw.

Veen, SMP, AM Ruissen, GAM Widdershoven 2020. Irremediable psychiatric suffering in the context of physician-assisted death: a scoping review of arguments. *Canadian Journal of Psychiatry* 65: 5933–5603.

Velleman, JD 1991. Well-being and time. *Pacific Philosophical Quarterly* 72: 48–77. Reprinted in Fischer ed. 1993.

Velleman, JD 1992. Against the right to die. *Journal of Medicine and Philosophy* 17: 665–681.

Velleman, JD 1999. A right of self-termination? *Ethics* 109: 606–628. Reprinted in Velleman 2015.

Velleman, JD 2006. *Self to Self: Selected Essays*. Cambridge UP.

Velleman, JD 2008. Beyond price. *Ethics* 118: 191–212. Reprinted in Velleman 2015.

Velleman, JD 2015. *Beyond Price: Essays on Birth and Death*. UK: Open Book Publishers.

Verhofstadt, M, K Assche, S Sterckx et al. 2019. Psychiatric patients requiring euthanasia: guidelines for sound clinical and ethical decision-making. *International Journal of Law and Psychiatry* 64: 150–161.

Verhofstadt, M, K Audenaert, K van den Broeck et al. 2020. Belgian psychiatrists' attitudes towards, and readiness to engage in, euthanasia assessment procedures with adults with psychiatric conditions: a survey. *BMC Psychiatry* 20: 274.

Verhofstadt, M, K Audenaert, K van den Broeck et al. 2021. Euthanasia in adults with psychiatric conditions: a descriptive study of the experiences of Belgian psychiatrists. *Science Progress* 104: 1–23.

Verkissen, MN, D Houttekiet, J Cohen et al. 2018. End-of-life decision-making across cancer types: results from a nationwide retrospective survey among treating physicians. *British Journal of Cancer* 118: 1369–1376.

Vezzoni, C 2005. *The Legal Status and Social Practice of Treatment Directives in the Netherlands*. Thesis, Rijksuniversiteit Groningen.

Vincent, J-L 2014. "Piece" (sic) of mind: end of life in the intensive care unit. Statement of the Belgian Society of Intensive Care Medicine. *Journal of Critical Care* 29: 174–175.

Vink, T 2013. *Zelfeuthanasie: een Zelfbezorgde Goede Dood onder Eigen Regie*. Budel: Damon.

Vink T 2016a. Hoe zo 'voltooid' leven? *Filosofie & Praktijk* 37 (4): 67–77.

Vink, T. 2016b. Self Euthanasia, the Dutch experience: in search for the meaning of a good death or eu thanatos. *Bioethics* 30: 681–688.

Vink, T 2017. *Een goede dood: euthanasie gewikt en gewogen*. Utrecht: Klement.

Vink, T 2018. *Onder eigen regie: zelfeuthanasie belicht*. Utrecht: Klement.

Vis, JTE, S Zuurveld 2021. *Dagvaarding rechtbank, civiel*, https://www.rechtspraak.nl/SiteCollectionDocuments/rbdha-clw-vs-de-staat-der-nederlanden.pdf.

Vlaamse Vereniging voor Psychiatrie 2017. *Hoe omgaan met een euthanasieverzoek in psychiatrie binnen het huidig wettelijk kader?* Adviestekst VVvP, https://vvponline.be/uploads/docs/bib/euthanasie_finaal_vvp_1_dec.pdf.

Vlastos, G 1962. Justice and equality. In: RB Brandt ed. *Social Justice*. Englewood Cliffs, NJ: Prentice Hall.

Vollmann, J, A Bauer, H Danker-Hoffe, H Helmchen 2003. Competence of mentally ill patients: a comparative empirical study. *Psychological Medicine* 33: 1463–1471.

van der Wal, G 1987. Een recht op sterven. In: G van der Wal red. *Euthanasie: Knelpunten in een Discussie*. Baarn: Ambo.

van der Wal, GA, A van der Heide, BD Onwuteaka-Philipsen, PJ van der Maas 2003. *Medische Besluitvorming aan het Einde van het Leven: de Praktijk en de Toetsingsprocedure Euthanasie*. Utrecht: De Tijdstroom.

van der Wal, GA, PJ van der Maas et al. 1996. *Euthanasie en andere Medische Beslissingen rond het Levenseinde: de Praktijk en de Meldingsprocedure*. Den Haag: SDU.

Waldron, J 2009. *Dignity, Rank, and Rights*. Oxford UP.

Wall, PD, R Melzack eds. 1999. *Textbook of Pain*. Edinburgh: Churchill Livingstone.

Walsh, E 2020. Cognitive transformation, dementia, and the moral weight of advance directives. *American Journal of Bioethics* 20: 54–64.

Walther, C 2010. Rechtliche Fragen zum beabsichtigten, vorzeitigen Versterben durch Verzicht auf Nahrung und Flüssigkeit, chapter 5. In: B Chabot, C Walther eds. *Ausweg am Lebensende: Selbstbestimmtes Sterben Durch freiwilligen Verzicht auf Essen und Trinken*. München/Basel: Ernst Reinhardt Verlag.

Washington State Department of Health 2009ff. *Death with Dignity Act* Annual *Reports*.

Watt, JB ed. 2004. *From Sin to Insanity: Suicide in Early Modern Europe*. Ithaca, NY: Cornell UP.

Watts, DT, T Howell 1992. Assisted suicide is not euthanasia. *Journal of the American Geriatrics Society* 40: 1043–1046.

Weijers, D, V Schouten 2013. An assessment of recent responses to the experience machine objection to hedonism. *Journal of Value Inquiry* 47: 461–482.

Weir, RF 1992. The morality of physician-assisted suicide. *Law, Medicine and Health Care* 40: 116–126.

Welie, SPK 2001. Criteria for patient decision making (in)competence: a commentary on some empirical approaches. *Medicine, Health Care and Philosophy* 4: 139–151.

van Wesemael, Y, J Cohen, J Bilsen et al. 2010. Consulting a trained physician when considering a request for euthanasia: an evaluation of the process in Flanders and the Netherlands. *Evaluation and the Health Professions* 33: 497–513.

van Wesemael, Y, J Cohen, J Bilsen et al. 2011. Process and outcomes of Euthanasia requests under the Belgian Act on Euthanasia: a nationwide survey. *Journal of Pain and Symptom Management* 42: 721–733.

Weyers, H 2004. *Euthanasie: het Proces van Rechtsverandering*. Amsterdam: Amsterdam UP.

White, N, F Reid, A Harris et al. 2016. A systematic review of predictions of survival in palliative care: how accurate are clinicians and who are the experts? *PLoS One* 11(8): a0161407.

WHO 2002. *World Health Organisation Definition of Palliative Care*.

Wicclair, MR 1991. Patient decision-making capacity and risk. *Bioethics* 1991: 91–104.

Widdershoven, GAM, RLP Berghmans 2001. Advance directives in dementia care: from instructions to instruments. *Patient Education and Counseling* 44: 179–186.

van Wijngaarden, EJ 2016. *Voltooid Leven: over Leven en Willen Sterven*. Amsterdam: Atlas Contact.

van Wijngaarden, E 2021. The darker side of ageing: towards an ethics of suffering that emphasizes the primacy of witnessing. *Journal of Population Ageing* 14: 323–342.

van Wijngaarden, EJ, CJW Leget, A Goossensen 2014. Experiences and motivations underlying wishes to die in older people who are tired of living: a research area in its infancy. *Omega Journal of Death and Dying* 69: 191–216.

van Wijngaarden, EJ, CJW Leget, A Goossensen 2015. Ready to give up on life: the lived experience of elderly people who feel life is completed and no longer worth living. *Social Science and Medicine* 138: 257–264.

van Wijngaarden, EJ, M Merzel, V van den Berg et al. 2020b. Still ready to give up on life? A longitudinal phenomenological study into wishes to die among older adults. *Social Science and Medicine* 284: 114180.

van Wijngaarden, E, G Van Thiel et al. 2020b. *Perspectieven op de Doodswens van Ouderen die niet Ernstig Ziek zijn: de Mensen en de Cijfers*. ZonMw.

Wijsbek, H 1999. De genoegens van het leven zijn enkel leegte. *Filosofie & Praktijk* 20: 16–30.

Wijsbek, H 2000. Mijn broeders hoeder. In: F Kortmann, G den Hartogh eds., *Weldoen op Contract: Ethiek en Psychiatrie*. Assen: van Gorcum.

Wijsbek, H 2012a. 'To thine own self be true': on the loss of integrity as a kind of suffering. *Bioethics* 26: 1–7.

Wijsbek, H 2012b. The subjectivity of suffering and the normativity of unbearableness. In: Youngner, Kimsma eds.

Wijsbek, H 2016. Beoordeling ondraaglijk lijden bij euthanasieverzoek. *Nederlands Tijdschrift voor Geneeskunde* 160(22): D160.

von Wildt, K, ST Laureys, F Gerstenbrand et al. 2012. The Vegetative State – a syndrome in search of a name. *Journal of Medicine and Life* 5(1): 3–15.

Wilkinson, TM 2003. Against Dworkin's endorsement constraint. *Utilitas* 15: 175–193.

Willems, D, E Daniels, G van der Wal et al. 2000. Attitudes and practices concerning the end of life: a comparison between physicians from the United States and from the Netherlands. *Archives Internal Medicine* 160(1): 63–68.

Williams, B 1973. The Makropulos case: reflections on the tedium of immortality. In: *Problems of the Self; Philosophical Papers*. Cambridge UP.

Williams, G 2001. The principle of double effect and terminal sedation. *Medical Law Review* 9(1): 41–53.

Willmott, L, B White, R Feeney et al. 2021. Intentional hastening of death through medication: a case series analysis of Victorian deaths prior to the Voluntary Assisted Dying Act 2017. *Internal Medical Journal* 51: 1650–1656.

Wilson, KG, HM Chochinov, CJ McPherson et al. 2007. Desire for euthanasia or physician assisted suicide in palliative cancer care. *Health Psychology* 26: 314–323.

Wilson, KG, ID Graham, A Viola et al. 2004. Structured interview assessment of symptoms and concerns in palliative care. *Canadian Journal of Psychiatry* 49: 350–358.

Winburn, E, P Mullen 2008. Personality disorder and competence to refuse treatment. *Journal of Medical Ethics* 34: 715–716.

Wittwer, H 2013. The problem of the possible rationality of suicide and the ethics of physician-assisted suicide. *International Journal of Law and Psychiatry* 36: 419–426.

Wolf, SM 1996. Gender, feminism, and death: physician-assisted suicide and euthanasia. In: SM Wolf ed. *Feminism and Bioethics: Beyond Reproduction.* Oxford UP.

Wood, AW 1999. *Kant's Ethical Thought.* Cambridge UP.

Wood, D 1980. Suicide as instrument and expression. In: MP Battin, DJ Mayo eds. *Suicide: the Philosophical Issues*, London: Peter Owen.

Wrigley, A 2007. Proxy consent: moral authority misconceived. *Journal of Medical Ethics* 33: 527–531.

Wyatt, M, I Jaussent, K Ritchie et al. 2016. Iowa Gambling Task performance in elderly persons with a lifetime history of suicidal acts. *American Journal of Geriatric Psychiatry* 24: 399–406.

van Wylick, E, G van Dijk 2015. Dokters hikken soms tegen euthanasie aan. *Medisch Contact* 70: 16–19.

Young, J, R Egan, S Walker et al. 2019. The euthanasia debate: synthesizing the evidence on New Zealander attitudes. *Kotuiti: New Zealand Journal of Social Sciences Online* 14: 1–21.

Young, R 2007. *Medically Assisted Death.* Cambridge UP.

Youngner, SJ, GK Kimsma eds. 2012. *Physician-Assisted Death in Perspective: Assessing the Dutch Experience.* Cambridge UP.

Yun, YH, K-N Kim, J-A Sim et al. 2018. Priorities of a 'good death' according to cancer patients, their family caregivers, and the general population: a nationwide survey. *Supportive Care in Cancer* 26: 3479–3488.

Yun, YH, TR Mendoza, IO Kang et al. 2006. Validation study of the Korean version of the M.D. Anderson Symptom Inventory. *Journal of Pain and Symptom Management* 31: 345–352.

Zorgnet Vlaanderen 2012. *Richtlijn Sedatie.*

Zylberman, A 2016. Human dignity. *Philosophy Compass* 11(4): 201–210.

Index

For Product Safety Concerns and Information please contact our EU
representative GPSR@taylorandfrancis.com
Taylor & Francis Verlag GmbH, Kaufingerstraße 24, 80331 München, Germany

www.ingramcontent.com/pod-product-compliance
Lightning Source LLC
LaVergne TN
LVHW021246011026
849160LV00010BA/751

* 9 7 8 1 0 3 2 2 4 9 9 5 7 *